D0953029

Interpreting Personality Theories

*Under the editorship
of Gardner Murphy
and Wayne Holtzman*

Interpreting

Personality

Theories

SECOND EDITION

LEDFORD J. BISCHOF

PROFESSOR OF PSYCHOLOGY
Northern Illinois University

HARPER & ROW, PUBLISHERS
New York, Evanston, and London

(m) 06·02·8· 0601_96°0/

INTERPRETING PERSONALITY THEORIES, SECOND EDITION
Copyright © 1964, 1970 by *Ledford J. Bischof*

LIBRARY OF CONGRESS CATALOG CARD NUMBER: 79–98200

Rededicated to Betty and Barbara

whose personalities, theoretical or not,
still continue to fascinate me.

And so that we can better understand ourselves,
this book is written.

CONTENTS

PREFACE

IT IS ALWAYS a pleasure and yet a serious responsibility to prepare a second edition. The pleasure comes from having a book which apparently has been received well enough to warrant it. The sense of responsibility is felt because a second edition should be an improvement over the first, eliminating the errors and sins of omission and commission, incorporating the newer approaches and current research when applicable, and in general being more worthwhile.

What has been happening in personality theory since the first edition was published in 1964? Because psychologists are energetic, conscientious, and hardworking, there has been much new research, not all of it particularly appropriate to a personality theory yet in many cases applicable to the general field of personality. It will be discussed in the chapters where it seems pertinent to testing specific theories.

Since publication of the first edition, personality as a field of study has been rather widely accepted by psychologists, social psychologists, sociologists, and even anthropologists. It is interesting to note that in some instances nonpragmatically oriented clinical psychologists have turned to studying the concept of personality.

The present writer finds it disturbing, however, that many experimentalists seem to be reluctant actually to investigate the theory. Too often the experimentalist thinks he is researching a concept of the theory without having taken the time and trouble to learn what the theory is about. Thus, there is still a need for a book which covers the primary factors of the leading theories of personality.[1]

Some of the changes in this second edition are as follows: The bibliography has been updated through 1969; Chapters 1 and 2 from the previous edition have been combined; some rearranging of chapters has been done; except in the chapter on Freud, the "Explanation" section in each major theorist's chapter has been deleted; the last chapter has been completely revised; and the major change has been in incorporating new research—the most relevant and recent approaches to theory testing have been digested in the sections called "Scientific or Laboratory Prediction." Two new theorists have been presented. The personal construct theory of the late George Kelly is so refreshing, so necessary, that it must be acknowledged in the present edition. Kelly adds an important dimension: The individual is just as concerned with controlling and predicting his own personal behavior as the psychologist, if not more so. Erik Erikson has brought a crucial developmental expansion to the psychoanalytical school and therefore has been included. Even though some personality theories are not currently productive in initiating research, there is a rise and fall in theory influence. The temptation to bring in other new theories is almost overwhelming. The subjective decision not to succumb to it rests on these bases: There still is much research to be done on the existing and generally accepted theories now in this book; newer approaches still appear too narrow, too mechanistic, and too parochial. Yet we would have liked to include Skinner's singular work, Rotter's social learning paradigms, or Angyal, or Dollard, Miller, Sears, or McClelland, or Maddi, or all the others. However, there is a limit to the size of this book, and other writers handle these contributions in an excellent, readable manner. The primary consideration on inclusion or exclusion revolves around how global

---

[1] J. P. Dashiell, The unreliability of secondary sources with examples from Jung, *Psychol. Rec.*, 1962, 12, 331–334.

the theory is. Obviously, exclusion does not mean that a theory has no value.

This edition retains its "benevolent eclecticism" despite the disenchantment and irritation of some of the newer works on personality theory and personality testing (see Introduction). Perhaps we all take our individual selves too seriously. Urgency, yes. Hasty solutions to the human personality problem, no. Thus, what we sometimes consider contemporary is too often contemptuous.

As any writer of a technical work knows, the preparation of a book is a corporate endeavor. It is with a deep feeling of pride, praise, and humble gratitude that I thank my small group of helpers. I am grateful to the talented Miss Linda Darner for typing, taping, pasting, and keeping the loose ends gathered up while this second edition was in preparation. My gratitude is equally sincere to Mr. Timothy I. Marcy for his understanding of the concept of the book and for the countless dedicated hours he has spent in reading and researching. Without their help the second edition would never have been possible.

Once again, my thanks go to my wife, Betty, and my daughter, Barbara, for their tolerance, support, and encouragement.

L. J. B.

Part

I

Introduction

ODDLY ENOUGH most people seem to feel more comfortable when a theory or a law becomes identified with the name of the man who originated the idea or even with the leading exponent of the theory, when its origins are confused or lost in antiquity. Thus, men's names are attached to theoretical positions in the areas of learning, or intelligence, or physical laws, or religious beliefs (such as Christianity, Mohammedanism, Buddhism, Zoroastrianism). This propensity to associate a person with a theory holds also for theories of personality.

The chapters in this book bear the names of originators of major theories of personality. Unfortunately the individual's name in no way identifies the main aspects of the theory. Nevertheless, it is enough to say, "That was a Freudian slip," for instance, to express the phenomenon of repression as it is found in Freud's theory. At first the name identifies the theory; then a turnabout takes place and the theory is identified by the name.

Theories can be studied in many ways. One may organize them historically or heuristically or hierarchically or homogeneously or geographically (that is to say, American vis-à-vis European) or not at all. The organization of the theorists for study in this book is purely the device of the author; if no serious distortion is done to the theory itself, the organization is worthwhile. Further explanation of the grouping of theorists into particular sections is presented in the introductory remarks to the sections. The strengths and weaknesses of each theory are also discussed.

The theories in the present text have been grouped into the following classifications for ease in studying their relationships to one another:

Part   I: Introduction
Part   II: Psychoanalytical–Psychophilosophical
Part III: Psychoindividual–Psychosocial
Part IV: Self-Integrative–Biosocial
Part   V: Psychobiological
Part VI: Psychostatistical
Part VII: Contributions of Other Theorists
Part VIII: Prospects for Personality Theory

The current state of affairs in personality seems to be represented by two opposing camps. Group A includes concerned individuals who are impatient, irritated, and almost angry about what is being done with, to, and for personality theories. One gets the impression that they are saying, "Let's get going. What are we waiting for? We have trained personnel, electronic computer devices, statistical know-how, and the need is there. Surely we can crack the code." The judgment is that study in the personality field has become unnecessarily stuck "in a prolonged infancy," so that no progress takes place. Personality theory, particularly theorizing about personalities, is a sort of "game, engaged in primarily for its value as a stimulant."

Those in group B feel less dissatisfied, less hurried, and more circumspect; they may even have a touch of humility toward the problem of studying human personality. They seem to be saying, "Man has many unsolved problems, though he has the training and techniques to resolve some of them." It looks as if "man's biggest problem to solve is the problem of his fellow man," and it will take much more time to solve than any one of us has left in his life-span. The urgency is there, but hurried solutions may not be possible.

So group A says, "We are wasting time nattering," while group B says, "Nattering at each other may be the essence of progress, and out of it will come much more progress in the understanding of the human condition."

If all the problems inherent in the issues of personality theory and personality understanding were finally and irrevocably solved, what would happen? When we have reached Valhalla in personality understanding, do we then move on to the solution of wars, pollution, and overpopulation; or has the human being by that time reached homeostasis and can exist with all his delightful flavors of differences?

Before proceeding with the theorists, we must note another problem: the direction being taken by research on personality theories. The first factor to be observed is the strong influence of journal editors in deciding what is to be published in the psychological literature. This, of course, is their duty and privilege. It may, however, determine the flow and direction of the research done. It stands to reason that an investigator, particularly under the current rules of academic life, will put little effort into research which he cannot publish. Thus, journal editors have perhaps too much control over research.

A second strong influence on the direction of research in personality theory comes from executives who operate the funding agencies—mostly, but not exclusively, federal agencies. Again, the psychologist interested in personality theory is much more inclined to do that kind of research for which he can get a budget and have financial support. It is hard to conduct research without adequate funds. Thus, we have a circular effect. The psychologist can only conduct research for which he has adequate funds. This can then be reported only in journals whose editors will accept his work. Between the two factors, personality research may be going not so much in the direction which will advance its cause as in the directions prescribed and circumscribed by them. Actually, getting any theoretical kind of paper published is most difficult. Some recognition of this problem can be found in the editorial position of Katz (*J. Pers. Soc. Psychol.*, 1967, 7, 341–344) and Melton (*J. Exp. Psychol.*, 1962, 64, 553–557).

Adelson, writing in the 1969 issue of *Annual Review of Psychology*, vol. 20, is acutely aware of the problems and the current status of research in personality and/or theories of personality. The flavor of his exhaustive search for literature in the field can be felt in the following excerpts even though they are out of context: "The field of personality these days is marked by abundance, diffuseness and diversity . . . hard to establish clear boundaries between personality and other psychologies . . . considerable overlap between social and personality psychology . . . matter of sheer caprice how we classify the many studies . . . research in personality [is] a disconcerting sprawl . . . movement is centrifugal . . . detailed exploration . . . impulse for synthesis . . . been set aside . . . controversies rarely center . . . substantive issues . . . usually involve internecine squabbling about this or that measure, method, or technique." He goes on to say, "It can be argued that these tendencies—scatter of research, the lag in theory, the fitful connection between theory and research—merely reflect the intractability of psychological phenomena to simplistic theoretical formulations and easy empirical answers. 'The simple and sovereign ideas of the past . . . are not strong enough to carry us very far' . . . our habits of inquiry and inference may be partly to blame . . . research emphasizes . . . hypothesis testing . . . tight designs which limit both stimulus conditions and the range of response . . . may need . . . revival of inductive naturalistic approaches . . . most of the theories we lean on are derived from disciplines and scholars (psychoanalysis, ethology, Piaget) whose inductive, naturalistic modes of inquiry we neither emulate nor tolerate" (*Annual Review*, 1969). Adelson speaks incisively and well. He is worth listening to.

1

PERSONALITY THEORY: PROBLEMS AND PROCEDURES

PROBLEMS OF DEFINITION

The words *personality* and *personality theory* are still in semantic flux. Despite "copious flow," research and theoretical formulations continue to grapple with the problem of definition and the problem of how to study the concepts scientifically. There seems to be no disagreement on the importance of personality in delineating behavior. The question is what to call it and what to do about it. On that score there is a profusion of disagreement.

In general, most, but not all, of the concepts regarding personality theory revolve around motives for man's behavior and behavior systems. Patricke puts it well: "The core that propelled the whole human machine. . . ." (Wepman and Heine, 1963, p. 389).[1] The delineation of human motives and behavior systems helps to bring together the multifaceted aspects of human behavior; thus the term *personality theory* is useful but should not be exclusive.

The term is the result of the need for orderliness of cumulative material about man's behavior rather than an a priori dictum on what should be studied under the rubric of "personality," theoretical or otherwise. Personality theory (as a term) should *free* man's efforts to understand himself, not *constrict* them. When we accumulate enough satisfactorily tested "operational definitions" of human behavior, we look around for a convenient hopper to hold the related material. This, then, often becomes a personality theory.

In contrast is the approach which states that "theory follows thought" without recourse to tested experience. Few choose to follow this trend except, perhaps, those philosophers who aspire to arrive at truth through reason sans empirical data. It appears that one of the most vile names a personologist can be called is "armchair theorizer." The illegitimacy of one's ancestors is more acceptable than the charge that one's theory was the result of introspective, quiet contemplation of the human scene without recourse to data. The emerging stance, particularly of psychologists, is "tough-mindedness" in dealing with the terminology of personality or personality theory.

Some workers would prefer to drop the term *theory* and deal with the term *personality* alone. *Theory* is misleading, they think, but not entirely useless; it can provide hypotheses or hunches for true empirical study in the very early stages of the game. What is more important is to gather data (our present state of affairs) and then integrate them (Sarason, 1966). Others feel that it is less vital to consider what we call theory than to discover what theory can do for us in ordering data (Rychlak, 1968).

Cattell wisely notes that "A widespread human tendency has been to believe that *because there is one word, there must be one thing.* . . ." In his opinion personality must be defined and studied via a multivarious process. To define personality with words alone can be grossly inefficient because words are imprecise instruments. He further feels that "Theories are all things to all men" (Wepman and Heine, 1963; italics added). It should be noted, perhaps, that antics with semantics may be the personologist's continuing curse: man communicates with man primarily by using words. Gestures, pictures, and mathematical symbols either are for the specialist, too loose in stereotyped understanding, or, in most instances, only need more words to reinforce them.

---

[1] Full bibliographical citations may be found at the end of the chapter in which they appear.

Many theories tend to become literary exercises because they have emerged from the pragmatic efforts of the therapist in the clinical setting rather than from the experimentally oriented academician dedicated to empirically deriving data out of replicable research (Rychlak, 1968). The former is faced with the pressing problem of alleviating emotional suffering. His interest is in a theory he feels is most efficient for his client's welfare. The latter manipulates operationally defined variables which may be tested statistically. The pragmatic value is secondary to protecting himself from attack by fellow researchers. Each takes a different stance, runs on a different track, and pursues a different goal. It is no wonder that personality and theory have many definitions.

The problem of defining terms is certainly not unique to the field of personality study. The word *electricity* appears to have no uniform definition, yet it is researched and used in our daily lives. The words *love, justice, learning, intelligence,* and many others fall prey to inconclusive definitions yet continue to be part of the language. Perhaps our efforts can best be expended in testing theory for the benefit of mankind rather than building word structures that are more fictional than factual. In the final analysis, there will be as many definitions of personality and its theory as there are personality theorists. The theories will continue to reflect the personalities of those who create them. On this factor alone a separate book could be written.

Some attempts have been made to classify definitions of personality, probably the earliest being Allport's in 1937. He suggested seven categories: biophysical, biosocial, unique, integrative, adjustment, differential essential, and omnibus (Allport, 1937). Other classifications differentiate between structure and dynamics, trait, and type, and idiographic/nomothetic series (*Annual Review,* 1965; Bischof, 1964; Hall and Lindzey, 1957; Schuh, 1966; Shaffer and Sinnett, 1964).[2]

No attempt is made in this text to discuss the basic propositions in theory formulation. Readers interested in this area are directed to the following sources: Allen, 1965; Bakan, 1967; Byrne, 1966; Farber, 1964; Horst, 1968; Hoxter, 1967; Kelly, 1964; Loehlin, 1968; Maddi, 1968; Marx, 1963; Marx and Hillix, 1963; Mehrabian, 1968a; Nash, 1965; Rychlak, 1968; Skinner, 1965; Spence, 1944; and Tamm, 1965. Especially recommended is Rychlak's *A Philosophy of Science for Personality Theory.*

One of the major problems in defining personality theory is the strong reluctance to acknowledge existing theories as true theories in a scientific model. Either they "cannot meet the criteria for truly scientific theory" (Sarason, 1966) or "existing theories are not theories at all" and therefore a

---

[2] As a graduate student the present writer once accumulated seventy-three different definitions of personality. Completing the assignment was the only satisfying element. Classifying the definitions proved to be of little value.

new language, new methods, and a "separate science of the person" is re-quired (Goldstone and Goldfarb, 1964; Shontz, 1965). The personologists now contemplate the question "When is a theory not a theory?" or "Is theory formulation to be different for each of the separations in science?" If these questions are accepted, it follows that definition is in the future.

On the other hand, Farber, in an extremely intuitive contribution, maintains that "any relatively comprehensive theory of behavior, especially if it contains variables of a motivational sort, qualifies as a theory of personality" (Farber, 1964).

The trend now may be toward the term *theory of behavior* or *behavior theory* rather than *personality theory*. Perhaps Allport is correct: we do not solve our problems, we only give new names to them (Bischof, 1964). Farber concludes his insightful discourse by looking forward to the day, which he does not expect to happen in his lifetime, "when personality theories are re-garded as historical curiosities." However, countering Allport's caustic com-ment, Farber anticipates that behavior theories will be more precise and com-prehensive and possibly replace the term *personality theory*, which he finds unable to incorporate empirical facts (Farber, 1964).

Does behavior theory grow out of facts while personality theory hopes to find facts to substantiate its existence? Only time and great effort will tell. In the meantime, definition is as elusive as ever.

Personality theories appear to be wider, looser, less organized, more complex, integumented, and deeply concerned with two facets of human life: individuality and motivation. Motivation is a core concept in many of the older formulations, which persist in asking "Why?" They are closer to a deductive rationale; they are rooted in experience with deviant populations.

In contrast are the behavior theories, expressed in operational terms with testable hypotheses, empirical orientation, and statistical treatment. They seem to ask the question "How?" They are closer to an inductive rationale and are rooted in learning theory and related interests.

Finally, the problem of definitions is compounded by the fact we do not even know what to call personality theorists. Very few, it appears, enjoy or seek *that* title. It smacks of armchair theorizing, which, as we have previously stated, is bad language in psychology. In the past, the theories grew out of experiences, primarily in therapy. Theory construction was the last thing in the minds of most therapists. Now the situation is taking a curious twist: some clinical psychologists appear to be disinterested in their training as therapists and wish strongly to ally themselves with more experimentally oriented psychologists, particularly clinical psychologists in academic settings. A researcher often receives more prestige and salary than a therapist on the university campus. Certainly he gets more free time, money in the form of grants, promotions, and the *sine qua non* of the professor's life: at least one journal article per year. Under this rather tight set of circumstances the professorial clinical psychologist promotes research in therapeutic techniques or in the broad but ill-defined area of personality. He produces journal articles in a manner well-nigh impossible for the therapist—except for the psycho-analytically oriented journals, where case studies still may appear. As a consequence, university course titles get changed from "Theories of Person-ality" (still a substantive field) to the euphemistic "Psychology of Person-ality" or just plain "Personality." A contradiction appears here because for years psychologists have striven to strike the prefix "Psychology of" from such curricular efforts in advertising, religion, individual differences, and even "Psychology of Learning."

The end result has been to re-create the title "personologist," which harks back to Murray and 1938. Still, to define what a personologist is, is as tricky and frustrating as to define personality or personality theory. *C'est la vie!*

PROBLEMS OF CONSTRUCTING AND USING PERSONALITY THEORIES

This section deals with problems in the kinds and functions of personality theories, what is wrong with personality theories, and what attempts have been suggested to purify them. Again, for the serious student interested in the intricacies of constructing scientific theories other sources are available. Two outstanding sources in this area are Byrne's *An Introduction to Personality: A Research Approach* and Rychlak's *A Philosophy of Science for Personality Theory.*

Most personality theories can be divided into two kinds: general or global theories and specific or small theories. The first attempts to generalize and bring together explorations and predictions of the whole human being in almost all situations at almost all levels of development; it wants to answer all the *why*'s of man. The second deals with specific and delimited behavioral acts so that an attainable goal of prediction may be reached.

The problems of the global theory are that it "breaks down of its own weight" and it is almost impossible "to pick out things to research in." The problem of the specific theoretical approach emphasizing data gathering is that it may "eventually just wind up gathering data but never finally come out with a theory" (Byrne, 1966; Rychlak, 1968; Sarason, 1966). The first is so broad that it becomes unusable and untestable. The second is like a mail-order catalogue: all the data are present but how do you categorize them? As stated previously, specific theory testing has more prestige because it is pub-lishable, receives grants, and provides the researcher with more satisfactory goals.

Cattell suggests that many a clinician "developed elaborate theories *all too soon* and they have plagued and misled him." Cattell introduces a continuum with "Skinner at one pole and philosophers at the other pole." He concludes by stating that theorizing is a must, "but it is a question of *when*" (Wepman and Heine, 1963; italics added).

Rychlak admits that the personologists have had an extremely difficult time "striving to remain within bounds of a type of science which did not completely meet their purposes." He feels that "man devised his scientific methods and he alone can adjust his thinking about how to use them most productively and usefully." Thus, we all must revise the way we think about the nature of scientific knowledge (Rychlak, 1968).

David Bakan's provocative but penetrating analysis concerns the all too frequent *a priori* assumptions that statistical analysis may demand. Bakan contends that research design and its consequent statistical treatment are a trap: It ignores data which do not fit the design, it is unable to contribute new knowledge, and it replicates only the most obvious (Bakan, 1967).

What should a theory do? What should it promote? How should it arrange the data? How should it function?

Maddi suggests that a good theory should be six things: important and not trivial, operational, parsimonious, stimulating, usable, and empirically valid (Maddi, 1968). Hall and Lindzey feel a theory should be simple and clear enough to be understandable, useful, able to bring data together in an orderly manner, able to clarify man's thinking, and able to predict events accurately (Hall and Lindzey, 1957).

Others suggest four functions of a theory: descriptive, delimiting, generative, and integrative (Rychlak, 1968). Idiographic and nomothetic approaches are emphasized, as well as typologies of extraversion/introversion and the usual classification of trait theories (*Annual Review*, 1965). N. M. Bradburn believes that an ideal personality theory should describe how personality forms and develops, how it functions in the adult, and what changes take place in it during the life cycle. He concludes that personality theory must also consider the cultural and social variables as well as the tasks (Wepman and Heine, 1963). Finally, Maddi finds most useful in personality theorizing the essentials of three kinds of models: conflict, fulfillment, and consistency (Maddi, 1968).

There appears to be no lack of critiques on what is wrong with current personality theories. Among major writers in the field, they range from Skinner's advocating that theory is unnecessary because facts speak for themselves (Skinner, 1965) to Spence's analysis that the fact that "theory construction has not always been intelligently pursued . . . is no reason for doing without theory" (Spence, 1944). Most writers on personality theory readily admit that this field is too ambitious, a mixture of hypotheses, generalizations, and loose specualtion, contemplative, romantic, a literary exercise, dramatic, overly concerned with deviancies, lacking in prediction, one-sided, frustrating, unamenable to research, irrelevant, overly eclectic, in prolonged infancy, a stimulating game, capricious, sentimental, and downright irritating! At the same time all responsible contributors are deeply concerned and are attempting to clarify the field in a truly dedicated sense (Byrne, 1966; Byrne and Hamilton, 1966; Farber, 1964; Lindzey and Hall, 1965; Laudin, 1961; Maddi, 1968; Mehrabian, 1968a, b; Mischel, 1968; Rychlak, 1968; Sahakian, 1965; Sarason, 1966; Shontz, 1965; Wepman and Heine, 1963).

Obviously, the living theorists are just as concerned, if not more so, with the refining of their own theoretical positions: Cattell and Eysenck (outstanding examples of productivity), Fromm, Maslow, Moreno, Mowrer, Murphy, Murray, and Rogers.

Purification or restructuring of personality theories and personality studies has not been wanting for lack of effort, as is evident from a few examples: Miller and Blum's models on information processing, ego psychology and all its exponents, including Hartmann's work on "conflict-free autonomous coping resources and Erikson's important concept of identity," Rogers and Angyal's self-concepts, and the newer work on the central nervous system functioning (*Annual Review*, 1967). In addition, we have the social learning system of Rotter, Janet Taylor Spence's interest in aligning learning theory and personality (Wepman and Heine, 1963), the prodigious efforts in multivariate approaches of Cattell (Chapter 12) and Eysenck (Chapter 13), and finally the mathematical models (Mehrabian, 1968b) and the emerging attempts to fit personality patterns into computer language and manipulation (Loehlin, 1968; Tomkins and Messick, 1963).

PROBLEMS OF THEORY TESTING

Assuming that the personologist has constructed a viable theory, what do he and others do with it? What are the problems in testing his or any other theory?

Whether the theory emerged from the cool comfort of the armchair theorizer or out of the hot, hurried harassment of the laboratory, there are problems. In this writer's opinion, one of the primary problems is the inability and/or reluctance of the researcher *adequately to study and learn the theory in the first place*. Too many theory testers have not bothered to master the theoretical concepts before they begin their experimental efforts. As we shall see in the subsequent sections on scientific prediction, this is unfair and regrettable. At least before one challenges the concepts of a theory he should understand the theory. *It is partially for this reason that the present text has been written.*

Probably the main difficulty in personality theory testing lies in the lack of researchable concepts in many theories. How could one responsibly create a research design to test Jung's synchronicity? Some theories border on the supernatural and metaphysical while others read more like fiction. The dedicated research psychologist is frustrated and irritated because his talents and tools are meant for something else.

A third problem emerges from the training most American psychologists receive. Emphasis, particularly in the doctoral dissertation, is often on replication. Too frequently this produces a stereotyped researcher, surrounded by instrumentation and statistical expertise, who sheeplike follows the academic crowd. It is almost impossible for him to break the training mold and still retain his hard-earned reputation in his narrow field. Often he has to conform in order to receive grants and have editors of professional journals accept his work. As mentioned before, he must get money and he must publish in order to survive professionally, especially in the academic field wherein most research takes place. Granting agencies and editors appear reluctant to support *avant-garde* experimentation. They too have professional status and reputations to maintain. The cycle locks the system into refinement of techniques and narrower and narrower replication. Advances may be limited.

As Gardner Murphy wisely pointed out, none of the new, revolutionary methods (cross-cultural, developmental, clinical, experimental, and quantitative) in studying behavior "was devised by a professional psychologist." "Most of the methods which have proved most novel and successful for personality study have come to us from biology, medicine, physiology, psychoanalysis, and mathematics." He feels further that our students are not taught as a rule to be creative in searching for methods. Also, "clinical training often can and does become a form of ossification. . . ." He concludes that we are reluctant to accept other contributions as psychological because a trained psychologist did not utter them. In short, "if it is published in the very newest edition of the *Journal of Experimental Psychology*, you can be very sure that it is psychology. Indeed now that we have a *Journal of Experimental Research and Personality*, we can be sure what is really psychology" (Norbeck *et al.*, 1968).

Other problems in theory testing revolve around the assumed dichotomy between the "gadget psychologist" and the "armchair theorist." Rychlak puts it this way:

> This is the image of the gadget psychologist—too busy collecting data to think, to deliberate, to question the usefulness of his research activity. Whereas the armchair theorist put the world together to suit his cogitations, *the gadget theoretician now puts the world together to suit his apparatus.* He multiplies his gadgets just as readily as his counterpart multiplies his homespun notions. Neither seems prepared to appreciate the orientation of the other. They do not understand each other, and fail to grasp that one errs on the side of the dialectic while the other errs on the side of demonstration. [Italics added]

One of them says all men are completely predictable scientifically, the other says man is too complex ever to be grasped fully by science.

It is not a question of which psychologist is right.

Complete reliance on either can only lead to emptiness of description and the decline of our science. Psychology will either slip into an inconsequential role as a minor technology waiting for some physical science to take the lead in explaining human nature or be completely swallowed up as a modern art form of some sort, related to literature and drama. (Rychlak, 1968)

Don Fiske notes a dichotomy between the theorist and the psychometrician in testing theories of personality:

It is unfortunate that the personality theorist usually has a temperament and a set of interests and values quite different from those of the psychometrician. There has been a lack of understanding and only a minimum of interaction between the people interested in measurement and those interested in studying personalities and in conceptualizing the personality domain.

Rarely is a theorist competent in measurement or a psychometrician sympathetic to the efforts of the conceptualizer.

Progress in the science of personality requires the rapprochement of theory and measurement. The theorist must define his constructs in explicit and complete form so that the experimental situation may be designed to assess them.

Only by close collaboration between the theorist and the methodologist can we determine to what extent it is possible to measure personality as it is construed today. (Wepman and Heine, 1963)

Cattell adds another dimension in theory testing by this timely contribution:

Theory-lovers think they have a final answer to this when they say, "People only investigate when they have a theory to test." They overlook the fact that the investigator may have several dozen theories or that his theories may be so broad as to amount virtually to a profound sense of curiosity.

Applying this observation to psychology, it can be argued that personality theory should be generated from dependable observations of correlational, quantitative, lawful relationships *when* they become visible in multivariant experimental data—rather than on the basis of casual, everyday observation and consulting on hunches.

The waste of putting new wine in old bottles is here to be avoided only if we recognize that new instruments require new theory, no longer confused with and tied down with the old. (Wepman and Heine, 1963)

Supporting a parallel position but with a dedicated feeling for Skinnerian operant and respondent conditions in that all personality follows S–R laws, Lundin makes this statement: "There is no reason to assume that the study of personality offers any new or unique problems for psychology. We can consider the study of personality to be a branch of the general field of learning which investigates, in particular, those processes significant to human adjustment" (Wepman and Heine, 1963).

In contrast to Lundin's position, we find another source with this statement:

> A sterner test is the theory's ability to interpret the behavior of persons over the whole range. For such a task, what is needed is not the isolation of presumed traits, but the specification of the conditions under which various tendencies are expressed.
>
> It is instructive to view the problem of specifying regulatory constancies from the stimulus-response perspective which has guided American psychology.
>
> The notion of a self-regulative, autonomous organism that is continuously in a state of activity violates the familiar premise that all behavior is a "response" and that a response is initiated by a stimulus from an initial baseline of rest.
>
> Psychologists find it difficult to conceive the possibility of an active tendency to perform a response without an immediately present stimulus, somewhere inside or outside of the subject, as the cause of trigger or instigation. Yet neurophysiologists . . . are beginning to yield a new picture, one in which an active brain selects what shall and shall not be the stimulus for it. (*Annual Review,* 1967)

Finally, J. McVickers Hunt finds testing theories must take into account the interactional approach because most of the variables in personality studies are attributable to situational factors (Hunt, 1965).

Thus, as we stated in the beginning of this section, there are problems in testing personality theories providing the researcher has the time and patience to learn the theory in the first place.

PROBLEMS OF RESEARCH METHODOLOGY

Admittedly there is not much difference between testing a theory (previous section) and methodology (this section). However, there are enough distinctions between (1) asking the questions and ordering the data and (2) the tools one uses to warrant a separate discussion.

One source highlights an interesting and provocative set of problems in personality research. In a section called "The Crisis in Methodology" the authors acknowledged the criticism as striking at the heart of methodology itself: "It challenges the validity of the experimental method itself; and it questions the ethics of contemporary research." One may assume that in too many representative studies in personality an experimenter "lies to" an undergraduate subject, who later is "debriefed," and presumably the damage to his self-esteem is corrected. Citing one study (Walster *et al.*, 1967) they find that "Subjects still behaved to some extent as though the de-briefing had not taken place." Aside from the question of ethics (not including invasion of privacy), the point is then made that an overwhelming number of investigations of personality use college undergraduates as subjects, admittedly not a representative group of human beings. The *Journal of Personality and Social Psychology* in four randomly selected issues in 1967 revealed that "90 percent of the papers published used undergraduates." A few papers about children were omitted. The remaining ones concerned subjects "equally atypical" and from captive groups. Thus, the cliché that "Psychology is the study of the college sophomore" may be a tired joke and almost an endearing eccentricity of the personality researcher, but it may mean that we "have insulated ourselves from an adequate recognition of the problem" of whether the subjects are volunteer or, in many cases, captive (*Annual Review*, 1969).

Fiske contributes a significant list of six "Problems in Measuring Personality." He states that "Measurement requires no theory." "Measurement is atheoretical but should not be anti-theoretical." In general, it is assumed that science (and particularly the concept of personality) "is a theoretical construction that exists in the minds of people, scientists and laymen." The six problems are as follows: inadequacies of defining personality, the fact that response tendencies are probabilistic and not yes/no responses, the specifistic nature of personality measurement, distortion caused by individuality, "the peculiar situation in which personality is measured," and how representative the population of subjects is (see preceding paragraph) (Wepman and Heine, 1963).

Byrne considers not so much the problems of research, although he wisely acknowledges all of them, but these five categories in personality as a field of research: measurement, development, structure, dynamics, and changes in personality. The personality psychologist as a researcher falls somewhere in between the clinician and the hard-core experimentalist. The orientation and methodology of the experimentalist is used, but the content is frequently different. Like the clinician, the personality psychologist is interested in the complex variables of persons but directs his efforts toward the normal rather than the abnormal (Byrne, 1966).

There exists also a unique reciprocity between theory and method—or at least there should. Theory may mandate method and method may delimit theory (*Annual Review*, 1967; Rychlak, 1968).

The methodological problems of measurement are also involved. Mischel points out that "a test may not measure anything beyond itself." Also, "personality is not capricious" although the research, the test, and the results may be. And finally, many personality tests are lengthy, expensive, and overly convoluted, hoping by an "inference process to generate descriptions or predictions that are readily available from cheaper, concurrent sources"[3] (Mischel, 1968).

Others feel that "psychometrists seem to have adopted no comprehensive theory of personality at all" although the situation may be changing and they now "show a far greater willingness to collaborate with personality theorists." If they do not, the result is a "proliferation of separate tests" that is no different from the "sum total scores on instruments catalogued in the Buros handbook" (Wepman and Heine, 1963).

Problems in personality research methodology do exist. The following listing highlights many of them.

1. Much research in personality takes place in the laboratory, and human beings do not act like experimental animals (Shontz, 1965).
2. The tendency to look for average performance "across individuals obscures the relevant variables that vary in effectiveness from person to person" (*Annual Review*, 1967).
3. ". . . methods and concepts have been borrowed . . ." from too widely divergent sources, so that personality may become "more a matter of sentiment rather than logic" (Mednick and Mednick, 1963).
4. Gardner Murphy reminds us that "science is made chiefly not by advance in content but by advance in method." Thus, there exists "a vast graveyard of psychological ideas stimulating and challenging in their own era but *without a method which could give them life* while even rather meager and humble experimentalists have proven capable of building a structure of experimental psychology" (Norbeck *et al.*, 1968; italics added).
5. ". . . our experiences in research seem to accumulate so much faster than our knowledge" (Borgatta and Lambert, 1968).
6. ". . . a computer simulation approach is not a theory in itself but it is rather a method using a computer as a tool to test and elaborate a theory of personality" (Mehrabian, 1968b).
7. ". . . there is a crisis in psychology . . . psychology should be empirical rather than experimental . . . good research means that one allows the investigation to be guided by the experiences of the investigator. This cannot be predicted. If it can be predicted, then there is little information to be obtained from the research; and considerable less reason to do the research . . . science should not presuppose what it is yet to discover" (Bakan, 1967).

In the final analysis perhaps physicist Niels Bohr's "concept of complementarity," which recognizes the existence of two explanations rather than one, is appropriate.

As yet, no one has improved upon Duhem's 1905 statement: "In physics the crucial experiment is impossible."

---

[3] The problem in psychology is not new. Many psychologists use a $25,000 piece of equipment to get a 25-cent answer, often with great statistical finesse. Others accumulate and hoard expensive equipment but are not always sure what to do with it.

METHODS OF PROCEDURE

The theories that follow have been presented within the general framework of description, explanation, and prediction. It will be obvious to the reader before he proceeds far in his study of the theories that description and explanation are much easier than prediction.

Description

The study of man's behavior often begins by attempts to describe accurately and adequately what man has done. Problems instantly arise. Most students of human behavior realize that if three people witness a single event, there are likely to be three different descriptions of what actually happened (Mehrabian, 1968b). Thus, this text has in its title the word *Interpreting* because it is trying to describe what each personality theory states in regard to human behavior. Other writers are concerned with description as a necessary first step to the "possible prediction of behavior rather than to elicit a feeling of understanding in those who read the description" (Byrne, 1966). Wallace feels that many theories of personality have failed to include the anthropological aspects of human behavior. He suggests that descriptions not be culturally restricted, that they be true for all species and not just human beings, that they be relevant to the group as well as the individual person, and that they be broad enough to include total representation (Norbeck *et al.*, 1963).

Explanation

Rychlak, in discussing the necessary functions of description in personality theory, further feels that "The descriptive function of theory encompasses explanation. To explain behavior is to describe fully the conditions under which it presumably varies. . . . Explanation is a matter of giving increasingly sophisticated descriptions of the empirical data at play before our eyes" (Rychlak, 1968).

Maddi deals with explanation and its justification as follows: "There is a very simple way to determine whether a theory is sufficiently precise. Try to use it for what it was intended. Try to apply to observations of people so as to understand them better. Or try to generate predictions concerning the behavior of particular kinds of people whom you have not yet observed" (Maddi, 1968).

Byrne adds to his very complete discussing of description, explanation, and prediction: "Explanation at any level of complexity is useful if it increases predictive accuracy" (Byrne, 1966).

Prediction (Control)

The stone wall of science has been and continues to be prediction. Knowledge which can deal with before-the-act predictions far outweighs in value to man knowledge which tells only why a certain act took place. We want to know whether the boat will stay afloat before we embark, not why it sank after we find ourselves immersed in water.

In the present text prediction, with its overtones of control—or in some specific instances replicability of the research—constitutes the latter portion of each chapter on the major theorists.

The words of the late great physicist Robert Oppenheimer, delivered to the American Psychological Association at its 1955 convention in San Francisco, are still extremely pertinent: "The psychologist can hardly do anything without realizing that for him the acquisition of knowledge opens up the terrifying prospects of controlling what people do and how they feel. . . . I can see that the physicist's pleas that what he discovers be used with humanity and be used wisely will seem trivial compared to those pleas which you will have to make and for which you will have to be responsible" (Oppenheimer, 1956).

Rychlak finds at least three misunderstandings which may arise in the personality psychologist's distinctions and the use of the terms *control* and *prediction:* problems of their being part of the theory of knowledge, problems of their being simply language in theoretical description, and the usual problems of controlling society, which borders on the realm of ethics (Rychlak, 1968).

One major contribution consists of an entire book written on the manipulation of human behavior (Biderman and Zimmer, 1961).

Finally, Mischel feels that self-prediction has often worked relatively well. He cites, for example, a person's ability to predict whether or not he can be hypnotized, cases in which psychiatric patients were able to predict the behavior of other patients almost as well as the professional psychiatric staff, and college students' predicting their own grades just about as well as did other available predictors. He thinks that possibly the best predictor of future adjustment is the individual's previous adjustment (Mischel, 1968).

BIBLIOGRAPHY

PRIMARY SOURCES

BOOKS

Allen, R. M., *Variables in Personality Theory and Personality Testing: An Interpretation*. Springfield, Ill.: Thomas, 1965.

Allport, G. W., *Personality: A Psychological Interpretation*. New York: Holt, Rinehart & Winston, 1937.

Bakan, D., *On Method Toward a Reconstruction of Psychological Investigation*. San Francisco: Jossey-Bass, 1967.

Biderman, A. D., and H. Zimmer, *The Manipulation of Human Behavior*. New York: Wiley, 1961.

Bischof, L. J., *Interpreting Personality Theories*. New York: Harper & Row, 1964.

Borgatta, E. F., and W. W. Lambert (eds.), *Handbook of Personality and Research*. Chicago: Rand McNally, 1968.

Byrne, D., *An Introduction to Personality: A Resea·ch Approach*. Englewood Cliffs, N.J.: Prentice-Hall, 1966.

Byrne, D., and M. L. Hamilton (eds.), *Personality Research: A Book of Readings*. Englewood Cliffs, N.J.: Prentice-Hall, 1966.

Farber, I. E., A framework for the study of personality as a behavior science, in P. Worchel and D. Byrne (eds.), *Personality Change*. New York: Wiley, 1964, pp. 3–37.

Hall, C. S., and G. Lindzey, *Theories of Personality*. New York: Wiley, 1957.

Horst, Paul, *Personality: Measurement of Dimensions*. San Francisco: Jossey-Bass, 1968.

Kluckhohn, C., H. A. Murray, and D. M. Schneider (eds.), *Personality in Nature, Society, and Culture*, 2nd ed., New York: Knopf, 1964.

Lindzey, G., and C. S. Hall (eds.), *Theories of Personality: Primary Sources and Research*. New York: Wiley, 1965.

Loehlin, J. C., *Computer Models of Personality*. New York: Random House, 1968.

    Compares to traditional theories.

Lundin, R. W., *Personality: An Experimental Approach*. New York: Macmillan, 1961.

Maddi, S. R., *Personality Theories: A Comparative Analysis*. Homewood, Ill.: Dorsey Press, 1968.

Marx, M. H. (ed.), *Theories in Contemporary Psychology*. New York: Macmillan, 1963.

Marx, Melvin H., and W. A. Hillix, *Systems and Theories of Psychology*. New York: McGraw-Hill, 1963, p. 489.

Mednick, M. T., and S. A. Mednick (eds.), *Research in Personality*. New York: Holt, Rinehart & Winston, 1963.

Mehrabian, A., *Personality Theories: Models for the Description, Prediction and Influence of Interpersonal Behavior*. Englewood Cliffs, N.J.: Prentice-Hall, 1968a.

Mehrabian, A., *An Analysis of Personality Theories*. Englewood Cliffs, N.J.: Prentice-Hall, 1968b.

Millon, T. (ed.), *Approaches to Personality*. New York: Pitman, 1968.

Mischel, W., *Personality and Assessment*. New York: Wiley, 1968.

Norbeck, E., D. Price-Williams, and W. M. McCord (eds.), *The Study of Personality, an Interdisciplinary Appraisal*. New York: Holt, Rinehart & Winston, 1968.

Rychlak, J. F., *A Philosophy of Science for Personality Theory*. Boston: Houghton Mifflin, 1968.

> Chap. 6 excellent on the enigmas of control and prediction.

Sahakian, W. S. (ed.), *Psychology of Personality: Readings in Theory*. Chicago: Rand McNally, 1965.

Sarason, I. G., *Contemporary Research in Personality*. Princeton, N.J.: Van Nostrand, 1962.

Sarason, I. G., *Personality, An Objective Approach*. New York: Wiley, 1966.

Shontz, F. C., *Research Methods in Personality*. New York: Appleton-Century-Crofts, 1965.

Skinner, B. F., *Science and Human Behavior*. New York: Free Press, 1965.

Tomkins, S. S., and S. Messick (eds.), *Computer Simulation of Personality*. New York: Wiley, 1963.

> Papers and critiques from a 1962 conference on the subject.

Wepman, J. M., and R. W. Heine (eds.), *Concepts of Personality*. Chicago: Aldine, 1963.

> An excellent survey of classic and contemporary personality theory. Includes chapters on basic processes—learning, perception, genetics, and drive theory; on the major analytical approaches to psychology and psychiatry; on anthropological and sociological contributions; and on the problems of measurement and assessment.

PERIODICALS

Bakan, D., The test of significance in psychological research, *Psychol. Bull.*, 1966, 66, 423–437.

Goldstone, S., and I. L. Goldfarb, Adaptation level, personality theory, and psychopathology, *Psychol. Bull.*, 1964, 61, 176–187.

Hoxter, A. L., Theory confirmation and the study of behavior: Some problems, *Alberta J. Educ. Res.*, 1967, *13*, 143–161.

> "The basic elements of theory formulation, the purpose of theories, the relationship of theories to the aims of science, and the role of models in psychological theory."

Hunt, J. McV., Traditional personality theory in light of recent evidence, *Amer. Scientist*, 1965, *53*, 80–96.

Kelly, G. A., The language of hypothesis: Man's psychological instrument, *J. Indiv. Psychol.*, 1964, *20*, 137–152.

Nash, H., Mixed metaphor in personality theory, *J. Nerv. Ment. Dis.*, 1965, *140*, 384–388.

> "Given the mixed metaphor's role in science it seems inadvisable to reject concepts and theories in haste merely because they are rooted in mixed imagery."

Oppenheimer, J. Robert, Analogy in science, *Amer. Psychologist*, 1956, *11*, 126–135.

Schuh, A. J., A synthesis of personality theories by cluster analysis, *J. Psychol.*, 1966, *64*, 69–71.

> Reduces Hall and Lindzey's eighteen variables (on seventeen personality theories) to four basic dimensions: (1) usefulness of self concept in changing behavior, (2) importance of self concept, (3) amount of change which is possible, (4) complexity of the process of change.

Shaffer, J. P., and E. R. Sinnett, A factor analysis of Hall and Lindzey's ratings of personality theories, *Acta Psychol.* (Amsterdam), 1964, *22*, 135–144.

> Finds five factors as meaningful orderings of personality theories.

Spence, K. W., The nature of theory construction in contempoary psychology, *Psychol. Rev.*, 1944, *51*, 47–68.

Tamm, U., Human personality, *Res. J. Phil. Soc. Sci.*, 1965, *2*, 38–49.

Walster, E., E. Berscheid, D. Abrahams, and V. Aronson, Effectiveness of debriefing following deception experiments, *J. Pers. Soc. Psychol.*, 1967, *6*, 371–380.

SUGGESTED READINGS

BOOKS

Annual Review of Psychology. Palo Alto, Cal.: Annual Reviews, Inc.

Sears, R. R., Personality, 1950, *1*, 105–118.
MacKinnon, D. W., Personality, 1951, *2*, 113–136.
Eysenck, H. J., Personality, 1952, *3*, 155–174.
Bronfenbrenner, U., Personality, 1953, *4*, 157–182.

Child, I. L., Personality, 1954, 5, 149–170.
Nuttin, J., Personality, 1955, 6, 161–186.

Personality study becoming a new approach to general psychology of human behavior.

McClelland, D. C., Personality, 1965, 7, 39–62.

Broad review of personality literature to 1955.

Eriksen, C. W., Personality, 1957, 8, 185–210.

Over 500 articles on personality between May, 1955, and April, 1956; author reviews 173 of them.

Jensen, A. R., Personality, 1958, 9, 295–322.

Review of entire field to April, 1957; extensive bibliography.

Blake, R. R., and J. S. Mouton, Personality, 1959, 10, 203–232.
Atkinson, J. W., Personality dynamics, 1960, 11, 255–290.
Messick, S., Personality-structure, 1961, 12, 93–128.
Jenness, A., Personality dynamics, 1962, 13, 479–514.
Christie, R., and F. Lindauer, Personality structure, 1963, 14, 201–230.
London, P., and D. Rosenhan, Personality dynamics, 1964, 15, 447–492.
Holtzman, W. H., Personality structure, 1965, 16, 119–156.
Klein, G. S., H. L. Barr, and D. L. Wolitzky, Personality, 1967, 18, 467–560.
Wiggins, H. S., Personality structure, 1968, 19, 293–350.
Adelson, J., Personality, 1969, 20, 217–252.
Barker, S. F., *Induction and Hypothesis: A Study of the Logic of Confirmation.* Ithaca, N.Y.: Cornell University Press, 1957.
Baughman, E. E., and G. S. Welsh, *Personality: A Behavioral Science.* Englewood Cliffs, N.J.: Prentice-Hall, 1962.
Bech, H. R., Personality theories and behavior therapy, in B. M. Foss (ed.), *New Horizons in Psychology.* Baltimore: Penguin, 1966, 349–358.
Blum, G. S., Programming people to simulate machines, in S. S. Tomkins and S. Messick (eds.), *Computer Simulation of Personality.* New York: Wiley, 1963.
Brand, H. (ed.), *The Study of Personality: A Book of Readings.* New York: Wiley, 1954.
Bronfenbrenner, U., Toward an integrated theory of personality, in R. R. Blake and G. V. Ramsey (eds.), *Perception: An Approach to Personality.* New York: Ronald, 1951.
Buckley, W. (ed.), *Modern Systems Research for the Behavioral Scientist.* Chicago: Aldine, 1968.
David, H. P., and J. C. Brengelmann (eds.), *Perspective in Personality Research.* New York: Springer, 1960.
Dreger, R. M., *Fundamentals of Personality.* Philadelphia: Lippincott, 1962.
Fiske, D. W., Problems in measuring personality, in J. M. Wepman and R. W. Heine (eds.), *Concepts of Personality.* Chicago: Aldine, 1963.

Helson, H., *Adaptation-Level Theory*. New York: Harper & Row, 1964.

Herrnstein, R. J., and E. G. Boring, *A Source Book in the History of Psychology*. Cambridge, Mass.: Harvard University Press, 1965.

Holt, R. R., A clinical-experimental strategy for research in personality, in S. Messick and J. Ross (eds.), *Measurement in Personality and Cognition*. New York: Wiley, 1962.

Janis, I. L. (ed.), *Personality: Dynamics, Development, and Assessment*. New York: Harcourt, Brace & World, 1969.

Kleinmuntz, B., *Personality Measurement, An Introduction*. Homewood, Ill.: Dorsey Press, 1967.

Kluckhohn, C., H. A. Murray, and D. M. Schneider (eds.), *Personality in Nature, Society and Culture*, 2nd ed. New York: Knopf, 1964.

Also contains contributions by Allport, Erikson, and Fromm.

Lecky, P., *Self-Consistency: A Theory of Personality*. New York: Island Press, 1945.

"Personality is the central fact of psychology."

Loehlin, J. C. A., Computer program that simulates personality, in S. S. Tomkins and S. Messick (eds.), *Computer Simulation of Personality*. New York: Wiley, 1963, pp. 189–211.

McCarey, J. (ed.), *Psychology of Personality: Six Modern Approaches*. New York: Logos Press, 1956.

Also issued by Grove Press.

Maher, B. (ed.), *Progress in Experimental Personality Research*, Vol. II. New York: Academic Press, 1965.

Notcutt, B., *The Psychology of Personality*. New York: Philosophical Library, 1953.

Critique of Anglo-American personality theories; attempts to develop a "theory of theories" in personality study.

Ruitenbeek, H. M. (ed.), *Varieties of Personality Theory*. New York: Dutton, 1964.

Sanford, N., Personality: Its place in psychology, in S. Koch (ed.), *Psychology: A Study of a Science*, 5. New York: McGraw-Hill, 1963.

Smelser, N. J., and W. T. Smelser (eds.), *Personality and Social Systems*. New York: Wiley, 1963.

Smith, H. C., *Personality Development*. New York: McGraw-Hill, 1968.

Southwell, E. A., and M. Merbaum (eds.), *Personality Readings in Theory and Research*. Belmont, Cal.: Wadsworth, 1964.

Spence, J. T., Learning theory and personality, in J. M. Wepmen and R. W. Heine (eds.), *Concepts of Personality*. Chicago: Aldine, 1963.

Stagner, R., *Psychology of Personality*, 3rd ed. New York: McGraw-Hill, 1961.

Thorpe, L. P., and A. M. Schmuller, *Personality: An Interdisciplinary Approach*. Princeton, N.J.: Van Nostrand, 1958.

Eclectic treatment of personality.

Vernon, P. E., *Personality Assessment: A Critical Survey*. New York: Wiley, 1964.

PERIODICALS

Alexander, P., Theory construction and theory testing, *Brit. J. Phil. Sci.*, 1958, 9, 29–38.

> Phenomenology is more than a means of testing a theory—it is something to be explained.

Atkinson, J. W., and D. Cartwright, Some neglected variables in contemporary conceptions of decision and performances, *Psychol. Rep.*, 1964, 14, 575–590.

Beck, S. J., The science of personality: Nomothetic or idiographic, *Psychol. Rev.*, 1953, 60, 353–359.

Beshers, J. M., Models and theory construction, *Amer. Sociol. Rev.*, 1957, 22, 32–3.

Blum, G. S., J. Geiwitz, and C. G. Stewart, Cognitive arousal: The evolution of a model, *J. Pers. Soc. Psychol.*, 1967, 5, 138–151.

Borgatta, E. F., Toward a methodological codification: The shotgun and the saltshaker, *Sociometry*, 1961, 24, 432–435.

> Theorizing may have to come after the fact.

Dreikurs, R., Are psychological schools of thought outdated? *J. Indiv. Psychol.*, 1960, 16, 3–10.

> Schools of personality theory are needed.

Fisher, J., The twisted pear and the prediction of behavior, *J. Consult. Psychol.*, 1959, 23, 400–405.

> Mathematics often inappropriate in predicting human behavior; human beings are too complex.

Fisher, M. B., and R. M. Roth, Structure: An essential framework for research, *Personnel Guid. J.*, 1961, 39, 639–644.

> Relates research to theory.

Fiske, D. W., Homogeneity and variation in measuring personality, *Amer. Psychologist*, 1963, 18, 643–652.

> "Let those of us who are interested in methodology work more closely with personality theorists. . . ."

Franck, I., The concept of human nature: A philosophical analysis of the concept of human nature in the writings of G. W. Allport, S. E. Asch, Erich Fromm, A. H. Maslow, and C. R. Rogers, *Dissert. Abstr.*, 1966, 27, 1079.

Grace, H. A., When is science? *Educ. Rev.*, 1957, 7, 93–101.

> Psychology uses three techniques: (1) discovery—laboratory experimentation; (2) uncovery—testing or interviewing; (3) recovery—symbol analysis: "An investigation is scientific when the method it employs is appro-

priate to the problem it seeks to solve." The scientist may choose any one but not all.

Holt, R. R., Individuality and generalization in the psychology of personality, *J. Pers.*, 1962, *30*, 377–404.

Kemeny, J. H., and P. Oppenheim, Systematic power, *Phil. Sci.*, 1955, *22*, 27–33.

The measure of the theory is its ability to explain and predict facts.

Krasner, L., Behavior control and social responsibility, *Amer. Psychologist*, 1962, *17*, 199–203.

New, important, useful development.

Levy, L. H., Personal constructs and predictive behavior, *J. Abnorm. Soc. Psychol.*, 1956, *53*, 54–58.

Research on predicting and controlling one's own behavior.

Lynn, D. B., The organism as a manufacturer of theories. *Psychol. Rep.*, 1957, *3*, 353–359.

All men learn by theories.

Malmquist, C. P., Problems of methodology and theory construction in psychoanalysis, *Psychoanal. Rev.*, 1963, *50*, 3–23.

Meehl, P. W., Theory testing in psychology and physics: A methodological paradox, *Phil. Sci.*, 1967, *34*, 103–115.

Morison, R. S., Gradualness, gradualness, gradualness, *Amer. Psychologist*, 1960, *15*, 187–197.

Pavlov's injunction to scientific method and theories; Morison asks for closer relations between theory and practice.

Rescher, N., On prediction and explanation, *Brit. J. Phil. Sci.*, 1958, *8*, 281–290.

Logically, prediction and explanation are vastly different.

Roby, T. B., An opinion on the construction of behavior theory, *Amer. Psychologist*, 1959, *14*, 129–134.

Rogers, C. R., Implications of recent advances in prediction and control of human behavior, *Teachers Coll. Rec.*, 1956, *57*, 316–322.

Rogers, C. R., The place of the person in the new world of the behavioral sciences, *Personnel Guid. J.*, 1961, *39*, 442–451.

Control of human behavior.

Rogers, C. R., and B. F. Skinner, Some issues concerning the control of human behavior: A symposium, *Science*, 1965, *124*, 1057–1066.

Rogers and Skinner disagree.

Rokeach, M., and S. H. Bartley, Some pitfalls in psychological theorizing, *Amer. Psychologist*, 1958, *13*, 283–284.

Think before you dream up a new term. Is it necessary or does it add to the confusion?

Rosenfeld, L. M., and N. Orlinsky, The effect of research on practice: Research and decrease in noncontinuance, *Arch. Gen. Psychiat.*, 1961, 5, 176–182.

> Keep a "research diary."

Rosenthal, R., Training students in personality theory, *Amer. Psychologist*, 1958, 13, 605–606.

> Personality theory course is fundamental in training clinical psychologists.

Royce, J. B., Toward the advancement of theoretical psychology, *Psychol. Rep.*, 1957, 3, 401–410.

> Desirable to have deducted experimentally verifiable mathematic equations for behavioral phenomena in mid-twentieth century, but present status indicates we are using methods that are inductive rather than deductive, qualitative vis-à-vis quantitative, empirical rather than removed from observations; need low-level elementary type of theorizing.

Rychlak, J. F., Reinforcement value: A suggested idiographic, intensity dimension of meaningfulness for the personality theorist, *J. Pers.*, 1966, 34, 311–335.

Scheffler, I., Explanation, prediction and abstraction, *Brit. J. Phil. Sci.*, 1957, 7, 293–309.

> Explanation and prediction are distinct from each other.

Sewell, W. H., Some observations on theory testing, *Rural Sociol.*, 1956, 21, 1–12.

> Need for empirical testing of complex behavior theories; Freud is tested and found wanting.

Shapiro, M. B., The single case in fundamental clinical psychology research, *Brit. J. Med. Psychol.*, 1961, 34, 255–262.

> Research should center on the individual, not groups.

Stephenson, W., Perspectives in psychology: A note on the methodology of clinical explanation, *Psychol. Rec.*, 1962, 12, 101–103.

Strunk, Orlo, Jr., Insights on human personality gained within psychology in the past seventy-five years, *Relig. Educ.*, 1964, 59, 283–294.

> Reviews experimental and theoretical research on human personality with a view to giving perspective in religious education.

Trankell, A., The psychologist as an instrument of prediction, *J. Appl. Psychol.*, 1959, 43, 170–175.

> Clinical prediction better than statistical for Swedish air pilots.

Ulrich, R. E., T. J. Stachnick, and S. R. Stainton, Student acceptance of generalized personality interpretations, *Psychol. Rep.*, 1963, 13, 831–834.

> College students took personality inventory, but all were given identical report and they agreed it was accurate.

Part

II

Psychoanalytical–
Psychophilosophical

THIS SECTION BEGINS with the work of Sigmund Freud. Any book on personality theory has to start with Freud or end with Freud. Although he is often referred to as the father of psychoanalysis, he may also be called the father of personality theory. Almost all the other theorists take off from the basic premises of Freud (Jung, Adler, Horney, Sullivan, etc.); they can often be best explained by the manner in which they depart from Freud.

Sheldon has been put into a separate section (Part V: Psychobiological). This change from the previous edition may appear more logical as time and research continue. It is the writer's belief that many advances may come through the efforts of psychobiologists and psychoneurologists, the point being that research on man's physical and neurological systems will supersede Sheldon's work. Meantime, as a personality theorist he stands alone: the body and behavior are uniquely related to each other.

H. A. Murray seems to fit comfortably between the theories of Freud and Jung. Murray knows how to use both yet creates a system all his own.

Again it must be repeated that the order of chapter presentation is a device, not a doctrine.

2

FREUD

Amoebas at the start
Were not complex;
They tore themselves apart
And started Sex.

      ARTHUR GUITERMAN
      Sex, Stanza 1*

SOME BIOGRAPHICAL DATA

Two excellent books contain perceptive biographies of Freud. The first is a short autobiography entitled *An Autobiographical Study,* which Freud wrote in 1935 and others revised in 1946. In this book Freud cleverly interweaves his adult years as a person and the development of his theories. The second is an outstanding work by one of Freud's closest associates, especially in his later years. Ernest Jones, who died in 1959 and who, some say, kept himself alive

* From *The Light Guitar,* Harper & Row, 1923, p. 15. Reprinted by permission of Mrs. Guiterman.

long enough to complete his task, wrote a brilliant and thorough account of Freud's life which was issued in three volumes (1953, 1955, 1958).

In Freud's words, "I was born on May 6th, 1856, at Freiberg in Moravia, a small town in what is now Czechoslovakia. My parents were Jews, and I have remained a Jew myself" (*An Autobiographical Study*). At the age of four Freud moved to Vienna, where he eventually became a medical student and received his medical degree in 1881. During his student days the severe ostracism he met as a Jew helped him in later years to withstand the gibes of the world because he had learned to inure himself to the displeasure of others. After a short period lacking direction he became a researcher in the Institute of Cerebral Anatomy and thus began to be interested in man's mental nature. He left the Institute because his growing family needed more financial support than his assistantship could provide and he went into private practice. Freud's friendship with Joseph Breuer, his year of work with Charcot in France in hypnotic techniques, which he found to be very limited, and his return to develop a cathartic, "talking out" technique with Breuer were all precursors of his psychoanalytic work. From about 1890 to 1900 Freud was a "loner," having broken with Breuer, who could not accept Freud's emphasis on sexual factors in the analysis of hysterics. Also, as a consequence of his holding stubbornly to his beliefs, he was eliminated from the ranking medical organization of his day. These were lonely years, but in his private practice he gained the autonomy of spirit which enabled him to depart from the thinking of the day and create his own theoretical position.

After 1900 Freud began to attract more and more attention, although most of it was negative, from the general populace. His fame, however, brought him the first of the dedicated followers who were to help him inaugurate in 1910 the International Psychoanalytic Association. Early associates with Freud were Carl Jung, assistant to Bleuler at the Burgholzli in Zurich, Switzerland, Alfred Adler of Vienna, Brill of New York, Jones of England, and Ferenczi of Budapest. In 1909 Freud and Jung were invited by G. Stanley Hall to attend the twentieth anniversary of Clark University in Worcester, Massachusetts, as guest lecturers. Freud says, "As I stepped on to the platform at Worcester to deliver my 'Five Lectures upon Psycho-Analysis' it seemed like some incredible daydream: psycho-analysis was no longer a product of delusion, it had become a valuable part of reality."

Later Freud faced the defections of Adler, Jung, Rank, and Stekel. The denial of Jung was an especially bitter blow.

In 1930 two events occurred which pleased Freud very much. Thomas Mann included him as an acknowledged influence in the history of modern thought. This recognition made Freud feel he was vindicated. The second event Freud describes as follows: "A little later my daughter Anna, acting as my proxy, was given a civic reception in the Rathaus at Frankfort-on-Main on the occasion of my being awarded the Goethe prize for 1930. This was the climax of my life as a citizen." Shortly afterward, with the advent of Hitlerian policies in Germany, Freud was forced to curtail his activities and eventually in regular spy-thriller manner to escape. Jones was instrumental in bringing him to London for his remaining years. From the middle 1920s on, Freud suffered from an advancing cancerous state of the throat. His last years were spent in considerable pain, but he was uncomplaining. He died on September 23, 1939, at 20 Maresfield Gardens, London, in a charming home where his daughter Anna continues to live. A plaque on the side of the home commemorates his residence and death there.

INTRODUCTION

There is a unique parallel between the careers of Freud and of other intellectual giants. Freud, Darwin, Einstein, Dewey all pioneered certain aspects of their professional fields, lived rather long and certainly productive lives, lived long enough to explain the "explainers" of their theoretical concepts, and in some instances went through periods of vilification and strong criticism of their then new ideas (Karier, 1963). Each attracted to himself a coterie of followers who became so dedicated as to approximate a cult of devotees. True, this was not so apparent in the case of Einstein, whose followers were more mentally *en rapport* than "worshipers in the temple."

It should be emphasized that the following is an interpretation of Freud's ideas circumscribed by the present author's viewpoint. The sophisticated reader will feel that many things have been left out of Freud's writings as they are here interpreted. This is certainly the case. The writer has used rough but definable criteria for the extraction of principles from Freud's works: (1) Does the theme of the principle actually occur in his writings and not in that of the neo-Freudians, who, although they have contributed invaluably to furthering his work, especially in the area of psychoanalytic practice, can also be classed as interpreters of his writing? (The term *writing* must be used here since that is the medium at the disposal of all of us.) Freud actually collaborated with no one in his development of personality theory in the present-day sense of our modern clinics, although he did correspond with and discuss his work quite intimately with a few close associates (Breuer, Jones, his daughter Anna, to name but a few). What we know mainly about his work and theoretical position is what he wrote about them. Some few authors suggest an intimacy with his thinking which in fact did not exist. They, too, are held to be interpreters of what he wrote despite disclaimers. (2) Does the principle help to weld together the ideas that he so interestingly presented in his numerous contributions and form them into a meaningful whole which advances the understanding of his theoretical concepts without undue distortion? (All interpreters distort to some degree. That is the nature of the beast—one religious sect vis-à-vis another in regard to the

Bible, the profuse interpreters of Shakespeare, etc.) (3) Is the principle of large enough proportions to be considered as such and not as simple explanatory material? (4) Does it concern itself primarily with a theory of personality, rather than with a theory of psychoanalytic therapy? (5) Does it meet the basic definition of a principle as traditionally accepted?

FREUD'S DESCRIPTION OF HUMAN BEHAVIOR

Although Freud did not set down any clear-cut principles in his brilliant and readable writing, the interpreter can deduce certain fundamental concepts so important to his theory as to constitute principles of man's behavior.

Pleasure Principle

Probably foremost of the so-called principles in Freud's approach is that of man as a pleasure-seeking animal. In this we do not use the concept in its hedonistic, philosophical connotation that it is a "duty" to seek pleasure, but rather in the broader psychological connotation that every act is *motivated* by the desire for pleasure and to some degree by the avoidance of pain.

Thus, man's *raison d'être* in this world is to make and keep things as pleasant as possible—not the same thing as the college sophomore's "Let's live it up, for you only live once." Freud would probably eschew the use of pleasure as a principle to excuse unrestrained appetites and gross immorality. For whatever his critics have leveled at Freud, the charge of immorality is a false charge. He was a highly moral individual who considered any use of sex not for procreation almost an act of perversion. Consonant with the desire to have as pleasant a life as possible is the underlying theme that man must consequently seek to avoid painful experiences. If he does meet painful experiences, he must reduce the pain or, failing this, avoid meeting them again if at all possible.

Being in a pleasant state of existence, then, is a basic principle of Freud's but it describes how man acts and not necessarily why. As the reader is aware, we shall attempt to develop the *why* in a later section devoted to explaining man's behavior, and subsequently to see whether this theory can help us *predict* man's behavior, either through personal experience (introspectively) or through the research which has been done in the behavioral sciences.

Psychologists call being happy a state of *euphoria*. Much has been written about man's wanting to be as happy as possible. The thought occurs even in the Preamble to the United States Constitution in the phrase *the pursuit of happiness*. To this we may assume that Freud would have agreed. Freud would possibly have agreed most heartily because of the word *pursuit*, which our early political scientists used. To Freud pleasure or happiness was not a goal so much as it was the motivating force behind human existence.

Without having to look far, we find examples in almost every minute of our waking life (and to Freud in our sleeping life, as we shall see later in touching upon dream analysis). All of the advertising efforts surrounding us, our most cherished contacts with family and friends, the television we watch, the movies we see, the sports we indulge in, the books we read, and the avocations we pursue seem to center around "having fun." Witness how the average public shuns a losing team, a "sad" play or movie, and pointedly avoids contact with people who "give us a bad time." Personnel psychologists overwhelmingly list as the number one reason for loss of job the inability to get along with people or make them like one.

Thus, to accept man in Freudian terms as a pleasure-seeking animal wanting to avoid pain does not stretch our imagination greatly. We shall find in studying Freud's polarity principle that pain itself may be a substitutive form for pleasure. At the moment this idea may stretch the imagination, but after studying it more carefully and examining illustrations from everyday life, we may be willing to accept this too.

Reality Principle

Not necessarily second in importance but the second to be examined is Freud's later principle that man not only seeks pleasure but is bound by limits of reality which tell him that upon occasion he must postpone an immediate pleasure in favor of a future, more important pleasure. He thus still seeks pleasure but is also realistic and creates a hierarchical ranking of pleasure: Later pleasures judged more important take precedence over current ones deemed less important. For example, take the present moment as you are reading these words. You would probably much prefer being at the student union with your friends, being home and making money, being at the movies, being with your fiancée, doing *anything* but reading about Freud because that is the assignment. Why then do you persist? Because, says Freud, you may be described as a reality-principle-motivated human being. You desire a college degree, a passing mark, some goal which keeps you at this page rather than allowing you to go toward a more immediate and possibly more pleasant objective. We all sense, therefore, that life is bounded by rules which, if followed, will create for us other pleasures.

Subsequent pages will introduce the concepts of instinct and learned behavior. For the present the principle of reality is regarded as learned and not inborn or instinctual. Whereas a child comes into life already equipped with the pleasure principle, only through the lessons of life and the guidance and direction of adults responsible for his upbringing does he acquire the sense of reality in his dealings with self and the environment. It may surprise some readers to discover that Freud did not ignore environment as an influence on human behavior. Thus, attaining a sense of reality applies both to man's inner appetites exclusive of the outer world and to those appetites admittedly within himself but fostered and given to him by his environment. By way of illustration: Hunger and thirst and sexual appetite may be considered to spring from the inner self. The desire for an automobile, for television, and for myriad other things may be considered to have been brought about by contact with one's environment. Hunger knows no social order or ethical flavor, but automobiles and television are components of environment. As any discerning reader may see, however, inner appetites can be and often are manipulated by outer factors—man's sexual appetites being aroused by sensual stimulae in the environment, for instance.

Tension Reduction Principle

Closely allied with the previous two principles (pleasure and reality) is the principle of *tension reduction*. Its closeness is evident when one realizes that some mechanism must be available for going between the extremes of pleasure and reality, especially when, in their most advanced forms, they conflict. Looking to the field of physics and the treatment of material things, we perceive that any object being pulled in two opposite directions will become taut or tense. Metallurgists use the term *tensile strength* in describing this property of steel. Pull a rope or rubber band, and you can see the same phenomenon operating more vividly. Consequently the Freudian principle subsumes that man will become tightened up in somewhat the same fashion when he too is being pulled from two diametric fields. In this sense, then, the material, man, is not in a happy state but in an unhappy one because pressure tears him apart. The way to avoid this painful force is to reduce it, to remove it, or to become so strong that the pressure becomes relatively weak and tolerable.

Because man cannot ignore that which came to him from birth (pleasure principle) and because man must face reality, both inner and environmental (reality principle), tension is a *sine qua non* of his existence. It becomes necessary for him to reduce this tension in the best way he can or succumb to it and be destroyed by it. He may be described as a tension-reducing animal.

Polarity or Duality Principle

At least for the writer the polarity principle has enormous possibilities for theorizing as well as for speculation about man. This particular principle derived from Freud's writing is not clearly labeled by him or apparent from his work. Rather it is our own device for interpreting and attempting to clarify Freud's theories. Weaving in and out of his writings is the concept of two opposing forces forever present in man's life. Everything in life, therefore, is manifest in two dissimilar qualities. Let us construct a list of these unlike characteristics that man seems to find in his everyday world:

right	wrong
good	bad
up	down
North Pole	South Pole
man	woman
inside	outside
good god	bad god
Jehovah	Satan
life	death
Eros	Thanatos
cathexis	anticathexis
white	black
positive	negative

No doubt the reader himself could construct hundreds more.

We are surrounded with polarities in regard to our actions. Imagine a student's typical day, which runs something like this. He begins with the fundamental decision to get out of bed or not to get out of bed. "Shall I sleep a little longer because it feels so nice here in bed or shall I get up and make my eight o'clock class?" The decision is either to do it or not to do it. One cannot be half out of bed very long. Clothes. "Shall I wear the brown or blue?" No matter how multiple the color choice it eventually descends to a choice of one. "Shall I brush my teeth now or after breakfast?" "Shall I walk with this person or go along by myself?" "Shall I or shall I not?" "Should I do it or should I not?" And so through the hours of the day goes life for all of us. We are continuously being confronted with and having to make decisions between pursuing or not pursuing certain activities. Decisions, decisions—this is the duality of life, or, its polarity (Bakan, 1966).

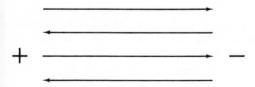

FIGURE 1. *The polarity of life.*

Let us assume that the positive and negative figures in the above drawing have the common properties of electrical charges. As we near the positive charge (the good things man does), we acquire its characteristics and become more positively charged or "good" minded. Here, however, we come under the laws of electrical properties; as all physicists know, opposites attract and similar charges repel. We are now in a dilemma. The closer we get to being good, and the more we try to be the best possible person, the more we are repelled. Then we may be heard to say that there are hypocrites in such and such organization, that one must be practical too, for it is not possible to be completely good all the time, everywhere. We finally reject the very characteristics of good and figuratively push away.

What happens then? Being repelled from one polarity, we go in the direction of the other, toward bad, immoral things. Fortunately or unfortunately, depending upon one's value system, we cannot approach this "bad" goal too closely either, for the same phenomenon operates here to repel us from complete emergence into the bad. The closer we get, the more like the characteristics we become, but at some point such a sameness is created that we are repelled from this opposing goal. Such is life, or to employ the Freudian phrase, this is the "life cycle."

The sophisticated reader might now ask, "Why not stay in the middle and be neither plus nor minus but neutral?" This is precisely what man does try to do to maintain some form of homeostasis, but he cannot. In the same sense that he cannot stay neutrally between being hungry and being satiated, he cannot remain in a stable state of neutrality to any of life's forces. His environment demands that he get off dead center. Pressures are exerted upon him that he cannot ignore. The urgencies of his own organic needs or those of society in the form of family demands, occupational demands and mobility, and other environmentally directed pressures keep him, so to speak, on the run. One of the things man cannot do is "freeze" activity, physical and/or mental, whether it be his own or that of the world surrounding him. It was this concept that made Freud the target for charges of pessimism.

Since we have extended Freud's theoretical position this far, let us move a few steps more in drawing out the life problems which may arise from the dilemma of polarity. To the quality of motion or direction of motion we may add one other dimension, that of *speed*. How fast we travel between opposite poles may have tremendous bearing on our mental state. This may be modern man's curse: He is required to make so many, many trips back and forth with no chance for a leisurely pace which would help him adjust to change. Concurrently we may assume that the quicker the trip between plus and minus in Figure 1, the quicker the rebound! Thus, the more rapidly we make up our mind about something, the more rapidly we find we have changed to the other side. Decisions quickly made about religion, jobs, or marriage partners may leave us with decisions to be just as quickly remade.

A reference was made above to "modern man's curse." If the reader wishes, he may now confront man in the historical sense and examine polarity from that point of view. Let us suppose that man in the early centuries of the Christian era was more agricultural than he now is. Historians would not quarrel with the assumption. Let us further suppose that in the pursuance of farming as a way of life things were done more slowly. While the farmer was plowing his field, a task which might take him days on end, he had little else to think about than to make straight furrows and possibly to wonder if there were not some faster and less arduous way of plowing. He seldom had to make quick decisions. All he did was plow all day long. Now we turn our attention to his descendant, who happens to work in an office, in a large metropolis, surrounded by telephones buzzing, voices calling, and all the accouterments of the commercial world. The higher he progresses in this world of work, the more rapidly do decisions demand his attention. No wonder he becomes bewildered, ulcered, and in need of emotional props. It is not that the twentieth-century man's decisions are necessarily bigger, or even that failure is more dramatic and painful; it is the rapidity of decisions that is his cross to bear. Death, injuries, loss of loved ones were all as hard to bear for fourteenth-century man as they are for twentieth-century man. It is the factor of rapidity between the poles of decision which perhaps makes our lives today so emotionally demanding.

Supposing, though, that through dint of sheer perseverance or through the exigencies of chance a person manages to approach one of the two poles and to remain there! The explanation for such an unlikely but not impossible phenomenon might be as follows: The human being has now managed to reverse the meaning of the poles for himself. What he has done is to make black white and white black. That which was positive is now negative and vice versa. Is this confusing state of reversal possible for any length of time? In the terminology of psychoanalysis the words *sadism* and *masochism* may help to explain the reversal of poles. Sadism (pleasure from making others suffer) and masochism (pleasure from making self suffer) are not farfetched emotional conditions. Psychoanalytic literature is replete with accounts of people who enjoy others being in pain, and certainly of people who enjoy their own sadness. Looking to our own introspective experience (which often proves little but is certainly vivid), we see that one may enjoy a sad song. Is it too hard to picture the victim of a broken love affair dedicatedly pursuing sad thoughts, even enjoying a fantasy of being injured saving the life of his ex-sweetheart's little brother and dreaming, as the now grateful girl stands beside the hospital bed, of turning his head to the wall with the murmur, "It was nothing. Really nothing." Hilarious as this sounds, it is certainly often used as a fictional device of the television program or film screen. Have not some of us enjoyed a gray day and having the blues and resented the intrusion of a boisterous voice that urged us to pep up? In the writer's own clinical experience he has met clients who like attending funerals and get happiness out of what is unquestionably a sad occasion. Probably the most advanced example of the reversal of poles is the condition known as the functional psychosis, hebephrenia, in which the patient giggles, laughs, and appears to have reached a truly happy state. Anyone familiar with this emotional disorder will readily testify that the person is sick and miserable despite what may appear as happiness.

In this way, then, man is still caught in a polar condition though he reverses the poles.

Repetition Compulsion Principle

No doubt one may extract from Freud's writing many other principles, depending upon the criteria employed; however, the principle of repetition compulsion will be the last to be treated here.

Like William James, whom he met and admired, Freud realized the role of habit in man's behavior. Once the human being has become accustomed to doing something a certain way, he is inclined to repeat the activity in much the same way until he can do it without much conscious thought. Though the similarity between James and Freud is so tenuous as to be almost nonexistent, both men gave to the behavior pattern of habit a major role.

Freud would describe man as a habit-following animal, and his extensions of this behavior syndrome are interesting to pursue. Since man is inclined to repeat that which is successful, the longer he does so the more fixed it becomes as his *modus operandi* in daily life. Because it is so thoroughly fixed, he follows this method of attacking problems *whether it leads to success or not*. Freud said that the human being was compelled to repeat that activity which once was successful in the past. Unlike James, Freud extended habit far beyond the organic and manipulative functions. In fact, as we shall see later on, he constructed an entire rationale for man's behavior from this proclivity to repeat past experiences. Although more fully spelled out by his daughter Anna under the name of *ego defense mechanisms,* it is in essence an extension of the repetition compulsion principle.

Dynamics of Behavior

To describe man's personality according to Freud involves much more than the previous principles. In subsequent pages we treat the more prominent dynamics of behavior in Freud's work. After describing *what* man does in exercising his personality we will attempt in the middle section of the chapter to explain *why* he behaves as he does, using for the most part anecdotal material where applicable. The third function of the chapter is to test the predictability of the theory.

ID

So much has been written concerning Freud's creation of the term *id* that it alone could furnish enough material for a book. After a while any student of psychoanalytical literature finds it difficult to winnow out what Freud said about the id and what later writers, both neo-Freudians and critics of Freud, have said.

Freud's approach was not to continue to discuss the id but to utilize the concept in further writings. Since he writes so extremely interestingly, we can almost parrot his words and come out with a fairly easily grasped understanding of the id.

Basic to every living human being, with him at the moment of birth and remaining with him throughout life, is the phenomenal energy system called by Freud the *id*. The id knows only the pleasure principle and cares naught for anything else. It is the raw, savage, undisciplined, pleasure-seeking, basic stuff that energizes man throughout life. It knows no laws, follows no rules, and considers only its own appetites. It gives man his will to continue and sparks all the other energy systems which might be imposed upon it. Contrary to a general opinion that the id is all bad and "isn't it a shame that man must have something that has to be held down all the time?", the id performs the invaluable task of keeping man going. Despite the proclivity of the id to go in any direction it wishes, it must conform to other systems, which conformity produces the need for the polarity and tension reduction principles. It is nonetheless the engine, or the power plant, for man's existence. Although closely allied with the organic systems, from which it derives its energy, the id is a "true psychic system" and does not have a physical place in the body such as the heart, cerebrum, or other organs. Where does it exist then? It exists probably in the same place that one's sense of love exists, or his feeling for God, or his trait of courage or cowardice.

One can never perceive the id in its raw state. Probably the closest he can come to finding out what the id appears to be is in the study of a small child or in the behavior of a psychotic individual. A child a year old squashes bugs, kills things if it so desires, makes entirely selfish demands on others, and in general disports itself in an id-motivated manner. The child apparently follows only the pleasure principle. A deeply disturbed psychotic individual may act in whatever way he chooses. Whether the psychotic flouts the customs of society is beside the point. He may spit, defecate, use foul language, harm others bodily, and make every attempt to satisfy only self, a true manifestation of the pleasure principle. Stripped of controlling devices, or not yet having developed controlling devices, the psychotic and the child may bring us closer to the realization of what Freud meant by the id.

LIBIDO

For many years the unlearned or undiscriminating reader of his works considered the libido Freud's total contribution. Even today, the layman reader and the public in general continue to regard his work as highly sexual in nature. This is only a part of his theoretical formulations; much of the misinformation arose out of the term *libido*.

The libido is that part of the id structure which seeks its gratifications from purely sexual activities. Since sexual appetites are as prevalent in the organic sense as other appetites, although not as strong as the food drive, they are obviously a factor in the psychic makeup of all people. Freud was probably the first to emphasize this phenomenon.

In Freud's earlier writings there was much emphasis on the libidinal content of man's personality, not because it was the major part of his makeup, but because Freud was so concerned with the sexual appetites and especially the aberrations of these appetites which he found in his patients. Freud did not feel he overemphasized the sexual aspects of man's behavior, although many of his professional contemporaries as well as numerous latter-day psychoanalysts did. Freud's split with Adler, the later work of Horney, and many other analysts' writings attest to this schism. And, of course, to the general public anything of a sexual nature became exaggerated.

The libido is not the largest part of man's id structure. It is, however, extremely important, for without a driving libidinal desire man would not be as prone to procreate. Instead of being something shameful, it is a factor in continuing the human species on earth. Freud's contention was that because man enshrouds the sexual aspects of his life with innumerable taboos he has magnified them in his life. Freud believed that he only explained what man does. Just as the police reporter does not create crime, but only writes of it, Freud felt he did not create the overemphasis on the sexual content of life, but only wrote of it.

EGO

We may suppose that if the raw id were left to its own devices it would destroy itself. Something is needed to police its energy and to direct it toward as much fulfillment as can be allowed under the exigencies of life without letting the id destroy itself. Freud said that the ego performs these functions and performs them well. The ego follows the principles of reality. It is the executive with veto powers of all that the id attempts to energize in seeking fulfillment of its desires. The ego makes no ethical value judgments. It is an extension of the id and is never independent of it. The ego is the organized part of the id and merely looks for outlets that serve the id's purpose without destroying it. Whereas the id may be considered the organic part of man's personality, the ego becomes its psychological part. It, the ego, enjoys all the gratifications that it permits the id to enjoy, but it acts with intelligence in controlling, selecting, and deciding what appetites will be satisfied and just how they are to be satisfied.

As we shall see in a moment, when introduced to the socialized part of the personality, the ego comes under great pressure. In trying to permit the id to express itself and, of course, receiving the benefits of that action and still keeping the action within the bounds of subjective, social reality, the ego is that portion of us which moves back and forth between the polarities mentioned previously. How the ego accomplishes this to the satisfaction of all concerned to a large degree determines our emotional state. The more it can allow the id to have, within the bounds of reality, the happier we apparently are in life.

SUPEREGO

As the reader has undoubtedly anticipated, there is a third component to man's personality, lying at the other end of the continuum from the id. Freud never called this the conscience except "in a whisper," but it comes closer to conscience than to any other term. The superego is the last to develop in Freud's trichotomized picture of the human personality. It must be understood, however, that the superego is internalized. It is within personality and not a set of governmental laws. Only when one develops a superego within himself does he have a fully developed personality. The superego is the ethical-moral arm of the personality. It is idealistic and not realistic. Perfection is its goal rather than pleasure. It makes the decision whether an activity is good or bad according to the standards of society which it accepts. Societal laws mean nothing to it unless it has accepted them and internalized them.

Although these personality characteristics may be listed and discussed separately, they are not separate entities within the personality. Id, ego, and superego are intrinsically interwoven in all that man does. Each has its own function but can never exist alone, being inextricably involved with the other components. Only in the case of the undeveloped neonate or during a psychotic episode do we find one of the elements, usually the ego–superego structure, malfunctioning.

INSTINCT

Basic to all of Freud's writings and theoretical positions, as well as to the rationale of his psychotherapeutic work, is the concept of instinct. Almost everything Freud did is predicated on the idea that man came into the world at birth equipped with certain instincts. These Freud did not spell out too definitively, for other instincts appear later on in life as new bodily needs develop. It is the latter part of this statement which makes the concept of instinct as most of us know it rather fuzzy. Later-developing instincts may be considered delayed instincts.

Possibly no other word in the language of the behavioral sciences has caused more controversy than the term *instinct*. Usually three positions are evident: One denies the term categorically; one is caught in the tendrils of defining the term and levels off at that plane; or one uses the concept as a valuable adjunct to psychoanalytic thought and pays little attention to its precise definition.

In point of fact Freud was more prone to use the concept than to expend effort in rounding out a neat and ironclad definition for it. This circumvention is not unusual. Witness the number of things written about personality while as yet no clear-cut definition has emerged for this word. The present text is an example. After more than thirty years of writing, during which time the *idea* of instinct is either directly used or subsumed in treating other material, Freud eventually delimited the term *instinct* to cover two phenomena: Eros—love or life instinct; and Thanatos—death or destruction instinct.

In a general way it is assumed that Freud would have accepted the following as a workable definition of *instinct:* "Any set of responses, shown by a great majority of the members of a species, that are associated together in time under specified environmental conditions and specified drive conditions" (English and English, 1958, p. 265). To this he would add that an instinct is a primary component of man's personality and cannot be reduced to lesser components.

Although Freud did think that instinct is irreducible, to him it had four features: source, aim, object, and impetus. For example, let us consider a person who is suffering from a painful toothache. He is directed by the homeostatic principle of tension reduction, as we previously discussed.

1. source: the pain of the aching, throbbing tooth.
2. aim: to remove the painful aching and return to the painfree state which existed prior to the aching.
3. object: arranging for an appointment with the dentist, going to the dentist, sitting in the dentist's chair, gripping the arm of the chair, etc.
4. impetus: how terrible is the ache; as it subsides during the day, the impetus value is lessened; as it grows unbearable during the early hours in bed at night, the impetus value increases tremendously until one swears he will see the dentist the first thing in the morning.

To most people interested in the behavioral sciences an instinct to be called such would have to be present in all the species, and there should be no opportunity to learn the characteristic behavior pattern. The toothache example cited above would probably meet some unanimity of agreement if that is what instinct is supposed to be. Obviously Freud, too, had his problems with the term *instinct,* for we see that, despite the four features he posited, he eventually refined his concept to include only two demonstrably clear-cut cases of instinct: the aforementioned life and death instincts. Again we find an example of the polarity or duality principle operating. However, within the polarity of life–death there is an umbrella-like effect. All other instincts may be lumped under either of these two opposing instincts. The crude term *lumped* is probably accurate since the listing of instincts becomes so disparate that any orderly classification is rendered nearly impossible.

We shall proceed as Freud did by using the underlying concept of instinct without defining the term.

EROGENOUS ZONES

One of the truly original ideas that Freud created in describing personality is that of erogenous zones, sometimes called erotogenic zones. An erogenous zone is any part of man's body where the inner and the outer skin meet, an area which may have the potential, when manipulated, of arousing pleasant and sensual feelings. These feelings may be either inborn or developed later in life. In a tangential sense they are all inborn, but they may be dormant as pleasure feelings if not given the opportunity to be aroused. Areas of emerging mucous membranes are highly sensitive to irritation. Thus, the lips are much more prone to respond to manipulation than is the small of the back, the point of the elbow, or the calf of the leg, for example. It would seem that the more protruding or outward the mucous membrane, the more highly susceptible it is to becoming an effective erogenous zone.

Naming the zones is a fairly routine organic census technique. They are (keeping in mind that the closer the mucous membrane to the outer skin, the more susceptible it is to sensual gratification): the ears, eyes, mouth (lips), the male and female genitals, and the anal aperture. The eyes and ears are often not considered strictly within the scope of erogenous zones; they do, however, meet the criteria of the definition.

If man can produce pleasure by manipulating the erogenous zones, it is not difficult to explain his perverted behavior within the Freudian frame of reference. Just how man exploits these zones will be treated in a subsequent section dealing with explaining his behavior. At the moment we will attend to the task of describing his personality.

DEVELOPMENTAL SEQUENCE

The term *sequence* is deliberately used to describe how Freud traced the development of man and his personality from birth to adulthood. *Sequence* connotes that the phenomenon is genetically determined, with the further implication that unless development suffers interference by abnormal conditions, it is exactly alike for all men. Further, the developmental sequence follows closely the discovery and utilization of the erogenous zones mentioned in the previous passages.

At this point some digression is in order so as better to explain the basic position of man as he develops in Freud's viewpoint. We will make an analogy of personality as a brick wall versus the concept of a tension system such as a kite. To Freud, "the child was father to the man." As a brickmason slowly constructs a wall, the structure is fixed in relation to the bricks at the bottom or the bricks originally used in construction. The form of the wall, its thickness, all of its characteristics are set. To change them appreciably is to destroy the structure (the personality). The personality, therefore, is set as it goes along. The foundation is unchangeable. Furthermore, it limits and restricts what can be built on top of it. If the bottom of the wall is shaky, poorly constructed, and uneven, the bricks that are placed upon it can be supported only in relation to the strength of the underlying structure. So the child becomes the father (guide, director, chief influence) to the man that eventually emerges in adult life. This does not imply that as the brick wall grows it cannot be changed. It is always being changed by newer kinds of brick, by slight alterations to the design, by extra embellishments of the original design, *but* it can never exceed the limits of load bearing as they are set by the underlying structure. Whenever such a thing does happen, and of course it can and does, the structure collapses (a psychotic personality results, or, in the case of a shaky structure, a neurotic personality). Normally most of us continue to vary as we grow up, but sensing the danger of complete collapse or the discomfort of a trembling structure, we are constrained from a departure too far beyond what our substructure will tolerate.

A moment ago mention was made of a *tension system* in contrast to the Freudian "brick-by-brick" analogy. By *tension system* we are referring to the concept of the architect Buckminster Fuller that a structure is best contrived when it is held together by tension and not constructed piece by piece, one brick on top of the other, a method which creates a heavy, inflexible edifice. The tension system creates a building which is far easier to manipulate, more economical of material and space, and able to withstand far greater stress and pressure than the heavier, set, inflexible, bulky building of masonry. The newer method of roof construction, in which vast areas may be covered without columnar support, the so-called "Dymaxion" house, is a tension system device. A kite is a tension system. It is held together by the tension of string, strips of wood, and taut paper. It is mobile. It can stand great stresses as the wind buffets it about the sky. This is the opposite to Freud's "brick-by-brick" concept of man and his developing personality. The controversy rages around these two questions: Is man held from future development by his first few years of life or is he capable of changing as life progresses? The kite may be recovered, strings changed, loosened, retightened, and even increased to some slight extent, without being destroyed. Equally true, the kite may be destroyed if the wind becomes too strong. But to change its basic features does not automatically bring destruction, the fate of the altered brick wall.

After our sojourn into analogy we may return with possibly a clearer concept of what Freud meant by considering the first five years of life as absolutely essential and decisive in the later formation of the personality. And we have seen what the other side of the door looks like to the deeply dedicated environmentalist who eschews the confinement of the Freudian position. Now we may return to terminology as we describe the sequence of development as Freud saw it.

Oral—The first sequence to develop in the formation of man's personality is related to the erogenous zone of the mouth and more precisely of the lips. Shortly after being born, the human animal uses his lips to ingest food. Food is pleasant (pleasure principle). Whether it be from the mother's breast or from a nippled bottle, the neonate (birth to one month of age) very soon learns (repetition compulsion) that the lips-tongue-oral cavity when manipulated on the mother's breast and/or bottle makes him happy (erogenous zone). Because there are so few conflicting things in his environment, the lesson of lips producing pleasure is quickly and lastingly learned. It is natural for him then to exercise his lips when he wishes to regain a happy state of being. When he is again hungry, the erogenous zone of the mouth comes into play, and he feels happy. When he has been reinforced enough times by this particular activity, lips-tongue-oral cavity automatically spells pleasure to his impressionistic existence. Ergo, if one wants to feel happy, let him use the lips. Being a creature of habit, the neonate uses the lips for pleasure no matter what the state of hunger happens to be. Consequently, having trained his lips for pleasure production, he may now stick his fingers, thumb, or any convenient device (toes!) into his mouth and thus receive pleasure whether he is hungry or not (tension reduction). From now on it will be possible to use the lips for pleasure, and food does not have to be a party to the exercise.

Somewhat akin to the generalization that the first things to go into a system are the last to leave (i.e., Jackson's law), the oral sequence and erogenous zone are the longest and the strongest of man's stages as he lives out his life. He will always seek his oral zone for pleasure and do so even if such activity is not efficient toward solving the problem and reducing the tension. We will explore this more thoroughly in relation to why man behaves in actual life as he does when we get to the section on the explanation of man's personality. Suffice it for the moment to describe what he has as equipment for his personality.

Anal—When enough food waste has accumulated in the lower digestive tract, a tension of the viscera is produced which causes discomfort or pain. When he is older, the human learns that the reality principle operates and that he must not defecate when the pressures become great but must learn to control the eliminative process. Control of bowel movements is far beyond the sense of reality of a tiny infant. The sphincteral muscles of the anal area operate to discharge the feces. With the mass removed and the pressure decreased, the neonate knows pleasure again. In this way the anal area becomes the second sequence to develop. It is likewise the second longest in duration and the second strongest of the erogenous zones.

The unique reciprocity of the zones is apparent since the action of one is allied to the action of another. Thus no erogenous zone in its function or in its development can exist independently from any other. Through a process intercorrelated but not necessarily sympathetic, the erogenous zones become sensitized to one another.

Phallic—Probably around the age of two the child has passed through the oral and anal stages of development and proceeds to discover and enjoy the remaining erogenous zones of his body. Primary among them are the sexual organs of penis and vagina although the nostrils and ears and eyes may come to be manipulated for pleasure. Anyone familiar with small children is aware that they put their fingers in their nostrils to remove encrusted mucus. Clinical cases in which small foreign objects are thrust into the nasal passages are not unknown.

From about the beginning of his sixth year until puberty, when the endocrine system regenerates an intense period of activity, the child is in a dormant aspect of the sequential development of his personality via the erogenous zones. The first three phenomena discussed are usually called the pregenital stages.

Genital—Reciprocity is the keynote of the genital stage. No new erogenous zones are discovered or employed. A synthesis or fusion of the preceding three sequences takes place and instead of directing their force upon the individual, they now become outer-directed, usually toward the opposite sex. The chief physical objective of the genital stage is to indulge in intercourse either for reproduction of the species or for reciprocal pleasure between the partners via use of the erogenous zones. Abortive attempts to consummate the sex act become the mode of behavior where society prohibits full intercourse because of lack of marriage status. Contrary to the belief of many, any sexual act not designed to propagate the species was almost an act of perversion to Freud. He attempted to describe and explain man's sexual behavior but never once condoned extramarital activity.

LOVE STAGES

On the basis of the previous material it is possible and we hope profitable to recast the Freudian material to create sequences in which the erogenous zones play only a background part. This rubric is a rank extension of Freud's work. Nowhere in his writings does he speak of it although others have made similar interpretations.

Consider man as a love-generating animal. Love is to be regarded as a reciprocal state of attraction in that to give love one must receive from the love object some satisfaction. This concept would differentiate love from passion (an emotional state so strong as to overrule good judgment) or infatuation (a short erotic attraction which contains no reciprocity; i.e., the love object does nothing of and by itself to foster the relationship toward any one individual). Probably the closest term to describe what we mean is the Greek word *agape*, which connotes that love goes *between* people. A person cannot love in only one direction but must be loved in return. It is a two-way proposition: I love you, you love me. Anything else would be considered infatuation, passion, or what have you.

Self-love—When the infant is born, he knows only one thing: himself. Since we may assume that he is not yet concerned with abstractions about himself, he can deal only with the concrete. There is nothing more concrete than his organic self. His body describes, defines, and circumscribes his total world. He can know only those things that are apparent to his senses. If he cannot touch, taste, see, hear, or smell a person or thing, it does not exist as far as he is concerned. In the beginning his body is the receptor and affector of learned things. Through it he senses and learns pleasure, pain, and some realization of other things. Since his body (himself in the most directive manner) is both a receptor and an effector, he has a reciprocal situation. Being able to reciprocate with himself, he is now able to make himself a love object because satisfaction and pleasure come from himself. He can suck his toes and fingers; he can find pleasure in his eating and his passing of feces; he can experience pleasure of bodily warmth. In short, he can find himself the most wonderful thing he has known so far in his very short existence. He loves himself because "himself" is the only thing he can know and know how to love. To this stage Freud gave the name *autoerotism*.

Because the infant is the first object of his own love and because it is so exclusively his own and he can never be apart from it, this love stage is the longest and strongest of them all. He starts life loving himself and ends life with the feeling of self-love being paramount. No other feeling of love will be quite as strong.

Parental love—Very soon after the infant finds in himself a love object and before he has even formulated self-love to a lasting degree, he finds an external object in the form of a mother, father, or some adult figure that does nice things for him. It feeds him, takes wet, uncomfortable clothes off him and replaces them with dry, warm clothes, holds him and comforts him through gastric pains, caresses him, sings to him, plays with him—in short, is a very nice thing to have around. Without much practice on the infant's part he is likely to discover that the ministrations to his needs may also be increased if he too does something like smile, laugh, or make responding noises to this figure. Consequently a reciprocal relationship is soon established and, as is the case in most infants' lives, it is with the mother, who is usually the purveyor of all these pleasant things. Of course, it also could be any parent surrogate.

The second strongest and longest-lasting love stage is related to the parent or parents. To the sophisticated reader familiar with Freudian literature this would seem to be an excellent place to introduce the concept of Oedipus complex and its concomitant operational devices of penis envy and castration complex. If not placed here it might profitably be included in the section on erogenous zones. With this the author does not quarrel. However, dealing with the erogenous zones is complicated enough without adding the exposition necessary to understand the Oedipus complex. Treating the latter here seems ill advised because this section is purely an extension and interpretation of Freud's work. Finally, the Oedipus complex is a phenomenon of identification, and to Freud a tremendously important one. It has, therefore, been postponed to the later section dealing with identification.

Fictional love—Before life progresses too far, the infant grown into a small child comes to the realization that his present two love objects have certain limits. The insurmountable problem with self is self. One cannot go beyond the bounds of what one is. There is only so much to be done with oneself and then one is circumscribed by his own talents and facilities. Parents present problems too. They scold. They set up what seem to be innumerable rules of conduct such as washing, eating certain foods, conducting self according to the rules of society, and so on. They may even inflict physical punishment in the form of spankings. Now that the child's world is expanding, he can see, and does, that there are other adult figures, and they perform magnificent feats like flying through the air, hitting home runs, always winning gun fights with the "bad guy," and doing many more exciting things than parent figures ever seem to do. Also, they do not spank or scold. As the child's mental capacity and concurrent fantasy life increase, he becomes more aware of the wonderful world of fictional heroes and what they can do for him. He falls in love, then, with fictional figures—be they real or characters from plays, books, films, television.

Having fictional love is a lasting behavioral pattern. We carry permanently some images of these personality forms which help us to live in fantasy what we cannot live in reality. Unfortunately, there is a drawback even with fictional love objects; the degree of reciprocity is very limited. They can do nothing for us unless we first initiate the action. A book with its hero stays on the library shelf until we make the effort for it to enter our lives. It is the same with films, television, the sports world. The burden of rapport is mainly ours. We find also that in time these love objects become stereotyped and really have restricted use despite the high moments of sharing vicariously their exploits.

Homosexual love—With a backward glance now to the Freudian sequence we can recapitulate some similarities between this departure from Freud and the extension into love stages that is being proposed.

As the child progresses through the oral, anal, and phallic sequences, he is developing a love for self by means of his body. The fuller emergence of the phallic period brings forth the fictional stage. Because fantasy is so strongly a part of the phallic period, the child casts fictional heroes for his pleasure more easily at this time than in the two previous (oral and anal) periods.

According to Freud, basic to all humans is an inborn bisexuality. All males have some characteristics of the female, and all females have some characteristics of the male. Current endocrine and biochemical research indicates the presence of androgens and estrogens in every human, the male hormone androgen being predominant in the male and estrogens being predominant in the female. Coupling this fact with the similarity in sexual organs lays the groundwork for the homosexual love stage. It should in no way be interpreted at this age level with any perversion whatsoever.

The boy of elementary school age becomes engrossed in cub scouting and having pals with whom he likes to wrestle and engage in bodily contact activities; he eschews the company of girls. The opposite sex is assigned the role of tolerable nuisance. On the other hand, little girls become members of the Brownies, have slumber parties with one other girl, play happily at dolls, swear lifelong allegiance to another girl and then confound parents with a new lifelong allegiance the following week, and in general assign to boys the role of "snails and puppy dog tails," accompanied by dirty hands, boisterous behavior, and insensitive manners.

Heterosexual love—Just as the genital sequence becomes the synthesis of the oral–anal–phallic periods, the heterosexual stage climaxes the self–parental–fictional–homosexual stages. Roughly speaking, the heterosexual and genital phases are comparable.

With the onslaught of puberty and the concomitant functioning of the endocrine system, the young boy or girl finds that there seems to be something deliciously nice in the form of the opposite sex. The first fumbling attempts at rapport are often amusing to the adult. The girl or boy does all the wrong things. The girl snatches caps hoping to be chased and tickled and yet protests vehemently that the "boys are bothering her." The boy acts like a puppy. To get the girl's attention, he waits until she is surrounded by friends on the school playground and then he backs off, runs at a galloping pace, plunges right through the middle of the group of girls, upsetting them, and stands off with a foolish grin. All this to get the girl's attention! Very soon the heterosexual byplay takes on more and more sophisticated expression until necking, petting, and deviant forms of physical expression of the sexual appetite are learned and exploited.

As economic and social status increases, the male and female of the species called man have matured through five love stages and have utilized all of them. Life continues through the selection of a marriage partner within the laws of society to the rearing of children, who in turn will progress through the love stages that their parents did and thus complete the cycle.

STATES OF CONSCIOUSNESS

One cannot do much with the Freudian approach to personality without incorporating in the descriptive system a treatment of the states of being conscious. It is so easy to become involved in a semantic squabble about the term *conscious* vis-à-vis *unconscious* that one is tempted to invent new words. This is impossible, however, when dealing with a Freudian scheme of things. The entire Freudian position is linked with the belief that something exists in man's mental state which is opposite to the state of being conscious. Rather than belabor the point of whether conscious-unconscious exists and in what manner the terms are abused, we may best bend our efforts to describing what Freud meant by the terms, their characteristics positively basic to his concepts, leaving the verbal infighting to the semantically minded.

Conscious—The conscious is that part of man's mental life of which he is fully aware. The state of being conscious enables us to know where we are, what is happening around us, who we are, how we are to go about doing what we are at present doing. When something happens, we become aware of it and can purposefully direct our attention to it; our senses tell us things, and we can properly interpret their afferent impulses and efferently respond to a demand through them (i.e., winking, blinking, motion of the body). In short, we are alive in the most acute sense of being. Running, swimming, eating, or any strenuous physical exercise in which mental activity is an integral part is probably the best example of being conscious. The more active we are, the more conscious we seem to be. The end of an exciting basketball game would find us at our highest, mentally conscious self. As you read these words, you may or may not be overtly conscious depending upon the energy with which you are attending to the task at hand. To Freud, consciousness meant being vitally and mentally alive and awake.

Preconscious—In descending order, we are next interested in that mental state of being called preconscious, which exists between the mental state of being conscious and the mental state of being unconscious. The preconscious is that shadowy land where our memories, for example, seek blindly for a bit of knowledge readily known in the past but now not immediately in our possession for use. Surely every student who has ever taken an examination has sat groping for a piece of knowledge when he can't remember the entire fact. When he walked out of the examination room or that evening shortly before falling asleep, it suddenly occurred to him. That piece of information was floating around in the preconscious, almost, but not quite, in the conscious. However, not all things of a mental nature that exist in the preconscious have to be teased out or are coyly unavailable until moments of stress are past. Facts, information, data, feeling tones, emotional states which may lie in the unconscious can be obtained from the preconscious with little or no effort, providing stress is not excessive. The preconscious acts more as a membrane than a repository. It actually stores little but acts as a device to keep the unconscious from interfering with the work that the conscious must do to keep us alert and attending to the day's activities. All mental content coming from the unconscious to the conscious must pass through the preconscious.

Unconscious—Somewhere in man's mental life, says Freud, there has to be a state of being which accounts for things that are not available to the mind at any given moment but that have occurred to the mind in the past. There must be some storehouse for all that man's mind has gone through. There must also be some area in which the mind can play as freely as it wishes in a pure pleasure principle sense without paying obeisance to the rules of the ego–superego. There must be some place for having mental fun without obeying any rules. This area lies in the unconscious. To put it another way, the unconscious is the mental storehouse of man's past and the mental playground of his present. All that has happened to him in the past is deposited in the mind whether he likes it or not. He may exercise many censoring powers over the contents of the unconscious mental self through use of the preconscious, but this censorship is a continuing process which never stops. When the censorship relaxes, as during sleep or moments of stress, the content of the unconscious may come bubbling up through the preconscious and cause emotional pain, especially when the repressed content is largely motivated by the pleasure principle.

Subconscious—Our treatment of the mental phenomenon called the *subconscious* is another extension of the Freudian theory which holds up nonetheless within the general framework of Freud's concepts (Benassy, 1967).

The present author has extracted that activity of man with which he enters life completely equipped and has given to it the term *subconscious*: what lies below or outside of consciousness but is not necessarily the opposite of the term *conscious*. One other distinction applies: Whereas everything in the unconscious has to have been at some time in the conscious past, the elements in the subconscious have not been in the mental past but are all present at birth. Man, therefore, comes into the world equipped with a subconscious mental factor. He has also an emerging conscious capacity which may or may not develop adequately (as with idiots and some imbeciles). He accumulates an unconscious mental area only after the conscious mental state has passed along an experience to it.

An illustration is that state of being which one undergoes during anesthesia. The usual experience is to feel that the anesthetist will not completely do his job prior to the actual surgery, and one counts to seven worrying that the surgeon will cut too soon. This is the last conscious thought, and then, without any seeming passage of time, the surgery is over and the attending nurse or surgeon is cautioning the patient to relax; "it is all over." The time during what could possibly be hours of existence with yet no feeling of time experienced was lived in the subconscious. Being in a coma or being unaware of anything takes place in the subconscious.

To the above description must be added the inborn mental processes which accompany man at birth and are largely autonomic in nature but do require some mental effort. Desire for water, hunger for food, attention to breathing all come out of the subconscious. They do not have to go through the conscious mental process in order to operate.

EGO DEFENSE MECHANISMS

Although Freud's daughter Anna reconstituted some of her father's work to develop the principle ego defense mechanisms, and many, many neo-Freudians have since expanded and utilized the concept, it was Freud who originated the basic tenets.

All three words are important to understanding what is meant by ego defense mechanisms. As we have seen, the ego is a central component of personality. We have also seen that man wishes to remain happy even though he realizes that certain realities of life may postpone happiness. In order to meet the vicissitudes of everyday life which care not at all for his ego, man must defend his ego against the outside world—in some cases against himself too, as we shall see later. This defense becomes mechanical through the repetition compulsion proclivity.

One of the chief characteristics of an ego defense mechanism is that it does not enter the conscious state of reasoning but operates in the unconscious. Hence, the personality is not aware that it is defending its ego. Somewhere in the past it learned this defense technique. Now the personality utilizes the technique even though at times it in no way solves the problem of supporting the ego.

Another chief characteristic of an ego defense mechanism is that it may distort, or even deny, reality. It is not outside the realm of possibility that man may lie to himself in order to protect himself from unhappiness. He may also so twist reality without realizing it that any resemblance to what actually happened and how he interprets what happened has disappeared. He may also be so disturbed by an incident which causes him great emotional discomfort as simply to pretend that it did not happen and do such a good job of pretending that he eventually comes to deny what truly existed. The outside world, his friends, and others stand confused.

The primary ego defense mechanisms are these: repression, regression, reaction formation, projection, and fixation. As previously mentioned, these five are primarily the formulations of Anna Freud, who continued to work somewhat in the vein of her father. Other defense mechanisms, although not as pointedly described by name, are sublimation, substitution, identification, and displacement. In the recent literature on psychotherapy and allied fields are still other ego defense mechanisms, some of which appear redundant but are possibly useful in describing man's personality. The concept of defense mechanisms apparently intrigues many therapists.

Repression—Repression may be considered a fundamental defense mechanism, the cornerstone for many of the others because it comes into play so early in life and influences or causes some of the other ego defenses to be brought into play. In fact, Freud, in his *An Autobiographical Study*, stated, "The theory of repression became the foundation stone of our understanding of the neuroses." And farther on, "It is possible to take repression as a centre and to bring all the elements of psychoanalytic theory into relation with it."

Basically, the definition of the word is quite like that in any dictionary. It means to hold back, to prevent from acting, to exclude, or to block. The unique characteristic of the Freudian definition is that *all* these things are done without the knowledge, in the conscious sense, of the personality. If they are done with the knowledge of the conscious mind, then we may call that *suppression*. Suppression is not a part of the present discussion.

Repression has two factors which must be considered:

1. Content coming up from the id for the first time, not having been previously in the conscious mind and gone back into the id level, is subject to *primal* repression. By this process certain inborn impulses to act via the pleasure principle are denied first entry into the conscious mind. That is not to say that they are permanently kept out. At the moment, in the present consideration of repression, they are denied entry, however.
2. *Primary* repression is the denial of a reentry of some past experience into the conscious mind, especially if the past experience would cause emotional pain.

Repression is an excellent example of the superego structure's imposing the reality principle upon the id substructure.

Regression—To regress is to go back to a previous state, place, or position. Whereas one could repress something which had not existed previously in experience, it is possible to regress only to what has already been experienced. One cannot *return* to some place he has never been.

Most of Freud's writing about regression concerned his patients' returning to behavior characteristic of their childhood. This became so prevalent in his therapy with patients that the word *infantilism* became almost the synonym of regression. It is possible, however, to regress to an earlier form of behavior which is not of childhood but of later maturity, as we shall see farther on.

Regression is a manifestation of the repetition compulsion mentioned previously. The human personality is again inclined to repeat an activity which was once successful or at least pleasant. Since it is a compulsion type of repetition (reasoning plays no part in a compulsion), the activity repeated may in no way solve the present problem and may even worsen it. Usually the regressive form of behavior does not re-create the entire past experience but only portions of it which reinforce the whole past episode. When a person is frustrated and regresses to an infantile form of behavior, such as pouting, sucking on objects (oral erogenous, pleasure zone), or hitting, he does not also dress, talk, or deport himself completely as a baby. Usually only vestiges of the earlier form of behavior are manifested.

Reaction formation—This defense mechanism often is one of the hardest concepts to grasp and is rejected vehemently by many beginning students of psychology. In essence, the reaction formation phenomenon is clearly seen if one remembers the duality or polarity principle, according to which man is doomed to wander back and forth between two poles of action. The reaction formation mechanism finds him doing just that but in a more subtle way, such that the preconscious keeps him from realizing the true meaning of his behavior.

Shakespeare's oft-quoted line "The lady doth protest too much, methinks" fits quite well into the concept of reaction formation. Thus a student may be everlastingly discussing cheating by other students, or someone is so set against something that the listener soon wonders what all the fuss is about. Reaction formation is exhibited by extreme behavior. The individual who appears to be frightened by absolutely nothing gives indications of unconsciously being afraid to such an extent that he must overplay the role of hero. Whereas most people come to a point of fearing some things and avoiding them as best they can, the reactive formation individual continuously seeks out situations most of us fear to enter. The American college football player who loudly exhibits aggressiveness may be considered an example.

Projection—The word *projection* receives a great deal of attention in the psychological literature. Much of its intent springs from Freud's introduction of it as an ego defense mechanism. Projection means the protection of one's own ego from feelings of guilt by casting them toward another individual and unwittingly blaming him for the very faults that one has himself. We project our anxiety-producing thoughts onto someone else, thereby not having to defend our own thoughts. Thus when the penurious person accuses the world of being stingy, he has unconsciously projected his own feeling of being tightfisted onto the world at large, making his own efforts to save a comparatively laudable endeavor. Another example of projection is called "comparing the irregular adjective." "I am thrifty, you are tightfisted, he is stingy"; "I am brave, you take chances, he is foolhardy"; "I like to relax from studying now and then, you haven't been very busy lately, he is going to flunk out of school if he spends all his time in the student union." These closely approach the mechanics of projection.

Fixation—Fixation is much like the ego defense mechanism of regression except that the individual who employs this ego defense mechanism does not necessarily go back (regress) to an earlier form of pleasant behavior in order to relieve a present emotional problem. One may fixate or remain at a current pleasurable activity whether or not it solves any problems in the future. The feeling is: I like doing this, I do it well, it makes me feel good when I do it, and therefore, why change? To the fixated person, flexibility leads only to unknown paths, and the unknown may present challenges which cannot be met.

In the usual Freudian sense, the mechanism of fixation describes the holding on to a past idea which was at one time successful in solving emotional problems; consequently, it is closely allied to regression. One regresses by returning to a fixated point.

The following defense mechanisms, though not found in Anna Freud's recapitulation, are nonetheless integral parts of Freud's concept and writings of the ego defense mechanisms.

Sublimation—That man has to hold down (repress) his libidinal desires and conform to the reality principle of the ego–superego structure does not necessarily mean that he can do nothing about his desires. Through the unconscious process of sublimation he may direct his thoughts and impulses into fields of expression which afford him some disguised outlet and which, most important, are accepted and at times prized by his fellow men. Traditionally, the artistic pursuits of sculpturing, painting, dancing, and the like have been assigned this role of release-serving agency for inhibited sexual desires. It is interesting to speculate on why the average layman has so often accepted this mechanism, all the while indignantly denying most of the other theories of Freud. One may suspect that individuals who do not create in the artistic sense feel pangs of jealousy about those who do. In addition to the creative arts, physical contact sports such as football, wrestling, and so on may be included as sublimated homosexual tendencies. This revelation is taken as blasphemy by the adherents of bodily contact sports; there is, however, no difference between painting and football as sublimatory releases because both fit the criteria.

Substitution—Substitution is closely allied to the defense mechanism of sublimation; both are directed toward goals accepted by society instead of goals not acceptable to society (or self). The basic difference lies in the part the conscious plays vis-à-vis the unconscious. Sublimatory activities are not known to the conscious self, whereas substitution may be a conscious process, although frequently it is not. There is the added difference that libidinal or sexual repressions are not as prevalent in substitution as they are in sublimation. Agreement with the two proceding statements is not universal by any means. Obviously, if the conscious self is operating, i.e., if the self knows what it is doing, the criteria of a defense mechanism of the ego have not been met. However, the ego defense mechanisms have been expanded greatly by post-Freudians, as was previously mentioned.

Substitution of the conscious type (and hence not entirely in the Freudian rubric) would be exemplified by a student's indulging in and excelling in sports or physical activities for a feeling of success and the pleasure principle because he is unable to gain satisfaction or success in academic pursuits. The opposite example is a strong emphasis on studying as a substitute for renown in athletics. The implied suggestion that highly qualified athletes cannot be successful students or vice versa is obviously sophistry and false.

Identification—In general, we may consider three meanings for the term *identification*. The last of these will be treated more fully than the others as it involves a fundamental and complex theory of Freud's which he called the Oedipus complex.

Identification in the first sense means recognition of something—a word, person, place, song. This is possible only if the subject has previously met or learned in the past the characteristics of the object which is recognized. Having once seen the past thing as familiar, one may place it in a serial order (classification or differentiation) or merely accept it.

When we react to a situation which reminds us of a similar situation, but one which we have not experienced directly in the past, we may then be identifying in the secondary sense of this word. Transfer of training comes within the scope of this meaning. Although the various meanings of the word tend to converge, they frequently lose preciseness in actual usage.

It is in the last definition of the word *identification* that the more accurate meaning is conveyed according to the Freudian theory. Whenever one person merges his personality deeply in the personality of another, the psychoanalytic definition of *identification* is exhibited. The word means, therefore, more than identifying something from the past or more than employing a past experience which is reminiscent of an analogous experience; it means that entering directly into the feeling tone of the object toward which one has cathexis. It is more than mere imitation of the other person, more than sympathy for him, and more than a strong empathic identification with his emotional states; it means feeling one *is* the other person. Obviously, this is not actually possible, for one never loses or supplants one's own ego (except perhaps in the psychotic states).

Oedipus complex—Using the previous definition of *identification* as a springboard but not a set of semantic rules, we may now consider the theoretical aspects of the Oedipus complex. Incidentally, this theoretical position was responsible for much of the furor and intense indignation directed toward Freud by other analysts, the clergy, and laymen in general. Freud himself states that he "stumbled" on the idea and that it took him long hours of pondering to accept it. Prior to his expounding the theory that children's lives are highly sexually oriented, he accepted and understood in others the historical position that children know nothing about sex and are completely innocent of sexual drives until well after puberty.

When a child is born, the first object it experiences other than itself is its mother, the human being who feeds it, clothes it, loves it, and answers to all its needs. If the mother does not perform her tasks in the traditional manner of devoted duty, the child transfers its love and trust to the mother surrogate, whoever that may be. In most societies it is, of course, a female figure. As the child develops, it identifies strongly with the mother figure. From this dependence for life and identification grows a feeling of love for the mother. Thus both the boy and girl baby begin the earliest years of life with a strong attachment to the mother.

Paralleling the development of love toward mother is the exploration and discovery by the child of its own body and how it functions. In the course of this learning the baby notices its sexual organs. At this point the development of the Oedipus process differs for boys and girls, and we must consider them separately. Up to now the organism has been called "it," but we refer henceforth to "he" or "she."

In conjunction with loving mother and discovering his own body, the boy becomes aware of the role his father plays in his life. Father is a stronger, larger, more powerful, less present, and like-sexed creature. Father also shares the mother, her attention, her love, her time, and in fact appears to have some priority for the mother's time and affection. The infant boy becomes aware of this pattern and finds that he and his ego must at times share the mother with the father. The natural outcome is a feeling of unexpressed rivalry and concomitant jealousy. In the initial stages of this awareness the infant boy does nothing to curb his jealousy. However, repression takes place as he develops. He also notices that he is physically more like his father than like his mother, a fact which leads him to identify with the father as well as the mother. Ambivalence (polarity principle) results from this cathexis toward two different individuals, both of whom are so largely instrumental to his well-being. He must share mother with father, which is not to his liking, but he is more like father than mother, which sense of identification brings him satisfaction. Since the reality principle is also developing, he now can fantasize a retribution from his father for usurping some of the father's prerogatives with the mother. Because knowledge of the world was originally confined and continues to be proscribed by his oral–anal–phallic education, it follows that whatever retribution his father will perpetrate upon him will be in an erotogenic zone. The one physical characteristic that definitely makes him different from his mother is his protruding sexual organ, the penis. This, then, becomes the focus of retaliation which he feels his father might make against him, the removal of the penis, which would make him more female-like but would also take away his one masculine feature. Equally important, the penis as the incestuous organ must be removed in order to eliminate the possibility of an incestuous and competing relationship. This fear Freud referred to as the *castration complex:* the male child fears both the removal of the organ which makes him masculine like father, with the consequent loss of his identification with father, and also his continued rivalry with father for mother's love and attention. The polarity principle creates an anxiety which he is unable to cope with until the reality principle introduces the ego defense mechanism of repression. Now at last he has a method of solving the problem despite its requiring the use of symbols and other devious means of gaining expression of the repressed desire for mother. The fictional love stage, later the homosexual and heterosexual love stages, and the gradual development of his superego all help to resolve the polarity.

The boy approximately three to five years of age is generally considered to be in the strongest throes of the polarity of the Oedipus complex. The complex, however, continues to be a vital factor throughout the remainder of his life and has much to do with his adult attitude about the opposite sex, figures of authority, and relationships with his own wife and children. No great significance is attached psychoanalytically to the word *Oedipus.* The exploits of the hero Oedipus of Sophocles' tragedy *Oedipus Rex* made this an appropriate name to Freud for the complex. Indeed it is, for Oedipus killed his father unknowingly and subsequently married his mother. Since the identities of his parents were unknown to him, the analogy fits well with Freud's theory; all the above behavior operates in the id (unconscious processes) of the infant boy.

Electra complex—The Oedipus complex as it operates in the female unconscious is called specifically the *Electra complex* although that term is not too
often found in current psychoanalytic literature.

As stated previously, a different set of forces operates for the girl infant.
She, too, finds the mother her primary and initial love object after her own
oral–anal–phallic narcissistic period, which Freud called autoerotism, has
developed. The ministrations of mother and the consequent feeling of love
are equally present in her case. However, after this point the similarities
between the male and female complexes diverge. Here the steps are much
more complicated. Freud based the Oedipal theory on his investigations of
and reflections on men and assumed that the female would be a complete
parallel, but "this turned out not to hold . . . [and] . . . revealed profound
differences between the sexual development of men and women" (*An Autobiographical Study*, p. 65). It is also true that he first formulated the Oedipal
theory from therapy with his adult male patients and only later in life was he
able to corroborate the theory to his satisfaction by working with small children as clients (*Analysis of a Phobia in a Five-Year-Old Boy*, the case of
Hans, 1909).

As the small girl becomes familiar with the father, she also notices the
relationship between her body and the father's. In conjunction with the
feeling of rivalry between the girl and her mother for her father's love, she
notices the lack of a male organ in herself. This causes the girl to blame her
mother for removing her penis or at least for her lack of a penis. She attributes the loss to the mother's jealousy, which in this way removes the child as a
love object with the father. Along with holding her mother responsible for
her castrated condition, she identifies quite strongly with the father because
he possesses the envied phallic organ. Her envy arises from the obvious
comparison of her body, which has nothing (or a cavity), to that of her
father, who possesses something neither she nor her mother has. Again the
polarity arises. Sharing the lack of something with her mother strengthens her
original identification with the mother, and the ambivalence brings emotional
anxiety. To this state of anxiety for the girl Freud gave the name penis envy.
The girl does not so readily resolve her polarity, as the boy solves his castration complex, with the result that numerous psychological differences exist
between the male and female. The girl continues the rivalry ("Daddy's girl")
much longer, represses it less strongly, becomes recalcitrant toward the
mother at puberty—approximately at age eleven—and modifies it gradually
until she, too, gains a marriage partner and then as a mother displays her
ambivalence toward both sexes in her roles as a mother to boys and girls and
as a sexual partner to a male.

It must be stressed at this point that the Oedipus–Electra complexes are
the result of the operation of the id in the unconscious areas of the psyche.

Children are *not* consciously aware of this behavior, a fact that is fundamental to a grasp of Freud's theory.

Displacement—In Freudian terminology *displacement* refers to man's inclination to select an object reminding him of an original object which elicited a
strong positive or negative effect, and then to respond to the second object
with all the intensity of feeling that the first object aroused. The use of
symbols is almost mandatory in the consideration of displacement. The
following incidents may serve as examples:

1. The undergraduate student becomes angry at his professor. Being unable
   to retaliate against the professor, the student "takes it out" on his roommate. The anger is therefore placed against another object even though
   that object is entirely innocent.
2. The motorist becomes upset by the driving of sports car enthusiasts. He
   displaces his annoyance at sports cars onto anything that reminds him of
   low-sweep automobiles. Any object resembling the sports car becomes a
   symbol of recklessness: berets worn by drivers, fast starts by other automobiles, etc.
3. A widow displaces all her thwarted love feelings for a lost husband upon
   the young son who resembles the departed husband.

All of the above examples are indicative of displaced feelings. From
displacement spring other types of behavioral patterns such as stereotyping,
displaced aggression, scapegoating, etc.

DELIMITATIONS

The foregoing description of Freud's system by no means includes all the
many contributions he made to psychoanalytic thinking. Reasons for restricting the material are (1) limitations of space; (2) concern with personality
theory rather than with methods of therapy; (3) the fact that no writing
explaining another work can be as inclusive as the first (one must go to the
original if he is to get the complete work); (4) the bibliography at the end of
the chapter, which lists many excellent sources for further study. The author
urges the student to go as far as he likes, especially in the writings of Freud,
who is an absorbing author.

Free association as a therapeutic technique, the analysis of dreams, the
phenomenon of forgetting, slips of the tongue during conversation—all of
these and many more of Freud's contributions are left to the work of other
authors. Freud's *A General Introduction to Psychoanalysis, The Psychopathology of Everyday Life,* and one of his very last, *New Introductory Lectures
on Psycho-Analysis,* are highly recommended. The conversational tone of
Freud's writings and the flow of style make them usable for the average
undergraduate student.

EXPLAINING HUMAN BEHAVIOR VIA
FREUD'S PSYCHOANALYTIC THEORY

Students of personality theory may reasonably question the worth of a theory if it does not explain some of man's behavior. To that issue this section has been primarily directed. As will be seen, the examples used do not always fit the theory to the theory's best advantage; in some cases other factors enter in.

Criteria for examples:

1. The example should be present in most known cultures or ethnic groups.
2. The examples should be within the actual experience or at least vicarious experience of most people.
3. The example should not necessarily favor the exposition of one theory over another.
4. The example should be useful and as practicable as possible in furthering the explanation of why man behaves as he does.

With the above criteria in mind the following examples are proposed:

1. Marriage: Why does man in most societies go through some kind of formalized ceremony? Why does man select a mate?
2. Perversions: Why does man engage in sexual perversions which in no way are designed to procreate the race? What promotes man's sexual appetites?
3. Suicide: What forces bring man to end his own life? Why does he purposefully and at times painfully put himself to death?
4. Lawbreaking: What causes man to construct laws with other men and then deliberately break some law every day (for example, exceeding speed limits, throwing debris on the sidewalk, jaywalking, etc.)? The emphasis is on the *deliberate* flouting of a law and not on casual or unwitting misdemeanors.
5. Supranatural being: Why do most societies worship a god figure of some kind?
6. Humor: Why does man laugh? What gives him a "sense of humor"?
7. Smoking: Why do most societal groups who have ever had the opportunity smoke pipes, cigars, cigarettes, and continue this custom?
8. Play and recreation: Why does man throughout the known world practice some form of participative or spectator recreation?
9. Psychoses–neuroses: Why does man lose his sense of identity and reality and become either psychotic or neurotic? What causes him to have compulsions, obsessions, phobias, and the like? (This section considers only the functional disorders, not the organically caused psychoses.)

Admittedly, constructing a list such as the above might be a fascinating sort of quiz game, and the endeavor could result in hundreds of "why" questions, bearing on stuttering, thumbsucking, masochism–sadism, thrift, dreaming, losing one's temper, etc. Those posed above are intended to draw out of the theory many possibilities for giving us practical information.

Even to the most unsophisticated reader it must now be apparent that any theory that could explain all the dynamics underlying these questions would be the answer to life itself! The questions are not intended to be metaphysical but merely to be a device to bring the reader closer to understanding the practicality of each theory.

Marriage

To explain marriage or the selection of at least one mate with whom to live and share we draw on some fundamental concepts in the Freudian theory. Man gets married because he seeks pleasure, assuming of course that marriage is considered a pleasant state. It is necessary for him to select one wife in most cultures, and in almost all cultures he goes through some sort of ceremony his society constructed and prescribing that the marriage partners be responsible to each other. Also, all this must be done publicly. Thus the latter part serves the reality principle as well as the pleasure principle. Other bases of the Freudian system may also be employed in examining the social custom of marriage and why man follows it. Through the libidinal appetites which he has now grown to direct toward the opposite sex, he most certainly needs a sexual partner. The erogenous zones have developed, the love stages have matured to the heterosexual stage, and since he wishes to reduce the tension created by unfulfilled wishes, it is a natural behavioral act for him to enter matrimony. The ego and superego direct him to a formalized approach to matrimony whenever his background has been such as to develop the concepts handed down by his ethnic group.

Perversions

The problem of perversion seems almost to be designed for the Freudian theory because there are so many readily available answers to the question of why man commits perverted acts upon himself or with others of his sex or the opposite sex. Probably the main reasons lie in the development of the erogenous zones. As the oral–anal–phallic–genital areas become sensitized, traumatic incidents may prolong or delay the natural sequence. Whatever the influence which changes normality, the zone is now ripe for exploitation beyond its normal developmental urgings. Consequently, a child not properly weaned through the phallic–genital period may indulge in masturbatory practices well into adulthood. In fact, much current psychoanalytic literature is devoted to explanations of deviant sexual excesses and their effect upon societal life. The temptation in this section is to overexplain rather than underexplain.

Any stimulation of an erogenous zone is considered a perverted act in Freudian theory if the stimulation is not in the natural course of marital cohabitation.

Suicide

According to the duality principle, man is forever going back and forth between two polarities. In suicide he has gone from Eros (life–love) to its opposite, Thanatos (death) and has managed to remain at the one pole until he has destroyed himself. In his later writings Freud made much of the "Death wish," and later writers have picked this idea up in light of psychoanalytic phenomena. That is to say that man gains satisfaction if not pleasure from destroying things including himself. Suicide is the greatest destructive act that man can perpetrate.

Lawbreaking

When the pleasure principle under pressure from the id is expressed in favor of self at the expense of society, laws may be broken, customs may be flouted, and the ego may rationalize its behavior in indulgence of the self. The laws, of course, have been created by the collective superegos of men who are guided by the reality principle that man must evolve controls for group behavior if he is not to destroy himself as a group. In fact, Freud, toward the latter part of his work, began to evince a deep interest in social psychology and the use of his theory in explaining collective behavior.

If confronted with his lawbreaking, man makes himself feel better by employing a few of the defense mechanisms—projection, for one. "Other people break far bigger laws than I do; why don't the police catch them and leave me alone?"

Supranatural Being

Freud's explanation of why man worships a god figure went through considerable change between his four essays collected in *Totem and Taboo* (1913) and his further investigations of the origins of religion and morality in *The Future of an Illusion* (1927) and *Civilization and Its Discontents* (1930). The publication of these works brought down the wrath of the current clergy and corroborated for them the concept of Freud as anti-Christ and an evil, sexually obsessed old man. Beginning in 1907 with a study of the similarity between obsessive acts and religious practices or ritual, especially in relation to "totemism," Oedipus complex, and incestuous repressions, Freud wrote: "I perceived ever more clearly that the events of human history, the interactions between human nature, cultural development and the precipitates of prime-val experiences (the most prominent example of which is religion), are no more than a reflection of the dynamic conflicts between the ego, the id, and the super-ego, which psychoanalysis studies in the individual—are the very same processes repeated on a wider stage" (*An Autobiographical Study*, p. 138).

Humor

By extending some of Freud's theses, we may explain humor as the sudden release of tension which involves the inflation of the ego structure and the enhancement of the ego. This may be brought about by identification with some individual in the humor-producing situation—the Chaplinesque person knocking a top hat off the head of a pompous individual who may be reminis-cent of the figure of authority, the father figure, thus revealing some involve-ment with the Oedipus complex. The obvious principle involved throughout the humor situation is the pleasure principle. (See especially, Jokes and their relation to the unconscious, in the Hogarth Standard Edition of Freud's *Works*, Vol. 8.)

Smoking

The pleasures of smoking are known throughout the civilized world. This universality of a habit is not difficult for the Freudian theorist to explain. Smoking is a form of tension reduction coupled with repetition compulsion based on the pleasure principle that utilizes the oral erotogenic zone. Aside from the manipulative pleasure of handling the instruments of smoking (the pipe, cigarette, the lighter, tamping the tobacco, turning the cigarette in the corner of the mouth), man regresses to using what was pleasant and con-tinues to give him pleasure: the oral cavity. When tensions mount or when one merely behaves repetitively, he reaches for his smoking instruments as a form of oral pleasure sometimes called the "nipple substitute." Picture the modern business executive faced with decisions involving dollars and jobs for his fellow men, caught in a vortex of strong penalties for failure, and sur-rounded by clattering typewriters and all the cacophony of the commercial world. The Freudian theorist finds no surprise in this man's seeking solace in a cigar, which he rolls around in his mouth, sucks, and usually does not smoke to completion. This oral activity returns him to an earlier form of infantile pleasure and thus helps to reduce his inner tensions, despite the fact that it does not help in a direct sense to solve any of his current problems. The college student in the midst of a difficult examination will frequently suck or chew the end of a pencil. Thus he seeks the oral zone to relieve his test-produced anxiety although, again, such mouthing of objects gives him no answers for the examination. The childhood propensity for thumbsucking and the almost automatic appeal of bubble gum for children are part of the return to the oral zone for pleasure.

Play and Recreation

At least six theories about play or combinations of these theories have been formulated by those unconcerned with Freudian theory.

1. Play is a phylogenetic aspect of man's development. Children recapitulate the progress of man's civilization in their play form. From the infant's nihilistic play where he squashes, kills, and plays as he pleases with no thought of consequences to others (doesn't take turns, pushes, hits, bites, etc.) to the more socialized forms of play in organized sports and games with highly involved sets of rules, the child goes through all the steps that man went through from his caveman savagery to his present mode of living.

2. Play is a preparation for adulthood. The child goes through all the necessary roles he may have to fulfill in later life as he makes believe he is one of his parents, or a hero, or a villain.

3. Play is simply the disposition of excess energy which the child builds up during the confinement of his more societally constricted roles. As children dash out to the playground for recess in a noisy exuberant manner, they are seeking release from pent-up feelings that have arisen out of the formality of a classroom situation. Recess and after-school play provide the chance to explode and do all the things that the teacher could not or would not allow to be done in the classroom.

4. Play is necessary as a change from whatever one has to do in most of one's existence. The academic person indulges in fishing and outdoor activities because they are different from his normal existence and thus add variety to life.

5. Play and recreation allow man to rest from the vicissitudes of everyday living. This factor applies especially to the more sedentary recreational forms such as spectator sports, television viewing, and the like. Play then is man's chance to rest his body and mind without resorting to sleep.

6. Play is that wonderful medium of life at all ages that allows us to work out our emotional problems under and with the approval of society's codes. If we are angry and disturbed about something in our workaday world, we may strike a golf ball as hard as we can, we may throw a bowling ball with all our might at ten inoffensive pins without retaliation, we may sing or act and take the roles that are not possible for us in regular life. Thus as we play we resolve inner conflicts that make us unhappy.

Freud's theory could accept all of the above possibilities in explaining play and why man seeks recreation no matter what his culture, background, or age. Recasting the preceding theories, the psychoanalytic explanation could be construed as follows.

1. The gradual development of the id structure into the ego and super-ego superstructures follows man's phylogenetic reasons for play. As he develops, the child indulges in biting (oral, sadistic outlet), pushes or hits other children (pleasure principle predominating), and eventually learns complicated rules for games (reality principle which tells him that by postponing the present pleasure of retaliation he may gain a more solid and higher pleasure of acceptance and approval from parents and playmates).

2. Many of the child's play and recreation agencies utilize the very developmental stages he is going through. The scouting organizations of Cubs or Brownies help him to express his normal homosexual appetites. Literature of a make-believe character helps to fulfill the fictional love stage and promote the fantasy level which he undergoes during the phallic–genital ages. His superego is tremendously strengthened during play because of the rules which others construct and which he discovers are useful and necessary.

3. The irrepressible id and libido are frequently allowed to follow the pleasure principle in, at times, thinly disguised recreational activities. The boy may hold a girl's body during dancing and gain some satisfaction for the libidinal appetites.

4 and 5. These non-Freudian theories of play follow the dictates of the duality principle. As he goes from work to its opposite, play, man follows the polarity of interests and living habits.

6. Catharsis and the value of working off emotional problems are highly allied with the therapy for children that is used by both Freudian and non-Freudian therapists as among their chief stocks in trade. Although Freud and, of course, others go far beyond the cathartic aspects and rightfully consider reinterpretation as a *sine qua non* of therapy, much of the technique of free association is involved in Freud's theory of play.

Psychoses–Neuroses

We will make no detailed exposition of why man becomes psychotic or neurotic within the Freudian framework simply because to do so is to summarize at this point the entire theory or to repeat the entire chapter, for Freud's theory concerns itself solely with, grew out of, and was constructed for the pursuance of the very question: Why does man become so deviant in his emotional behavior as to be psychotic or neurotic? Theorists to be explained in later chapters lend themselves more to this treatment because their theories did not grow originally from an explanation of man's deviant behavior. The reader then must content himself with a review of the previous portions of this chapter or a reading of the summary to follow.

PREDICTING HUMAN BEHAVIOR VIA
FREUD'S PSYCHOANALYTIC THEORY

Prediction of actions or the *when* question can be directed in two ways: at the single individual or at a group of individuals. To predict the behavior of the former is almost impossible; to predict the actions of the latter comes closer to being possible. One person has so many variables floating around his behavior that we may never come to recognize, let alone control, them in order to predict his actions. It might be supposed that the variables would increase in proportion to the size of the group, and they do to some extent. But the individuals contained in a group will tend, as the size of the group increases, to have more and more of the same variables operating. Thus, group prediction becomes somewhat simpler only because the variables become more identifiable. But the true ease in comparing individual with group predictability lies in the factor of deviation from the average. Some individuals will always be at the extremities, but most will cluster in the middle as the size of the group is extended. In dealing with predictability of personality theories for groups, we have size unlimited. We are speaking of all men, not just a restricted population of college students, agricultural workers, or the like. Our task is now easier, for we want to predict when most of the group will conduct itself in a prescribed manner. The bigger the "most" group, the more successful we are in prediction.

Although prediction of an individual's behavior is complicated by intangible variables, we cannot beg the question. The latter would be the safest thing to do for many reasons. First, the individual is primarily concerned with himself. He will test all theories on the basis of his own experience. Second, meaningful discussion of human behavior always descends to "It depends upon the individual." This rejoinder soon becomes habitual and stops any further consideration of one human's behavior. We do not quarrel with the assumption that it is good to know all we can concerning one human being, but complete knowledge is never possible, even for ourselves. Another factor arises from the "depends upon the individual" cliché. If each individual is different from all other individuals, which he is, then by the process of *reductio ad absurdum* we must construct as many laws or theories of behavior as there are people in the world. This, too, is partially true but manifestly absurd when one is trying to promote some definitive considerations of man's behavior. Either we always deal with people in groups, a limited approach, or we are restricted to dealing with each individual in the confines of his individual *gestalt*. But there must be some middle ground in which certain constants hold for most individuals. We have, then, taken out of the group study the largest part of their numbers and looked at them as single people operating under similar responses to life's demands.

Personal Prediction

Two factors are involved in this classification. One is the student reader's own introspective feeling regarding prediction of human behavior; the idea either makes sense to him or it does not. The other is the evidence as it has been accumulated by investigators, who sometimes call themselves scientists, and their work in a particular theory. Even after weighing the scientific data, the individual alone makes the final decision as to its acceptability as a personality theory leading to prediction.

This first section is concerned primarily with the individual reader's acceptance or rejection of Freud's theory and its worth in predicting human behavior.

If Freud's theory is accurate, we may expect all men to, for example, progress through the erogenous zones of oral–anal–phallic–genital. We may further expect them to regress to an oral fixation of sucking or mouthing some object when anxiety and stress are present. Can we predict that man will always have some supreme being to worship and fear because, as Freud states, he needs a supranatural father figure? Under the psychoanalytic theory man will always be prone to psychotic and neurotic episodes as long as there are pressures in the world and in himself which upset the polarity of his existence. Does it make sense to the reader to accept the thesis that man is forever to go back and forth between two polarities of action or decision and only by being an extreme deviate ever to remain at one of the poles? These are but some of the behaviorisms of man that we may predict if the Freudian theory is correct.

It may be of interest to reexamine some of the defense mechanisms to evaluate their predictability. Suppose, for example, that a child reverses the Oedipus–Electra complex; instead of feeling strong but unconscious rivalry with his father for his mother's love, a boy feels no rivalry with his father but undergoes an overwhelming attachment and identification with his father, ignoring or even hating his mother. Will he be a homosexually perverted adult?

Let us presume that whenever an individual must repress a libidinal desire he or she will turn to one of the forms of substitution and paint or draw or engage in activities that bring proximity to others' bodies.

Can we accurately say that man, when he is deeply frustrated and cannot retaliate openly to the object of frustration, will displace his anger at a secondary object only remotely akin to the original object?

Is it possible for the reader through introspection to recognize, only tangentially of course, the stirrings and urgings of an id as Freud described it? What proof does one need to find in himself to sense the pulling and tugging of the duality principle of life?

All the above queries are directed at the individual reader with no attempt to decide scientifically whether they are meaningful or not. The reader either answers them to his satisfaction or he does not, just as he either accepts the reports of research concerning Freud's work or does not accept them.

Scientific or Laboratory Prediction

A concerted effort to continue the work of Freud is now being made by his daughter Anna in the Hampstead Child-Therapy Clinic, Maresfield Gardens, in London. The Hampstead Clinic is primarily devoted to training lay analysts in child therapy and to conducting research. It is well staffed although small compared to many American training institutions. Almost all of its output is reported in the annual volumes of *The Psychoanalytic Study of the Child*. Miss Freud is one of the senior editors of this interesting journal. No attempt is made here to evaluate the quality of prediction of their work. The reader is urged to make an independent judgment after having read the journals.

As will be the case throughout this text, no attempt is being made to cover exhaustively all the research pertaining to any theory including the Freudian or psychoanalytic theories of personality. Instead, the focus is on representative or unique studies and on the most recent research being done on a theory. Exclusion is mandated because the size of the book must be controlled. Recency is emphasized because older works most adequately covering research were published prior to 1960 (Blum, 1953; Munroe, 1955; Sears, 1943; Whiting and Child, 1953). A later source is Lindzey and Hall, 1965.

By far the majority of articles and books about Freud are not concerned with research but center on Freud the person (including minutiae about his personal life and family), semantic affirmation and rebuttals of his theory and therapy, his friends and foes, and ramifications of the entire psychoanalytic history and movement.

Investigation of method has been suggested as of prime concern before much progress can be made in modern research on psychoanalysis. Methodology will clarify the theory (Ramzy, 1963).

In a very difficult research area, dreams, some work has been accomplished with, at times, modest and conflicting results (MacKenzie, 1965). The concepts of manifest and latent dreams as well as rapid eye movements are not always researched along psychoanalytic lines; however, "Freud's dream theory has been by no means discredited" (Glick, 1967a). The most ambitious research by a dedicated scientist is that of Calvin Hall. He and others have compared the Freudian and Jungian approaches to dream analysis (Hall and Domhoff, 1968) and aggression in dreams (Hall and Domhoff, 1963);

have compared the superego in men and women and found a "modest confirmation" that women suffer more aggressive dreams while men dream more often of misfortunes (Hall, 1964); and have determined that the erogenous zones are implied in dream content. This last study indicated that men have more dreams about castration anxiety while women dream more often of castration wish and penis envy (Hall and Van de Castle, 1965).

Some "animal studies" support (but do not prove) Sigmund Freud's theories of psychosexual development which emphasize that a child's infantile experiences—especially his affinity to his mother—meticulously fashion his adult sexual behavior (Cohen, 1969). One well-publicized example is Harlow's maternal deprivation research with rhesus monkeys. When the animals were reared in isolation, there was gross maladaptive heterosexual behavior with sexual aberrations. Later contacts with other infant monkeys appeared to ameliorate the condition (Harlow, 1962; Harlow and Harlow, 1962).

Possibly the greatest volume of research and the most clear-cut involves infants and children. The studies, both experimental and correlational, range from an analysis of fairy tales interpreted in a Freudian sense (Heuscher, 1963) to the effect of infant sexuality on later development (Broderick, 1966; Chodoff, 1966; Kreitler and Kreitler, 1966). These studies for the most part challenge the basic Freudian positions on psychosexual forces in early life. Additional work on early ego development stress the neurological influences (Bronson, 1963), relationship to learning theory (Rohde, 1967), abnormality in development (Saul and Wenar, 1965), and the meaning and measurement of ego development (Loevinger, 1966a).

Two studies were concerned with castration complex. One, reported in 1963 on forty amputees, found tentative evidence validating castration anxiety (Block and Ventur, 1963). The other, an anthropological investigation, speaks of Coro, a mental derangement peculiar to southeast Asia, in which the patient "is afraid that his penis will withdraw into his abdomen resulting in his death." The anxiety is intense and sudden and may be prolonged for days or weeks. Excessive masturbation or overindulgence is blamed for the condition. "To prevent the withdrawal of the penis, the afflicted holds his penis in a vise-like grip and is assisted in doing so by his wife, friends, and relatives. To release the penis, even for an instant, in their belief would be fatal. Some clamp the penis in a wooden box or tie a red string around it" (Wittkower and Dubreuil, 1968).

In an older study using sixty-one college women as subjects and the Blacky Pictures as a measuring device it was suggested that anal-retentive subjects indicated greater superiority in memory than anal-expulsive subjects (Adelson and Redmond, 1958). A more recent study supported the psychoanalytical hypothesis that phallic, latency, and genital stages would be revealed in symbolic shape preferences (Cameron, 1967).

For many years most psychoanalysts supported Freud's hypothesis that male paranoids had strong delusional homosexual tendencies. Case histories dating back to World War I appeared to support this contention. Carefully conducted research substantiated some of the hypotheses: Paranoid delusional males "tend to have stronger homosexual impulses than male psychotics who are relatively free from these delusions"; they avoid homosexual object preference and have a "primary attraction toward men as sexual objects" (Zamansky, 1958).

A representative analysis of suppression–repression supported the Freudian position (Worell, 1965).

The following studies indicate how broad is the research interest in proving or disproving the psychoanalytic theory of personality in structural aspects or dynamics. They range from chemical homologues (Bernhard, 1964) to a support of Freud's thesis that aggressive humor disguises the real reason one laughs (Gollob and Levine, 1967). Continuing the spectrum of research interest we find a "clear distinction" between the superego and ego-ideal (Adcock and Adcock, 1967) and speculative analogy between Cattell's third-order factors and the id–ego–superego concepts (Pawlick and Cattell, 1964). "Recent literature suggests that the superego is beginning to come of age" although the "overwhelming majority of studies have focused on ego and to a lesser extent on id factors." Although the majority of studies begin with a tangential reference to Freud, "the remainder of the study bears little resemblance to the psychoanalytic conception of the superego" (Bortner, 1963; Higashimachi, 1963; McCord and Clemes, 1964; Shore *et al.*, 1964). And finally an investigation by Corman and associates found a method of examining the relationship between visual imagery and preconscious processes (Corman *et al.*, 1964).

As is now well known by students of Freudian theory, Freud had his patients lie down on a couch during therapy. Interestingly one small recent study found that forty-two college undergraduates were able to recall more early childhood memories in a "lying down position" than in a "sitting up position" (Berdach and Bakan, 1967).

Thus it is refreshing and encouraging to note that some attempts have been and are continuing to be made to test a theory, in this case Freud's vast contribution to a theory of personality. It is good to be critical of the above research contributions. It is even better to work hard and to do research of one's own to add to man's knowledge of the Freudian concepts both in his theory of human behavior and in his therapeutic dynamics.

■ SUMMARY

Figure 2 is a diagrammatic attempt to summarize the main features of Freud's theory regarding personality and its formation in man.

The id lies at the bottom, is the largest portion of the personality, and supports the entire structure. Basic to the id is the bottom layer of subcon-

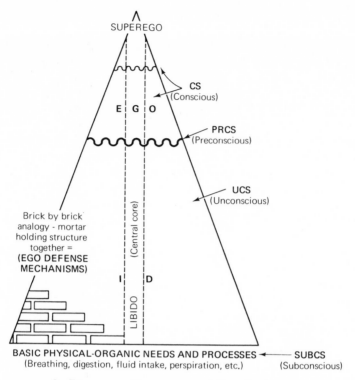

FIGURE 2. *Diagrammatic summary of Freud's theory.*

scious processes upon which all of life depends. The physical, sensory, and ongoing organic functions operate out of the subconscious. One does not have to think consciously about breathing, for example, in order to breathe. The id also permeates the unconscious. Only those activities which have been in the conscious and go through the preconscious may be considered in the unconscious. The subconscious, on the other hand, is innate and operates from birth.

The ego, which must deal with reality because it operates in the conscious state, is separated from the id by only the small membrane of the preconscious. The preconscious acts as a doorkeeper rather than as a repository of mental activity. It can only facilitate or limit and restrict passage of mental material from the id to its component, the ego.

The superego, being the last to develop, lies at the top of the structure well within the realm of the conscious. It is the smallest component of the personality structure as well as the latest. If the structure is to collapse, it does so from the top down: The superego defaults first, followed by the ego. The last characteristic of the personality to cease operating is the subconscious level of breathing, digestion, and organic functioning.

Central to the entire structure of the personality (as given in Figure 2) is the libido, which runs up through the middle of the structure to diminish at the apex of the superego and thus be the core of much that is within man's personality and is affected by it.

Around the entire structure, protecting it from the pressures and weathering of the outside world, is a brick façade held together by the mortar of the ego defense mechanisms. Consequently, although the ego defense mechanisms may change the outward appearance of the structure, they may never alter the fundamental structure.

Outline

EROGENOUS ZONES	CHARACTERISTIC BEHAVIOR	LOVE STAGES
Oral		Self
Anal		Paternal
Phallic		Fictional
Latent period		Homosexual
Genital		Heterosexual

BIBLIOGRAPHY

PRIMARY SOURCES

BOOKS

Freud, S., *The Standard Edition of the Complete Psychological Works*, trans. James Strachey, 24 vols. London: Hogarth, 1953–55.

> The most complete and definitive compilation of Freud's writings. Because of its size—24 volumes—it must usually be read in reference libraries and hence does not lend itself to browsing at leisure.

Freud, S., *Collected Papers*, Vols. I–V. London: Hogarth, 1925–1950.

> A secondary source if the complete volumes are not available.

Freud, S., *Collected Papers*. New York: Basic Books, 1959.

> First American edition of 5 vols. *Collected Papers*, published in London.

Freud, S., *The Basic Writings of Sigmund Freud*, ed. A. A. Brill. New York: Random House, 1938.

> Probably the most available book covering most of his important writings; also the least expensive.

Freud, S., *A General Selection from the Works of Sigmund Freud*, ed. J. Rickman. New York: Liveright, 1957.

> Indicates change and development of Freud's work from 1910 to 1926.

Freud, S., *The Case of Dora and Other Papers*. New York: Norton, 1952.

> Nine essays taken from previous writings.

Freud, S., and D. E. Oppenheim, *Dreams in Folklore*. New York: International Universities Press, 1958.

Breuer, J., and S. Freud, *Studies on Hysteria*. New York: Basic Books, 1957.

> Reprint of Vol. XI of Standard Edition.

Freud, S., *The Origin of Psychoanalysis: Letters to Wilhelm Fliess, Drafts and Notes: 1887–1902*. New York: Basic Books, 1954.

> Also as a paperback published by Doubleday (Anchor), Garden City, N.Y., 1957.

Freud, S., *On Aphasia: A Critical Study* (1891). New York: International Universities Press, 1953.

Freud, S., *The Interpretation of Dreams* (1900). London: Hogarth, 1953.

> Also as a Basic Book, New York, 1955.

Freud, S., *Psychopathology of Everyday Life* (1904). New York: New American Library, 1951.

> Also as a paperback published by Norton, New York, 1966.

Freud, S., *Leonardo da Vinci: A Study in Psychosexuality* (1910). New York: Random House, 1947.

Freud, S., *Totem and Taboo* (1913). New York: Random House.

> Modern Library paperback with no publication date.

Freud, S., *A General Introduction to Psychoanalysis* (1917). Garden City, N.Y.: Doubleday, 1953.

> Permabook paperback. Also published as a Perma Giant in 1949; Garden City Deluxe and Star Editions in 1938, 1943.

Freud, S., *Beyond the Pleasure Principle* (1920). London: Hogarth, 1948.

> Also as a paperback published by Bantam Books, New York, 1963.

Freud, S., *Group Psychology and the Analysis of the Ego* (1921). New York: Bantam Books, 1960.

Freud, S., *The Ego and the Id* (1923). London: Hogarth, 1947.

Freud, S., *On Creativity and the Unconscious* (1925). New York: Harper & Row, 1958.

Freud, S., *Inhibitions, Symptoms and Anxiety* (1926). London: Hogarth, 1936, 1948.

Freud, S., *The Question of Lay Analysis* (1926). New York: Norton, 1950.

Freud, S., *Civilization and Its Discontents* (1930). London: Hogarth, 1930.

Also as a paperback published by Norton, New York, 1962.

Freud, S., *New Introductory Lectures on Psychoanalysis* (1933). New York: Norton, 1933.

Freud, S., *An Autobiographical Study* (1935), rev. ed. London: Hogarth, 1946.

Also as a paperback published by Norton, New York, 1963.

Freud, S., *An Outline of Psychoanalysis* (1938). New York: Norton, 1949.

Also as a paperback published by Norton, New York, 1963.

Freud, S., *Moses and Monotheism* (1939). New York: Knopf, 1947.

Freud, S., *Delusion and Dream*. Boston: Beacon Press, 1956.

Freud, S., *Three Contributions to the Theory of Sex*. New York: Dutton, 1962.

Freud, S., *Character and Culture*. New York: Crowell-Collier, 1963.

Freud, S., *Dora, an Analysis of a Case of Hysteria*. New York: Crowell-Collier, 1963.

Freud, S., *Early Psychoanalytic Writings*. New York: Crowell-Collier, 1963.

Freud, S., *General Psychological Theory*. New York: Crowell-Collier, 1963.

Freud, S., *The History of the Psychoanalytic Movement*. New York: Crowell-Collier, 1963.

Freud, S., *Jokes and Their Relation to the Unconscious*. New York: Norton, 1963.

Freud, S., *On Dreams*. New York: Norton, 1963.

Freud, S., *The Sexual Enlightenment of Children*. New York: Crowell-Collier, 1963.

Freud, S., *Sexuality and the Psychology of Love*. New York: Crowell-Collier, 1963.

Freud, S., *Studies in Parapsychology*. New York: Crowell-Collier, 1963.

Freud, S., *Therapy and Technique*. New York: Crowell-Collier, 1963.

Freud, S., *Three Case Histories: The Wolf Man, the Rat Man, and the Psychotic Doctor Schreber*. New York: Crowell-Collier, 1963.

Freud, S., *The Future of an Illusion*. New York: Doubleday (Anchor), 1964.

Freud, S., *Leonardo da Vinci and a Memory of His Childhood*. New York: Norton, 1964.

Freud, S., *The Problem of Anxiety*. New York: Norton, 1963.

Freud, S., and O. Pfister, *Psychoanalysis and Faith*. New York: Basic Books, 1964.

Freud, S., *New Introductory Lectures on Psychoanalysis*. New York: Norton, 1965.

Freud, S., *On the History of the Psychoanalytic Movement*. New York: Norton, 1966.

PERIODICALS

Freud, S., Report on my studies in Paris and Berlin (1886), *Int. J. Psycho. Anal.*, 1956, 37, 2–7.

Breuer, J., and S. Freud, On the psychical mechanism of hysterical phenomena (1893), *Int. J. Psycho. Anal.*, 1956, 37, 8–13.

Freud, S., On the teaching of psychoanalysis in universities (1918), *Int. J. Psycho. Anal.*, 1956, 37, 14–15.

Freud, S., Memorandum on the electrical treatment of war neurotics (1920), *Int. J. Psycho. Anal.*, 1956, 37, 16–18.

Freud, S., Three letters to America, *Psychoanalysis*, 1952, 1, 5–6.

Freud, S., An unpublished letter on parapsychology, *Psychoanalysis*, 1954, 4, and 5, 12–13.

Freud, S., Four unpublished letters of Freud, *Psychoanal. Quar.*, 1956, 25, 147–154.

SUGGESTED READINGS

BOOKS

Abraham, H. C., and E. T. Freud (eds.), *A Psychoanalytic Dialogue: The Letters of Sigmund Freud and Karl Abraham, 1907–1926.* New York: Basic Books, 1966.

Amacher, P., *Freud's Neurological Education and Its Influence on Psychoanalytic Theory.* New York: International Universities Press, 1965.

Andreas-Salomé, Lou, *The Freud Journal of Lou Andreas-Salomé.* New York: Basic Books, 1964.

Arlow, J. A., *The Legacy of Sigmund Freud.* New York: International Universities Press, 1956.

Bakan, D., *Sigmund Freud and the Jewish Mystical Tradition.* Princeton, N.J.: Van Nostrand, 1958.

> Also available in paperback, Schocken Books, New York, 1965.

Bakan, D., *The Duality of Human Existence, An Essay on Psychology and Religion.* Chicago: Rand McNally, 1966.

Bergmann, T., *Children in the Hospital.* New York: International Universities Press, 1966.

> In collaboration with A. Freud.

Bertocci, P. A., and R. M. Miller, *Personality and the Good.* New York: McKay, 1963.

> In Part I the concepts of Freud, Jung, Adler, Horney, Fromm, Maslow, and G. Allport are examined for their contributions to the nature of the good life.

Blum, G. S., *Psychoanalytic Theories of Personality.* New York: McGraw-Hill, 1953.

Bolles, R. C., *Theories of Motivation*. New York: Harper & Row, 1966.

> Includes Freud, Murray, and Lewin.

Brill, A. A., *Basic Principles of Psychoanalysis* (1921). New York: Washington Square Press, 1960.

> Also issued as Garden City ed., 1949, and now reissued as a paperback. See especially Chap. 5, "Wit: Its Technique and Tendencies," an adaption of Freud on wit and humor.

Brill, A. A., *Psychoanalysis, Its Theories and Practical Application*, 3rd ed. Philadelphia: Saunders, 1922.

Brill, A. A., *Freud's Contribution to Psychiatry*. New York: Norton, 1944.

Brown, I. A. C., *Freud and the Post-Freudians*. Baltimore: Penguin, 1961.

> Horney, Fromm, and Sullivan also included.

Choisy, M., *Sigmund Freud: A New Appraisal*. New York: Citadel, 1963.

> Suggests that anxiety of death and concern for the unknown were key concepts in Freud's thought.

Cohen, J., *Personality Dynamics*, Series 17, Eyewitness Series in Psychology. Chicago: Rand McNally, 1969.

Costigan, G., *Sigmund Freud: A Short Biography*. New York: Macmillan, 1965.

Eissler, R., A. Freud, and E. Glover (eds.), *The Psychoanalytic Study of the Child*. New York: International Universities Press, 1965.

English, H. B., and A. C. English, *A Comprehensive Dictionary of Psychological and Psychoanalytical Terms*. New York: Longmans, Green, 1958.

Fine, R., *Freud: A Critical Re-evaluation of His Theories*. New York: McKay, 1962.

Fliess, R., *Erogeneity and Libido: Addenda to the Theory of the Psychosexual Development of the Human*. New York: International Universities Press, 1957.

Freeman, P., *An Introduction to Sigmund Freud, M.D., and Psychoanalysis*. Englewood Cliffs, N.J.: Prentice-Hall, 1965.

Freud, A., *Psychoanalysis for Teachers and Parents*. New York: Emerson, 1935.

Freud, A., *The Ego and the Mechanisms of Defence*. New York: International Universities Press, 1946.

Freud, A., *Normality and Pathology in Childhood: Assessments of Development*. New York: International Universities Press, 1965.

Freud, A., and others (eds.), *The Psychoanalytic Study of the Child*, Vol. 1, 1945, to current Vol. 15, 1960. New York: International Universities Press.

> A yearly publication—Anna Freud's chief agency for publishing. Reflects thoroughly the new Freudian approach.

Freud, E. L., *Letters of Sigmund Freud*. New York: Basic Books, 1961.

> His son's collection of 315 letters Freud wrote between 1873 and 1939.

Freud, M., *Sigmund Freud: Man and Father*. New York: Vanguard, 1958.

> Personal memories of Freud's second child and eldest son.

Friedman, P., *On Suicide: With Particular Reference to Suicide Among Young Students.* New York: International Universities Press, 1967.

Fromm, E., *Sigmund Freud's Mission: An Analysis of His Personality and Influence.* New York: Harper & Row, 1959.

> Also published by Grove Press, 1963.

Glover, E., *Freud or Jung.* New York: Norton, 1950.

> Compares Freud with Jung; Freud wins. Also as a Meridian Pocketbook, 1956.

Grollman, E. A., *Judaism in Sigmund Freud's Work.* New York: Appleton-Century-Crofts, 1966.

Guntrip, H., *Personality Structure and Human Interaction.* New York: International Universities Press, 1961.

> Psychoanalysis a true theory of personality.

Hall, C. S., *A Primer of Freudian Psychology.* Cleveland: World Publishing, 1954.

> Also published by Mentor Books, 1955.

Hall, C. S., and G. Lindzey, *Theories of Personality.* New York: Wiley, 1957, pp. 29–75.

Heuscher, J. E., *A Psychiatric Study of Fairy Tales.* Springfield, Ill.: Thomas, 1963.

> Fairy tales from various parts of the world analyzed and interpreted psychiatrically. Interpretations made in terms of Freudian and Jungian analytic theories.

Higgins, M., and C. M. Raphael, *Reich Speaks of Freud.* New York: Noonday Press, 1967.

Hilgard, E. R., and H. Bower, *Theories of Learning,* 3rd ed. New York: Appleton-Century-Crofts, 1966.

> Freud's reality and pleasure principles in the learning theory framework.

Hoffman, F. J., *Freudianism and the Literary Mind,* 2nd ed. Baton Rouge: Louisiana State University Press, 1957.

> Also Grove Press, 1959.

Holland, N. N., *Psychoanalysis and Shakespeare.* New York: McGraw-Hill, 1966.

Hollitscher, W., *Psychoanalysis and Civilization: An Introduction to Sigmund Freud.* New York: Grove Press, 1963.

Johnston, T., *Freud and Political Thought.* New York: Citadel, 1965.

Jones, E., *The Life and Work of Sigmund Freud:* Vol. I (1856–1900), *The Formative Years and the Great Discoveries,* 1953; Vol. II (1901–1919), *Years of Maturity,* 1955; Vol. III (1919–1939), *The Last Phase,* 1957. New York: Basic Books.

> All of the series dedicated to "Anna Freud, True daughter of an immortal sire."

Jones, E., *Sigmund Freud: Four Centenary Addresses*. New York: Basic Books, 1956.

Klein, G. S., H. L. Barr, and D. L. Wolitzky, Personality, in *Annual Review of Psychology*, Palo Alto, Cal.: Annual Reviews, Inc., 1967, pp. 518–519.

Kohut, H., and P. F. D. Seitz, Concepts and theories of psychoanalysis, in J. M. Wepman and R. W. Heine (eds.), *Concepts of Personality*. Chicago: Aldine, 1963.

Kubie, L. S., Problems and techniques of psychoanalytic validation and progress, in E. Pumpian-Mindlin (ed.), *Psychoanalysis as Science*. Stanford, Cal.: Stanford University Press, 1952, pp. 46–124.

LaPiere, R., *The Freudian Ethic*. New York: Duell, Sloan & Pearce, 1959.

Lauzon, G., *Sigmund Freud: The Man and His Theories*. New York: Eriksson, 1965.

Lee, R. S., *Freud and Christianity*. Middlesex, Eng.: Penguin, 1967.

Lesser, S. O., *Fiction and the Unconscious*. Boston: Beacon Press, 1957.

Levitt, M., *Freud and Dewey on the Nature of Man*. New York: Philosophical Library, 1960.

They stood "shoulder to shoulder" in some respects.

Lindzey, G., and C. S. Hall (eds.), *Theories of Personality: Primary Sources and Research*. New York: Wiley, 1965.

MacIntyre, A. C., *The Unconscious: A Conceptual Analysis*. New York: Humanities Press, 1958.

Some promise in the unconscious concept but may be more metaphysical than scientific.

MacKenzie, N., *Dreams and Dreaming*. New York: Vanguard, 1965.

Madison, P., *Freud's Concept of Repression and Defense: Its Theoretical and Observational Language*. Minneapolis: University of Minnesota Press, 1961.

Meng, H., and E. L. Freud (eds.), *Sigmund Freud. Psychoanalysis and Faith: Dialogues with the Reverend Oskar Pfister*. New York: Basic Books, 1964.

Milton, K., *Freud and Hypnosis and the Interaction of Psycho-Dynamics and Hypnosis*. New York: Matrix House, 1966.

Munroe, R. L., *Schools of Psychoanalytic Thought*. New York: Holt, Rinehart & Winston, 1955.

Analysis and integration of Freud, Adler, Jung, Rank, Fromm, Horney, Sullivan, *et al.*

Murphy, G., *Psychological Thought from Pythagoras to Freud: An Informal Introduction*. New York: Harcourt, Brace & World, 1968.

Nelson, B. (ed.), *Freud and the 20th Century*. New York: World Publishing (Meridian), 1957.

Notenberg, M., *The Case History of Sigmund Freud: A Psycho-Biography*. Chicago: Regents, 1955.

Nunberg, H., and E. Federn (eds.), *Minutes of the Vienna Psychoanalytic Society*, Vol. 1, 1906–1908. New York: International Universities Press, 1962.

Rapaport, D., On the psychoanalytic theory of motivation, in M. R. Jones (ed.), *Nebraska Symposium on Motivation*. Lincoln: University of Nebraska Press, 1960.

Read, H., *Art and Society*. New York: Schocken Books, 1966.

Relationships between art and Freud.

Rieff, P., *Freud: The Mind of the Moralist*. New York: Viking, 1959.

Rieff, P., *The Triumph of the Therapeutic: Uses of Faith after Freud*. New York: Harper & Row, 1966.

Roazen, P., *Freud: Political and Social Thought*. New York: Knopf, 1967.

Roback, A. A., *Freudians: Including Unpublished Letters from Freud to Havelock Ellis, Pavlov, Bernard Shaw, Romain Rolland, et al.*, Cambridge, Mass.: Sci-Art Publishers, 1957.

Robert, J., *The Psychoanalytic Revolution: Sigmund Freud's Life and Achievement*. New York: Harcourt, Brace & World, 1966.

Roheim, G. (ed.), *Psychoanalysis and the Social Sciences*. New York: International Universities Press, 1948.

Ruitenbeek, H. M., *Freud and America*. New York: Macmillan, 1966.

Ruitenbeek, H. M. (ed.), *Heirs to Freud: Essays in Freudian Psychology*. New York: Grove Press, 1966.

Schoenwald, R., *Freud: The Man and His Mind, 1856–1956*. New York: International Universities Press, 1956.

Sherman, M. H., *Psychoanalysis in America*. Springfield, Ill.: Thomas, 1966.

Sherwood, M., *The Logic of Explanation in Psychoanalysis*. New York: Academic Press, 1969.

Stafford-Clark, D., *What Freud Really Said*. New York: Schocken Books, 1967.

How Freud came to see myth and legend as repositories of truth about basic human situations.

Teevan, R., and R. Birney (eds.), *Theories of Motivation in Personality and Social Psychology*. Princeton, N.J.: Van Nostrand, 1964.

Toman, W., *An Introduction to Psychoanalytic Theory of Motivation*. New York: Pergamon Press, 1960.

An attempt to systematize Freudian theory.

Waelder, R., *Basic Theory of Psychoanalysis*. New York: Schocken Books, 1964.

Wells, H. K., *The Failure of Psychoanalysis: From Freud to Fromm*. New York: International Publishers, 1963.

Whiting, J. W. M., and I. L. Child, *Child Training and Personality: A Cross-Cultural Study*. New Haven, Conn.: Yale University Press, 1953.

Wittkower, E. R., and G. Dubreuil, Cultural factors in mental illness, in E. Norbeck, D. Price-Williams, and W. McCord, *The Study of Personality*. New York: Holt, Rinehart and Winston, 1968.

Wortis, J., *Fragments of an Analysis with Freud*. New York: Simon and Shuster, 1954.

Diary and notes of a former patient analyzed in winter, 1934–35.

PERIODICALS

Adams, L., Sigmund Freud's correct birthday: Misunderstanding and solution, *Psychoanal. Rev.*, 1954, *41*, 359–362.

Adcock, N. V., and C. J. Adcock, A factorial study of the ego reference system, *J. Genet. Psychol.*, 1967, *110*, 105–115.

> Finds a "clean distinction" between these two "superego" factors and the "sentiment of self-regard."

Adelson, J., Freud in America: Some observations, *Amer. Psychologist*, 1956, *11*, 467–470.

Adelson, J., and J. Redmond, Personality differences in the capacity for verbal recall, *J. Abnorm. Soc. Psychol.*, 1958, *51*, 244–248.

Alexander, F., Unexplored areas in psychoanalytic theory and treatment, *Behav. Sci.*, 1958, *3*, 293–316.

Angel, R. W., Jackson, Freud, and Sherrington on the relation of brain and mind, *Amer. J. Psychiat.*, 1961, *118*, 193–197.

Ansbacher, H. L., The significance of the socio-economic status of the patients of Freud and Adler, *Amer. J. Psychother.*, 1959, *13*, 376–382.

Ansbacher, H. L., Was Adler a disciple of Freud? A reply, *J. Indiv. Psychol.*, 1962, *18*, 126–135.

> The answer is no.

Aronoff, J., Freud's conception of the origin of curiosity, *J. Psychol.*, 1962, *54*, 39–45.

> Curiosity is somatically based during anal–sadistic stage and copes with sibling rivalry.

Atlantic, 208, No. 1, 61–111, special supplement on psychiatry in American life.

Bach, G. R., Freud's time bounded group concepts, *Group Psychother.*, 1956, *9*, 301–304.

Bailey, P., Janet and Freud, *A.M.A. Arch. Neurol. Psychiat.* (Chicago), 1956, *76*, 76–89.

Bakan, P., Some thought on reading Augustine's "Confessions," *J. Sci. Stud. Relig.*, 1965, *5*, 149–152.

> The Oedipal elements in Augustine's life and writings.

Balint, M., Letter to the editor, *Int. J. Psycho. Anal.*, 1968, *49*, 99.

Beets, N., Ego psychology and the meeting face-to-face in psychotherapy, *Rev. Exist. Psychol. Psychiat.*, 1967, *7*, 72–93.

Bellak, L., Freud and projective techniques, *J. Proj. Techn.*, 1956, *20*, 5–13.

Benassy, M., Psychoanalye théorique (Theoretical psychoanalysis), *Bull. Psychol.* (Paris), 1967, *20*, 563–567.

> There is a difference between Freud's concept of the subconscious and the concepts of psychologists and psychophysiologists.

Berdach, E., and D. Bakan, Body position and the free recall of early memories, *Psychother. Theor. Res. Pract.*, 1967, *4*, 101–102.

Bernfeld, S., Freud's studies on cocaine: 1884–1887, *J. Amer. Psychoanal. Ass.*, 1953, *1*, 581–613.

Bernfeld, S., and S. Bernfeld, Freud's first year in practice: 1886–1887, *Bull. Menninger Clin.*, 1952, *16*, 37–49.

Bernhard, R., Chemical homologue of the model presented in Freud's "project," *Psychoanal. Quart.*, 1964, *33*, 357–374.

Blanton, S., Freud and theology, *Pastoral Counselor*, 1963, *1*, 3–8.

Block, W. E., and P. A. Ventur, A study of the psychoanalytic concept of castration anxiety in symbolically castrated amputees, *Psychiat. Quart.*, 1963, *37*, 518–526.

> Evidence validating castration anxiety was found.

Bonime, W., The psychic energy of Freud and Jung, *Amer. J. Psychiat.*, 1955, *121*, 372–374.

Bortner, R. W., The relationship between age and measures of id, ego, and superego functioning, *J. Geront.*, 1963, *18*, 286–289.

Brams, J., From Freud to Fromm, *Psychol. Today*, 1968, *1*, 32–35, 64–65.

Brandt, L. W., Process or structure? *Psychoanal. Rev.*, 1966, *53*, 50–54.

Broderick, C. B., Sexual behavior among pre-adolescents, *J. Soc. Issues*, 1966, *22*, 6–21.

> Main contention is that normal heterosexual development seems to be borne out by the available data.

Bronson, G., A neurological perspective on ego development in infancy, *J. Amer. Psychoanal. Ass.*, 1963, *11*, 55–65.

Bruner, J. S., Freud and the image of man, *Amer. Psychologist*, 1956, *11*, 463–466.

Burchard, E. M. L., Mystical and scientific aspects of the psychoanalytic theories of Freud, Adler, and Jung, *Amer. J. Psychother.*, 1960, *15*, 289–307.

Cameron, P., Confirmation of the Freudian psychosexual stages utilizing sexual symbolism, *Psychol. Rep.*, 1967, *21*, 33–39.

Canning, J. W., A logical analysis of criticism directed at Freudian psychoanalytic theory, *Dissert. Abstr.*, 1966, *27*, 1078–1079.

Carroll, J. B., and H. Levin, A method for determining the polarity of behavior items, *Child Developm.*, 1956, *27*, 427–438.

> Objectivity in scoring polarity, as love–hate, masculine–feminine, etc.

Chertok, L., From Liebeault to Freud, *Amer. J. Psychother.*, 1968, *22*, 96–101.

Chodoff, P., A critique of Freud's theory of infantile sexuality, *Amer. J. Psychiat.*, 1966, *123*, 507–518.

> Serious reservations about the original Freudian construct.

Colby, K. M., On the disagreement between Freud and Adler, *Amer. Imago*, 1951, *8*, 229–238.

Conkling, M., Sartre's refutation of the Freudian unconscious, *Rev. Exist. Psychol. Psychiat.*, 1968, *8*, 86–101.

Corman, H. H., S. Escalona, and M. F. Reiser, Visual imagery and preconscious processes, *Arch. Gen. Psychiat.* (Chicago), 1964, *10*, 160–172.

Cornyetz, P., Panel discussion: Psychoanalysis and social reality, *Psychoanal. Rev.*, 1967, *54*, 61–65.

Cumes, J., Contrasting systems of explanation in psychology, *Psychol. Scene*, 1967, *1*, 30–33.

Daley, J. W., Freud and moral philosophy, *Dissert. Abstr.*, 1967, 27, 3487.

Dement, W., The effect of dream deprivation, *Science*, 1960, *131*, 1705–1707.

Deri, F., and D. Brunswik, Freud's letter to Ernest Simmel, *J. Amer. Psychoanal. Ass.*, 1964, *12*, 93–109.

Desmonde, W. H., G. H. Mead and Freud: American social psychology and psychoanalysis, *Psychoanalysis*, 1957, *4* and *5*, 31–50.

Eissler, K. R., Freud and the psychoanalysis of history, *J. Amer. Psychoanal. Ass.*, 1963, *11*, 675–703.

Ellenberger, H., The unconscious before Freud, *Bull. Menninger Clin.*, 1957, *21*, 3–15.

Eng, E., Freud and the changing present, *Antioch Rev.*, 1956–57 (winter), pp. 459–468.

Engler, B. O., The concept of knowledge in the thought of Sigmund Freud, *Dissert. Abstr.*, 1967, *28*, 1845–1846.

Erikson, E. H., Freud's "The origins of psychoanalysis," *Int. J. Psycho. Anal.*, 1955, *36*, 1–15.

Feldman, A. B., Freudian theology, *Psychoanalysis*, 1952, *1*, 31–52.

Feldman, B., Sidelights on Freud's *Psychotherapy of Everyday Life*, *Amer. Imago*, 1960, *17*, 47–60.

  Extending the analysis of Freud's book.

Federn, E., Was Adler a disciple of Freud?, A Freudian view, *J. Indiv. Psychol.*, 1963, *19*, 80–82.

Fizer, J., Errata of Freud, *Amer. J. Psychol.*, 1956, *69*, 309–311.

Fodor, N., Freud and the poltergeist, *Psychoanalysis*, 1955–1956, *4*, 22–28.

Fodor, N., Jung, Freud and a newly discovered letter on the Poltergeist theme, *Psychoanal. Rev.*, 1963, *50*, 119–128.

Frailberg, L., Freud's writings on art, *Int. J. Psycho. Anal.*, 1956, *37*, 82–96.

Fromm, E., Teoria Freudiana de la agresividad y la destructividad (Freudian theory of aggressiveness and destructiveness), *Rev. Psicoanal. Psiquiat. Psicolog.*, 1968, *8*, 19–48.

  Challenges Freud's assumption on the presence of a constant amount of aggressive–destructive behavior between individuals and between different groups.

Galdston, I., Eros and Thanatos: A critique and elaboration of Freud's death wish, *Amer. J. Psychoanal.*, 1955, *15*, 123–134.

Geil, R., Freud and the devil in Ethiopian psychiatry, *Psychiat. Neurol. Neurochir.: J. Netherlands Soc. Psychiat. Neurol.*, 1968, *71*, 177–183.

Gervais, T. W., Freud and the culture-psychologists, *Brit. J. Psychol.*, 1955, *46*, 293–305.

Gladston, L., A midcentury assessment of the residuum of Freud's psychoanalytic theory, *Amer. J. Psychother.*, 1957, *11*, 548–559.

Glick, B. S., Freud, the problem of quality and the "secretory neuron," *Psychoanal. Quart.*, 1966, *35*, 84–97.

> Freud made some brilliant stabs into the neurophysiology of the future.

Glick, B. S., Freud's dream theory and modern dream research, *Amer. J. Psychother.*, 1967a, *21*, 630–643.

Glick, B. S., A note on Freud's "empty" neuron, *Brit. J. Med. Psychol.*, 1967b, *40*, 159–162.

Gollob, H. F., and J. Levine, Distraction as a factor in the enjoyment of aggressive humor, *J. Pers. Soc. Psychol.*, 1967, *5*, 368–372.

> Supports Freud.

Goshen, C. E., The original case material of psychoanalysis, *Amer. J. Psychiat.*, 1952, *108*, 829–832.

> Freud misinterprets because of his own personality.

Grotjahn, M., Psychoanalysis twenty-five years after the death of Sigmund Freud, *Psychol. Rep.*, 1965, *16*, 965–968.

> Proved: its value in investigating UCS. Has greatest value as a technique for training psychotherapists.

Hall, C. S., A modest confirmation of Freud's theory of a distinction between the superego of men and women, *J. Abnorm. Soc. Psychol.*, 1964, *69*, 440–442.

> In dreams women more often suffer aggression, men more often suffer misfortune.

Hall, C. S., and B. Domhoff, Aggression in dreams, *Int. J. Soc. Psychiat.*, 1963, *9*, 259–267.

Hall, C. S., and B. Domhoff, The dreams of Freud and Jung, *Psychol. Today*, 1968, *2*, 42–45, 64–65.

Hall, C. S., and R. L. Van de Castle, An empirical investigation of the castration complex in dreams, *J. Pers.*, 1965, *33*, 20–29.

Harlow, H. F., The heterosexual affectional system in monkeys, *Amer. Psychologist*, 1962, *16*, 1–8.

Harlow, H. F., and M. K. Harlow, Social deprivation in monkeys, *Sci. Amer.*, Nov. 1962, 136–146.

Hartmann, H., The development of the ego concept in Freud's work, *Int. J. Psycho. Anal.*, 1956, *37*, 425–437.

Higashimachi, W. H., The construct of the Progressive Matrices as a measure of superego strength in juvenile delinquents, *J. Consult. Psychol.*, 1963, *27*, 415–419.

Hiltner, S., Freud, psychoanalysis and religion, *Pastoral Psychol.*, 1956, *7*, 9–21.

Hitschmann, E., Freud correspondence, *Psychoanal. Quart.*, 1956, *25*, 357–362.

Holmes, R., Freud and social class, *Brit. J. Sociol.*, 1965, *16*, 48–67.

Holt, H., Existential analysis, Freud, and Adler, *J. Exist.*, 1967, *8*, 203–222.

Holt, R., A critical examination of Freud's concept of bound vs. free cathexis, *J. Amer. Psychoanal. Ass.*, 1962, *10*, 475–525.

Ichheiser, G., On Freud's blind spots concerning some obvious facts, *J. Indiv. Psychol.*, 1960, *16*, 45–55.

Jones, E., Freud's early travels, *Int. J. Psycho. Anal.*, 1954, *35*, 81–84.

Kanzer, M., Freud's use of the terms "autoerotism" and "narcissism," *J. Amer. Psychoanal. Ass.*, 1964, *12*, 529–559.

Kardiner, A., A. Karush, and L. Ovesey, A methodological study of Freudian theory: Part I. Basic concepts, *J. Nerv. Ment. Dis.*, 1959 (July), *129*, 11–19; Part II. The libido theory, 1959 (Aug.), 133–143; Part III. Narcissism, bisexuality and the dual instinct theory, 1959 (Sept.), 207–221; Part IV. The structural hypothesis, the problem of anxiety, and post-Freudian ego psychology, 1959 (Oct.), 341–356.

Kardiner, A., A. Karush, and L. Ovesey, A methodological study of Freudian theory, *Int. J. Psychiat.*, 1966, *2*, 489–544.

> An imposing body of creative theory has demonstrated its vitality and usefulness over and over again.

Karier, C. J., The rebel and the revolutionary: Sigmund Freud and John Dewey, *Teachers Coll. Rec.*, 1963, *64*, 605–613.

Kaul, R. N., Freud's contribution to ethical theory, *Psychoanal. Rev.*, 1964, *51*, 72–78.

Kaywin, L., Problems of sublimation, *J. Amer. Psychoanal. Ass.*, 1966, *14*, 313–334.

> "Sublimated behavior" can't be distinguished from normal behavior.

Keiser, S., Freud's concept of trauma and a specific ego function, *J. Amer. Psychoanal. Ass.*, 1967, *15*, 781–794.

Knight, J. A., Conscience, *J. Pastoral Care*, 1964, *18*, 132–139.

Kreitler, H., and S. Kreitler, Children's concepts of sexuality and birth, *Child Develpm.*, 1966, *37*, 363–378.

Kubie, L. S., Pavlov, Freud, and Soviet psychiatry, *Behav. Sci.*, 1959, *4*, 29–54.

> The Russians don't like Freud.

Kuehn, J. L., Encounter at Leyden: Gustav Mahler consults Sigmund Freud, *Psychoanal. Rev.*, 1965, *52*, 5–25.

Laffal, J., Freud's theory of language, *Psychoanal. Quart.*, 1964, *33*, 157–175.

Lehmann, H., Two dreams and a childhood memory of Freud, *J. Amer. Psychoanal. Ass.*, 1966, *14*, 388–405.

Levin, R. B., The psychology of women: An empirical test of a psychoanalytic concept, *Dissert. Abstr.*, 1963, *24*, 837.

Lewis, N. D. C., and C. Landis, Freud's library, *Psychoanal. Rev.*, 1957, *44*, 327–354.

> Included are 814 titles of 1200 items.

Lindzey, G., Some remarks concerning incest, the incest taboo, and psychoanalytic theory, *Amer. Psychologist*, 1967, *22*, 1051–1059.

Lipton, S. D., Freud's position on problem solving in dreams, *Brit. J. Mec Psychol.*, 1967, 40, 147–149.

> Freud says problem solving is not part of the "dream-work."

Loevinger, J., The meaning and measurement of ego development, *Amer. Psy chologist*, 1966a, 21, 195–206.

Loevinger, J., Three principles for a psychoanalytic psychology, *J. Abnorm Psychol.*, 1966b, 71, 432–443.

> Freud's cathexis theory is less parsimonious than other theories in ex plaining some things.

McCord, J., and S. Clemes, Conscience orientation and dimensions of personality *Behav. Sci.*, 1964, 9, 18–29.

Mann, T., Freud and the future, *Int. J. Psycho. Anal.*, 1956, 37, 160–115.

Mart-Ibanez, F., A. M. Sackler, and R. R. Sackler, The quest for Freud, *J. Clin Exp. Psychopath.*, 1956, 17, 117–127.

Marx, O. M., Freud and aphasia: An historical analysis, *Amer. J. Psychiat.*, 1967 124, 815–825.

Maslow, A. H., Was Adler a disciple of Freud? A note, *J. Indiv. Psychol.*, 1962 18, 125.

May, R., The problem of will and intentionality in psychoanalysis, *Contemp Psychoanal.*, 1966, 3, 55–70.

> Conceptualizations are integrated with Sullivanian theory via symboli processes, interpersonal acts, identity, and empathy.

Menninger, K., Freud and American psychiatry, *J. Amer. Psychoanal. Ass.*, 1956 4, 614–625.

Moreno, J. L., The psychodrama of Sigmund Freud, *Psychodrama Monogr.*, 1967 42, 12.

Mullen, F. G., Jr., Estimation of the universality of Freudian and Jungian sexua symbols, *Percept. Mot. Skills*, 1968, 26, 1041–1042.

> "Examines the sexuality of 36 nouns in French, German, and Spanish. "Results suggest that universality of Jungian or Freudian sexual symbol in terms of their power to predict gender of nouns is lacking."

Munsford, R. S., Traditional psychiatry, Freud and H. S. Sullivan, *Compr Psychiat.*, 1961, 2, 1–10.

Murphy, G., The current impact of Freud upon psychology, *Amer. Psychologist* 1956, 11, 663–672.

Nameche, G. F., Two pictures of man, *J. Humanist. Psychol.*, 1961, 1, 70–88.

> Freud and Rogers on man.

Nash, H., Freud and metaphor, *Arch. Gen. Psychiat.* (Chicago), 1962, 7, 25–29

Nikelly, A. G., Parsimony in Freud and Adler, *Psychiat. Quart. Suppl.*, 1962, 36 100–106.

> Adler is more parsimonious, ergo better.

Nikelly, A. G., The Adlerian concept of the unconscious in psychotherapy, *J. Indiv. Psychol.*, 1966, 22, 214–221.

O'Connell, W. E., The adaptive functions of wit and humor, *J. Abnorm. Soc. Psychol.*, 1960, 61, 263–270.

> Freud on wit and humor differences is valid.

Parsons, T., Social structure and the development of personality: Freud's contribution to the integration of psychology and sociology, *Psychiatry*, 1958, 21, 321–340.

Pawlick, K., and R. B. Cattell, Third order factors in objective personality tests, *Brit. J. Psychol.*, 1964, 55, 1–19.

Racker, H., On Freud's position towards religion, *Amer. Imago*, 1956, 13, 98–121.

Ramzy, I., Research aspects of psychoanalysis, *Psychoanal. Quart.*, 1963, 32, 58–76.

> It is method that defines problems and clarifies theory.

Rank, O., The psychological approach to personal problems, *Otto Rank Ass.*, 1966, 1, 12–25.

> Rank's theory is contrasted to the theories of Jung, Adler, and Freud.

Reik, T., Freud and Jewish wit, *Psychoanalysis*, 1954, 2, 12–20.

> Based on Freud's 1905 book, *Wit and Its Relation to the Unconscious*.

Rohde, K. J., Effect of early experience on the child: Possible solution to controversy, *Psychol. Rep.*, 1967, 20, 134.

> A suggestion to resolve the controversy between Freudians and learning theorists.

Rosenfield, I., A study of Freud's theory of unconscious motives, *Dissert. Abstr.*, 1967, 27, 3912–3913.

Roth, N., Freud and Galton, *Compr. Psychiat.*, 1962, 36, 77–83.

> Did Galton influence Freud?

Rychlak, J. F., The motives to psychotherapy, *Psychother. Theor. Res. Pract.*, 1965, 2, 151–157.

> Discusses the scholarly, ethical, and curative motives and clarifies them through the use of theories of Freud, Rogers, and Wolpe.

Saul, L. J., and S. Wenar, Early influences on development and disorders of personality, *Psychoanal. Quart.*, 1965, 34, 327–389.

> Research findings implicit in and central to Freud's concept of the lasting effects of early influence.

Schlessinger, N., *et al.*, The scientific style of Breuer and Freud in the origins of psychoanalysis, *J. Amer. Psychoanal. Ass.*, 1967, 15, 404–422.

Schmid, F., Freud's sociological thinking, *Bull. Menninger Clin.*, 1952, 16, 1–13.

> Freud was an inadequate sociologist!

Schneck, J. M., Countertransference in Freud's rejection of hypnosis, *Amer. J. Psychiat.*, 1954, *110*, 928–931.

Schneck, J. M., Dostoyevsky and Freud on criminal psychopathology, *Psychiat. Quart. Suppl.*, 1966, *40*, 278–282.

Schusdek, A., Freud's "seduction theory": A reconstruction, *J. Hist. Behav. Sci.*, 1966, *2*, 159–166.

Schwartz, B. J., An empirical test of two Freudian hypotheses concerning castration anxiety, *J. Pers.*, 1956, *24*, 318–327.

Sears, R., Survey of objective studies of psychoanalytic concepts, *Soc. Sci. Res. Council*, 1943, Bull. 51.

Serban, G., Freudian man vs existential man: The spirit of the age in the formulation of the concept of man in modern psychiatry, *Arch. Gen. Psychiat.* (Chicago), 1967, *17*, 598–607.

Sewell, W. H., Infant training and the personality of the child, *Amer. J. Sociol.*, 1952, *58*, 150–159.

Shakow, N., and D. Rapaport, The influence of Freud on American psychology, *Psychol. Issues*, 1964, *4*, 1–243.

Shor, J., A well-spring of psychoanalysis, *Psychoanalysis*, 1953, *2*, 27–33.

Shore, N. F., J. L. Massimo, and R. Mack, The relationship between levels of guilt in thematic stories and unsocialized behavior, *J. Proj. Tech. Pers. Assess.*, 1964, *28*, 346–349.

Simon, R. I., Great paths cross: Freud and James at Clark University, 1909, *Amer. J. Psychiat.*, 1967, *124*, 831–834.

Slap, J. W., Freud's view on pleasure and aggression, *J. Amer. Psychoanal. Ass.*, 1967, *15*, 370–375.

Slavson, S. R., Freud's contributions to group psychotherapy, *Int. J. Group Psychother.*, 1956, *6*, 349–357.

Stagner, R., and J. W. Moffitt, A statistical study of Freud's personality types, *J. Clin. Psychol.*, 1956, *12*, 72–74.

> No statistical differences were found.

Stark, S., Rorschach movement, fantastic daydreaming, and Freud's concept of primary process: Interpretive commentary, *Percept. Mot. Skills*, 1966, *22*, 523–532.

> Conceptual framework showing what meaning Freud's concept of primary process has for Maslow.

Starr, A., Psychoanalysis and the fiction of the unconscious, *Sci. Soc.*, 1951, *15*, 129–143.

Steiner, C. M., An investigation of Freud's attention cathexis theory in the context of a concept formation task, *Dissert. Abstr.*, 1966, *26*, 7448–7449.

Stenzel, E., A reevaluation of Freud's book, *On Aphasia* its significance for psychoanalysis, *Int. J. Psycho. Anal.*, 1954, *35*, 85–89.

Stevenson, I., Is the human personality more plastic in infancy and childhood? *Amer. J. Psychiat.*, 1957, *114*, 152–161.

> Doubts Freudian theory that childhood is overly formative.

Sulzberger, C. G., Epicurus, Luther, and Freud, *Psychoanalysis*, 1953, *1*, 70–72.

Sulzberger, C. F., Two new documents on Freud, *Psychoanalysis*, 1955–1956, *4*, 9–21.

Swanson, G. E., Mead and Freud: Their relevance for social psychology, *Sociometry*, 1961, *24*, 319–339.

> Neither one seems to be relevant.

Trueblood, W. E., The challenge of Freud, *Pastoral Psychol.*, 1958, *9*, 37–44.

Turiell, E., An historical analysis of the Freudian conception of the superego, *Psychoanal. Rev.*, 1967, *54*, 118–140.

Tyson, A., and J. Strachey, A chronological hand list of Freud's work, *Int. J. Psycho. Anal.*, 1956, *37*, 19–33.

> Complete list of all Freud's writings published prior to November, 1955.

Viereck, G. S., An interview with Freud, *Psychoanalysis*, 1957, *4*, and *5*, 1–11.

Waelder, R., Freud and the history of science, *J. Amer. Psychoanal. Ass.*, 1956, *4*, 602–613.

Walker, N., Science and the Freudian unconscious, *Psychoanalysis*, 1957, *4*, and *5*, 117–124.

> Freudian unconscious belongs with respectable scientific models.

West, R., The social significance of the uncompleted father analysis of Sigmund Freud, *Psychother. Psychosom.*, 1967, *15*, 69.

Wheelock, L. F., Sigmund Freud and James J. Putnam: An addition to the Sigmund Freud Collection, *Bull. Menninger Clin.*, 1968, *32*, 178–183.

Wieck, D. T., Funny things, *J. Aesthet. Art Crit.*, 1967, *25*, 437–447.

> Freud's theory (aim of the comic is to return to infantile euphoria) is much too simple.

Wolpe, J., and S. Rachman, Psychoanalytic "evidence": A critique based on Freud's case of little Hans, *J. Nerv. Ment. Dis.*, 1960, *131*, 135–148.

> Freud was wrong about little Hans.

Worell, L., The ring of punishment: A theoretical and experimental analogue of repression-suppression, *J. Abnorm. Psychol.*, 1965, *70*, 201–209.

Zamansky, H. S., An investigation of the psychoanalytic theory of paranoid delusions, *J. Pers.*, 1958, *26*, 410–425.

Zetzel, E. R., 1965: Additional notes on a case of obsessional neurosis: Freud 1909, *Int. J. Psycho. Anal.*, 1966, *47*, 123–129.

Zilboorg, G., Freud's fundamental psychiatric orientation, *Int. J. Psycho. Anal.*, 1954, *35*, 90–94.

Zilboorg, G., Freud's one hundredth anniversary, *Psychoanal. Quart.*, 1956, *25*, 139–146.

> Freud was a Lamarckian and prone to forget his sources.

✺

3

MURRAY

No brain, no personality . . .

HENRY A. MURRAY
article in *Dialectica*, Volume V, page 267

Human hopes and human creeds
Have their roots in human needs.

E. F. WARE
"Ironquill," *The Washerwoman's Song**

SOME BIOGRAPHICAL DATA

Henry Alexander Murray was born on May 13, 1893, in New York City. He
acquired his education on the eastern seaboard, graduating from Harvard in
1915. In 1919 he received his doctorate in medicine from Columbia College
of Physicians and Surgeons. During the following seven years he was primarily
concerned with research in the areas of chemistry, biology, and biochemistry.
The climax of his professional training came in 1927 when he was awarded a
Doctor of Philosophy degree in biochemistry by Cambridge University.

* From *Some Rhymes of Ironquill*, copyright 1903 by Putnam & Co. Reprinted by permission of Putnam's & Coward-McCann.

England. Thus for approximately twelve years Murray was a student of high standing in the fields of medicine and biology.

It was during his years of European training that Murray first began to be seriously interested in the world of psychological endeavor. Much of this interest he attributes to a dramatic effect of the literature of Jung and especially of personal visits with Jung in Zurich. In Murray's words, "The great flood-gates of the wonder-world swung open," through his personal conversations with Jung. After that Murray was a psychologist first and other things second.

From 1927 until 1943, Murray was occupied at Harvard University in roles of ever increasing responsibility and influence. Starting as an instructor in psychology without formal training in the academic psychology of the time, he rose rapidly to become director of the newly created Harvard Psychological Clinic.

In 1943 Murray became an officer in the Army Medical Corps for the purpose of creating screening and selection methods for candidates in the Office of Strategic Services. Much depended upon the correct choice of men to do counterespionage work, and Murray and his coworkers were able to devise ingenious methods for selecting the men. The project was relatively successful, and Murray was awarded the Legion of Merit for his work on it.

Returning to Harvard after the war, he continued to work at that institution. Dr. Murray retired during the winter of 1962 as a Professor of Clinical Psychology. In September, 1961, at the American Psychological Association meeting in New York, he was awarded the APA Distinguished Scientific Contribution Award.

If a student read nothing else of Murray's, he should by all means read his autobiography as it appears in the *History of Psychology in Autobiography*. It is a fey, whimsical, penetrating document that is a delight, especially in these times of ponderous scientific "psychologese."

With genuine regret this writer reports that Murray's latest treatment of his theory (*Encounter with Psychology*) is being published too late to be included in the second edition of the current book. Apparently his newest contribution is to reify his earlier work and incorporate such concepts as "Keith's group theory of evolution, role theory . . . general systems theory . . . adoption of the on-going process of metabolism (the anabolic composition Co, and the catabolic decomposition De, of energy-binding substances) as the *sine qua non* of the givenness of life, the source of psychic energy (psychometabolism) and the *core* (with additional variables) of basic paradigm for a host of analogous phenomena at different levels . . . the problem of life from non-life, to the theory of the creative (emergent) evolution of genetical systems . . ." (Murray, 1967a, 1968). It is easy to see that even seven years after his retirement Murray continues to be intellectually curious and a concerned contributor to man's knowledge of man.

In my most recent contact with Murray he states, however, "I am astonished at your conscientiousness in accurately representing the gist of what I said by way of definition of this and that concept . . . in the few instances in which you have written [it] does not correspond very well with what I had in mind, I have been taught what was lacking or confused in my original presentation. In this way you have helped me very much" (personal communication, January 21, 1969).

INTRODUCTION

If the reader wonders what kind of theory would evolve if a university professor were to construct a theory of personality, perhaps he will find the answer in Henry A. Murray. Murray has been associated with universities most of his professional life with short but interesting digressions during World War II (*Assessment of Men*, 1948) and, prior to that, as an intern in surgery for two years. He did work in biochemistry, had a practice in psychoanalysis and psychotherapy, and took four years' leave of absence to work on the life of Herman Melville. His theory is quite synthesistic. It incorporates the unconscious, an emphasis on the physiological, and a great emphasis on naming things; it is always developing, it does not ignore sociological aspects of man, and it covers the full range of human behavior.

Murray's theory could very well be placed in Part IV because of its integrative emphasis. It seems, however, more apt to place his work in this section. The integration is less apparent than is the gathering together of various theoretical positions regarding man's behavior. That is, across-the-board synthesism is more characteristic of his work than is the integration of ideas into salient features.

There are some close parallels between Sheldon and Murray. Oddly enough, during his medical training days Murray once did a cursory study of twenty-five of his fellow medical students in an attempt to correlate anthropometric measures with behavioral traits. However, he pursued the idea no farther. Murray also is widely trained and traveled, as was Sheldon, both having earned doctorates in medicine and philosophy and both having studied abroad and come under the influence of such great figures as Jung and Freud. Murray, in a very moving passage, credits Jung with the major emphasis that brought him into the field of psychological study (Murray, 1940b). Both men emphasized the unity of experience, but both were willing to "take man apart" in order to study his personality and then reconstruct the pieces into a unified theoretical position. In describing man's behavior Murray and Sheldon have also created long taxonomic lists, Sheldon through his Scale for Temperament and somatotyping and Murray through his needs–press–thema approach.

However, it is not the intent here to link Murray and Sheldon but to introduce Murray to the reader and to justify the inclusion of his work in the section on biophysical–biophilosophical theories of personality.

MURRAY'S DESCRIPTION
OF HUMAN BEHAVIOR

Despite the device used by this book, description–explanation–prediction, Murray strongly denies that personality can be described, especially in a diagnostic sense. To Murray, description connotes a static, immobile, fixed quality which denies the moving, changing, ever-in-flux nature of personality. Murray prefers the term *formulation* in defining personality. However, it is felt by the writer that the devices used here in no way subvert the work of Murray, and it is hoped that the present organization will help the reader better to understand the taxonomic nature of Murray's work by emphasizing certain of his primary concepts.

Extracting principles from Murray's large production is somewhat like trying to organize the dictionary into major and minor words, for Murray's penchant for taxonomy has caused him to use many terms and phrases to divide and subdivide man's behavior into multiple facets. Once again, as in all the theorists presented here (none of whom created principles per se), the salient features of Murray's work have been extracted and labeled *principles* so as to provide a better look at the theory and how it describes man's personality.

Regnancy Principle

At the beginning of this chapter is a noteworthy quotation from an article of Murray's: "No brain, no personality." This theme runs throughout his writings from the earliest to the most current. Fundamentally he is speaking of the basic function of the physiological process which governs and pre-scribes what the personality can do, but in this section we shall interpret this concept to include also the brain as an administrator of all that the person-ality does. Thus the brain, and only the brain, gives unity to the behavior of man. The brain is an organic entity, but it must be regarded as more than a physiological process of the body. With its complex and adaptive functions it is also the seat of the personality. We must carry some of our interpretations beyond the realm of operant behavior stemming from the locus of the brain.

The question becomes intriguing if we consider quality, for example. What are the differences between the imbecilic and the highly gifted brain? One cannot at this juncture equate Murray's statement with intellectual ability, although that seems a neat and comfortable thing to do. Dr. Murray said to me, " 'No brain' does not mean 'no brains' (no intelligence). It means 'no organ in the cranial capacity,' a commonplace to stress the location of processes of personality." More to the point are the differences between one brain and the other in all its capacities to adjust and solve problems. Thus the brain of limited ability has less a personality than the brain of high adaptability and power. We may even ponder whether "no brain" might mean that the lowest idiot would have so marginal a personality as to seem to have no personality at all. Were one to observe the idiot in a number of situations calling for response of some kind by the personality (brain), he would perforce agree that "No brain, no personality" appears a fruitful contribution to the world of personality study. Again it must be emphasized that quality of brain is *not* concomitant with intelligence as measured by the usual intelligence test. What is connoted is the aptitudinal approach: that the brain with the greatest amount of skill in many areas is the brain likely to be adjoined to the best personality. Interpretations such as the above immediately bring forth the rebuttal that "brainy" people many times are duds in life situations. Therefore, "No brain, no personality" is a false concept. Again, what is meant is total brain strength, not popularity. The wider, the stronger, the more penetrating, the more adaptable, and the more spontaneous the brain is in handling problems which arise in *all* areas of life, the greater the personality. This is but one interpretation that can be deduced from Murray's statement "No brain, no personality."

Two other points which are less interpretive of Murray's words must be taken up: the interdependence of physiological and neurological processes and the factor of constitutional types somewhat as Sheldon approached them. To Murray any ongoing behavioral process must have in the brain an ongoing neural excitation which has hierarchical dimensions. It is the brain which "rules" the needs and demands of the moment. The demands may be mainly organic (hunger), mainly symbolic (reading), or any of the multiple combinations of both (continuing to read an assignment although the reader is bothered by hunger for some food). The brain makes the decisions regarding subsequent action. The hierarchy of alternative actions to be taken is determined by the brain. These single units of experience come so rapidly and in such uninterrupted succession that regnancy ("ruling") is considered to be in multiples. A single unit happens so quickly as to defy examination. We shall see more of this phenomenon in the study of serials.

Also involved in regnancy as an element in personality and its behavior is Murray's acceptance of constitutional types as having differing modes of regnancy in responding to situations. This concept has not been spelled out in his writings, but it is fundamental in much of his description of the regnant process.

In summary, all behavioral processes of a strictly organic type, or of a psychological nature, or both, are processes of a functioning brain. One final word: A regnant process may be conscious or unconscious. We shall deal with Murray's concept of the unconscious in a later section.

Motivation Principle

Perhaps the most important feature of Murray's theory is his intense interest in and development of motivation and how it affects human behavior. Above all Murray is a motivational psychologist, by which one means a psychologist who studies the *direction* of man's endeavors in the mental, physical, or verbal realm. As we shall see, his taxonomic bent is given full rein in this aspect of his theory. He has not, as yet, taken the one step back, to study where the motivation originates. In his system the "motivator" is met as if it came full-blown into man's existence.

Within the concept of motivation principle we shall deal with five components of his system: (1) tension reduction, (2) needs, (3) press, (4) vector–value, (5) thema.

TENSION REDUCTION

Like many other theorists Murray does not believe man lives in a tensionless state, but both biologically and psychologically Murray finds room for tension reduction. Homeostasis (maintaining an equilibrium between body states) is a true biological phenomenon, and Murray uses it in his theory to explain his first position in regard to tension reduction. Man desires to avoid pain and get pleasure as a mode of existence; therefore, he wants to correct hunger states, organic disunity, and all other biological conditions of imbalance in order to return to a state of no tension or no pain. Thus, as he is hungry, he eats food and dissipates the feeling of discomfort that comes from hunger. This is, incidentally, the position of Freud and, of course, others. But to Murray the organic homeostasis is but half the picture describing tension reduction states. From the subsequent sections on needs, presses, etc., we shall see that neither does man care for a *completely* tensionless condition. As a completely tensionless organism he would progress not at all. Thus, Murray feels that, while homeostasis of the organism leads to conservation of its properties, it in no way brings the organism to construct anything. Homeostasis alone leads to a vegetable-like existence. Man is, then, possessed by the "divine discontent." He feels that progress is a natural state of existence. The desire for better living, more material property, and all of the motivations for going beyond the present state of being are also of major importance in reducing tension.

To the formula of tension ⟶ reduction of tension, which he would refer to as the traditional homeostatic condition of man, Murray adds the valuable concept that is expressed in the formula: *generation* of tension ⟶ reduction of tension. Man has a need for positive thrust, for excitement, for movement even though it may not evolve into forward progress and success, for zest, appetite, and being with his fellow men. The constructive need systems lead to advancement in the total scene of life, while the conservative need systems lead to maintaining the status quo of our existence.

We may now consider the avenues by which man is motivated. In his theoretical system, tension reduction, need, press, and the other factors in the motivational scheme are not independent of one another but highly coordinated complexes which become inseparable in action. It is only in the studying of these phenomena that we are able to pull them apart for more intensive understanding of their importance.

NEED

By a very close scrutiny of a small number of subjects and by intensive study of their needs Murray has developed a rather involved taxonomy of *needs*. Much of his need theory emerged early in the construction of the theory. Although he has since redeveloped and reemphasized the fundamental concept of need in his theory, probably still the best source for his rationale is his first major text, *Explorations in Personality*, which he published in 1938.

Criteria: In studying the need structure of man, Murray found that he required criteria in order to establish that a need existed. This was, of course, an inference on his part because he was not studying his own needs via introspection but attempting to study and later to classify those of his subjects. The criteria he established were as follows: (1) response to a particular object or to a series of like objects which seemed to serve as stimuli, (2) kind of behavior involved, (3) consequences or end result of that behavior, (4) amount and kind of emotional response connected with the behavior, (5) amount of satisfaction or dissatisfaction when the total response is achieved. Having thus set up criteria for recognizing a need in others, Murray also provided a definition for need. Defining terms is a task not very often done by theorists of personality, as we have stated in Chapter 1.

Definition: Inherent in Murray's definition are at least six major points, accompanied by corollary actions (Murray, 1938).

1. "A need is a construct," i.e., a term made by man,
2. "which stands for a force," i.e., there is power and strength within the person,
3. "In the brain region," i.e., the regnancy idea that personality stems from the brain,
4. "which organizes . . . action," i.e., it is more than just haphazard activity,
5. "so as to transform in a certain direction," i.e., the person is going to be different as the result of a need,
6. "an existing, unsatisfying situation," i.e., need grows out of dissatisfaction to lead to a goal of satisfaction.

Corollaries on a minor level are as follows:

1. The need may be "provoked by internal processes" or "more frequently by . . . environmental forces."

2. "Need is accompanied by a particular feeling or emotion."
3. "It may be weak or intense."
4. It may be "momentary or enduring."
5. It "usually persists and gives rise to a certain course of overt behavior or fantasy."

Number: With the criteria that Murray set up, and with his definition and its major and minor factors in mind, we may study the taxonomic efforts of Murray as he considered the number and types of needs that motivate man. The present list has been modified in his later work and also modified by others interested in his theoretical concepts of need. The original list of twenty terms holds the basic components of Murray's need concept.

The needs are listed in alphabetical order (as adopted from Murray's *Explorations in Personality,* pp. 152–226); Murray originally gave no emphasis or priority to one need over another as man uses them.

1. abasement: be resigned to fate; seek and enjoy pain, illness, misfortune; blame or belittle self; confess and atone; surrender, admit inferiority.

2. achievement: overcome obstacles; rival and surpass others; accomplish something difficult; master, manipulate, or organize physical objects, human beings, or ideas; increase self-regard by successful exercise of talent.

3. affiliation: please and win affection; approach, enjoy, and reciprocate with like persons; adhere and remain loyal to a friend.

4. aggression: overcome opposition forcefully; oppose forcefully or punish another; revenge an injury.

5. autonomy: avoid or quit activities prescribed by domineering authorities; resist coercion and restriction; be independent and free to act according to impulse; defy convention.

6. counteraction: overcome weakness; repress fear; efface a dishonor by action; maintain self-respect and pride on a high level; search for obstacles and difficulties to overcome.

7. defendance: defend the self against assault, criticism, and blame; vindicate the ego.

8. deference: emulate an exemplar; conform to custom; admire and support a superior.

9. dominance: influence or direct the behavior of others by suggestion, seduction, persuasion, or command; control one's human environment.

10. exhibition: make an impression; be seen and heard.

11. harmavoidance: take precautionary measures; escape from a dangerous situation; avoid pain, physical injury, illness, and death.

12. infravoidance: refrain from action because of the fear of failure; avoid humiliation.

13. nurturance: give sympathy and gratify the needs of a helpless object; assist an object in danger; feed or help or support or console or protect or comfort or nurse or heal others.

14. order: achieve cleanliness, arrangement, organization, balance, neatness, tidiness, and precision.

15. play: seek enjoyable relaxation of stress; act for "fun" without further purpose.

16. rejection: exclude, abandon, expel, or remain indifferent to an inferior object.

17. sentience: seek and enjoy sensuous impressions.

18. sex: form and further an erotic relationship; have sexual intercourse.

19. succorance: remain close to a devoted protector; always have a supporter; have one's needs gratified by the sympathetic aid of an allied object.

20. understanding: be interested in theory; speculate, formulate, analyse, and generalize.

As man is motivated by these needs, he uses them in accordance with certain methods, some of which are discussed below.

Prepotency—When two or more needs demand satisfaction at the same time by the same person, a priority for action must occur. Some needs are of more urgent character, or, as Murray states, there is a prepotency factor inherent in the need itself which mandates that it receive first attention by the subject. Hunger, for example, which is a primary or viscerogenic need, has a built-in prepotency which requires it to be satisfied before such a need as play. Thus, there is a hierarchy of needs, and the level is ordered less by the subject than by the need itself.

Fusion—Not all needs are contradictory or come into conflict. Needs which are complementary become fused as motivating devices. Although the needs themselves are not identical, they may be satisfied by a single course of action. Thus, one may satisfy his need for protection and dominance by the same act. It is the behavior which is fused although the two needs are not similar in basic character.

Subsidiation—Some needs may be met only through meeting the demands of lesser but necessary way needs. For example, to the need for achievement one may first have to satisfy the need for deference. The college student may wish to achieve a certain degree of success on his campus. In order to do so he must first perhaps exercise deference by adopting and conforming to the customs of the local campus in his manners, speech, forms of recreation, and general demeanor.

Conflict—The last special consideration of the list of needs is the obvious fact that needs are often in conflict. As we have seen, man is a tension-reducing animal. When he comes upon two, or possibly three, conflicting needs, he produces tension. Murray feels that if one is to know more about the human being, he must know specifically what needs the person has that are in direct conflict. This idea resembles the Freudian polarity or duality principle. Most often conflict needs are dichotomized, with only two being involved, and no third or fourth needs in chainlike conflict. Such a complex of more than two conflicting characters is not at present under discussion.

According to Murray, not all of the twenty needs listed are present in all people. Some of us never experience certain ones in our lifetimes while others may run the gamut of the entire list and do so in a relatively short period of days or weeks. Still others of us may have favorite needs to which we pay attention rather constantly, having regard for other needs only occasionally. To understand how we use these needs one may find the following section useful.

Types—There are five different types of needs:

    primary and secondary
    proactive and reactive
    overt and covert
    focal and diffuse
    effect and modal—with process activity

Oddly enough, types of needs, as Murray deals with them, seem to be dichotomized, and one wonders what effect the Freudian duality principle has had upon the typology which deals with apposites.

Primary and secondary types of needs—The primary needs of man, sometimes called the *viscerogenic needs,* are those of an organic–biologic nature, as for food, water, air, elimination of bodily wastes, and, in Murray's opinion, sexual activity, which are mainly organic for both sexes.

The secondary or *psychogenic needs* come from the primary needs but in a diffuse and indirect manner. Many of the needs listed would be properly considered secondary needs—for example, achievement, affiliation. They are not to be thought unimportant because they are called secondary. The term refers rather to state of development. Primary needs develop first, followed by the secondary or psychogenic needs. The latter, as we shall see, may become quite important and even take precedence over the primary, or organic, needs in times of great stress. The nomenclature refers, then, to sequence rather than to dominance.

Proactive and reactive types of needs—Once again the word *apposites* describes Murray's need types as the terms are not distinctly in opposition to each other but exist in a side-by-side relationship.

In some sense this distinction between types of needs seems redundant to the primary–secondary classification since the proactive need means the one that originates within the person, the reactive need the one that originates outside the person. Under the proactive need the person merely reacts to the stimulus. However, Murray is speaking here of relationships between people and not just processes. Thus, in a group of two or more people, the individual may begin the action of the group through some need within himself. In this case he is meeting a proactive need. On the other hand, the proactor needs someone to react to his stimulus, which situation Murray called the *reactive need*. Both needs are intricately interwoven in something of a cause–effect relationship. In clapping hands one cannot produce an effect with only one component, i.e., with only one hand.

Overt and covert types of needs—Again referring to the list of needs, we find that some needs can be openly expressed. Society will sanction them and even give prizes of one kind or another for successfully meeting them. Such needs would be called overt or open. They are openly expressed and openly met. Examples are achievement, defendance, and counteraction. A study of the list of needs also brings out those which must be fantasized or dealt with in a dream stage or obtained through devious means: the covert, or secret, hidden needs. Examples (depending upon the society in which one were operating) might be aggression, sentience, and succorance. To meet these needs one might perforce be quite secretive about his activities or achieve the need fulfillment through daydreaming.

Focal and diffuse types of needs—As we shall see in a later section which considers Murray's longitudinal principles with their proceedings and serials, there are needs which can be satisfactorily met by closeness to an environmental object. These needs are *focal*, and they can be met by only one object, or, in a few cases, by very few objects. Thus, in the need for deference one might want only to admire and support one person. This is a focal need. On the other hand, in the need for harmavoidance he wishes and needs to avoid *all* kinds of pain. Pain has a universal quality of hurt that everyone wants to avoid. True, one may construct a high and low order of pain-reducing stimuli, but past a certain point of excitation, pain is pain and our subject needs to avoid all of it. A toothache in full, throbbing state brings the need of harm avoidance. At the moment, it might seem that a burned finger would be much the easier pain to bear, but when the burned finger begins to hurt, it has the value of the aching tooth. One has the diffuse need to avoid pain, be it in any part of his body or in his societal contacts.

Effect and modal types of needs—The fifth and last types of need that Murray outlined are called *effect* and *modal*. An effect need is one that leads to a direct and identifiable goal object. In an automobile trip we have the need to arrive at a definite goal. We depart from one place and drive in the most direct and practicable route to our destination. There is a direct need involved. In the process of driving, however, Murray acknowledges the joy of manipulating the automobile. The sheer pleasure of physically operating the car is what he called a *process activity*, or the *sheer function pleasure*. Out of this grows the need to function with a high degree of excellence. The expert manner in which we operate the automobile goes beyond the pleasure of operating it, and this is what Murray called the *modal need*. In short, the mode of operation in which we satisfy need may be as important as the goal we strive for.

PRESS
Still within the concept of motivation principle, we find Murray's corollary term *press*, which he applied to the external factors of man's life. The term *press*, which is used in reference to an object or a person, means that attribute which either gets in the way of or aids a person in satisfying his needs. It presses him into one form of action or another. *Press potency* is "what can be done ' . . . to the subject or for the subject—the power it has to affect the well-being of the subject in one way or another' " (*Explorations in Personality*, p. 121). The press comes from the environment, while the need comes from within the person.

A typical list of press concepts follows. The press itself is of no value in understanding the personality of the subject. The subject's subjective view and impression of the press makes it significant in further understanding the human personality.

Murray, in *Explorations in Personality*, presents long lists of press terms which he has evolved from working with a selected group of subjects. The terms may be applicable to an explanation of the dynamics of behavior for an individual through techniques Murray has developed, and may, as well, give a measure of the relative importance or quantitative characteristics in the study of an individual:

1. **p** Family insupport
    a. cultural discord
    b. family discord
    c. capricious discipline
    d. parental separation
    e. absence of parent:
        father
        mother
    f. parental illness:
        father
        mother
    g. death of parent:
        father
        mother
    h. inferior parent:
        father
        mother
    i. dissimilar parent:
        father
        mother
    j. poverty
    k. unsettled home
2. **p** Danger or Misfortune
    a. physical insupport, height
    b. water
    c. aloneness, darkness
    d. inclement weather, lightning

e. fire
f. accident
g. animal
3. p Lack or Loss
   a. of nourishment
   b. of possessions
   c. of companionship
   d. of variety
4. p Retention, Withholding
   Objects
5. p Rejection, Unconcern and
   Scorn
6. p Rival, competing contemporary
7. p Birth of sibling
8. p Aggression
   a. maltreatment by elder male,
      elder female
   b. maltreatment by contempo-
      raries

c. Quarrelsome contemporaries
9. Fp Aggression–Dominance, Punishment
10. p Dominance, coercion and pro-
    hibition
11. Fp Dominance–nurturance
    a. parental ego idealism:
       mother
       father
       physical
       econ, vocation
       caste
       intellectual
    b. possessive parent:
       mother
       father
    c. oversolicitous parent
       fears: accident, illness, bad
       influences

Murray shows two ways for considering the press quality of persons or objects: *Alpha press* is the objective and real characteristic of the press. In this there is no distortion or subjective interpretation of the press. It is what the outside observer not involved in the ramifications of the press object would consider it to be. *Beta press* is the subjective personal interpretation the individual makes of those objects which influence him. Obviously his behavior is most influenced by the beta aspect of the press since that is what he sees and feels and responds to. There may be, of course, a wide disparity between the alpha and beta aspects of the same press concept.

In addition to alpha and beta aspects of press Murray describes the capacity of the press object to attract or repel the individual, using Freud's term *cathexis* for this. Cathexis may be described as the emotional charge which can attract or repel and which is within the object itself. Contrary to this is the sentiment of the person toward the press object, the sentiment being, according to Murray, negative or positive, short or long term but usually long term, and always conditioned by the capacity within the person rather than within the object.

VECTOR–VALUE

Murray as well as many others interested in his theoretical work have been aware of the inadequacy of the need concept to explain why man behaves as he does. The need, according to some observers of his theoretical system, seems to appear full-blown and with little to help one understand where it comes from. The significance of what need does is what Murray has most adequately dealt with, in the view of these observers. Lacking is the origin of the needs. As has been stated, Murray is aware of this problem. The lack is not a weakness in his theory but a sign that his is a developing theory, with the aspect of primary and original sources as yet undeveloped. To complete the picture, Murray has in writings subsequent to his original thesis of 1938 (*Explorations in Personality*) expanded the need–press idea to include the vector–value theme.

The word *vector* has long had psychological respectability, especially in the work of Lewin. Murray uses this term, which means *a force going in a defined direction*. The force may be weak or strong. The direction is prescribed by the other variables which impinge on the one vector force. Although the term is probably most widely used in the field of statistics, it has been adopted by others than Murray to connote an emotional charge directed toward some given object. *Value* bears the usual meaning: that of "the worth or price or power inherent in an article," a price which is determined by man. That is, the article has the value but does not declare its own value: man sets the price.

Again preoccupied with taxonomic efforts to better understand man, Murray has begun to create a list of values and vectors which he feels help to explain the need concept and the entire motivational life of man.

The basis (values) for man's needs which help bring about the direction and strength of desire (vector) that he will utilize to achieve tension reduction and to explain his motivational existence *in toto* are incorporated in a matrix which Murray hopes to use further in laboratory work and experimentation.

In addition to the above reason for the use of value–vector (to get deeper into fundamental causes) Murray is primarily interested in the *interaction* between factors which create behavior patterns in man. Thus, if a man has a need to do a certain thing, he will, or can be expected to, behave in a somewhat circumscribed way. In practice this interactional study of behavior is beginning to emerge from Murray's laboratory work. As yet it is not refined.

What follows is his tentative list of vectors and values as he has worked them out to date:

VECTORS	VALUE
(how you do it, activity, etc.)	(why you do it, worthwhileness, etc.)
acquisition	aesthetic value
avoidance	affiliation
conservation	authority
construction	body
defendance	ideology
destruction	

expression   knowledge
expulsion   property
reception
rejection
transmission

THEMA

One further idea remains to be presented in Murray's motivational principle. The idea of *thema* refers to the totality of the sequence from press to need. This may be a simple one-to-one relationship: a singular press which leads to a singular need. Murray finds, however, that the theme, or plot, or sequence, of presses and needs is chiefly plural. Thus, themes may be in serial order. One may lead to another, which leads to still another, all of them of a complex nature. *Thema* is Murray's method of handling more than one need–press relationship but not in as direct a manner as he has attempted recently with the value–vector method, which he feels is more definite in ordering behavior along dynamic and descriptive lines.

Thus we find the major components of the principles which underlie motivation, according to Murray, to be tension reduction, needs, press, vector–value, and thema.

Longitudinal Principle

Although short in length, this is also one of the primary components of Murray's theory of personality. In his frequently quoted "The history of the personality *is* the personality" we have the key thought to the longitudinal principle. Like many psychoanalysts, Murray believes that the "child is father to the man," but not perhaps in the inflexible way that many neo-Freudian analysts have interpreted the statement. Murray feels with numerous other personality theorists that much of what man does is recurrent and that many of his behavior patterns are enduring. Man operates out of habits he forms as he goes along in life. Expressed in still another way, man's life consists of a series of events which he follows from day to day. With the statement "The trouble with life is that it is so daily" Murray would agree and would add that, if one is to study what a person is and how he became that way, he must examine past daily experiences. Murray feels that the ideal case study would begin at birth and include all of an individual's experiences up to the moment of study.

COMPLEXES

As part of the study of the development of man, Murray has paid strong attention to the erotogenic zones emphasized by Freud; Murray, however, has a somewhat different rationale for them from Freud's. Taking them as complexes to be adjusted to and worked through, Murray finds five of these complexes to operate in the developmental process of man. He describes them as enjoyable conditions, all of which are roughly and rudely interrupted by external forces beyond the control of the child. The first is the feeling of safety and dependent existence within the womb, a state which is interrupted by the act of birth. The second is the sucking activity as food is ingested from the mother's breast or the bottle, with all that accompanies this process in the warm and loving ministrations of the mother or nurse; this labial pleasure, too, is halted by the adults' persistent efforts to wean the child. The third is the exercising of the anal muscles in the free and pleasurable sensation of defecation and consequent release of visceral pressure. This pleasure is delimited by persistent toilet training. The fourth pleasant sensation is that of urination, which comes within the same pleasure sense and curbing sense as defecation. The fifth complex of pleasure which the child enjoys, and which is denied him, is the genital friction of the penis or vagina, with much the same explanation from Murray that Freud gave to the phallic period of development. Murray names the complexes in order: *claustral*—passive feeling of warmth and protection in the womb; *oral*—enjoyment of taking in food; *anal*—the pleasure of bowel and tension release with concomitant pleasure of the exercise of sphincteral muscles; *urethral*—the feeling corresponding to the anal complex; and *castration*, which he expands beyond the Freudian approach. All of these complexes play a large part in the longitudinal development of the child, as he is denied each pleasure by society for reasons which he may not support.

Those developmental aspects which revolve around the erogenous zones Murray has evolved and expanded beyond the work of Freud, or some of the neo-Freudians like Rank, into a rich and meaningful description. The entire longitudinal work of Murray gives much emphasis to his thesis that the child is father to the man and that those who would study the personality at any given period must perforce study the background of the individual, a thesis which is not unpopular with most of the current personality theorists.

PROCEEDINGS AND SERIALS

In addition to the infantile complexes introduced in the previous section, Murray has added to the longitudinal picture of man the concept of *serials* and *proceedings*. He uses the term *proceedings* to indicate that man is forever moving in his life, that man is dynamic and not static, that whatever man does must be considered in a sequence of actions. Proceedings, therefore, are those activities of man by which he interacts with another object (dealing with an automobile that refuses to start, for example) or with another human being (asking a girl for a date). Both examples indicate an interaction between the subject (man) and an object (car) or another subject (girl).

Proceedings help Murray to cast man in a time sequence rather than in a frozen, snapshot description of his behavior.

Proceedings may be internalized (the subject reasons through a problem within his own mind) or externalized (the subject talks with a companion, sells an article, or engages in any other external activity in which overt action takes place).

Proceedings may also be of short or long duration. Short proceedings are exemplified by a momentary conversation or an activity such as a social gathering of an evening's length. The *durance* Murray's term for a proceeding longer than a conversation) may be illustrated by an individual's service in the armed forces, a four-year college period, the total event of being a teen-ager, and the like.

In addition to interior–exterior and length aspects of proceedings, Murray also has presented the possibility that proceedings may conflict, or more accurately overlap, in their functions. Mealtime for a husband and wife who also function as the father and mother of a small child is an excellent example of overlapping proceedings. While they are eating and attempting to talk to each other, the child may be demanding immediate and continual attention. Thus the proceeding is both overlapping and conflicting for the parents.

Serials are, in a sense, the accumulated proceedings of man with the additional provision that a serial has a history behind it; it has a goal of finite or indefinite characteristic to be met; in other words, the entire serial is purposive. The three aspects of a serial are ordination, programs, and sched-ules. By *ordination* is meant the establishment of programs and schedules in a hierarchical form to give greater or less importance to them. Hence a priority or order is given to the establishing of serial activity. *Programs* are the attempts of man to create subgoals which help him to arrive eventually at the total goal. *Schedules* help him to avoid or at least to minimize conflicting programs. In effect, all three aspects of serials are tightly interwoven in many of man's activities and cannot be considered apart from one another. For example, the student who wishes to make his living eventually as a medical doctor is in the process of creating a serial. Through ordination, he selects an undergraduate course of studies designed for obtaining admission to a medical school. He must bear in mind the type and location of the medical school he hopes to enter. At this point he considers the past in relation to what he must do at the present in order to regulate the future. Having made an orderly serial of activities for himself, the student must follow a program which is designed to bring about the desired end. He thus studies courses and arranges subgoals within the major goal structure. As he proceeds in his program, he will quite probably encounter conflicts such as lack of money, or a deep interest in getting married. He might then, via the schedules which he creates or which have been created for him by outside pressures, decide to drop out of school until he has accumulated enough money to continue his premedical education. Or he might make the decision and schedule events so that he does or does not get married as a result of his need–press–thema demands. If he gets married, he brings certain consequences and changes to his life. If he decides against marriage, that decision minimizes the schedule changes he must make toward fulfilling his total goal structure.

In all, the entire aspect of the longitudinal principles of man's life are of utmost importance to the basic cloth of Murray's system.

Physiological Processes Principle

Deeply embedded in Murray's entire theoretical scheme is the dedication to the idea that man is an animal and controlled and motivated by animal needs. This is not intended to mean that man is coarse or rough or crude in his behavior but that he is foremost a biologically functioning organism. His need structure is founded first upon his physiological appetites. After these are met, he becomes more than an existing organism: he becomes a societal creature.

First, it is necessary to repeat the primary or viscerogenic needs that Murray found essential to the motivational structure of man. Why does man do the things he does? Because, in Murray's view, he is an organic entity. He does what he does for air, water, food, eliminative pressures, etc.

Second, in some of Murray's definitions for personality is this statement concerning man's organic self: "Personality may be biologically defined as the governing organ, or superordinate institution of the body. As such it is located in the brain" (*Dialectica*, 1951, 5, 267).

Third, his entire concept of tension reduction is predicated in the organic, biological field.

Fourth, the idea of priority of needs and a hierarchy of motivators is spelled out in his concept of prepotency, as discussed earlier in this chapter.

Fifth, there is, in the contribution of the regnant processes principle, the basic foundation that the physiological and neurological processes are first. Stated in other terms: there is no personality if the fundamental stuff which makes up personality is reduced or affected in some way. In its widest application of the term *regnant processes* the idiot, the person existing in complete coma, or the deceased has no personality.

Finally, Murray does not deny in any of his writings, and even openly supports at times, the value of Sheldonian approach. Murray feels that one's constitutional type may indeed have much to do with the formation and future functioning of his total personality. For to Murray, a synthesistically oriented theorist, it is ill advised to deny another theory that may be valuable in helping to explain man's diffuse nature.

Abstract Principle

Murray has been heavily influenced by the psychoanalytically oriented theorists, but in an unorthodoxy of his own he has created, in some respects, a parallel system; in other respects a contradictory system. As basic to Murray's system as the physiological processes is the undertone of the unconscious operating. Personality is of an abstract nature just as much as it is of an observable organic nature. Murray first recognized the defense mechanisms of repression and reaction formation in 1938, some time before it was fashionable for orthodox psychologists to maintain a position of acceptance toward Freud's psychoanalytic theories of personality. Although some clinicians had used his therapeutic techniques as their *modus operandi*, the background of Freud's theory as it applied to personality dynamics was not as readily accepted. Murray received it as meaningful, and he further incorporated it into his own system of personality theory.

Roughly, two areas of acceptance can be found in Murray's use of psychoanalytic theory: the levels of unconscious, preconscious, conscious and a deep and elaborated recognition of the id–ego–superego structure of personality.

In a magazine article published in 1936 (*J. Gen. Psychol.*, 1936, *15*, 241–268), Murray acknowledged that all of man's behavior is *not* on the surface. At that time he was uncertain (and in good professional company) as to where the unconscious determinants of personality lie within the lower regions of man's unseen behavior, but he was nonetheless convinced that the regnant processes are not all in awareness. Thus an individual may be a mystery not only to others but also to himself because he cannot find logical reasons for his own behavior. The claustral, oral, anal, urethral, and castration complexes mentioned earlier are based on the abstract nature of man. Murray further accepted the idea that man as a being with hidden motives and unconscious drives and needs is man in the natural state and needs no explanation founded on psychotic behavior. All men operate partially under unconscious motivators.

In extending the abstract nature of man, Murray uses the Freudian *id*, *ego*, and *superego* concepts but introduces refinements. Murray's chief departure from the Freudian id is to give it the capacity for good as well as for evil. Id motivation can as well be acceptable to the child, as he develops, as to his parents and society. The energy, ebullience, and playfulness displayed by a child and both pleasing to himself and endearing to his parents come out of the id structure, which also creates in him the undesirable and unacceptable behavior that disturbs the self and the exterior world. Murray further feels that the id content differs in humans. One person has a larger id than another, and consequently his problems, and his strengths for energizing action, are greater. How an individual adjusts to life is partially determined by the amount of id he has to motivate him and must likewise learn to control. The smaller the id, then, the less the person can accomplish. The larger the id, the more he may accomplish providing he is able to channel the id strength toward acceptable goals.

The ego is also considered more than a police force which forever controls the raw id impulses. Murray feels that the ego as it organizes, tests, and seeks opportunities for id expression can and does find exhilaration from goals approved by self and society. Rather than cast the ego in an ever repressant role, Murray chooses to think of it as a wise and many times benevolent administrator. With id strength behind it, the ego creates as much pleasure for the id as it represses pleasure for the id. In essence, Murray's contribution to psychoanalytic theory (not unlike that of other neo-Freudians) is more encouraging than depressing.

In addition to the regular concept of the superego as a conscience system imposed by parents and figures of authority on the child, Murray feels that symbolic figures from literature and other forms of nonhuman contact are equally effective in creating the superego structure for the child. Moreover, the child's friends and acquaintances can and do help to create the superego for one another. Parallel to the superego is the ego-ideal, which is Murray's device for adding a goal for the superego. The superego does not try merely to adjust to society day by day but has long-time goals to strive for. This is man's way of arriving "at his future best."

Murray is guided then, by a principle that man is an abstract entity not entirely controlled by surface phenomena but much motivated by inner dynamics—dynamics not always understood by himself or by the society in which he operates.

Uniqueness Principle

Briefly stated, this principle is that each human being is an individual like no other human being who ever was or who ever could be. Murray's strong conviction of the individuality of man is accepted by most current personality theorists and is the foundation for much of the research Murray has done. He prefers to work intensively with small groups in order best to discover the complex and different nature of each subject in the study.

In addition to the uniqueness principle and as part of it, Murray has paid strong attention to the varying aptitudes and achievements of his subjects in research. He is strongly disposed toward the aptitudinal picture of man's intellectual, physical, and social abilities. He supports the contention that man has not just one area of general ability in the Spearman sense but many abilities such as physical agility, memory factors, spatial factors, and the like.

Role Concept Principle

The last of the principles which we shall attribute to Murray (though certainly others not so central could be extracted) is man's need to assume a role in society. This need to achieve status and definition in the society in which he operates is a necessary component of man's existence. It is further necessary for an individual to be able to define all the roles he is placed in, and in some sense to be able to accept at least most of them as his society defines them.

Murray has continued to rethink and bring forward his theory, as this statement indicates (personal communication, April 4, 1962):

> The emphasis on need is OK, but without the idea of cathexis one doesn't arrive at a formulation of the particular aims towards which the needs are oriented. I think at the time *Explorations* was written I was stressing needs, any one of which might manifest itself in a great variety of ways. But now I am more inclined to put the emphasis on aim (or goal) which may serve as a fulfilment of several needs. An individual is usually aware of his aim but not of all the needs that might be satisfied by the realization of that aim. Also, the means or mode of progress towards the aim is a decisive component of the individual's endeavor.

EXPLAINING HUMAN BEHAVIOR VIA MURRAY'S PERSONOLOGY THEORY

Murray's theory, which he called *personology*, lends itself well to the format of this book as it attempts to explain why man does the things he does. Part of the strength of Murray's work in this kind of application lies in the breadth of his theory. Being essentially a synthesist, he has tried to bring some order into what can be described as a loose and amorphous direction of effort. With his skill in organizing and highlighting data under a taxonomic system he produces work which is useful in the effort to explain man's behavior.

The student may now try his hand at explaining behavior via the personology theory of Murray. The examples, as used throughout the book, are marriage, perversions, suicide, lawbreaking, supranatural being, humor, smoking, play and recreation, and psychoses–neuroses.

PREDICTING HUMAN BEHAVIOR VIA MURRAY'S PERSONOLOGY THEORY

Murray feels that, fundamentally, predicting human behavior is an impossible task. Yet one finds a remarkable degree of success in predicting human behavior from Murray's own work. All prediction needs a full set of underlying facts, and one's knowledge of facts is always incomplete or fragmentary. To claim to depict completely all human behavior at all times is absurd. Nothing could chill life more utterly than to know one's future irrevocably. Predicting, however, the *tendency* to act in certain ways in selected situations is well within the partial scope of the psychological world. Some aspects of the commercial world (advertising, purchasing materials, etc.), most efforts of the psychological therapist, and indeed the normal hopes and dreams of the layman are predicated on some educated hunches for the future. In brief, all the world continues its life on the prediction that the future is sufficiently worthwhile for us to continue the efforts of today. To believe otherwise would be to cease today's efforts.

Personal Prediction

Once again it is the reader who makes the primary decision as to the predictability of life, according to Murray. After examining Murray's list of needs, the reader may or may not agree that these needs reflect his own. If the majority of the items do coincide, we may expect that the reader's needs will continue to function much as they did in the past. Following Murray's suggestion that man is a habituated animal, we find that the needs of the past will probably continue in the future, especially if they have been satisfactorily met often enough for the establishing of a pattern of behavior. Needs, important in the past and satisfactorily met, may be expected to be important in the future.

The reader may further assume that certain of his needs have a higher priority than others. Some may conflict and these will conflict in the future. Some conflicts may have been allayed by fusing them into another avenue of approach; success in this endeavor will ensure its continuance, and hence some success in the fusion of needs for the future.

From a personal frame of reference, then, the reader decides the predictability of needs as Murray proposes them. We shall assess in the next section to what extent the evidence of research indicates predictability.

Scientific or Laboratory Prediction

How does one test Murray's personology theory? Actually, the theory has been undergoing research since 1938 and the introduction of his major work, *Explorations in Personality*. However, the major thrust of the investigations centered in two areas: the Thematic Apperception Test (TAT) and two of the needs, need for achievement (n Ach) and need for affiliation (n Aff). Thus, it is difficult to proclaim that Murray's personality theory has been adequately researched. Aspects of it, yes; the global ramifications, no.

First of all, the enormous effect and use of the TAT is almost equal to that of another projective device, the Rorschach Ink Blot Test. But the TAT is a method or device, not a component of the theory. Any recent issue of the *Buros Mental Measurements Yearbooks* will strikingly illustrate the vast efforts in diagnosis with the TAT. Anastasi's or Cronbach's measurement books also attest to the work done with and on the TAT as a projective device. Again we repeat, this is a method and not the essence of Murray's theoretical position.

On the other hand, primarily through the efforts of one man, McClelland, one particular need (n Ach) as espoused originally by Murray has had an enormous quantity of investigative research. The amount of study of this one aspect of personology is overwhelming. It must be remembered that McClelland was not specifically putting Murray's theory to the test; he used need for achievement only as his avenue for research.

For the student interested in McClelland's work on achievement the literature is easy to find (McClelland, 1951, 1961, 1965; McClelland *et al.*, 1953). It illustrates his long dedication, from 1947 to the present, and the wide variety of his correlating achievement to all of the following: arousal, individual differences, parental attitudes and child training, academic performance, occupational goals, national economic growth, cross-cultural dynamics, risk taking, and the special problems of women. The list is impressive. However, this is a chapter on Murray, not McClelland.

McClelland has not been the sole investigator of achievement. Others too have been interested (Birney, 1959; Hunt, 1964; Heckhausen, 1967; Megargee and Parker, 1968; Merbaum, 1962; Mischel, 1961). In the final considerations of the personology approach to Murray's theory of personality one gets the feeling that much of the research is follow-the-leader, the leader being McClelland. Some diversity can be found in the eighteen essays which were written by his former students and colleagues to commemorate Murray's seventieth birthday. These are primarily positional and procedural papers rather than refined research reports.

Obviously Murray has been a valuable and lifetime stimulator in the field of personality theory. It will be interesting to see whether his other contributions are also productive in provoking research. For example, would it be equally fruitful to conduct experiments on the needs for abasement or autonomy or infravoidance or sentience? Certainly the longitudinal principle ought to receive further examination.

■ SUMMARY

The major part of Murray's theory of personality is based on man as a motivated animal. The author has extracted seven principles from Murray's theory which seem to highlight its major factors. The seven principles are these:

1. Regnancy principle: highlighted by Murray's statement "No brain, no personality."

2. Motivation principle: based on man's making a continuous effort to reduce the tensions in his life which are caused by the needs he feels from within and the press of society from without. The amalgamation of these needs–press phenomena does more than reestablish status quo; it also creates newer tension areas to be reduced, so that man moves forward toward constructive goals rather than merely conserving goals. The methods by which man handles his need–press life may lead to conflict or fusion of needs or to subsidiating them into a hierarchical structure. Needs may have characteristics within themselves. They may be primary or secondary, originate within the self or be brought into the personality from society, openly expressed (overt) or disguised in expression (covert), directed toward one object (focal) or toward many objects (diffused). Finally, needs may be exercised for an immediate purpose (effect) or purely for enjoyment of the process of the activity with no goal object in mind (modal). Murray has recently attempted to classify needs into vectors (how you do it) and value (why you do it).

3. Longitudinal principle: characterized by his statement "The history of the personality *is* the personality." One cannot study personality and ignore the past life of the personality. Involved in the developmental aspects of man is the emergence of the erotogenic zones and their effect on man's future behavior, the zones being much the same as those Freud suggested, but interpreted somewhat differently by Murray. The zones are the claustral, oral, anal, and urethral; in addition there is a castration complex revolving around the Freudian phallic theory. Longitudinally speaking, man also arranges his life in terms of short-time goals (proceedings), which may be overtly or covertly expressed, and long-time goals (serials), in which the activities or proceedings must progress along orderly lines in order to achieve the end goal.

4. Physiological processes principle: allied to the regnancy principle but with the additional emphasis that man is first and foremost an organic being.

5. Abstract principle: Murray approaches the neo-Freudians in accepting the id, ego, superego structure as Freud introduced it, but with important deviations of his own similar to those of all the neo-Freudians. Murray is convinced that not all behavior is surface phenomenon.

6. Uniqueness principle: typified by the expression "No man is like any other man in some respects and is like all other men in other respects." Each man is unique.

7. Role concept principle: one of Murray's newer incorporations in his theory of personality, possibly influenced by his work with Kluckhohn. Illus-

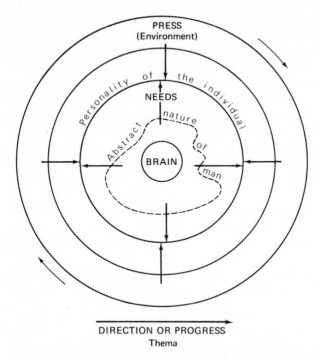

FIGURE 3. *Diagrammatic summary of Murray's theory.*

trated by the oft-quoted line from Shakespeare's *As You Like It,* "All the
world's a stage, / And all the men and women merely players: / They have
their exits and their entrances; / And one man in his time plays many parts."

Figure 3 summarizes the effects of the needs and press on the personality.
Needs, coming partially from within the conscious and partially from without, attempt to keep the personality in formation, with the help, but sometimes hindrance, of the press (environment). The structure is always and
recurrently lopsided to the right, affording motion off dead center and
connating tension reduction as more than a state of equilibrium: as a force for
movement. Like the wheel that is always slightly off center and retains its new
off-center position with each turn, the personality is always moving in only
one direction, the future. The conflicts and victories of the past have either
weakened or strengthened it; their necessity as a foundation cannot be denied
(longitudinal principle).

Central to the entire structure of man's personality is the brain. Without
that hub, the structure collapses or disintegrates, and thus fails to function.

The route over which the wheel has passed and its future route are
described as thema, proceedings, and serials.

BIBLIOGRAPHY

PRIMARY SOURCES

BOOKS

Murray, H. A., *Explorations in Personality*. New York: Oxford University Press, 1938.

Murray, H. A., *Thematic Apperception Test*. Cambridge, Mass.: Harvard University Press, 1943.

Murray, H. A., Assessment of the whole person, in *Proceedings of the Meeting of Military Psychologists and Psychiatrists*. College Park: Maryland University Press, 1945.

Murray, H. A., *Assessment of Men*. New York: Holt, Rinehart & Winston, 1948.

Murray, H. A., Research planning: A few proposals, in S. S. Sargent and M. W. Smith (eds.), *Culture and Personality*. Beloit, Wis.: Viking Fund, 1949.

Murray, H. A. (ed.), Introduction, in H. Melville, *Pierre or The Ambiguities*. New York: Hendricks House, 1949.

Kluckhohn, C., and H. A. Murray, *Personality in Nature, Society, and Culture*. New York: Knopf, 1950.

Murray, H. A., Toward a classification of interactions, in T. Parsons and E. A. Shils (eds.), *Toward a General Theory of Action*. Cambridge, Mass.: Harvard University Press, 1951.

Kluckhohn, C., H. A. Murray, and D. M. Schneider, *Personality in Nature, Society, and Culture*, 2nd ed. New York: Knopf, 1953.

Murray, H. A., Versions of man, in *Man's Right to Knowledge*. New York: Columbia University Press, 1955.

Murray, H. A., Introduction to A. Burton and R. E. Harris (eds.), *Clinical Studies of Personality*, Vols. 1–2. New York: Harper & Row, 1955.

Murray, H. A., Introduction to Methods, in G. G. Stern, M. I. Stein, and B. S. Bloom, *Personality Assessment*. New York: Free Press, 1956.

Murray, H. A., Drive, time, strategy, measurement, and our way of life, in G. Lindzey (ed.), *Assessment of Human Motives*. New York: Holt, Rinehart & Winston, 1958.

Murray, H. A., Preparations for the scaffold of a comprehensive system, in S. Koch (ed.), *Psychology: A Study of a Science*, Vol. 3. New York: McGraw-Hill, 1959.

Murray, H. A., Vicissitudes of creativity, in H. H. Anderson, (ed.), *Creativity and Its Cultivation*. New York: Harper & Row, 1959.

Murray, H. A., Historical trends in personality research, in H. P. David and J. C. Brengelmann (ed.), *Perspectives in Personality Research*. New York: Springer, 1960.

Murray, H. A., The possible nature of a "mythology" to come, in *Myth and Mythmaking*. New York: Braziller, 1960.

Murray, H. A., Two versions of man, in H. Shapley (ed.), *Science Ponders Religion*. New York: Appleton-Century-Crofts, 1960.

Murray, H. A., Beyond yesterday's idealisms, in C. Brinton (ed.), *The Fate of Man*. New York: Braziller, 1961.

Murray, H. A., Definitions of myth, in R. M. Ohmann (ed.), *The Making of Myth*. New York: Putnam's, 1962.

Murray, H. A., Prospect for psychology, in G. Nielson (ed.), *Proceedings of the Fourteenth International Congress of Allied Psychology*. Vol. 1, *Psychology and International Affairs*. Copenhagen, Denmark: Munksgaard, 1962.

Murray, H. A., and C. Kluckhohn, Outline of a conception of personality (pp. 3–49), and Personality formation: The determinants (pp. 53–72), in C. Kluckhohn, H. A. Murray, and D. M. Schneider (eds.), *Personality in Nature, Society, and Culture*, 2nd ed. New York: Knopf, 1964.

Murray, H. A., Dead to the world, or the passions of Herman Melville, in E. S. Shneidman (ed.), *Essays in Self-destruction*. New York: Science House, 1967a.

Murray, H. A., In E. G. Boring and G. Lindzey (eds.), *A History of Psychology in Autobiography*, Vol. V. New York: Appleton-Century-Crofts, 1967b, pp. 283–310.

Murray, H. A., Personality: II. Contemporary viewpoints, components of an evolving personological system, in D. Sills (ed.), *International Encyclopedia of the Social Sciences*. New York: Macmillan and Free Press, 1968, Vol. 12, pp. 5–13.

Murray, H. A., *Encounter with Psychology*. San Francisco: Jossey-Bass, 1969.

PERIODICALS

Murray, H. A., Ten publications on research on physiological ontogeny. Summarized (with A. E. Cohn) in: Physiological ontogeny: Vol. I, The present status of the problem, *Quart. Rev. Biol.*, 1925–1927, 2, 469–493.

Murray, H. A., A case of pinealoma with symptoms suggestive of compulsion neurosis, *Arch. Neurol. Psychiat.* (Chicago), 1928, 19, 932–945.

Murray, H. A., H. Barry, Jr., and D. W. MacKinnon, Hypnotizability as a personality trait, *Hum. Biol.*, 1931, 3, 1–36.

Murray, H. A., The effect of fear upon estimates of the maliciousness of other personalities, *J. Soc. Psychol.*, 1933, 4, 310–329.

Murray, H. A., The psychology of humor: Vol. II. Mirth responses to disparagement jokes as a manifestation of an aggressive disposition, *J. Abnorm. Soc. Psychol.*, 1934, 29, 66–81.

Murray, H. A., H. A. Wolff, and C. E. Smith, The psychology of humor, *J. Abnorm. Soc. Psychol.*, 1934, 28, 341–365.

Morgan, C. D., and H. A. Murray, A method of investigating fantasies, *Arch. Neurol. Psychiat.* (Chicago), 1935, 34, 289–306.

Murray, H. A., Psychology and the university, *Arch. Neurol. Psychiat.* (Chicago), 1935, 34, 803–897.

Murray, H. A., The Harvard Psychological Clinic, *Harvard Alumni Bull.*, Oct. 25, 1935.

Murray, H. A., Facts which support the concept of need or drive, *J. Psychol.*, 1936a, 3, 27–42.

Murray, H. A., Techniques for systematic investigation of fantasy, *J. Psychol.*, 1936b, 3, 115–143.

Murray, H. A., Some concepts for a psychology of personality, *J. Gen. Psychol.*, 1936c, 15, 240–268.

Murray, H. A., and D. R. Wheeler, A note on the possible clairvoyance of dreams, *J. Psychol.*, 1936, 3, 309–313.

Wolf, R., and H. A. Murray, An experiment in judging personalities, *J. Psychol.*, 1936, 3, 345–365.

Murray, H. A., Visceral manifestations of personality, *J. Abnorm. Soc. Psychol.*, 1937, 32, 161–184.

Murray, H. A., Sigmund Freud: 1856–1939, *Amer. J. Psychol.*, 1940a, 53, 134–138.

Murray, H. A., What should psychologists do about psychoanalysis? *J. Abnorm. Soc. Psychol.*, 1940b, 35, 150–175.

Murray, H. A., and M. Stein, Note on the selection of combat officers, *Psychosom. Med.*, 1943, 5, 386–391.

Murray, H. A., and C. D. Morgan, A clinical study of sentiments, *Genet. Psychol. Monogr.*, 1945, 32, 3–311.

Murray, H. A., and D. W. MacKinnon, Assessment of OSS personnel, *J. Consult. Psychol.*, 1946, 10, 76–80.

Murray, H. A., Time for a positive morality, *Surv. Graphic*, 1947b, 36, 195 ff.

Murray, H. A., Problems in clinical research: Round table, *Amer. J. Orthopsychiat.*, 1947c, 17, 203–210.

Murray, H. A., America's mission, *Surv. Graphic*, 1948, 37, 411–415.

Murray, H. A., Uses of the TAT, *Amer. J. Psychiat.*, 1951a, 107, 8.

Murray, H. A., Thematic Apperception Test, *Milit. Clin. Psychol.*, 1951b, 45, 54–71.

Murray, H. A., *In nomine diaboli*, New Eng. Quart., 1951c, 24, 435–452.

Murray, H. A., Some basic psychological assumptions and conception, *Dialectica*, 1951d, 5, 266–292.

Murray, H. A., Poet of creative dissolution (Conrad Aiken), *Wake*, 1952, 11, 95–106.

Murray, H. A., Science in two societies, in *The Contemporary Scene*. New York: Metropolitan Museum of Art, 1954.

Davids, A., and H. A. Murray, Preliminary appraisal of an auditory projective technique for studying personality and cognition, *Amer. J. Orthopsychiat.*, 1955, 25, 543–554.

Murray, H. A., Morton Prince: Sketch of his life and work, *J. Abnorm. Soc. Psychol.*, 1956, 52, 291–295.

Murray, H. A., Religion in an age of science, *Christian Reg.*, 1956, 135.

Murray, H. A., Individuality: The meaning and content of individuality in contemporary America, *Daedalus*, 1958, 87, 25–47.

Murray, H. A., Myth and mythmaking, *Daedalus*, 1959, 88, 211–380.

Murray, H. A., H. Cantril, and M. May, Some glimpses of Soviet psychology, *Amer. Psychologist*, 1959, 14, 303–307.

Murray, H. A., Commentary on the case of El, *J. Proj. Tech.*, 1961, 25, 404–411.

Murray, H. A., Unprecedented evolutions, *Daedalus*, 1961, 90, 547–570.

Murray, H. A., Prospect for psychology, *Science*, 1962a, 136, 483–488.

Murray, H. A., The personality and career of Satan, *J. Soc. Issues*, 1962b, 18, 36–54.

Murray, H. A., Studies of stressful interpersonal disputations, *Amer. Psychologist*, 1963, 18, 28–36.

Hall, M. H., A conversation with Henry A. Murray, *Psychol. Today*, 1968, 4, 56–63.

SUGGESTED READINGS

BOOKS

Hall, C. S., and G. Lindzey, *Theories of Personality*. New York: Wiley, 1957, pp. 157–205.

Heckhausen, Heinz, *The Anatomy of Achievement Motivation*, trans. R. C. Birney, K. C. Balter, and D. McClelland. New York: Academic Press, 1967.

McClelland, D. C., *Personality*. New York: Holt, Rinehart & Winston, 1951.

McClelland, D. C., *The Achieving Society*. Princeton, N.J.: Van Nostrand, 1961.

McClelland, D. C., J. W. Atkinson, R. A. Clark, and E. L. Lowell. *The Achievement Motive*. New York: Appleton-Century-Crofts, 1953.

Maddi, S. R., Humanistic psychology: Allport and Murray, in J. M. Wepman and R. W. Heine (eds.), *Concepts of Personality*. Chicago: Aldine, 1963a, pp. 162–205.

Tyler, L. E., Toward a workable psychology of individuality, in M. T. Mednick and S. A. Mednick (eds.), *Research in Personality*. New York: Holt, Rinehart & Winston, 1963b, pp. 22–31.

White, R. W. (ed., *The Study of Lives: Essays on Personality in Honor of Henry A. Murray*. New York: Atherton Press, 1963c.

PERIODICALS

Bellak, L., and H. A. Murray, An appreciation, *J. Proj. Tech.*, 1958, 22, 143–144.

Birney, R. C., The reliability of the achievement motive, *J. Abnorm. Soc. Psychol.*, 1959, 58, 266–267.

Chambers, J. L., and L. J. Broussard, The role of need-attitudes in adjustment, *J. Clin. Psychol.*, 1960, 16, 383–387.

Edwards, A. L., Edwards' Personal Preference Schedule, *Psychol. Corp.*, New York, 1953.

> Two hundred and twenty-five paired comparisons based on fifteen of Murray's needs.

Faith, H. W., Jr., The discrepancy between self-ideal self concepts as needs projected to thematic apperception test pictures, *Dissert. Abstr.*, 1961, 21, 1999–2000.

Hunt, H. F., Discussion: Explorations in personality, *J. Proj. Tech. Pers. Assess.*, 1964, 28, 169–171.

> Twenty-fifth anniversary of Murray's *Explorations in Personality*.

McClelland, D. C., N achievement and entrepreneurship: A longitudinal study, *J. Pers. Soc. Psychol.*, 1965, 1, 389–392.

McClenahan, M. L. P., The relationship of test-defined needs to illuminance matches of need-related pictures, *Dissert. Abstr.*, 1961, 21, 3862–3863.

McCreary, J. K., The problem of personality definition, *J. Gen. Psychol.*, 1960, 63, 107–111.

Megargee, I. I., and G. V. Parker, An exploration of the equivalence of Murrayan needs as assessed by the Adjective Check List, the TAT and Edwards' Personal Preference Schedule, *J. Clin. Psychol.*, 1968, 24, 47–51.

Merbaum, A. P., Need for achievement in Negro and white children, *Dissert. Abstr.*, 1962, 23, 693–699.

Mischel, W., Delay of gratification, need for achievement, and acquiescence in another culture, *J. Abnorm. Soc. Psychol.*, 1961, 62, 543–552.

4

JUNG

Every cradle asks us, "whence?" and every coffin, "whither?"
The poor barbarian weeping above his dead can answer
these questions as intelligently as the robed priest of the
most authentic creed.

ROBERT G. INGERSOLL
Address at a Little Boy's Grave

SOME BIOGRAPHICAL DATA

Carl Gustav Jung was born in Kesswyl, on the shores of Lake Constance in Switzerland, on July 26, 1875. He continued to reside in Switzerland, where he maintained a residence and clinical practice in the small town of Küsnacht, south of Zurich, on Lake Zurich.[1] Jung obtained a Doctor of Medicine

[1] The author is indebted to the late Dr. Jung for his hospitality and guidance during a visit to his home in Küsnacht in the spring of 1960. In response to this chapter he said, "I don'

degree from the University of Basel and began his psychiatric work as an assistant in the famed Burghözli Mental Hospital in Zurich. Through his work and contacts at the mental hospital he later met and worked with Eugen Bleuler and also Pierre Janet in Paris. Prior to World War I he gave up his teaching and research posts, first at the Burghölzli Mental Hospital and in 1913 at the University of Zurich, in order to devote full time to his then large private practice. He also conducted training seminars for many years and, of course, continued to write voluminously about his theoretical system and case studies. Shortly after his semiretirement in the immediate post-World War II years, he accepted a created chair of medical psychology for him at the University of Basel. Prior to his semiretirement Jung traveled extensively throughout the world in pursuance of the history of man as he found it in Oriental and Occidental cultures.

Jung's association with Freud started in 1906 through correspondence concerning the validity Jung found for Freud's dream analysis techniques. At the founding of the International Psychoanalytic Association in 1910 Jung had been elected its first president. So close was the relationship between the two men that Freud considered Jung his successor, and, in fact, they traveled amicably together to give the famous Clark University lectures at the twentieth anniversary celebration in Worcester, Massachusetts, arranged by G. Stanley Hall. The friendship lasted until 1914 when Jung withdrew from the International Psychoanalytic Association and further contacts with the then Freud-dominated organization. Many accounts have been written of their disaffection with each other. Probably the most complete, though likely to be one-sided, is that of Ernest Jones in his three-volume series on Freud (Jones, 1953, 1955, 1957).

More recent biographical accounts which soften the Freud-oriented references come mainly from adherents and admirers of his analytical theory (Bennet, 1966; Douglas, 1961; Evans, 1964; Fordham, 1964). Just as Freud and Adler have people dedicated to their work, Jung too has left a legacy of devoted adherents. Some of the most loyal to him and to the continuation of his work are Michael Fordham, Sir Herbert Read, Gerhard Adler, Jolande Jacobi, and particularly his personal secretary, Aniela Jaffe. Whether American psychology grants Jung much status or a place in its annals, his work will continue to be perpetuated by these and many others. The primary maintenance of analytic psychology centers around two well-established institutions: the C. G. Jung Institute in Zurich, Switzerland, and the Bollingen Foundation, founded in 1941, which continues to publish his work through the Princeton University Press.

On June 6, 1961, Dr. Jung died at his home in Küsnacht, Switzerland, an occasion noted by the whole intellectual world with deep regret.

---

believe a word of it, but I can't disagree with anything you have said." Then he laughed merrily. He was a delightful conversationalist and host.

INTRODUCTION

In many ways Carl Gustav Jung was the "grand old man" of personality theorists. He lived through the earliest era of personality theory, wrote voluminously, gathered many honors, and continued until his death to write, treat a few patients, and excite the psychological world with his work. Jung's influence has been unique. His theories are not popular in the sense that many papers at the psychological meetings are oriented toward them. Most psychologists are bothered by Jung. They cannot ignore him. The usual reaction is an attack on his theory; then, with a feeling that all has been put in its proper place, the psychologist continues with his main thesis. But to ignore Jung does not seem to satisfy psychologists. Jung irritated them because he was different, mystical, circuitous in writing style, provocative. He led one to accept vigorously or totally reject his theories on personality. There seems to be little room for halfhearted responses. Although Jung was quite aware of the world of psychologists, his position in it left him unimpressed, as he continued to feel that truth is truth whether it happens to be popular or not.

Perhaps one clue to the influence of Jung was his deep and, among psychologists, rarely duplicated erudition in fields far beyond the usually cultivated areas of psychology. He went back to the historical aspects of man's existence in both written and artifactual records in an attempt to provide clearer answers to the ubiquitous question of why man does the things he does. Jung delved deeply into alchemy, mythology, religion, archeology, rituals, symbols, Sanskrit and other forgotten languages, as well as into the newer ideas in psychoanalysis, all in a dedicated attempt to learn more about the personality of man as he exists today. If a new language had to be learned to trace a remote source of information, Jung learned it rather than accept translations or ignore the thread he felt to be a promising lead. Jung's learning and erudition were impressive and honest.

None of Jung's positive influence appears to be direct, although in the writings of Allport, Rogers, Murphy, and Maslow, as well as in the writings of the nonpsychologists Arnold Toynbee and Philip Wylie, one finds oblique references to, and a strong flavor of, the Jungian point of view. Here is one comment made by Feifel in a chapter he wrote about death: "Any personality theory worth its salt must make meaningful place for the entire continuum of human existence" (Fiefel, 1963).

Jung's theory is different from others in that it is shadowy, metaphysical, of a nature almost impossible to test in a laboratory situation, and appears to reverse the current trend for statistical treatment of psychological data.

It is a hopeful theory: Man is gradually becoming through the ages a better and more civilized human being, operating within better and better frames of reference. The theory gives encouragement to the middle and later years of life, an attitude which runs counter to the modern trend of emphasis on child psychology. Although Jung was originally attracted to Freud and his work to the extent of being Freud's announced successor, as we have seen, he broke sharply with Freud in 1914. Freud's theory is inclined to emphasize the dreary, inescapable polarity of life; Jung treated the improving aspect of man's existence.

As is the case with many original and provocative writers, Jung at times was accused of supporting a position when in fact he was attempting to explain it. This, Jung felt, led to unfairness in the evaluation of his own work and was the obstacle to objective reporting.

JUNG'S DESCRIPTION OF HUMAN BEHAVIOR

One finds it easy to oversimplify Jung's theoretical position into principles, although Jung speaks of only two principles as such, using terms which he borrowed from the field of physics: *entropy* and *equivalence*. The temptation to discern more is strong because of the great volume of his writings. Jung felt that his work was not theoretical but based on observable and identifiable facts evident to all who take the time to discover them in the world of today, and in what we know of the world of yesterday.

The author presents Jung's work by means of four principles, which seem to help the undergraduate student digest the written work and apparently do no great injustice to the core of his ideas. To gain a greater grasp of all that is Jungian, one must read Jung for years, preferably in the original German text. Since such an endeavor is obviously impossible for all but a few undergraduates, it is hoped this book will afford considerable understanding.

The four principles are polarity, self-actualization, unconscious states, and teleology. The order is unimportant. All four principles as used in this text apply equally well to Jungian psychology. Because they apply more to psychoanalysis as a technique than to understanding the basics of personality, we shall not treat Jung's analytic methods, such as sentence completion or dream analysis, even though these are basic and interesting; they concern themselves more with operational factors than with systems of thought.

Polarity Principle

Probably one of the most universal ideas extant among personality theorists is that of polarity. Jung is no exception, and much of what his theory contains has been grouped within the principle of polarity in this text. Also, as with many other theories, discussing and emphasizing one idea at a time creates the impression that it is a singular factor in the theory with no relationship to other factors. This is not the case; almost all of the polarity principles discussed herein are directly related to some other aspect of Jung's work. But, as always, they must be discussed singly, so that they may be better understood. Relationships will be developed as the text continues.

After many years of study, concentration, and reflection Jung became convinced that all the world and perhaps the universe, animate and inanimate, exists because of opposition. There is and always must be opposites, and opposites beget conflict. Without conflict, life is nothing. Conflict is the basic stuff of life. Conflict generates progress. Without conflict nothing happens because only through conflict can one thing or another emerge beyond the point at which conflict began. Progress, movement, change of position, therefore, are possible only under conditions of stress. Wishing to remove the stress of conflict with an opponent motivates the original object to action. Opposition, conflict, resultant stress, and the removal of stress are the *sine qua non* of the world we live in. In a rather metaphysical way Jung said that whatever exists has an opposite even if that opposite is the lack of existence of the original condition: life–no life, hunger–no hunger, love–no love, house–no house, clothes–no clothes. In most cases what exists has an existing counterpart. In the case of life–no life, however, one can only assume that the opposite of life is no life, a state called death. Other oppositions, such as water eroding rock, two nations at war, or two automobiles in collision, obviously indicate factually real quantities countering each other.

In contrast to the Freudian position that life consists of the eternal going back and forth *of one object* between two poles, and thus the evolution of a perpetually frustrated, vacillating object, never able to settle at any point, Jung suggested a happier ending to the story of opposition and its resolution into equilibrium. True equilibrium is of short duration, but it is a sign of progress. All is not a "vale of tears." Opposition not only moves the object off dead center, and thus prolongs its existence, but may be resolved into progress within itself by three actions. The actions are *compensation, union,* and the aforementioned *opposition*.

When the personality feels that it is in conflict because it cannot reach a desired goal, it may seek another goal equally attractive and in so doing remove the conflict. This form of compensation moves the personality toward a new position, even though the advanced position may not be in the direction of the original goal. The important factor to Jung was that the personality has done something to shift itself from its first position. Symbolic action is not as important as physical action in a compensatory move. Simply dreaming about conquering an objective (although dreaming was most important as a behavioral phenomenon to Jung) is not a true compensatory action. For example, think of the student who desires athletic recognition but cannot make the team and who therefore redoubles his efforts in the classroom and achieves scholastic recognition instead of athletic recognition. The unfortunate connotations of this oft-repeated example are that all good students are assumed to be compensating for failure in athletics, their real goal. It ignores the fact that some students study because they want to learn. The opposite is just as fallacious when misused: athletes are athletes because they cannot be scholars. A more meaningful example may be found in the case of a student who uses color and design to compensate in dress for a deformity in stature and figure. But to Jung compensation which grows out of conflict is a favorable factor for man's personality. It helps him go forward.

In the second type of action, opposing forces may unite in seeking a resolution satisfactory to both. Once again, progress has been made, and the value of opposition in life is demonstrated. Although this appears paradoxical, the following example may help to clarify it. Have you ever witnessed or been involved in a fight with two members of the same family? Frequently interference in this type of battle only brings the wrath of both opponents down upon the peacemaker. Thus, the conflict of the brothers is united against another object, the peacemaker, a result which leads to a mutual feeling between the kin toward a third object. Peace reigns, amicability between brothers is reestablished, the frustrated energy has been expended on a third force, and some progress in relationships in the family ensues. It is true that the resolution of conflict may not always be morally correct, as we see in the case of two nations that loathe and suspect each other but are quite willing to unite against a third nation which seeks to attack them both. The union of opposing forces, then, according to Jung, may be a way of merely resolving opposition.

The third type of action, in which opposition leads to movement and possible progress, is best typified by the rivalry of two students for grades or scholastic status. Spurred on by their conflict with each other, both extend themselves far beyond the limits of learning the subject matter. Much of the commercial world refines its product, price, and service because of the impetus of commercial rivals.

To Jung opposition was good. Only by action can man possibly make forward steps.

With the above as a general introduction to Jung's concept of polarity as exemplified by opposition in life, we may now examine more closely the specific polarities that he felt exist in man's personality.

Principle of Equivalence

As was stated previously, the use of the term *principles* was used only twice by Jung and then in a borrowed sense. The inclusion of the polarity aspects of Jung's work at this point connotes not so much that they are opposing forces but that they represent opposite ends of a scale of behavior.

The principle of equivalence comes from the field of physics, the first law of thermodynamics. Sometimes called the *conservation of energy principle*, it means that energy used to change the condition of some object is not lost but will reappear in another form in another object. For instance, the energy used in the burning of an object is not lost but transformed into the energy of heat. Jung uses this principle to apply to man's personality dynamics. As the desire for one object diminishes, an equal amount of desire may be directed toward another object. The principal feature regarding man's behavior is that desire is not lost entirely; it is merely diverted to another objective. Desire remains constant if it is present at all; the goals change. The student who desires a social life in college does not lose the desire when he ceases to date one coed; he seeks another as his dating partner. Athletically motivated students who desire the outlet of sports may transfer their activities from football to basketball to baseball as the academic year progresses. Students who engage in only one sport and come to the end of that season must use the energy and time formerly expended in long practice sessions in moving toward fresh goals. Desire shifted from one activity may be directed toward diverse activities, such as more studying, socializing with friends, and trips home, all of which were not possible during the season when energy was expended only in playing on a varsity team.

What happens when a desire is repressed? This question was most important to Jung, for out of it comes the symbolic life of man through which he must dream or fantasize his activities toward the desired goal. The answer is that the energy conserved is redirected toward the desired object through the dream world, whether it be by diurnal or nocturnal dreaming. Much of what man is, Jung stated, he is because he can dream his way toward the resolution of a conflict.

Principle of Entropy

The principle of entropy, which is the second law of thermodynamics, states that the properties of one body when placed in juxtaposition to another that is similar in kind but different in degree will tend to assume the characteristics of the more highly charged body. It is important to note that the bodies must be of the same species or type. Man to man or animal to animal fits this specification. When the bodies are in contact, the more highly charged body loses some of its charge, until the two are equal in respect to the exchanged characteristic. Two bodies of water of different levels, when connected, will eventually be equal in level. The result is a loss of energy as the two bodies reach a state of equilibrium. As Jung applied this law of physics to the dynamics of personality, certain extensions of the theory also apply. Since the personality is not a closed system, it is never possible to achieve a true state of balance or equilibrium between two people or within one person engaged in two activities. Society and inner changes create constantly changing conditions and feed energy into the dynamics of personality, thereby tending to keep the person's behavior off balance while he continuously attempts to keep himself in balance. However, in spite of the fact that man can never win the battle of balancing his conflicts, the nearer he comes to doing so, the nearer he comes to peace and tranquillity. This state of true harmony does not necessarily accomplish anything, as we will recall from the previous discussion on the value of conflict. To illustrate: It is only because one body of water is placed higher than a second, receiving body of water that power can be produced through a hydroelectric dynamo system. Two lakes of equal altitude produce no power or movement between their respective waters.

We shall see more of these two systems as they operate within the personality in the following sections of the chapter. To repeat: All of Jung's system is highly interrelated.

REGRESSION VS. PROGRESSION

As Jung believed, the personality either goes forward or goes backward. It is not possible to stay happily but unproductively in the middle. Progression obviously connotes movement forward, and such movement further connotes some kind of change which is beneficial to the personality. In the meantime, what good can come out of regression, or backward movement, according to Jung? Much, he said, because not all that man accomplishes is done in a direct to-the-target manner. More times than man realizes, he attains goals by returning to a previous position, reorienting himself, and possibly finding a better pathway than the first to attain the hoped-for goal. The strategic withdrawal is often the wisest maneuver. As we shall see, withdrawal is sometimes made through symbols and in the unconscious areas of the personality, but the value of regression is not to be minimized. Again, this is in contrast to the Freudian doctrine, which holds that the personality forever vacillates between two polarities but does not necessarily move forward or learn new methods of approach.

PERSONAL UNCONSCIOUS VS. COLLECTIVE UNCONSCIOUS

The full treatment of this concept is given later in the chapter, but at the moment it is deemed important to introduce the concept briefly because of the polar nature of Jung's two states of unconsciousness: *personal* and *collective*.

The *personal unconscious,* somewhat akin to Freud's unconscious, is the storehouse of all that has happened to the individual. All previous conscious material which is now not available to the conscious mind because it has been forgotten or repressed, or was not strong originally in a subliminal sense, resides in the personal unconscious.

The *collective unconscious* is one of Jung's most controversial contributions to the field of personality theory. Essentially, what Jung suggested is that man is born with a predisposition through his racial past to act in certain ways. As man has evolved through the centuries, he has accumulated knowledge and feelings. These, plus the accumulated predispositions of the present generation, do not disappear but are handed down via inheritance to each succeeding generation. All these—knowledge, feelings, superstitions—may never be triggered to action if no opportunity presents itself as a stimulus. Certain seemingly universal fears known to all men—feelings about mother, aspirations toward a supranatural figure, worship of gods and deities—are examples of the collective unconscious. It is as if men through the ages share an increasingly complex repository of memories collectively passed down from one generation to the next. This phenomenon, stated Jung, has continued to be active for all the centuries of man's existence. Jung gave various names to the collective unconscious, sometimes calling it primordial images, imagos, behavior patterns, but most often he referred to the collective archetypes.

The personal vis-à-vis the collective unconscious operates sometimes independently and sometimes in coordination but always is a different phenomenon within the personality. At times, when the personal unconscious is incapable of reducing pressures, the collective unconscious through the richness of its accumulated past can solve present problems. Conversely, as men acquire rich experiences in the present life, these are passed on to future generations in the form of predispositions to act in prescribed ways found to be useful, or strong enough not to be ignored.

CONSCIOUS VS. UNCONSCIOUS

A polarity also exists between the conscious and the unconscious aspects of man's behavior. The latter, despite its being of two kinds (personal and collective), is different from the state of awareness or consciousness of the world. The conscious has as its core the ego. The ego is that part of man's personality which has feelings, perceptions, and thought processes helping the personality to attend to the business of everyday living. However, it never operates alone, for there is much byplay between it and the two areas of the unconscious. To the ego falls the task of directing life's processes. The direction is always a vacillating proposition between the ego in the conscious, and the tug and pull and influence of the unconscious. Much of what goes on is governed by the principles of entropy and equivalence. Thus, what conflicts the conscious mind cannot resolve are often resolved by the unconscious impinging subtly upon the conscious. The total effect again creates a polarity in life which does not always connote direct struggle between the two forces but may aid the ongoing life of the personality. Progress results eventually through the byplay of the two states of being.

EXTRAVERSION VS. INTROVERSION

Very few original concepts of Jung have been adapted by the modern psychological world, but his suggestion that the personality moves in two different directions, either extraverted or introverted, is one of those few. The extraverted personality moves in the direction of people, toward the objective, nonreflective world and a life centered on action. The introverted personality moves in the opposite direction; his world is quiet, free from people, and centers on subjective experiences which are quite personal. Although current psychological research has discovered a third position of ambiversion, many lay people still adhere to the extraversion–introversion description of personality. Where the conscious self or ego is oriented toward extraverted behavior, the principle of polarity causes the unconscious realism of the personality to be oriented toward introversion. The individual who is brash, bold, and direct in behavior utilizes dreams and fantasies which make him into the image of the quiet, reflective scholar, the opposite of his known personality to the world. The converse, of course, applies to the introverted personality. His dreams and aspirations in fantasy form are desires to be more forthright and direct in contacts with people. By the reciprocity of these two forces, said Jung, the total personality comes nearer the middle of the two polarities than the external personality would suggest. Perhaps, after all, Jung was not truly in disagreement with the research which indicates a middle point called *ambivert*, although he did not create or use the term.

SUPERIOR FUNCTIONS VS. INFERIOR FUNCTIONS

In a following section on the self-actualization principle more will be said about the four functions. At the moment we may consider these functions as being of superior or inferior strength. The four functions are as follows:

Intuition: why it is (theory)
Sensation: what it is (recognition)
Feeling: what it is worth (value)
Thinking: what it means (understanding)

Most personalities utilize one function more comfortably and continuously than the other three. This becomes the superior function. A person may be looking at an oil painting and see it primarily for its value or worth. His superior function in reacting to oil paintings is what Jung called the *feeling* or *value* of the painting. It is, or is not, valuable. The other three functions at this time will be inferior, although one of the three may act in an auxiliary or supportive capacity. For example, besides his feeling for the painting, a man may consider oil paintings through his sensation function. The sensation function tells him that he recognizes it as a painting of the seashore. Assuming that the painting is an *avant-garde* work and he can sensate nothing because he can recognize nothing in the picture, the auxiliary aspect of the sensation function influences his feelings. The primary feeling function now places a lower value on the picture as far as he, the viewer, is concerned because he cannot recognize or receive an identifiable sensation from it. The other two functions in this situation (thinking and intuition) are inferior. Inferior functions usually express themselves via symbols in dreams and fantasies. In our example, the viewer may express via the unconscious a feeling of rejection and disturbance about the painting because he cannot understand it. He is unable to think about it or know what it means. He is therefore irritated and angry about such pictures, but he cannot express this feeling well because he cannot understand them.

Again, the aspects of polarity, so important to Jung's system, are illustrated by the superior and inferior functions of the personality.

PHYSICAL ENERGY VS. PSYCHIC ENERGY

From the libido comes all energy for the individual. Although the term *libido* is at times used in a confused sense by Jung, we may assume that, as in the Freudian system, this is a wellspring for energy. Jung did not consider the term to mean primarily sexual energy. (It was partially on the accusation of Jung that Freud's work overemphasized the sexual content in the personality that they parted ways.) From the libido emerge two types of energy: psychic and physical. Since both use the same source of energy, there may at times be conflict in their demands upon it. The polarity of physical energy (walking, muscular working, etc.) to psychic energy (thinking, feeling, perceiving, etc.) creates a reciprocity which keeps the individual somewhat in balance between the poles.

ORGANIC NEEDS VS. CULTURAL NEEDS

Somewhat similar to the previous polarity is Jung's suggestion that organic needs and cultural needs are in conflict for the basic energy provided by the libido. A priority system exists here, so that the organic needs take precedence in obtaining the libidinal (psychic) energy. After they have been satisfied, the psychic needs may use whatever energy remains. The primary demands to maintain life (eating, sleeping, eliminating, etc.) must be met before the person can hope to pursue the cultural needs (reading, creating art forms, pursuing hobbies, worship, etc.). Jung pointed out that man is progressing as a living thing because, as he better meets his organic needs, he spends less and less energy and time on these needs; therefore, man is able to create higher and better forms of culture. Jung is saying that bread comes first; then man may have Bach, Beethoven, and books.

ANIMA VS. ANIMUS

It will be recalled from the previous discussion regarding the collective unconscious that all individuals inherit a characteristic from their ancestors which is universal. This archetype, when referring to man's bisexuality, is called the *anima* or the *animus*. In males the feminine characteristic is called the anima. In females the masculine characteristic is called the animus, revealing Jung's feeling that there is something of the opposite sex in each of the sexes. Although this concept has wide acceptance in the present day, Jung boldly announced it long before it was ready to be accepted. He departed, however, from the generally approved biological theory of androgens and estrogens. Jung credited the bisexuality of man to primordial influences, admitting the influence of the sex chromosomes but insisting that they are the result of racial experience and not of genetically organic evolution as such. He stated that "the whole nature of man presupposes woman . . . ," and, of course, the reverse would be equally true. By this archetype, which has accumulated over the ages, man and woman are able to appreciate and understand each other's role. We may assume further that, as Jung believed, man and woman are progressively becoming more and more in tune with the sex roles of each other. The ultimate of this trend was not discussed by Jung directly.

SUBLIMATION VS. REPRESSION

The reader will remember that, according to the principles of entropy and equivalence, energy does not just disappear but finds another form of expression. Jung felt that this outlet is definitely important when psychic energy from the libidinal source is not permitted full expression. As usual in his system there seem to be only two directions or polarities in which the frustrated psychic energy can move: upward into fields of expression which are socially acceptable and can be pursued openly, or downward into hidden avenues of expression which are not always acceptable to society. The former method is called *sublimation*; the latter, *repression*.

In sublimation the personality moves forward because the outside world encourages its motives. Being given encouragement, the sublimated psychic energy can be put to rational use and coordinate its strength to bring about the desired goal. The energy is there because of the principles of entropy and equivalence. The only real factor which has changed is the goal. Unmarried women may, for example, sublimate their very understandable desire for children and the role of motherhood into valuable roles in society by being teachers of the young. Through this avenue they may "mother" children, be kind to them, be responsive, warm—all of which society holds in high esteem. This is not to say that all unmarried teachers are using sublimated psychic energies. The reasons for entering and remaining in an occupation are varied. In this example we are merely pointing out a method of sublimation which transplants the energy directed toward one goal, motherhood, to that of another, entering the teaching field, although this may not be directly within the conscious reasoning of the teacher. Sublimation often hides its real reasons from the sublimator.

Repression is disturbing. The psychic energy is blocked. It cannot disappear, according to the principles of entropy and equivalence. Therefore it descends into the deepest recesses of the unconscious to boil and roil about, creating tighter tensions the more it is repressed. Having no place to go but into the ego forms of consciousness to which it is denied access, the repressed feeling causes pain and irrational behavior. Not being coordinated, because its goal is unobtainable, it can only create pressure. This causes the personality to behave in odd and neurotic ways. Sudden mood shifts, headaches, irritability, lack of concentration—all or any of these may be the result of repressed psychic energy. In most cases the individual is largely unaware of what is happening. Usually only through deep insight and psychotherapy is he able to uncover the dynamics of repressed psychic energy. All is not hopeless, however, according to Jung, because, as we have discussed in the section on regression *vs.* progression, "strategic withdrawal" may be the wisest move. By allowing the personality to move backward, one may be able to find other goal structures, or an acceptable sublimatory action. If the pain of repression is high enough, the psychic energy may perforce do something about relieving the situation. The deepest forms of repressed behavior may eventuate in psychotic behavior, a poor adjustment, according to society, but one which may satisfy the personality because no other method of solving the problem has been found. The catatonic in deep, trancelike state has "solved" his problem to some degree by complete withdrawal.

CAUSALITY VS. TELEOLOGY

Teleology is important enough in Jung's work to be considered a principle later in these pages, but for the present it represents such a major polarity (with causality at the other pole) that we have included it here.

Although almost no personality theorists deny that man is a goal-seeking creature of some kind, few place as much emphasis on the distant future as Jung did. *Teleology*, a term more often encountered in philosophy and theology than in psychology, means essentially "that the present can be *explained* in terms of the future." This carries it beyond the concept that man goes along seeking immediate goals, to the idea that he seeks and is strongly influenced by goals and aspirations in the very far future.

In contrast to the teleological viewpoint as an explanatory factor in the dynamics of behavior is the currently popular mode of explaining man's behavior by what he has been in the past. His past is irrevocable. It has happened and cannot be undone. If you wish to know why a person behaves as he does now, you must explore and examine his past.

Jung did not deny the causality of the past as a determiner of the present, but he accepted causality as only a part of the picture for describing present behavior. Aside from feeling that concentration on the past leads only to discouragement (you are stuck with your irrevocable past), Jung believed that all people conduct themselves in the present according to a forward-looking philosophy. The college student, for example, works and dreams and plans for the day when he will graduate, get a job, get married, and achieve wealth and success. This dream of the future, stated Jung, explains better why he studies and remains in college in the present than does any description of his background. Jung was willing to admit that man's progress may be curtailed by his habits of the past, but he insisted also that man has his eye to the future.

Thus, to Jung a polarity exists between what a person has been and what he is trying to become. Only the interplay between these two factors can explain why he acts as he does in the present. The past is prologue, the present is action, while the future determines behavior.

PROCESS OF INDIVIDUATION

In summary, all of the previous personality factors and others we shall write about must be balanced in equality if a true self is to emerge. Governed by the principles of entropy and equivalence, the system cannot be in a state of equilibrium while one factor is greater than another. Tension and conflict result, causing unhappiness and frustration. The true goal in life is to seek full development of all the component parts, be they psychic or organic, conscious or unconscious. However, Jung declared, such a perfect state of affairs is impossible, for man is not a closed system existing only within himself. The human being cannot avoid the storms and stresses of the exterior world any more than he can keep his interior organic self in a balanced state between hunger and satiation or sleep and wakefulness. The demands of society, friends and foe, also continuously tip the balances. Only because man has to keep working continuously to equate the polarities in his life does he move forward, although progress may not be easy.

Self-Actualization Principle

Jung was an optimist about man and his future. Although he read and studied extensively the unwritten and written past, his main interest was in the future of man, which he found good. It is good because it is better than the past, and all indications are that it will continue to improve just as it has in the past. Modern man, he felt, is an improvement over primitive man. There is no reason to suspect that with all the past vicissitudes of life—famine, pestilence, disease, methods of warfare which man was able to surmount—progress will cease. The very struggle that man must go through to survive strengthens him and assures that the race will continue. The polarity of man's existence guarantees struggle, out of which comes progress.

Gradual improvement does not come out of a mass effort but only through individuals. Individuation within the self (seeing that all parts of the self attempt equalization) and also individuals as single identities are the keystones of progress for man as a whole. A person acts in concert with others primarily for reasons of well-being and mutual aid, but any group improvement is only the accumulation of its variegated parts, the part being the individual.

The emphasis, then, for Jung was the single personality. How does the personality reach its highest level of self-actualization? What are the basic components of the personality system one has to use, and how does he go about using them?

THE COMPONENTS OF SELF-ACTUALIZATION

The personality consists of various parts or systems, some of which are the ego, the self, the states of conscious and unconscious, the functions, the persona, the attitudes of introversion and extraversion, the psychic and physical energy systems, and the culmination of all of these into the *self*, as it is fully actualized through the polar quality of existence. Synonymously with the term *personality* Jung uses the term *psyche*, although at times in a confused way. The highest level of interaction within the psyche is the *self*.

EGO

As Jung developed his theory of personality through the years, he refined and confined the concept of ego to include only the conscious mental activities of man. The ego structures the external and, in part, the internal world for the individual. Through the ego he knows himself. The ego attends to the conscious processes of thinking, perceiving, and identifying sensations. It is the ego which man knows best and at the level of which he operates in his daily life. It gets him up, dresses him, remembers for him the things he must do, and makes his primary decisions of the day. To Jung the ego exists in the center of man's conscious world. However, because it is in the center of his conscious world it must, therefore, be in conflict with the unconscious world. People who live primarily at the ego-conscious level sometimes resent and become angry at the suggestion that a part of their personality or psyche may exist outside of the conscious. This is defensible, according to the Jungian theory. The conscious and the unconscious are in opposition. The primarily consciously oriented individual resents the intrusion of the unconscious. He feels it is a sign of weakness or witchcraft, lacking any proof in substance or fact as he knows them in his conscious world. But there is, said Jung, an attempt by the unconscious to manifest itself through dreams, autistic thinking, and heavy dependence upon symbols in life. Ritual and fantasy in personal life or a strong reaction amounting to reaction formation absorbs the doubted of the unconscious. In this way the psyche is attempting to bring balance to the ego through pressure created by the unacknowledged unconscious. The more strongly the consciously oriented ego denies and vehemently scoffs at the idea of an unconscious, the more the unconscious is proving its existence. Eventually the ego gives way (usually in life after the forties) to the self. In the self we have the full acknowledgment and use of both conscious and unconscious states of being. The self inherits the role of the old ego.

SELF

The self, lying "midway between the conscious and the unconscious," is able to give equilibrium to the total personality: the psyche. It does more than balance the psyche; it also keeps the psyche in a relatively stable position. Man achieves this stability only, in most cases, in later life after he has emerged from the brashness of adolescence and the worldly orientation of early adulthood. The attitudes of extraversion gradually are replaced by the attitudes of introversion as the individual lives through middle age. The middle-aged person no longer needs the physical energy he once used to make a start in life, and thus, following the precepts of entropy and equivalence, he displaces physical energy with psychic energy to balance out the life picture. Likewise, the organic needs become less important, especially if he has managed to accrue some wealth and position, thus freeing more of his mental and physical energy. To take the place of organic needs, he may pursue and enjoy the cultural activities of later life. (At this time the individual may wish he had received more education and had acquired college degrees and the like while he was younger. But he could never have done so unless his earlier years had been saturated with a physical energy which more than fulfilled his organic needs. If it were possible to reverse this individual's life, the chances are strong that he would repeat the same pattern.) The total result of these readjustments is a balanced psyche, due to the ability of the self to change from one pole to another, arriving at the midpoint if the self is actualized in most of its potential. As we have seen, the personality never fully achieves a state of balance and fulfillment because of the outer and unpredictable influences of life.

Jung felt that only in very rare instances, in some religious figures, such as that of Jesus of Nazareth and certain religious men of the Orient, has a psyche come near to being in perfect harmony. Jung's interest in religion and in rituals and the theory of Nirvana resulted in much of his writing about the balanced psyche.

CONSCIOUS AND UNCONSCIOUS STATES

These two states of being are primary components of man's existence. When his psyche is able to use and live in both states to the profit of the psyche, then it is in equilibrium. So many of the observable characteristics of man are in the conscious state, for that is what we see and feel in both ourselves and others, that Jung spent relatively little time in discussing it as a single entity. Most of his writings deal with the reciprocity of the conscious to the unconscious. The unconscious is divided into two parts: the personal unconscious and the collective unconscious. The personal unconscious contains such phenomena as the persona and the complexes. The collective unconscious contains the concepts of archetypes, shadow, and synchronicity. The line between conscious and unconscious behavior by the psyche is amorphous, and there is much free flow between the two states in daily life. A more complete exposition of these states follows later in the chapter. At this point it is necessary to note that they are the chief components of the psyche. Because they constitute a major contribution in themselves, they are treated separately, as fundamental principles of Jungian psychology.

FUNCTIONS

One of the few articles of Jung's theory that do not lend themselves readily to polarities is his concept of four fundamental, mental functions. Although the functions were employed to illustrate superior and inferior functions, it is only by extension that the four activities align themselves into opposing groups. Here again we see the polarity or dualism of Jung's ideas.

The chief objective of the functions is to develop equally well so that the psyche may be in full balance, as was previously described in the discussion on polarity. When the functions do not array themselves equally within the system, superior and inferior functions result. Usually each of the superior and inferior functions is supported by an auxiliary function. The personality is rarely able to create a state of equal power among the functions although this is the end goal for their existing. Jung mentioned precisely four functions and firmly held to the view that these four, and no more, exist in man's psyche. Whenever the superior function is in full sway, it is always in the conscious realm, while its counterpart, the inferior one, is in the unconscious, where it has a highly disturbing effect on the mental processes. As man develops in all his potential and as he gets older and more mature, two, three, or rarely all four functions perform with equal efficiency.

The illogical and nonrational mental functions are intuition and sensation. The logical and rational functions are feeling and thinking. All four are necessary for man's mind to perform if he is to know and live in this world.

Intuition—When a student makes a decision and is unable to give reasons for it, he is often said to have acted intuitively. Intuition goes beyond the senses of sight, hearing, and so on, to lower levels of consciousness. Thinking is not a part of intuition. We come upon our decision without any conscious activity of which we are aware. Obviously, subliminal cues are used, but because they are subliminal, we cannot reconstruct our thought processes.

Jung felt that intuition is as important to man's mental life as is any of the other three functions. Only by intuition is man able to solve some of his problems. Sensating, feeling, and thinking may bring him no nearer to a solution, because the facts do not lend themselves to the five senses, to a personal commitment of emotion, or to the orderly arrangement of facts. He then may be able to arrive profitably at some sort of conclusion by intuition, which employs none of these mental functions. But intuition, like sensation, knows no rules of logic. The answers come from the inner recesses of the unconscious through patterns and processes that cannot be traced.

Sensation—Although this term has been a point of contention in the field of philosophy to the detriment of its psychological meaning, Jung felt no confusion in its use as applied to one of the nonrational mental functions. Sensation "establishes what is actually given." Sensation is seeing, hearing, smelling, tasting, and feeling.

Through the avenue of our senses we know about the world around us. They tell us what is. The fact that the senser does not have to think through his reaction to color, flavor, painful touches, and so on makes this mental function a nonrational one. He may have to think through whether he recognizes a certain fruit taste and then further whether he likes it or not, but he does not have to think about whether he is tasting the substance. He is stimulated either to taste or not to taste. This phenomenon requires no thought but only a substance strong enough to excite the taste buds.

Feeling—To most semanticists and psychologists, *feeling* is a term with multiple meanings, most of them not clearly defined. Furthermore, psychologists in general consider feeling to be a nonrational, emotional state. That is, if one judges situations by his feelings, it is assumed that his judgment is based primarily on emotions and can be influenced by emotions in a direction contrary to what wisdom and facts would indicate. To Jung feeling is a subjective concept which connotes "the value an individual places upon a person, place, or event." How he feels about something tells us how important it is to him. If the individual states he feels strongly about an object, he is indicating that the object is of great importance to him. Weak feeling indicates passivity or lack of interest and, hence, of value. Rarely do two persons have an identical value of feeling toward the same object because feeling arises from the self's inner, individualistic judgment. Feeling is one of the most subjective experiences of man.

Jung considered feeling a rational state of mind—an unusual attitude in comparison with other professional and/or lay interpretations. However, his position was that feeling tells us the value of an object. One cannot place value upon an object without comparing it with one or more other objects. The moment a comparison is made, the thought processes growing out of the emotions involved are employed. Thought processes, or the use of mental energy, are forms of rational behavior. Therefore, accepted or not by others, to Jung feeling is a rational function of the mind. The mind has to make judgments. No matter if the basis for judging is the emotions, the values which derive from judgment are as rational as any other form of evaluation made by an individual.

Feeling as a mental function is essential to man's existence. Through feeling man derives the goals he strives for. Feeling helps him to raise or lower himself depending on the total benefit of the value–goal. However, all of this, because he has feeling, helps man to move away from dead center.

Thinking—Thinking is the fourth of the functions as proposed by Jung. Thinking is also rational. When one thinks, he makes an orderly arrangement of facts as he knows them. His senses may not necessarily come into play. Relationships are especially important because thinking requires an establishment of order for more than one set of propositions. Thus, to Jung thinking neatly fills out the roster of the four mental functions which are so important to man's existence.

PERSONA

Jung adapted the Greek term *persona*, which means "mask," to describe the "face" man presents to society. This face may be quite alien to his real feelings and intentions. Man derives his persona partially from the roles that society decides for him and partially from his own acceptance, creation, and change of society's concept of his role. The individual who lives primarily behind a public mask is called the *personal man*. He may deviate so widely from his own personal feelings as to become alienated from them. Such action destroys his ability to reach a true self-actualization. Jung believed that this is one of the major causes of man's becoming emotionally distraught in the modern day. The personal man lives by false aims and purposes. His real self and his public self are so widely separated that it becomes impossible for him to create a genuine self, true to his own ideals. The further man deviates from self-actualization, the more mentally sick he becomes. The man who minimizes the persona and thus comes closer to genuine self-actualization, Jung called the *individual man*. Life is a struggle between the polarities of personal man and individual man as characters within the same personality.

EXTRAVERSION–INTROVERSION

The self contains both factors: extraversion and introversion. As discussed in the polarities section, the extravert aspect of the self is oriented toward people. The extravert displays emotion, is inclined to be volatile, and favors action over contemplative thought. The introvert hides feelings and seeks solutions to problems through passivity. To achieve true self-actualization, man must bring both introvertive and extravertive characteristics into proper and lasting balance. Although this is never totally possible because the personality is not a closed system, Jung felt that the struggle for this goal is worthwhile, for it gives man a more interesting facet both to himself and to others.

THE MECHANICS OF SELF-ACTUALIZATION

Man achieves self-actualization by various methods, some incompatible with each other, some complementary to each other.

1. Primary to all of the mechanisms of self-actualization are the factors of polarity: regression *vs.* progression, personal unconscious *vs.* collective unconscious, conscious *vs.* unconscious, extraversion *vs.* introversion (carried into action), superior functions *vs.* inferior functions, physical energy *vs.* psychic energy, organic needs *vs.* cultural needs, anima *vs.* animus, sublimation *vs.* repression, and causality *vs.* teleology. All, of course, operate within the principles of equivalence and entropy.

2. Basic to the methods by which man gains a more complete self is the machinery he inherits in the form of his body and all of its mammalian characteristics. Through heredity he has two valuable factors which, as life progresses, enable him better to achieve self-actualization than can the lower forms of animal life. He inherits a biological system fully equipped with instincts. The main function of his instincts is to preserve life and to reproduce his own kind. He also inherits the potentiality of racial experiences, which Jung called *primordial images,* or *archetypes,* or *imagos,* or *behavioral patterns.* This controversial contribution of Jung's states that the human being does not lose all the knowledge and experiences that his ancestors learned, at such length and so painfully. Man inherits a potential fear of harmful animals and frightening natural phenomena, such as lightning and thunder, for example.

3. Man is more than an accumulation of his past experiences. He is also a collection of dreams and hopes for the future. Through the dynamics of the present life and the effect of his past he fashions a plan of some sort for the future. By this method he becomes a forward-looking creature, a fact which Jung regarded as being of primary importance in achieving self-actualization. Man can never become fully self-actualized without purposive behavior.

4. It is very rare in the Jungian theory for an adolescent or young adult to achieve full self-actualization. As the individual develops through his span of years, his primary energy source is organic and exists at the vulnerable, conscious level. Not until he develops the counterpart of organic energy (psychic energy) can he come near to a true self. The extraverted, impulsive behavior of children and youth must make room for the spiritual, more introverted behavior of adults, with their accumulated wisdom and value systems based on deeper philosophical grounds. Actual chronological years are not the most important factors in this type of self-actualization through stages of development, but Jung considered that most people in our civilization reach this revaluation around the age of forty or fifty. The age may vary in differing cultures. This aspect of Jung's personality theory can hardly be expected to appeal to younger people.

5. In some sense the more experience the personality gains, the better able it is to broaden and achieve full selfhood. Jung felt that only as the various components of the personality are developed can the personality obtain self-actualization. Since development grows out of profitable experience, the human who has the most experiences in life and who can make them profitable is the one who can come the closest to selfhood or self-actualization. Through this process, called *individuation,* the personality reaches the highest level of development of all its parts. All the polarities come near to balancing one another. When this level has been approached, man has developed into the best person he can possibly become, Jung felt. Through the transcendent function all spiritual systems come to the flowering which is man's goal of life.

6. Symbols are basic to Jung's theory of personality. Man is fortunate in that he can operate in life with symbols, whereas lower forms of animal life must conduct all of their operations through concrete facts. Much of man can exist at the symbolic level through pictures, words, dreams, music, and art forms, the symbolism of clothing and speech, while animals must live off actual flesh and food and actual physical contact with the earth's goods. Symbolism helps man to achieve a higher and more differentiated self than that possible for animals. In a general way, as man regresses in behavior, he loses more and more of his capacity to operate with symbols. The gross human being is one who uses very few symbols.

Symbols perform two basic functions for man. First, they serve as a repository for his ancestors' experiences. Here the symbol helps him to overcome instinctual behavior which he cannot express openly. Second, they represent his aspirational levels as he progresses through the ages. Here man develops through higher and higher forms of symbols, never fully aware of a symbol's full meaning as he uses it. Jung felt that there is tremendous importance in the hidden meanings of symbols. Much of his writing has delved deeply, and at times esoterically, into the symbology of man's existence throughout recorded history.

If man is to use symbols wisely, he should attempt to find those which help him to discharge repressed desires in more and more productive ways. Progress in a civilization may be partially marked by that civilization's capacity to create and maintain symbols which help it to release overpowering libidinal drives, drives which would harm its constituents.

Unconscious States Principle

Like Freud, Jung placed great emphasis on the power and effect of the unconscious upon man's behavior. To try to ignore the unconscious is to invite mental and emotional trouble through delusions, compulsions, and phobic difficulties. The unconscious part of man's psyche will not be ignored, even though one may deny that such an amorphous state exists in the personality makeup.

Unlike Freud, Jung divided the unconscious into two categories, each important to the behavior of man. He did not include the preconscious or subconscious states in his theory. Below the level of the ego, which lies in the conscious state of being, are the personal unconscious and the collective unconscious. They may operate singly or in harmony. Some parts of the collective unconscious have been so well identified and studied by Jung that these are discussed as separate systems: anima and animus, persona, symbols, and the shadow.

PERSONAL UNCONSCIOUS

All experiences which man undergoes are not forgotten, nor do they disappear. They become instead part of the personal unconscious. This region of the mind is the storehouse of experience. Each individual, therefore, has a different personal unconscious from that of any other individual. Material may get into the unconscious because it is forgotten or was of such a subliminal nature as not to be noticed in the first place, or it may be deliberately suppressed because it is a painful and disturbing memory of a past experience. There is always much reciprocity between the ego in the conscious state and the material in the personal unconscious. In living each day, man uses much of the material from the unconscious, which he deliberately brings up from that region to aid him in the problems of the day. As with Freud's treatment of repression, here, too, man may be unable to bring out a repressed thought or piece of information because it is associated with a painful past experience. However, the flow is usually quite free between the conscious and the personal unconscious. Jung felt that man does not fully appreciate the value of the personal unconscious in his daily life.

Complexes—As man gathers experiences in many areas, he begins to build cores of memories, emotions, and residual feelings around certain phenomena. These centers of experience are called *complexes*. One may have, for example, a mother complex, a father complex, a power complex, a complex dominated by an overpowering desire to live in a meticulously kept home, or any kind of complex which has a core of experiences forceful enough to remain in the ego field. As complexes evolve out of repetitive experience which is both satisfying and strong enough to have residuals in the ego, they also perform the function of attracting and interpreting new experiences around the former complex. This is called the *constellating power of a complex*. To some degree, and depending upon the drive of the complex's constellating power, almost any experience can be interpreted and gathered into the complex as being appropriate to it. For example, people with complexes centered around outdoor life and primitive living may twist and turn any experience to interpret it in their direction. Musicians, painters, professional athletes, and the like are possible examples of the constellating power of a complex. Mothers often have a strong complex regarding their mother role.

Most of the time the complex and its core operate in the personal unconscious. The individual is not aware that he interprets and utilizes extraneous phenomena in the service of his complex. The complex may, however, merge into the ego-conscious level. Frequently, at such a time, the individual will rationalize his stereotyped interpretation of all events in the light of his complex, especially if it is pointed out to him by others not so complex minded. By and large, however, the complex will make use of similar experiences, rather than dissimilar ones. Individuals whose complexes are directed by the same type of constellating power frequently band together in organizations.

The personal unconscious and the collective unconscious may also aid each other in regard to man's use of complexes. Not infrequently the personal unconscious has reawakened some past archetype which belongs to the collective unconscious. Camping and the outdoor life, for example, may be derivatives of man's early existence on this planet. In reciprocation, the outdoor life of fishing and hunting may reinforce this archetype as it has been handed down through the ages through the collective unconscious. One gives the complex a background of inherited potentials, while the other advances and enriches the background for future generations which may inherit the archetype. It should be remembered that the personal unconscious is man's past as actually lived and experienced in his lifetime. Should there be no opportunity, for example, for camping, it is hardly possible to reawaken the primordial experiences of outdoor living even though these experiences may lurk in the collective unconscious as archetypes.

Jung suggested three ways of studying the constellating power of a complex: (1) by assessing the degree of emotional expression displayed by the individual when in pursuit of or engaged in a complex; (2) by observing the behavior of the individual directly and indirectly (indirect observation Jung called *analytical deduction,* by which he meant that the observer must infer from peripheral data the power of the complex); and (3) by noting any behavioral disturbances such as forgetfulness, or strong emotional reactions, when something (a word, gesture, article of clothing, etc.) is presented to the individual's attention. The incitor is called a *complex indicator.*

COLLECTIVE UNCONSCIOUS

It seemed as logical to Jung to attribute accumulated past experiences to all men collectively as it did to attribute the same phenomenon to a single individual, as he did in the personal unconscious. If one man can store in the unconscious experiences out of his past personal life, why cannot man as a generic total accumulate and hand down to his progeny all of the collected experiences lived and learned through the ages? To Jung the answer was that man does, both singularly and collectively, accumulate experiences, which are not lost but retained and are available for further use should the opportunity arise. Because man does not change radically (i.e., he keeps the same cerebral system, does not have two heads; breathes air, does not revert to gills; continues to procreate in the same manner, does not lay eggs), it stands to reason that most of his experiences are going to be repetitive. As generation after generation goes through similar acts of eating, sleeping, obtaining food, procreating, defending itself from harm, valuable experiences are stored up and kept extant.

It was obvious to Jung that man transmits and communicates skills, attitudes, and customs to his children, who in turn transmit them to their children. But this was no explanation for the tremendous potency and staying power of certain concepts found in almost all civilizations. Surely, Jung felt, some of these ideas would have died out generations ago had they been restricted to only direct communication. There must be more than mouth-to-mouth, ritual-to-ritual, and symbol-to-symbol transmitting of the past. Through digging into the lore of the past and through dedicated study of many, many cultures, Jung became convinced that man's cerebral system inherits the richness of his ancestors' past experiences. The inheritance as such is not direct. The tendency or predisposition is always inherited with the brain, but if no event occurs which can reinforce the predisposition, it may never be fulfilled in the lifetime of any single individual.

The collective unconscious includes accumulated experience back through prehuman existence, providing that experience has been repeated often enough to leave memory traces in the brain. Consequently, the collective unconscious is universal. Some cultures in the present day may have less opportunity to release the memory than do other cultures because of variant conditions. The collective unconscious is the fundamental base for man's psyche or personality. Whatever the individual does in his modern world grows out of his primordial past. This gives to man many commonalities—fear of the dark, worship of power and status, as seen in nations at war, worship of some sort of deity figure, and especially the care and nurture of offspring. Reasoning that such universal phenomena cannot have been transmitted through each generation by custom and law alone, Jung suggests that man inherits these behavior patterns through his brain. The universality of some collective unconscious patterns is the result of repeated reinforcements from animal life on up to present man. The relatively few deviates from the collective unconscious pattern are pathological cases whose ego in the conscious and, more often, whose personal unconscious run counter to the strengths of the collective unconscious. Because the collective unconscious is so powerful and omnipresent, any gross deviation from it is bound to cause abnormalities in the psyche. Child abandonment, for example, is a personality deviation not because the law says it is but because it is against man's collective unconscious. To defy too strongly the collective unconscious is to invite into one's personality strife and unhappiness. Mother love, to illustrate, is not taught by example but inherited from one's past through the collective unconscious. Animals do not care for their young out of a sense of duty and societal pressure but out of their own forms of collective unconscious. Man is a higher form of life than are animals, and he too inherits the same tendency. Again, when he ignores this tendency or has not had it reinforced into his own personal unconscious, he will be the victim of emotional stress.

Archetypes—Archetype is the name usually given to the kind of image from his collective unconscious that man uses most frequently. Other names for it are *behavior pattern, imago,* and *primordial image.* An archetype always carries great emotion. Jung and some of his coworkers named a few of the archetypes and suggested that there are many more, as yet unidentified, that are equally forceful in man's personality makeup. A few named are these: God, Devil, mother and father figures, the child, birth, death, reincarnation or life after death, world's end, and the hero and villain figures.

Archetypes often become interwoven with each other, as illustrated by the Christian phrase "God the Father." Crime movies and western films, as well as many sporting events, follow archetypal patterns by which the audience constructs a "good" guy and a "bad" guy within the situation. A hero without the counterpoint of a villain is unpalatable, fictional fare for most people. Each complements the other in the welding of archetypal figures. As an example, there is the spectator to an athletic contest who begins the game with a completely nonpartisan viewpoint but soon succumbs to the archetypal images of a hero team and a villain team. He wishes one team to win, despite his attitude at the beginning of the game. "May the best team win" is a cliché which means "I" shall pick the best team as the contest develops. One is unable to keep from identifying with an athletic team if his emotions are involved. (It must be remembered that all archetypes are charged with emotion.)

In place of the Freudian id or libidinal forces in the unconscious, Jung proposed the term *shadow* to represent the raw, savage, animal instincts in man. Morally bad, reprehensible conduct comes out of the vestigial collective unconscious that man inherits from his animal ancestry. However, differing from Freud, Jung felt that this shadow, the animalistic side of man, helps him to develop the polarities so necessary to his existence and to his eventual progress. Only through bad does man get to know good and try to achieve the good life.

Another kind of phenomenon, which Jung called *synchronicity,* applies to archetypes. A thought and event may occur simultaneously but neither one being caused by the other. Most present-day thinking has it that for every event there must be a corresponding cause. Jung went beyond the causal relationship and suggested that a different plane of relationships may exist. His exhaustive study of parapsychology and its manifestations in poltergeists, clairvoyance, and mental telepathy led him to feel that something operates in the universe beyond the probability of chance. Actions which we do not fully understand but can only observe may take place at the same period of time in which we are thinking about them, but neither thinking nor action caused the other to happen. Dreaming of a death and discovering later that the death actually occurred is an illustration of synchronicity. The dream did not cause the death. The death, since it was not communicated to the dreamer at the time of the dream, did not cause the dream.

As synchronicity applies to archetypes, we often find one archetype emerging in two different parts of the world simultaneously. Occidental and Oriental cultures sometimes evolve the same archetype at the same time in history with no communication of the archetype from one to the other. Sun worship, reincarnation, and similar archetypes may be considered as examples. Moreover, synchronicity can occur within a single personality. An individual may dream of his own death (an archetype) and experience that death just as it was dreamed.

Teleology Principle

Originally, the term *teleology* came from the field of philosophical theology, where it comprises a considerable body of study concerned with the doctrine that "a universal purpose pervades all reality and that all events tend to its ultimate fulfillment." As Jung used the term, its meaning varies to include a number of things. Basically, it means that man is improving all the time and will eventually have achieved true self-actualization. Admittedly, this path of improvement must take thousands upon thousands of years, but Jung felt, without being facetious, that man has the time. As discussed in the previous pages, man has already taken steps toward selfhood. He has the necessary equipment in the polarities, brain structure, and life energy eventually to reach self-actualization. However, progress seems so slow that modern man feels defeated when considering his teleological end. To hasten the process, then, he assumes a life after death and/or a resurrection process at the end of the world which could achieve perfect selfhood in a heaven to come constructed by forces other than man. Jung felt that man constructs his own Nirvana, has already made initial steps, and will eventually achieve it, but that the longevity of the process depresses and frustrates present-day minds. All lives which are lived to the nearest point of achieving selfhood help to advance the cause through the inheritance of the archetypes.

How does man achieve this state of Valhalla or heaven on earth?

Obviously, thought Jung, only through the passage of millennia, because of man's unequal polarities—not only within each psyche but between psyches. Since the psyche is not a closed system but is influenced by other psyches, true selfhood cannot come to any one psyche until the other psyches have reached selfhood. Man attempts to create short cuts to selfhood. He is irritated by results which are not immediately open to his knowledge. Many of the short cuts are in the forms of religious beliefs and practices. By utilizing better balancing and loftier symbols, man has invaluable tools with which to achieve ultimate self-actualization. In the final summation, what he considers a form of perfect life is to be reached by the efforts of each individual psyche first bringing itself into harmonious balance and then repeating somewhat the same process in interpersonal dealings with the psyches of others. Nothing can be achieved without the initial efforts of the singular personality, Jung felt. Individuation starts from self and moves to others. From the polarities principle, true harmony in self and others would bring no progress because progress is achieved through the balancing of all forces. Harmony, in some degree, is the cessation of all movement, the resolving of all action-producing imbalance.

The end result of man's teleological frame of reference is to give him purpose and plans for the future. Man is guided by more than the immediate goals of day-to-day and year-to-year living; he is guided also by a sense of responsibility to future generations and to mankind as a whole. To deny this, Jung felt, is to deny the existence of man through the past ages of fire, famine, pestilence, war, and all the vicissitudes of living. Man would have given up ages ago were it not for his teleological frame of reference. The present concern to keep the world alive despite nuclear warfare is an example of teleological thinking.

DELIMITATIONS

This chapter has not covered the work Jung has done with sentence completion tests or with serial dream analysis. These seem more fitted to a text on therapeutic and analytic techniques. Much of Jung's work on mythology, the occult sciences, religion, and symbology in literature has also been omitted for the same reason. A complete discussion of his vast written contribution would require at least two volumes.

EXPLAINING HUMAN BEHAVIOR
VIA JUNG'S ANALYTIC THEORY

Jung's theory can either explain the behavior of man totally or is completely incapable of explaining some facets of it. The usual behavioral activities of man's life may be used as indexes to test the theory's applicability. These nine activities are as follows: marriage, perversions, suicide, lawbreaking, supra natural being, humor, smoking, play and recreation, and psychoses–neuroses. The reader is now invited to attempt an explanation using the aforementioned criteria.

PREDICTING HUMAN BEHAVIOR VIA JUNG'S ANALYTIC THEORY

As one considers Jung's thoughts on teleology, one sees that much of his system concerns itself with prediction. Jung predicted that man is going to be a better and better species. He predicted that man will increase in his potentialities for improvement just as he has in the past. However, as far as definitive prediction is concerned, the system comes nowhere near to establishing any kind of predictability except on the broadest of bases.

Personal Prediction

Much of Jung's theory concerns broad, metaphysical aspects of man's behavior over thousands of years of time. Little of it deals with the day-to-day problems with which the student reader can involve himself. Essentially, again, only the reader in his own personal way can make the decisions that will convince him of the value of Jung's theory for prediction.

As a point of departure, it is interesting to speculate on the predictability of the things that man will fear. Consider, for example, the archetypes of things man fears. If it were possible to raise at least two generations of children with no knowledge of snakes, would they continue to hold the snake in derision and to fear it universally? Any reader of a basic psychology book knows that some children have been reared to love and fondle snakes. Jung's point is that this is so unusual that it becomes a *cause célèbre*. He regards the snake as an inherited archetype, so firmly implanted in man's background that it takes little experience to re-create the imago. The experience may be actually physical, or it may be symbolic—through the printed page and the spoken word. Jung further postulated that the snake universally represents evil and becomes an object of revulsion and scorn for most people in most cultures. Even the small snake bears the stigma of being a snake, whereas the puppy, fawn, or bear cub are lovable creatures, even though they may become objects of fear and distrust as they grow older, stronger, and more threatening. Fear of the dark, fear of thunder, fear of lightning also are imagos inherited from the past. All it takes for these phenomena to become fears is a slight contact, physical or symbolic. Fears of dogs, water, high places have to be learned through more prolonged experiences because they apparently are not imagos from man's past to be freed at the least contact with them. Such fears as mentioned above were questions of susceptibility to Jung. He asked, for example, why man seems so universally to fear a "boogeyman" if the susceptibility to it is not inherited. Parents who stringently rear their children to have no concepts of "spooks" or similar imaginary creatures often complain that their child seems to create the imaginary characters by himself with absolutely no reinforcement or with only the slightest shred of experience. Cursory experiences with other phenomena which later produce fear do not seem to "take" so immediately. Many fears have to be learned. Fear of the supernatural seems to be ready, full-blown and available, to control behavior with scarcely any symbolical reinforcement. This, said Jung, is because of the difficult-to-explain archetype which the child inherits. Now it is the task of the reader to determine whether it can be predicted that man will continue to harbor certain archetypes such as fear of snakes or fear of a supernatural figure, as found in the child's "boogeyman."

Scientific or Laboratory Prediction

Although Jung felt strongly that he was dealing with factual materials, there are relatively few studies designed around the material of his work. Most of the current reactions, as stated in the beginning of the chapter, are rebuttals of Jung's work, and understandably so, as little of his theory lends itself to experimentation of a statistical or laboratory nature.

Jung's earliest research, preceding and during World War I, concerned itself with the relationship between the free association test (now generally referred to as the <u>word association test</u>) and the concomitant organic responses. Jung may be considered a precursor of the lie detector devices now used in many psychological and police laboratories, though he was by no means directly responsible for its current development. The free association method itself, however, preceded Jung by many years with the work of Wundt in Leipzig and Galton in England. Jung also predated some of the work of Murray and his Thematic Apperception Test. Again, we do not know the direct influence Jung had upon Murray and his coworkers in their TAT work, although Murray expresses a tremendous admiration for Jung and acknowledges the influence Jung had upon his own entry into the field of psychology. The association of the TAT and Jung's work comes about through the method Jung originated, of having the patient use what he called "active imagination" in describing all his responses to a dream image or self-created visual image. In the beginning Jung carefully noted changes in respiration and perspiration as measured by the pneumograph and galvanometer prompted by the patient's subconscious during the process. He later became extremely intuitive and untangled complex cases through the method of "active imagination" without the use of apparatus.

Self-actualization as a concept was fully expounded by Jung. Many, many others have since written and designed research around this concept although no direct evidence seems to be present that they were following leads given by Jung. Allport, Angyal, Maslow, Murphy, and especially Rogers have made self-actualization a major part of their theories.

H. Gray, for a very short period in the late 1940s, was one of the most directly involved current investigators of Jungian psychology. His main emphasis was on the psychological types as he interpreted them in Jung's writings (Gray, 1947a,b; 1948; 1949a,b). Other writers have been fairly thorough in investigating the development of personality and the emergence of archetypes through case study material (F. Fordham, 1953; M. Fordham, 1947, 1949, 1951, 1956; Wickes, 1966). None of them, however, have conducted appreciable research within the framework of Jung's position but rather have cast themselves into the role of interpreters.

At least in volume of published research Jung's concepts of introversion/extraversion and the functions (intuition, sensation, feeling, thinking) appear to have stimulated the most research since 1960.

Indeed, H. J. Eysenck, the most prolific of experimentalists (aside from Cattell), has produced an enormous array of factorial studies on introversion/extraversion. In no way is Eysenck trying to prove a Jungian idea, but it seems most odd that Eysenck, who has great disdain for psychoanalysis, should employ the analytical terms *introversion* and *extraversion*. We are not suggesting here that he uses them in the same way Jung did (Eysenck, 1962a,b; Eysenck and Eysenck, 1963, 1964 a,b). "Even such a staunch experimentalist as Eysenck in 1961 has based a moderate amount of his work on theories developed by Jung" (Garfield, 1963). Incidentally, three studies find "no support" for Eysenck's rubric of introversion/extraversion as it applies to authoritarian attitudes (Siegman, 1963), reactive inhibition as measured by a pursuit rotor (Yates and Laszlo, 1965), and judgment of time (Du Preez, 1964). Other studies revolving around the Eysenckian approach have dealt with aesthetic preference for painting, supporting Eysenck's hypothesis that extraverts vary more in choices (Mohan and Mohan, 1965), the finding that introverts work more efficiently in the morning or when isolated (Colquhoun and Corcoran, 1964), and the proposition that introverts salivate more than extraverts! (Corcoran, 1964; Eysenck and Eysenck, 1967).

Cattell's work has also been related to Jung's introversion/extraversion dichotomy. Some direct relationship was found (Marshall, 1967).

In the one study directly pertaining to Jung's typology there was no significant difference between extraverts and introverts in reactions to perceptual isolation (Tranel, 1962).

Ball's dissertation dealt with a factor analytic investigation of the relationship between introversion/extraversion and the functions of thinking and feeling. The results were that "the dimensions postulated by Jung have some utility, making possible the conceptual organization and understanding of many divergent behaviors" (Ball, 1968). Another study also related the personality typology with the functions. Tentative conclusions were that, for men, introversion correlated with dreaming in color and sensation related to vividness in color dreaming. For women, there was a significant relationship between intuition and vividness in color dreaming (Suinn, 1966).

Research on only the functions has indicated the following to date: Sensation-oriented college students prefer movies and television; intuitives prefer the "printed page in novels and magazines" (Anast, 1966). Relating the four types to judgment of time indicated that thinking types considered time in a linear fashion; sensation types, in terms of the present; feeling types, in terms of the past; and intuitive types, in terms of the future (Mann *et al.*, 1968). The self-reports of individuals seemed to corroborate the Jungian typologies (Gorlow *et al.*, 1966). Analyzing the four functions conceptually also appeared to substantiate Jung's work (Marshall, 1968).

We come now to what appears to be the strongest and most concerted effort to measure the four functions that Jung felt man possessed. The ten studies noted in this paragraph are all outgrowths of one test designed to measure the four functions of sensation, intuition, thinking, and feeling as well as introversion/extraversion and a factor of judgment versus perception. The authors, Katherine Briggs and Isabel Briggs Myers, constructed two forms (F, Fs), having begun their test work around 1943. The test is called the Myers–Briggs Type Indicator (MBTI). It is a forced-choice, self-report test which takes approximately fifty to fifty-five minutes to administer. Despite the authors' reliability and validity work of nineteen years, particularly for the 1962 revision, the corroborative investigations of other studies are mixed. Some support the MBTI; others do the opposite. The question of support and nonsupport is confusing because some investigators felt that their primary function was to verify the MBTI itself, while others felt that in verifying the MBTI they were also testing the power of Jung's function concept. Questions of validity and reliability further weaken the instrument's applicability to analytical personality theory verification (Gorlow *et al.*, 1966; Insel *et al.*, 1968; Knapp *et al.*, 1962; Knapp and LaPuc, 1965; Richek and Brown, 1968; Ross, 1966; Stanfiel, 1966; Stricker and Ross, 1963, 1964a,b).

Perhaps this all reflects Byrne's concern that "We should note that several of Jung's assumptions about introversion/extraversion are quite often ignored by those who have adopted the terms . . ." (Byrne, 1966). And not a similar comment that "although reporting details of experimentation is given strict adherence, scientists take *unintentional license with a man's theory*" (italics added) (Dashiell, 1962).

A side trip from a research point of view should be taken in reflecting on the collective unconscious. One geneticist acknowledges that great strides have been made in recent years on the nature of inherited characteristics in infrahumans and a few forward steps in discovering the inheritance of an extra chromosome for mongoloids; however, "given the appropriate skills and time, the problem of the genetic determination of behavior potentials can be cracked, and we will achieve a quite complete explanation in *mechanistic* terms. Let me point out that this represents only the physical part of the psycho-physical parallelism. The 'psycho' part overlaps it, as has been pointed out by another geneticist, Professor Sewall Wright (1953), by 100 percent, and one can only be in the pure psychological realm by *introspection*" (Ginsburg, 1963; italics added).

■ SUMMARY

The author has chosen to interpret Dr. Jung's theories about personality on a polar basis. Using this approach, one can assume all of Jung's work to be a struggle between two opposing forces that man has gone through since time began. The tensions arising from the struggle, the resolution of these tensions, the new strength and direction that result from successful resolving of polarities, and the immense effect of man's past as he inherits behavioral traits have been discussed in this chapter.

Once again a diagram will highlight the major features of Jung's system concerning personality. Figure 4 is only a means of thinking about Jung's system and is not to be taken too literally.

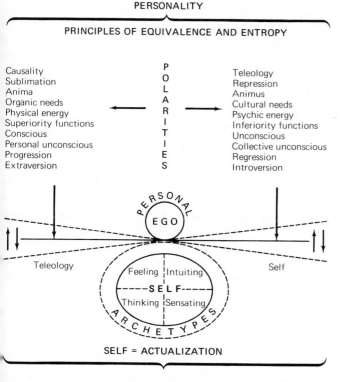

FIGURE 4. *Diagrammatic summary of Jung's theory.*

The main features of the diagram represent the process of balancing that the ego-self structures must maintain, despite the constant downward pressures exerted by the polarities. The full state of equilibrium shown is called self-actualization. The self operates as a fulcrum, bearing all the weight of the polar factors and making the adjustments to keep the entire structure in balance. The ego, lying above the self and covered by the façade of the persona (which is all that other men see), is more prone to move back and forth quickly when the polarities exert undue pressure. The width of the horizontal line can be interpreted as the individual differences found from man to man. Some personalities are "wider" than others, and thus easier to stabilize. In the act of balancing or achieving equilibrium, ego and self must be in direct alignment one above the other. Any other position produces an imbalance. The persona, by taking precedence over the true ego, may so alter the structure as to create an imbalance. Further imbalance may result if one or more of the four mental functions (feeling, intuition, etc.) becomes superior to the others. All four mental functions should be in equal parts, as shown in the diagram, if one is to achieve full self-actualization. The archetypes surrounding the self structure are also important to the stability of the entire process. As life progresses, the size of the self and ego circumferences should increase. The larger and more experienced the four mental functions become, the easier it is to keep the system in balance. Differing polarities shown above may be emphasized at different times in life. Some polarities, hardly ever being of unequal weights, rarely cause a lack of balance, while others may be continuously out of proper proportion to each other, thus causing the ego and self to move constantly back and forth in an attempt to compensate for the unequal pressures from above. Through the ages man has teleologically been able to smooth the exterior structure of the self. The smoother this surface, of course, the easier it is to bring about movement and to achieve balance when difficulties arise between the polarities. Regression is any downward or upward movement which disturbs equilibrium of the life plank. Progression is the leveling out of the life plank. It should appear obvious that true balance for any appreciable length of time would be quite rare because of the tremendous number of variable conditions which must be met to bring it about. Neuroses and psychoses result when any of the numerous factors become more permanently out of balance. Life ceases, supposedly, when the ego-self structures are deflated to nothing.

BIBLIOGRAPHY

PRIMARY SOURCES

BOOKS

There are two major sources: Jung's own works and those of other authors edited and published through the Bollingen Foundation established in 1941. (Bollingen is the name of his home in Kusnacht on the shores of Lake Zurich.) The foundation publishes through Pantheon Press.

Jung, C. G., *The Collected Works of C. G. Jung*, Bollingen Series, H. Read, M. Fordham, and G. Adler (eds.): Vol. 1, *Psychiatric Studies*, 1957; Vol. 3, *The Psychogenesis of Mental Disease*, 1960; Vol. 4, *Freud and Psychoanalysis*, 1961; Vol. 5, *Symbols of Transformation*, 1956; Vol. 7, *Two Essays on Analytical Psychology*, 1953 (also published as Meridian paperback, 1956); Vol. 8, *The Structure and Dynamics of the Psyche*, 1960; Vol. 9, Part II, Aion: *Researches into the Phenomenology of the Self*, 1959; Vol. 10, *Civilization in Transition*, 1964; Vol. II, *Psychology and Religion: West and East*, 1958 (also published as a paperback by Yale University Press, 1960——, based on Terry Lectures given at Yale in 1937); Vol. 12, *Psychology and Alchemy*, 1953; Vol. 13, *Alchemical Studies*, 1967; Vol. 14, *Mysterium Coniunctionis*, 1963; Vol. 15, *The Spirit in Man, Art, and Literature*, 1966 (also published as a paperback by Princeton University Press); Vol. 9, Part I, *The Archetypes and the Collective Unconscious*, 1959; Vol. 16, *The Practice of Psychotherapy*, 1954; Vol. 17, *The Development of Personality*, 1954.

Jung, C. G., *The Theory of Psychoanalysis*. New York: Nervous and Mental Disease Publishing Company, 1915.

Jung, C. G., *Analytical Psychology*, New York: Moffat-Yard, 1916.

Jung, C. G., *Collected Papers on Analytical Psychology*. New York: Moffat-Yard, 1917.

Jung, C. G., *Studies in Word Association*. London: Heinemann, 1918.

Jung, C. G., *Psychology of the Unconscious*. New York: Dodd, Mead, 1925.

Jung, C. G., *Contributions to Analytical Psychology*. New York: Harcourt, Brace & World, 1928.

Jung, C. G., and R. Wilhelm, *The Secret of the Golden Flower*. New York Harcourt, Brace & World, 1931.

Jung, C. G., *Modern Man in Search of a Soul*. New York: Harcourt, Brace & World, 1933.

Also as Harvest Book paperback.

Jung, C. G., *Psychological Types*. New York: Harcourt, Brace & World, 1933.

Also published as a Pantheon Book—the 1923 translation by H. G. Baynes.

Jung, C. G., *Psychology and Religion*. New Haven, Conn.: Yale University Press, 1938.

Also published in Bollingen Series, No. 11.

Jung, C. G., *The Integration of Personality*. New York: Holt, Rinehart & Winston, 1939.

Jung, C. G., and C. Kerenyi, *Essays on a Science of Mythology*. New York: Pantheon, 1949.

Jung, C. G., *Psychological Reflections: An Anthology from the Writings of C. G Jung*. New York: Pantheon, 1953.

Selected and edited by J. Jacobi—thirty-first in Bollingen Series.

Jung, C. G., *Answer to Job*. London: Routledge, 1954.

Jung, C. G., and W. Pauli, *The Interpretation of Nature and the Psyche*. New York: Pantheon, 1955.

Fifty-first publication in Bollingen Series, translated from 1952 German edition. Jung on synchronicity and physicist, Pauli on Kepler's theories

Jung, C. G., *Two Essays on Analytical Psychology*. New York: World Publishing (Meridian), 1956.

Two essays, "On the psychology of the unconscious" and "The relations between the ego and the unconscious," first published in 1912 and 1916 Also appear as Vol. 7 in Bollingen Series.

Jung, C. G., *The Undiscovered Self*. Boston: Little, Brown, 1958.

Jung, C. G., *Psyche and Symbol*, V. de Laszlo, ed. Garden City, N.Y.: Doubleday (Anchor), 1958.

Contains commentary on "The Secret of the Golden Flower."

Jung, C. G., *The Basic Writings of C. G. Jung*, V. de Laszlo, ed. New York: Random House, 1959.

Jung, C. G., *Symbols of Transformation: An Analysis of the Prelude to a Case of Schizophrenia* (trans. by R. F. C. Hull). New York: Harper & Row, 1962.

Original version published in 1912.

Jung, C. G., *Memories, Dreams, Reflections*. New York: Pantheon, 1963.

Jung, C. G., *Mysterium Coniunctionis: An Inquiry into the Separation and Synthesis of Psychic Opposites in Alchemy*. New York: Pantheon, 1963.

ung, C. G., and C. Kerenyi, *Essays on a Science of Mythology*. New York: Harper & Row, 1963.

> A paper edition of the book originally published in 1949.

ung, C. G., *Man and His Symbols*. New York: Doubleday, 1964.

> The essence of his work, first chapter by Jung. His trusted and selected collaborator Joseph Henderson, Marie-Louise von Franz, Aniela Joffe, and Jolande Jacobi complete the chapters. Strikingly illustrated. Least technical of Jungian expositions.

PERIODICALS

Jung, C. G., Psychotherapists or the clergy, *Pastoral Psychol.*, 1956, 7, 27–44.

SUGGESTED READINGS

BOOKS

Adler, G., *Studies in Analytical Psychology*. New York: Norton, 1948; New York: Putnam's, 1966.

> Technical aspects of Jungian treatment, dream analysis, and case studies—first put out in 1949 by Jung Foundation.

Bennet, E. A., *What Jung Really Said*. New York: Schocken, 1966.

Bertine, E., *Jung's Contribution to Our Time: The Collected Papers of Eleanor Bertine*. New York: Putnam's, 1968.

> Ambiguous position of modern women, relationships between man and woman, meaning of evil.

Byrne, D., *An Introduction to Personality: A Research Approach*. Englewood Cliffs, N.J.: Prentice-Hall, 1966.

Clark, R. A., *Six Talks on Jung's Psychology*. Pittsburgh: Boxwood Press, 1953.

Cox, D., *Jung and St. Paul: A Study of the Doctrine of Justification by Faith and Its Relation to the Concept of Individuation*. New York: Association Press, 1959.

Dry, A. M., *The Psychology of Jung: A Critical Interpretation*. New York: Wiley, 1961.

Eisler, R., *Man into Wolf: An Anthropological Interpretation of Sadism, Masochism, and Lycanthropy*. New York: Philosophical Library, 1952.

> Based on Jung's archetypal ideas.

Evans, R. I., *Conversations with Carl Jung and Reactions from Ernest Jones*. Princeton, N.J.: Van Nostrand, 1964.

Fierel, H., Death, in N. L. Farberow (ed.), *Taboo Topics*. New York: Atherton Press, 1963.

Fordham, M., *The Life of Childhood*. London: Routledge, 1947.

Fordham, F., *An Introduction to Jung's Psychology*. Baltimore: Penguin, 1953.

Fordham, M. (ed.), *Contact with Jung*. Philadelphia: Lippincott, 1964.

Freud, S., *An Autobiographical Study*. London: Hogarth, 1935.

Freud, S., The history of the psychoanalytic movement, in A. A. Brill (ed.), *The Basic Writings of Sigmund Freud*. New York: Random House, 1938.

Garfield, S. L., The clinical method in assessment, in J. M. Wepman and R. W. Heine (eds.), *Concepts of Personality*. Chicago: Aldine, 1963.

Ginsburg, B. E., Genetics and personality, in J. M. Wepman and R. W. Heine (eds.), *Concepts of Personality*. Chicago: Aldine, 1963.

Glover, E., *Freud or Jung?* New York: Norton, 1950.

> Compares Freud to Jung. Freud wins. Also as a Meridian paperback, 1956.

Goldbrunner, J., *Individuation: A Study of the Depth Psychology of Carl Gustav Jung*. New York: Pantheon, 1956.

Goldbrunner, J., *A Study of the Depth Psychology of Carl Gustav Jung*. Notre Dame, Ind.: University of Notre Dame Press, 1964.

Hall, C. S., and G. Lindzey, *Theories of Personality*. New York: Wiley, 1957.

Hostie, R., *Religion and the Psychology of Jung*. New York: Sheed & Ward, 1957.

Jacobi, J., *The Psychology of C. G. Jung*, rev. ed. New Haven, Conn.: Yale University Press, 1951.

Jacobi, J., *Complex/Archetype/Symbol in the Psychology of C. G. Jung*. New York: Pantheon, 1959.

Jones, E., *The Life and Work of Sigmund Freud*: Vol. I (1856–1900), The formative years and the great discoveries, 1953; Vol. II (1901–1919), Years of maturity, 1955; Vol. III (1919–1939), The last phase, 1957. New York: Basic Books.

> See especially Vol. II.

Lindzey, G., and C. S. Hall, *Theories of Personality: Primary Sources and Research*. New York: Wiley, 1965, pp. 57–93.

Martin, P. W., *Experiment in Depth: A Study of the Work of Jung, Eliot, and Toynbee*. New York: Pantheon, 1955.

Munroe, R. L., *Schools of Psychoanalytic Thought*. New York: Dryden, 1955.

> Analysis and integration of Freud, Adler, Jung, Rank, Fromm, Horney, Sullivan, *et al.*

Neumann, E., *The Archetypal World of Henry Moore*. New York: Harper & Row, 1965.

Philipson, Morris, *Outline of a Jungian Aesthetics*. Evanston, Ill.: Northwestern University Press, 1963.

Pollard, W. G., *Physicist and Christianity*. New York: Seabury Press, 1961.

> Tridimensional life and heaven as possibilities of synchronicity. Noncausality in behavior; the world of anti-matter.

Progoff, I., *Jung's Psychology and Its Social Meaning*. New York: Grove Press, 1953.

> A paperback edition.

Progoff, I., *The Death and Rebirth of Psychology: An Integrative Evaluation of Freud, Adler, Jung, and Rank and the Impact of Their Culminating Insights on Modern Man*. New York: Julian Press, 1956.

Scott, T. A., Jung and Piaget: A study in relationships, in J. L. Philbrick (ed.), *Contemporary Studies in Social Psychology and Behavior Change*. New York: Academic Press, 1966, pp. 51–70.

Teilhard de Chardin, P., *The Phenomenon of Man*. New York: Harper & Row, 1959.

> The Omega-point, "imagined end state."

Wickes, F. G., *The Inner World of Choice*. New York: Harper & Row, 1963.

Wickes, F. G., *The Inner World of Childhood: A Study in Analytical Psychology*. New York: Appleton-Century, 1966.

PERIODICALS

Adler, G., A discussion on archetypes and internal objects: III. A contribution of clinical material, *Brit. J. Med. Psychol.*, 1949, 22, 16–22.

Ajmal, M., Some considerations concerning the concept of archetype, *J. Psychol*, 1965, 2, 109–121.

Anast, P., Personality determinants of mass media preferences, *Journalism Quart.*, 1966, 43, 729–732.

> "Sensation oriented persons prefer the well-structured media of television and movies; intuitive persons prefer the more ambiguous stimulus of the printed page in novels and magazines."

Arluck, E. W., Training facilities of the C. G. Jung Institute, Zurich, *Amer. Psychologist*, 1960, 15, 626–629.

Assagioli, R., Jung and psychosynthesis, *Psychosynthesis Res. Found.*, 1967, No. 19.

Ball, E. D., A factor analytic investigation of the personality typology of C. G. Jung, *Dissert, Abstr.*, 1968, 28, 4277–4278.

> "The dimensions postulated by Jung have some utility, making possible the conceptual organization and understanding of many divergent behaviors."

Bash, J. W., Einstellungstypus and Erlebnistypus: C. G. Jung and Herman Rorschach, *J. Proj. Tech.*, 1955, 19, 236–242.

Belford, A., A consideration of C. G. Jung's psychology of the feminine and its implications for Christian theology, *Dissert. Abstr.*, 1967, 28, 1689–1690.

Bonime, W., The psychic energy of Freud and Jung, *Amer. J. Psychiat.*, 1955, 112, 372–374.

Burchard, E. W. L., Mystical and scientific aspects of the psychoanalytic theories of Freud, Adler, and Jung, *Amer. J. Psychother.*, 1960, 15, 289–307.

Burt, Cyril, Baudouin on Jung, *Brit. J. Psychol.*, 1964, 55, 477–484.

Clark, R. A., Jung and Freud: A chapter in psychoanalytic history, *Amer. J. Psychother.*, 1955, 9, 605–611.

Colquhoun, W. P., and D. W. J. Corcoran. The effects of time of day and socia'
isolation on the relationship between temperament and performance, *Brit. J
Soc. Clin. Psychol.*, 1964, 3, 226–231.

    Introverts work better in the A.M. or where isolated.

Corcoran, D. W. J., The relation between introversion and salivation, *Amer. J
Psychol.*, 1964, 77, 298–300.

    Evidence that introverts salivate more.

Dashiell, J. F., The unreliability of secondary sources with examples from Jung
Psychol. Rec., 1962, 12, 331–334.

    Scientists commonly take unintentional license with a man's theory.

Douglas, W., Carl Gustav Jung: 1875–1961, *Amer. J. Psychol.*, 1961, 74, 639–641
Du Preez, P. D., Judgment of time and aspects of personality, *J. Abnorm. Soc
Psychol.*, 1964, 69, 228–233.

    Refutes several of Eysenck's hypotheses on extraversion and judgment o
time.

Eysenck, H. J., Conditioning and personality, *Brit. J. Psychol.*, 1962a, 53, 299-
305.
Eysenck, H. J., Reminiscence, drive, and personality—revisions and extensions o
a theory, *Brit. J. Soc. Clin. Psychol.*, 1962b, 1, 127–140.
Eysenck, S. B. G., and H. J. Eysenck. On the dual nature of extraversion, *Brit
J. Soc. Clin. Psychol.*, 1963, 2, 46–55.
Eysenck, S. B. G., and H. J. Eysenck, Personality of judges as a factor in the
validity of their judgements of extraversion-introversion, *Brit. J. Soc. Clin
Psychol.*, 1964a, 3, 141–148.
Eysenck, H. J., and S. B. G. Eysenck, An improved short questionnaire for the
measurement of extraversion and neuroticism, *Life Sci.*, 1964b, 3, 1103-
1109.
Eysenck, S. B. G., and H. J. Eysenck, Salivary response to lemon juice as a measure
of introversion, *Percept. Mot. Skills*, 1967, 24, 1047–1053.
Fodor, N., Jung's sermons to the dead, *Psychoanal. Rev.*, 1964, 51, 74–78.
Fordham, M., A discussion on archetypes and internal objects: On the reality o
archetypes, *Brit. J. Med. Psychol.*, 1949, 22, 3–7.
Fordham, M., The concept of the objective psyche, *Brit. J. Med. Psychol.*, 1951
24, 221–231.
Fordham, M., Symposium on Jung's contributions to analytical thought and
practice: 1. The evolution of Jung's researches (pp. 3–8); 2. On Jung'
concept of the symbols (by R. Moody, pp. 9–14); 3. The transference in
analytical psychology (by A. Plant, pp. 15–19), *Brit. J. Med. Psychol.*, 1956
29.
Fordham, M., The relation of the ego to the self, *Brit. J. Med. Psychol.*, 1964, 37
89–102.

    Compares Jung and Federn.

Friedman, P., and J. Goldstein, Some comments on the psychology of C. G. Jung, *Psychoanal. Quart.*, 1964, *33*, 194–225.

Ginsburg, B. E., Genetics as a tool in the study of behavior, *Perspect. Biol. Med.*, 1958, *1*, 397–424.

Gorlow, L., N. R. Simonson, and H. Krauss, An empirical investigation of the Jungian typology, *Brit. J. Soc. Clin. Psychol.*, 1966, *5*, 108–117.

Five of the eight types postulated by MBTI were found.

Gray, H., Psychological types and changes with age, *J. Clin. Psychol.*, 1947b. *3*, naire, *J. Gen. Psychol.*, 1947a, *37*, 177–185.

Gray, H., Psychological types and changes with age, *J. Clin. Psychol.*, 1947b, *3*, 273–277.

Gray, H., Jung's psychological types in men and women, *Stanford Med. Bull.*, 1948, *6*, 29–36.

Gray, H., Jung's psychological types: Ambiguous scores and their interpretations, *J. Gen. Psychol.*, 1949a, *40*, 63–88.

Gray, H., Freud and Jung: Their contrasting psychological types, *Psychoanal. Rev.*, 1949b, *20*, 22–44.

Harms, E., Carl Gustav Jung—defender of Freud and the Jews, *Psychiat. Quart.*, 1946, *20*, 199–230.

Harms, E., Carl Gustav Jung, *Amer. J. Psychiat.*, 1962, *118*, 728–732.

Obituary.

Hawkey, M. L., The witch and the bogey: Archetypes in the case study of a child, *Brit. J. Med. Psychol.*, 1947, *21*, 12–29.

Henderson, J. L., Jung and education, *Educ. Psychol. Baroda*, 1954, *11*, 196–202.

Illing, H. A., C. G. Jung on the present trends in psychotherapy, *Hum. Relat.*, 1957, *10*, 77–83.

Ingham, J. G., and J. O. Robinson, Personality in the diagnosis of hysteria, *Brit. J. Psychol.*, 1964, *55*, 276–284.

Insel, S. A., C. S. Reese, and B. B. Alexander, Self-presentations in relation to internal and external referents, *J. Consult. Clin. Psychol.*, 1968, *32*, 389–395.

Jackson, M., Jung's "archetypes" and psychiatry, *J. Ment. Sci.*, 1960, *106*, 1518–1526.

Jacobi J., Pictures from the unconscious, *J. Proj. Tech.*, 1955, *19*, 264–270.

Jaeger, M., Reflection on the work of Jung and Rank, *J. Psychother. Relig. Proc.*, 1955, *2*, 47–57.

Kawai, H., Professor Carl G. Jung and Japanese psychology, *Psychologia* (Kyoto), 1962, *5*, 8–9.

Knapp, R. H., An experimental study of a triadic hypothesis concerning the sources of aesthetic imagery, *J. Proj. Tech.* 1964, *28*, 49–54.

Knapp, R. H., H. Gewirtz, and J. D. Holzberg, Some personality correlates of styles of interpersonal thought, *J. Proj. Tech.*, 1962, *26*, 398–402.

Myers-Briggs test and projective tests used to create interpersonal inventory.

Knapp, R. H., and P. S. LaPuc, Time imagery, introversion and fantasied pre-occupation in simulated isolation, *Percept. Mot. Skills*, 1965, 20, 327–330.

> Time view correlated with introversion on Myers-Briggs type indicator.

Lewis, A., Jung's early works, *J. Anal. Psychol.*, 1957, 2, 119–136.

Mace, C. A., On the eightieth birthday of C. G. Jung, *J. Anal. Psychol.*, 1956, 1, 189–192.

McLaughlin, R. J., and H. J. Eysenck, Extraversion, neuroticism and paired-associates learning, *J. Exp. Res. Pers.*, 1967, 2, 128–132.

> Moderate anxiety facilitates learning an easy list; low anxiety facilitates learning a difficult list.

MacLeod, R. B., Teleology and theory of human behavior, *Science*, 1957, 125, 477–480.

> Social sciences should think teleologically and in more global terms.

Mandler, George., Subjects to think: A reply to Jung's comments, *Psychol. Rev.*, 1965, 72, 323–326.

Mann, H., M. Siegler, and H. Osmond, The many worlds of time, *J. Anal. Psychol.*, 1968, 13, 33–56.

> "Jung's psychological types and their different ways of perceiving or experiencing the world also correlate with 4 basic temporal orientations."

Marshall, I. N., Extraversion and libido in Jung and Cattell, *J. Anal. Psychol.*, 1967, 12, 115–136.

> "Some correspondences are suggested between Jung's clinical descriptions of extraversion/introversion and Cattell's experimental studies of the same."

Marshall, I. N., The four functions: A conceptual analysis, *J. Anal. Psychol.*, 1968, 13, 1–32.

> Suggested definitions and a conceptual analysis of Jung's four functions are offered.

Mindess, H., Analytical psychology and the Rorschach test, *J. Proj. Tech.*, 1955, 19, 243–252.

Mohan, J., and V. Mohan, Personality and variability in aesthetic evaluation, *Psychology: Int. J. Psychol. Orient*, 1965, 8, 218–219.

> Uses aesthetic preferences for paintings. Extraverts vary more because of higher level of suggestibility. Supports Eysenck's theory of personality.

Nelson, B., Hesse and Jung, *Psychoanal. Rev.*, 1963, 50, 11–16.

Progoff, I., The psychology of Lee Harvey Oswald: A Jungian approach, *J. Indiv. Psychol.*, 1967, 23, 37–47.

Richek, H. G., and O. H. Brown, Phenomenological correlates of Jung's typology, *J. Anal. Psychol.*, 1968, 13, 57–65.

MBTI gives information on selection and training of prospective teachers, but further research is "necessary to specify the parameters of this contribution."

Ross, J., The relationship between a Jungian personality inventory and tests of ability, personality and interest, *Aust. J. Psychol.*, 1966, *18*, 1–17.

Siegman, A. W., A cross-cultural investigation of the relationship between introversion-extraversion, social attitudes and anti-social behavior, *Brit. J. Soc. Clin. Psychol.* 1963, *2*, 196–208.

No support for Eysenck's hypothesized position correlation between extraversion and tough-minded or authoritarian attitudes.

Spiegelman, M., Jungian theory and the analysis of thematic tests, *J. Proj. Tech.*, 1955, *19*, 253–263.

Stanfiel, J. D., The Jungian typology, neuroticism, and field-dependence, *Dissert. Abstr.*, 1966, *27*, 618.

No clear resolution of the issue.

Stein, L., Analytical psychology: A "modern science," *J. Anal. Psychol.*, 1958, *3*, 43–50.

Strauss, F. H., Interpretation of thematic test material: A Jungian approach, *Bull. Brit. Psychol. Soc.*, 1954, *23*, 12–13.

Stricker, L. J., and J. Ross, Intercorrelations and reliability of the Myers-Briggs type of indicator scales, *Psychol. Rep.*, 1963, *12*, 287–293.

Extraversion–introversion, sensation–intuition, and thinking–feeling scales were independent of each other, but judging–perceiving was moderately related to S–I and T–F scales.

Stricker, L. J., and J. Ross, An assessment of some structural properties of the Jungian personality typology, *J. Abnorm. Soc. Psychol.*, 1964a, *68*, 62–71.

"There is little support for any of the structural properties attributed to Jung's typology."

Stricker, L. J., and J. Ross, Some correlates of a Jungian personality inventory, *Psychol. Rep.*, 1964b, *14*, 623–643.

"Extraversion-introversion and judging-perceiving scales may reflect something quite different from their postulated dimensions."

Strunk, O., Biographical sketch of Carl Gustav Jung, *Time*, 1952, *60*, 37.

Strunk, O., The old wise man, *Time*, 1955, *65*, 62–70.

Strunk, O., Psychology, religion, and C. G. Jung: A review of periodical literature, *J. Bible Relig.*, 1956, *23*, 106–113.

Suinn, R. M., Jungian personality typology and color dreaming, *Psychiat. Quart.*, 1966, *40*, 659–666.

For males: introversion correlated with color dreaming.
        sensation type correlated with vividness.
For females: intuition type correlated with vividness.

Toynbee, A., The value of C. G. Jung's work for historians, *J. Anal. Psychol.*, 1956, *1*, 193–194.

Tranel, Ned, Effects of perceptual isolation on introverts and extraverts, *J. Psychiat. Res.*, 1962, *1*, 185–192.

> Results "were not inconsistent with Jungian theory on which hypothesis was based."

Valett, R. E., Jung's effect on psychology, *Bull. Brit. Psychol. Soc.*, 1962, *46*, 58–66.

> Possibilities of research by the analytic procedure.

Weigert, E. V., Dissent in the early history of psychoanalysis, *Psychiatry*, 1942, *5*, 349–359.

Yates, A. J., and J. I. Laszlo, Learning and performance of extraverts and introverts on the pursuit rotor, *J. Pers. Soc. Psychol.*, 1965, *1*, 79–84.

> Found no support for Eysenck's theory that there is a difference between introverts and extraverts in the rate of growth of associative connections or reactive inhibitions.

Part

III

Psychoindividual— Psychosocial

THREE THEORISTS, Adler, Horney, and Moreno, fit most comfortably in Part III, which we have called "Psychoindividual–Psychosocial." In the present edition the work of Sullivan has been inserted in Chapter 15, "Contributions of Other Theorists: Neo-Freudian." This rearrangement is absolutely not because his work is any the less important but only because the present edition stresses the productivity of research that each theory seems to generate. An exhaustive search of the literature since 1960 has uncovered very little ongoing experimentation stemming from Sullivan's interpersonal theory.

Alfred Adler's theory encompasses the uniqueness of the individual, the striving for superiority through a style of life, and a core of social concern or social interest: *Gemeinschaftsgefühl*. There has been an interesting renascence of some of the concepts Adler espoused in his lifetime. The primary research interest is in birth order, therapy, and the life style.

Karen Horney, generally considered the only woman personality theorist, still retains a position in the field despite a very small amount of research concerning her theory. No one else quite duplicates her work and certainly she upholds the feminine aspects of personality theory, particularly with the issuing of her former papers in the 1967 book *Feminine Psychology*. That and her originality earn her a place in Part III.

Finally we come to the highly original theories of J. L. Moreno and his dedicated, action-oriented coworkers, especially Zerka Moreno. Rarely do J. L. Moreno's concepts receive adequate recognition despite the creative contributions of a fresh approach. One can only conjecture as to the reasons: Since little if any of his work appears in the "traditional" APA-sponsored psychological journals, many researchers are unaware of the psychodramatic theories; psychological experimentalists are prone to yield to centripetal professional forces rather than to seek out new concepts (until a "name" person introduces the material through one of the "traditional" journals); the entire approach of psychodrama *demands direct physical and emotional involvement* of the experimenter—and not as a passive manipulator of subjects via questionnaires, psychogalvanometers, one-way vision screens, and so on, all operated by graduate research assistants. Much research (but not all) in psychodrama requires the experimenter to be *in* the experiment himself. Most research psychologists have been trained with animal studies and employing highly statistical analyses and would rather not bother. In any case, Moreno's theories have received scant experimentation in the academic psychological world. For the emerging research psychologist looking for new worlds to conquer, they are, then, wide open.

5

ADLER

*Men's weaknesses are often necessary
to the purposes of life.*

MAURICE MAETERLINCK
Joyselle, Act II

SOME BIOGRAPHICAL DATA

On February 7, 1870, when Freud was fourteen years old, Alfred Adler was born in Vienna, Austria. The two men were destined to meet and for a short time work closely together. Both were graduated from the same medical school. Freud received his doctorate in medicine in 1881 from the University of Vienna, Adler the same degree in 1895.

For a time after receiving his degree Adler specialized in eye diseases but he soon went into the practice of general medicine and, like Freud, became interested in the mental aspects of his practice. Before long he too took up the practice of psychiatry. The two men were mutually attracted and joined forces with others through the founding of the Vienna Psychoanalytic Society, of which Adler later became president. Jung parted company with Freud in 1914, while Adler had already cooled toward Freud's pansexualism and had left the Freudian group in 1911.

Adler continued to practice psychotherapy and develop his own concepts and techniques on an individual basis. Gradually there grew around him a coterie of believers in his system, which he named *individual psychology,* in contrast to Freud's psychoanalysis. During the 1920s and 1930s neither man had much to do with the other professionally, although both practiced in Vienna. Their split in 1911 was never healed.

Adler left Vienna in 1935 during the regime of the Nazis; Freud left in 1938. Adler came to the United States, where he continued his private practice as a psychiatrist and lectured widely. During this time he accepted the position of Professor of Medical Psychology at the Long Island College of Medicine and attracted many followers.

Alfred Adler died suddenly, at the age of 67, on May 28, 1937, while on a tour and lecturing in Aberdeen, Scotland.

INTRODUCTION

One of the chief characteristics of Adler was his capacity to change. From the time he first began to formulate theories about human behavior until his death in 1937, he exhibited a continued evolution of his ideas which has been interesting and in many cases logical. Though he never contradicted his previous work, he showed the metamorphosis of his thinking from an original idea to ideas more complex and inclusive of more complete behavioral phenomena. This strengthened his theoretical position considerably.

The evolution in Adler's thinking is reflected by the following changes he made in the theoretical structure of human behavior. Beginning with an increased absorption in man as an aggressive animal, a concept which gradually weaned him away from sex as the prime mover of man, he moved to considering man as a complex of characteristics seeking primarily power. Finally, Adler came to the conclusion that the true motivator in man was his seeking to be superior.

In the same vein, Adler changed from regarding man as a lustful animal, driven by opportunities to express his lustful desires, to what amounts to almost a complete reversal: regarding man as a socially responsible animal. He believed that man is imbued at birth with social awareness and needs only to be awakened to his responsibilities to other men for their welfare as well as to his own personal welfare. In the end, Adler was convinced that the human animal had a deeply embedded social interest in his fellow human animals.

Other changes are reflected in his development of the organ inferiority complex to the broader and more comprehensive theory that man is essentially governed by a feeling of inferiority and thus moves forward in life to achieve new and finer things, motivated by the desire to overcome his basic weakness. Organ inferiority means that man is born with a basically inferior organ in his body. The fact that it is weaker than the other parts of his body serves as a compensation device for overcoming obstacles. More important is the role of the weaker organ in providing a rationalization for failure to perform difficult or onerous tasks. Migraine headaches, asthma, weak eyes, ulcers, and the like may be evidences of organs of inferiority.

Adler did not conceive a theory and spend the remainder of his professional life defending it. He continued to refine his work before criticism demanded it. He was an excellent example of his own theory, continuously striving for superiority in his work, being motivated by a feeling that his present position was inferior to what he could eventually reach by more effort. In essence, this behavior epitomizes the hard core of Alfred Adler's personality theory. It is in deep contrast to the impression one frequently receives in studying the personalities of personality theorists. What the theorist does as a personality at times seems to be in direct contradiction to what the theorist states as a theory.

Adler's followers are centered mainly in New York, Chicago, and Los Angeles, where branches of the American Society of Adlerian Psychology exist. The term *individual psychology* is one that Adler used, and it has become identified with his work especially through the title of his definitive book, *The Practice and Theory of Individual Psychology*. Publications of Adler's were primarily collections of his lectures, often compiled into books either by Adler himself or by those interested in disseminating his ideas. Probably the best and most devoted work being done in the Adlerian field is by the gifted team of Heinz and Rowena Ansbacher, whose *Individual Psychology of Alfred Adler* is a compendium and excellent collection of Adler's writings. The Ansbachers represent the academic approach to Adlerian psychology. Rudolph Dreikurs may be said to be a leader in the Adlerian methods of Adlerian diagnosis and therapy. Two of Adler's children, Drs. Kurt and Alexandra Adler, qualified psychiatrists, continue to carry on their father's tradition by active practice in New York City. Adler's widow, Raissa, died at the age of eighty-eight on April 23, 1962.

ADLER'S DESCRIPTION
OF HUMAN BEHAVIOR

Not many of the theories discussed in this book lend themselves as readily as does Adler's to a description of human behavior. Many of his ideas are clear-cut and describe well what it is that man does as he pursues a life pattern. Part of the ease in using Adlerian psychology in descriptive ways lies in his few well-defined concepts. Unlike Jung, and particularly Freud, both of whom spun out multiple variations on a theme, Adler was economical in the same sense as Sheldon: A few well-formulated and basic unitary concepts sufficed.

Adler was a master at separating the meaningful from the trivial in reporting his case studies. Not infrequently the reader has the feeling of knowing almost at firsthand the case being studied. Adler wrote voluminously, and the writings translated thus far display this facility of description.

The reader will note that Adler was a humanist in the tradition of Jung. Later theorists, such as Carl Rogers and Gordon Allport, are in the same camp. Unlike Freud, Adler felt that man has a chance to be better and move upward in life, to reduce his problems and eventually (though not as distinctly and teleologically as Jung puts it) to arrive at a nearly perfect adjustment to the life process.

The author has abstracted seven principles of human behavior, as he interprets them, from Adler's work. Some interpreters may find fewer, some more. These seven seem to represent accurately the salient features: (1) inferiority, (2) superiority, (3) style of life, (4) creative self, (5) conscious self, (6) fictional goals, and (7) social interest. Upon these seven hooks the author hangs the cloth of Adler's theoretical work on man's personality.

Inferiority Principle

Adler believed that man is born into the world feeling incomplete and unfulfilled, with a deep sense of inferiority. Everything that lies before the newborn babe is better, bigger, and more competent than he. To a neonate, this state of affairs hardly makes any difference in his struggle for existence. As he grows, however, his perceptive system makes him aware of his inferior role in society. As he moves through his first, second, third, and fourth years, he is continuously reminded that most of the creatures around him can reach things, throw things, prepare things, and control things much better than he can. Feeling inferior, he wishes to emulate the strengths and capacities of others. In a few abnormal cases, the child remains at an inferior level, is unable to try anything new, or reverts to an even more inferior role, but most humans want to go beyond where they are, as does the child who desires to be more complete than he is at any given moment in his early development. Plateaus in development, although quite natural, do not last long. Once having attained a plateau in his development toward more and better skills and powers, one has only a temporary feeling of satisfaction and success. The moment he can see something bigger and better beyond where he is at the moment, he again feels inferior, unfulfilled, or incomplete. The entire process starts again, a process that leads from inferiority to efforts for new attainments, to achievement of the new level (either symbolically or actually), to recognition of a still higher level, and hence to the inevitable feeling of inferiority once again. This, said Adler, is the stuff of life. The feeling of inferiority introduced at birth is what keeps man living through the ages. Biologically and psychologically he inherits the feeling of inferiority.

The idea of man as an inferiority-driven being first came to Adler when he was practicing general medicine in Vienna early in this century. Many of his patients, he noticed, seemed to localize their complaints and illnesses toward specific regions of the body. In a time which preceded psychosomatic medicine Adler discovered, too, that man turns to illness to solve certain nonphysical problems. Frequently, the complaints and syndromes which Adler studied were not associated with the actual condition of the organic system of the patients he was seeing. Out of these experiences Adler evolved a theory which he referred to as *organ inferiority*. At that time (though he was later to expand the concept), he felt that man is born into the world with a potentially weak organ in his body. Stress, the natural course of events in life, or various combinations of causes could make the potentially weak organ break down. The result was an attempt to compensate for it by trying all the harder to succeed. Compensation for an inferior organ frequently determined the style of life and the manner in which the human would strive for superiority in life: Individuals with weak bodies in childhood who would exercise prodigiously to build stronger bodies, and then become professional athletes: Demosthenes and his pebbles to cure stuttering; Franklin Delano Roosevelt and his political career after his attack of poliomyelitis—all these can be considered examples of this inferiority-motivated response.

Organ inferiority became interpreted later as a device used to evade painful and insurmountable tasks as the individual conceived them within his personal frame of reference. Under this interpretation also, man was born with a potentially weak organ which would come to his rescue whenever the pressures of life became too strong for him to surmount. If the striving for superiority became blocked or the goal remained totally inaccessible to the individual, he could seek solace and excuse his inferiority by claiming sickness of the weak organ. Thus, some businessmen in highly competitive and pressure-racked occupations develop ulcers, others develop migraine headaches, and still others find solace in sinus difficulties or asthmatic problems, or any type of organic breakdown which allows them to rationalize failure or withdraw from failure-producing situations. The inferior organ, of course, varies from individual to individual.

Having associated inferiority with organic conditions, Adler then created what he called the *masculine protest*. By a somewhat devious route in his thinking, he connected being inferior with weakness and femininity. Inferiority, then, was akin to femininity. Both males and females were considered to be in protest against weakness, women because of their inherent weakness as the female of the species and males for the association with femaleness which connoted inferiority. Adler himself was dissatisfied with this truncated concept. Gradually he widened and strengthened it to include the generalized idea that all mankind is inferior at birth and that the inferiority has nothing to do with femininity but is the result of a hereditary condition, followed after birth by a feeling of being incomplete.

In summary, then, Adler's concept of the inferiority principle developed through the years from 1897 to 1911, when he left the Freudian group under protest, and even strong criticism, from the Vienna Psychoanalytic Society, of which he was president at the time. His ideas on inferiority feelings developed through organic inferiority to masculine protest to the generalized concept that all men are inferior and weak at birth and thus begin a lifelong struggle to elevate themselves from their present levels.

Superiority Principle

To treat this principle as an entity separate from the principle of inferiority feelings would be wrong, since both are so entwined that to speak of one immediately brings the other into play: they are mutual and highly complementary principles. However, because Adler's thinking on *superiority* as a principle was somewhat different from his thinking on *inferiority*, we shall separate these principles. As they operate in man's life, the semantic separation is not possible.

After starting with an acceptance of Freud's emphasis on sexuality as a prime motivator in life, Adler soon became disenchanted with the monotony of the approach. As he defended his ideas before the Vienna Psychoanalytic Society, he stressed that man is an aggressive animal and must be so in order to survive. During the "masculine protest" phase, he gradually evolved through his therapy with clients a belief in man as more than an aggressive animal, as one who seeks power in the physical and/or symbolic sense in order to survive. Too many patients he was seeing then appeared to lack totally aggressive qualities and might be described as power-less human beings. By a reverse process, Adler reasoned that the opposite of power-lessness is power. Therefore, what man wants is power. This idea, too, had a short life with Adler. Soon he came to the concept which he continued to develop throughout the remainder of his professional life: that man simply wishes to be superior and that this superiority wish grows out of feelings of being inadequate or inferior. With the newer concept of *superiority*, Adler continued to feel that wanting to be superior is a universal and timeless property of man's personality.

The softening of Adler's approach through the sequence of sexuality–aggressiveness–power and superiority is interesting to note. Running parallel to this, as we shall see later in the chapter, is his emerging concept of man's social interest.

To Adler, there are no separate drives or needs such as those Murray incorporated in his theory. There is only one drive, and that is the desire for superiority, which Adler felt grows out of feelings of inferiority. The two principles are inseparable. It should be noted that superiority does not mean power over other men. It does not mean that one human is necessarily more gifted than another (though Adler readily admitted and strongly advocated the uniqueness of persons), but that each human is striving to be superior within *himself* and not necessarily in competition with other men. *Superiority* means, to the Adlerian, "superiority over self." The prime mover in life, the dynamic that describes why he does the things he does, is man's striving for superiority.

Style of Life Principle

In order for man to achieve superiority out of his feelings of inferiority, it is necessary for him to conduct his life in a certain prescribed way. This Adler called the *style of life*. The style of life that each human being pursues is a combination of two things: his inner self-driven and -dictated direction of behavior, and the forces from his environment which aid, interfere, or reshape the direction the inner self wishes to take. The most important part of this two-way system is the inner self. A singular event may produce an entirely different reaction within the inner selves of two humans. The main feature is that behavior is caused primarily within the self but always in counterplay with the environment. Adler did not feel that man is a free-floating chip on the waters of life, rising and falling, advancing and retreating according to the dictates of other forces. Man has and always will have the capacity to interpret exterior forces for himself. He further has the capacity to avoid, attack, or be defeated by outside forces. Defeat may call for new directions. Direct attack upon outside forces may strengthen or weaken the inner structure. Avoidance may call for entirely new directions of effort. The salient feature of any of the variables which man may endure from outside forces is, however, his ability to conduct his own affairs. To Adler, man has enough will power, not always fully free, to make and arrange a life of his own. Adler, although one of the very first to acknowledge the effects of environmental forces and thus aid the struggling field of social psychology at that time, could not accept the purely environmentalistic viewpoint that man is solely a product of his environment. To Adler there is too much material born and developed within man: the self-operated system he called the *style of life*.

Each human being's style of life is unique. Probably, thought Adler, no two human beings ever lived who had, or could have, identical styles of life. At least two forces demand a unique style of life for each individual. The first force comes from the individual's hereditary past with all of the variable components inherent in the system at birth. The second force comes from the variant environment that each human being enters immediately upon being born. Since no two human beings can occupy the same space at the same time, the environment for each must, therefore, be different. Even Siamese twins do not look at themselves from the viewpoint of the other. With different environments and different inherited systems, no two human beings can be expected to behave in the same way. To the Freudian, sex is the *sine qua non* of all men's behavior. To the Adlerian, sex may or may not be the *sine qua non* of any man's behavior. It would depend upon his individual style of life.

Despite the fact that each life is unique, Adler believed there are certain strong threads which are common to people. Just as each human being requires the organic functions of heart, lungs, and liver, he also has feelings of inferiority and superiority and a distinctive life style.

Each person has the same goals which he hopes to reach through his creative self, but the paths to these goals are always different. His behavior on the way to these goals is always dissimilar; however, the mainsprings of action are always feelings of inferiority and superiority.

Just as there is consistency in everyone's feelings of inferiority and superiority, so there is a tremendous amount of consistency within one person's style of life. The style of life frequently prescribes a singular interpretive quality for all of the experiences that a human being may encounter. The individual whose style of life revolves around feelings of neglect and being unloved interprets all his experiences from that frame of reference. Activities which are not subject to such interpretation are ignored or twisted into forms appropriate to the desired interpretation. The unloved child feels that all human contacts substantiate his role of being unloved; contacts with people who do give him love prove that that is what life might be for him if he were not unloved. The individual whose style of life centers on feelings of aggression and power considers any display of counterpower a challenge to self, while displays of cooperation or weakness indicate his own strength. Most human beings, however, do not have styles of life in such strong tones of black and white. As we shall see later, the style of life is ameliorated by the creative self and particularly by social interest. The majority of people follow a style of life that is tempered by broader goals than the examples just cited. The basic style of life, however, is not an amorphous thing centering on vague concepts, such as wanting, in a nebulous way, to be a good fellow. It is a strongly interpretive and bonding agent: It controls all actions of life in a determined way. It continues to operate throughout life and remains constant to its core. It is the sole unifying force in life.

From birth to about the age of five or six, the style of life is becoming fixed. Based on the inherited capacities of the child and, equally important, on the child's use and interpretation of these capacities, the style of life is being formed during these years—and, according to Adler, it rarely changes.

What may and frequently does change is the form of expression the individual utilizes to bring about his desired ends. To change deliberately another's style of life is well-nigh impossible. To change one's own style of life (which is essentially the only way it can change) is painful, since for the moment of change one has no style of life—an intolerable situation. Adler feels the most practical way of change is to divert the basic style toward ends that meet with less and less frustration. Basically, then, the style of life remains constant throughout life. What changes is the ways of achieving goals and the interpretation machinery used to satisfy the style of life. Thus, to the unloved child whose style of life is being unloved, it is more practical to form fictional goals where love is not so important than to attempt to convince him that the past of being unloved is not important and that the possibilities for love in the future will make up for the past. It is possible to change the basic style of life, Adler felt, but the cost in emotions and the effort in energy frequently rule against it. Besides, the successes that accrue to even a faulty style of life make change hazardous. It is far easier to continue on the old and known style, which becomes more mechanical and fixed through the years, than to change. Adler felt so strongly about the formative years in man's childhood that he wrote volumes about educational methods. He was one of the very first to establish child guidance clinics. He directed a great deal of energy also to improving schools and in particular to educating parents to the risks involved in faulty early childhood training.

Precisely how does one develop a style of life? What forces create an almost immutable way of living? Why are there so many differing styles of life in the children of the same family, whose environments may be so closely parallel? The answer might lie in the universal feeling of inferiority with which all men are born and in the ensuing striving for superiority. However, since these are universal characteristics, the individual shadings must come from other sources. These sources, which Adler felt account for the uniqueness in men's personalities, grow out of the different physical, psychological, and sociological conditions for each human. In trying to deal with a differing set of these three influences, each person emerges as different from all other people. Some specific factors which lead to a faulty style of life causing men to differ are childhood experiences, number of brothers and sisters, and order of birth in the family—this latter status being called ordinal position.

Through his work with individuals in therapy, Adler felt there are three factors which, unless checked or compensated for, will create styles of life inoperable in society and causing, for the individual and others, a lifetime of unhappiness and grief. These factors are inferiorities of an organic or mental nature, pampered and indulged childhood, and neglect in childhood.

The physically impaired child may understandably have much greater feelings of inferiority than the able-bodied child. Whether he fails to achieve superiority or achieves it with resounding success, the fact remains that his physical disability is highly instrumental in formulating his style of life. Some children with organic weaknesses never surmount their inferioirty feelings and succumb to a style of life defeated and subjected to all the perils of existence. Other children (and many biographies remind us of this) compensate so strongly for an inferior organic weakness that they achieve a degree of superiority far beyond what one might expect from their otherwise normal talents. Examples may be found everywhere. Small-statured people who themselves consider their size an organic defect, although society may not, can be found to have gained outstanding success—for example, in athletics, the arts, or the industrial world. Chronically ill children have been known to strive valiantly to compensate for their afflictions and sometimes become more successful than they would have been had they possessed physically normal bodies. Obviously the compensation of the organically weak does not lead automatically to success. The pathways from inferiority to superiority may bring them only to the level of normal-bodied human beings. The gradient of improvement itself, however, may be quite unusual. The outstanding feature, to Adler, of these cases was that the style of life becomes formulated through the organic weakness of the individual. In some cases a faulty life pattern results from an organic inferiority that is too restricting to overcome. In other cases the organic inferiority gives added strength and compensatory goal activity, resulting in superiority within self.

Mental impairment as an inferiority feeling source has a somewhat more severe result in our society, for several reasons. (1) Compensation is far more difficult to attain by a limited brain than by a normal one, because of difficulty in understanding. (2) The variety of avenues for compensation is more limited for mental activities than it is for physical activities. (3) Modern society operates more on brain power than it does on muscular power. (4) Society understands less and tolerates less the compensatory activities of the mentally inferior than of the physically (but mentally normal) inferior. (A child on crutches presents a far more sympathetic picture than does a moron.) One might expect to find, therefore, and does find, more faulty life styles in the mentally impaired than in the physically impaired. But whatever he does, the mentally impaired personality sets his life style by the incapacities he inherits and the strivings toward superiority he makes from them.

The degree to which both types (physically and mentally impaired) achieve superiority, according to Adler, depends on the amount of encouragement and realistic guidance the child receives from his parents or other adult parent figures. Adler felt it particularly important that the parents serve as excellent models. It is not so much in the techniques they use as in the parents' own style of life that the child who is physically or mentally impaired gains his greatest strength in trying to achieve superiority over the self's inferiorities. Because each child has a different style of life anyway, the techniques are as varied as the number of children they are applied to.

Consequently Adler stressed the parental model as the basic feature for the child's superiority strivings.

Passing from the physical to the psychological conditions which create uniqueness in the style of life, we find a more fundamental environmental force operating, although Adler never denied the basic instinctual predispositions to act that we find in Freud's and Jung's work. Still keeping within the rubric of childhood experiences, we see that a faulty life style may result from the behavioral patterns formed in the early years. Adler felt very strongly that the pampered and indulged child is a psychological cripple headed for a life utterly lacking in true superiority of self. He was vehement in his disapproval of parents or any figures of authority who allow the child to be petted and pampered. Yielding too often to the wishes of the child, he felt, deprives the child of the invaluable opportunity to exercise and develop a feeling of superiority within self. Having been sufficiently deprived of the one challenge which could bring him growth, the child becomes saddled with a style of life that is good for nothing. He is now of no real value to himself and of less value to the world at large. Adler's condemnation was directed toward the parents. The child, he believed, can in no way develop a life style of his own completely independent of those who care for him. When a human being has nothing to struggle for because all hurdles have been removed or minimized, he cannot possibly learn how to surmount the hurdles he is forced to meet later in life. The essential relationship between inferiority and superiority is subverted by the artificial superiority supplied by the well-meaning parents. Adler considered the pampered personality the scourge of society. Innumerable times he spoke out against the egocentric demands of the pampered person whose style of life revolves around taking from others to achieve a false superiority rather than developing within himself the great struggle to emerge from inferiority to superiority. People like this, whose demands upon others do not cease at adulthood, are often potentially dangerous. It will be remembered that the style of life is continuous throughout life and that the longer the style continues, the more deeply embedded it becomes.

The neglected child suffers equally in developing a style of life. Although his faulty life style is as harmful and painful to himself as is that of the pampered person to *him*self, he acts with less friction toward society. His contribution to society is less, but the real loss comes with the lack of triumph in his life. Neglect commits him to having only himself as a model. The trial and error of self-direction may be so costly to his strivings that he ultimately ceases to struggle upward. Even the successes he manages to achieve do not seem to be reinforced by others. The end result is a lackadaisical style of life which brings neither joy to himself nor pleasure to other persons.

Sociological conditions may exert equal force in molding a defective style of life despite the normality of the physical and psychological conditions. As an example, stultifying poverty may operate so severely on the style of life as to deprive it completely of any enrichment and opportunities for growth. Conversely, an enriched and stimulating early environment may foster a style of life adaptable to all sorts of conditions in later life. The reciprocity between self and social forces is a never ending one, Adler stated.

In summary, then, man creates a style of life out of the physical, psychological, and social conditions under which he develops. The previous passages used the criteria of faulty development to illustrate the three conditions. In addition, the factors of mental–physical inferiorities, pampering, and neglect were employed to bring out the affect of creating the life style. We turn now to positional psychology, which Adler considered could bring further insight into how a style of life comes into being.

Positional psychology has not met with great acceptance as a fruitful avenue of research, although many employers, lay people, and psychological clinics often give thoughtful consideration to the order in which one was born into the family. Only children, children coming from very large families, and children who have many siblings not of their sex are considered in light of these familial facts. The value of positional psychology is not under consideration here. The following material is presented in an interpretive sense to promote understanding of how a style of life may be created out of the psychological and social forces surrounding the human at birth. Interpretive liberties have been taken with Adler's original theme in order to demonstrate fully the positional phenomena.[1] The writing style is deliberately journalistic and novel-like.

> Mr. and Mrs. Jones have three boys, John, Harry, and Larry, now well advanced into their adult years and married. John is the oldest son, Harry was born four years later, and Larry was born four years after Harry. The spread in ages, then, is eight years between John, the oldest, and Larry, the youngest, with Harry in the middle.
>
> The Joneses can still remember John's birth. They lived at that time in a small flat and had been married about a year and a half. The birth was a thrilling event. Both sets of grandparents were deeply involved, for this was the first time that they were grandparents. John came into life to face six adults: a set of parents completely unlearned in the role of parenthood and two sets of grandparents uninitiated in grandparentry but with definite ideas, learned from being parents, on just how a baby should be reared. Some rivalry existed between the two grandmothers about the best methods to be used. At times the rivalry became more than subtle. John gradually became aware of this and made good use of it. What one grandma might refuse could often be wheedled out of the other one, who was inclined (in a nice way, of course) to take an opposite view to that of the first.
>
> John's biggest problems were with his parents, however. They never

[1] No family such as that described here actually exists. The illustration is a montage drawn from the author's clinical experience with clients mainly in therapy. No professional confidences are violated.

seemed to know exactly how to act. Mom and Dad were learning from him how to be parents. Every single little thing he did got noticed. They always seemed to overdo or underdo everything. Life got to be a series of stresses, but a fellow learned how to manipulate Mom and Dad fairly soon. There was plenty of practice, too, because if you couldn't work on the folks, there was usually at least one grandparent visiting the house and being proud and contradictory. John got very good at manipulating human beings who were adults. Children were different. There were none in the house at all, and the kids in the neighborhood were either too big or too selfish or too little to be interesting.

But life to John was wonderful. Dad took him everywhere and promised he would be famous some day. They took hundreds and hundreds of pictures of him, even buying an expensive movie camera, and there was a tape recorder, which he broke. Every one of the toys in the house was his. It was lonesome many times but make-believe can create a pal out of any teddy bear. It was lonesome, that is, until Harry, his brother, came into the house.

John will never forget the day Harry came home. Things were very mixed up then. His grandma and his dad argued once about the way he should eat. It was absolutely wonderful to have Mom home again, and it was even better than before because now it wouldn't be lonesome at all with a baby brother to play with. But he should have known better. The first time John met Harry, he got scolded and yelled at. Naturally he had to see if Harry was built as well as his teddy bear, so when he pushed Harry's eye in to see if the other one popped out as it did in his teddy bear and when he wanted to see if Harry's leg would turn completely around, too, everyone yelled. His father said, "What are you trying to do?" Harry wasn't very satisfactory as a playmate, and Harry was very, very selfish about his mother and wouldn't share her at all.

Now, Harry always said he lived in a world of "hand-me-downs." Even his parents at times seemed secondhand. It seemed that he got things like bicycles and ice skates only after John had thoroughly wrecked them. Then John would get new bikes and new skates, and Harry would have to do with the old ones. Even his bed and most of his clothes at first were John's old things. His folks didn't take so many pictures of him as they had taken of John. They didn't even telephone long distance to Grandma and Grandpa when he said his first words the way they did for John. One time Grandma even forgot his birthday. She said there were beginning to be so many grandchildren that "My goodness, it's hard to keep up with them all." The biggest fights came with John, who wouldn't share anything. All the old toys Harry now had John still felt were his, and John would get the new ones, too. Mom kept saying over and over to his brother John, "Remember he's smaller than you are," as if being small were a penalty. But the kids in the neighborhood were wonderful. John would never let Harry play with his friends, but there were plenty of kids the right size who didn't keep on bossing him around the way a bigger brother did.

Larry, right from the start, was called "Lovable." There were some fights in the beginning between John and Harry as to who was going to take care of

Larry. He was cute, like a real doll. John usually won, of course, and would get to change Larry and do other things so that Harry went out to play. Larry loved life. There was always someone to play with in the house and give him extra turns at bat and chase for him and stick up for him in fights, and there were new things to play with (the old bike had worn out, and Dad had done well in business, and they had moved to a nice big house). Mom and Dad let him do lots of things John and Harry never, never got to do. They always told him so, too. Mom was very sentimental. She always called him her "Baby."

John married a local girl he had met at the church fellowship groups. He went to junior college for two years and then decided not to go on to state university because his part-time work at the shoe store brought good money, and his dad at that time couldn't help very much with two other brothers to feed and clothe. John married a girl very much like himself, a solid person. She had helped raise her brothers and sisters, too, after her mother had died, so she knew what life was about. She often helped John with the accounting for the shoe store he now owned for himself. John never moved away and he still sees a lot of the folks. Almost every weekend or Sundays they spend together. He's the treasurer of the church, and lots of people call him "good, solid, conservative stuff."

The folks haven't seen Harry for two years now. He's a real go-getter. He not only finished college with a tremendous reputation as an athlete and student, too, but he went on for a law degree. He did it all himself with practically no help from his dad. Dad would have been glad to help, but Harry moved fast and never seemed to confide in Dad what he was doing. It seemed to be done by the time the folks knew of it. He even eloped with a girl they say is brilliant but somewhat erratic. She was an actress. Actually Mom was hurt about Harry running away like that, but all things work out. His old room fit nicely for the sewing room she had always wanted, and she was terribly proud of his business success. Some say that he could buy and sell his brothers.

Poor Larry has had a hard time of it. He's been divorced once, and his present marriage doesn't seem to make either of them very happy. His mother still calls him her "Baby" and this infuriates Larry. At his wedding she cried and cried all the way through. In college, Larry was tremendously popular and got to be the fraternity president two years in a row, something which had never happened before. It took him a little longer to graduate because he transferred colleges twice and he changed his major many times. His first wife was a "Homecoming Queen" and very popular. She was an only child, and her folks spent a lot of money on her. People liked her a lot even though she seemed awfully contradictory at times. She's remarried now to a widower with two children, and the marriage is a model of marital happiness. Larry remarried shortly after the divorce to an older friend of his first wife. He has been a salesman for some time but keeps changing companies. Larry has many friends and has been quite famous in a way because he has won the state amateur golf title three times. His mother keeps the cup because his present wife makes caustic comments about the cup being worth a hundred customers for each year. Most people like Larry at parties but he hasn't seemed to keep many friends over the years.

This fictional account of the three boys in the Jones family serves as a demonstration of the forces which may occur in constructing a style of life out of the common fabric of a single family. Each son grew to pursue a unique style of life, possibly out of the inferiorities which he surmounted from early childhood. John perhaps developed his conservative style of life partially out of experiences in an adult world in childhood. Harry turned to the outside world from the home; in the outside world, he learned to be aggressive and to fend for himself. Larry was never given a true chance to develop a style of life and thus emerged with a faulty one based on strong relationships with people but with an incapacity to struggle for himself toward a superiority based on his own achievements.

Adler, however, felt dissatisfied with the mechanistic aspects of the style-of-life approach for man's pathway from inferiority to superiority. Returning to some of the earlier ideas of man as a dynamic, *unifying*, highly interpretive self-structure, Adler went a step farther and evolved the concept of the creative self.

Creative Self Principle

Man is more than a product of his environment. Man is more than a totally predisposed animal confined by his instinctual, inherited past. Man is an interpreter of life. By this Adler meant that the human animal creates a self-structure out of his inherited past, interprets the impressions he receives from his ongoing life, searches for new experiences to fulfill his desires for superiority, and puts these all together to create a self that is different from any other self and that describes his own peculiar style of life. The creative self is a step beyond style of life. The latter is reactive and mechanical. The creative self, however, is more than that. It is original, inventive, and makes something that never existed before: a new personality. It creates a self. To Adler, the term was very accurate in all its connotations. Adler felt that this concept was the capstone to his career. For his remaining days, he subordinated all other concepts within his theoretical system to the power and unifying force of the creative self. It was as if toward the end of his life he had created his own personal creative self. The concept left him satisfied and contented with his own work.

Conscious Self Principle

Adler never discoursed on his belief that man is a conscious, aware animal, but the belief is evident through all of his work. He felt that man is aware of everything he is doing and upon self-examination can deduce why he has acted in certain ways. Consciousness is the core of personality. The human animal is fully aware of what he is doing every day, and nothing like the unconscious, preconscious, or subconscious lurks beneath his personality ready to erupt at any moment. The fact that man may not attend at any given moment to a memory of the past did not mean to Adler that the unnoticed past is buried in a sea of repressed vestigial forces.

The human animal with his type of brain can perform only so many mental processes at one time. Those things which are not in a state of awareness at any given moment may become so at the will of man. Memory is a mechanism of the mind, and, like all processes, it may not operate efficiently. Inefficiency of the mind or forgetfulness is a product of the lack of organic well-being, coupled with poor training, or lack of training, of the memory functions of the brain. Individual differences also come into play. Consequently, that which man is not aware of can be brought into awareness if the mental functions are efficient.

Adler did not accept the Freudian preconscious and unconscious. As a social psychologist, Adler thought they seemed akin to mysticism. He felt that man knows quite consciously what he is doing; he knows where he is going, he has the ability to plan and direct his own behavior toward goals he consciously selects. This is in such direct contradiction to Freud's theory that it is understandable that the two men parted and never reestablished a professional relationship.

Fictional Goals Principle

Although Adler believed that the past is tremendously important, since out of it grows man's style of life and his creative self, it is the future which shapes what man will do with his creative self at any given moment. The past may set the stage and thus limit the actions of the actors, but the future determines what the players will do. The past is prologue, but the future is the scene. Adler says, "The final goal alone can explain man's behavior." For example, the undergraduate student is not motivated by his record, good or bad, in elementary school. He is not in college to perpetuate that record if it is good or to correct it if it is bad. He is, paraphrasing Adler, in college to get a degree. This motivates him to study to remain in college, and to pursue all the necessary tasks that college life demands. The undergraduate is not necessarily motivated by the subject matter of the day as much as by the final grade in the course.

To continue with the college student as an example, his grade and his degree are creations of fiction. Grades and degrees do not represent anything material or concrete. They are semantic devices or fictions representing a larger composite of future goals. Although man is motivated by organic needs for food, clothing, and shelter, these basic needs become represented in fictional ways. An automobile to the adolescent means more than transportation. It means the symbols of prestige, equality with other, adult motorists, freedom, and possibly many fictional goals far beyond the simple end of being transported from one place to another by the automobile.

In quite another sense, the goal may be a fiction because it is fabricated as an ideal to strive for; it is removed from reality and will be unattainable to the creative self striving for superiority. One may find examples of this in the phrases "perfect husband" and "always tell the truth." Noteworthy phrases that they are, the individual may find it impossible to reach them as the fictional goals of life.

Fictional goals are inseparable from style of life and creative self. Man moves toward superiority via his style of life and creative self out of feelings of inferiority always pulled and attracted by his fictional goals.

Fictional finalism, as Adler sometimes termed *fictional goals*, is an operating force in man's day-to-day behavior. It is not an ideal floating beyond his reach, as a star in the sky. Through his creative self man makes his own fictional goal from native ability and self-experiences. The human personality is fully aware of his fictional goal and will continuously interpret the daily happenings of life in the perspective of his fictional goal.

Social Interest Principle

This final principle extracted from Adler's work sheds further light on the growth in his thinking. Starting from his initial interest in the aggressive characteristics of man, passing through his theory that man is a power-hungry animal to his final principles of the human being as an inferiority-to-superiority-driven personality exhibiting a style of life and creative self progression, Adler expanded his theory in 1929 to proclaim that man is also socially interested. He reasoned that man is born with an interest in social beings; it is a universal interest. Like all instincts, it needs a contact to bring it into action. This contact with other human beings, Adler stated, is an automatic condition. Man has to be brought up by man just as definitely as he has to be born out of man. To start with, a human being is predisposed to be interested in like-appearing human creatures. The interest is in the societal environment surrounding him; it is not yet social interest as later developed. The child notices a mother, a father, other similar-appearing human beings surrounding him, and the important fact that they do things for him. They (people in general) feed him, bathe him, clothe him, give him solace when pain interferes with his normal state of existence. Adler reasoned that this care of the child must make an impression upon him and that the impression is most logically one that the world is good and that one helps one's fellow man.

Gradually, as the child is reared from his animal state, the predisposition toward other persons is educated into a concern for the welfare of other persons. Being reared by socialized animals turns the baby into a socialized animal.

The process of socialization takes a great deal of time and continuous effort. Taking turns on slides, helping mother with the housework, receiving high praise for ineffective efforts, sharing with siblings the food and comfort of the common home have their effect upon the child's natural bent to grow from natural feelings of inferiority to greater heights of superiority. The aggressive qualities of superiority become socialized through the efforts of the surrounding environment.

After the formative years to four or five, and continuing through the elementary school experiences, the child begins to identify with social groups of his own. Much of the world at that time is designed to help him. Schools have been constructed and operated, toys have been purchased, opportunities for recreation are provided, all of which maintain and strengthen the feeling of social interest and concern for fellow man. The child enters the world inadequate to cope with his needs. He notices inadequate characteristics in his peers. Through a sense of empathy, he learns what it is like to be weak and have others help him. He in turn wishes to exercise his emerging feeling of superiority so that when the opportunities arise he, too, turns back to help the less fortunate. The process both enriches his own feelings of superiority and strengthens the social interest he is beginning to develop. Through identification, empathy, and cooperation he discovers that a unique reciprocity exists within the world: Help others as you may need help yourself in achieving superiority.

Because man never fully achieves superiority (as soon as one goal is reached the next one beckons), he retains a feeling of inadequacy. The feeling is universal and thus becomes a common bond between men. Held to others by bonds of inadequacy, man trusts that a strong and perfect society can help him achieve for himself a fuller feeling of superiority. Possibly the perfect society will lift him along with it and through association fulfill his inner desire for superiority. The style of life and its more encompassing creative self now incorporate a principle of social interest that permeates his behavior throughout life.

Adler in his own life was a strong believer in social causes and democratic principles—a theorist who appears to have lived much more closely by his theory than have some of the others.

To summarize, we have discussed Alfred Adler's theory of personality by using the device of seven principles; each principle is entwined with another and all operate within the dynamics of man's personality. The seven principles used are (1) inferiority, (2) superiority, (3) style of life, (4) creative self, (5) conscious self, (6) fictional goals, and (7) social interest.

EXPLAINING HUMAN BEHAVIOR VIA
ADLER'S INDIVIDUAL PSYCHOLOGY THEORY

Possibly the main point in this section can be succinctly put in Adler's own statement: "The final goal alone can *explain* man's behavior." The temptation to expand exists, nevertheless; there are extrapolations one may make from his theory which come close to explaining the dynamics of man's behavior in certain functions. In other cases the theory is found wanting as an explanatory tool. Let the reader use the above quotation as a preface to his answers to the *why* of the nine activities: marriage, perversions, suicide, lawbreaking, supranatural being, humor, smoking, play and recreation, and psychoses–neuroses.

PREDICTING HUMAN BEHAVIOR VIA
ADLER'S INDIVIDUAL PSYCHOLOGY

Prediction is not the strength of Adler's theory. Two reasons for this assertion are drawn from the core of his system. On the one hand, the Adlerian system is built around the uniqueness of man; on the other hand, the emphasis is on man not only as highly individual and personalized but as a being in a highly therapeutic climate.

Although it is almost impossible to draw out prediction from Adler's theories because of the personalized style of life, it is easy to make one solid prediction: Every individual will continue to be different from every other individual that has ever lived or is now living.

Adler worked and did research in a clinical setting, not in a laboratory. He was a highly individual worker like Freud, and a solitary one, engaging only in small collaborative efforts with others.

Personal Prediction

The judge of any theory is the reader and student of the theory. As judge, the student must weigh the theory for himself, accept whatever evidence seems meaningful to him, and reject the rest. It may be possible for him to accept Adler's ideas about the patterns of behavior which emerge into the style of life, especially those concerning the influence of one's position in the family. Maybe Adler could anticipate certain behavior patterns from an only child in the family. Possibly the youngest of three sons will turn out to be a rather soft, easygoing, socialized human with not too much striving for superiority. Perhaps the reader has known in others, or is himself addicted to, some kind of organic inferiority to which he can ascribe a will to succeed that might not have been present otherwise. Or he can recognize behavior which seeks and uses an organic weakness to evade pressure points in life. These are the things the student of a theory ultimately decides for himself, contrary to or in substantiation of evidence gathered in life.

Scientific or Laboratory Prediction

One part of Adler's theory seems to have been involved in a disproportionate amount of research, as compared, at least, to his other contributions. We say involved because few research studies have stemmed from Adler's theory per se. We refer here to the concept of birth order and its effect on the life style.

There is absolutely no direct obligation on any researcher to follow the precepts of any personality theory. He is free to pursue his own interests with no debt to any theory, past, present, or future. It is intellectually dishonest, however, to claim one has done research on a precept which never was in the theory and then claim the theory was "wanting." What is wanting is that the research psychologist sit down and read and understand the theory before attacking it. It is not fair to demean a theory particularly when the research did not apply to the theory. This sharp criticism is directed to much of the research cited in the present book for all the theories.

The most striking example is found in the plethora of reports on the effects of order of birth in the family. Adler stated that firstborn children *could* be the same from family to family. He did not say they *would* be. The same for lastborn children. To maintain that firstborn children will be similar in personality structure and dynamics in all families is categorically to deny the very essence of Adler's theory, revealed by its name: *individual* psychology. The theory is about how each individual pursues a personal pattern in structuring a life style, no two life styles possibly being similar. How, then, can the researcher assume that firstborns or lastborns are going to have common characteristics? Adler did say that your order of birth in your particular family would have a powerful effect on the development of *your* personality. But it would always depend upon your *individual* family circumstances. Firstborns may be inclined to be somewhat alike, but again the similarity would depend upon the individual circumstances and not operate as a fixed conditional set.

This status of research on birth order may be a concomitant of the "nature of things" in psychological experimentation. One factor in the situation is the "follow-the-leader" or replicative study. It is unfortunate when a few of the original studies erroneously assume a relationship to a theory. If this happens, and it frequently does with Freudian and Adlerian theories, the studies that follow commit the same error. (Ambitious investigators soon learn what journal editors will accept and what areas of research are publish

able whether they have an abiding interest in the subject or not.) A second
factor pertains to the ease of conducting the research. If the psychologist
happens to have access to or own comparable equipment, it is easier to
replicate another's published study than branch out into newer fields. In the
case of birth-order studies the ease is of a different kind. Data on order of
birth are fairly easy to obtain. Correlating them with an already standardized,
accepted, published psychological test is all that is needed to conduct a study.
Thus, research reports roll out (Kammeyer, 1967).

A case in point may be found all the way back in a 1931 review of
approximately 250 birth-order studies for the years 1881–1931. Birth order was
compared to intelligence in eighty-eight of these works (Jones, 1931). A more
recent review of the literature on birth order contains a 153-item bibliography
covering the years 1897 to 1964. The author, Sampson, credits Koch and
Schachter (*The Psychology of Affiliation,* 1959) with shifting the efforts from
simple correlational studies to more precise psychological experimentation.
Sampson's chapter on the "study of Ordinal Position" is a refreshing contribution and clarification of research on birth order. It is our opinion that this
is must reading for psychologists who intend future research in the area
(Sampson, 1965).

The following research studies run the gamut from good to bad and
relate birth order to just about anything the imagination could conceive.
Many of the reports are correlational studies and not straightforward experimental work. The categories are not necessarily pure but grouped in a general
way. The latter part of the listing deals more with discussion papers but not
exclusively so.

Behavior, adjustment, and maladjustment
   Allman and White, 1968; Brock and Becker, 1965; Cushna *et al.*, 1964; De-
   Lint, 1964; Gormly, 1968; Lessing and Oberlander, 1967a,b; Smith and
   Goodchilds, 1963
Attitudes, affiliation, and achievement
   Demeber, 1964; Greenberg *et al.*, 1963; Hall and Barger, 1964; Harrison,
   1964; Mukherjee, 1968; Rhine, 1968; Taylor and Eisenman, 1968; Weiss,
   1966
College attendance
   Alexander, 1968; Schachter, 1963; Smelser and Stewart, 1968; Warren, 1966
Cross-cultural effect
   Altus, 1965, 1967; Diab and Prothro, 1968
Therapy and treatment
   Dinkmeyer, 1968; Dreikurs, 1957; LaPorte, 1966; Nelson and Haberer,
   1966; Nikelly, 1967; Papanek, 1965; Sivadon, 1964; Vandette, 1964
Style of life
   Corval, 1965; Dreikurs and Mosak, 1966, 1967; Ferguson, 1964; Harms,
   1965; Mackler and Shoutz, 1964; Williams, 1966; Winetrout, 1968

Social interest
    Ansbacher, 1968a; Brennan, 1966, 1967; Clark, 1967; Nikelly, 1963;
    O'Connell, 1965
Existentialism
    Adler, 1963; Farau, 1964; Johnson, 1966a,b

There are also some studies, hardly experimental, which deal with the
aspects of Adler's life and his relationship to others, personal or theoretical.

Adler's personal life
    Anon. editorial, 1966; Ellenberger, 1966; Farau, 1967; Shoobs, 1967
Adler and others
    Ansbacher, 1959a,b, 1962a, 1965a; Berger, 1964; Brennan, 1968; Deutsch,
    1966; Morris, 1965; Mosher, 1968; Rom, 1963; Rom and Ansbacher, 1965;
    Shulman, 1965; Stern, 1965

■ SUMMARY

The grand staircase of life in Figure 5 is a diagrammatic summary of the
personality theory of Alfred Adler as the author interprets it.

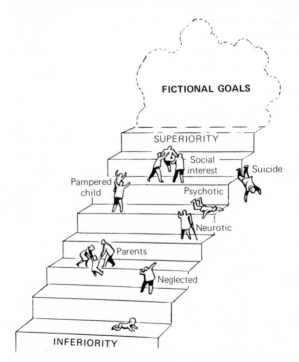

FIGURE 5. *Diagrammatic summary of Adler's theory.*

It seems to the author that Adler's main rationale is man's lifelong struggle to emerge from inferiority feelings to superiority feelings, only to find himself repeating the process all over again because there is always another step above his present level to which man aspires.

Many figures are represented on the staircase in an attempt to portray the versatility and uniqueness of each individual's style of life. The path of progress for most figures is upward to the next higher level of superiority. At the very top of the long climb is the fictional finalism that man continuously aspires to. The course of one's life may be thought of as the climb up the staircase.

Certain figures show the versatility of man's approaches. On the right side near the top of the drawing a figure is shown in the act of suicide. The struggle has been too difficult, and this personality is destroying his life by leaping off. Just below are a psychotic and a neurotic who are unable to advance because of faulty style or because of a complete inability to move to the next higher step. In the center of the staircase are shown the social interest aspects of man's behavior with three figures climbing together. Each helps and gives comfort to the others. Also shown in the drawing are the neglected child, the child whose parents help him in his initial steps, and the pampered child on his father's shoulders. The pampered child is unable to learn how to climb because he rides freely on the efforts of someone else.

Other factors, of course, enter the picture. Some individuals may excuse their inability to go upward because of an organic inferiority. This disability may moderate their gait. It may cause them to strive harder and thereby develop faster and easier ways of achieving the next rungs. Positional psychology may also give more aid to certain children born first or last in the family. The firstborn may have a difficult time. His parents have to learn how to help him. They may overplay or underplay their roles. As more and more children enter the family, the parents have to divide their time between the many children for whom they are responsible. An only child may have a hard time trying new steps and new ways for himself. His parents overemphasize everything he does.

Life, therefore, as summarized here by Adler's theory, is a struggle upward from life to death, each traveler using his own method, each traveler aware of others, each traveler pulled by many common goals, and each traveler exposed to all the vicissitudes of the trip.

BIBLIOGRAPHY

PRIMARY SOURCES

BOOKS

Adler, A., *The Neurotic Constitution*. New York: Moffat, 1917.

Adler, A., *Study of Organ Inferiority and Its Psychical Compensation*. New York: Nervous and Mental Diseases Publishing Co., 1917.

Adler, A., *Practice and Theory of Individual Psychology* (1920). Totowa, N.J.: Littlefield, Adams, 1959.

Adler, A., *Understanding Human Nature* (1927). New York: Premier Books, 1957.

Adler, A., *The Case of Miss R.: The Interpretation of a Life Story*. New York: Greenberg, 1929.

Adler, A., *Problems of Neurosis* (1929). New York: Harper Torchbooks, 1964.

Adler, A., *The Science of Living*. New York: Chilton, 1929. Also in paperback, Doubleday Anchor Books, 1969, with introduction by H. L. Ansbacher.

Adler, A., *The Education of Children*. New York: Greenberg, 1930.

Adler, A., Individual psychology, in C. Murchison (ed.), *Psychologies of 1930*. Worcester, Mass.: Clark University Press, 1930, pp. 395–405.

Adler, A., *The Pattern of Life*. New York: Holt, Rinehart & Winston, 1930.

Adler, A., *The Problem Child: The Life Style of the Difficult Child as Analyzed in Specific Cases* (1930). New York: Capricorn Books, 1963.

Adler, A., *The Case of Mrs. A.: The Diagnosis of a Life Style* (1931). Chicago: Alfred Adler Institute, 1969.

Adler, A., *What Life Should Mean to You*. Boston: Little, Brown, 1931.

Adler, A., *Social Interest*. New York: Putnam, 1939.

Adler, A., *The Individual Psychology of Alfred Adler: A Systematic Presentation in Selections from His Writings*, H. L. and R. R. Ansbacher (eds.). New York: Basic Books, 1956. Also a Harper Torchbook, 1964.

Adler, A., *Superiority and Social Interest: A Collection of Later Writings*, H. L. and R. Ansbacher (eds.). Evanston, Ill.: Northwestern University Press, 1964.

PERIODICALS

Adler, A., Characteristics of the first, second, and third child, *Children*, 1928, 3, 14–52.

Adler, A., The fundamental views of individual psychology, *Int. J. Indiv. Psychol.*, 1935, *1*, 5–8.

Adler, A., The significance of early recollections, *Int. J. Indiv. Psychol.*, 1937, *3*, 283–287.

Adler, A., Physical manifestatons of psychic disturbances, *Indiv. Psychol. Bull.*, 1944, *4*, 3–8.

Adler, A., How I chose my career, *Indiv. Psychol. Bull.*, 1947, 6, 9–11.

Adler, A., The progress of mankind, *J. Indiv. Psychol.*, 1957, *13*, 9–13.

> Originally published in 1937—first English translation.

Adler, A., Suicide (1937), *J. Indiv. Psychol.*, 1958, *14*, 57–61.

> You hurt others by hurting yourself.

Adler, A., Fortune-telling and prophecy, *J. Indiv. Psychol.*, 1965, *21*, 41–43.

Adler, A., The psychology of power, *J. Indiv. Psychol.*, 1966, 22, 166–172.

Adler, A., Two letters to a patient, *J. Indiv. Psychol.*, 1966, 22, 112–115.

SUGGESTED READINGS

BOOKS

Adler, A., *Guiding Human Misfits*. New York: Philosophical Library, 1948.

Adler, K., and D. Deutsch (eds.), *Essays in Individual Psychology*. New York: Grove Press, 1959.

Ansbacher, H. L., Suicide: The Adlerian point of view, in N. L. Farberow and E. S. Shneidman (eds.), *The Cry for Help*. New York: McGraw-Hill, 1961.

Ansbacher, H. L., Introduction to Torchbook edition, in A. Adler, *Problems of Neurosis: A Book of Case Histories*. New York: Harper Torchbooks, 1964a.

Ansbacher, H. L., and R. R. Ansbacher, *The Individual Psychology of Alfred Adler: A Systematic Presentation in Selections from his Writings*. New York: Harper Torchbooks, 1964b.

Ansbacher, H. L., and R. R. Ansbacher (eds.), *Superiority and Social Interest: A Collection of Later Writings with a Biographical Essay by Carl Furtmuller*. Evanston, Ill.: Northwestern University Press, 1964c.

Ansbacher, H. L., The structure of individual psychology, in B. B. Wolman and E. Nagel (eds.), *Scientific Psychology: Principles and Approaches*. New York: Basic Books, 1965.

Beecher, W., and M. Beecher, *Beyond Success and Failure: Ways to Self-reliance and Maturity*. New York: Julian Press, 1966.

Beecher, M., and W. Beecher, *Parents on the Run*. New York: Julian Press, 1955. Also in paper, Agora, 1966.

Bottome, P., *Alfred Adler: A Portrait from Life*. New York: Vanguard, 1957.

> Originally published in England, 1939—very thorough and devoted biography.

Brachfield, O., *Inferiority Feelings in the Individual and the Group*. New York: Grune & Stratton, 1951.

Dinkmeyer, D., and R. Dreikurs, *Encouraging Children to Learn: The Encouragement Process*. Englewood Cliffs, N.J.: Prentice-Hall, 1963.

Dreikurs, R., *Fundamentals of Adlerian Psychology*. New York: Chilton, 1950.

> Excellent source and equal to Ansbacher's tome.

Dreikurs, R., *Psychology in the Classroom*. New York: Harper & Row, 1957.

Dreikurs, R., *The Challenge of Parenthood*. New York: Duell, Sloan & Pearce, 1964.

Dreikurs, R., *Children: The Challenge*. New York: Duell, Sloan & Pearce, 1964.

Dreikurs, R., R. J. Corsini, and M. Sonstegard, *Adlerian Family Counseling: A Manual for Counseling Centers*. Eugene: University of Oregon Press, 1959. Paper.

Friedman, P., *On Suicide: With Particular Reference to Suicide Among Young Students*. New York: International Universities Press, 1967.

Ganz, M., *The Psychology of Alfred Adler and the Development of the Child*. New York: Humanities Press, 1953.

Gondor, E. I., *Art and Play Therapy*. New York: Random House, 1958. Paper.

Hoff, H., and W. Ringel, A modern psychosomatic view of the theory of organ inferiority by Alfred Adler, in A. Jores and H. Freyberger (eds.), *Advances in Psychosomatic Medicine*. New York: Brunner, Inc., 1961.

Jones, E., *The Life and Work of Sigmund Freud: Vol. II, Years of Maturity (1901–1919)*. New York: Basic Books, 1955.

> The Adler–Freud split from the Freudian viewpoint.

Jones, H. E., Order of birth in relation to the development of the child, in C. Murchison (ed.), *Handbook of Social Psychology*. Worcester, Mass.: Clark University Press, 1931, pp. 204–241.

Munroe, R. L., *Schools of Psychoanalytic Thought*. New York: Holt, Rinehart & Winston, 1955.

> Analysis and integration of Freud, Adler, Jung, Rank, Fromm, Horney, Sullivan, *et al.*

Orgler, H., *Alfred Adler: The Man and His Work*. New York: Liveright, 1963; Capricorn Books, 1965, paper.

Ray, M. B., *The Importance of Feeling Inferior*. New York: Harper & Row, 1957.

> Wonderful imaginary conversation between Adler and Freud—also utilizes Alderian concepts.

Sampson, E. E., The study of ordinal position: Antecedents and outcome, in B. A. Maher (ed.), *Progress in Experimental Personality Research*, Vol. 2. New York: Academic Press, 1965.

> Excellent summary on ordinal position.

Schachter, S., *The Psychology of Affiliation*. Stanford, Cal.: Stanford University Press, 1959a.

> "First time ordinal position took its place among the legitimate foci of psychological investigation."

Schachter, S., Ordinal position and fighter pilot effectiveness, in *The Psychology of Affiliation*. Stanford, Cal.: Stanford University Press, 1959b.

Senn, M. J. E., and C. Hartford (eds.), *The Firstborn*. Cambridge, Mass.: Harvard University Press, 1968.

> ". . . describes and interprets the experiences of 8 representative families with their firstborn children, concentrating on parental expectations, sociocultural factors, and the family pattern which emerges."

Way, L., *Adler's Place in Psychology*. New York: Macmillan, 1950.

Wile, I. S., and R. Davis, The relation of birth to behavior, in C. Kluckhohn, H. A. Murray, and D. M. Schneider (eds.), *Personality in Nature, Society and Culture*, 2nd ed. New York: Knopf, 1964.

PERIODICALS

Adler, A., Historical review, *Amer. J. Indiv. Psychol.*, 1952, 10, 80–82.

> Alexandra Adler, president of the American Society of Adlerian Psychology, describes its beginning.

Adler, A., The concept of compensation and overcompensation in Alfred Adler's and Kurt Goldstein's theories, *J. Indiv. Psychol.*, 1959, 15, 79–82.

Adler, A., Adlerian psychotherapy and recent trends, *J. Indiv. Psychol.*, 1963, 19, 55–60.

> Drug treatment, changes in patient symptoms, group therapy, existentialist and religious psychotherapy.

Alexander, C. N., Jr., Ordinal position and social mobility, *Sociometry*, 1968, 31, 285–293.

> Previous findings that firstborns exceed later borns in rates of college attendance are explained in terms of the greater dependency needs of the firstborn.

Allman, T. S., and W. F. White, Birth-order categories as predictors of select personality characteristics, *Psychol. Rep.*, 1968, 22, 857–860.

> Significant differences appeared between firstborn only and second born and youngest as well as between firstborn only and third born *Ss*.

Altus, W. D., Birth order and its sequelae, *Science*, 1965, 151, 44–49.

> In England and the United States there is an "indubitable relationship" between achievement of eminence and ordinal position (firstborn).

Altus, W. D., Birth order and its sequelae, *Int. J. Psychiat.*, 1967, 3, 23–29.

Angers, W. P., Achievement motivation: An Adlerian approach, *Psychol. Rec.*, 1960, 10, 179–186.

Anonymous, Adler and the Vienna College of Professors, *J. Indiv. Psychol.*, 1966, 22, 235–236.

> An editorial on the rejection of Adler's application to lecture at Vienna University Medical School.

Ansbacher, H. L., Adler's place today in the psychology of memory, *J. Pers.*, 1947, 3, 197–207.

Ansbacher, H. L., Causality and indeterminism according to Alfred Adler, and some current American personality theories, *Indiv. Psychol. Bull.*, 1951, 9, 96–107.

Ansbacher, H. L., Purcell's "memory and psychological security" and Adlerian theory, *J. Abnorm. Soc. Psychol.*, 1953, 48, 596–597.

Ansbacher, H. L., The alienation syndrome "and Adler's concept of distance." Also A. Davids, some comment on Ansbacher's note on the "alienation syndrome" and Adler's concept of "distance," *J. Consult. Psychol.*, 1956, 20, 483–486.

Ansbacher, H. L., Anomie: The sociologists' conception of lack of social interest, *J. Indiv. Psychol.*, 1959a, 15, 212–214.

> Adler and Durkheim compared.

Ansbacher, H. L., The significance of the socio-economic status of the patients of Freud and of Adler, *Amer. J. Psychother.*, 1959b, 13, 376–382.

Ansbacher, H. L., Rudolf Hildebrand: A forerunner of Alfred Adler, *J. Indiv. Psychol.*, 1962a, 18, 12–17.

Ansbacher, H. L., Was Adler a disciple of Freud? A reply, *J. Indiv. Psychol.*, 1962b, 18, 126–135.

> The answer is no.

Ansbacher, H. L., and P. Rom, An Adlerian case or a character by Sartre? *J. Indiv. Psychol.*, 1965a, 21, 32–40.

Ansbacher, H. L., Sensus Privates versus Sensus Communis, *J. Indiv. Psychol.*, 1965b, 21, 48–50.

Ansbacher, H. L., and P. A. Stone, Social interest and performance on the Goodenough Draw-a-Man Test, *J. Indiv. Psychol.*, 1965c, 21, 178–186.

Ansbacher, H. L., Review of Lou Andreas-Salome, *The Freud Journal* (New York: Basic Books, 1964), *J. Indiv. Psychol.*, 1965d, 21, 93–94.

Ansbacher, H. L., Review of Henri Baruk, *Hebraic Civilization and the Science of Man* (London: World Federation for Mental Health, 1961), *J. Indiv. Psychol.*, 1965e, 21, 221.

Ansbacher, H. L., Love and violence in the view of Adler, *Humanitas*, 1966a, 2, 109–127.

> There is only one dynamic force: a striving for growth, expansion, success, completion, perfection. When the aptitude for social interest is developed, the resulting behavior is love; when undeveloped, violence.

Ansbacher, H. L., *et al.*, Lee Harvey Oswald: An Adlerian interpretation, *Psychoanal. Rev.*, 1966b, 53, 379–390.

Ansbacher, H. L., *et al.*, What's in a dream? *Voices*, 1966c, 2, 37–42.

Ansbacher, H. L., Review of Hubert Bonner, *On Being Mindful of Man: Essay Toward a Proactive Psychology* (Boston: Houghton Mifflin, 1965), *J. Indiv. Psychol.*, 1966d, 22, 243–244.

Ansbacher, H. L., Review of Benjamin B. Wolman (ed.), *Handbook of Clinical Psychology* (New York: McGraw-Hill, 1965), *J. Indiv. Psychol.*, 1966e, 22, 131–132.

Ansbacher, H. L., Gemeinschaftsgefuehl, *Indiv. Psychol. Newsltr.* (London), 1966f, 17, 13–15.

Ansbacher, H. L., Life style: A historical and systematic review, *J. Indiv. Psychol.*, 1967a, 23, 191–212.

Ansbacher, H. L., Review of Alvin R. Mahrer (ed.), *The Goals of Psychotherapy* (New York: Appleton-Century-Crofts, 1967), *J. Indiv. Psychol.*, 1967b, 23, 246–247.

Ansbacher, H. L., The concept of social interest, *J. Indiv. Psychol.*, 1968a, 25, 131–149.

Ansbacher, H. L., Adler and the 1910 Vienna Symposium on Suicide: A special review, *J. Indiv. Psychol.*, 1968b, 25, 181–191.

Arnold, N., What is an Adlerian? *Indiv. Psychol. Bull.*, 1951, 9, 144–146.

Arnold, N., An Adlerian evaluation of methods and techniques in psychotherapy of adults, *Amer. J. Indiv. Psychol.*, 1954, 11, 34–46.

Bakan, D., The relationship between alcoholism and birth order, *Quart. J. Studies Alcohol*, 1949, 10, 434–440.

Baldwin, A. L., Differences in parent behavior toward three- and nine-year-old children, *J. Pers.*, 1947–1948, 16, 143–165.

Beecher, W., and M. Beecher, What makes an Adlerian? *Indiv. Psychol. Bull.*, 1951, 9, 146–148.

Berger, E. M., Antithetical thinking in personality problems, *J. Indiv. Psychol.*, 1964, 20, 32–37.

> Author points out similarity of his research findings and Adler's theory.

Brennan, J. F., Friendship: The Adlerian mode of existence, *J. Indiv. Psychol.*, 1966, 22, 43–48.

Brennan, J. F., Self-understanding and social feeling, *J. Indiv. Psychol.*, 1967, 23, 53–57.

> "The process of self-understanding viewed in the light of Adlerian 'social feeling,' defined, and exemplified."

Brennan, J. F., Upright posture as the foundation of individual psychology: A comparative analysis of Adler and Strauss, *J. Indv. Psychol.*, 1968, 24, 25–32.

Brock, T. C., and G. Becker, Birth order and subject recruitment, *J. Soc. Psychol.*, 1965, 65, 63–66.

> Birth order is unrelated to whether students in an experiment prefer to work alone or with other students.

Burchard, E. W. L., Mystical and scientific aspects of the psychoanalytic theories of Freud, Adler, and Jung, *Amer. J. Psychother.*, 1960, 15, 289–307.

Clark, K. B., Implications of Adlerian theory for an understanding of civil rights problems and action, *J. Indiv. Psychol.*, 1967, 23, 181–190.

> The author, Negro psychologist and civil rights leader, expresses how from the beginning he was inspired and guided by Adlerian psychology.

Colby, K. M., On the disagreement between Freud and Adler, *Amer. Imago*, 1951, 8, 229–238.

Colver, T., and D. F. Kerridge, Birth order in epileptic children, *Neurol. Neurosurg. Psychiat.*, 1962, 25, 59–62.

> Epilepsy more frequent in firstborn than second born.

Connors, C. K., Birth order and needs for affiliation, *J. Pers.*, 1963, 31, 408–416.

> Firstborn have less expectancy of affiliative reward.

Corval, P., Themes de la psychologie Adlerienne, *Bull. Psychol.*, 1965, 19, 30–39.

> Organ inferiority, will to dominate, style of life are discussed.

Cushna, B., M. Greene, and B. C. F. Snider, First born and last born children in a child development clinic, *J. Indiv. Psychol.*, 1964, 20, 179–182.

> Firstborn had more functional disorders and more withdrawal problems.

DeLint, J. E. E., Alcoholism, birth order, and socializing agents, *J. Abnorm. Soc. Psychol.*, 1964, 69, 457–458.

> The absence of one or both natural parents is "strongly indicated as a variable meaningfully intervening between birth order and alcoholism."

Demeber, W. N., Birth order and need affiliation, *J. Abnorm. Soc. Psychol.*, 1964, 68, 555–557.

> Firstborns had higher average need affiliation scores.

Deutsch, D., An instance of Adlerian psychotherapy, *Case Reports, Clin. Psychol.*, 1956, 3, 113–130.

Deutsch, D., Alfred Adler and Margaret Mead: A juxtaposition, *J. Indiv. Psychol.*, 1966, 22, 228–233.

> Illustrates the influence of Adler's ideas on contemporary thinking.

DeVries, S. J., Some basic principles of Adlerian psychology, *Indiv. Psychol. Bull.*, 1951, 9, 149–151.

Diab, L. N., and E. T. Prothro, Cross-cultural study of some correlates of birth order, *Psychol. Rep.*, 1968, 22, 1137–1142.

> In three groups of Arab undergraduates, results do not corroborate previous findings on birth order.

Dinkmeyer, D., Contributions of teleoanalytic theory and techniques to school counseling, *Personnel Guid. J.*, 1968, 46, 898–902.

Dreikurs, R., The international picture of individual psychology, *Indiv. Psychol. Bull.*, 1951, 9, 1–3.

Dreikurs, R., Adler's contribution to medicine, psychology, education, *Amer. J. Indiv. Psychol.*, 1952–1953, 10, 83–86.

Dreikurs, R., Adlerian analysis of interaction, *Group Psychother.*, 1955, 8, 298–307.

Dreikurs, R., Psychotherapy as correction of faulty social values, *J. Indiv. Psychol.*, 1957, 2, 150–158.

Dreikurs, R., What is psychotherapy?: The Adlerian viewpoint, *Amer. Psychother. Monogr.* 1959, No. 1, 16–22.

Dreikurs, R., and H. H. Mosak, The tasks of life: I. Adler's three tasks, *Indiv. Psychol.*, 1966, 4, 18–21.

Dreikurs, R., and H. H. Mosak, The tasks of life: II. The fourth life task, *Indiv. Psychol.*, 1967, 4, 51–56.

Ellenberger, H. F., Alfred Adler: Two letters to a patient, *J. Indiv. Psychol.*, 1966, 22, 112–115.

Farau, A., The influence of Alfred Adler on current psychology, *Amer. J. Indiv. Psychol.*, 1952–1953, 10, 59–76.

Farau, A., Individual psychology and existentialism, *Indiv. Psychol.*, 1964, 2, 1–8.

> Individual psychology seen as most similar to early existentialist, except more optimistic in outlook for the future.

Farau, A., A few personal memories of Alfred Adler, *Indiv. Psychol.*, 1967, 4, 42–45.

Federn, E., Was Adler a disciple of Freud? A Freudian view, *J. Indiv. Psychol.*, 1963, 19, 80–82.

Ferguson, E. D., The use of early recollections for assessing life style and diagnosing psychopathology, *J. Proj. Techn. Pers. Assess.*, 1964, 28, 403–412.

> Life style formulations based on earliest recollections were shown to be reliably communicable to a wide range of professional workers.

Gelfand, S., The relation of birth order to pain tolerance, *J. Clin. Psychol.*, 1963, 19, 406.

> No relationship was found.

Glass, D., C. M. Horwitz, I. Firestone, and J. Grinker, Birth order and reactions to frustration, *J. Abnorm. Soc. Psychol.*, 1963, 66, 192–194.

> Contradictory findings from previous studies suggest birth order is ecological, not psychological.

Gormly, R., Birth order, family size, and psychological masculinity–femininity, *Proc. 76th Annu. Conv. Amer. Psychol. Ass.*, 1968, 3, 165–166.

Greenberg, H., R. Guerino, M. Lasken, D. Mayer, and D. Piskowski, Order of birth as a determinant of personality and attitudinal characteristics, *J. Soc. Psychol.*, 1963, 60, 221–230.

> Some slight difference primarily affecting the youngest child.

Grey, L., A comparison of the educational philosophy of John Dewey and Alfred Adler, *J. Indiv. Psychol.*, 1954, 11, 71–80.

Grunwald, B., The application of Adlerian principles in the classroom, *Amer. J. Indiv. Psychol.*, 1955, 11, 131–141.

Hall, E., and B. Barger, Attitudinal structures of older and younger siblings, *J. Indiv. Psychol.*, 1964, 20, 59–68.

Harms, E., Inferiority and superiority as psychological concepts, *Stud. Gen.*, 1965, *18*, 361–364.

Harrison, L. B., The relationship between ordinal position and dependency, dominance, affiliation, affection and task-orientation, *Dissert. Abstr.*, 1964, *26*, 3688.

Hoch, P., Influence of Alfred Adler on psychoanalysis, *Amer. J. Indiv. Psychol.*, 1952–1953, *10*, 54–58.

Holt, H., Existential analysis, Freud, and Adler, *J. Exist.*, 1967, *8*, 203–222.

James, W. T., K. Horney, and E. Fromm, In relation to Alfred Adler, *Indiv. Psychol. Bull.*, 1947, *6*, 105–116.

Johnson, E. L., Existential trends toward individual psychology, *Indiv. Psychol.*, 1966a, *3*, 11–13.

Johnson, E. L., Existential trends toward individual psychology, *J. Indiv. Psychol.*, 1966b, *22*, 33–42.

> The more recent existential trends are becoming congruent with individual psychology.

Kammeyer, K., Birth order as a research variable, *Soc. Forces*, 1967, *46*, 71–80.

> The literature reflects confusion. There is a need for some system that will aid in the evaluation of existing findings and also indicate areas for future research.

Koch, H. L., Some personality correlates of sex, sibling position, and sex of sibling among five- and six-year-old children, *Genet. Psychol. Monogr.*, 1955, *52*, 3–50.

Langman, L., Adlerian thought in Asch's social psychology, *J. Indiv. Psychol.*, 1960, *16*, 137–145.

> Parallels between Adler and Asch.

LaPorte, G. H., Social interest in action: A report on one attempt to implement Adler's concept, *Indiv. Psychol.*, 1966, *4*, 22–26.

Ledermann, E. K., A review of the principles of Adlerian psychology, *Int. J. Soc. Psychiat.*, 1956, *2*, 172–184.

> Differences between Freud, Jung, and Adler.

Lessing, E. E., and M. Oberlander, Developmental study of ordinal position and personality adjustment of the child as evaluated by the California Test of Personality, *J. Pers.*, 1967a, *35*, 487, 497.

> Firstborns had superior adjustment.

Lessing, E. E., and M. Oberlander, Ordinal position and childhood psychopathology as evaluated from four perspectives, *Proc. 75th Annu. Conv. Amer. Psychol. Ass.*, 1967b, *2*, 179–180.

Lilienfeld, A. M., and B. Pasamanick, 1. The association of maternal and fetal factors with the development of mental deficiency. 2. Relationship of maternal age, birth order, previous reproductive loss and degree of mental deficiency, *Amer. J. Ment. Defic.*, 1956, *6*, 557–569.

Long, L. M. K., Alfred Adler and Gordon W. Allport: A comparison on certain topics in personality theory, *Amer. J. Indiv. Psychol.*, 1952–1953, *10*, 43–53.

Long, L. M. K., Alfred Adler and the problem of the unconscious, *Amer. J. Indiv. Psychol.*, 1955, *11*, 163–166.

McArthur, C., Personalities of first and second children, *Psychiatry*, 1956, *19*, 47–54.

> First child serious and adult-oriented. Second, peer-oriented with laziness and friendliness.

McKeown, T., and R. G. Record, Maternal age and birth order as indices of environmental influence, *Amer. J. Hum. Genet.*, 1956, *8*, 8–23.

> Must be taken with clinical and other evidence to be useful.

Mackler, B., and F. C. Shontz, Life styles and creativity: A review, *J. Psychol.*, 1964, *58*, 205–214.

Maslow, A. H., Was Adler a disciple of Freud? A note, *J. Indiv. Psychol.*, 1962, *18*, 125.

> Maslow says Adler said no.

Minton, H. L., Contemporary concepts of power and Adler's views, *J. Indiv. Psychol.*, 1968, *24*, 46–55.

Montagu, M. F. A., Sex order of birth, *Amer. J. Orthopsychiat.*, 1948, *18*, 351–353.

Moore, M., Alfred Adler—creative personality, *Amer. J. Indiv. Psychol.*, 1954, *11*, 1–8.

Morris, C., Alfred Adler and George H. Mead, *J. Indiv. Psychol.*, 1965, *21*, 199–200.

Mosher, D. L., The influence of Adler on Rotter's social learning theory of personality, *J. Indiv. Psychol.*, 1968, *24*, 33–45.

Mukherjee, B. N., Birth order and verbalized need for achievement, *J. Soc. Psychol.*, 1968, *75*, 223–229.

> Birth order and economic class are joint determinants of verbalized need achievement.

Nelson, M. O., and M. H. Haberer, Effectiveness of Adlerian counseling with low achieving students, *J. Indiv. Psychol.*, 1966, *22*, 222–227.

Nikelly, A. G., Democratic assumptions in Adler's psychology, *J. Indiv. Psychol.*, 1963, *19*, 161–166.

> The concepts of universal striving and of ability for social interest are consistent with democratic principles.

Nikelly, A. G., The Adlerian concept of the unconscious in psychotherapy, *J. Indiv. Psychol.*, 1966, *22*, 214–221.

Nikelly, A. G., Maternal indulgence and neglect and maladjustment in adolescents, *J. Clin. Psychol.*, 1967, *23*, 148–150.

O'Connell, W., Humanistic identification: A new translation for Gemeinschaftsgefuehl, *J. Indiv. Psychol.*, 1965, *21*, 44–47.

> "Social interest" is an "uninspiring" translation of Adler's concept. Sug-
> gests "humanistic identification."

Orr, J. K., and F. Risch, Is the order of birth a factor in epilepsy? *Neurology*,
1953, *3*, 679–683.

Overton, R. K., Experimental studies of organ inferiority, *J. Indiv. Psychol.*, 1958,
14, 62–63.

Papanek, H., Adler's concepts in community psychiatry, *J. Indiv. Psychol.*, 1965,
21, 117–126.

Papanek, H., and E. Papanek, Individual psychology today, *Amer. J. Psychother.*,
1961, *15*, 4–26.

Peller, L. E., Character development in nursery school, *Ment. Hyg.*, 1948, *32*,
177–202.

> The oldest child takes care of the youngest.

Phillips, E. L., Cultural vs. intropsychic factors in childhood behavior problem
referrals, *J. Clin. Psychol.*, 1956, *12*, 400–401.

> Firstborn referred more often for psychological help.

Rank, O., The psychological approach to personal problems, *J. Otto Rank Ass.*,
1966, *1*, 12–25.

> Rank's theory is contrasted to the theories of Jung, Adler, and Freud.

Raychaudhuri, A. K., Are the first born more susceptible to functional mental
diseases? *J. Nerv. Ment. Dis.*, 1956, *124*, 478–486.

> Heredity does not affect firstborn but physical and sociofamilial condi-
> tions may.

Rayner, O., Adler and his psychology, *Ment. Hlth.* (London), 1957, *16*, 58–62.

Rhine, W. R., Motivational and situational determinants of birth order differences
in conformity among preadolescent girls, *Proc. 76th Annu. Conv. Amer.
Psychol. Ass.*, 1968, *3*, 351–352.

Rom, P., Adler and Goethe, *Indiv. Psychol.*, 1963, *1*, 2–4.

> Adler's partial indebtedness to Goethe, which he acknowledged, is exem-
> plified.

Rom, P., and H. L. Ansbacher, An Adlerian case of a character by Sartre, *J. Indiv.
Psychol.*, 1965, *21*, 32–40.

> Sartre's "Herostratus" is used to illustrate the similarity between Sartre
> and Adler.

Rotter, J. B., An analysis of Adlerian psychology from a research orientation, *J.
Indiv. Psychol.*, 1962, *18*, 3–11.

Schachter, S., Birth order, eminence, and higher education, *Amer. Soc. Rev.*, 1963,
28, 757–767.

Shafer, V. W., A construct validation of Adler's social interest, *Dissert. Abstr.*, 1959, *19*, 3374–3375.

Shoobs, N. E., Individual psychology and psychodrama, *Amer. J. Indiv. Psychol.*, 1956, *12*, 46–52.

How to be an Adlerian and still use psychodrama.

Shoobs, N. E., The formative years of Adlerian psychology in the United States: 1937–1943, *Indiv. Psychol.*, 1967, *4*, 49–51.

Shulman, B. H., Adler's place in psychology, *Indiv. Psychol. Bull.*, 1951, *9*, 31–35.

Shulman, B. H., The family constellation in personality diagnosis, *J. Indiv. Psychol.*, 1962, *18*, 35–47.

A guide expedites measuring the style of life.

Shulman, B. H., A comparison of Allport's and the Adlerian concepts of life style: Contributions to a psychology of the self, *Indiv. Psychol.*, 1965, *3*, 14–21.

"Adler's 'life style' and Allport's 'proprium' are compared with regard to aspects of bodily sense, self-identity, ego enhancement, ego-extension, rational agent, self-image, propriate striving, and the knower."

Sivadon, P., Alderian psychology and mental hygiene, *J. Indiv. Psychol.*, 1964, *20*, 194–195.

Smelser, W. T., and L. H. Stewart, Where are the siblings? A re-evaluation of the relationship between birth order and college attendance, *Sociometry*, 1968, *31*, 294–303.

"The overrepresentation of first born in college is thus a function of not only ordinal position, but also sex of the subjects and sex of the sibling."

Smith, E. E., and J. D. Goodchilds, Some personality and behavioral factors related to birth order, *J. Appl. Psychol.*, 1963, *47*, 300–303.

Stern, A., Existential psychology and individual psychology, *J. Indiv. Psychol.*, 1958, *14*, 38–50.

Sartre and Adler are more alike than we may realize.

Stern, A., Adler and Sartre: Comment, *J. Indiv. Psychol.*, 1965, *21*, 202–203.

Stotland, E., and R. E. Dunn, Empathy, self esteem, and birth order, *J. Abnorm. Soc. Psychol.*, 1963, *66*, 532–540.

Tendency for later borns to empathize more readily.

Stotland, E., and J. A. Walsh, Birth order and an experimental study of empathy, *J. Abnorm. Soc. Psychol.*, 1963, *66*, 610–614.

Later born children are more sympathetic.

Taylor, R. E., and R. Eisenman, Birth order and sex differences in complexity–simplicity, color–form preference and personality, *J. Proj. Techn. Pers. Assess.*, 1968, *32*, 383–387.

Firstborn males and later born females prefer more complexity than their respective sex groups.

Thorne, G. L., Conforming behavior as related to birth order, anxiety, and rejection, *Dissert, Abstr.*, 1962, 22, 3280.

Ullman, M., Dreaming, life style, and physiology: A comment on Adler's view of the dream, *J. Indiv. Psychol.*, 1962, *18*, 18–25.

Vandette, J., Application of Adlerian principles to speech therapy, *J. Indiv. Psychol.*, 1964, 20, 213–218.

Von Dusen, W., Adler and existence analysis, *J. Indiv. Psychol.*, 1959, *15*, 100–111.

Adler and phenomenology complement each other.

Warren, J. R., Birth order and social behavior, *Psychol. Bull.*, 1966, *65*, 38–49.

Overproportion of firstborns in college; firstborns more susceptible to social pressure than later borns.

Weiss, R. L., "Acquiescence" response set and birth order, *J. Consult. Psychol.*, 1966, *30*, 365.

Werner, H. D., Adler, Freud, and American social work, *J. Indiv. Psychol.*, 1967, *23*, 11–18.

White, R. W., Adler and the future of ego psychology, *J. Indiv. Psychol.*, 1957, *13*, 112–124.

Williams, R. H., A concept of style of life induced from a study of aging, *J. Indiv. Psychol.*, 1966, *22*, 100–103.

Winetrout, K., Adlerian psychology and pragmatism, *J. Indiv. Psychol.*, 1968, 24, 5–24.

6

HORNEY

Love conquers all.

VIRGIL
Eclogues, **X**, line 69

This is the Law of the Yukon,
that only the strong shall thrive.

ROBERT SERVICE
*The Law of the Yukon**

I never found the companion that
was so companionable as solitude.

HENRY THOREAU
Walden, Chapter V, Solitude

SOME BIOGRAPHICAL DATA

Like many of the theorists discussed in this book, Karen Horney was German-born. On September 16, 1885, she was born in the city of Hamburg in the northern part of Germany, of a Norwegian father and a Dutch mother. She attended medical school at the University of Berlin and while there became interested in psychoanalysis. She was a resident physician at a Berlin psychi-

* From *The Law of the Yukon*, in *The Complete Poems of Robert Service*. With the permission of Dodd Mead & Company, Inc.

atric hospital for four years, then became a practicing analyst in Berlin and a teacher for two years in the Berlin Psychoanalytic Institute.

In 1932 she was invited to Chicago to become assistant director of the Institute for Psychoanalysis there. In 1934 Dr. Horney went to New York where for a time she trained analysts at the New York Psychoanalytic Institute. She also gave lectures at the New School for Social Research, practiced as an analyst, and did extensive writing. Later she became Dean of the American Institute of Psychoanalysis, a position she held until her death December 4, 1952.

She was deeply influenced by Freud, having studied with Dr. Karl Abraham, a well-known pupil of Freud. However, Horney found herself unable to accept all Freudian tenets and considered Freud's work a foundation upon which further concepts could be built. Unlike Freud, she emphasized cultural factors as an influence on personality and contended that man is essentially a constructive creature rather than one ridden by the destructive drives posited by Freud.

Karen Horney reflected in her own life the constructive attitude she proclaimed. In addition to her extremely heavy professional obligations, she maintained a balanced personal life. In 1909 she was married to Oscar Horney, a lawyer; they were divorced in 1937. They had three daughters: Brigitte, Marianne, and Renata.

INTRODUCTION

Karen Horney is the only woman theorist in the present text. Overtones of feminine protest are discernible in her theoretical concepts, but they are protests against Freud's concepts of the female role rather than against being a female herself.

Horney was, and readily admitted to it, a neo-Freudian in her approach to the dynamics of man's behavior. There is much in Freud's work to which she subscribed. Her early training and the analysis she underwent were strongly in the Freudian tradition. In her later years, however, as a practicing psychoanalyst and then as a writer and theorist, she desexed Freud's theory. The denial of pansexualism as she interpreted Freud's work developed from her experiences in the United States as a therapist and her deep conviction that man and his personality are derivatives of the culture.

Beyond her professional contacts she gained popular attention through the publishing of five books: *Neurotic Personality of Our Times,* 1937; *New Ways in Psychoanalysis,* 1939; *Self-Analysis,* 1942; *Our Inner Conflict,* 1945; and *Neurosis and Human Growth,* 1950. Recently Kelman and others compiled most of her earlier German articles on female sexuality, which Kelman then edited. Published in 1967, this work is called *Feminine Psychology.*

Karen Horney had the deep conviction not only that mankind has the capacity for change but that change in man's behavior, both singularly and collectively is for the better. She felt that man has a positive nature. Her last statement in her last book is indicative of hope for the future: "Our [philosophy], with all its cognizance of the tragic element in neurosis, is an optimistic one" (*Neurosis and Human Growth*, p. 378).

Besides the early, strong influence of Freud upon her thinking, Horney also had a deep appreciation of the ideology of Erich Fromm, whom she quoted frequently in her last two books and for whom she expressed a profound respect. She also quoted liberally from the Danish philosopher and theologian Sören Kierkegaard, whose writings appear to have had an effect on her theorizing.

Like many other theorists, Horney improved and added to her theory, never being quite satisfied with her position. As one reads her books, starting with her publication of 1937, one is impressed with the progression of her ideas. Each book builds upon the material of the previous ones until a clear picture of evolutionary thinking becomes apparent. The progression, however, seems not to emerge as clearly in her last book, *Neurosis and Human Growth*, as in the previous ones. Here she presented a recapitulation of the total theory rather than a step beyond the previous works.

The author recalls with pleasure hearing Dr. Horney as a platform speaker describe the disillusionment she felt in her initial attempts at psychoanalysis shortly after arriving in this country from Berlin in 1932. In a somewhat humorous vein she related in detail the initial interviews she had had with her clients. Having been trained as a Freudian, she naturally expected and tried to elicit responses which would bring out the psychosexual problems of the client. Time after time the client appeared confused or irritated when questioned about sexual problems. He felt fine about his sexual life. Things were going great between him and his wife. No, he didn't hate his mother when he was a baby, and his dad was a pretty good pal of his until the day he died. What was he worried about? Then Horney discovered that her clients were understandably worried and troubled and sick about "losing my job" or "I hate my foreman," or "I have no money to pay the rent and my kid has tuberculosis." Suddenly, Horney stated in her talk, she discovered that in the Depression years in the United States people were not worried about sex. If anything, sex was helping them and was not a source of deep-seated neurosis. Her clients were behaving neurotically because of societal pressures, economic inadequacies, or occupational pressures. She related that the disenchantment she felt, which led to a reorientation in her thinking, was one of the first steps toward departing from the traditional Freudian approach in psychoanalysis, an approach that she was to reexamine and restructure for the rest of her professional career.

It should be noted that Horney at no time wrote about personality theories. She wrote and taught and worked on the neurotic aspects of man's behavior. However, in so doing she successfully developed a rationale for man's behvaior that helps to explain why man does the things he does. Only by attenuating Horney's theories on neuroses have others, including the author, been able to construct a theory of personality from a theory designed to explain neurotic behavior. It is for the reader to decide how closely a general theory of behavior has been created out of a specific theory of neurotic behavior.

HORNEY'S DESCRIPTION
OF HUMAN BEHAVIOR

A reader of the literature of Karen Horney may be impressed with the similarity between the three kinds of behavior that Sheldon discovered through research and the three methods of reacting to people—moving toward, against, or away from them—that Horney posited. To the writer's knowledge there was no direct influence of one upon the other. Only conjectural reasons for the likeness of the two systems of thought are possible. Even the descriptions of behavior in the Sheldon and Horney typologies, as we shall see in subsequent sections, appear to be quite similar. (Horney, however, eschewed the typology approach.) One possible reason for this resemblance of theories is the inclination that Horney had for trichotomizing her concepts. Even the most cursory reading of her material brings out the remarkable number of times she chose to phrase her ideas in three forms.

Again, in order to distill Horney's work into principles for the purposes of this book, one needs to examine the amount of agreement and disagreement between her concepts and those of Freud. This approach is logical in that Horney is, and wanted to be, considered a neo-Freudian. It is also to be understood that, since she based her work on that of Freud, we must examine those Freudian concepts which lie at the bottom of her own theoretical position. The following schematic presentation highlights the basic agreements and disagreements she had with the work of Freud.

Agreement with Freud	Disagreement with Freud
1. Psychic determinism—The cause and effect of man's behavior is primary to understanding the dynamics of man. For every action there must be a preceding causal reason. Behavior does not happen haphazardly; lying beneath behavioral acts are precursors of a causal nature.	1. Id, ego, superego—The disagreement is not so pronounced as are the extensions she makes to his primary mechanisms.
	2. Repetition complex—Man does not repeat infantile behavior in a blind fashion but rather reacts to situations of anxiety out of a character structure which he de-

2. Unconscious motivation—At one point Horney claimed that this takes first place as a contribution of Freud.
3. Emotional drives—Emotions are the primary driving mechanisms of man's behavior. Man is a non-rational animal.
4. Ego defense mechanisms—Though she added her own particular flavor in using the ego defenses, Horney, after extending their meanings in her own terms, considered them an invaluable tool to therapy.
5. Therapeutic techniques—Although this is a book on theories, not techniques, one should note that Horney "value[d] most highly" the instruments of therapy such as transference, free association, dream analysis, which Freud introduced.

rives from all of his earlier life. (See "Character-Structure Principle," below.)
3. Oedipus complex—This is not an exclusively sex-oriented behaviorism but a parentally induced anxiety wrought from feelings of punishment, indulgence, or rejection that are a part of the child's environment; it does not necessarily develop in all children.
4. Penis envy—The same disagreement holds true as for the above. Horney says it is just as sensible to say that the boy child envies his mother's capacity to "make babies" as to say that the girl child envies her father's penis and thus becomes involved with rejection of mother.
5. Libido—Horney preferred to consider libido as an emotional drive rather than an animalistic sex impulse that forever plagues man. "All is not gold that glitters, all is not sexuality that looks it" (*Neurotic Personality of Our Time*, p. 157). She further felt that sexual problems are the effect, *not* the cause of anxiety. Man turns to sexual behavior as a method of reassurance for insecure feelings.

In summary, Horney felt that Freud's real contribution was not that he solved problems but that he "made them accessible to understanding." This contribution she prized highly and credited him richly for. While her debt to Freud was openly expressed and warmly given, she further felt that "We find what we may expect to find" when reading Freud.

A brief review of her publications is helpful not only in tracing the changing concepts she followed but in advancing the basic assumptions of her theory.

In *The Neurotic Personality of Our Time* (1937) the main contention is that neuroses are brought about by cultural factors, meaning more specifically that neuroses are generated by disturbances in human relationships. Horney felt that compulsive drives are specifically neurotic, born out of feelings of isolation, helplessness, fear, and hostility, and that man aims at safety more than sexual satisfaction.

New Ways in Psychoanalysis (1939), unlike the first book, which was primarily intended for the educated lay person as well as for the professional therapist, "is not to show what is wrong with psychoanalysis, but, through eliminating the debatable elements, to enable psychoanalysis to develop to the height of its potentialities." Horney followed with a reappraisal built around Freud's terminology. Each concept was examined. None was rejected outright, but some concepts were rephrased to include her ideas regarding sex as other than a prime motivator of human behavior, the cultural effect upon man's behavior, the character structure rather than infantile repetitions of adults, and the spontaneity that the normal person must possess in order to handle the cause and effect aspects of his development.

Self-Analysis (1942) became a controversial book in some circles, where it was interpreted as a "self-help do-it-yourself book" for neurotics. Horney rejected this criticism by stating that man had to solve his problems for himself. The analyst was only a skilled professional who could help but never, by his own efforts, without the cooperation of the patient, resolve conflict. She felt that psychoanalysis was not the only cure, but that "Life itself is the most effective help for our development."

Our Inner Conflicts (1945) is considered by many, including the author, her magnum opus. In this book she summarized her development and came to the conclusion that there are three ways of responding to life situations—moving toward people, or moving against people, or moving away from people—and that most of us utilize all three. The response depends upon the situation that confronts us, and as we develop from infancy into adulthood, we grow through the manifestations of all three interpersonal methods.

Neurosis and Human Growth (1950) concerns itself with man's striving to be his idealized self, a condition which, of course, man cannot sustain at all times in all places. Horney thought that "it involves a fundamental problem of morality—that of man's desire, drive, or religious obligation to attain perfection."

Feminine Psychology (1967), an edited book of her early German papers, adds very little to her basic tenets. Some existential themes seem to be present. The first paper was written in 1917. Most of the papers are her interpretations of the Freudian concepts of penis envy, castration complex, and Oedipus complex.

The following six principles extracted from her writings are pertinent to an understanding of Horney's social-psychological theory of personality: optimism–positivism, society–culture, character structure, self-concept, complementation–conflict, and self-analysis. The order in no way indicates the degree of importance as this interpreter sees it but provides a sequential treatment necessary for better understanding.

Optimism–Positivism Principle

Karen Horney had faith in mankind's ability to change for the better. She was optimistic about the evolution of the human being from the levels of the past. She was encouraged by the positive qualities in mankind and felt her theory was constructive because eventually it might lead to resolving neuroticism. Since in all her thinking neurotic behavior is central, the resolution of neurotic behavior would, she felt, lead to a happier and healthier society.

Two quotations from *Our Inner Conflicts* attest to this optimism. The first is from the beginning of the book and the last from near the end. In between the two statements is repeated, with equal emphasis, the same theme of optimistic positivism.

> My own belief is that man has the capacity as well as the desire to develop his potentialities and become a decent human being, and that these deteriorate if his relationship to others and hence to himself is, and continues to be, disturbed. I believe that man can change and go on changing as long as he lives. And this belief has grown with deeper understanding [p. 19].

> Our daring to name such high goals rests upon the belief that the human personality can change. It is not only the child who is pliable. All of us retain the capacity to change, even to change in fundamental ways, as long as we live. This belief is supported by experience [p. 242].

In a slightly different vein Horney approached the problem of human growth and striving for perfection via the idealized image with a reference to the Christian injunction "Be ye perfect." Her point was not that man should be "goody-goody" but that he must strive for perfection if happiness is to be attained and neurotic behavior brought under control. Her feeling was that without this approach man's existence would be a shambles and, in fact, that man would probably long ago have ceased to exist. "Would it not be hazardous, indeed ruinous, to man's moral and social life to dispense with such dictates?" (*Neurosis and Human Growth*, p. 14). Horney was far from naive, and she realized the impact of life's problems upon man as he strives for perfection. This causal factor in neurotic behavior is discussed in the principle entitled self-concept. We wish merely to introduce the idea here because it does deal with the positive aspects of man's behavior as Horney sees it.

Society–Culture Principle

To Horney man is more than a product of interactions with other men in a social order, he is also refined and molded by the particular mores, customs, and roles that his particular culture impresses upon him. Thus the principle here emphasizes more than interpersonal relationships, incorporating as well the *rules* by which man plays the game of life. What methods he employs to achieve a better and more productive life will be further explored under "Complementation–Conflict Principle." For the present it is the formulative effect of the interaction of man and man and the general and specific rules by which it takes place that concern us.

The reader may recall the effect of American culture and particularly of the Depression of the early thirties that so impressed Karen Horney when she first began to practice psychoanalysis in Chicago. In her second published work after this experience, *New Ways in Psychoanalysis,* she characterized the change from Freudianism to social–cultural thinking by stating, ". . . the entire emphasis falls on the life conditions molding the character," and later, "A prevailingly sociological orientation then takes the place of a prevailingly anatomical–physiological one" (p. 9). With statements such as these Horney departed from the dedicated Freudian camp and set out in new directions with her own interpretations.

Horney felt that our present culture generates a great deal of anxiety and that neuroses are natural under the industrialism of today. Influenced by Fromm, she also thought that man's loss of security when he left the medieval system gave rise to a struggle for status and the longing to be "somebody." This cultural attitude surrounded by a civilization that was built upon individual competitiveness (and one might assume group competitiveness) ranked first in her thinking as a cause of neuroses. Almost the entire theme of her first book, *Neurotic Personality of Our Time,* deals with the conflict in culture, the struggle in society, and the tremendous amounts of endeavor one must face in adjusting to life conditions.

So deep was Horney's feeling about the imprint of society and culture upon man that she agreed with some sociologists that no such thing as normal psychology existed for all of mankind. One could only define psychological principles from the frame of reference of the culture within which the human operated. In the same sense she felt that "Thus, the term neurotic, while originally medical, cannot be used now without its cultural implications" (*The Neurotic Personality of Our Time,* p. 14). In dealing with aspects of normality, she later states, "The conception of what is normal varies not only with the culture but also within the same culture, in the course of time." As cultures changed, so did the concept of normality. All the above, of course, is to be found repeatedly in the literature of sociology.

It is obvious that Karen Horney was speaking primarily of anxiety as it manifests itself in neurotic behavior and not directly about character formulation as it is seen in personality theory. Without being guilty of any attenuations, however, one sees that she also spoke of an underlying personality formation beneath the syndromes of neuroses. Again, although not writing directly about personality theory, she continuously subsumed a basic set of motives *which, when disturbed,* create neuroses. It is out of this phenomenon that most writers find a personality theory in the work of Karen Horney.

Character Structure Principle

A third major theme which departs from Freud is important to the full development of Horney's theoretical position. Horney began the formulation by denying the pervasive effect of the repetition compulsion motive by which man is subconsciously driven to repeat earlier infantilisms throughout his life hoping to re-create the pleasures that the behavior once gave him. The fallacy of this position, she felt, is that one might just as well call anxiety in the child, for example, a precocious grown-up attitude as call anxiety in the adult an infantile reaction. In no way does Horney ignore the experiences of early childhood. To her, "Genetic understanding is useful only as long as it helps the functional understanding" (*The Neurotic Personality of Our Time*, p. 33). Although she admitted that a complete understanding of human behavior in the present is not possible without tracing behavior back to infantile conditions, she strongly believed the genetic approach confused the issue rather than clarified it. This, she felt, is particularly the case with the purist Freudian approach which leads the analyst to neglect existing conditions of society and culture which are so forceful in analysis.

Horney preferred to consider that ". . . the entirety of infantile experiences combines to form a certain *character structure*." (My italics.) *Character structure* means the total experiences the adult accumulates during his lifetime, experiences which in turn circumscribe his capacities. The character structure not only limits his abilities but may also increase his potentialities, effects which depend upon the accumulated experiences. Horney's idea is that the personality is not set by early infantile experiences, but that these are only a part of the always ongoing structuring of the personality. Events may happen when one is twenty or thirty, for example, that are as crucial to the individual's welfare as any earlier experience. Man is a product of his environment, and as his environment is always with him, it continues to change him. Life conditions mold the character. The crux of all character structure is human relationships. As we shall see later, character is not shaped by natural phenomena such as stars, storms, or seawater. Other people, and only other people, are instrumental in creating a human personality out of the stuff with which man enters the world at birth.

Man, however, does have the capacity for inner-directedness. He is more than a chip floating freely on the sea of life. In her final book, *Neurosis and Human Growth*, Horney deliberately used *neurosis* in the singular, for here she was concerned about what the analyst can do to help the single individual to grow and develop. "Self knowledge, then, is not an aim in itself, but a means of liberating the forces of spontaneous growth." Spontaneity is an inner personal characteristic and not a societally derived force. Self-knowledge is supremely important in the formulation of the personality, which she termed character structure. This is something no society can build for one but each person must build for himself. Man has a moral obligation and a moral privilege to seek self-knowledge. Horney chose to call this striving the *morality of evolution*. This means that man has the evolutionary forces within him to realize his greatest potential. Evolution comes from within and not from society.

Self-Concept Principle

This main theme from Horney's work is highly involved. The convolutions of the theme of the self-concept are woven throughout her writings and although unclear they nevertheless constitute a major aspect of her theory. The word *self* is most difficult to define technically. The Englishes in their extremely competent dictionary give the word *self* an extensive treatment and mention that there must be nearly one thousand combination forms of *self*.[1] Consequently, because of the divergent general usage and because of Horney's gradual development of the concept of self throughout her work, the ideas do not always emerge as plainly as one would wish.

The accompanying diagram traces the self-concept principle of Horney in its major aspects only. The ramifications of the concept must be left to the reader of her original work.

Starting with the real or actual self, man hopes to achieve a full realization of all his potentialities and to reach the maximum development. This dynamic, Horney feels, is universal. However, in order to achieve self-realization, man must have, or feels he must have, an idealized self before him to follow as a model. Thus he too frequently bypasses the genuine goal of self-realization and constructs behavioral activities patterned after the idealized self. He is therefore, seeking an unobtainable goal and is certain to end up with neuroticisms in his behavior. The idealized self (the perfect person) is never possible. Instead of returning to the "spontaneity" of the real self, man continues to drift away from what he actually is and to follow the image of what he would like to be. An image is false, illusory, and never true to reality. The farther man drifts toward an illusory goal, the more alienated he becomes from his actual self. The result is inner conflict, which leads to neurotic behavior through vain attempts to resolve the conflict. Somewhat akin to the Freudian superego, which tells man he must be the best person he can be, is the self-abnegation to which the neurotic turns, self-abnegation which makes him feel he "should" be doing this or he "should not" have done that. One of the mechanisms the neurotic employs in his futile effort to be like his idealized image is externalization. There are other mechanisms which we shall study in the principle of complementation–conflict, but for the moment we follow Horney's emphasis. *Externalization* means more than projection (the process of ascribing to others one's own unacknowledged desires or faults).

[1] H. B. English, and A. C. English, *A Comprehensive Dictionary of Psychological and Psychoanalytical Terms*, Longmans, 1958, pp. 484–485.

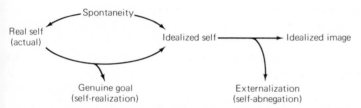

The externalizing individual not only shifts the responsibility toward some other object but actually *feels* that all these things take place outside himself. He has become so alienated from his actual self by trying to live in his idealized image that he can blame all his failures upon outside forces. Horney saw the process of externalization in many neurotic manifestations.

Horney's self-concept principle states that unless man "retains his spontaneity" or holds to being the "spontaneous individual" his real self becomes alienated and emotionally sick. Her plea was that through analysis, either by self and/or by the professional analyst, the individual can regain his will power and objective judgment, so that decisions he makes for himself will be reinstated in dignity.

Finally, as was stated previously in the character structure principle, a morality of evolution helps man to realize his true potentials and freely plays upon the constructive evolutionary forces with which he is endowed. Horney rejected the Freudian belief in the necessity of taming the *status naturae* in seeking the real self. The second alternative, of employing supernatural aids or of resorting to the strenuous ideal of reason and will, she felt is the proper endeavor of theology and philosophy, but not of herself, since she was unqualified to speak in these areas. The third possibility, of moral evolution, was the one she advocated—finding and using the real self as a directing force in life. This, she felt, is not only a moral privilege but also is a moral obligation for the individual himself and posterity.

Complementation–Conflict Principle

We come now to what the author considers Horney's most original and strongest theme. It is also the most renowned of her contributions to the field of personality theory. This theme appears in her fourth book, *Our Inner Conflicts*, 1945.

Although it may seem to the reader that the three types of reactions to life situations are typologies, Horney denied being a typologist. "I definitely do not intend in this chapter or the following to establish a new typology. A typology is certainly desirable but must be established on a much broader basis" (p. 48). Her advice is well taken. Her position was that all of us use all three methods of reacting to people. Only the highly neurotic individual utilizes one method to the exclusion of the other two. We (are we not all normal?) play all three melodies, our choice depending upon the situation and upon our individual talents; we slide from one effort to another in response to our fellow man. Horney, too, felt that it would be convenient to have a typology. It makes things so much easier to understand. Behavior can be categorized, then readily identified for therapy and also for the reactions necessary to everyday living. However, a broader base is necessary, a base which incorporates more than neurotic actions. In true typology there would be some who would use each of the ways of reacting to people—moving toward, against, or away from them—as their ordinary way of doing things. Since there are no normal people who use one of these reactions exclusively, a typology is not possible. The broad base is missing.

MAJOR ADJUSTMENT TECHNIQUES

The schematic presentation that follows is highly economical, verbally. Each word represents an involved extension of meaning that we now hope to portray.

(helpless)	moving	toward	people	(infant)
(hostile)	moving	against	people	(adolescent)
(isolate)	moving	away from	people	(adult)

Originally Horney became interested in the neurotic's inclination to be either helpless or hostile in conflict situations. This is the theme, somewhat, of her first three books. In *Our Inner Conflicts* she developed a third type of reaction: isolation from self and from others. The first type says, "If you love me, you won't hurt me." By accepting his helplessness to resolve conflict, he hopes desperately to win the affection of others and have them resolve conflicts for him. The second type states, "If I have power, no one can hurt me." He assumes that the world is hostile; therefore, the best way to reduce conflict and tension is to control the hostile elements of life. The third type has as his slogan, "If I withdraw, nothing can hurt me." His way of resolving conflict is to isolate himself from it both physically and mentally. Thus, we have the three types of neurotic behavior as Horney saw them: the helpless, the hostile, and the isolate.

The next term to consider is the word *moving* in the schematic presentation above. Horney considered life to be always moving, never static. Living things change, grow, develop, mature, get older, get bigger, never remain the same. Specifically, Horney felt this way about the human being. In the very few seconds, for example, that it has taken the reader to read these few sentences he has aged and therefore changed, imperceptibly, but nonetheless changed. Expanding this minute example to all the aspects of life, Horney believed that movement is a vital criterion of life. An assumption might be, therefore, that a definition of death is the cessation of movement. Consequently the living human personality must always be considered in terms of movement. Man's personality is forever in a state of flux. The motion may not be, and rarely is, a continuous flowing motion toward any specific goal. Possibly it is like that of the water fly skittering about the surface of a pond. A hummingbird in flight may even more accurately exemplify it, for the human personality is multidirectional. Whatever he does, Horney felt, man is never still. He cannot be. To live is to be in motion physically, mentally, emotionally, socially, or in any combinations of these.

Horney identified three general directions in which the personality moves. However, the directions of toward, against, and away from will not be discussed at the moment but postponed to a later section. The goal of movement is people. The trouble with man is man. The conflicts, anxieties, worries, neuroses that plague man's existence have their roots in his fellow men. His deepest concern is his relationships with the human beings that surround him. It matters not whether he knows them personally. It may be a matter of his reputation with the public at large that causes him anxiety. The few worries man may have about lightning, tornadoes, and extremely violent physical forces are transitory. The importance of external violence may be in the impression his conduct leaves upon others during the frightening experience. He may be terribly concerned about an act of nature, but in the end it is his reputation for bravery or cowardice that may dictate his behavior. The human being does not worry about trees or grass or houses. He worries about what others may say about his Dutch elm disease, his weedy and crabgrassed lawn, and his seedy and unpainted house. Weather doesn't worry him. Weather either promotes or delays his social outdoor contacts, such as swimming, golfing, or picnicking. Horney's entire rationale is pointed toward the only goal that man could possibly have: his fellow man.

Chronologically, the human personality goes through the three types of adjustive techniques as they are listed in the schematic presentation from infancy through adolescence to adulthood, each age level being oriented toward the corresponding method as shown. As an infant the human is more inclined to win with love. "If you love me, you won't hurt me," than to try hostility or isolation. The reason seems obvious. The young of any species (with possibly the exception of snakes!) is generally considered to be cute, cuddly, and attractive. Puppies, kittens, lion cubs, and so on appear to be lovable objects, and so, we may presume, does the human baby. It is natural for the baby to use his strongest asset: his loveableness. It is unnatural for the baby to be hostile simply because he is so very dependent upon others for food and sustenance. For the same reason it is unnatural for the baby to attempt to isolate himself.

Upon reaching adolescence the human may seem to act aggressively. He may become hostile toward the parents who nurtured him and found him so lovable in his babyhood. Being neither man nor child, the adolescent may move against people as he searches for the role he wishes to fulfill as an adult.

Especially in the later years of adulthood we may find the adjustment technique of moving away from people much more prominent than it ever was before. The older citizen feels he does not need to circulate in society as freely as he once did. A few good friends and quiet pastimes are preferable to the old noisy country club parties. He reasons that since he has lived this long and not been able to change the world dramatically, there is no use now trying to change it by participating in drives, and clubs, and movements of an uplifting nature. He will let the younger men with more energy do those things he once was so actively engaged in. The general pattern of behavior for the later adult is along the lines of withdrawal or isolation.

In summary, then, we may extend Horney's three types of neurotic adjustment techniques to follow a chronological pattern from moving toward people to moving against people to the isolationist desire to move away from people.

Before beginning a detailed analysis, we do well to remind ourselves that most people utilize all three techniques in handling the vicissitudes of everyday living. And we must always keep in mind that no human is entirely free from irregular behavior which either is neurotic or borders upon the neurotic. Thus, each of us singles out one of the three modes of behavior whenever conflicts become too difficult to resolve in an ordinary way. Supplementary methods of resolving conflicts are discussed in a subsequent section, "Minor Adjustment Techniques." However, it must be emphasized again that even though most of us employ all three techniques we are always inclined to utilize one more than the other two when anxiety becomes overpowering, a situation which occurs more often than we would wish.

We shall now examine the dynamics of neurotics who either move toward, against, or away from people, keeping in mind that we are also looking at ourselves when we are in deep stress. We complement the aspects of our personalities by the judicious use of the adjustment techniques. Conflict arises immediately when we begin to use any one technique exclusively. Our real self becomes unable to use spontaneously the most comfortable method based on our strongest assets. Conflict within ourselves (which grows out of conflict with our fellow man) may also arise when all three methods are so nearly equal in strength that a trivalence emerges. The result is a stalemate of action. This latter conflict is rare and is a neurotic trait rather than a behavioral pattern.

Complementation and conflict of the trichotomized adjustment techniques occupy a major position in the principles of Horney's work.

MOVING TOWARD PEOPLE (HELPLESSNESS)

The slogan that best identifies this technique is "If you love me, you will not hurt me. If I give in, I shall not be hurt." Beginning with the premise that we do not hurt the things we love, the individual makes supreme efforts to win the affection of all who surround him. Love protects. He concludes that if he cannot beat them, it is best to join them. The following points summarize his behavior when inner conflicts upset the equilibrium of life.

1. He has tried and tried to be superior. All the methods he has used have seemed to bring unsatisfactory results and to leave him dissatisfied. At length he accepts his own helplessness to cope with conflict within himself and conflict as it has developed toward others. By accepting helplessness he can use it as a device to win the approval of others. He is the "nice guy," the one we all love. We enjoy his company because, always affable, he makes every effort to win us over. His own vanity is subjugated to the will and pleasure of his friends, for he must have friends. "Love conquers all."

2. Once he has accepted his helplessness to cope with figures stronger than himself, the person who moves toward people makes a strong effort to feel safe by attaching himself to the strongest person and/or group willing to accept him. Because of the feeling of belonging and support which the group gives him, actually or vicariously, he feels stronger and more capable of confronting life.

3. If he fails, others in the group will come to his rescue. Even if no particularly identifiable group will accept him and protect him, this individual still persists in making supreme efforts to gain favor with all. He suffers bitterly if rejected. His psyche cannot stand lack of love and affection. Almost nothing is too much to ask of him. He will do favors, lend or give his property, be slavishly attentive to the desires and wants of others, always be alert to kindnesses he may perform, and never lose sight of the objective for which he seeks: to make others obligated to him through what he does for them. That he does this in so dedicated a manner is unknown to him. The golden rule is his meat and drink, for by following it he not only gets credit for being a "good guy" but buys affection by making people indebted to him for past favors. "Do unto others as you would have them do unto you" is his way to win friends and influence people.

4. Failure to achieve his goal of winning affection frequently turns him into a hypochondriac or a victim of multiple psychosomatic complaints. He reasons that society always commiserates with an invalid. He realizes that society frowns upon kicking an underdog. He finds comfort in the phrase "poor little ol' me."

5. When he marries or seeks a dating partner, he overwhelms his loved one with dedicated affection. The relationship is based upon long selfless service to win the affection of the affianced. He is inclined to date and marry a stronger individual than himself because such a one can give him strength and protection. Relationships with others as weak as he is soon collapse. How can one lean on a reed? He finds it impossible to do for another what he himself wants done for him. Each one in this situation clings to the other, but the relationship cannot sustain itself; the one who moves toward people consumes them with his love. Two such people simply cancel each other out.

If such a marriage does come about (mainly through the efforts of others), it may end in divorce. This causes their friends to be highly confused, for "they both seem to be such nice people." As a slogan to describe the love seeker the reader may pick one of the following song titles: "All of me, why not take all of me" or "I can't give you anything but love, Baby."

6. We may assume that the helpless individual with the preemptive desire for affection developed in somewhat the following manner. One warm Sunday afternoon when he was a small child the ice-cream truck with its tinkling bell came past his home. At the moment his father was recovering from a heavy Sunday dinner by lying half-asleep on the living-room sofa listening to the baseball broadcast. Suddenly the father is awakened by the child's insistent coaxing for an ice-cream cone. The child continues aggressively to demand a treat. The father refuses. The child repeats his demands, howling louder and louder. The father is thoroughly irritated. The child gets a slap on his bottom. The next attempt to get ice cream is through sulking and withdrawal. The isolating approach is no more successful than the aggressive maneuver. This time his father goes back to sleep. Finally, the youngster tiptoes up to his daddy and gives him a big kiss. "Shucks," says the father. "What a sweet kid. Why not let him have some ice cream right after dinner? After all, you're only young once!" Using love and affection wins the prize of ice cream. Having tried all three methods, the child may eventually perfect the love approach. "I get a lot of ice cream that way." The above anecdote is imaginary, but it illustrates how one becomes successful in using one adjustment technique, after having tried all three. The motto is "You can catch more flies with sugar than you can with vinegar."

MOVING AGAINST PEOPLE (HOSTILITY)

The individual committed to this technique says, "If I have power, no one can hurt me." Although, according to Horney, all of us use the technique at times when we feel it is appropriate to the situation, this type of neurotic overemphasizes aggressiveness in contacts with people. The following summary brings out the most salient rationale for his behavior.

1. He accepts and takes for granted that he lives in a hostile world. Consciously or subconsciously, he is determined to fight and resist the hostility around him. To the personalities who move against people "It's a dog-eat-dog world."

2. The primary feeling here is a desire to be strong and defeat the opposition, whoever and wherever it may be. Because there is an implicit distrust of others—"What's their angle?"—the defenses are always up. All human motives are suspect. "What's in it for him?" The desire to protect oneself at all times and to come out fighting overemphasizes power and strength in all situations. The wisest philosophy is "Might makes right."

3. Not all aggressive actions are overt, however. The hostile individual may try hard to help others by the most humanitarian methods, but implicit in the help he gives others is an unacknowledged gift to himself of power and control over them. This individual may be attracted to social welfare work without realizing that his job satisfaction derives from feeling superiority and control over welfare patients. Ministers and teachers and doctors may be following this dynamic of feeling superior by helping others less fortunate than themselves. These neurotically motivated individuals may be quite unaware of the inner motivations of their actions, or, by appearing to help others, they may be quite openly striving for superiority over those weaker than themselves. Serving on club committees to win the approval of others may serve a person well until he can be elected to the top office in the organization and *then* change things to suit himself. The lures, devices, and gimmicks he uses to influence people may be based on the slogan "Never give a sucker an even break."

4. The hostile person's regard for the first type, who strives to move toward people and be loved by them, is touched with a mixture of contempt and amusement. The affectionate one is so soft and vulnerable. He typifies him as a "sloppy sentimentalist."

5. His behavior in dating and in marriage have much the same characteristics. He dates only the best on the campus. For his social partner he wants either the beauty queen or the girl with money, privileges, and a convertible. Again, his method of obtaining these may be to use subtle flattery, but the end in view is to become associated with someone who will enhance *his* status with others. In marriage he also seeks a partner who has beauty, brains, charm, or money, all of which reflect *his* good taste in a wife and will bring to the marriage more than a fair share of success. He eschews the weak and clinging partner who longs to be protected, unless she has money or prestige which he can share. Although the masculine pronoun is used it is to be understood that this kind of neuroticism applies to women as well as to men. All in all, "It costs so little more to go first class" in love and marriage.

6. In reviewing the development pattern of this type we refer again to the small child desiring ice cream. This time he raises so much furor with his father that the father finally digs into his pocket for the necessary money just to "Keep the kid quiet for a minute and get a little peace around here." Enough successes with the aggressive method gradually develop the technique in dealing with people. Thus the child reasons, knowingly or unknowingly, "You may as well get your fair share of things. Everybody else does, so why not watch out for number one?"

MOVING AWAY FROM PEOPLE (ISOLATION)

The isolation may be either physical or mental, or both. According to Horney and others, one does not have to be removed physically in order to be isolated from a group of people. Isolation of a mental nature is probably most pronounced in the schizophrenic, catatonic type. The individual who isolates himself to the point of neurotic behavior to solve his problems says, "If I withdraw, nothing can hurt me."

1. The individual who has the tendency to withdraw or the neurotic who follows this pattern exclusively wants neither to belong nor to fight. His strongest wish is to remain apart. Because people are the main sources of unhappiness and conflict, his overwhelming desire is to be entirely free of entanglements. Complete independence guarantees for him no heartbreaking involvements. If he can establish that he is not dependent upon others and especially that others may not look to him for support, he keeps trouble out of his life. He lives for himself and by himself. He feels that he has not much in common with others and that they do not understand him anyway. If questioned about his aloofness and his general pattern of nonparticipation in society, he responds with, "Am I my brother's keeper?" His answer is, "No."

2. Lacking the normal amount of social participation, the isolationist looks to books, dreams, fantasies, and art forms for recreation and relaxation. Thus he builds up a world of his own, and because it is his exclusive property, he can do with it what he wants. He can change it, expand it, or destroy it and build another. The democratic process or the fight for survival he can ignore. What he has is his alone because he made it that way. Consequently, much of his manipulation must come through vicarious means. He writes, he dreams, he reads literature for the stuff with which to make his world immune from attack. His slogan: "There's nothing so companionable as a good book."

3. In order to exist apart from others, either mentally or geographically, one must be strong enough to support one's own demands. The weak and those who bore themselves, therefore, cannot adopt this mode of adjustment. The isolationist is self-sufficient. He has to be. There is no one else to fall back upon in time of need or crisis. If he cannot be proficient in many things, he restricts his existence to the few things he can do well. He takes up gardening, or the hermit existence of caretaker, or any type of occupation and avocation which he can hold for himself, though it may be limited in scope. Whether his strengths are broad or narrow, he becomes an expert for his own pleasure, contrary to what the crowd may be doing. He feels popularity is a fool's game. Popularity is given by others, and they can take it away any time they want to. His response is, "Only the strong can stand being unpopular."

4. To perpetuate the role of individuality he becomes an extreme individualist. The moment the crowd discovers his private hideaways, he deserts them for even more remote places. It matters not that his "Shangri-La" is inconvenient and inaccessible. He wants to be out of season all year long. To be different is to harbor jealously one's own uniqueness. To follow the crowd is anathema. "The public be damned."

5. Dating is a matter of convenience. He dates because that is the only way he will be admitted to certain activities he might enjoy. In dating he seeks a partner much like himself who can also withdraw into silence for the evening's engagement. He avoids the affectionate type who moves toward people as an incessant talker and table hopper. Under no circumstance does he care to date an aggressive individual, even if it means missing the event. The first type as a date might make strong overtures toward getting involved as a steady companion, a situation which would threaten his control of life. The second type is the very kind of companion he hates, for by that person he is controlled and manipulated. Marriage is postponed until the late twenties or thirties if it occurs at all. The single life is to be preferred, but he may chance upon another companion who also treasures solitude and withdrawal from people. For them the sexual aspects of marriage are transitory and solely for the satisfaction of a physical appetite. Intimacy in the sex act requires a state of emotion impossible for them to sustain. Marriage is a contractual agreement to live together, arrived at because living together is convenient. The long-time single male reasons that restaurant food is monotonous and expensive. Laundries are costly and bothersome. The regimentation of daily living bores him and creates inconveniences which keep him from enjoying other things. The services he now needs, if his parents are no longer living and he has to fend for himself, become a burden. Thus, if he can find someone who does not make too strong a demand upon his emotions, he is inclined to marry as a convenient means toward easier living. On the opposite side, the female who is an isolate by choice, be it conscious or subconscious, arrives at a marriage through somewhat similar circumstances. For one thing, marriage will eliminate her having to work for a living in a world of people. Perhaps she reasons that a husband is away most of the day in his occupation, a fact which gives her even more time than before to enjoy her own solitary pursuits. If the right, nondemanding male comes along, she might be very attracted to marriage. Being supported, having a secure economic future, and having fine things of her own which she does not have to share with a mother or roommate appeal to her very much. Or perhaps the marriage will not interfere with her chosen occupation, since her husband, too, is willing to make it a working partnership, much like a business agreement. By pooling resources, each can have fine records, furniture, books, paintings, and the art forms they both enjoy so much. Children in such a marriage are upsetting. If children do result, they are quickly channeled into proper slots, with a minimum of affection. Isolation-driven people usually utilize contraceptive devices with practiced regularity.

6. The rigidity of isolating one's feelings from the control of others may have had its source in the following: In his earliest years the child gives his love unstintingly to a mother, father, or some other person. In the person he

loves are all the virtues and sustenance he needs for love and understanding. Perhaps he loves not wisely but too well. In the course of events the object of his love may at some time deny him. In his own mind the denial is brutal and open. He finds that his favorite love object—Mommy, Daddy, or both—also loves his baby brother or sister. Or there was a divorce and in the proceedings they bandied him about like a piece of property. Whatever the cause, he discovers that his emotions, his trust, his faith, his hopes, his objects of unquestioning love are now denied him. We may assume that the experience is so terrifyingly traumatic that he vows never again to give his heart to another person, never again to lose control over his feelings. Once caused pain by having another in possession of his emotions, he insulates himself from further harm. Perhaps as he pursues an isolated pathway from people, he discovers that loneliness is preferable to heartache. The result is a determination not to have a hasty heart for anyone, and to "never wear your heart on your sleeve."

In the preceding discussion of Horney's three types of adjustment techniques the illustrations have been overdrawn to highlight the deeper neurotic kinds of behavior. Overemphasis of neurotic reaction in moving toward, against, or away from people may make easier an understanding of some of the basic concepts of Horney's theory of neuroses from which we have drawn a general theory of personality.

The conflict that arises out of inability to utilize the three types of adjustment techniques was originally presented as ten neurotic needs in her 1942 publication, *Self-Analysis*. The difference between the ability of the normal person to integrate these needs and avoid conflict, and the lack of ability of the neurotic to do the same, is a matter of degree. Even though the normal personality is able to complement one or more of the following ten needs with others of the ten needs, he has more success with some of them than with others. The deeply involved neurotic fails with most of them in trying to integrate them into a life pattern (character structure) and consequently drifts farther and farther toward an unrealistic, idealized image. Despite his many failures with the ten needs the neurotic, too, has better success with some than with others. As a final result, for both the neurotic and the normal individual, adjustment is a matter of degree: variable degrees of the needs and variable degrees of success in complementation between the normal and neurotic.

TEN NEUROTIC NEEDS

Following are the ten needs from which Horney evolved her three basic adjustment techniques: moving toward, against, and away from people. All personalities have these needs to some extent. The neurotic has them to an overpowering degree. Most of us complement these needs. The neurotic cannot.

Neurotic Need	Salient Feature	Tendency of Moving in Relation to People
1. affection and approval	live to please others and win love	toward
2. dominant partner in life	give in and be protected by strong mate in exchange for pervasive love	toward
3. narrowly confined limits of life	to be ultrareactionary, conservative, retain status quo, retire to background	away from
4. power	glorify power and strength, despise weakness	against
5. exploitation of others	win at games, always be dominant	against
6. prestige	have name in the newspapers, be recognized	against (?)
7. personal admiration	have others see you as your idealized image	against
8. ambition in personal achievement	have a consuming desire to be rich, famous, important regardless of cost to self and others	against
9. self-sufficiency and independence	go to extreme lengths to avoid being obligated to anyone	away from
10. perfection and unassailability	be flawless because of hypersensitivity to criticism	away from (?)

Thus, out of her rich background of experience in psychoanalysis and using the above ten neurotic needs, Karen Horney drew out the three types of reactions toward people which man may use as he lives his life.

MINOR ADJUSTMENT TECHNIQUES, AUXILIARY
APPROACHES TO ARTIFICIAL HARMONY

In addition to the trichotomized approach discussed previously Horney suggested a lower level of effort which man employs to integrate the opposing forces he meets in dealing with people. Although the following techniques are false attempts to reduce conflict, Horney felt that they are more common than the deeper neurotic levels of moving toward, against, or away from people. To some extent, then, more of us use the auxiliary approaches to artificial harmony than use the ten neurotic methods and the three subsequent techniques.

Karen Horney did not deny Freud's ego defense mechanisms, and her approaches are supplementary to Freud's contribution. Horney called the seven approaches the *protective structure*, which the personality erects to ease the basic conflicts relating to self and others.

1. *Blind spots*—When a basic inner conflict becomes unmanageable, we may be inclined to ignore the conflicting force. Disregard of behavior which does not fit the picture of our idealized self is an artificial attempt to bring balance into life. Because the self is oblivious to the true situation, there is no direct solution to the problem. Because the attempted solution is artificial, it cannot be expected to last very long. Conflict once again emerges. Blind spots occur, for example, when a mother is unable to tolerate the thought of being a poor mother. By ignoring the reports she hears of her son's poor behavior she spares herself, for the moment at least, the revealing truth of her own inadequacies as a mother. Students who ignore the devastating effect that not studying can have upon grades may have a blind spot. The utilization of this particular protective structure is generally a matter of degree. Depending on the amount of conflict involved, we may develop stronger blind spots for some phenomena than for others. Between individuals there may also be differing degrees of blind spots. False though the success of the method is, by simply ignoring an unhappy fact we are temporarily persuaded that it does not exist.

2. *Compartments*—Compartmenting aspects of life is, according to Horney, the result of inability to integrate the various roles we must sustain in life, so that one has two or more sets of rules which are contradictory. The professor who is adamantly opposed to cheating by the students in his classroom, and yet cheats at golf or bridge, is guilty of compartmentalizing his values about honesty. The ruthless businessman who is in turn a devoted religious worker, espousing the highest Christian principles on Sunday, is also guilty of making compartments in his life. Because it is difficult always to follow a clear-cut policy, individuals may turn to acting one way in one kind of situation and a reverse way in another kind of situation. This Horney called *compartmenting*.

3. *Rationalization*—To Horney, as to many other writers, *rationalization* means to be "giving *good* reasons to excuse conduct, rather than giving the *real* reason" to explain conduct. Somewhat as an extension of externalization, rationalization is a low form of self-deception based upon erroneous reasoning. Its damage to the personality's ability to complement the forces of life is not to be underestimated, she felt, because of the pervasive use of this artificial approach to harmony. Horney saw a wide range in what is rationalized as well as in the methods employed. The breadth of the technique and its adaptability make it one of the most popular of all seven protective structures.

Also, because it requires a conscious mental process akin to reasoning, the practitioner feels he is fully justified in its use and hence it becomes difficult to control. Rationalization is a primary method of trying to eliminate the discrepancy between the actual (real) self and the sought-after, idealized self. Examples from the activities of everyday life are numerous. The football team that lost because it rained (failing to realize that it also rained on the opponent), the student who fails examinations because he gets "nervous" (failing to realize that practically no serious student takes an examination calmly), the housewife whose home is a shambles because she has children (failing to realize that some control can be exercised over children and that millions of housewives who also have children manage to keep some semblance of order in the home) illustrate the phenomenon of rationalization.

4. Excessive self-control—Originally Horney was so impressed with the power of this auxiliary device to achieve artificial harmony that it was included as a part of the ten neurotic needs. The openness of the technique and the tremendous willpower needed to sustain excessive self-control have, however, brought it into the realm of the artificial devices. Horney is not speaking against the value of willpower and control of self in a civilized society. She is concerned with slavish rigidity, conscious or subconscious, with excessive self-control which grows out of the feeling of panic the personality may have if he lets himself go even once. Most of us must in the ordinary course of living control our appetites and desires. When we relax this control of self, we do not lose all self-control. In many cases we gain a renewed and more successful control of self for use in the future. Moreover, the punishment following lack of self-control frequently teaches us the value of control. Not so, however, for the individual who practices compulsive self-control, for the prospect of one failure is so truly frightening to him that he must at all costs maintain rigid self-control or collapse.

5. Arbitrary rightness—To the person utilizing this device he can do no worse than be indecisive about something. By settling an issue once and for all he gives himself a double-barreled protection of being free from doubt and free from outside influences. Once he has made the decision that something is wrong, for example, he no longer need worry about that. It is wrong. It will always be wrong. To him, equivocation is a sign of weak, vacillating, simple minds. To be doubt-free is to be strong. Reopening a question is the surest road to conflict. Conflict leads to unhappiness, and with his fear of losing his idealized image, he cannot tolerate conflict. Positiveness is synonymous with purity. In Horney's opinion this state of being arbitrarily right grows stronger with each apparent success the personality feels it has obtained by refusal to entertain doubts. If uninfluenced by others, the person becomes more and more positive about everything until no doubts remain about anything—anything, that is, which has been "reasonably" thought out. The personality having an equal desire to move against people and to move away from people can be expected to use the minor adjustment technique of arbitrary rightness. To have opinions one must necessarily be strong enough to come to conclusions and to hold them regardless of the opinions of opposing forces. This is a characteristic of moving against people. Likewise, to avoid conflicting data one must remove himself from the influences of others. This is a characteristic of moving away from people. Both types of behavior assure a protection for the response of arbitrary rightness, such as we may find in an aged male who has a foreign background where males are strong and unquestioned. Being in a strange country he retires from its invidious influences and develops stronger and stronger opinions, substantiated by the conflicting dynamics of his background.

6. *Elusiveness*—Opposite to the above protective structure is the defense of never making up one's mind about anything, simple or complex. The value in this method is that if one never commits himself to anything he can never be wrong. If he is never wrong, he can never be criticized for being wrong. When one is faced with decisions, the obvious diversion is to reexamine the past, discuss the enormous variations which may be drawn from any set of circumstances, and postpone a decision until all the facts are in. Since it may be impossible to gather all available data, a decision is therefore unwarranted and impossible to make at this time. By being elusive one subverts any and all decisions for which one may eventually be held to account. The extension of elusiveness operates in the following manner: A student will say, "I could get good grades *if* I studied." The student will not, however, study. Studying commits him to taking a position. Once he has taken a position to study and does so, he no longer can be elusive. If he should fail *now*, there is no one to blame but himself! The criticism that may follow concerns his lack of mental ability. Prior to this one might criticize him for being lazy, which he considers in a quasihumorous way to be regrettable, but all too human. The criticism now maligns his intelligence, an aspersion his ego may not be able to accept. Thus the student may be elusive about trying in college. If he tries and fails, he has no excuse. If he never commits himself to study, he always has the excuse that he could get good grades if he tried. In the end he fails college anyway but *not* on the grounds of his lack of mental ability. Horney feels evasion is the dullard's device.

7. *Cynicism*—The last protective structure in Horney's treatment of the auxiliary approaches to artificial harmony as a minor adjustment technique deals with the denial of moral reality. The cynic plays it safe by not believing in anything with an ethical or moral structure. If he follows a pattern of total disbelief, he is then disappointed in nothing. Because he believes in nothing,

he avoids the heartaches that come from having believed in something that ends in failure. The device he uses is to deprecate any value which seems to hold forth hope. Probably growing from a background of repeated failure, his decision is never to believe in a value system again. In this way he avoids the failures of the past. By denying and deriding man's pet goals he relieves himself of the tortuous task of deciding what he believes in himself. Better be sneering than sorry.

SUMMARY

All of the preceding methods come within the framework of man's attempt to integrate the complementary forces in his life in order to achieve the actualization of a real self and in so doing to avoid the pain of conflict. Horney sees most of these devices as neuroses, but the line between normality and neuroses is variable. The neuroses may exist within the self or within interpersonal relationships. The result of using protective devices is a reduction of the inner conflicts that beset man. We may now examine the final principle of self-analysis as the author perceives it in Horney's work.

Self-Analysis Principle

Karen Horney believed that life itself gives balance to man's existence. Although this idea appears to be an off-theme to the dynamics of man, it was not so to Horney. Adjustment to problems is as much a part of the core of man's existence as are the deeper inner dynamics he may possess. All of the above are part of her answer to the question of why man behaves the way he does and as such belong in a general theory of behavior.

Horney asked the provocative question How did man ever solve his emotional problems before psychiatry and psychology came on the scene? In no way did she demean the role of these two, but she did hold to the proposition that man must have had some success in solving his own problems before the refinements of psychiatry and psychology developed. Otherwise he would have perished. Using the premise that the human race has within it certain alleviating factors, Horney proposed that we not lose sight of the tremendous value of self-analysis as an aid to emotional problem solving. Although she did not deny the extra benefits which may come from professional help, her primary thesis was that we must hold to past benefits while we continue to improve current practices. In order to clarify her position as well as to aid those interested in self-analysis, she brought out her third book in 1942, *Self-Analysis.*

In support of her thesis, Horney felt that all of us who are not psychotically involved do some elementary analysis of our own behavior, possibly every day. Rather than ignoring this prevalent phenomenon she advocated training it so that it may operate more efficiently and with greater insight.

Ultimately, Horney suggested, all therapy involves self-analysis, and the true role of the therapist is to make analysis and manipulation of self easier and more profitable. No therapist can change human behavior without the involvement of the client. Just as no one can learn for another (teaching is basically preparing the ground), neither can a therapist take the client's place in analysis. The client analyzes himself.

Horney was prompt in admitting that extreme neurotics and psychotics are unable to help themselves in the initial stages of therapy. Operation "bootstrap" is not possible for those deeply mired in emotional problems. What she hoped to do with her severest cases was to bring them to the point of taking responsibility for their own therapy through insight into their own dynamics. But, although severe neuroses should be in the hands of experts, man can go a long way in disentangling his own conflicts.

In some ways self-analysis may be less dangerous to the patient's welfare than analysis controlled exclusively by the therapist. There will be times when the client wishes to avoid painful references to past injuries. If the therapist can do no more than uncover old scars with no improvement in their condition, Horney felt the client's wisdom might be the better guide. Not all problems which the therapist may uncover are amenable to therapy. The very act of digging around in the client's past may bring out more problems than the therapist can possibly handle. For reasons such as these Horney believed a tremendous value should be placed on helping the client develop his capacities for self-analysis.

Horney further proposed that a valuable advantage might be gained for future problem areas if the client were led to develop his own techniques of analysis. Patients who become overly dependent upon their therapist because of prolonged leaning upon him are poor prognostic risks. The moment a new problem arises, they can hardly wait to get back to the therapist for more help. Karen Horney felt that the client is much farther along the road toward emancipation from the therapist if he is given the skills to analyze his own behavior.

It should be added that Horney was discussing analysis of one's own development, conduct in daily life, resolvement of restrictive problem areas, and skills necessary to live in concert with fellow man. The practice of deep therapy she reserved for the professionally trained expert. The crucial point of her position is that living in this world as we know it contains factors which build man up as well as tear him down. A loving spouse, children laughing, a lovely fall day, all are factors in bringing therapy to man's problems without recourse to psychiatric help. By analyzing our dynamics, she felt, we can go a long, long way toward keeping emotionally intact and toward solving minor emotional problems. This we have done in the past; to lose its benefits would serve man poorly.

EXPLAINING HUMAN BEHAVIOR VIA
HORNEY'S SOCIAL PSYCHOLOGICAL THEORY

The reader may now attempt to use Horney's theory to explain human behavior in marriage, perversions, suicide, lawbreaking, belief in a supranatural being, humor, smoking, play and recreation, psychoses–neuroses. Three different explanations for specific behavior may arise, corresponding to the three directions of movement in relation to people suggested by Horney.

PREDICTING HUMAN BEHAVIOR VIA
HORNEY'S SOCIAL PSYCHOLOGICAL THEORY

Like most other theories, Horney's does not lend itself to predictions that one can make either personally or objectively through scientific and laboratory work. There is an undercurrent of prognostic feeling running through the statements of her published work. The general tone is that we may expect neurotic behavior from individuals who behave in ways which Horney discusses. One may assume that in the ongoing daily therapy of their profession all psychoanalysts proceed perforce on some basis of better-than-guessing what the future holds for their clients. Just as the physician conducts his practice along lines of predictable (within limits) patient behavior under the influence of prescribed medicines, the psychoanalyst presumes through diagnosis that certain therapeutic approaches will bring forth desired and predictable patient behavior. However, these are pragmatic facets of clinical insight coming out of the practice of therapy, and consequently one does not find such predictions in the published work of a therapist although it is a part of his practice of therapy.

Personal Prediction

The reader must ask for himself whether man goes through helplessness, hostility, and isolation as he lives through infancy, adolescence, and the middle and later years of adulthood. May we assume that this is a predictable course of an individual's life? This question and others to follow may have for the reader in his own personal prediction a modicum of face validity although no evidence may exist from research directed toward these phenomena.

We as individuals interested in our own personalities may predict that some or all of the following will apply in our lives:

1. The seven auxiliary approaches to artificial harmony—blind spots, compartments, rationalization, excessive control, arbitrary rightness, elusiveness, and cynicism—operate and will continue to operate.

2. The historical evidence of the past is that humanity is getting better and will continue to improve in the future.

3. All of us strive to create an idealization of ourselves which, if over-emphasized, may become too illusory and lead us to follow an image of what we think our idealized selves are.

4. When we are in deep stress and have exhausted the usual means of resolving our conflicts, we ultimately move toward people, or against them, or away from them.

5. Man will continue to solve many of his emotional problems and thus avoid deeper neuroses by self-analysis and by his own capacity to change his behavior.

Scientific or Laboratory Prediction

The direct influence of the work of many outstanding theorists upon scientifi-cally rigorous research is not easily determined. There appear to be no con-spicuous studies of the three types of neurotic behavior, yet one must believe that Horney's influence has been strong among psychoanalysts nonetheless. Perhaps her strength may be in operational factors during therapy.

Whatever the predictive success of Horney's work, the results are probably buried in the success she and her students have had in the ongoing business of improving behavior through psychoanalysis.

■ SUMMARY

Departing from its original content as Freudian-indoctrinated psychoanalysis, Karen Horney's work can probably be best summarized by referring to the six principles extracted from her work, with special emphasis upon the three types of neurotic maneuvers that are possible when man fails to integrate the conflicting forces in his society.

Optimism–Positivism Principle. Mankind has the capacity to change. The human personality is not rigidly held to the formations of early childhood.

Society–Culture Principle. Man's personality is a product of his inter-actions with other men. These interactions are bounded by the society in which he lives, as well as the past societies in which he lived, and the cultural rules he has had to follow.

Character Structure Principle. Throughout his life man creates a struc-tured character, which may be changed. In general it remains constant within any given environment and is inclined to remain constant through life. Rather than prescribing how an individual will behave, it sets the limits within which he has free choice to behave.

Self-Concept Principle. *Self-concept* means, first, "an awareness of one-self as a human being," and second, the "importance or significance of oneself in the roles of life." It also distinguishes the person's self from all other selves he sees around him. The actual or real self is all that we have to operate with in life. Because we would like to be better than we are, or more important than we are, we may construct idealized pictures of ourselves. If these pictures become more important than the real self, we may depart too widely from the real self and establish an unobtainable image. Inability to reach the idealized image may cause us to blame others by the process of externalization.

Complementation–Conflict Principle. The writer considers this the major theme and contribution of Horney's theory. There are two divisions: the major adjustment techniques and the minor adjustment techniques. The prominent features of the major adjustment techniques are highlighted in Figure 6.

Out of the following ten neurotic needs Horney felt that the individual tends to respond in one of three ways to other individuals—toward, against, and away from them. The ten neurotic needs are these: affection and approval, dominant partner in life, confined limits of life, power, exploitation of others, prestige, personal admiration, ambition in personal achievement, self-sufficiency and independence, and perfection and unassailability.

Figure 6 indicates the three types of reactions to people that all of us have a tendency to duplicate. When we are unable to complement their

"Wait for me"

"C'mon get going"

"Leave me alone, I'm thinking"

FIGURE 6. *Diagrammatic summary of Horney's theory.*

forces to ease conflicts, we become fixed at one of the three types into a
neurotic pattern.

The minor adjustment techniques call for auxiliary approaches to artificial harmony in order to complement the conflicting forces of life. Horney
discusses seven of these: blind spots, compartments, rationalization, excessive
self-control, arbitrary rightness, elusiveness, and cynicism.

Self-Analysis Principle. Horney feels that man has the capacity to analyze his own dynamics with enough skill to solve many, but not all, of his own
problems. Man has always done this with some measure of success and he will
continue to do so in the future. Life itself has many curative powers. Man
must learn to use these through developing the ability to analyze his own
role.

BIBLIOGRAPHY

PRIMARY SOURCES

BOOKS

Horney, K., *The Neurotic Personality of Our Time.* New York: Norton, 1937.
Horney, K., *New Ways in Psychoanalysis.* New York: Norton, 1939.
    Reprint in paper of 1964 ed.
Horney, K., *Self-Analysis.* New York: Norton, 1942.
    Reprint in paper, 1968.
Horney, K., *Our Inner Conflicts.* New York: Norton, 1945.
Horney, K., *Neurosis and Human Growth.* New York: Norton, 1950.
Horney, K., *Are You Considering Psychoanalysis?* New York: Norton, 1962.
    Paperback of original 1946 paper.
Horney, K., *Feminine Psychology.* New York: Norton, 1967.
    Many of Horney's original German papers edited by H. Kelman; per-
    mission granted by Horney's three daughters.

PERIODICALS

Horney, K., Culture and neurosis, *Amer. Sociol. Rev.*, 1936, *1*, 221–230.
Horney, K., Values and problems, *Amer. J. Psychoanal.*, 1952, *12*, 80–81 (ab-
    stract).

Kelman, H. (chairman), F. A. Weiss, P. Tillich, and K. Horney, Human nature can change: A symposium, *Amer. J. Psychoanal.*, 1952, *12*, 62–68.

Horney, K. (moderator), Constructive forces in the therapeutic process: A round table discussion, *Amer. J. Psychoanal.*, 1953, *13*, 14–19.

Horney, K., Culture and aggression: Some considerations and objections to Freud's theory of instinctual drives toward death and destruction, *Amer. J. Psychoanal.*, 1960, *20*, 130–138.

Horney, K., The technique of psychoanalytic therapy, *Amer. J. Psychoanal.*, 1968, *28*, 3–12.

> Horney's first paper (originally published in 1917) on psychoanalytic technique.

TAPE RECORDINGS

Horney, K. *Can Human Nature Change?* (G. W. Kisker, ed.), Sound Seminars, No. 101, Cincinnati, Ohio.

SUGGESTED READINGS

BOOKS

Brown, I. A. C., *Freud and the Post-Freudians.* Baltimore: Penguin, 1961.

> Horney, Fromm, and Sullivan also included.

Kelman, H., *New Perspectives in Psychoanalysis: Contributions to Karen Horney's Holistic Approach.* New York: Norton, 1965.

Kelman, H. (ed.), *Advances in Psychoanalysis: Contributions to Karen Horney's Holistic Approach.* New York: Norton, 1964.

Munroe, R. L., *Schools of Psychoanalytic Thought.* New York: Holt, Rinehart & Winston, 1955.

> Analysis and integration of Freud, Adler, Jung, Rank, Fromm, Horney, Sullivan, *et al.*

Sahakian, W. S., *Psychology of Personality: Readings in Theory.* Chicago: Rand McNally, 1965.

> Neo-Freudianism and sociology with an excerpt from Horney's writings.

Saltzman, L., *Developments in Psychoanalysis.* New York: Grune & Stratton, 1962.

> The innovations of Horney and Sullivan.

Sarason, I. G., *Personality: An Objective Approach.* New York: Wiley, 1966.

> Treats Fromm and Horney as equals.

PERIODICALS

Cameron, D. E., Karen Horney: A pioneer in the science of human relations. *Amer. J. Psychoanal.*, 1954, *14*, 19–29.

Cantor, M. B., Karen Horney on psychoanalytic technique: Mobilizing construc tive forces. *Amer. J. Psychoanal.*, 1967, *27*, 188–199.

> "Compiles and edits Horney's lectures on the subject, material from her writings, and publications of her colleagues."

Endler, N. S., A behavioristic interpretation of the psychotherapy system of Karen Horney, *Canad. Psychologist*, 1965, *6*, 188–200.

James, W. T., K. Horney, and E. Fromm, In relation to Alfred Adler, *Indiv Psychol. Bull.*, 1947, *6*, 105–116.

Kelman, N., Karen Horney, M.D., 1885–1952, *Psychoanal. Rev.*, 1953, *40*, 191–193.

Kelman, N., In memoriam: Karen Horney, M.D., 1885–1952, *Amer. J. Psycho anal.*, 1954, *14*, 5–7.

Kelman, N., What is psychotherapy? The viewpoint of the Karen Horney group, *Ann. Psychother. Monogr.*, 1959, No. 1, 37–43.

Kelman, N., Karen Horney of feminine psychology, *Amer. J. Psychoanal.*, 1967, *27*, 163–183.

Lussheimer, P., N. Kelman, E. Kilpatrick, H. Gershman, E. A. Gutheil, and C. Oberndorf, Tributes to Karen Horney, *Amer. J. Pychoanal.*, 1954, *14*, 8–13.

Oberndorf, C. P., Dr. Karen Horney, *Int. J. Psycho. Anal.*, 1953, *34*, 154–155.

Robbins, I., An analysis of Horney's concept of the real self, *Educ. Theor.*, 1958, *8*, 162–168.

Rose, D., Application of Karen Horney's theories to group analysis, *Int. J. Group Psychother.*, 1953, *3*, 270–279.

Salzman, L., Sociopsychological theories in psychoanalysis: Karen Horney and Harry Stack Sullivan, *Amer. J. Psychoanal.*, 1964, *24*, 131–144.

Sheiner, S., Karen Horney on psychoanalytic technique: Free association, *Amer. J Psychoanal.*, 1967, *27*, 200–208.

Tillich, P., Karen Horney: A funeral address, *Pastoral Psychol.*, 1953, *4*, 11–13.

Vollmerhausen, J. W., Alienation in the light of Karen Horney's theory of neurosis, *Amer. J. Psychoanal.*, 1961, *21*, 144–155.

> Conflict in self-alienation.

Weiss, F. A., Karen Horney: A bibliography, *Amer. J. Psychoanal.*, 1954a, *14*, 15–18.

Weiss, F. A., Karen Horney: Her early papers, *Amer. J. Psychoanal.*, 1954b, *14*, 55–64.

Wilkins, J. W., Jr., An experimental investigation of certain aspects of the per sonality theory of Karen Horney, *Dissert. Abstr.*, 1959, *19*, 3359.

Wolman, B., Psychoanalysis without libido: An analysis of Karen Horney's contri bution to psychoanalytic theory, *Amer. J. Psychother.*, 1954, *8*, 21–31.

7

MORENO

All the world's a stage,
And all the men and women merely players:
They have their exits and their entrances:
And one man in his time plays many parts . . .

WILLIAM SHAKESPEARE
As You Like It, II, 7

SOME BIOGRAPHICAL DATA

Jacob L. Moreno was born in Bucharest, Rumania, on May 22, 1892.[1] He was first a student at the University of Vienna, later a member of the philosophy faculty, and still later a medical student. He received his M.D. from this

[1] In preparing the manuscript, I sent this chapter to Dr. Moreno for his comments. I am extremely grateful to him for his suggestions. The present treatment does not incorporate all of his remarks although he found, "It is fascinating reading and it documents that you have a high spontaneity quotient." His other comments follow in the chapter where appropriate.

institution in 1917. After this time he was successively Superintendent, Mittendorf State Hospital, near Vienna and health officer of Voslau, Austria, and, concurrently with the latter post, a psychiatrist in private practice. During his professional life in Vienna he displayed a deep interest in psycho-drama, founding *Das Stegreiftheater* (The Spontaneity Theatre) and even developing in 1922 a stage especially adapted to spontaneity work. The dates for his beginning work in these areas were: group psychotherapy, 1913 (Spittelberg, Vienna); sociometry, 1915–1916 (Mittendorf, near Vienna), role playing, 1909–1911 (Viennese Gardens).

In 1925 he came to the United States where he was licensed as a physician in New York in 1927. He became a naturalized citizen of the United States in 1935. His years since then in this country have been filled with an increasing interest in psychodrama, sociometry, and group psychotherapy. His efforts and accomplishments in these areas can be only partially recounted here. He has engaged in private psychiatric work since 1928. This same year he began psychodramatic work with children at the Plymouth Institute in Brooklyn, Mt. Sinai Hospital, New York City, and later did the same type of work at Grosvenor Neighborhood House and Hunter College. In 1931–1932 Moreno made sociometric studies at Sing Sing Prison and Public School 181, Brooklyn, New York, and from 1932 to 1938 did the first long-term socio-metric work at the New York Training School for Girls in Hudson, New York. The Moreno Sanitarium, formerly known as Beacon Hill, was founded by him in 1936. He has taught at the New School for Social Research and at Teachers College, Columbia University, and has been on the faculty of New York University since 1951.

Throughout his professional life Moreno has been a prolific writer of articles, many of them appearing in *Sociometry*. He has written a number of books, edited others, and made films on psychodrama. Altogether, he has led a prodigiously full and fruitful professional life.

Moreno was married in 1949 to Zerka Toeman. He has two children, Regina (by a previous marriage) and Jonathan. The Morenos reside at Beacon, New York.

INTRODUCTION

The figure of Jacob L. Moreno as a personality theorist is not as clear as that of some of the previous theorists in the present text.[2] Most students of the

[2] Moreno himself says: "I question the first statement, and wish to refer you to my major work on personality development, Spontaneity Theory of Child Development, especially the Introduction, pp. 89–90, *Sociometry*, Vol. VII, 1944, first paragraph from which I quote herewith: 'The theoretical structure of every empirical science needs from time to time a thorough overhauling. New findings, and perhaps, still more than this, new dimensions of investigation require and demand new supporting hypotheses. A *theory of personality*, for instance, is needed, especially a theory of child development, which is in better accord with

field of personality have emphasized Moreno's techniques of sociodrama, psychodrama, and the related sociometric devices which he has so cleverly created as a major contribution to the psychological world. Others have felt that he is primarily a sociological thinker, dealing chiefly in group behavior with little or no relevance to the psychological manifestations of man's behavior. Still others consider Moreno a practitioner of the art of therapy in his role as the guiding light of the theater for role playing at Beacon, New York. To many educators he is the originator of the sociogram, which was introduced to them through the publication, by the Horace Mann–Lincoln Institute, of the pamphlet "How to Construct a Sociogram" (1947, Teachers College, Columbia University). Some know Moreno as the originator and long-time editor (1937, Vol. I, No. 1, to 1956, Vol. XVIII, No. 4) of the periodical *Sociometry*. Moreno is all these things and a good bit more.[3]

Moreno began his professional life as a medical doctor in Vienna. His dynamic and forceful personality soon led him into greater concerns for the welfare of his fellow men, concerns that go beyond the realm of the medical sciences. Feeling that "No [science] is an island of itself," Moreno turned his fertile mind in any direction that appeared fruitful for a wider understanding of the dynamics of man's behavior.

Moreno is a prodigious writer. Starting in 1914 in Austria, he has continued to the present day to produce many, many articles, some in joint authorship with members of his family: Florence B., Zerka T., and Jonathan Moreno. Other articles were done in collaboration with members of his staff at his institutes in New York. Most of his writing, however, has been his own singular effort. The primary source of Moreno's written work may be found in the issues of *Sociometry*, especially during the years of his editorship, 1937–

---

the dimensions of study in which an increasingly large number of child psychologists, social psychologists, analysts, and therapists are engaged. They still carry on with antiquated concepts which do not quite meet new situations. The theories of child development, as evolved by behaviorism, the Gestalt School, and psychoanalysis have lost their magnetism in some quarters, probably because they have lost their usefulness in empirical and experimental study. The appeal of concepts such as spontaneity, warming-up process, spontaneity training, auxiliary ego, role-playing, and tele (mental distance-receptors) is growing in momentum.'

"Indeed, my ambition was to construct 1. a *personality theory* which is superior to that of Freud—psychodrama, 2. a *social theory* which is superior to that of Marx—sociometry, and 3. a cosmic theory which is superior to that of the Old and the New Testament, the Koran and the Speeches of Buddha—The Words of the Father, published in 1920 in German as 'Das Testament des Vaters,' in English as 'The Words of the Father' in 1941."

[3] Moreno states, "He [Moreno] introduced the first systematic *theory of interpersonal relations*, see *Sociometry*, Vol. I, No. 1, 1937, pp. 1–74—one year before H. S. Sullivan who duplicated it in his *Psychiatry*, Vol. I, No. 1, 1938. He introduced the concept of 'The Encounter' ten years before Martin Buber, in 1914. He created the scientific foundations of group psychotherapy and coined all the terms pertinent to it: group therapy, group psychotherapy, group cohesiveness, group catharsis, acting out and the concept of self realization which, as an 'actual' process comes to life in psychodramatic presentation."

1956. Frequently these articles have been reprinted as monographs of his institute's publishing house, Beacon House. Currently, a major outlet for his work is the journal *Group Psychotherapy*, which has inherited the mantle of *Sociometry* but with an avowed international flavor. Besides his chief book, *Who Shall Survive* and his editorship of the eighteenth volume of *Sociometry* (published as a book under the title *Sociometry and the Science of Man*) and recently of *The Sociometry Reader*, Moreno has created motion pictures on the practice and techniques of his work, *Introduction to Psychodrama*. The pioneer project of Moreno in using television as a medium is uniquely described by his wife Zerka (Z. Moreno, 1965a, 1967) and others (Vogeler and Greenberg, 1968).

Currently, Zerka Moreno is deeply involved in the training of psychodramists at the Moreno Institute in Beacon, New York, and in New York City. Her talented contributions to the work of her husband have been lively and dedicated. Many others have also advanced the concepts of psychodrama. There is an American Society of Group Psychotherapy and Psychodrama as well as its international counterpart. The latter draws members from every continent and most of the larger nations on the globe; meetings have been held in Paris, Barcelona, Baden–Prague, Vienna, Milan, and the Orient. The Morenos travel widely in the United States and throughout the world to universities and hospitals demonstrating and training therapists in their techniques.

Since approximately 1937 the expansion and adaptation of Moreno's basic tenets have had an intriguing, cumulative effect on the minds of sociologists, psychiatrists, and psychologists alike. Moreno himself has broadened the application of his concepts, but the original tenets remain essentially unchanged. For example, Moreno frequently states that everything in life is in the "here and now." His is the psychology of the moment. This and the concepts of spontaneity—creativity—cultural conserve, tele, warming up, role playing, the social atom, and sociogenetic laws have remained virtually as Moreno first proposed them. The applications of Moreno's theories widen with each new devotee, but the basic theory continues to hold.

Since the very earliest role playing, first attempted in the Komoedian Haus in Vienna on April 1, 1921, Moreno has amplified his concepts into sociodrama, psychodrama, sociometry, group psychotherapy, and the Theoretical framework of the trichotomized idea of spontaneity–creativity–cultural conserve. Gardner Murphy, himself one of the world's renowned personality theoreticians, has called Moreno's work more than a technical trick or device: "the beginning of a new way of viewing human relationships," a social theory in its own right (Murphy, 1956). Moreno is most creative. Thus, "A person such as Moreno apparently did not borrow much from anyone in his system of personality. . . ." In comparing Moreno to Freud and Rogers Corsini makes an interesting observation: "And, why did Moreno, with his

mpestuous Psychodrama, develop a technique so different from these other
wo? The answer may be that these therapists' manifest personality domi-
ated their procedures, that how they conduct therapy is the way they have to
ecause of their own nature" (Corsini, 1956). Probably one of the most
nique and powerfully dramatic descriptions of role playing, particularly role
eversal, is Moreno's quotation from his earliest work, *Einladung zu einer
Begegnung* (1914): "A meeting of two: eye to eye, face to face, and when
ou are near I will tear your eyes out and place them instead of mine, and you
vill tear my eyes out and will place them instead of yours, then I will look at
ou with your eyes and you will look at me with mine" (p. 3).

Although Moreno eulogized Freud on the occasion of the hundredth
nniversary of Freud's birth in 1956, he felt that his own techniques were far
nore advanced than Freud's because at last they freed the therapist from the
ouch and the chair. Through the spontaneity of psychodrama both the client
nd the therapist could actively participate in lifelike situations that really
hanged human behavior *in situ*. Also Moreno felt that the heavy emphasis
vhich Freud placed upon the unconscious states of man was in error. Moreno
referred to regard the formulations of spontaneity–creativity as the root-form
f all behavior—indeed, of the entire behavior of the universe itself. "Spon-
aneity–creativity is *the* problem of psychology." In comparing his theory with
he theories of the big three—Freud, Jung, and Adler—Moreno found his
ystem superior. He rejected Freud's repetition compulsion principle on the
rounds that man does not continue slavishly to repeat infantile behavior but
lways builds his roles on the success or failure of past roles. He felt the "big
hree" neither had a theoretical foundation based on a logical approach nor,
n their clinical methods, went much beyond the understanding of the one
erson being analyzed, whereas Moreno's own treatment of interpersonal
roups was wider and included total understanding of human behavior.
Moreno also felt that it is far more efficient to deal with groups in sociodrama
ituations than to spend time in the one-to-one relationship that individual
osychotherapy demands. Moreno was a precursor to Lewin in regard to the
ositional diagrams which Lewin so brilliantly espoused. As far back as 1916
Moreno used diagrams to indicate the space and movements between the
osychodrama actors, much in the same way that Lewin was to adopt them in
936. Moreno published these diagrams in his first book on the theater for
pontaneity (*Stegreiftheater*) in Berlin, Germany, in 1923.

Jiri Nehnevajsa, in *Sociometry and the Science of Man* (p. 49), feels
vith many others, including Gardner Murphy, that Moreno has created a
'theory of human behavior." Moreno's work is a combination of theory,
herapy, and research. This text makes no attempt to deal with the "how to
lo it" aspects of psychodrama or sociometry. It is the intent here to treat only
he theoretical aspects of Moreno's work as they apply to the dynamics of
nan's personality. In short, *why* does man do the things he does?

MORENO'S DESCRIPTION
OF HUMAN BEHAVIOR

In searching for Moreno's main themes or principles, one is tempted to divide his personality theory into three main sections: spontaneity, creativity, and cultural conserves. There are, however, as we shall see, many concepts of his that do not fit comfortably in any of these three categories. Contrary to almost all the other theorists considered in the present book, Moreno does consider himself a personality theorist. In many ways he sees himself as primarily concerned with "social reconditioning." His work revolves around this core. With others (Murphy, Nehnevajsa, *et al.*), the author feels that the breadth and depth of Moreno's work are admirably adapted to a theory about why man behaves as he does. In short: A theory of personality is involved in Jacob Moreno's writings.

As the present author interprets the contributions of Moreno, at least ten major themes, concepts, or principles appear. The order of their presentation here has no special significance. Other interpreters may, of course, be more comfortable with more or fewer than ten principles. For the present, the ten that follow adequately cover the basic structure of Moreno and his theoretical considerations of man's complex personality. Admittedly some principles are more important than others, but the reader may best rank them for himself. The ten principles are: social atom, tele, warming up, role playing, spontaneity, creativity, cultural conserves, group development, sociogenetic law, and measurement.

Social Atom Principle

By definition, the social atom is the "smallest living social unit," one which cannot be subdivided. The relationship between the social atom and tele is very close, as we shall see later. Social atoms, when reduced to their basic nature in man's behavior, are the mastic that holds society together. Although tele has characteristics of positive and negative human relationships, the social atom is neither positive nor negative. It is a state of relationship between one human being and another. Beneath the tele relationship is the social atom. The key word in regard to social atoms is *reciprocity*. Thus, there may be attraction or repulsion in any reciprocal relationship between two people, but the social atom does not lend itself to negative or positive relationships. The attraction or repulsion comes from the feeling tone of the reciprocating human beings, not from the social atomic structure. The social atom describes the structure; the human beings involved bring into the structure their feelings of attraction or repulsion to each other. The concept of tele is reserved for describing the action involved in the reciprocity of human to human

Little of man's personality in actual behavioral examples is explained thus far. We must proceed with the concept of the social atom.

The social atom has two distinct perspectives as it operates in human behavior: psychological and collective. The social atom in the former case refers to one person and his relationship with others. Thus, the one-to-one relationship of a husband to his wife is a form of the psychological social atom. In the collective perspective the social atom is viewed as the smallest part of human society: the casual encounter of a customer with a salesclerk, for instance. This relationship between two people cannot be further reduced. From the viewpoint of the psychological social atom there is implied a previous feeling tone between the two reciprocating human beings. Collective social atoms imply no previous condition of feeling tone between the individuals involved. Psychological social atoms, therefore, have longer histories and more definable reciprocal relationships. Collective social atoms are generally of short duration with little or no previous history, and the reciprocity is more difficult to define. Putting it another way, we may better predict what a husband and wife will do than what a salesclerk and customer will do.

Social atoms do not exist in isolation from other types of human behavior. In a sense, social atoms are the building bricks of all human encounter. As the child grows into adulthood, the social atomic structure also grows, and with growth it changes. The roles each human must play and the roles he chooses to emphasize require stronger or weaker social atomic structuring. Individuals who are unable to handle their roles in a manner satisfactory to themselves and to society have an unbalanced social structure. Neurotics, for example, may be considered to have an unbalanced social structure.

A further distinction is made between social atoms and the cultural atom. Just as personality disorders may be due to an unbalanced social atom formation, they may also be caused by a poor adjustment between the cultural atom and the social atom of an individual. Cultural atoms are formed by the irreducible role that one receives in the culture within which he operates. The difficult role of the Negro in contemporary American society may serve as an illustration. Although the man with black skin may have a strong affective social atomic structure with an individual whose skin is white, the cultural atomic structure is restricted to such a stringent degree that personality disorders may result. There are limits on whom they may marry, with whom they may attend church or enter a business relationship, as well as multiple other cultural atomic relationships. World War II gave examples of the difficulties of adjustment for social atom versus cultural atom: One man might be an officer while his brother was an enlisted man; or two friends would find their social atom structure restricted by the prescribed relationship of officer to enlisted man. Neither the social atom nor the cultural atom may be reduced. In the military services an officer is an officer, not part officer and part enlisted man. Likewise in cultures which assign a colored person the irreducible role of being colored there are no halfway points. What the individual does with his role and how he reacts to it is, of course, a matter of individual difference. This we shall study more explicitly in the sections on role playing.

When two or more social atoms combine, the combination results in what Moreno calls *social molecules*. As two or more social molecules combine the result is a classoid or a socoid. The entire structure is now the psychosocial network. Such a network may have sympathetic relationships with other networks in other communities; even throughout the world. So far the discourse appears to be a matter of words combined into a large definition, but with little practical significance. For better understanding an example of gossip on a college campus may be used. Let us assume that two fraternity brothers or two sorority sisters (social atoms) whisper an item of gossip that they have heard or read. The rumor concerns the annual trek many college students make during the Easter vacation to Ft. Lauderdale or similar places in Florida. It is said that the white students will attempt to stage sit-in strikes at various places during the vacation week as a supportive measure condemning segregation of black and white in the South. As many rumors do, this one soon spreads throughout the Greek-letter organization (social molecule). Before long it permeates the entire campus, both to other fraternities and sororities and to students who do not belong to fraternities or sororities. The Greek letter organizations might be termed *classoids*; the nonmember students, *socoids*. As the rumor gains force and wider circulation on other college campuses (psychosocial network), it may even be publicized throughout the world by newspapers and television. Thus we have an example of the development of the progress from social atom through all the stages to psychosocial network.

Tele Principle

It is not possible to deal with Moreno's works without coming repeatedly upon the concept of tele, or "t," or telic sensitivity. Even a reader who scans his writings will have his eye caught by the term *tele*. The concept is basic to Moreno's theory of personality. It is one of the central themes in sociometry. A true grasp of the meaning of tele helps to explain the social atom, because tele is a part of the social atom. Whereas the social atom is considered the smallest indivisible unit of action between humans, tele is the *process* of action between individuals. Therefore, to get a deeper understanding of the social atom one must also study the tele in the structure of the social atom.

Moreno feels that man does more than act; he coacts. This coaction between individuals is called the *tele factor*. By definition *tele* means, ". . . the simplest unit of feeling transmitted from one individual towards another . . ." (*Who Shall Survive?* p. 159). And as Moreno wrote to me:

. . . it represents a two-way process, a process of the reciprocation. In contrast empathy has been defined by Lipps as a "one-way nonreciprocal feeling into an esthetic object"; transference, according to Freud, is a "one-way projection," from one individual to another, a delusionary process. Tele is responsible for the two-way and multiple feelings of several individuals into each other's private worlds and the socio-emotional structure resulting from them. Tele is a binder; transference is a disintergrator. A transference relation eventually either vanishes or changes into a tele relation. Therefore tele is conceived as the main stem with two branches, transference and empathy.

Tele is the true basis of interaction between humans. As we shall see in later paragraphs, Moreno speaks of "t" as having some sort of physiological basis. Out of the primordial organic or biological manner of acting toward other humans (as used by animals, unable to communicate with involved symbolic speech) man has evolved a method of acting toward individuals beyond the human physiological systems. Man can function physiologically without outside stimulation (feeling, hunger, breathing, elimination of body wastes, etc.), and because these functions are the forerunners of telic sensitivity, tele is more than reacting to other people. Tele has a built-in self-starter. The self-energizing characteristics of tele may, therefore, initiate a feeling tone within the individual, even before anything has happened to cause a reaction to another person. Man's personality is more than a reactive agent like the surface of a body of water when a pebble strikes it. Man has the capacity to create his own waves. In this sense, then, he coacts with other human beings as well as reacts to them.

Just as man has an aversion–affection continuum of biological feeling within himself (he likes or dislikes certain foods, certain odors, etc.), he also has a flow of affection and disaffection between himself and others, be they single persons or groups. Thus tele becomes the "flow—to and fro—of affectivity between individuals" (*Sociometry and the Science of Man*, p. 62). This like–dislike emotional tone is no respecter of bivariant groups. White may like black; male, female; Republican, Democrat; German, French; and vice versa. There is, of course, always the reactive factor in tele. The essential feature of tele is that an emotional feeling tone exists in almost all human relationships. The exceptions are so few as to be insignificant.

In using the Greek word *tele*, meaning "far" or "far off," Moreno intends it to mean "distance." This meaning holds for him more than time and space connotations; etymologically it carries a connotation of "emotional tone between two human objects." The origin of the word is *telencephalon* or endbrain, the neurological term meaning "the anterior subdivision of the embryonic brain in which are developed the olfactory lobes, the cerebral hemispheres, and the corpora striata." Moreno felt that tele begins as the infant gradually develops ideas of nearness and distance, both within and without himself. The physical distance receptors of the visual and auditory

senses help him little by little to differentiate objects from persons. This lead
to his liking and disliking objects and persons, a reaction called *positive o
negative tele*. Tele also develops into a sensitivity for real objects and fo
imagined objects. When tele begins in the human system, it is a psycho
organic level of expression of feeling and is inarticulate. As the human
mechanisms mature, the tele sensitivity becomes psychosocial and develops t
a highly articulate level.

Other attributes of tele follow.

Intensity. The intensity of accepting or rejecting another human bein
is variable within the single human subject. At times he may have a stron
feeling of tele toward another human, whether it be acceptance or rejection
at other times the intensity of his feelings may be quite low.

Sensitivity. The degree of sensitivity varies considerably between two
individuals. A telic relationship implies more than empathy or counter
empathy. The ability to "penetrate and understand" another individual is im
plied in telic sensitivity. A therapist and his client will be operating at a loss i
there is no high degree of telic sensitivity. In like manner a marriage may b
only a formal agreement if the marriage relationship lacks a high degree o
telic sensitivity.

Simple tele. This results when both the subject and the object of the tel
relationship have an unimpeded flow of emotional tone toward each other

Infra tele. This is the incompatibility of two related individuals wh
have contrary feelings for each other.

Ambivalent tele. Two related individuals have mutually ambivalen
feelings.

Projective. This is an aspect of tele not entirely clear, but apparently i
signifies that one individual in the tele relationship "projects" a stronge
feeling tone than the other individual. Some aspect of the future in teli
relationships is also probably implied by the term.

Retrojective. This is a perplexing concept of tele which means that on
individual takes unto himself the feeling tones of other individuals "and in
fuses them with new intensity, throwing them back upon the others, a teli
feedback."

Tele for persons, objects, and symbols. These represent a trichotomy o
tele affectivity within the individual that has developmental and societal over
tones. As man matures from infancy to adulthood, the sensitivity and intense
ness of his tele relationships may proceed from persons to objects to symbols
in that order. A truly matured adult, we may further assume, has all three
tele feelings developed to such a degree that they complement one anothe
in his personality. The child is more successful with people as he begins life
than he is with objects or symbols. Gradually, as he grows through child
hood and adolescence into adulthood, he also becomes skilled in tele fo
things, such as bicycles and toys; later for the printed word, spoken word
and all other forms of symbolic tele relationships. Because tele is affected b
its six previously named attributes (intensity, sensitivity, simple and infra

tele, projective, and retrojective) it may be that an individual or group of individuals becomes more successful and more oriented toward one of these three forms of tele. Something like the following would then be expected to happen: Societies which overemphasize tele for persons evolve great emotionality in their relationships; object tele in its extreme forms creates a technologically oriented society which has little sympathy for people or symbolic ideation; and overtly symbolic tele societies become withdrawn in a contemplative Buddha-like organization with little or no thought of the people in the society or of the use of objects such as food, clothing, and shelter in making everyday existence comfortable. Presumably one aspect of therapy is helping the client to bring all three aspects of tele into complementary order.

Negative, neutral, positive. These are attributes of tele which are pretty well expressed by the terms. One who has a negative tele toward persons, objects or for symbols. In short, the comparison is not always between per-automobiles or dislikes reading and other forms of symbolic behavior. Neutral tele indicates a feeling of apathy toward any of the three referent qualities. Positive tele obviously conveys the idea of an enthusiastic devotee of persons or objects or symbols. Within the same frame of reference the individual may have negative or neutral or positive tele feelings toward different persons without a comparison with objects or symbols. The reverse would hold true for objects or for symbols. In short, the comparison is not always between persons and objects or symbols. It may be between persons, objects, or symbols.

"*Tele–Transference–Empathy.* Tele is the binding, constant, integrating forces of reciprocation with two branches: transference, the pathological dissociating aspect, and empathy, the esthetic one-way aspect. As a construct they are separated from tele but *in vivo* they are interwoven."[4]

Telic sensitivity is the smallest unit of feeling that can be measured by a sociometric device (sociogram). However, as is the case with intelligence, tele cannot be measured directly. The sociometrist can measure only the manifestations of telic sensitivity. Moreno feels that by itself tele has no social existence. It is an abstraction. To be understood it must be considered always as a process within the social atom. "Tele is the fundamental factor underlying our perception of others. We see them, not as they are; nor yet as we are; but as they are in relation to ourselves" (*Sociometry and the Science of Man*, p. 275).

Warming Up Principle

It would be difficult to find an adult who has not witnessed at some time or other an act of warming up. An automobile engine warms up; track athletes warm up prior to racing; some people make circular motions before signing an

Personal communication to the author, May 15, 1962.

important document; singers vocalize before singing a solo. As we shall see Moreno attaches great importance to *warming up*. It is essential to his theory of man's behavior exemplified in the personality structure.

GENERAL IMPORTANCE

Almost every act of man begins with warming up. In the morning he emerges from a state of sleep in a gradual way, warming up for the process of leaving his bed and assuming the state of wakefulness. Even after he gets out of bed he may need a prolonged period of warming up to the activities and demands of the day. He yawns, he stretches, he scratches himself, and he ponders the immediate problems which have to be met and solved, such as the choice of clothing and the consuming of breakfast. All of this activity can be called *warming up* for the business of conducting life through one day. At the end of each day he begins to unwind; in order to prepare for the cessation of mental and organic activity, he must reverse the process he went through that morning and begin to warm up for sleep. His program of settling down for the night may incorporate certain techniques. Prior to getting into bed he may snack, or smoke, or read, or watch television, or deliberately turn his mind to the habitual orderly habits of "putting the house to bed" by locking doors, adjusting the thermostat, and the like. In between the warming up processes of waking from sleep and putting himself to sleep, he has a day full of activities almost all of which must be preceded by warming up procedures.

There is a circular quality in the relationship of warming up and spontaneity. Warming up creates spontaneity. Spontaneity in turn shortens the period of warming up. Moreno feels that at times he does not know which comes first, warming up or spontaneity, because each is so entwined with the other as to seem to be both cause and effect. Moreno likens this to the ancient dilemma about the chicken and the egg.

The usual definition of warming up does not, however, include the many ramifications of its effect upon the personality. In a sense the shorter and more controlled the process of warming up becomes, the greater the degree of spontaneity. Also the shorter the period of warming up, the more efficient the personality becomes in meeting the situations of life. The more quickly one can make adjustments prior to beginning a task, the less trial and error is involved in "shifting gears," especially in proceeding from one task to another. Consequently one of life's goals in creating a good personality is to be aware of and to appreciate the effect of warming up. Efficient warming up may also reduce emotional anxiety. Take, for example, the ubiquitous intrusion of the telephone call. Answering a telephone permits very little opportunity for warming up to the voice on the other end of the line. The usual reinforcement clues such as the speaker's appearance and the location of the conversation (one expects to talk of bowling in a bowling alley) are absent; the abrupt interrupting ring of the telephone, the voice not always clear and the face unseen, and the disruption of the activity prior to the ringing are not designed to aid the answering party in warming up to the conversation. Emotional anxiety may result, therefore, if the individual does not possess adequate spontaneity and an efficient warming up technique suited to telephone conversations.

Warming up exists before and *in the course of* any act whether the act is creative or not. As we have seen, warming up and spontaneity have a circular effect (one reinforces the other). Later we shall observe the high degree of reciprocity that exists in the triad of spontaneity–creativity–cultural conserve. Consequently, warming up does not mean the same thing as conditioning. Conditioning implies a set relationship between a stimulus and a response. Although the term *conditioning* has been so widely stretched in usage that it approaches ambiguity, it is not synonymous with our present term *warming up*. To use the telephone example, it is true that an individual may become conditioned to respond to the telephone's ringing by arising and answering the call with little or no thought immediately apparent. However automatic that response becomes, he is still confronted with a warming up task the moment he picks up the telephone. From then on it is demonstrated that in the act of conversation the individual makes preliminary adjustments and that the manner in which he makes them produces reciprocal adjustments in the respondent. Thus, both prior to the call and during the call, the warming up process is operating. A conditioned response would produce only a singular behavior pattern. Warming up both prepares the subject for the act and is highly involved in structuring the act as it proceeds from singular act to singular act. As the individual warms up to the telephone conversation, he becomes more spontaneous. As he becomes more spontaneous, he continues to warm up to the situation. In summary, therefore, warming up exists before and in the course of any act whether the act is creative or not, and it is not synonymous with conditioning.

Purely as a sidelight to Moreno's theory it is interesting to note that the current well-publicized high-speed electric computers do not possess this fundamental concept of personality which Moreno calls warming up, nor its corollary, spontaneity. The gigantic electric brains possess phenomenal conditioned responses but lack the ingenuity of man's reciprocity to situations.

THE DEVELOPMENT OF WARMING UP

How does man gain his capacity for warming up? Moreno feels that the infant, in a developmental sense, is an actor who does not "know his lines." One of the miracles of life, moreover, is how the newborn baby enters life with so little warming up time other than the nine-month gestation period. From the dark, quiet, wet world of the womb, protected by constant temperature and assured of a continuous flow of nourishment, the tiny infant is plunged into a bright, dry, noisy, hot and cold world where he must adjust to irregular feedings regulated by outside forces. Moreno feels the infant need immediately all the help he can get in developing a minimum of warming u procedures. At best the neonate has only imperfect physical self-starters. I the birth act itself the beginning movements for freedom from the uterus ar initiated by the infant, but they must always be aided by others, primarily th mother, the midwife, or the attending physician. The very first warming u that the human being attempts in life are inadequate for the occasion: H must be helped to be born. Life begins with the physical self-starters such a breathing (though the neonate may need help in this by a slap on th bottom), elimination, pulse, and first sucking motions. These soon grow int the realm of interpersonal relations. In a sense all of childhood and adoles cence is a warming up period just as is the intrauterine life. What Moren calls the mental and interpersonal starters (mother, obstetrician, nurses come to the rescue of the physical starters (sucking, eating, passing ga breathing, etc.). Mental starters aid the neonate in developing a level o mentation, or the mental processes which actually go along with the signif cant physical starters. Soon, therefore, the neonate recognizes outside force which aid his own physical self-starters.

Mentation leads to the development of an auxiliary ego which is a extension of the self, or a substitute for the self. Persons who feed, clothe, an minister to the neonate become identified as auxiliary egos. The human bein retains auxiliary egos throughout his life in the form of husband or wife mother and father, friends, teachers, leaders, employers, governments, and th like. Parallel with the development and retention for life of one or mor auxiliary egos is the development and lifetime retention of auxiliary objects The bottle which replaces the mother's breast, the thumb which may replac the bottle, the blanket which may replace the uteral warmth, the doll whicl may replace the past period of protected infancy and so become a pseud auxiliary ego, and the toy which recaptures uncomplicated childhood may a become auxiliary objects. The importance of auxiliary egos and objects lies i their capacity to shorten the warming up period. If one is dealing with th familiar or its symbol, one does not need to go through a bothersom warming up period for the new and unknown.

ADULT IMPLICATIONS

According to Moreno each warming up process has an organic locus o greatest strength. He differs from Freud in his concept of the erogenou zones, because to Moreno the locus is more than the skin itself. As an illustra tion, the oral zone or locus represents also the condition or type of nippl (mother's breast or rubber nipple), the condition of the milk, the air, anc proximity of the infant to the source of milk, all of which are contributin factors to the locus. In like manner hands, feet, and other areas of the bod may coact or interact with the original oral zone. The final result is that th

cation of a warming up process may lie well outside the body itself and be
iented to places, objects, or other human beings.

Warming up for an act may express itself in three ways.

1. Somatic: in which the preliminary steps to adjustment are basically organic, with little or no relationship to the next two methods of expression.
There is, however, usually a relationship between the methods of expression, although it may be operating covertly. (A miler in a track meet may
appear to be jogging around the track merely as a somatic warming up,
but we may presume he is also concerned with the psychological and
sociological ramifications of winning or losing the race.)

2. Psychological: which is a warming up time to prepare for the question
"What does it mean to me?" In the above example, a win or a loss in the
mile event must be prepared for, along with the physical behavior of the
miler during the event.

3. Social: which attempts to prepare for the question "How does it affect
others?"

Moreno distinguishes five types of warming up: undirected, directed,
:neral state, immediate, and chain. The undirected type is vague, chaotic,
ıd confused in its direction. It may involve individuals or groups. A college
udent called before the dean for reasons not known goes through the
·ocess of undirected warming up. There is an alertness to action or response,
ıt the reason and direction for the action are obscure or unknown. The
sult is a feeling of tenseness with highly undifferentiated behavior.

The directed type of warming up may also be of an individual or group,
ıt the entire action moves toward a specific goal. There is little or no
eviation in the progress of the warming up. Football teams suited up and
aiting in the dressing room for the game to begin demonstrate the directed
·pe of warming up. The coach's preliminary remarks, the previous week's
·actice, the pep rally, the scouting reports are all pointed toward the un-
eviating goal of victory. What the team is warming up for is no mystery.
he efficiency of the warming up process may lead to perceptual spontaneity.
or example, films of the opponent's team may make it possible to discover
ew ways of meeting the situation by developing counterplays and counter-
efensive measures.

In the general state of warming up, the person knows that a novel
·sponse will be required, but the specific goal is lacking or unclear. A young
·ed who is about to embark on an arranged blind date may be expected to
·hibit the general state of warming up. She knows something about what is
·ing to happen and dresses and prepares herself cosmetically for a social
·gagement, but the reciprocity and further warming up that depend upon
·er date are unknown.

Any kind of emergency situation usually gives rise to the immediate type
f warming up. Because little or no warming up is possible in this situation,

the individual must warm up at once with whatever residual capacity he brings from similar situations. If there have been no previous experience comparable to the emergency situation, he will probably utilize a symbolic approach. Lacking any past experiences similar to the present emergency situation, he may warm up in an entirely inappropriate way. For example being told that a person you love dearly has just died calls for an immediate warm-up to what the news means and how one is to adjust to it. If one has had past experience in losing a friend, the warm-up will probably follow the last pattern. However, because the event is fortunately a rare one, the announcement of a sudden death usually leaves one unprepared. Probably small children give the best examples of the inappropriate response in warming up to the expected social reaction. Their questions may be irrelevant or even crude.

The last type of warming up that Moreno mentions is the chain. The response of an audience to a comedian can be used for an example. As the comedian tells his jokes to a new audience he gradually builds up laughter as one person after another gets warmed up to his particular kind of humor until finally there is a cumulative effect of one audience member upon another. Actors in a play may have the same chain warming up in regard to each other as they proceed from the first to the last act.

Moreno speaks of some things, such as the conceptual trichotomy of truth–beauty–love, which do not require a warming up process. In a metaphysical way he feels that whatever is good has beauty and truth in it. Similarly, truth is both beautiful and good, and beauty contains truth and goodness; hence the spontaneity and creativity which follow these stimuli do not need a warming up period.

In the final analysis, life cannot be lived without one's warming up to all of its endeavors. The process is significant in the roles we play in our everyday living as well as in the roles that are played in Moreno's therapeutic techniques of psychodrama.

Role Playing Principle

Moreno's name has become identified with the term *role playing*, primarily as a psychotherapeutic technique. As we shall see, however, the theoretical aspects of role playing have contributed much to personality theory. To Moreno the roles that man plays and must play in life are more than artificially staged psychodrama; they are attempts at self-realization but are often frustrated. There is an equal emphasis upon how we get our roles and how we feel about them.

Actors in early Greek drama literally read their lines from scrolls or rolls. Hence, with extension of meaning and change in the spelling of the word one who takes a role is an actor. We now define role almost synonymously with role playing as "the characteristic function and contribution of an individual in a group, as well as the expected behavior and position defined by the group for the individual." Because everyone is supposed to live up to his official role in society, conflict may arise between the self and the roles man has to play in society. Adolescents, for example, can be expected to have role confusion and contradiction in their behavior as they are trying to learn their roles. At other times a half-learned or poorly learned role may cause one to have anxiety. Viewing the human personality from the role playing frame of reference, we may say that man strives for sociostasis (to maintain his status in the group) rather than homeostasis (maintaining his status within himself as a person).

In the Morenian sense role playing is a subform of psychodrama and sociodrama. Although the terms psychodrama and sociodrama are frequently used interchangeably (Read Bain even coined the term psychosociodrama), there are some subtle and not so subtle differences between them. Generally speaking, psychodrama implies a deeper level of therapy than sociodrama. In methodology they are more nearly the same. Other differences may be roughly summarized as follows: Psychodrama concerns itself with an individual's depth diagnosis and therapy while sociodrama deals more often with group diagnosis and therapy; psychodrama emphasizes the individual while sociodrama emphasizes the group and the individual's place in the group. Psychodrama is the older word; psychodrama primarily attempts to change individual behavior while sociodrama primarily attempts to change group behavior. The concern in the former is "Individual, heal thyself"; in the latter, "Community, heal thyself." Psychodrama is a measure of the individual while sociodrama is a measure of the group; in psychodrama the actors represent individual personalities while in sociodrama the actors represent the group. And in the final analysis, all depends upon the viewpoint: One may look at a group interacting and interpret it as a psychodramatic event while another viewing the same scene may interpret it as an example of sociodrama. The writer does not wish to convey the thought, "You pays your money and takes your choice," but often in usage the terms do become confused.

HISTORICAL BACKGROUND

Jacob Moreno was not the first writer to employ the concept of role or role playing, although the term has been tightly associated with his name. The Shakespearean quotation which introduces this chapter indicates a prior use.

Starting around 1911 Moreno began to experiment and work out his theoretical ideas on role playing and allied concepts. The first sessions were conducted in the gardens of Vienna in a highly informal atmosphere. These sessions culminated in the first structured performance, which took place on April 1, 1921, at the Komoedian Haus, a theater for drama in Vienna. Between 1911 and 1924 Moreno was also involved in other activities which had strong sociodramatic overtones, such as the vast effort, in 1916, to relocate southern Tyrol natives who were being displaced from their mountain homes by the threat of advancing Italian troops during World War I. How Moreno and others attempted to reform these people in Mittendorf, a settlement adjacent to Vienna, makes a fascinating account and one which helped him further to formulate his theories. Finally, role playing through the avenue of psychodrama and sociodrama found a home in the Stegreiftheater of Vienna in 1923. Moreno's work with role playing was continued in the United States with the establishment of the Impromptu Group Theatre performing at Carnegie Hall, New York City, 1923–1931, and the first theater for psychodrama, in Beacon, New York, 1935.

GENERAL THEOREMS

None of the following general theorems is stated directly by Moreno although he does refer to general theorems. They have been culled out of his writings in order to present a clearer position of the "role" of role playing in his work.

1. Roles may be imaginary or real, based on fantasy or fact.
2. Through the medium of play one may personify other forms of life by taking and acting out roles.
3. The personality can be taught to expand itself and to explore the unknown through the avenue of role playing.
4. Role playing can change personality as well as study personality.
5. Role playing may bolster the individual's ego.
6. Role playing, especially through the method of sociodrama, can be an effective technique for reducing the distance between two variant ethnic groups.
7. The more roles one learns to play, the greater flexibility one has in dealing with the problems of life.
8. Roles which are learned efficiently reduce the warming up period necessary to changing life conditions. (Note Polonius' advice to Laertes, "To thine own self be true. . . .")
9. The individual learns about society primarily through the roles he plays.

DEVELOPMENT

With a rather sophisticated phrase Moreno described the child as, "*Megalo mania 'Normalis'—Dosim Repetatur.*" Thus, using his previous training as a medical doctor, Moreno diagnosed the child's first role as a megalomaniac and then stated that the prescription to retain this inner core of the first role is to repeat it. Out of this super-self-centered role that the infant first plays he must gradually and at times painfully learn all the other roles that society demands of him as well as the new roles he desires for himself. The latter may run counter to society's demands, or they may be ignored by society, especially when they are played at the fantasy level. (Perhaps James Thurber's "Th

Secret Life of Walter Mitty" exemplifies fantasy at the adult level.) Through all of the developmental process of role playing runs the central theme of the infant and his normal megalomania. The core of his personality is supported by continuous reference to his own self, or by "repeated doses," as Moreno phrases it. All other roles revolve around this core, and all other roles are subordinate to it. The *modus operandi*, as we shall see in the next section, by which man learns to expand his roles is the technique of role reversal.

ROLE REVERSAL

Moreno places a heavy emphasis on role reversal, which is important both as a learning technique for children and adults and as a method of therapy for individuals and social groups. To a pointed degree, role reversal is the heart of role playing theory as demonstrated in psychodrama and sociodrama. It is the foundation of a balanced personality although, as we shall see later, the individual can never completely reverse a role. By being able to look at the world through other eyes (through role reversal) one can, for limited times, break the terrible trap of always being one's self. We get bored with ourselves. We are restricted in our self-perceptual systems. We need the viewpoint of others to correct our own myopia concerning the world. In a larger sense, Moreno feels that man may be able to achieve a lasting peace between nations if he can cultivate and maintain the capacity to reverse roles with the peoples of all nations. Thus, role reversal may also be the *sine qua non* of a balanced society on earth.

Moreno poses some hypotheses about the indispensable nature of role reversal. Some of these grew out of his experience with his son Jonathan when the son was between the ages of two and three. Others are extracted from his work in psychodrama and sociodrama both in the United States and in Europe. The following listing or role reversal hypotheses is only partial, and the order of presentation is not significant.

1. Role reversal is a technique of socialization and self-integration.
2. Role reversal is an indispensable requirement for establishing a psychodramatic community.
3. Role reversal may be a corrective for unsocial behavior.
4. Role reversal is an invaluable teaching and learning device.
5. Role reversal may go through three critical stages: (1) inferior subhuman beings such as animals or insects, (2) nonhuman objects such as machines, trees, stones, water, automobiles, and (3) superior and powerful beings like parents, teachers, God, or a devil.
6. Role reversal tends to decrease the dependency of a child on his parents.
7. Role reversal is most effective when the psychological distance between the two individuals is small.
8. Role reversal increases role perception.
9. The more roles the individual plays in life, the greater his capacity to reverse roles.

10. Children use their parents as a natural untrained auxiliary ego object in role reversals.
11. Role reversal requires specific techniques which must be mastered in order to benefit from the viewpoint of the other person.

Moreno concedes that complete role reversal is not possible. Reciprocity is a necessary function of role reversal (that is, the other object must give some response in turn), so that in hypothesis 5 above, for example, the child has trouble getting a stone, dog, or authority figure to respond to its efforts.

ROLE PLAYING RELATIONSHIP TO SPONTANEITY AND CREATIVITY

There is a close reciprocal relationship between role playing and spontaneity-creativity. Role playing is the avenue to the making of a truly spontaneous individual. Out of spontaneity comes the creativity that man needs to exist in this world. However, if an individual tightly structures his role, he creates one form of the phenomenon that Moreno calls *cultural conserve*. By "storing up" his capacity to play a role in which he does not deviate from a set pattern of behavior, he loses the advantage of further spontaneity–creativity.

According to Moreno, the past structures man's roles, the present governs the action of the roles, and the future sets the goals for the roles. If spontaneity and the resultant creativity are allowed to be an integral part of all roles, he may automatically play each one in full concert with the past, present, and future. Without spontaneity–creativity a role may be frozen into the past, the present, or the future. Roles which are structured in the past emphasize regressive infantile behavior, while roles structured only in the present lack a central core of behavior and vacillate wildly according to the stimuli present at the time. Roles cast in the future are inclined to remain at the fantasy level with little or no application to problems of the moment. Therefore, without spontaneity which helps create new roles, man is unable to develop through life a personality suited to his highest potential.

KINDS OF ROLES

Moreno differentiates three kinds of roles: psychosomatic, social, and psychodramatic. Psychosomatic role taking emerges out of the functions of reality and the functions of fantasy that the infant copes with from birth. If he merges his reality and fantasy roles successfully, the child is able to accept and use the one set of roles Moreno calls *psychosomatic roles*. Once this is done successfully, the individual may orient himself toward persons, things, and goals that actually exist outside of himself. This orientation is called the *social role*. Psychodramatic roles grow out of orientation toward persons, things, and goals which the individual imagines are outside of himself. "They are called respectively *social roles* (the parent) and *psychodramatic roles* (the god)' (*Sociometry and the Science of Man*, p. 152).

ABUSES OF ROLE PLAYING

Moreno condemns the practice of collecting various people into a situation and encouraging them to start a conversation about anything they want in the hopes that something significant will emerge from just talking. The assumption is that, if enough people talk about enough things, an idea will result beneficial to all, merely through statistical probability. He terms this practice the *role playing fallacy*. It may occur in a social setting, in an educational classroom as a teaching technique, or in an advertising agency as a method called *brainstorming*. Wherever it occurs, Moreno feels it cannot achieve its objective of creativity because an adequate warming up period is assumed to exist in the operation itself. Without sufficient warming up the spontaneity which should follow is lacking, and without spontaneity one cannot hope for creative results. What usually results in free play discussion is a potpourri of words leading to confusion and a feeling of disenchantment among the participants.

Spontaneity Principle

If man is ever to move beyond his present position, Moreno feels, he must act spontaneously toward the problems of life. Acknowledging Bergson's contribution of the *élan vital*, Moreno has moved far beyond the concept of a vital and creative force which is in all living things and has been the root of all evolutionary progress. Beginning with this Bergsonian concept, Moreno has evolved a dynamic design to describe the human personality.

Spontaneity may be described as "the self-initiated behavior of man." Moreno calls it a hypothesis, an entity that no one actually sees. Difficulty in defining *spontaneity* does not relieve the personality theorist of asking its meaning. Spontaneity is the "here and now," and not a mere time sequence. To Moreno it is "Man in action, man thrown into action, the moment *not* a part of history but history as a part of the moment" (*Sociometry and the Science of Man,* p. 60). Because of spontaneity, Moreno feels that in his therapeutic practices he works forward while the psychoanalyst works backward.

Spontaneity, or the *s-factor*, is inseparably and strategically linked with creativity, yet they are distinct. Similarly the s-factor is inextricably mixed with the process of warming up. In all considerations of spontaneity this interdependence must not be ignored. Warming up begets spontaneity, which in turns begets creativity. As we shall see later, the resultant condition is the cultural conserve.

Although spontaneity has a degree of novelty, it is far more than a novel response to a new situation. Psychotics are capable of giving a novel response, but the result may be chaotic. The individual who is highly spontaneous, but not at all creative, is what Moreno calls a *spontaneous idiot*. In addition to being novel, the response must be adequate to the situation. To avoid the adequate response which is stereotyped, the s-factor must contain (1) appropriateness to the situation, (2) a degree of competence for a solution to the situation, and (3) immediacy to the here-and-now situation. A genius, Moreno feels, exemplifies at times complete spontaneity.

IMPORTANCE OF SPONTANEITY

Moreno states that spontaneity and its corollary, creativity, are of such immense importance that they are *the* problem of psychology and indeed of the universe. Without the s-factor, man is reduced to stereotyped behavior which paralyzes the personality. "Robotism is the opposite of spontaneity." The individual or group in any species that insists upon perpetuating the same response to a situation soon faces extinction. The dinosaur perished because it was unable to create spontaneously new modes of behavior to adjust to changing conditions. The imbecile with the stereotyped behavior of banging his head on the floor would soon cease to exist without the gentle help of others.

Spontaneity releases the latent genius in mankind. Because he can be spontaneous and create new things, man moves off dead center and accumulates the cultural conserves that enable him to be healthier, more productive, and better able to meet new situations. Through spontaneity man exercises the right to a free society. Through group spontaneity society can change some of its conditions through referendum or through the rejection and selection of its elected officials. In a group, the self-initiated capacity, which is Moreno's spontaneity, pushes its leaders forward. Dictatorships quell spontaneity; democracies are founded upon spontaneity and can exist only as long as their constituents spontaneously create new methods to move forward. The American Revolution may be an example of this phenomenon. Gardner Murphy credits Moreno not only with contribution of tele as a personality factor but also with establishing spontaneity testing and especially spontaneity training as indispensable adjuncts of the human personality.

The importance of spontaneity also rests on the premise that a certain degree of unpredictability always exists in life. If we knew the future, we should not need spontaneity. Since the future is unknown or half-known, the individual and/or the human race must possess flexibility. If the future were known, a fixed pattern of behavior might be worked out to meet its problems; but since the future is not known, it is incumbent upon the collective personality or the singular personality to prepare for the future by acknowledging spontaneity as a key tool to change, and by training, as adequately as possible, the capacity to meet changing conditions. Through spontaneity training, the individual and the group may better prepare themselves for adjusting to whatever the future may bring.

DEVELOPMENT OF SPONTANEITY

Moreno states that fortunately for man birth is not a trauma but a good beginning for spontaneity. The s-factor begins at birth or even before birth through the built-in medium of act-hunger. Even before the infant is born, he moves his body, squirms, and at times causes the mother some discomfort. Thus the genesis of self-initiated behavior is first noticed. Immediately after birth the s-factor begins to expand at a greatly increased rate as the neonate initiates the demand for food, begins to eliminate urine, and responds to its new environment. Moreno claims the infant could not survive without a built-in s-factor. The obstetrician, the nurse, and the mother can do only so much for the newly emerged human being; the remaining effort to stay alive is up to him. Later as he develops through infancy and childhood, he continues to exercise the s-factor. Spontaneity training and spontaneity testing proceed as he increases in locomotion, response to parents, siblings, and others, and efficiency of organic system. "Lack of spontaneity generates anxiety. Anxiety increases as spontaneity decreases."

The development of spontaneity becomes a course in reality testing. To test reality the child tentatively initiates actions to see if something will work. These reality testings are things which no other can do for him. Gradually the child begins to distinguish between himself and external reality. Although spontaneity is bounded by the institutional setting, there is always room for individual freedom of expression of the spontaneity core. Through the s-factor the human personality learns to differentiate between his psycho-somatic roles (eater, sleeper, sex roles), his psychodramatic roles (god, angel, Santa Claus, etc.), and his social roles (father, policeman, doctor, etc.).

Individual differences emerge in the amount of s-factor each human possesses. Starting at birth with his nipple behavior and his ability or lack of ability to relate to his environment, as well as his nature-given inner drive, the human personality reaches adulthood with varying amounts of spontaneity. Consequently the s-factor is distributed unevenly in the human race and probably in all other species. Some of us have a high amount of s-factor while others have little. The s-factor is also unevenly distributed throughout the lifetime of one person. The following summary presents the rise and fall of spontaneity within one person:

Infancy: at birth a great increase proportionately, but low output in general.
Childhood: highest the s-factor will ever be.
Adolescence: high, but fluctuates extremely, because of environmental pressures to conform and also role confusion.
Early adulthood: diminishing.
Adulthood: a true plateau stage.
Later adulthood: fading and highly stereotyped with little or no s-factor prevalent.

TYPES OF SPONTANEITY

Moreno finds it useful to differentiate three types of spontaneity. In the first type, there is a novel response to a situation but a response not adequate to the situation. Psychotics, for example, may state that two times two is five, certainly a novel response but hardly one that is adequate. Children also are prone to give novel but inadequate responses. Novelty without adequacy becomes an undisciplined or pathological spontaneity.

The second type is the spontaneous response which is quite adequate to the situation but lacks sufficient novelty or significant creativity to be fruitful to the situation. Such spontaneity soon descends to a stereotyped response and becomes trite. The comedian's repetitive reaction to a situation loses its novelty, and although it may continue to provoke some laughter, it soon ceases to be a spontaneous response. Cultural conserves in the form of art, music, and literature may also lack spontaneity although they may serve as warming up procedures for further spontaneity.

The first two types of spontaneity are false; the third type Moreno considers to be true spontaneity. In this type there is an adequate response always accompanied by characteristics that are both novel and creative. The resulting phenomenon may be in the form of an act or a substantive article such as a poem, story, art object, or piece of machinery. To be truly spontaneous the results must be in some way new and the results must be useful for some purpose.

FORMS OF SPONTANEITY

In somewhat the same fashion as he delineates types of spontaneity, Moreno postulates three forms of spontaneity: the *pathological variety*, the *stereotype variety*, and the *high-grade creativity variety*. In the pathological form there is novelty but negligible adequacy and very little creativity. In the stereotype form there is adequacy but negligible novelty and very little creativity. In the high-grade creativity form there is a harmonious conbination of novelty and adequacy leading to productive creativity.

SPONTANEITY—CREATIVITY—CULTURAL CONSERVE

Spontaneity does not exist in a vacuum. It must be *for* something. As previously intimated, the s-factor in its truest form always leads to creation. Creativity may produce a new way of behaving for the individual, a new way of behaving for the group, or a new building, poem, story, oil painting, industry, or form of government. The product of the spontaneity–creativity continuum is called a *cultural conserve.*

The relationship is reciprocal between spontaneity, creativity, and cultural conserve. Assume that an artist has gone through the warming up procedures in painting a picture by erecting his easel, mixing the paints, and casting about for an appropriate subject. From this point he utilizes whatever degree of spontaneity he possesses to create the picture. The result of his creative efforts is a cultural conserve. Now the process may be reversed, so that the finished painting serves to warm the artist up to do another painting on the same subject using different techniques. In still another way, the completed painting may serve to warm up and cause a degree of spontaneity in a second artist, who in turn will create a cultural conserve. Thus the trichotomized concept of spontaneity–creativity–cultural conserve moves back and forth and has done so throughout the history of man.

Moreno makes the plea, however, that a cultural conserve can "freeze" the best efforts of the human personality to be spontaneous and creative. If the cultural conserve becomes too sacred and too immutable in the minds of men, it will thwart their best efforts to create behavioral patterns to meet the changes that time inevitably brings. Old facts are good only in the sense that they can be applied to new, demanding current situations. To worship the old simply for its reliquary value is fruitless, Moreno believes. Philosophers, for example, can oversell the cultural conserve value of Socrates, Plato, or Aristotle when they regard them as sacrosanct idols of the past with no capacity to influence the present. In the same vein man is held back by the provincialisms of the medieval past just as much as by the chauvinistic national fervor of the present—cultural conserves that stultify the future needs of such organizations as the United Nations and its service adjuncts like UNESCO and WHO. The human personality cannot afford to cling to outmoded cultural conserves which block the spontaneous efforts to create newer things.

Fortunately for mankind, the "mortar" of spontaneity holds together the "bricks" of the cultural conserve which man has created to build a life and a civilization. To Moreno the Sermon on the Mount is an excellent example of a cultural conserve which can create a better personality if it is not relegated to the past as an untouchable law but is spontaneously used to foster current thinking. "The conserve has done a great deal to encourage the alienation of the self from total self-realization, the technological alienation of Marx is only a small part of it. More than any other single factor the conserve has stimulated the development of the robot."

Creativity Principle

"Creativity is a separate entity from spontaneity and a separate entity from cultural conserve but strategically linked to both," Moreno has said to me.

Moreno considers spontaneity the chief catalyzer of creativity. Here he means that ideas are brought together by spontaneous action, and, if one is lucky and/or persistently spontaneous about his output, a creative act may occur. Like all other catalyzers, the spontaneity is not changed. It may bubble off in all directions, as it does in what he termed the *spontaneous idiot*. However, if the spontaneous output is genuine and persistent, there usually occurs a creative act. As we shall see later, the resulting creativity may produce not a phenomenal work of art but only a new tele relationship between two human personalities. Moreno suggests that creativity can be defined better operationally and pragmatically by its results than semantically. Traditionally creativity is defined as "bringing something new into being," whether it be an act of behavior or a construct such as a building, work of literature, or form of government. However one defines the word *creativity*, Moreno feels that the results may be new to the individual but not necessarily to the rest of the world, as we see in a child creating for himself a new relationship to others; or new to the individual and new to the world at large. The crux of creativity to Moreno is not the discovery of something that man has never known before or that has never to man's knowledge ever existed before, but the creation in most cases of a new relationship which did not exist before.

IMPORTANCE OF CREATIVITY

In Moreno's book *Who Shall Survive?* (1934) the implication is that only the creative man or animal can survive, especially in a world of technocracy. (The student of history may recall that during the depths of the Depression much of the blame for unemployment was directed at machines which were replacing men.) It is readily seen what immense importance Moreno attaches to the creative act. To be creative means more than to be adaptable. The springs in a sofa are adaptable; they depress and adapt to the weight of a person's body. What is crucial here is that the creativity factor leads humanity to respond constructively to new situations rather than merely to adapt to new situations.

Moreno likens the personality that is not creative to the robot. The robot conserves and reacts to situations but cannot create new situations. It is in the treachery of assuming too much from automatons that the personality is likely to defeat itself and fail to survive in a changing world. The personality must not only *meet* new situations but *create* them, a task for which it can be prepared.

Creativity is of such importance that Moreno uses the concept to explain how some societies are better able to provide a higher standard of living than are others. He coins the word *creatocracy* to describe the scientific democracy which he feels the United States has become in order to emerge as a world power. Admitting that Americans live in a continent blessed with tremendous resources, we still see that they would be unable to use these resources if it were not for their creativity. In contrast, Moreno feels the European nations have held too conservatively to the cultural domains of the past.

GENERALITY OF CREATIVITY

The true value of creativity is to be found in daily living, not in producing the usual cultural conserves such as operas, best sellers, and huge edifices. Creativity is the core of human behavior as it occurs from day to day.

Moreno said to me: " "The future of a culture is finally decided by the creativity of its carriers. If a disease of creative functions, a creativity neurosis, has afflicted the most primary group, the creative men of the human race, then it is of supreme importance that the principle of creativity be redefined and that its perverted forms be compared with creativity in its original states' [1939, 2]. There are higher and lower forms of creativity. The highest forms of human creativity are manifest in the lives and works of prophets, poets, saints, and scientists."

It is erroneous, Moreno believes, to assume that only the mentally gifted are capable of being creative. The housewife as she prepares a meal for her family may be highly creative in the combinations of foods she serves. The salesman is perforce creative as he exercises the tele component and social atomic structure in dealing with a tremendous variety of clients' personalities. The schoolteacher employs creativity as she adjusts the curricular material to meet the differing abilities of her students. In fact, it would be difficult to live a normal life without being creative because maintenance of normality requires one to be spontaneous enough to create behavior adequate to the inevitable changes in life. The neurotic and the psychotic fail to make adjustments because of their noncreative stereotyped behavior. It is true, however, that people of small talent need longer warming up periods to be creative than the aristocrats of the mind, as Moreno names them. Creativity is the core of all organic existence. Trees, flowers, vegetables, paramecia, and people must be creative in order to survive.

It is for these reasons that Moreno emphasizes the therapeutic technique of spontaneity–creativity. If we accept the assumptions that the more creative the personality, the more problems it can solve, and that the more creative it is, the better it can structure and predict the future, then it seems mandatory to Moreno that we must train for creativity.

FORMS OF CREATIVITY

As with spontaneity, Moreno differentiates three forms of creativity: (1) chance—the type of creative act that happens by pure luck and can rarely be duplicated (the person who performed the act may be unable to appreciate or use what he created); (2) spontaneous creativity—bringing something new into being from a feeling of spontaneity which is designed to meet an immediate purpose; (3) conservable creativity—wherein the thing created does not necessarily meet an immediate purpose (for example, a painting, poetry). There is little, if any, feedback in conservable creativity. Feedback is always inherent in the second type.

Cultural Conserve Principle

The last of the spontaneity–creativity–cultural conserve triad to be discussed as a principle is the cultural conserve. Although in a sense cultural conserve is the end product of the entire process which begins with the warming up period, the flow is not always in one direction.

By definition, a cultural conserve is anything that preserves the values of a particular culture. It is the finished product of the creative process. Normally the cultural conserve is considered a material object such as a film, book, building, or musical composition. However, it may take the form of a stylized ballet, a religious ceremony, or any highly set pattern of behavior. The Viennese salutation "*Grüss Gott*" is a cultural conserve. Fraternity initiation ceremonies are cultural conserves, as are the inaugural ceremonies for the President of the United States.

STRENGTHS OF CULTURAL CONSERVES

Cultural conserves perform an important function in the development of civilization. Without them man would be reduced to creating spontaneously the same forms to meet the same situations, day after day. Dictionaries, for example, are highly useful cultural conserves. Because of them man does not have to redefine his word every time he wishes to use it.

As a repository of the past, cultural conserves preserve and continue man's creative ego. When they are used properly, as we shall see later, they give continuity to the heritage of human personality. The vestigial qualities of cultural conserves represent the past power of an organization which holds it together until newer forms of creativity once again give it the vigor it needs to move forward. When actual power or superiority ceases to exist in the human personality, for instance, it may coast on the accumulated strengths of the past until new spontaneous creative behavior begins to take hold. A recently widowed woman is sustained by the cultural conserves of the past, money, status, and living accommodations, until she gradually warms up to her new role and is able once again to meet spontaneously the new situations in which she finds herself.

The proper use of a cultural conserve is that of a springboard for enticing new spontaneity toward creativity. When the pianist interprets "Clair de Lune," for example, he brings to it a modified degree of spontaneity in his playing, which is probably different from the composer's, and thus he creates a new impression upon his audience with each playing of the composition. When an actor portrays Shakespeare's Macbeth, he, too, adds spontaneity and creativity to the well-known characterization. Every cultural conserve has the capacity to arouse new spontaneity and creativity if the new cultural conserve form is not a strict replication. A correct attitude toward a cultural conserve allows all of us to enjoy symphonies, records, fiction, paintings, and ceremonies, and to enjoy them as a boost toward further creativity.

WEAKNESSES OF CULTURAL CONSERVES

Moreno states, however, that the world is full of "lovers of conserves" who deliberately or unconsciously freeze the conserve into an untouchable, sacred form. The danger of the cultural conserve lies both in its state of finality and in the abuse of it by mankind. In the first place, once spontaneity and creativity have been conserved in the culture of a people, the twin factors no longer exist as an actuality in the universe. In the second place, the sanctification of conserves is a hard habit to break. The conserve is comforting and maternal. To idealize it is to regress. Weak personalities in particular are prone to seek the security of the conserve and shy from the unpredictability of creating something new from the old. Consequently such valuable conserves as the Bible, great books, great symphonies, and so forth may become objects of worship in themselves and be ignored for the good they can accomplish as warming up stimuli and spontaneity agents for current creative living.

FORMS OF CULTURAL CONSERVES

Moreno mentions three forms that cultural conserves may take:

1. Burned-out. This is a cultural conserve which has lost its value but continues to be. The pyramids of Egypt, the many-staired Inca temples, old political campaign songs, and stereotyped nineteenth-century portraits are possible examples of the conserve which has lost its ability to create spontaneity. Outdated textbooks should not be ignored in this category, either.
2. Inflammable. This conserve has the capacity to excite interest and attract devotees. Examples may be found in current best-seller books; in popular musical comedies like My Fair Lady (which came from another cultural conserve that had the capacity to foster spontaneity and creativity, Pygmalion); in the political figure with a "new" face and a creative program in the tradition of Franklin Roosevelt in the Depression of the early thirties, or Winston Churchill during World War II.
3. Eternalized. The Talmud, the Koran, the Bible are examples of this third class of idolized conserve. To be eligible the conserve must still possess the ability to arouse new enthusiasms, and have the freshness and appeal and vitality to meet current situations.

Although it may appear at this point that cultural conserves have little or nothing to do with the human personality operating in daily life, quite the opposite is true. An individual's pattern of day-to-day living may itself be harmed or helped by the conserve he preserves. Anachronistically dressed U.S. senators are a cultural conserve of the personal sort. All of us, Moreno asserts, may have hide-bound roles which we slavishly play in duplication of the cultural conserve. This conservation of a role may help or harm us in the work our personalities must do in normal living. The scientist who perpetuates his role in sloppy research, the minister who fails to unbend and recognize current issues, the middle-aged woman who frantically and ludicrously tries to preserve an unpreservable youth, and even the perpetual college freshman are all illustrations of the cultural conserve as it applies to the human personality.

On the other side of the coin, we may look to the marine who plays a role of heroism out of a long tradition of heroism in the Marine Corps. As he conserves the role his culture has given to him, he somewhat automatically acts brave whether he feels brave or not; according to his culture, he is supposed to act brave in battle. Other examples of the culture's conserving a role to benefit the role player and others are the autocratic stance of teachers of recalcitrant children, the deterrent effect of the policeman's uniform in a riot, the willingness to help the infant, and the quality of humility and fellowship in a devout church congregation.

Group Development Principle

The last three principles (group development, sociogenetic law, measurement) that are extracted from Moreno's work by the present author are not as vital as the previous ones but are, nevertheless, basic to an understanding of his system.

In a previous discussion dealing with the social atom the concept of the psychosocial network was presented. The principle of group development is an extension of the psychosocial network.

Because Moreno is primarily a therapist, the group development principle can be interpreted as a philosophy of adjustment. He feels that his work in psychodrama and sociodrama which center on role playing have at last broken the secretiveness that has too often surrounded psychotherapy. His techniques are out in the open and, in fact, can only operate with others in an open fashion. In contrast, the psychoanalyst works in a sensitive one-to-one relationship that almost defies study by a third party. The student of personality may wonder what place the study of group development has in the investigation of individual human personality. There is the implication in Moreno's work that weaknesses in society have the same causal factors as weaknesses in the individual personality. Just as individuals have personalities, so do societies. And, of course, there is the known sociological position that a society, an ethnic group, or a culture is a composite of individuals: an obvious fact. Essentially the principle means that a philosophy of adjustment applies equally well to societies as to individuals.

We may now address ourselves to the question Moreno poses: Do societies (and/or individuals within it) change somewhat in the Marxian economic frame of reference, or do they grow and then decline in the tradition of Spengler's or Toynbee's theses? Moreno indicates that both positions are assumptions that may or may not be accurate and that further sound research along the lines of sociodramatic techniques is needed. It may be that societies do both. Certainly, Moreno feels, the individual personality grows from a simple organism into a highly complex and highly differentiated one. Therefore, if society parallels individuals in their matrices, we may conclude that society has a natural development of growth and decline, and as it develops it influences its constituent individuals. Whatever we say of the individual may be an interpretation of his society. Both individuals and groups develop according to the same pattern.

One more introductory theme is needed prior to discussing the periods, chronology, and characteristics of individuals as they develop into groups and groups as they develop from the effect the individuals have upon them. Using Greek mythology, as he so often does, Moreno employs the gods Eros (god of love), Eris (god of discord), and the lesser known brother of Eros, Anteros, the god of mutual love, to exemplify the forces of attraction and repulsion among men. As the personality develops in groups, it demonstrates all the capacities of Eros, Eris, and Anteros. Between personalities there is attraction in the form of love, repulsion in the form of hatred, and mutual attraction in the form of reciprocal fellowship, compassion, sympathy, and empathy. Their development is treated in the next section.

PERIODS OF GROUP DEVELOPMENT

The reciprocity of maturing sociability that exists between individuals and their groups follows somewhat certain patterns as Moreno distinguishes them.

Presocialized period—From birth to around 7 or 9 years of age individuals singly and in groups show a diffuse pattern. Most of the action is independent and uncoordinated. Roles are poorly structured. Toward the latter part of the period strong telic relationships may be found, but the incidence of developing attraction, repulsion, and mutual attraction patterns is spasmodic. The social atom structure is probably the strongest factor, with the exception of unbridled spontaneity. The value of the warm-up and the recognition of strong tele feelings are missing. In short, the child up to the ages of 7 or 9 has a poorly formed personality, as does the age group he belongs to.

First socialized period—From 7 to 9 years to around 13 or 14 years of age there is a rapid increase in both individual and group socialization. The children are now capable of organizing and operating independent social groups without adult help. Each child now has the capacity to develop and use a telic relationship based on real properties of aversion and affection, and from the tele content strong role structures are being created by the peer society and by himself.

Second socialized period—The last period runs from 13 to 14 years of age into full maturity. Whereas in the first socialization period there was a cleavage between adult and child groups, these differences are now disappearing, especially as the adolescent takes on more and more adult values. At the beginning of the period the sexual cleavages and the racial cleavages are emerging to become, at the adult level, a fully developed split. If a full personality emerges, there is then a full set of principles operating through the Morenian frame of reference: tele, warm-up, role playing, spontaneity–creativity–cultural conserve, and especially the sociogenetic law that will be introduced in a coming section.

STAGES OF GROUP DEVELOPMENT

Moreno includes these stages as a part of the first socialized period, but they are discussed separately here for clearer understanding. The period from birth to about the ages of 6 to 8 years is the intersexual stage. The period from 8 to 13 years is the first homosexual stage. From age 13 to 15 Moreno feels there is a parallel set of stages called the second intersexual stage and the second homosexual stage. Obviously he is not talking about sex per se, in the Freudian term of reference, but saying that groups are developed with like-sexed or heterosexual emphases. In this case *intersexual* means "between sexes" and *homosexual* means "between the same sex."

CHARACTERISTICS OF GROUP DEVELOPMENT

As previously mentioned, Moreno feels that one of the characteristics of groups as they develop is the cleavage between racial groups. This cleavage is the result of prejudicial attitudes which children get from adults. Because children wish to meet the approval of their elders, it does not matter whether the adults are controlling factors (parents, teachers, etc.) or environmental figures with no direct control of the child's behavior. The effect is the same.

Another characteristic of group development is the horizontal and vertical vectors of development. By *horizontal vectors* Moreno means "inter-relatedness in a group with no individual at the top or bottom." By *vertical vectors* he means "a feeling in the group of a hierarchical order from top to bottom in relation to one or more factors." Moreno first began to study this phenomenon by arranging nine babies in a circular position equidistant from each other for about the first year of life. Until approximately the ages of 20 to 28 weeks the infants existed in organic isolation, each infant absorbed in itself. After about 20 to 28 weeks the babies began to react to each other. At this stage psychological distance was highly correlated with physical distance. One baby would respond to the crying or emotional tone of another baby. Moreno gave the name *horizontal differentiation* to the reciprocity of emotional feeling and believed that it continued to influence the personality for the remainder of life. At about the 40th to 42nd week the differences in physical strength or mobility and mental alertness began to affect the organization of the group. There began to develop leaders and followers for short periods of time. Moreno called this the *vertical arrangement* in the group organization. It, too, continued to affect the personality for life. Although he did not work with the same group of infants for the entire study, the result with each group studied was that it contained three types of formations: organic isolates, horizontal and homogeneous groupings, and a vertical structure running from the strongest to the weakest, with the strongest exerting powerful influences on the behavior of the weaker members of the group.

Out of all of this and innumerable studies with larger and older groups and in a variety of settings, Moreno evolved something akin to a sociogenetic law.

Sociogenetic Law Principle

The sociogenetic law, like the previous principle, group development, is not a major part of Moreno's theoretical position. Its contribution is great enough, however, to merit consideration as a factor in molding personality.

The variable personalities in a group do not destroy the entity of the group, Moreno maintains, but seem to create a synthesis. If all personalities were stamped in the same mold, not a group but a monotonous line of robots would emerge. From these automatons no spontaneity or creativity could ever be hoped for. What Moreno terms the *crisscrossing of personality currents* or *telic systems* synthesize and produce a dynamic group that makes sense to him.

Similar to biogenetic law, the sociogenetic law states that higher group organizations develop from lower group organizations. The parallel, Moreno feels, is quite close and quite accurate. Essentially the sociogenetic law states that ontogenetically all groups go through some modifications of form, as did ancient and primeval societies in the historic evolution of man. That is, there is a law of developmental sequence from simple to complex in the formation of every group. As a basis for supporting his thesis Moreno cites the following:

1. Children and adolescents spontaneously develop groupings from year to year; these groupings get more complex, with rituals and rules as the organization integrates, until such final touches as constitutions and rules of order appear.
2. The above groups always have vestiges of the previous periods of growth and development. Each stage of growth has both the shades of the past and the portents of the future, which can be discerned by careful study of the group in its current form.
3. Retarded adolescents and early school classes are comparable in their groupings.
4. Primitive societies and children's societies are remarkably similar in many of their formal attributes.

The basic importance of the sociogenetic law to personality theorists is threefold. Individual personalities go from simple to complex, thereby providing a parallel kind of study. Individuals comprise groups and are both controlled by the group and in control of the group. Whatever happens to the singular human personality is of interest to the personality theorist.

SOCIODYNAMIC EFFECT

"A distortion of choice distribution in favor of the more chosen as against the less chosen is characteristic of all groupings which have been sociometrically tested" (*Who Shall Survive?* p. 639). "The hypothesis of the sociodynamic effect claims that a number of persons of a group will be persistently left out of a productive contact and communication; the persistent neglect of some individuals is far beneath their aspirations and persistently favors others, out of proportion to their requirements" (personal note, spring, 1962).

Measurement Principle

There is no doubt that an entire text could be written (and has been!) concerning Moreno's measurement principles.

Much of Moreno's work and especially that of the neo-Morenians has been grouped together under the subject of sociometry, which deals primarily with sociograms, spontaneity tests, and sociometric matrices. But actually the measurement principle is not a principle of personality dynamics but a method of measuring these dynamics. Moreno is chiefly noted for sociometry, a method of structuring and graphically portraying group organization. However, as the reader has no doubt observed, Moreno has more to say than how to draw lines from one circle to another. His is a way of thinking about personality and thus becomes a theory of personality.

With his emphasis on graphic presentation of human behavior Moreno has at times been criticized for studying closed systems of societal orders. The renowned anthropologist Margaret Mead has felt that sociometry has been guilty of this charge. Moreno's rebuttal is probably best stated by the opening sentence of *Who Shall Survive?*: "A true therapeutic procedure cannot have less an objective than the whole of mankind."

No less famous a figure in psychology's past than E. L. Thorndike has said that "Whatever exists at all, exists in some amount," and practically the entire psychometric world has added, "Whatever exists in some amount can be measured directly or indirectly." Along the same line, but *not* as a direct result of Thorndike's statement, Moreno, too, feels that human behavior can be analyzed structurally. In his sociometric tests, for example, horizontal sociograms reflect little or no reasons for the respondent's choices while the vertical type of sociogram reveals strong reasons for positive or negative choices. This small example of sociograms (the field and its implications are tremendous) indicates something of Moreno's emphasis on the value of graphic presentation. It is interesting that in the opinion of some of Moreno's followers Moreno predated Lewin in the diagrammatic attempt to portray human behavior.

Now, however, the question must be answered: What does measuring personality have to do with the dynamics of personality structure? It is precisely for the reason that personality does have a structure that sociometrists feel they are dealing with the basic stuff of personality. In what appears to be an inversion of cause and effect, they say that personality has dimensions, the social atom, telic sensitivity, role taking, spontaneity testing, creative activity, and cultural conserves and that whatever exists in some amount can be measured. To approach the thesis tangentially, we may say that one cannot measure that which does not exist. The sociometrist can get measurements of the dimensions of personality; ergo, personality exists because it can be measured directly or indirectly. It is a way of saying that man has a dynamic personality which does things for him because it can be measured. If this is the case, then measurement is part and parcel of man's personality both as that being measured and as that which measures.

DELIMITATIONS

This chapter does not include a discussion of the techniques of psychodrama or sociodrama, nor does it cover the other aspects of therapy. It confines itself to Moreno's description of why man does the things he does rather than discussing how we can measure these processes (except, of course, for the short treatment of measurement as a principle).

Other valuable contributions of the sociometric approach which have been omitted are these: act centers and content centers in forgetfulness, dream hunger, first and second universes, psychosocial networks, and the six types of tele. The reasons for omission are twofold: First, although Moreno is highly skilled in theory, therapy, and research, the current text is interested only in the theoretical aspects of his work; second, many of the ideas listed above are those of Moreno's followers and not exclusively those of Moreno. As was stated in the beginning of the present book, it is not the purpose here to be an interpreter of an interpreter.

EXPLAINING HUMAN BEHAVIOR VIA MORENO'S SOCIOMETRIC THEORY

No two interpreters of Moreno's work would probably ever agree completely on how to use his theory in explaining certain of man's behavioral problems: marriage, perversions, suicide, lawbreaking, supranatural being, humor, smoking, play and recreation, and psychoses–neuroses. This is not unusual because neo-Freudians, neo-Sullivanians, or neo-Rogerians do not use a theory in accordance with each other's interpretations. The reader may now interpret Moreno's work in attempting to explain for himself why the nine behavioral phenomena occur.

PREDICTING HUMAN BEHAVIOR VIA
MORENO'S SOCIOMETRIC THEORY

Some aspects of the sociometric theory seem to lend themselves admirably to forecasting what the human personality will do. Because Moreno is a therapist first and a theorist second, he operates as all therapists must and indeed do, on the basis that their therapeutic work is going to change the client's behavior and that the change will be in a desired direction. The specific details may not be predictable, but certainly the overall behavioral pattern is. To assume that therapists do not do this is to level the charge that therapy is completely trial and error manipulation. Any therapist who has no prognostic idea of what he is doing to the client's future had best leave the business. Thus, the emphasis in sociometry with its psychodramatic and sociodramatic techniques of changing human personalities is on predicting what these techniques will do to the client's future.

Personal Prediction

Many of the ideas represented in this chapter are pragmatically oriented. They are based on ordinary people in ordinary circumstances. Whereas Freud extracted his concepts from deviant individuals and Jung dealt with the entire panoply of human existence from its earliest beginnings to its ultimate teleological end, Moreno works *in situ* (in the life situation where the behavior actually happens) from normal origins or *status nascendi* ("the emerging condition," *status*; "of things that may be in the unpredictable future," *nascendi*; i.e., the experience is new to the child although not to others, or, the child feels he is creating an experience which is new not only to him but to the world).

Personal prediction, it may be recalled, has two connotations as it is used in this book. One is that no matter what research has indicated or what empirical evidence is at hand, each of us subjectively accepts or rejects the evidence from a personal frame of reference. In short, what is predictable proof to Sheldon may be poor evidence to others. We all predict from a personal bias. The second meaning of personal prediction is that the reader is allowed the privilege of using the theory to predict his own future.

On the basis of the second meaning the reader is now invited to test Moreno's theory in predicting his own behavior. For example, it may be a convenient exercise and a fruitful one to take, for a point of referral, the nine problems mentioned in the section on explanation. The reader may predict success in his own marriage and in others he knows through a consideration of the roles involved. In a good marriage there must be a strong telic relationship. If the wedded couple cannot reverse roles either symbolically or actually, the marriage may end in divorce, or at best as a very unhappy contract. Children used as idolized cultural conserves will restrict the new roles the husband and wife can play, and there may result a poorly constructed personality for the child. All of these outcomes can be predicted by the reader if he believes in the efficacy of the Moreno theory.

In like manner, perversions may be role confusion, suicide may be collapse of the role structure, and lawbreaking may be role stereotyping accompanied by complete inability to reverse roles. If the a priori conditions exist, then we may be able to predict the consequent behavior pattern. One may predict that human personality will always have and worship a supranatural being, that man will always laugh, that he will smoke, that he will play, and finally that he will continue to become neurotic and psychotic.

Scientific or Laboratory Prediction

The literature by Moreno and on Moreno's work is voluminous. However, as is true with most theorists, the bulk of his work concerns itself with therapeutic techniques and devices. Moreno is involved with the "here and now," which nevertheless does not make him ignore the future. Predictability, for Moreno, is tied up with constancy. "If there is constancy, then there should also be predictability" (*Sociometry and the Science of Man*, p. 114). From still another viewpoint, spontaneity without the conservability of the cultural conserve will of necessity lead to unpredictability in human behavior. On the other hand we may assure ourselves of predictability if we create and acknowledge the power inherent in the cultural conserve.

Prediction in sociometry is concerned with the role playing situations in psychodrama or sociodrama. Such being the case, prediction is of the greatest importance to Moreno. He feels that low- and middle-range levels of creativity can be adequately predicted in the psychodramatic theater or laboratory if the warming up stage is long enough to cause the spontaneous creation of individual behavior. Plunging an actor in one of his sociodramas into a role before the actor has had sufficient time to warm up to the role will bring unpredictable results. Extending this thought out of the laboratory into real life we find that an individual's behavior may be predicted more and more accurately, the longer the warming up time prior to the spontaneous creativity of an act. In like manner predictability increases with knowledge of the roles one is expected to play and amount of experience gathered in actual life roles. If an individual pursues a stereotyped role, we may predict his or her behavior with an extremely high degree of accuracy. The more rigidly a stereotyped role is played, the less effect society and other influences have upon behavior. The result is prediction and control of the highest order.

Moreno himself acknowledges the difficulties inherent in validating research on psychodrama.

The question as to the validity of psychodrama has aroused considerable controversy in the course of the years. There have been two opinions. One emphasizes that the usual measures of reliability and validity do not seem to be particularly appropriate for psychodrama. If each person acts out his life honestly, the data are perfectly reliable and valid. The second opinion is that the current methods of measuring validity can be applied. The *two opinions do not exclude one another*. The two methods of validation can be combined.

But it is accurate to say that the validity of psychodrama does not require proof beyond its face value. It is a statement of the persons themselves, what they experience at a certain moment in respect to a given activity. Psychodrama deals with primary acts and bits of behavior, and not with "factors" like intelligence, genes, or any other hidden factor. A choice is not more honorable because it is statistically valid. There is no need for further validation as long as the members of the group and their behavior are taken as they are expressed in the present tense and as long as no pretense is made that the future of the participants can be predicted from the events which have been produced or that generalizations can be drawn from whatever the events demonstrated. But one can state with certainty that what matters is that the actions and decisions are valid for the participants themselves at the time when they are experienced. *In such a case, one may talk about an "existential" validation, and it should be definitely separated from "scientific" validation.* But when one thinks of existential validation, one must guard against automatically thinking that this must be an impulsive and irrational kind of behavior. It may be behavior of the highest and most well-organized kind (Moreno, 1968a; italics added).

Despite what appears to be a growing interest in psychodrama as a research field in the academic world (see the following studies), a careful screening of studies on personality as they are found in the reviews of research contained in *Annual Review of Psychology* for the years 1964 to 1969 reveals no mention of Moreno's name or psychodrama as a tool for studying human personality. Perhaps the omission will be corrected in the ensuing volumes.

Nevertheless, research has been and is being done both here and abroad to test some of the psychodramatic theories. Most of the studies are reported in *Group Psychotherapy*, the "Official Organ of the American Society of Group Psychotherapy and Psychodrama." As yet research reporting on Morenian concepts is sparse in the established academic psychological journals, particularly those under the aegis of the American Psychological Association.

The following studies represent some of the investigative efforts on psychodrama as a theory and as a technique to change behavior. What happens after a person has participated in an intensive three-day psychodramatic session? In one study, the attitudinal changes appeared to last for many weeks (Dean and Marshall, 1965). (It would be refreshing to see a similar study of "T" groups or sensitivity marathons.—i.e., Who picks up the pieces?) Contrary to what may be general opinion, the most-liked person in a group may have little influence upon the group or helping the group to achieve its goals (Hashmi, 1968). Creative adolescents do not seek each other's company but have friendships that are "evenly distributed" (Yamamoto, 1964). For many years educators and others have used sociograms to arrange students in some desired order. One study indicated that sociometric devices are "not genuine indicators of real play preferences." A student may indicate a preference but actually play out of school with a nonchosen classmate (Sutton-Smith, 1965). Sociometry as an approach to understanding individuals has also been studied (Tokita, 1960; Waisman, 1964). The telic structure between racial groups indicates a strong rejection of blacks by whites, but in one study orphans were more often rejected than black classmates (Morgan and Nussel, 1967). A second study in the same racial problem substantiated Moreno's principle of sociostasis (Hart, 1964). And finally, the inventive use of television by Moreno, who was the first to mention and use it in therapeutic settings, has been chronicled and replicated (Z. Moreno, 1967; (Vogeler and Greenberg, 1968).

■ SUMMARY

The main theme of Moreno's sociometric theory revolves around the concept of role playing. The actors portrayed in Figure 7 suggest that man plays roles

FIGURE 7. *Diagrammatic summary of Moreno's theory.*

both for himself and for an audience. The social atom is suggested by the proximity of the members of the audience to each other. The feeling of tele also operates between members of the audience and the cast on the stage. The cast on the stage is in a state of flux, as is shown by a member of the audience climbing the steps to take part in the drama. In fact, the action of members of the audience in responding to each other is as important as their response to the action on the stage. Children are shown in the theater to suggest an undeveloped group who will eventually stop playing and, through the sociogenetic law, begin to take the place of the adult figures in the audience as they die and pass out of the theater.

The stage itself represents a cultural conserve just as much as does the play on it. The two actors in this scene (one shown by dotted lines) look alike to indicate role reversal. From the time that the play was first cast a period of warming up has been going on between the actors and the audience, which had been aware of the play through previous publicity. As each actor enters the scene, engages in action, and leaves the scene at an appropriate time, the full panoply of spontaneity–creativity–cultural conserve is demonstrated. Even if two actors play the same character, they will portray the role differently. The impression an actor leaves of the role he played, whether it be the star or a spear carrier, can be considered a cultural conserve. Later actors playing the same role may wish to emulate the first one or try desperately to revise the role.

Thus, the quotation which began this chapter is perhaps the best single-sentence summary of Moreno's theory of personality.

> All the world's a stage,
> And all the men and women merely players:
> They have their exits and their entrances:
> And one man in his time plays many parts.

BIBLIOGRAPHY

PRIMARY SOURCES

BOOKS

Moreno, J. L., *Homo Juvenis*, in *Einladung zu einer Begegnung*. Berlin: G. Kiepenheuer, 1914, p. 19.

Moreno, J. L., *Das Testament des Vaters*. Berlin: G. Kiepenheuer, 1920. Trans., *The Words of the Fathers*. New York: Beacon House, 1941.

Moreno, J. L., *Das Stegreiftheater*. Berlin: G. Kiepenheuer, 1923. Trans., *The Theater of Spontaneity*. New York: Beacon House, 1947.

Moreno, J. L., *Who Shall Survive?* New York: Beacon House, 1934.

Also reprinted 2nd ed. and revised in 1953.

Moreno, J. L., *Mental Catharsis and the Psychodrama*. New York: Beacon House, 1944.

Moreno, J. L., *Sociodrama: A Method for the Analysis of Social Conflicts*. New York: Beacon House, 1944.

Moreno, J. L., and F. B. Moreno, *Spontaneity Theory of Child Development*. New York: Beacon House, 1944.

Moreno, J. L., *Psychodrama*, Vol. I. New York: Beacon House, 1946.

Moreno, J. L. (ed.), *Group Psychotherapy*. New York: Beacon House, 1946.

Moreno, J. L., *A Sociometric Guide for Teachers*. Washington: American Council on Education, 1947.

Moreno, J. L., *The Theater of Spontaneity: An Introduction to Psychodrama*. New York: Beacon House, 1947.

See earlier German work in 1923.

Moreno, J. L., *Sociometry: Experimental Method and the Science of Society*. New York: Beacon House, 1951.

Moreno, J. L., *Preludes to My Autobiography*. New York: Beacon House, 1955.

Moreno, J. L., Psychodrama and sociatry, in A. A. Roback (ed.), *Presentday Psychology*. New York: Philosophical Library, 1955, pp. 679–686.

Moreno, J. L. (ed.), *Sociometry and the Science of Man*. New York: Beacon House, 1956.

Also considered as Vol. 18, No. 4, of *Sociometry*, 1955.

Moreno, J. L., and L. Yablonsky, Progress in psychodrama, in D. Brower and L. E. Abt (eds.), *Progress in Clinical Psychology*, Vol. II. New York: Grune & Stratton, 1956, pp. 216–222.

Fromm-Reichmann, F., and J. L. Moreno (eds.), *Progress in Psychotherapy*. New York: Grune & Stratton, 1956.

Moreno, J. L., *The First Book on Group Psychotherapy*, 3rd ed. New York: Beacon House, 1957.

Moreno, J. L. In J. E. Fairchild (ed.), *Personal Problems and Psychological Frontiers*. New York: Sheridan House, 1957.

Masserman, J. H., and J. L. Moreno (eds.), *Progress in Psychotherapy*: Vol. II, *Anxiety and Therapy*. New York: Grune & Stratton, 1957.

Moreno's introduction discusses global psychotherapy and prospects of a therapeutic world order.

Moreno, J. L., and Z. T. Moreno, *Psychodrama*, Vol. II. New York: Beacon House, 1959.

Masserman, J. H., and J. L. Moreno (eds.), *Progress in Psychotherapy*: Vol. V, *Review and Integration*. New York: Grune & Stratton, 1960.

Moreno, J. L., *The Sociometry Reader*. New York: Free Press, 1960.

Moreno, J. L., *Code of Ethics for Group Psychotherapy and Psychodrama: Relationship to the Hippocratic Oath.* New York: Beacon House, 1962.

Appeared originally in *Group Psychotherapy*, 1955, 8, 357.

Moreno, J. L., *The First Psychodramatic Family.* New York: Beacon House, 1964.

Moreno, J. L., The sociometric approach to personality, in W. S. Sahakian (ed.), *Psychology of Personality: Readings in Theory.* Chicago: Rand McNally, 1965.

Excerpts from Moreno's writings.

Moreno, J. L. (ed.), *The International Handbook of Group Psychotherapy.* New York: Philosophical Library, 1965.

A truly global survey of trends and achievements in group psychotherapy; has contributions from more than 150 authors in five languages—English, French, German, Italian, and Spanish.

PERIODICALS

Moreno, J. L., Group method and group psychotherapy, *Sociometric Monogr.*, 1932, No. 5.

Moreno, J. L., Who shall survive? *Nerv. Men. Dis. Monogr.*, 1934, No. 58.

Moreno, J. L., and H. H. Jennings, Spontaneity training, a method of personality development, *Sociometric Rev.*, 1936.

Moreno, J. L., Interpersonal therapy and the psychopathology of interpersonal relations, *Sociometry*, 1937, 1, 9–76.

Moreno, J. L., and H. H. Jennings, Statistics of social configurations, *Sociometry*, 1938, 1, 342–374.

Moreno, J. L., Psychodramatic shock therapy: A sociometric approach to the problem of mental disorders, *Sociometry*, 1939, 2, No. 1, 1–30.

Moreno, J. L., Creativity and cultural conserves with special reference to musical expression, *Sociometry*, 1939, 2, No. 2, 1–30.

Moreno, J. L., Mental catharsis and the psychodrama, *Sociometry*, 1940, 3, 209–244.

Moreno, J. L., Psychodramatic treatment of marriage problems, *Sociometry*, 1940, 3, 1–23.

Moreno, J. L., Psychodramatic treatment of psychoses, *Sociometry*, 1940, 3, 115–132.

Moreno, J. L., H. H. Jennings, and J. Sargent, Time as a qualitative index to interpersonal relations, *Sociometry*, 1940, 3, 62–80.

Moreno, J. L., Foundations of sociometry, an introduction, *Sociometry*, 1941, 4, 15–35.

Moreno, J. L., The philosophy of the moment and the spontaneity theatre, *Sociometry*, 1941, 4, 205–226.

Moreno, J. L., The prediction and planning of success in marriage, *Marriage Fam. Liv.*, 1941, 3, 83–84.

Moreno, J. L., and W. S. Dunkin, The function of the social investigator in experimental psychodrama, *Sociometry*, 1941, *4*, 392–417.

Moreno, J. L., and J. K. Fischel, Spontaneity procedures in television broadcasting with special emphasis on interpersonal relation systems, *Sociometry*, 1942, *5*, 7–28.

Moreno, J. L., and Z. Toeman, The group approach in psychodrama, *Sociometry*, 1942, *5*, 191–195.

Moreno, J. L., The concept of sociodrama, *Sociometry*, 1943, *6*, 434–449.

Moreno, J. L., Sociometry and the cultural order, *Sociometry*, 1943, *6*, 299–344.

Moreno, J. L., A case of paranoia treated through psychodrama, *Sociometry*, 1944, *7*, 312–327.

Moreno, J. L., Psychodrama and therapeutic motion pictures, *Sociometry*, 1944, *7*, 230–244.

Moreno, J. L., Spontaneity test and spontaneity training, *Psychodrama Monogr.*, No. 4, 1944.

Moreno, J. L., and F. B. Moreno, Spontaneity theory of child development, *Sociometry*, 1944, *7*, 89–128.

Moreno, J. L., and F. B. Moreno, Spontaneity theory in its relation to problems of interpretation and measurement, *Sociometry*, 1944, *7*, 339–355.

Moreno, J. L., and H. H. Jennings, Sociometric methods of grouping and regrouping: With reference to authoritative and democratic methods of grouping, *Sociometry*, 1944, *7*, 397–414.

Moreno, J. L., Psychodramatic treatment of marriage problems, *Psychodrama Monogr.*, No. 7, 1945.

Moreno, J. L., Psychodrama and therapeutic motion pictures, *Psychodrama Monogr.*, No. 11, 1945.

Moreno, J. L., Psychodramatic treatment of psychoses, *Psychodrama Monogr.*, No. 15, 1945.

Moreno, J. L., Psychodrama and the psychopathology of interpersonal relations, *Psychodrama Monogr.*, No. 16, 1945.

Moreno, F. B., and J. L. Moreno, Role tests and role diagrams of children, *Sociometry*, 1945, *8*, 426–431.

Moreno, J. L., Psychodrama and group psychotherapy, *Sociometry*, 1946, *9*, 249–253.

Moreno, J. L., Situation test, *Sociometry*, 1946, *9*, Nos. 2–3.

Moreno, J. L., Contributions of sociometry to research methodology in sociology, *Amer. Soc. Rev.*, 1947, *12*, 287–292.

Moreno, J. L., Discussion of Snyder's "The Present Status of Psychotherapeutic Counseling," *Psychol. Bull.*, 1947, *44*, 564–567.

Moreno, J. L., and H. H. Jennings, Sociometric control studies of grouping and regrouping, *Sociometry Monogr.*, No. 7, 1947.

Moreno, J. L., How Kurt Lewin's "Research Center for Group Dynamics" started and the question of paternity, *Group Psychother.*, 1952, *5*, 1–6.

Moreno, J. L., Psychodramatic production techniques, *Group Psychother.*, 1952, *5*, 243–273.

Moreno, J. L., How Kurt Lewin's "Research Center for Group Dynamics" started, *Sociometry*, 1953, *16*, 101–106.

Moreno, J. L., Interpersonal therapy, group psychotherapy and the function of the unconscious, *Group Psychother.*, 1954, 7, 191–204.

Moreno, J. L., Old and new trends in sociometry: Turning points in small group research, *Sociometry*, 1954, 17, 179–193.

Moreno, J. L., Sociometry and experimental sociology, *Sociometry*, 1954, 17, 358–363.

Moreno, J. L., Transference, counter transference, and tele: Their relation to group research and group psychotherapy, *Group Psychother.*, 1954, 7, 107–117.

Moreno, J. L., First note on the sociometric system, *Sociometry*, 1955, 18, 88–89.

Moreno, J. L., The significance of the therapeutic format and the place of acting out in psychotherapy, *Group Psychother.*, 1955, 8, 7–19.

Moreno, J. L., Z. Moreno, and J. Moreno, The discovery of the spontaneous man: With special emphasis upon the technique of role reversal, *Group Psychother.*, 1955, 8, 103–129.

See also *Sociometry*, 1956, 18, 411–438.

Moreno, J. L., American culture-in-transition, *Sociometry*, 1956, 18, 351–355.

Moreno, J. L., The dilemma of existentialism, daseinsanalyse and the psychodrama: With special emphasis upon "existential validation," *Sociometry*, 1956, 18, 55–63.

Moreno, J. L., Freud's hundredth birthday, *Group Psychother.*, 1956, 9, 251.

Moreno, J. L., The sociometric school and the science of man, *Sociometry*, 1956, 18, 271–279.

Moreno, J. L., Theory of spontaneity and creativity, *Sociometry*, 1956, 18, 361–374.

Moreno, J. L., and F. B. Moreno, Spontaneity theory of child development, *Sociometry*, 1956, 18, 393–411.

Moreno, J. L., Code of ethics of group psychotherapists, *Group Psychother.*, 1957, 10, 143–144.

Moreno, J. L., The dilemma of existentialism, daseinsanalyse and the psychodrama with special emphasis upon existential validation, *Int. J. Soc. Sociatr.*, 1957, 1.

Moreno, J. L., Ontology of group formation, *Group Psychother.*, 1957, 1, 346–348.

Moreno, J. L., Psychodrama of Adolf Hitler, *Sociometry*, 1957, 1, 71–80.

Moreno, J. L., Psychodrama of Adolf Hitler, summary and evaluation of the significance of the psychotic Hitler drama, *Int. J. Soc. Sociatr.*, 1957, 1.

Moreno, J. L., Replies to Medard Boss, Jiri Kolaja and Jiri Nehnevajsa on existentialism, *Int. J. Soc. Sociatr.*, 1957, 1.

Moreno, J. L., Sociometry of the Soviet Purges, *Int. J. Soc. Sociatr.*, 1957, 1.

Moreno, J. L., Sputnik and the psychodramatic space traveler, *Int. J. Soc. Sociatr.*, 1957, 1.

Moreno, J. L., The story of Johnny Psychodramatist, *Int. J. Soc. Sociatr.*, 1957, 1

Moreno, J. L., The role concept, a bridge between psychiatry and sociology, *Amer. J. Psychiat.*, 1961, *118*, 518–523.

Moreno, J. L., Czechoslovak Psychiatric Congress with photographs, *Int. J. Soc. Sociatr.*, 1962, 2.

Moreno, J. L., The first national Cuban Neuro-Psychiatric Congress, *Int. J. Soc. Sociatr.*, 1962, 2.

Moreno, J. L., The place of group psychotherapy, psychodrama and psychoanalysis in the framework of creativity and destruction, *Group Psychother.*, 1962, *15*, 339–341.

Moreno, J. L., Political prospects of sociometry, *Int. J. Soc. Sociatr.*, 1962, 2.

Moreno, J. L., Psychiatric encounter in Soviet Russia, *Int. J. Soc. Sociatr.*, 1962, 2.

Moreno, J. L., Role theory and the emergence of the self, *Group Psychother.*, 1962, *15*, 114–117.

Moreno, J. L., The "united role theory" and the drama, *Group Psychother.*, 1962, *15*, 253–254.

Moreno, J. L., The actual trends in group psychotherapy, *Group Psychother.*, 1963, *16*, 117–131.

Moreno, J. L., Genesis of sociometry, *Int. J. Soc. Sociatr.*, 1963, *3*, 21–25.

Moreno, J. L., Z. Moreno, and J. Moreno, The first psychodramatic family, *Group Psychother.*, 1963, *16*, 203–249.

Moreno, J. L., Psychodrama of murder, a joint trial of Lee Harvey Oswald and Jack Ruby, *Group Psychother.*, 1964, *17*, 61–62.

Moreno, J. L., The third psychiatric revolution and the scope of psychodrama, *Group Psychother.*, 1964, *17*, 149–171.

Moreno, J. L., Z. Moreno, and J. Moreno, New Moreno legends, *Group Psychother.*, 1964, *17*, 1–35.

Moreno, J. L., Psychodrama in action, *Group Psychother.*, 1965, *18*, 87–117.

Moreno, J. L., Therapeutic vehicles and the concept of surplus reality, *Group Psychother.*, 1965, *18*, 211–216.

Moreno, J. L., The creativity theory of personality: spontaneity, creativity and human potentialities, *N.Y. Univ. Bull.*, 1966, *66*, 18–24.

Moreno, J. L., Psychiatry of the twentieth century: Function of the universalia: time, space, reality and cosmos, *Group Psychother.*, 1966, *19*, 146–158.

Moreno, J. L., Psychodrama of a marriage: A motion picture, *Group Psychother.*, 1966, *19*, 49–93.

Moreno, J. L., The roots of psychodrama. Autobiographical notes: A reply to Sarró *Group Psychother.*, 1966, *19*, 140–145.

Moreno, J. L., Cervantes, Don Quixote and psychodrama reply to Professor Francisco Garcia-Valdecasas, *Group Psychother.*, 1967, *20*, 15–24.

Moreno, J. L., The validity of psychodrama, *Group Psychother.*, 1968a, *21*, 3.

> "Existential" validation and "scientific" validation are not mutually exclusive.

Moreno, J. L., Universal peace in our time, *Group Psychother.*, 1968b, *21*, 175–176.

FILMS

Moreno, J. L., *Introduction to Psychodrama*, 16 mm., black and white, sound, 10 min. New York: Beacon House, Therapeutic Film Prod., Inc.
Moreno, J. L. (director), *Psychodrama and Group Psychotherapy in Action*, 16 mm., black and white, sound, 60 min. New York: Beacon House, 1964.
Moreno, J. L. (director), *Psychodrama of a Marriage*, 16 mm., black and white sound, 100 min. New York: Beacon House, 1964.
Haas, Robert B. (director), *Role Playing in Guidance*, 16 mm., black and white sound, 17 min. New York: Beacon House, 1966.

SUGGESTED READINGS

BOOKS

Biddle, B. J., and E. J. Thomas, *Role Theory, Concepts and Research*. New York Wiley, 1966.

> Acknowledges Moreno's pioneering in role theory and role playing tech niques.

Corsini, R. J., Counseling and psychotherapy, in E. F. Borgatta and W. W Lambert (eds.), *Handbook of Personality Theory and Research*. Chicago Rand McNally, 1968, chap. 23.
Kahn, S., *Psychodrama Explained*. New York: Philosophical Library, 1964.

PERIODICALS

Allport, G. W., Comments on: J. L. Moreno, transference, countertransference and tele—their relation to group research and group psychotherapy, *Group Psychother.*, 1954, 7, 307–308.
Aucilino, J., Critique of Moreno's spontaneity theory, *Group Psychother.*, 1954, 7 148–158.
Bain, R., Science, art, ethics, and spontaneity, *Sociometry*, 1956, 18, 296–303.

> Creative act is both unique and uniform, and interdependent and inter active.

Borgatta, E. F., Role playing specification, personality and performance, *Soci ometry*, 1961, 24, 218–233.

> College students and role playing.

Corsini, R., Freud, Rogers, and Moreno: An inquiry into the possible relationship between manifest personality, theory, and the method of some eminen psychotherapists, *Group Psychother.*, 1956, 9, 274–281.

> Calls Moreno the man with capacity for immediate action.

Corsini, R. G., and L. J. Putzey, Bibliography, *Group Psychother.*, 1956, 9 177–249.

Dean, W. N., and E. B. Marshall, A validation study of psychodrama group experience: A preliminary survey, *Group Psychother.*, 1965, 18, 217–240.

A follow-up on attitudinal change after an intensive three-day psychodrama institute.

eLatil, P., Sociometry, the science of human groups, *Int. J. Soc. Sociat.*, 1963, 3, 39–42.

Greenberg, M. S., Role playing: An alternative to deception? *J. Pers. Soc. Psychol.*, 1967, 7, 152–157.

Iart, J. W., Rejection patterns and group maintenance: Rejection between racial subgroups, *Int. J. Soc. Sociat.*, 1964, 4, 26–32.

Moreno's principle of sociostasis applied to white and Negro boys.

Iashmi, H., Determinants of the sociometric pattern in an educational group, *Group Psychother.*, 1968, 21, 49–61.

The most-liked person may not influence the group and its goals.

zard, C. E., The effects of role-played emotion, intellectual function and evaluative ratings of the actress, *J. Clin. Psychol.*, 1964, 20, 444–446.

ebovici, S., Psychoanalytical applications of psychodrama, *J. Soc. Ther.*, 1956, 2, 280–291.

Psychodrama not better than psychoanalysis but both have common goals and principles.

Iann, J. H., Experimental evaluations of role playing, *Psychol. Bull.*, 1956, 53, 227–234.

Some evidence that valid role playing tests can be developed.

Meyer, H. J., The sociometrics of Dr. Moreno, *Sociometry*, 1952, 15, 354–363.

Moreno, Z. T., The "reluctant therapist" and the "reluctant audience" technique in psychodrama, *Group Psychother.*, 1958, 11, 278–282.

Moreno, Z. T., A survey of psychodramatic techniques, *Group Psychother.*, 1959, 12, 5–14.

Moreno, Z. T., An objective analysis of the group psychotherapy movement, *Group Psychother.*, 1960, 13, 233–237.

Moreno, Z. T., The twenty-fifth anniversary of the American Theatre of psychodrama, *Group Psychother.*, 1962, 15, 5–20.

Moreno, Z. T., Sociogenesis of individuals and groups, *Int. J. Soc. Sociat.*, 1963, 3.

Moreno, Z. T., Psychodramatic rules, techniques, and adjunctive methods, *Group Psychother.*, 1965a, 18, 73–86.

Moreno, Z. T., Saga of sociometry, *Group Psychother.*, 1965b, 18, 275–276.

Moreno, Z. T., The seminal mind of J. L. Moreno and his influence upon the present generation, *Group Psychother.*, 1967, 20, 218–229; also in *Int. J. Soc. Sociat.*, 1968, 5, 145–156.

Moreno, Z. T., Eye witness account of the Doctor Honoris Causa awarded to J. L. Moreno, Oct. 14, 1968, at Barcelona University, *Group Psychother.*, 1968, 21, 180–183.

Morgan, W. P., and E. S. Nussel, A sociometric study of play preference and play behavior in a group of third grade children, *Group Psychother.*, 1967, *20*, 74–87.

> Found rigidly structured system in parochial classroom, highest rate of rejection—orphans, 67%; Negroes, 57%.

Munzer, Jean, The effect on analytic therapy groups of the experimental introduction of special "warm-up" procedures during the first five sessions, *Dissert. Abstr.*, 1962, *22*, 2896–2897.

Murphy, G., New evaluation of sociometry, *Sociometry*, 1956, *18*, 293–294.

> More than technique or technical device; a new way of viewing human relationships.

Oeser, O. A., and F. Harary, A mathematical model for structural role theory, *Hum. Relat.*, 1962, *15*, 89–109.

Renouvier, P., The group psychotherapy movement and J. L. Moreno its pioneer and founder, *Group Psychother.*, 1958, *11*, 69–86.

Sarbin, T. R., and C. D. Hardyck, Conformance in role perception as a personality variable, *J. Consult. Psychol.*, 1955, *19*, 109–111.

> Some evidence that normal people and schizophrenics vary in role perception.

Shoobs, N. E., Individual psychology and psychodrama, *Amer. J. Indiv. Psychol.*, 1956, *12*, 46–52.

> Using psychodrama and not losing Adlerian status.

Sutton-Smith, B., Play preference and play behavior: A validity study, *Psychol. Rep.*, 1965, *16*, 65–66.

> Play preference on sociometric device not genuine indicator of real play preferences.

Teele, J. E., M. J. Schleifer, L. Corman, and K. Larson, Teacher ratings, sociometric status, and choice-reciprocity of antisocial and normal boys, *Group Psychother.*, 1966, *19*, 183–197.

> Moreno's suggestion that accuracy of teacher judgments declines as grade level increases not confirmed.

Tokita, T., Sociometric criteria for psychodramatic exercises: A research note, *Int. J. Soc. Sociat.*, 1962, *2*, 97–98.

> Simple questions must be supplemented.

Vogeler, E. S., and I. A. Greenberg, Psychodrama and audience with emphasis on closed-circuit television, *Group Psychother.*, 1968, *21*, 4–11.

Waisman, M. M., Sociometric perception and self-other attitudes, *Int. J. Soc. Sociat.*, 1964, *4*, 43–50.

> Sociometric perception and tele.

Warner, W. J., Sociology and psychiatry, *Brit. J. Sociol.*, 1954, 5, 228–237.

A critical appraisal of Moreno's *Who Shall Survive?*

Wolfe, L. A., Moreno and Mowrer: Or the new group therapy, *Group Psychother.*, 1965, *18*, 171–176.

Claims Mowrer should have read Moreno first.

Yamamoto, K., Creativity and sociometric choice among adolescents, *J. Soc. Psychol.*, 1964, *64*, 249–261.

Creativity and friendships evenly distributed. Creatives do not necessarily seek other creatives.

Part

IV

Self-Integrative—
Biosocial

GORDON ALLPORT, Carl Rogers, and Gardner Murphy seem to have a general and integrated approach to personality theory. They comprise the theorists in Part IV.

One of the most influential, most quoted, and oldest of personality theories is that of the late Gordon Allport of Harvard University. Many current theorists begin their own work by citing Allport's 1937 book, *Personality*. Allport specialized in commenting on the general world of personality theory formation. He was both a personality theorist and a theorist of theories about personality. His work was also original and integrative.

Rogers, whose personality theory is not fully formulated, stresses the integrative power of the self. To Rogers, all things belong to the self, are interpreted by the self, and are integrated by the self. His work has been developed as a full chapter primarily because of his tremendous influence in the field of therapy and also because of the research he has stimulated.

Gardner Murphy, who has wide influence through his leadership in research and as an educator of many renowned psychologists, has perhaps the most eclectic approach to personality theory of any now extant.

8

ALLPORT

He is great who is what he is from Nature,
and who never reminds us of others.

RALPH WALDO EMERSON
Representative Men, Uses of Great Men

SOME BIOGRAPHICAL DATA

Gordon Willard Allport was born on November 11, 1897, in Montezuma, Indiana,[1] one of the four sons of Dr. John Edwards and Nellie Edith (Wise) Allport. Allport received his early education in the public schools of Cleveland, Ohio, and majored in economics and philosophy at Harvard, where he was awarded the A.B. degree in 1919. He taught English and sociology at Robert College, Istanbul, Turkey, during the next academic year,

The author is most grateful to the late Dr. Allport for his patience and help in refining this chapter prior to his death in 1967.

1919–1920. Allport then returned to Harvard and received his A.M. in 1921 and his Ph.D. in psychology a year later. He studied at the University of Berlin and at the University of Hamburg during the school year 1922–1923 and spent the next year in England at Cambridge University. He again returned to Harvard and taught as an instructor in the Department of Social Ethics for the two following years. Allport accepted the position of assistant professor at Dartmouth College and stayed there until 1930, at which time he returned to Harvard as an assistant professor, then became a full Professor of Psychology in the Department of Social Relations at Harvard University, a position he held from 1942 on. In 1958 Boston University awarded him an honorary L.H.D. degree.

Gordon Allport married the former Ada Lufkin Gould of Lincolnville, Maine, on June 30, 1925. Their son, Robert Bradlee Allport, is a pediatrician.

The world lost a beloved psychologist on October 11, 1967, when Gordon Allport died at the age of 69.

Allport held office and membership in a great number of professional and honorary societies. He was a member of both the American Psychological Association (member of the council, 1936–1938; president, 1939) and the Eastern Psychological Association (president, 1943). He was a past member of the National Commission for UNESCO. He was president of the Prospect Union Association, past director of the National Opinion Research Center, and executive secretary of the Ella Lyman Cabot Foundation. In addition, he was a member of the Social Science Research and National Research councils, a member of the Society of Colonial Wars, and a member of the Harvard Club of New York. He was an honorary fellow of the British Psychological Society and an honorary member of the Deutsche Gesellschaft für Psychologie, the Osterreichische Ärztegesillschaft für Psychotherapie and the Société Française de Psychologie. Allport was a member of Phi Beta Kappa. During the period 1937–1949 he served as editor of the *Journal of Abnormal and Social Psychology*. In 1956 he was visiting Overseas Consultant to the Institute of Social Research, University of Natal, South Africa. The world of personology will never be quite the same since his passing.

INTRODUCTION

Gordon W. Allport advocated the open approach in considering the problems of personality theory. To him man's personality is not only a self-enclosed entity but also open to the world in general. Allport felt that psychology has no right to exclude contributions to personality theory, whether they come from the refined methods of science or are the insightful, behavioral descriptions of literature and philosophy.

Allport had the happy faculty of saying and writing provocative thoughts on personality theory without becoming overly controversial. He entertained no bitter recriminations against any man's theory. He did, however, plant very harp barbs in the hides of zealous workers whose systems and theories eemed to him to have proceeded too far in one direction. Such a phrase as person-destroying psychologists," as well as the following phrases, indicates his capacity to deflate the one-sidedness of some psychological efforts: "edifice omplex"; "We never seem to solve our problems or exhaust our concepts, we nly grow tired of them"; "Personality evaporates in a mist of method"; human personality . . . is . . . captive into some autistic paradise of methdology" (meaning that much is done because it is fit for testing or research lthough in essence it has little or nothing to do with human behavior); and Some of us model man after the pigeon." In advocating "person-centered sychology," Allport felt that "The greatest failing of the psychologist at the present time is his inability to prove what he knows is true."

Personality theory lives by controversy, according to Allport, and alhough personality theory itself cannot be cumulative (i.e., a theory built rom bits and pieces like beads on a string), research on personality can be umulative.

ALLPORT'S DESCRIPTION OF HUMAN BEHAVIOR

'ersonality is the "natural subject matter" of psychology; "one of the outtanding events in psychology of the present century has been the discovery of ersonality" (*Personality and Social Encounter*, p. 5 and p. 146). It is obvious hat to Allport the study of personality and the creation of an adequate heory concerning its dynamics are endeavors of the first magnitude for sychologists. However, because he promoted the open-ended method of peronality study, Allport also firmly believed that an emerging theory of peronality must be considered from the viewpoint of, and must come to terms vith, literature (Who else can present the most understandable descriptions of behavior?), philosophy (Why ignore the oldest field of personality tudy?), the natural sciences (Who have so much to contribute to methodolgy?), and the biological sciences (Is not man an animal?). Allport's rationale s more than an open-ended approach; it is also a plea for a system blended rom the work of all who can contribute to the greater understanding of nan's personality.

In his *Personality: A Psychological Interpretation* (1937), Allport wove in interesting history of the word *personality* out of the original Greek word ersona. He used the writings of the Roman statesman, orator, and author, Cicero, who found four distinct meanings of *persona:*

1. The external appearance but not the true self.
2. The character or role someone plays in life.
3. The collection of highly individual qualities that enables one to live an adequate life.
4. The distinction and dignity with which one fulfills his role in life.

From these four definitions of Cicero, Allport ferreted out fifty defini tions for the word *personality*, ending the list with his own, which is one of the most copied and discussed of all definitions: "Personality is the dynamic organization within the individual of those psychophysical systems that de termine his unique adjustments to his environment" (*Personality: A Psycho logical Interpretation*, 1937, p. 48; changed slightly in *Pattern and Growth in Personality*, 1961, to "characteristic behavior and thought," p. 28).[2]

The key phrases in Allport's definition are important for an understand ing of his conception of the term *personality*.

1. *dynamic organization:* meaning that man's personality is more than a loose collection of behaviors, that it is organized, and further that this organized human is constantly evolving and changing in motivation and self-regu lation.
2. *psychophysical systems:* meaning that man is both brain and body.
3. *determine:* meaning that "Personality *is* something and *does* something" of and by and for itself, which removes personality from being a mere ploy of others.
4. *unique:* meaning that every human being is unique in time, place, person, and adjustment quality, and is unlike any others in these characteristics.
5. *adjustments to his environment:* meaning that "Personality is a mode of survival."

In a later work Allport stated that personality has three essential char acteristics: locus, uniqueness, and inner congruence. These appear to be an excellent summary of his 1937 definition of personality in *Personality and Social Encounter*, 1960, p. 21.

Before considering the description of human behavior via Allport's system, we may profit from noting his five requirements for an adequate theory of personality. An adequate theory of personality will (1) regard the human personality as integumented—that is, as centered in the organism; (2) regard the organism as replete, not empty; (3) regard motivation as normally a fact of present structure and function, not merely as an outgrowth of earlier forces; (4) employ units of analysis capable of living synthesis; and (5) allow adequately for, but not rely exclusively upon, the phenomenon of self-con sciousness.

Like many other theorists, personality and otherwise, Allport continually expanded his concepts regarding the personality of the human. His writing style is highly readable and anything but pedantic. He presents his theory of personality primarily in four books: *Personality: A Psychological Interpreta tion* (1937), *Becoming: Basic Considerations for a Psychology of Personality* (1955), *Personality and Social Encounter* (1960), and a revision of his 1937 book, of which he changed the title to *Pattern and Growth in Personality*

---

[2] "*Pattern and Growth in Personality* changes the definition slightly: not 'unique adjust ments to his environment' but 'characteristic behavior and thought'" (personal letter March 19, 1962).

(1961). In this revision "The outlook, scope, and emphasis are not greatly changed" (Preface, p. ix), and the "basic problem remains unchanged" (Preface, p. x), but the book is a complete rewriting, includes citations of current research, and gives his expanding ideas of cognition, culture, and the self. The greatest change is his delineating more completely the process of functional autonomy.

As a personality theoretician, Allport was basically tender-minded about the foibles of man. He had a strong, humanitarian orientation toward the behavior of his fellow human beings. He did not take an extreme position, as we have seen, and he was eminently fair in considering the value of contributions from all disciplines. Consequently, he was neither pessimistic about man as a species nor unfair to the work of other theoreticians. Allport liked and cared about people, about personality theorists on all continents (his international reputation is excellent and well deserved), and in turn was liked by all who know him and his work.

In many respects Allport talked more about personality theory than he defined what personality theory actually is. His role seemed to be that of a judge of personality theories, and in this role he began to create interpretations which soon became personality theories of his own, as is demonstrated in his work printed in 1961, which offers critiques of the motivational concepts of homeostasis, instincts, needs, basic drives, tension reduction, etc. In his critical analysis he found them wanting because they are unchanging motives. Having judged these theories and found them inadequate, although somewhat helpful, he developed his own motivational theory of functional autonomy beyond the position that he took in 1937. (See later section.)

Continuing in 1961, Allport still found his original definition of personality a usable and valuable concept. The term *character*, he felt, could be largely dispensed with since it deals, from his frame of reference, with methods of evaluation of personality and is not directly connected with a definition of personality. As we shall see later, he found the term *temperament* a useful one.

In 1961 Allport was maintaining his "true eclectic" position. He agreed with Gardner Murphy that most of the potentialities of man have never been truly realized by man or by the personality psychologists who study this aspect of man.

Gordon Allport was one of the very, very few American psychologists to acknowledge Asiatic psychology. Within the subject matter of this book, Carl G. Jung is probably the only other personality theorist to pay much attention to Oriental thinking. Allport believed it inexcusable provincialism for psychologists in our culture to neglect the wisdom of the East. He examined briefly the four central desires of Hindu psychology: please, success, duty, and liberation from the pleasure–success–duty periods of existence (*Pattern and Growth in Personality*, p. 565).

One of Allport's central themes was his strong desire to occupy an inter-

mediate position between generalities and individualities about personality
However, he could not but lean toward the individualistic interpretations o
personality. He was like a skier going downhill between two mountains, suc
cessfully maintaining a position in the middle of the valley. But, as the skie
may always turn to the right, Allport always turned to the right toward
individualism as he came to the end of the journey.

In his last book Allport continued to disagree with Freud although he
saw much value in Freud. Freud "smudged the boundary lines between
neurotic and normal mental functioning" (*ibid.*, p. 155), but he made a
brilliant contribution to the world of psychology in his concept of the ego
defense mechanisms such as repression, denial, rationalization, projection
fixation, regression, and reaction formation.

Allport considered the raw materials of personality to be physique, intel
ligence, and temperament. He gave credit to Sheldon and his work with body
types and felt that there may be a close relationship between body constitu
tion and temperament. The raw material of intelligence is idiographic—that
is to say, basically unique to the individual. It is the interplay between the raw
materials of physique, intelligence, and temperament that eventually makes a
personality.

We now turn to an examination of the seven principles or major themes
that the present writer has extracted from the writings of Gordon Allport:
motivation, learning, contemporaneity, uniqueness, ego or self, continuity-
discontinuity, and traits–trends–tendencies. (There is a strong inclination at
this point to include "becoming" as an eighth principle. It is not included
only because the author believe it is adequately covered in the above seven
major themes. However, Allport emphasized the essential nature of man to
"be somebody," to become a human being worthy of the self-image in all
respects, to achieve a true "life-style" in the fullest Adlerian sense.)

Motivation Principle

According to Allport, "There is no problem in psychology more difficult to
handle" than the problem of motivation (*Personality: A Psychological Interpretation*, p. 110). Motivation theory, including his own, is incomplete: "All
theories of motivation fail to provide a full solution" (*Personality and Social
Encounter*, p. 144). "The problem of motivation is central to the psychological study of personality" (*Pattern and Growth in Personality*, p. 196).

There appears to be an overemphasis on reactive quality in motivational
theory, whereas we need more proactive motivational theory. The "re" has
been grossly overplayed at the expense of the dynamics of the "pro" factors in
motivation and, in fact, in the total picture of psychology.

> Motivation is the "go" of personality, and is, therefore, our most central prob-
> lem. Psychologists are not agreed in their accounts of what internal conditions

induce action and thought. Some say that all conduct is instigated by un-changing instincts or by drives. Such theories stress the reactive side of man's behavior. Severe restrictions must be laid on theories of this order (whether of the psychoanalytic or stimulus-response order). They fail to allow for the extensive transformation in motives from infancy to maturity, or for the extreme diversity of motives that we find in adulthood. Current theories are tending to allow for an additional principle: they claim that competence, self-actualization, and ego autonomy are equally basic features of human motivation. A final theory of motivation will have to admit the truth that lies in all of these views (*Personality and Social Encounter,* p. 218).

Allport held to the integumented view of motivation, in which a blending of factors leads to motivating man. Actually, there are only a few major motives in any well-integrated personality. They are often "surprisingly well focused and well patterned." The number of motives, "indeed, in a well-integrated adult may be adequately indicated on the fingers of two hands, perhaps one." Thus, in motivation the important factor is the individual's systematized design for living. To understand better the motivational aspects of man's behavior, we must study his private worlds of desire, appreciation, and conscience.

In his 1961 book, Allport found four requirements for an adequate theory of motivation: (1) acknowledgment of the contemporary nature of motives, (2) allowance for motives of diverse types, (3) allowance for the dynamic forces of cognitive processes, i.e., planning and intention, and (4) constant allowance for the concrete uniqueness of motives.

In this system, traits and motivation are highly similar, although they are, of course, treated separately in the present text. It is those traits which are driving, dynamic, and directional of effort that help to create motivation.

In rebuttal to the learning theorists, Allport felt that not all drives are equally potent for learning, although he believed that many theorists in that field make this assumption. In his last work Allport gave the name *quasi-mechanical view* to this type of approach.

Despite the fact that humans often strive for goals not clearly identified, that they seem to reach hungrily and to have "aspirations meshed into no gear," motivation is not Freudian, goal-inhibited sexuality. It is more meaningful to speak of what an individual's intentions are, or what he is trying to do, than of the painful repressions of sexual urges as the mainspring in life. Similarly, the phylogenetic continuity of man and animal appetites for food and shelter is only a fraction of the total motive structure.

Allport differentiated between activity and participation as behavioral factors in motivation. The student who attends class regularly may not be very motivated because this activity is task-involved. It becomes habitual to attend class. The motivation gradient is low. On the other hand, when participation is ego-involved, it is usually based upon much stronger motivational patterns. For example, the college man who goes out for the football team has a large amount of ego-involvement in his attempt to make the team. Participation in practice every day and the possibility of playing on the varsity team each Saturday stimulate a tremendous amount of ego-involvement. The same individual, however, may have little or no ego-involvement in attending classes on the campus. Only as he becomes ego-involved by participating in a class recitation or oral report may we expect more than the minimal amount of motivation to be present. The moral, therefore, is that if the instructor wishes to increase motivation in classrooms, he must involve the student's ego by creating opportunities for full participation in the classwork.

To carry the point farther, we see that there are two forms of motivation: one ego-involved and the other not. The latter is called *routine motive* and the former *ego motive*. Routine motives are a result of previously rewarded behavior. They help to maintain self-esteem. The father who daily goes to his job in order to provide for his family does so under a routine motive. Routine motives may be adequate for lower animals, but they are likely to cause boredom in the human animal. The human being demands new responses in changing goals. As an illustration, we are not likely to repeat successful research, or repeat conversations, or replay a bridge hand that has ended successfully. To do so would be highly boring. In contrast to the routine motives, ego motives thrive on a degree of frustration. The unmade hand in bridge, the unsold customer in business, and the reciprocation of a new conversation bring forth much more motivation. Succinctly put, the greater the ego demand, the higher the level of aspirations, and the higher the level of aspirations, the more fully are we motivated. Repeated success brings boredom and little motivation. Continuous challenge to the ego brings stimulation and high motivation. In this capacity, Allport maintains, we are different from the lower forms of living things. On this score, as well as some others, he finds fault with the work of the comparative and stimulus–object–response research psychologist.

Finally, "all units of motivation are at the same time units of personality, but not all units of personality are simultaneously units of motivation" (*Personality and Social Encounter*, p. 118). Thus, although motivation is an essential characteristic of human behavior, it is by no means the whole story of man's personality.

NORMAL–ABNORMAL MOTIVES

There is a difference in the motivational patterns of children and adults and of emotionally stable and emotionally unstable people. The character of motives changes from infancy to maturity. Adult motives supplant infant motives. The infant is motivated by organic demands of food, body warmth, elimination. The adult goes far, far beyond these elemental motives and indeed may deny himself food in order to lose weight, may dress his body only for style and suffer lack of warmth or too much warmth, and may regulate his elimination functions to fit social demands to the point of considerable visceral discomfort. In addition to these extensions of former motivating mechanisms are the mature motives that regulate the adult's existence.

There is also a discontinuity between the motivations of normal and abnormal people. Motivation which is simple tension reduction is pathological. The ordinary human wants much more than to return to mere status quo. He may sentimentally regard the "good old days," but he wants more to have and own the newer things in life: automobiles, job advancement, travel to other lands, success for his children. Parents who are motivated to keep their children at an infantile level are pathological. It is the neurotic and the psychotic who strive for complete homeostasis in life. The normal personality is vigorous and dynamic enough to want and demand change.

CONTEMPORANEITY IN MOTIVES

Allport was certain that motivation is always a contemporary process. An individual's current self-image is far more important than whatever he has been in the past (except for pathological cases, as previously discussed). No central motive, even for the abnormal personality, is ever totally independent of the contemporary ego structure. The most withdrawn catatonic will, upon recovery, speak of events which occurred and to which he attempted to respond, although unable to do so, even during the deepest states of his catatonic condition.

Not only are motivational processes current in their dynamics, but most of them can be taken at their face value. Allport mentioned, for example, that if we were to ask a hundred individuals who had raided the icebox for a midnight snack why they did so, they would quite truthfully answer, "Because I was hungry." Only one person out of the one hundred snackers might be guilty of compulsive oral regression in the Freudian sense. Why then, Allport asked, do so many theorists base motivational processes on the single case? Because one person does have an unconsciously operating motive, it is false to assume that all the others have an unconscious desire for oral regression, especially with the further assumption that it is necessary only to dig around deep enough to uncover the repression. To Allport it is erroneous to say that a condition exists universally despite the fact that it can be found in only a few of the species. It is erroneous to state, "It is there all right, only we cannot find it." Along this line, Allport made some devastating comments in regard to the overuse of, and overdependence upon, the projective type of clinical psychodiagnostic tests. "Motivation is always contemporary" (*Pattern and Growth in Personality*, p. 227).

FUNCTIONAL AUTONOMY

One cannot consider motivation from an Allportian frame of reference without special consideration of the term he coined: *functional autonomy*. This theme has caught the interest of many theorists. Functional autonomy has been criticized, examined, discussed widely, and above all closely associated with the name of Allport as a personality theorist.

Functional autonomy is a shorthand phrase representing the present "go" of interests and tendencies that initiate and sustain current behavior. As customarily defined, it means a strong inclination for a motive system to develop which becomes highly independent of the primary drive first originating an action. Thus, a given activity may become an end or goal itself, or we may continue to pursue an activity for its own sake.

The traditional example from Allport is that of the employee who prides himself on the quality of his workmanship. Originally it was necessary for him to learn a skill in order to obtain the position. Since then he has been doing satisfactory work, but the autonomous (ruling) nature of the function compels him to do clean-cut work of the highest standards because he enjoys doing it that way. The actual job demands may be far less than his self-imposed standard. Further illustrations may be found in (1) maternal behavior, which began as a necessary task to keep the child alive, but is continued for the sheer enjoyment of motherhood, long after the child needs protection and nurturance; or (2) the sailor who has spent his working years on the sea and who enjoys his retirement near the sea; or (3) an original hunger drive which becomes a motive of acquisition for objects completely unrelated to hunger. It is interesting to note that within the dynamics of functional autonomy college students may take a course for the credit alone but, through participation where there is ego-involvement rather than mere attendance of lectures with routine motivation, come to learn for the sheer pleasure of knowing something new. Few activities have an a priori built-in motivation. Motivation comes out of participation where the ego is involved.

Allport distinguished between two types of functional autonomy. *Perseverative functional autonomy* is a closed or an almost-closed system which continues primarily under its own power with little or no outside reinforcement. It is a self-sustaining circuit mechanism and is of a lower order than the next type. *Propriate functional autonomy* is an open system which presupposes that the individual is constantly bombarded with stimuli. Although both types are essential to motivation, the second type is the more important. Because of the open system, the personality is led to achieve progressively higher levels of behavior.

Perseverative functional autonomy gives consistency and coherence to man's personality, while propriate functional autonomy causes him to respond appropriately to life's challenges so that he can produce greater and greater things.

The following Allport statement summarizes functional autonomy. "The doctrine of functional autonomy helps to express the uniqueness of motives that confer distinctiveness to a person's characteristic adjustments" (*Person-*

ality and Social Encounter, p. 146). In this book Allport expanded the concept of functional autonomy but left the core essentially untouched. The reader of Allport's work gains the impression that he continues to answer the critics of his concept of functional autonomy even though some of the criticisms were made as far back as 1940 (Bertocci, 1940). This particular reference occurs and reoccurs in all the Allport books written since the 1937 edition.

In *Pattern and Growth in Personality* (1961) Allport buttressed his argument in support of functional autonomy. "We turn now to one general law of motivation that allows fully for the concrete uniqueness of personal motives, and observes all other criteria for an adequate theory of motivation" (p. 226). However, Allport did not claim that the concept of functional autonomy is the only valid principle in developing human motives or that it explains all the motivational aspects of man. What he did add to his theory is a rebuttal to the critics and a further development of the processes which are not functionally autonomous.

Allport suggested eight processes which are *not* functionally autonomous.

1. Biological drives: air, sleep, hunger, elimination.
2. Reflex action: eye blink and knee jerk.
3. Constitutional equipment: raw materials of physique, intelligence, and temperament.
4. Habits: since habits are motivational in Allport's view.
5. Primary reinforcement: behavior that stops after the goal is gained.
6. Infantilisms and fixations: "behavior due to repressed infantile motives in the Freudian sense when and where these actually occur (which is seldom)." [Allport's note to author.]
7. Some neuroses: those in which therapy, by going backward, traces the original causal behavior to create a cure.
8. Sublimation: "If a primary drive or early fixation is being sublimated it is not a case of functional autonomy (but this too is a rare situation)." (Note to author.)

In regard to the eight processes, Allport felt that it is a question of degrees of yes or no and not an either/or proposition.

There are two major methods in which functional autonomy may be created in the personality pattern of the human: the quasi-mechanical and the propriate. In the quasi-mechanical way, functional autonomy may grow out in a gradual sense from stimulus–object–response or from the learning theory methods. Functional autonomy may also come about through propriate means in which the self attempts to enhance itself. In this case, the self-image demands a continuation of ego-involvement.

Most of the transformations from basic drives, basic needs, basic motives, as considered by many theorists, to the Allport concept of functional autonomy are very gradual. Only in rare cases such as traumatic (sudden and painful) events is a transformation from basic drives to functional autonomy sudden, highly emotional, and dramatic.

Learning Principle

In keeping with the general trend of emphasizing learning and therapeutic work, Allport emphasized learning as a personality development factor. He found that learning is highly involved as a mode of motivation. Self-actualization (the philosophical term is *teleological functions of mankind*) helps to advance man toward his goals. Although the dual pathways of (1) mechanical determinism and (2) self-actualization ("becoming") may appear to be contradictory, man learns to do things and to create a personality because of these two factors. By mechanical determinism Allport referred to the stimulus–response, conditioning, and reinforcement theories of learning. By "becoming" meant not the philosophical definition but the psychologically oriented definition of an advance toward goals. As man learns how to have a personality, he does so through the avenues of differentiation and integration. The serious student of personality theory will see a relevance here to the theory of Gardner Murphy.

"How personality develops is basically a problem in learning." It is evident, then, that man gains a sense of self by learning. In his first two years of life man employs essentially the "quasi-mechanical ways (condition, reinforcement, and repetition)."

Allport, however, made strongest use of the term *proprium* as the main source of learning about the self and finding the personality. *Proprium* has become uniquely an Allport word, meaning "the aspects of personality which together seem singularly one's own." These aspects taken together make for individuality and inward unity. In other words, one seeks goals to develop what he wants to be and does not necessarily wait on circumstances to develop goals for him. The personality creates and seeks conditions in life which are favorable to its own purposes.

Not only does man learn how to have a personality and how to use it; he must also learn the roles which he finds compatible in society and the roles which he finds society has given or made for him. The human personality must learn how, when, and why to play the roles of life.

COGNITION

Cognition, mental set, and perception, as well as the term *procept*, seem to fit most comfortably into this major theme of learning

In *Pattern and Growth of Personality* (1961), Allport recognized the voluminous research which has been done in the area of perception, well over three hundred studies in the decade 1946–1956. Nearly all of these indicate that personality influences perception. Consequently Allport gave the latter some consideration.

Despite the emphasis on perception, Allport used *procept* as a wider and more valuable concept in personality study. He felt that perception is uniquely tied in with sensory processes, whereas *procept* connotes the sensory processes plus the past, present, future, as well as the imagery, judgment, reason, remembering, forgetting, and reporting that are ongoing activities of any human personality.

> Personality, it is said, is an individual's unique way of perceiving his environment, including himself.
>
> This definition has the merit of raising cognitive operations to a level of primary importance. It counteracts the common misconception of higher mental processes as mere shadows (servants and rationalizations) of underlying motives. There is nothing secondary about cognition. The hunger to know, to comprehend our environment, is a basic motive in life.
>
> It would be still more accurate to say that all motives are an inextricable blend of feeling and cognition. The root factor in both is a "set" or "tendency" (both cognitive and affective). The most important sets are personal traits which are basic modes of striving—and—thinking. These sets direct our perceptions, images, judgments (in short our proceptions) of our personal world.
>
> There results for each individual a "cognitive style." To some extent culture slants this style, thus accounting for much of uniformity in people's thought and behavior. But, in the last analysis, each person is unique in the way he blends veridicality, culture, and his own personal existence (*ibid.,* p. 274).

Contemporaneity Principle

Allport firmly believed that man lives and thinks in the present and not the past. Motivation is always contemporary. What the individual intends for the future (immediate or distant) is best explained by his behavior in the present. The links between past and present are historical not functional. For example, the human personality does not strive for a goal successfully achieved any more than a student who earns an "A" grade in a course wants to repeat the course, the individual who solves a puzzle wants to do it again. Although Allport did not deny a continuity at all times with the past, the past is inadequate to explain present drives. A modern city is historically related to its past (the buildings, streets, facilities did not spring up overnight), but it is naive to assume that the modern city is not living for the present day's activities and planning for future activities.

Whereas to Freud and his followers the term *preconscious, unconscious,* and *subconscious* were of extreme importance, Allport felt that the unconscious has been grossly overplayed and overestimated as a dynamic factor in life. Although there may be infantilisms, the unconscious mental states are primarily malfunctions of the abnormal personality. Normal human beings are not prisoners of the past. The fully mature adult is one who exercises traits that are rational, conscious, and appropriate.

Therapists in particular are highly prone to exaggerate the client's past, according to Allport. Too often the psychologist and his subject for therapy face in different directions. While the therapist looks back, the individual with a problem looks forward with hopes for a happy future. One is oriented toward the past, and the other is interested only in his future. There has been an excessive dependence on geneticism in all its forms, contrary to the feeling of Allport that man has subjective values and not only reactive tendencies. The most important question anyone can ask a client is "What do you want to be doing five years from now?"

Allport continued this theme: "Adult motives are infinitely varied, self-sustaining, contemporary systems. They are not fossils." It will be remembered from the aforementioned requirements for an adequate theory of motivation that the first one is to acknowledge the contemporaneity of motives. There can be no doubt, according to Gordon Allport, that man lives in the present and looks to the future and is not bound to the past in the Freudian sense.

Uniqueness Principle

Some personality theorists consider the study of single humans the fruitful way of learning more about man's personality. Allport felt very strongly about this and based much of his work on the unique aspects of each human personality. The uniqueness of each human is a cornerstone in his theoretical framework of personality.

Personality is never general in nature but must always be particular to a single human. Consequently, whatever experimenting the behaviorist psychologist may do with animals such as rats, hamsters, or rhesus monkeys will have very little, if anything, to do with any human being. Further, Allport maintained that the affective units of personality are peculiar only to an individual. Percentile scores, standard deviations, and the like are extremely poor units of description for the human personality. The intelligence quotient may also be considered in the same light.

Allport advocated the use of traits for descriptive purposes (see "Traits–Trends–Tendency–Temperament Principle" later in this chapter). Each individual can be described by a different cluster of traits. No cluster would hold true for more than one person, and thus a universal cluster for all people of even a few traits such as self-preservation and desire for love would be an impossibility. Traits are Allport's favorite descriptive tool because they are enduring and meaningful and lend themselves to accurate personal description. Thus, if psychology deals only with universals (i.e., general laws of earning or behavior) and not with particulars, it cannot be dealing adequately with the human personality. So strongly did Allport feel about uniqueness of personality that he sharply criticized the studies of human behavior which he called a "particular hash" of all the participants in the study. The study has little to do with any single person. Important as it may be to measure a group's total amalgamated response, the study should never be utilized to measure the individual. The individual is lost the moment he becomes a statistic in the total data, and he can never be extracted from the data or meaningfully compared to the total result of the group. At this point it should be obvious that Allport had little use for many of the measures of personality that are nonprojective. His attitude toward projective techniques, which is equally critical, will be discussed in a later section.

In defense of his use of traits as descriptive devices, Allport said that most adjectives used in the current psychological world cut across people rather than applying within the single person. The novelist, the poet, and the biographer frequently are much superior to the psychologist in using meaningful descriptive language for human behavior. In short, frequently we know more about a person after reading a passage from the biographer's page than after studying a Rorschach analysis or the traditional case study used in the guidance clinic. All too often the recipient of the information wonders, "Yes, I know, but what is he really like?"

Allport likened his position that no two human beings have the same set of traits to that of the ancient Greek philosopher Heraclitus, who said we cannot step into the same river twice. Although the banks of the river, the bottom of the river, and the surrounding area may be very similar with each step, the river is different from what it was before. It is the same with individuals. Although they may be surrounded by many identical things, each person is different from another.

Allport made wide use of the terms *idiographic* and *nomothetic*, which he ascribed to Windelband, a German writer who first used them in 1904. Allport was very much in favor of the term *idiographic* to describe man's personality. Idiographic means one's own. Nomothetic means seeking universal laws.[3]

Allport did believe there are similarities between personalities. However,

[3] Allport wrote: "I now prefer the term 'morphogenic' (because people misuse and misspell 'idiographic'). I introduce the term occasionally in *P & G* (especially preface and last paragraph. Am sending a more recent paper that makes use of it. . . . An improved version of this paper will appear in the September, 1962 number of the *J. Personality*, probably under the above title. See, *Image of Man, Proceedings of the 1961 Summer Conference*, Vol. 14, Western Washington State College, Bellingham, Washington, December, 1961, especially page 26 as follows, 'The science of molecular biology shows us that life-substances are identical across species. The building blocks of life—vegetable and animal—turn out to be strikingly uniform in terms of nucleic acids, protein molecules, and enzymatic reactions. Yet an antelope differs from an ash tree, a man from an antelope, and one man is very unlike another. The challenge of morphogenesis (accounting for pattern) grows more acute as we discover the commonalities of life.' " (Personal communication to the author, March 19, 1962.)

they are due to species, culture, differing stages of development, climatic conditions, and so on. Although these factors reveal some resemblances, the resemblances are mere approximations and do not constitute one-to-one general laws of behavior for mankind.

Whatever we are in the way of personality, we must always be considered as peculiar to our own selves. The laws of behavior that interested Allport are the laws that are possible within one given person.

Allport frequently used the term *personal nexus* or *patterned personality* or *person centered* as the most important consideration for a theory of personality.

Repeatedly he said that there is far too much research of an exclusively nomothetic nature. He especially berated factor analysis, which attempts to extract characteristics of man's personality which are poorly defined and may not have existed in the original person in the first place. Some of his sharpest questions were directed at factor-analysis-minded personality theorists who, he felt, cannot take out of their statistical data any more than was put in. Measuring instruments for personality are also regarded as nomothetic. Allport made a plea for the use of case records, life histories, and biographical data, facts which concern the singular human being. Only as these instruments are perfected will we have more valuable predictive tools for purposes of helping mankind. The psychologist who is interested in personality research should also direct his efforts at "the pattern of events within the single personality."

Allport likened some aspects of personality to the molecular theory of chemistry. Although common molecules may exist in trees, animals, clouds, it is obviously an error to assume that all of these things are the same. Similarly, common properties or molecules of human behavior do not necessarily make human beings alike. Hydrogen and oxygen exist in many forms of organic matter. The commonalities between these forms, however, are far apart. It is just as ridiculous to assume that commonalities such as courage and other attributes of human behavior, although they are found in many individuals, mean that these individuals will be very much alike. It is nomothetic fantasy to find common units which alone make common personalities.

Having stated this position in 1937, Allport repeated the plea for individuality or uniqueness twenty-four years later in *Pattern and Growth in Personality*. In both cases he quoted Goethe: "Nature seems to have staked everything on individuality." Innumerable times he came to the conclusion that the major dilemma haunting the house of clinical psychology is the uniqueness of man. Every time the clinical psychologist feels he has a strong theme running through human behavior, he meets client after client who defies classification. Although, as we shall see later, Allport did entertain the concept of *traits*, he did so in a highly idiographic manner. He admitted some limited value in a psychogram but felt that too few psychologists acknowledge the overwhelming limitations of profiling an individual's strengths and weaknesses. One limitation is that it gives us only a diagram of the things we chose to investigate. It tells us nothing beyond what questions we have asked of the client. A second and even stronger limitation is that it gives nothing of the inner organization and dynamics of any individual. A profile is only a silhouette. All we can see of the human being is a dark outline against a white background. "The fact of the matter is that psychography *cannot* synthesize. It can only string beads."

Ego or Self Principle

In many ways Allport used the term *ego* as synonymous with the term *self*. Consideration of the subjective, or feeling about oneself or one's own person, is most difficult. However, personality theorists cannot shelve this problem.

In Allport's opinion there may be an overemphasis on the self. He hazarded a guess that many people go through an entire day without being aware of self at all. Each may pursue his daily chores in a somewhat automated way, without spending many reflective moments upon who he is, what he is, why he is, where he is, and how he got there. His life consists of minutiae.

Allport admitted that, despite the difficulty of describing the nature of self, the concept of self is essential in the study of personality. Historically this may be attributed to the strong influence of the work of Sigmund Freud, who died before completing his theory of the ego, Allport believed. Allport's concept is that the ego has within itself a dynamic process of great positive power; in the Freudian concept the ego is a "rider on a horse." It may be remembered by the reader that in the Freudian sense the ego sits upon the id and tries to control it as the executor or administrator of id impulses. In Allport's terms, the ego and/or the self is the unifying force or mastic for all the habits, traits, attitudes, sentiments, and tendencies of a human being.

Historically, psychology has gone from the soul to the self to the ego. The current emphasis seems to be upon ego-involvement, wherein the ego serves as knower, organizer, observer, status seeker, or socialized being, or, most often, a combination of all five. Moreover, whenever the ego is involved in human behavior, it affects the confidence, judgment, memory, frame of reference, learning aptitude, and all of the motivational aspects of any human being. It is essential, then, Allport felt, in studying anyone to study the ego structure. Where the ego is involved, there is usually a total participation of the self. Ego-involvement or the absence of ego-involvement makes a critical difference in human behavior.

If democracy is ever to be a success, in Allport's view, it is essential that its constituents be ego-involved. It will be recalled that ego-involvement was an important factor in motivation in a previous section.

The self-image leads to the ego-ideal. However, the ego-ideal does not automatically allow the self to be a mover, motivator, or agent toward further action. Primarily the self-image is only the individual as he is known to himself. The self-images may often be completely inaccessible to any other human. Although self-images grow out of good intentions, and intentions are important in the theory of Allport, we cannot say that intentions will necessarily motivate, or lead to, changed behavior.

Allport considered that there are eight historical conceptions which have led toward the concept of the ego. All eight have three things in common: (1) the ego is never the entire personality; (2) one must always consider ego-involvement in degrees; (3) whatever one considers about the ego, it is always operating in the present and is highly preoccupied with the future.

Eight Historical Concepts Toward Ego Formation

1. Ego is the knower.
2. Ego as the object of knowledge.
3. Ego as a source of primitive selfishness.
4. Ego as the prime dominant drive.
5. Ego as the passive organizer of mental processes.
6. Ego as "fighter for ends" (purposive and forceful).
7. Ego as the variable set of forces which lead to a behavioral system.
8. Ego as the subjective organizer of culture (social values).

PROPRIUM

Much of Allport's discussion of the ego or self culminates in the proprium. The proprium is more than a style of life; it is the understanding that man wants to become something for himself and not just to survive on a tension-reduction basis. Allport adroitly presented the view that man wants to become something in his *Becoming: Basic Considerations for a Psychology of Personality* (1955). The proprium includes all the collected aspects of an individual's personality that are uniquely his own. These are what make him different from all other individuals and give him some inward unity. The proprium includes bodily sense, rational thinking, propriate striving, and the concepts of self-image, self-identity, self-extension, and self-esteem. The proprium does not develop automatically, nor does it develop very quickly. At least partially Allport agreed with Jung that man does not have a full-blown sense of self or ego until he reaches the middle years and has acquired all the above characteristics. The proprium initially develops through the usual laws of learning: conditioning, reinforcement, habits, and so on. However, in adulthood man needs to develop and learn a self-image, a great deal of cognitive insight, a true identification of self and closure (bringing together the figure of himself and the background into a unity). Allport considered the mature person a true extension of all the self-concepts he has gained in achieving adulthood. The mature adult is also able to objectify himself in the world scene. To Allport two components are highly significant in objectifying the self: insight and humor. To be able to see oneself in his true position in life and, further, to see oneself as not overpoweringly important in the world order of things are key components in objectifying, or seeing oneself objectively.

Pattern and Growth in Personality discusses the steps which lead up to a development of the proprium.

1. The first aspect is developing a sense of one's own body and organic and physiological systems.
2. The second aspect has to do with continuing the sense of self-identity, that is to say, who one is, the relationship of an individual to others, and the position one holds in life.
3. The next step is fulfilling a sense of pride in one's self, or a feeling of self-esteem. (Aspects 1, 2, and 3 are the first three years of life.)
4. Now one begins to extend the limits of the self as he sees more of the world, meets more people, and experiences deeper levels of contact with things and people.
5. The individual gradually gains a greater self-image. (Aspects 4 and 5 are ages four to six.)
6. Beginning with approximately the age of six, the individual develops his self as a rational "coper." The self as a coper hopes to find solutions and to cope with life's problems as they occur at this age level. (Ages 6–12.)
7. The last aspect to develop out of the beginnings of life occurs at the adolescent level.[4] These seven steps are necessary before the proprium is fully developed at the adulthood level.

The proprium may develop ineffectively under two subjective conditions: feelings of inferiority and deeply involved feelings of conscience. When these two feelings are present in the concept of the self, Allport felt that they affect negatively all of the functioning and especially all of the structuring of the personality.

ROLES

Being a true eclectic, Allport did not ignore the value of roles in the development of the personality. He followed somewhat the accepted conception of roles as structured modes of indulging in the social life: ". . . it is what society expects of an individual occupying a given position in a group." Although one cannot question the importance of roles, they are all too frequently overemphasized by the social psychologist, Allport believed.

There is considerable latitude in the way each person plays his roles. "We cannot agree that personality is a mere colligation of roles."

---

4 Allport stated further: "One does not strive for a proprium. His ego-involved functional autonomous interests are 'propriate striving.' " (Note to author.)

Four factors are involved in the consideration of roles. First, there are the roles one is expected to take. These constitute "the rules of the game" and are what society expects from us. Second, much depends upon how each of us conceives the role that society may want to ascribe to us. We all define our role from our own perceptual system. Consequently, two fathers or two college-aged sons may not conceive of their roles in exactly the same way. As a matter of fact, it is highly unlikely that two fathers conceive of their father role in an identical manner. Third, there is the factor of the degree to which each one of us decides to accept the roles determined for us by society and seen by us in differing ways. It is quite possible that radicals are inclined not to accept roles which they find untenable, whereas conservatives are more likely to accept their socially assigned roles. Fourth, the performance of each of us in our roles varies tremendously. This is another manifestation of the uniqueness of personality. It was obvious to Allport, as it is to many others, that the levels of ability are so varied that so-called equal roles will never produce equal results. Thus, the captain of one football team can never be compared in his performance of that role to the captain of the same football team for the second game of the season. Each of us can play the role only to the best of our ability—a quality that must differ from person to person.

Allport asked this provocative question and spent considerable time discussing it: What is the fully developed self or what may we call a mature personality? (chap. 12, "The Mature Personality," *Pattern and Growth in Personality*, p. 307). He admitted that neither he nor any other psychologist can tell us completely what normal, or healthy, or mature personalities are. However, there is a practical aspect which in our Western culture does lead to substantial agreement on what can be considered the mature personality or the fully developed self. Allport found six criteria that all of us may agree upon. "The mature personality will 1. have a widely extended sense of self; 2. be able to relate himself warmly to others in both intimate and nonintimate contacts; 3. possess a fundamental emotional security and accept himself; 4. perceive, think, and act with zest in accordance with outer reality; 5. be capable of self-objectification, of insight in humor; 6. live in harmony with a unifying philosophy of life." Allport claimed no originality for the six criteria but did feel that too often psychotherapy and counseling ignore these factors and overstress one or two. Also involved, and not too well handled, are our habits and developmental techniques in training children to become adults. It is the well-rounded individual who can meet the above six criteria.

Continuity–Discontinuity Principle

In this principle, as interpreted by the writer, Allport ran counter to the generally accepted current practice of assuming that all behavior has a con tinuum basis. Many aspects of life are not on a continuum, in other words, what we do is not always a matter of degree but one of difference in kind.

Allport felt that there is confusion between symptoms and processes. Where there appears to be a continuum, it is a continuum of symptoms and not processes. Appearances may be deceiving. When persons judge an individual or measure outward appearances by response to a psychological test, these appearances (performances) may very well distribute themselves along a continuum. But the underlying basis which brings about appearances (performances) is definitely not continuous. The dynamics or processes in mechanisms are frequently polar in nature.

Allport found a great gulf between the lives of different human beings. Each human being is not a continuum toward the next human being but must be considered an entity of and by himself. As we have stated before, Allport rejected Freud's idea of tying all adult motivations to infant biological ones. The normal personality does not drag its infantile expressions around but leaves them behind, grows out of them. Allport agreed that there may be some instinctive behavior in the infant or some reflexive form of behavior throughout life. However, the mature personality is essentially a postinstinctive behavior pattern. The tiny infant is a creature of heredity, motivated primarily by primitive drives, and has a high degree of reflex existence. As such, the infant is a biological model. The adult is also a biological model plus a sociological member of society plus a fully integrated ego culminating in the aspect of functional autonomy. Allport almost suggested a discontinuity between the child and adult motivational structure, which creates in effect two theories of personality. The theory of personality for the child is based on tension reduction, avoidance of pain and seeking of pleasure, and a biological model. The adult personality operates from a matrix or radix of organized and highly focused traits. The adult, then, no longer derives his power from organic, primitive sources but from the functional autonomy motivating system. Allport repeated this theme again in 1961, having first posited it in his 1937 book. In one section (p. 196) he used the phrase *the adult vs. the infant*. It is almost as if there were two worlds, a childhood world and an adult world. The theme is a recurrent one that normal people are not prisoners of the past (*Personality and Social Encounter,* p. 145).

In still another sense, Allport approached the problem of continuity *vs.* discontinuity by quoting from Julian Huxley: "Man stands alone." It is partially for this reason that Allport questioned the value of using rats or primates as models to study personality. Although he readily admitted that mice and monkeys are not used directly in personality studies, he objected primarily to the extension of research data on animals to human beings.

As we have previously stated, Allport felt that Freud "smudged" the boundary lines between the behavior of a neurotic and that of a normal human being, stating that "there is, in a restricted sense, a discontinuity between normal and abnormal motivation, and that we need a theory that will recognize this fact. Discontinuities are distinctly unpopular in psychological science." There is a difference between the normal and the abnormal human being. Allport was willing to admit borderline cases or a linear continuum in behavior. He was also willing to admit a relative shifting from culture to culture in man's behavior and some abnormal behavior. However, he insisted there is a vast difference in the motivational structures, in the perceptual systems, and in the behavioral processes of normal and psychotic human beings. In 1937 he delineated some of the characteristics he felt normally behaving people possessed. In a sense, therefore, he was saying that the abnormal person or the psychotic has different behavioral processes. (See especially p. 154 in *Pattern and Growth in Personality*.) The normal human being is able to do at least some or all of the following three things: (1) There is a capacity to make an ego-extension beyond the self. To be interested in more than the self is a normal behavioral activity. (2) Self-objectification, which includes the capacity for self-insight and also the capacity for humor or laughter about oneself, is also in the normal behavioral pattern but not in the abnormal one. (3) The normal individual almost always has a unifying philosophy of life. By this Allport meant there is a frame of meaning and a feeling of responsibility as a human being. In 1958 he added three more factors which he felt the normal human being possessed: "the capacity for a warm, profound relationship of oneself to other people; . . . realistic skills, realistic abilities," and a realistic perceptual system for solving the practical problems of everyday living; and "a compassionate regard for all living creatures" (*Personality and Social Encounter*, p. 162).

The process of going from normality to abnormality is not continuous. There is a difference between a preponderant anabolic process which the normal human being builds, or attempts to build, for the future and a catabolic process in which the abnormal human being is attempting to destroy or forestall a forward motion.

To Allport there is a need for something like a moral philosophy in determining continuity and discontinuity in human behavior. This again reflects his willingness to admit all aspects of personality study as valuable. He did not profess to have settled the issue of continuity–discontinuity but felt strongly that psychologists and philosophers working together may come much closer than we are at present.

Allport entertained the idea that there may be two ways to divide the normal from the abnormal: statistical and ethical. The ethical quality obviously belongs to the psychologist-philosopher. We have not progressed far enough in admitting an ethical standpoint in delineating normality from abnormality; there may well be a basis for considering behavior as either right or wrong. It is, however, the statistical approach which he feels creates many more problems than it solves. Psychologists are too much in love with the beauty of the normal distribution curve. The normal distribution curve fails psychology in the field of personality study because the curve is only a label. Whenever one works with numbers or quantified data, the scales and the test scores automatically distribute continuously. This creates a situation in which measurement dictates the behavior of man, bimodal data not being possible because of the instrument used. Scores on a single instrument which measures personality will fall on a continuum. It might be far better to use a number of measurement devices and compare the results of the devices to find out what dichotomies exist. Despite the fact that traits, even though intercorrelated positively, may fall on a continuum as recorded by a single testing instrument, Allport felt that traits are distinct from each other. Studies of averages among differing subjects which must be treated statistically often lead to creating false continua. Allport did not deny the value of statistics and quantitative measurement. But in using such techniques their weakness must be acknowledged. It is a weakness to measure human beings and allow the measuring instrument to determine the quality of human behavior.

Another tool that does not support the theory of continuity in behavior is Allport's tool of functional autonomy. If one accepts the concept of functional autonomy, he must realize that it permits a relative divorce from the person's past. Thus, "as the individual matures, the bond with the past is broken" (*Pattern and Growth in Personality*, p. 227).

Traits–Trends–Tendency–Temperament Principle

This principle reflects a high degree of evolution in the thinking of Allport. The primary theme is that of traits. The terms *traits, trends, tendency,* and *temperament* are not intentionally alliterative. Not represented in the title but contained in the body of the principle, however, is another word beginning with *t: types.* As we shall see later, Allport did not use this concept of types.

In studying the human personality, Allport asked quite sensibly, Which units shall we use? In his 1958 essay he discussed ten current possibilities as units of study ("What Units Shall We Employ?").

1. Intellectual capacities. Measuring and analyzing intellectual ability may some day be a fruitful approach, but at present the field is not well enough developed to give many cues to motivation and personality.

2. Syndromes of temperament. The work of Sheldon, Thurstone, Catell, Guilford, and others has made a valuable contribution to personality theory.

3. Unconscious motives. This is the dimension with the Freudian flavor in the study of personality.

4. Social attitudes. This is a method of personality study primarily practiced by the social psychologist.

5. Ideational schemata. Personality study is conducted through generalizing the forms of thought.

6. Interests and values. Personality is studied through the structuring of motives such as those measured by the Allport-Vernon-Lindzey Study of Values Test.

7. Expressive traits. Primarily postures, but also gestures, and possibly graphology, are studied.

8. Stylistic traits. This is a field, not too well studied, which considers those behavioral traits lying on the surface of human behavior.

9. Pathological trends. This unit of study of personality has received wide emphasis. Such tests as the MMPI are instruments for measuring the pathological trends. (Unit of study for personality.)

10. Factorial clusters. In this Allport included the work of Cattell, Eysenck, and others who use primarily a statistical approach as a unit of study of personality. In regard to factorial clusters, "psychology cannot synthesize. It can only string beads," meaning that the factorial analysis unit of study may not derive true units of human behavior.

Allport repeated the question "What unit shall we use?" especially in his *Pattern and Growth in Personality.* After much consideration of the value as a unit of study of the terms *trait, trend, tendency, temperament,* or *type,* he held the strongest argument for the concept of trait. It is "the only approach possible if we wish to compare people." He did not deny the value of tendency, or trends, which he later developed as personal dispositions. Temperament, he felt, has a strong hereditary flavor. The use of types as a unit of study does not seem feasible because types are assigned by others, and the individual loses his unique characteristics. The type is more a classification system than a unit of study.

In addition to the five kinds of units of study mentioned above, there are attitudes and character. Character is difficult to cope with as a unit of study because of the judgment of moral rightness and wrongness involved. On the other hand, attitudes are a disposition to an object or toward an object or value. There may be in this sense a retraction or a repulsion for the object. Also involved is an emotional response from the very narrow range of stimuli toward the object of value. Attitude, too, evaluates, while a trait does not evaluate but simply exists within the individual. Since attitudes are very changeable, attitude is difficult to work with as a unit of measurement. As we shall see later, Allport considered attitude a somewhat difficult unit of study. He eventually employed the term *values* as a unit of study for the unique individual. (See Allport-Vernon-Lindzey, *A Study of Values,* rev. ed., Houghton Mifflin, 1960.)

In his 1961 work, Allport still found it hard to discover the fundamental units that psychology may use in studying personalities. Historically, we have progressed in the following manner:

A. Units of the	(black bile—melancholic)
humors:	(yellow bile—sanguine)
	(red bile—choleric)
	(white bile—phlegmatic)
B. Faculties:	(powers of the mind)
C. Instincts:	(Freud and McDougall)
D. Drives:	(behaviorists)
E. Needs:	(H. A. Murray)
F. Current themes:	(habits, S–R, value–vectors, sentiments, syndromes, ergs, personal constructs, dimensions, schemata, and factors)

Having considered Allport's struggles with adopting a comfortable and profitable unit of study, we shall now review the most tenable units he found. They are presented not in order of importance or chronological development but simply as a pedagogical method.

TRAITS

Allport's consideration of the term *traits* as a unit of study for personality continued for many years. "My first paper on trait was, 'What is a trait of personality?' published in 1931 (as you show in your bibliography). Actually this paper was given at the International Congress in 1929 (at Yale). So my interest dates back over thirty years" (note to author). In that time he did not change his essential position but simply added more and more detail to the picture. In fact, Allport's treatment of this term has so much depth that it will be the device of the writer to enumerate some (but not all) of the factors Allport dealt with under the term *trait*.

Eight criteria define trait: (1) A trait has more than nominal existence (habits of a complex order). (2) A trait is more generalized than a habit (two or more habits which are organized and coherent). (3) A trait is dynamic, or at least determinative (plays a motivating role in each act). (4) The existence of a trait may be established empirically or statistically (evidence of repeated reactions or statistical treatment). (5) Traits are only relatively independent of each other (usually correlate positively to some degree with each other). (6) A trait of personality, psychologically considered, is not the same as moral quality (may or may not coincide with conventional social concept). (7) Acts and even habits that are inconsistent with a trait are not proof of the nonexistence of the trait (may be contradictory traits in the same personality—neatness and carelessness—plus behavior acts under stress which temporarily belie the trait). (8) A trait may be viewed either in the light of the personality that contains it or in the light of its distribution in the population at large (traits are unique and traits are universal).

The following list covers some, but certainly not all, of the elements that Allport saw in trait as a comfortable and meaningful unit of study for personality.

1. Traits have the capacity to motivate, inhibit, or select appropriate human behavior. A trait is a combination of motives and habits.

2. Mutually interdependent traits are the main elements in behavior.

3. Traits help to explain the consistencies that we find in personality Although, as we have stated, traits are highly interdependent and highly consistent, they are not completely interdependent or consistent.

4. Traits are not directly observable but must be inferred. As such, traits are difficult to classify.

5. A trait begins with a neuropsychic system.

6. There are two kinds of traits: individual and common. The individual trait is a true trait while the common trait is simply a measure of a number of individual traits as found in a number of people. Allport said: ". . . might add to 'individual trait' (called in 1961 'personal disposition'). It is just a shift in terms because no one fully understood the sharp difference between my conceptions (1937) of 'common' and 'individual' trait" (note to author).

7. As we have stated, a trait is a combination of two or more habits. However, habits no longer have the capacity to dominate traits, but traits may force a creation of new habits. These new habits, then, must be compatible to the trait. Traits may be regarded as stylistic and dynamic. The stylistic trait tells how one goes about behaving; the dynamic trait tells why one behaves as he does. The first gives style whereas the second gives motivating factors.

8. Traits may drive as well as direct. They may push as well as dictate the path. Traits guide and initiate behavior.

9. Traits have a strong connotation of contemporaneity or a state of being and a "nowness" of things. Traits do not exist directly from the past.

10. The question of what to call traits is interesting. Allport and Odbert (1936), for example, made a search of the dictionary and other works and found 17,953 trait names! In his 1937 book, Allport gave four solid columns of trait names, divided approximately into true dispositions, present activities, evaluative terms, metaphorical, and other trait names. The following are obviously only a very few of the names for true traits: *punctuality, aggressiveness, cheerfulness, competitiveness, fancifulness, gregariousness, vigor.*

11. Despite the fact that there are thousands of traits, Allport made rough classification of traits for a given individual into cardinal, central, and secondary traits. The cardinal traits are all-pervasive and are few. They are the dominant traits and become almost "ruling passions." Central traits are the "building blocks of personality." They bring focus to the primary aspects of the individual's behavior. The secondary trait is less important in the scheme as Allport saw it. Secondary traits are not as evident to others, and one must study an individual quite thoroughly in order to discern what they are.

12. Each existing trait may not have an opposite trait. For example, the absence of a trait does not guarantee the presence of its opposite. Allport, in short, did not believe in the polarity of behavior.

13. The value of common traits is that all of us can compare approximate modes of adjustment of similar individuals in similar societies. A minor value of common traits is that they help train young psychologists in a common language and in analytical procedures with common factors.

14. Clusters of traits were often called *syndromes* by Allport.

15. Expressive traits and stylistic traits are two of the units often sought in personality assessment in a clinical situation. Expressive traits, for example, are extraversion, persistence, and traits which denote degrees of sociability. Stylistic traits center on manners of behaving, such as politeness or hesitancy.

16. In an essay derived from a symposium in which Allport participated in 1946, he argued strongly that acquired traits may become primary motivational units. This is an introduction in a sense to his concept of functional autonomy. It is also a rebuttal to the Freudian concept of the ego as executor of the id. Allport preferred to consider the ego as having a "go" of its very own and not having to be responsible to the id for primary moving forces (*Personality and Social Encounter*, pp. 137–151).

Allport continued to pursue this trait system idea in his 1961 book, asking, "Are traits veridical (really true to the individual) or are traits fictional (made up for convenience' sake)?" He answered by saying, "We have voted in favor of the veridical view of traits" (*Pattern and Growth in Personality*, p. 337).

Allport emphasized the common traits as a necessary aspect in studying human behavior to the point of defining the term and then giving two other statements which, in a sense, are redefinitions and reinforcements of the original definition:

Common traits are, then, those aspects of personality in respect to which most people within a given culture can be profitably compared.

A common trait is a category for classifying functionally equivalent forms of behavior in a general population of people. Though influenced by nominal and artifactual considerations, a common trait to some extent reflects veridical and comparable dispositions in many personalities who, because of a common human nature and common culture, develop similar modes of adjusting to their environments, though to varying degrees (*ibid.*, pp. 340, 349).

Finally, Allport gave a simpler though less precise definition of a common trait as "*generalized disposition in respect to which people can be profitably compared.*"

Allport himself was not satisfied with the common trait approach. It creates many ambiguities, and the difficulties we have are necessary ones because we are forced to use them. We have nothing better at the moment than common traits. As we have said, Allport felt that the trait approach is the only sensible one if we are to compare one individual to another.

PERSONAL DISPOSITIONS

This term seems much more comfortable to Allport than the term *individual traits*. A personal disposition, or PD, is defined as "a generalized neuropsychic structure (peculiar to the individual), with the capacity to render many stimuli functionally equivalent, and to initiate and guide consistent (equivalent) forms of adaptive and stylistic behavior."

Borrowing the terms *phenotypical* and *genotypical* from Lewin, Allport found them convenient in distinguishing between personal dispositions. Phenotypical personal dispositions attempt to describe behavior in terms of the present or ongoing behavior. Genotypical personal dispositions are of much the deeper nature. It is the genotypical with which the psychoanalyst wishes to deal. Because the genotypical personal disposition is so difficult to get at, it is possible that the therapist is dealing with pseudo traits.

Carrying over his former discussion of cardinal, central, and secondary traits, Allport used these three classifications in regard to personal dispositions. The definitions and explanation for these three is essentially the same as given for traits in the above section.

Purely in a hypothetical manner, Allport asked, "How many dispositions has a person?"

"When psychology develops adequate diagnostic methods for discovering the major lines along which a particular personality is organized (personal dispositions), it may turn out that the number of such foci will normally vary between five and ten. We state this proposition as a hypothesis subject to eventual scientific testing."

We now end our major consideration of traits as a behavioral phenomenon or descriptive or comparative phenomenon of human behavior. Allport worked with these traits for over twenty-four years, weaving in and out clarifying a little more closely what his concept of the trait system in personality theory is. We turn our attention to a short discussion of trends as a necessary part of personality structure.

TRENDS

The question of trends in human behavior is somewhat synonymous with style of life or the tendency to action, or, as Allport finally worked it out, the personal dispositions of each individual. Gordon Allport's brother, Floyd H. Allport, now retired from the Maxwell School for Citizenship, Syracuse University, is credited with the principle of life purposes or teleonomic trends. The idea here is that principal themes or trends or constructs are highly involved in any given life. To Gordon Allport probably the best solution to what units may be profitably used in studying personality lies in identifying the unique dynamic *trends* peculiar to the structure of each individual life (*Personality and Social Encounter*, p. 111).

TENDENCY

The term *tendency* also occurs frequently in the thinking of Allport. It is almost synonymous with *trends,* and both *trends* and *tendency* ultimately become the *personal dispositions* which Allport created in his work of 1961. The term *tendency* appears to mean a long-range mental set toward behavior, or some kind of disposition for readiness to act, and in a certain prescribed way.

Both *trend* and *tendency* are overtures of the prologue to the theme of personal dispositions as Allport treats it.

TEMPERAMENT

Allport found the term *temperament* useful and defined it in the following way.

> *Temperament refers to the characteristic phenomena of an individual's emotional nature, including his susceptibility to emotional stimulation, his customary strength and speed of response, the quality of his prevailing mood, and all peculiarities of fluctuation and intensity in mood, these phenomena being regarded as dependent upon constitutional makeup, and therefore largely hereditary in origin (Pattern and Growth in Personality, p. 34).*

Temperament, intelligence, and physique are the "raw materials" from which personality is fashioned.

Temperament as a hereditary factor cannot be ignored although it is changeable, as are all the considerations of Allport concerning personality. It will be remembered that Allport's is an open-ended system of personality theory.

We have now covered the primary themes or principles, as they are called in this book, of Gordon Allport's theory of personality. These seven principles around which we find it most convenient to group his ideas are motivation, learning, contemporaneity, uniqueness, ego or self, continuity–discontinuity, and traits–trends–tendency–temperament.

DELIMITATIONS

As must be true with all eclectic personality theorists, there is much of Allport's theory or considerations regarding personality that is not covered in this chapter. The omission is unavoidable in any attempt to condense the writings of well over twenty years and the thinking of so active and intellectually curious a mind.

The chapter ignores, except as an introduction, the fascinating development of how to approach personality theory through literature and psychology, philosophy and psychology, religion or ethics and psychology, for instance. The primary reason for not including the approach theory is that it seems to concern *how* to consider personality rather than the dynamics of *why* man behaves as he does.

Also missing is Allport's discussion of morale as a dynamic force, as well as his various methods of assessment (chaps. 17 and 18 in his *Patterns and Growth in Personality*).

Although much more could be said, because Allport was a prolific and exciting writer, in the final analysis some of his writing is, of course, not directly applicable to personality theory as it is covered in the present text. Any student deeply interested in the work of Allport is urged to make a thorough study of the Allport-Vernon-Lindzey *Study of Values Test*, previously mentioned. The six values measured by this test are theoretical values, economic values, aesthetic values, social values, political values, and religious values.

For good fun in reading and stirring exposition, the student is urged to try at least one work of Gordon Allport (see bibliography at end of chapter).

EXPLAINING HUMAN BEHAVIOR
VIA ALLPORT'S THEORY

Once again we come to that section of the theorist's work in which the reader may test by extrapolation how well the theory can explain certain phenomena in life. As may be expected, the work of Gordon Allport and his personality theory are eclectic in explaining why man does the following things: gets married, commits perversions, commits suicide, breaks laws, believes in a supranatural being or practices a religious custom, has a degree of humor or laughs, indulges in smoking any form of tobacco, indulges in play or the pursuit of some recreational activity, and succumbs to psychotic or neurotic behavioral patterns.

PREDICTING HUMAN BEHAVIOR
VIA ALLPORT'S THEORY

Personal Prediction

Allport himself felt that *self-confrontation* is necessary in psychological thinking, but felt it is barely beginning to be applied to the productions of psychology. Thus, the student is invited through self-confrontation to examine his own predictions regarding his own behavior from the framework of Allport's theory of personality. "It is a good idea to invite students to apply the theories to their own lives, and see which theories are the 'best fit'" (note to author).

Probably none of us would disagree with Allport that the problem of motivation is central to the study of personality, especially our own personal ies. If we know why we do what we do, we have gone a long way toward understanding ourselves. Consequently, if we are to predict our own behavior, it is necessary that we understand how we learn to develop a personality, for this is central to the theme of Allport's theory of personality.

If we accept Allport's ideas of self-love and pride as being universal, we may find it easier to predict our own behavior, providing we have self-love and pride. "My statement is that although self-love and pride are universal, they *need not be sovereign* in a life. This qualification is very important" (note to author).

And finally we must decide for ourselves, because no one else can decide for us, whether the traits, the trends, the temperaments, the tendencies, and particularly the personal dispositions that each of us have will help in predicting something of what we are going to do in the future.

Scientific or Laboratory Predictions

How usable is Allport's personality theory of the individual? What research has it stimulated? As far as research is concerned, not much if any. Does this render the theory valueless? As we hope to indicate, the answer is essentially up to the reader interested in personology and depends on what he hopes to gain from a theory of personality.

Two sophisticated sources in personology seem to agree that Allport has stimulated almost no research directly stemming from his theory, but they qualify their statements in regard to the effect both Allport and Murray have had on personality theories. Maddi, in Wepman and Heine's book, after an exhaustive search of the literature, concludes that "Neither theory . . . has yet achieved useability" although both have had a "general stimulus value for other psychologists," and that "there has been a paucity of research designed to test specific predictions generated from the theories. . . ." But Maddi concludes that "they are genuine theoretical endeavors." In the same source Wepman and Heine make almost a nostalgic statement: "Perhaps the domain of psychology is now too wide and too complex to permit the kind of scholarly, insightful explanation and speculation which characterizes the writings of Allport and Murray. If indeed they are among the last proponents of comprehensive theory building and scholarly commentary which characterized the second half of the nineteenth century and the early twentieth century, it marks a change in the profession *in which more will be lost than will be gained.*" Finally, Maddi argues that a theory may be usable for stimulus value "to the degree that it provokes others to thought and investigation. Legitimate and important as stimulus value is, theory will probably not make a lasting specific contribution to understanding in an empirical discipline like psychology unless it achieves adequate useability and proves to have considerable empirical validity" (Wepman and Heine, 1963; italics added). On the latter score, Allport does not meet the test of usability, but stimulation is another matter.

If numerous citations in major books on personality is a criterion of stimulus value, Allport passes with colors flying. This author has just scanned the name index of twenty-four personality books, all of which have no less than eight citations for Allport. He may not stimulate research, but other writers seem unable to ignore him. There is a similarity here to other modern American theorists. Rogers, Maslow, Murphy, and particularly Allport appear in just about everyone's book of readings and anthology. Is this stimulus value? The reader will have to decide.

On another level, the difficulty in translating Allport to modern research methodology is plain. The reasons range from the valid to the peripheral. Some become irritated because of Allport's critical remarks; Allport stressed the idiographic above all (not a fruitful or popular field for statistical analysis, which analysis is *de rigueur* for publication in psychological journals); Allport emphasized normal individuals, not a popular group for research; his morphogenic eclecticism frustrates even the cleverest methodologist; and, particularly in the latter part of his career, Allport (like Mowrer) wrote often about the value and dynamics of one's religious concepts (never an area of interest for experimentally oriented psychologists). Allport himself may have the best reason for his failure to stimulate researchable ideas in his 1964 article, "The Fruits of Eclecticism: Bitter or Sweet?" " . . . The theoretical issue is not the truth or falsity of any particular formulation for some particular occasion. The question is rather *where do the primary dynamics of human life lie?* Shall we say that our patient suffers from a biochemical imbalance or from an intolerable loss of self-respect? Both statements may be true, but to science it seems more objective, less animistic, and mystical to attack a problem at a biochemical level where cause and effect are easier to perceive." (Italic added.)

On the other hand, maybe Allport has given guidelines for an enormous amount of research even though little of it grew directly out of his theory as such. We have in mind his emphasis on the functions of the proprium, part of which are a sense of body, self-identity, self-esteem, self-extension, rational coping, self-image, and propriate striving. Even a cursory examination of an issue of *Psychological Abstracts* will attest to the volume of research in these areas. But they are never accredited to or allied with the proprium or Allport's psychology of the individual.

The Allport-Vernon-Lindzey Study of Values scale has a respectable body of research literature to its credit (see Buros, *Sixth Mental Measurements Yearbook*). The third edition, 1960, is still based on Spranger's six types: theoretical, economic, aesthetic, social, political, and religious.

Allport certainly was not unaware of the analysis and assessment of personality. In truth, he spent a considerable number of words in *Pattern an*

Growth in Personality delineating eleven rubrics for studying personality, a few of which badly needed further research efforts. They are:

1. Constitutional and physiological diagnosis.
2. Cultural setting, membership, role.
3. Personal documents and case study.
4. Self-appraisal.
5. Analysis of conduct.
6. Ratings.
7. Tests and scales.
8. Projective techniques.
9. Depth analysis.
10. Expressive behavior.
11. Synoptic procedures.

Allport concludes that "There is no 'one and only' method for diagnosing personality."

Maddi, in his own comprehensive book *Personality Theories: A Comparative Analysis* of 1968, willingly credits some research as relevant to Allport. Maddi cites studies on the criteria of maturity, self-esteem, homor, expressive movements, and McClelland's work on the differentiation of motives and traits as possibly Allportian oriented (Maddi, 1968).

At this point we too would like to suggest at least five possible research suggestions which definitely stem from Allport's work.

1. Allport emphasized in 1964 that a person proceeds in life through steplike phases of development similar to Erik Erikson's Eight Stages of Development. What relationship is there between these two systems? (Allport, 1964b)

2. In view of the current unrest on the American and world scene, is it not appropriate to further utilize Allport's many concepts concerning prejudice?

3. Is it still true that "catastrophic social change fails to alter the basic expressive styles," as Allport, Bruner, and Jandorf found among Jewish victims of Nazi oppression? Would the same thing hold for the Viet Cong and Vietnam citizens and for other people throughout the world who must endure long violent periods of stress? (Allport *et al.* 1941).

4. In his graduate classes at Harvard, Allport would frequently ask his students to analyze the "Letters from Jenny" (Allport, 1965a) according to Freud, or Jung, or Adler, or any type of personality theory. With this theoretical framework, how valuable is the idiographic approach to studying other individuals' collective writings? Is it worth a try?

5. Although expressive movement seems to be passé in psychological literature, Turner in his doctoral dissertation found that body movements (knee, arm, foot) had higher predictive values than most scores on personality inventories! Even though all of us judge each other and have done so for

years by expressive movements, perhaps it is time to move back into this area for research that Allport and Vernon utilized way back in 1933 (Turner, 1963).

Allport fervently and continuously advocated the uniqueness of man, his individuality, his self-ness. Whether because of Allport or not, are there many studies of the single person? One extremely exhaustive review of research literature found at least 246 studies from 1940 to 1965 using single cases for the data. The conclusion was that "the usefulness of $N = 1$ studies in psychological research seems . . . to be fairly well established" (Dukes, 1965).

In conclusion, we must state that although Allport's stature with experimentalists, particularly learning theorists, is indeed not high, and others may feel he is both poet and metaprophet, they continue to quote him extensively. To ignore Allport seems akin to ignoring the general flow of psychology.

Allport has earned his place in the world of human behavioral studies, replication or no.

■ SUMMARY

Figure 8 diagrams the major themes of Gordon Allport's theory of personality. One note of caution is in order. There is no attempt to consider Allport's theory as atomistic. Although the structures are atomic structures, they are used as a convenience in highlighting his theory.

The outstanding feature of all of the models is that no one is like any other. This is a portrayal of the uniqueness of man. Again, the traits are very few in number in each individual. Some traits can be seen linked to others. These would be cardinal traits. Some traits are central and have other traits attached to them, while still other traits are out by themselves: secondary traits. Children, it will be seen, do not have many traits, and those they do have should be regarded as instinctual or drive-need traits, whereas adults have more traits because they have learned more things. Clusters of traits can be considered to be the style of life.

It should be noticed that no two traits blend with each other. There is a continuity–discontinuity between the individual "chemical compounds" as represented in the drawing. Some traits which are in the background and can hardly be seen could be thought of as the unconscious or preconscious dynamics of behavior, while others are more nearly on the surface or closer to the reader's eye. If the personalities as represented by the chemical compounds in Figure 8 do not possess an adequate perseverative or propriate functional autonomy, they can be seen to have fallen apart; i.e., they are the psychotics or neurotics.

> Psychology is truly itself only when it can deal with individuality. . .
> We study the human person most fully when we take him as an individual

He is more than a bundle of habits, more than a point of intersection of abstract dimensions. He is more than a representative of his species, more than a citizen of the State, more than an incident in the movements of mankind. He transcends them all. The individual, striving ever for integrity and fulfillment, has existed under all forms of social life—forms as varied as the nomadic and feudal, capitalistic and Communistic. No society holds together for long without the respect man shows to man. The individual today struggles on even under oppression, always hoping and planning for a more perfect democracy where the dignity and growth of each personality will be prized above all else (*Pattern and Growth in Personality*, p. 573).

Allport found it refreshing that psychologists are beginning to ask philosophical questions and also that philosophers are beginning to ask questions of a psychological nature. Only as all the arts and sciences work together can we really have a true dimension and a true theory of personality.

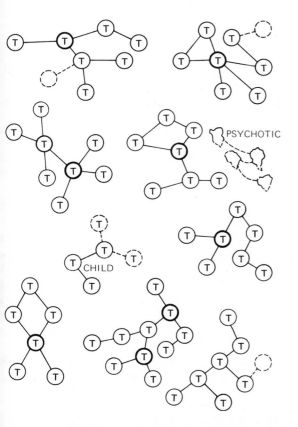

FIGURE 8. *Diagrammatic summary of Allport's theory.*

BIBLIOGRAPHY

PRIMARY SOURCES

BOOKS

Allport, G. W., and F. H. Allport, *A-S Reaction Study* (1928), rev. ed. Boston: Houghton Mifflin, 1949.

Allport, G. W., and P. E. Vernon, *A Study of Values* (1931), rev. ed. with G. Lindzey. Boston: Houghton Mifflin, 1951; 3rd ed., 1960.

Allport, G. W., and P. E. Vernon, *Studies in Expressive Movement*. New York: Macmillan, 1933.

Allport, G. W., Attitudes, in C. C. Murchison (ed.), *A Handbook of Social Psychology*. Worcester, Mass.: Clark University Press, 1935, chap. 17.

Allport, G. W., and H. Cantril, *The Psychology of Radio*. New York: Harper & Row, 1935.

Allport, G. W., *Personality: A Psychological Interpretation*. New York: Holt, Rinehart & Winston, 1937.

Allport, G. W., Dewey's individual and social psychology, in P. A. Schilpp (ed.), *The Philosophy of John Dewey*. Evanston, Ill.: Northwestern University Press, 1939, chap. 9.

Allport, G. W., The nature of democratic morale, in G. Watson (ed.), *Civilian Morale*. Boston: Houghton Mifflin, 1942, chap. 1.

Allport, G. W., *The Use of Personal Documents in Psychological Science*. New York: Social Science Research Council, 1942, bull. 49.

Allport, G. W. (ed. and author of Foreword), *ABC's of Scapegoating*, Central YWCA College, Chicago, 1944 (rev. ed.), Freedom Pamphlet Series. New York: Anti-Defamation League of B'nai B'rith, 1948; rev. 1959.

Allport, G. W., and L. Postman, *The Psychology of Rumor*. New York: Holt, Rinehart & Winston, 1947.

Allport, G. W., Psychology, in *College Reading and Religion*. New Haven, Conn.: Yale University Press, 1948, chap. 3.

Allport, G. W., How shall we evaluate teaching? in B. B. Cronkhite (ed.), *A Handbook for College Teachers*. Cambridge, Mass.: Harvard University Press, 1950, chap. 3.

Allport, G. W., *The Individual and His Religion*. New York: Macmillan, 1950.

Allport, G. W., *The Nature of Personality: Selected Papers*. Reading, Mass.: Addison-Wesley, 1950.

Allport, G. W., A psychological approach to the study of love and hate, in P. A. Sorokin (ed.), *Explorations in Altruistic Love and Behavior*. Boston: Beacon Press, 1950, chap. 5.

Allport, G. W., The role of expectancy, in H. Cantril (ed.), *Tensions That Cause Wars*. Urbana: University of Illinois Press, 1950.

Also in *New Outlook*, 1955, 8, 82–87.

Allport, G. W., Basic principles in improving human relations, in K. W. Bigelow (ed.), *Cultural Groups and Human Relations*. New York: Teachers College, Columbia University, 1951, chap. 2.

Allport, G. W., The situation we face: A psychological analysis, in A. W. Loos (ed.), *Religious Faith and World Culture*. Englewood Cliffs, N.J.: Prentice-Hall, 1951, pp. 35–48.

Allport, G. W., An evaluation of AFSC volunteer work service camps in Germany, in H. W. Riecken (ed.), *The Volunteer Work Camp: A Psychological Evaluation*. Reading, Mass.: Addison-Wesley, 1952, Append. A, pp. 185–220.

Allport, G. W., Reading the nature of prejudice, *Claremont* (Cal.) *College Reading Conference, Seventeenth Yearbook*, 1952, pp. 51–64.

Allport, G. W., Resolving intergroup tensions, an appraisal of methods, in L. A. Cook (ed.), *Toward Better Human Relations*. Detroit: Wayne State University Press, 1952, chap. 3.

Allport, G. W., J. S. Bruner, and E. M. Jandorf, Personality under social catastrophe: Ninety life-histories of the Nazi revolution, in C. Kluckhohn *et al.* (eds.), *Personality in Nature, Society and Culture*. New York: Knopf, 1953.

> "Even catastrophic social change does not succeed in effecting radical transformations in personality."

Allport, G. W., The historical background of modern social psychology, in G. Lindzey (ed.), *Handbook of Social Psychology*. Reading, Mass.: Addison-Wesley, 1954, chap. 1.

Allport, G. W., *The Nature of Prejudice*. Reading, Mass.: Addison-Wesley, 1954; Boston: Beacon Press (abr. ed.); Garden City, N.Y.: Doubleday (Anchor), 1958.

Allport, G. W., Techniques for reducing group prejudice, in P. A. Sorokin (ed.), *Forms and Techniques of Altruistic and Spiritual Growth*. Boston: Beacon Press, 1954, chap. 24.

Allport, G. W., *Becoming: Basic Considerations for a Psychology of Personality*. New Haven, Conn.: Yale University Press, 1955.

Allport, G. W., The limits of social service, in J. E. Russell (ed.), *National Policies for Education, Health and Social Services*. Garden City, N.Y.: Doubleday, 1955, pp. 194–213.

Allport, G. W., and J. M. Gillespie, *Youth's Outlook on the Future*, Doubleday Papers in Psychology. New York: Doubleday, 1955 (distributed by Random House).

Allport, G. W., The participant citizen, *The Sixth Annual George Denny Lecture*, Natal Technical College, Durban, South Africa, 1956.

Allport, G. W., Prejudice in modern perspective, *The Hoernle Memorial Lecture* South African Institute of Race Relations, Durban, South Africa, 1956.

Allport, G. W., European and American theories of personality, in H. P. David and H. von Bracken (eds.), *Perspectives in Personality Theory*. New York Basic Books, 1957, chap. 1.

Allport, G. W., What units shall we employ? in G. Lindzey (ed.), *Assessment of Human Motives*. New York: Holt, Rinehart & Winston, 1958, chap. 9 (Reprinted as paperback. New York: Grove Press, 1960.)

Allport, G. W., Normative compatibility in the light of social science, in A. H Maslow (ed.), *New Knowledge in Human Values*. New York: Harper & Row, 1959, pp. 137–150.

Also in *Relig. Educ.*, 1958, *53*, 62–68.

Allport, G. W., Preface to V. E. Frankl (trans.), *From Death-Camp to Existentialism*. Boston: Beacon Press, 1959.

Allport, G. W., *Personality and Social Encounter*. Boston: Beacon Press, 1960.

Allport, G. W., Psychology and religion, in J. Clark (ed.), *The Student Seeks an Answer*, Ingraham Lectures in Philosophy and Religion. Waterville, Me. Colby College Press, 1960, chap. 2.

Allport, G. W., Uniqueness in students, in W. D. Weatherford, Jr. (ed.), *The Goals of Higher Education*. Cambridge, Mass.: Harvard University Press 1960, pp. 57–75.

Allport, G. W., *Pattern and Growth in Personality*. New York: Holt, Rinehart & Winston, 1961.

Allport, G. W., *The Individual and His Religion*. New York: Macmillan, 1962.

Religion persists in human development.

Allport, G. W., The emphasis on molar problems, in M. H. Marx (ed.), *Theories in Contemporary Psychology*. New York: Macmillan, 1963.

Allport, G. W., Foreword, in N. L. Farberow (ed.), *Taboo Topics*. New York. Atherton Press, 1963.

Allport, G. W. (ed.), *Letters from Jenny*. New York: Harcourt, Brace & World 1965a.

Allport, G. W., Personalistic psychology: A trait approach to personality, in W. S Sahakian (ed.), *Psychology of Personality: Readings in Theory*. Chicago: Rand McNally, 1965b.

Bits and pieces of Allport's original writings.

Allport, G. W., In E. G. Boring and G. Lindzey (eds.), *A History of Psychology in Autobiography*, Vol. V. New York: Appleton-Century-Crofts, 1967.

Allport, G. W., *The Person in Psychology*. Boston: Beacon Press, 1968.

PERIODICALS

Allport, G. W., Personality and character, *Psychol. Bull.*, 1921, *18*, 441–455.

Allport, G. W., and F. H. Allport, Personality traits: Their classification and measurement, *J. Abnorm. Soc. Psychol.*, 1921, *16*, 6–40.

Allport, G. W., Germany's state of mind, New Republic, 1923, 34, 63–65.

Allport, G. W., The Leipzig Congress of Psychology, Amer. J. Psychol., 1923, 34, 612–615.

Allport, G. W., Eidetic imagery, Brit. J. Psychol., 1924, 15, 99–120.

Allport, G. W., The standpoint of Gestalt psychology, Psyche, 1924, 4, 354–361.

Allport, G. W., The study of the undivided personality, J. Abnorm. Soc. Psychol., 1924, 19, 132–141.

Allport, G. W., Concepts of trait and personality, Psychol. Bull., 1927, 24, 284–293.

Allport, G. W., The eidetic image and the after-image, Amer. J. Psychol., 1928, 40, 418–425.

Allport, G. W., A test for ascendance-submission, J. Abnorm. Soc. Psychol., 1928, 23, 118–136.

Allport, G. W., The composition of political attitudes, Amer. J. Sociol., 1929, 35, 220–238.

Allport, G. W., The study of personality by the intuitive method: An experiment in teaching from The Locomotive God, J. Abnorm. Soc. Psychol., 1929, 24, 14–27.

Allport, G. W., Change and decay in the visual memory image, Brit. J. Psychol., 1930, 21, 133–148.

Allport, G. W., The neurotic personality and traits of self-expression, J. Soc. Psychol., 1930, 1, 524–527.

Allport, G. W., Some guiding principles in understanding personality, Family, June, 1930, pp. 124–128.

Allport, G. W., and P. E. Vernon, The field of personality, Psychol. Bull., 1930, 27, 677–730.

Allport, G. W., What is a trait of personality? J. Abnorm. Soc. Psychol., 1931, 25, 368–372.

Allport, G. W., and P. E. Vernon, A test for personal values, J. Abnorm. Soc. Psychol., 1931, 26, 231–248.

Allport, G. W., The study of personality by the experimental method, Char. Pers., 1933, 1, 259–264.

Allport, G. W., and H. Cantril, Recent applications of the study of values, J. Abnorm. Soc. Psychol., 1933, 28, 259–273.

Allport, G. W., H. Cantril, and H. A. Rand, The determination of personal interests by psychological and graphological methods, Charact. & Pers., 1933, 2, 134–151.

Allport, G. W., and H. Cantril, Judging personality from voice, J. Soc. Psychol., 1934, 5, 37–55.

Allport, G. W., The nature of motivation, Understanding the Child, Jan., 1935, pp. 3–6.

Allport, G. W., The radio as a stimulus situation, Acta Psychol. (Amst.), 1935, 1, 1–6.

Allport, G. W., and H. S. Odbert, Trait-names: A psycho-lexical study, Psychol. Monogr., 1936, 47, No. 211.

Allport, G. W., and R. L. Schanck, Are attitudes biological or cultural in origin? Charact. & Pers., 1936, 4, 195–205.

Allport, G. W., The functional autonomy of motives, *Amer. J. Psychol.*, 1937, 5 141–156.

Allport, G. W., The personalistic psychology of William Stern, *Charact. & Pers.* 1937, 5, 231–246.

Allport, G. W., The Journal of Abnormal and Social Psychology: An editorial, in *J. Abnorm. Soc. Psychol.*, 1938, 33, 3–13.

Allport, G. W., William Stern: 1871–1938, *Amer. J. Psychol.*, 1938, 51, 770–774

Allport, G. W., The education of a teacher, *Harvard Progressive*, 1939, 4, 7–9.

Allport, G. W., and R. Ruggles, Recent applications of the A-S Reaction Study, *J Abnorm. Soc. Psychol.*, 1939, 34, 518–528.

Allport, G. W., Liberalism and the motives of men, *Frontiers of Democracy* 1940, 6, 136–137.

Allport, G. W., Motivation in personality: Reply to Mr. Bertocci, *Psychol. Rev.* 1940, 47, 533–554.

Allport, G. W., The psychologist's frame of reference, *Psychol. Bull.*, 1940, 37 1–28.

Allport, G. W., and J. S. Bruner, Fifty years of change in American psychology *Psychol. Bull.*, 1940, 37, 757–776.

Allport, G. W., and J. M. Faden, The psychology of newspapers: Five tentative laws, *Publ. Opin. Quart.*, 1940, 4, 687–703.

Allport, G. W., Liabilities and assets in civilian morale, *Ann. Amer. Acad. Pol Soc. Sci.*, 1941, 216, 88–94.

Allport, G. W., Morale: American style, *Christian Science Monitor* (weekly magazine section), April 26, 1941, pp. 1–2, 13.

Allport, G. W., Psychological service for civilian morale, *J. Consult. Psychol.* 1941, 5, 235–239.

Allport, G. W., J. S. Bruner, and E. M. Jandorf, Personality under social catastro phe: Ninety life-histories of the Nazi revolution, *Charact. & Pers.*, 1941, 10 1–22.

Allport, G. W., Defense seminars for morale study and morale building, *J. Soc Psychol.*, *SPSSI Bull.*, 1942, 15, 399–401.

Allport, G. W., Morale and its measurement, *Public Policy* (Cambridge, Mass. Littauer School of Public Administration), 1942, 3, 3–17.

Allport, G. W., The ego in contemporary psychology, *Psychol. Rev.*, 1943, 50 451–478.

   Also published in C. L. Stacey and M. F. DeMartino (eds.), *Understand ing Human Motivation.* Cleveland: Howard Allen, 1958, pp. 140–158.

Allport, G. W., The productive paradoxes of William James, *Psychol. Rev.*, 1943 50, 95–120.

Allport, G. W., Psychological considerations in making the peace: Editorial note *J. Abnorm. Soc. Psychol.*, 1943, 38, 131.

Allport, G. W., Restoring morale in occupied territory, *Publ. Opin. Quart.*, 1943 7, 606–617.

Allport, G. W., Test tube for rumors, *Coronet*, 1943, 14, 136–140.

Allport, G. W., This clinical supplement: Editorial note, *J. Abnorm. Soc. Psychol.*, 1943, 38, 3–5.

Allport, G. W., and G. R. Schmeidler, Morale research and its clearing, *Psychol. Bull.*, 1943, *40*, 65–68.

Allport, G. W., and H. R. Veltfort, Social psychology and the civilian war effort, *J. Soc. Psychol., SPSSI Bull.*, 1943, *18*, 165–233.

Allport, G. W., and E. C. Winship, Do rosy headlines sell newspapers? *Publ. Opin. Quart.*, 1943, *7*, 205–210.

Allport, G. W., The bigot in our midst, *Commonweal*, 1944, *25*, 582–586.

Also published in *Catholic Digest*, 1944, *9*, 93–96.

Allport, G. W., This clinical number: Editorial, *J. Abnorm. Soc. Psychol.*, 1944, *39*, 147–149.

Allport, G. W., and G. R. Schmeidler, Social psychology and the civilian war effort, *J. Soc. Psychol., SPSSI Bull.*, 1944, *20*, 145–180.

Allport, G. W., Catharsis and the reduction of prejudice, *J. Soc. Issues*, 1945, *1*, 1–8.

Allport, G. W., Human nature and the peace, *Psychol. Bull.*, 1945, *42*, 376–378.

Allport, G. W., Is intergroup education possible? *Harvard Educ. Rev.*, 1945, *15*, 83–86.

Allport, G. W., The psychology of participation, *Psychol. Rev.*, 1945, *52*, 117–132.

Allport, G. W., and L. Postman, The basic psychology of rumor, *Trans. N.Y. Acad. Sci.*, 1945, *8*, 61–81.

Also published in G. E. Swanson, T. M. Newcomb, and E. L. Hartley (eds.), *Readings in Social Psychology* (rev. ed.). New Cork: Holt, Rinehart & Winston, 1952, Pt. IIb, pp. 160–171. Also in D. Katz, D. Cartwright, S. Eldersveld, and A. McC. Lee, *Public Opinion and Propaganda*. New York: Holt, Rinehart & Winston, 1945, pp. 394–404.

Allport, G. W. (ed. and author of Foreword), Controlling group prejudice, *Ann. Amer. Acad. Pol. Soc. Sci.*, 1946, *244*.

Allport, G. W., Effect: A secondary principle of learning, *Psychol. Rev.*, 1946, *53*, 335–347.

Allport, G. W., Geneticism versus ego-structure in theories of personality, *Brit. J. Educ. Psychol.*, 1946, *16*, 57–68.

Allport, G. W., Personalistic psychology as science: A reply, *Psychol. Rev.*, 1946, *53*, 132–135.

Allport, G. W., The priest and the psychologist, *Bull. Gen. Theol. Sem.*, Sept., 1946.

Allport, G. W., and E. G. Boring, Psychology and social relations at Harvard University, *Amer. Psychologist*, 1946, *1*, 119–122.

Allport, G. W., and B. M. Kramer, Some roots of prejudice, *J. Psychol.*, 1946, *22*, 9–39; rev. ed., *Roots of Prejudice*, New York American Jewish Congress, Pamphlet Series, *Jewish Affairs*, 1946, *1*, 13.

Allport, G. W., and L. Postman, An analysis of rumor, *Publ. Opin. Quart.*, 1946–1947, *10*, 501–17.

Also published in *Sci. Dig.*, 1947, *22*, 58–61.

Allport, G. W., The genius of Kurt Lewin, *J. Pers.*, 1947, *16*, 1–10.

>   Also in *J. Soc. Issues*, 1948, *4*, 14–21, Suppl. Ser. I.

Allport, G. W., Guidelines for research in international cooperation, *J. Soc. Issues*, 1947, *3*, 21–37.

Allport, G. W., Scientific models and human morals, *Psychol. Rev.*, 1947, *54*, 182–192.

>   Also in T. H. Pear (ed.), *Psychological Factors of Peace and War*. London: Hutchinson, 1950, chap. 7.

Allport, G. W., J. M. Gillespie, and J. Young, The religion of the post-war college student, *J. Psychol.*, 1948, *25*, 3–33.

>   Also in J. Seidman (ed.), *The Adolescent: A Book of Readings*. New York: Holt, Rinehart & Winston, 1953.

Allport, G. W., Psychology and the fourth R, *New Republic*, Oct. 17, 1949, pp. 23–26.

Allport, G. W., Prejudice: A problem in psychological and social causation (Kurt Lewin Memorial Lecture), *J. Soc. Issues*, 1950, Suppl. Ser.

>   Also in T. Parsons and E. A. Shils (eds.), *Toward a General Theory of Action*. Cambridge, Mass.: Harvard University Press, 1951, Pt. 4, chap. 1.

Allport, G. W., The individual and his religion, *Andover Newton Bull.*, 1952, *44*, 3–10.

Allport, G. W., The mature personality, *Pastoral Psychol.*, 1952, *2*, 19–24.

Allport, G. W., The resolution of intergroup tensions, *Intergroup Educ. Pamphlet*. New York: National Conference of Christians and Jews, 1952.

Allport, G. W., What is in the student's mind? *Proceedings of the Thirtieth Annual Meeting, American College Health Association*, Bull. No. 32 (Stanford University Press), 1952.

Allport, G. W., Why do people join? Interview in *Adult Leader*, 1952, *1*, 10–12.

Allport, G. W., The psychological nature of personality, *Personalist*, 1953, *34*, 347–357.

Allport, G. W., The teaching-learning situation, *Publ. Hlth Rep.*, 1953, *68*, 875–879.

Allport, G. W., The trend in motivational theory, *Amer. J. Orthopsychiat.*, 1953, *25*, 107–119.

Allport, G. W., Comments on: J. L. Moreno, transference, countertransference and tele: Their relation to group research and group psychotherapy, *Group Psychother.*, 1954, *7*, 307–308.

Allport, G. W., A psychologist views the Supreme Court ruling on segregation, *Nieman Rep.*, 1954, *8*, 12–13.

Allport, G. W., and T. F. Pettigrew, Cultural influence on the perception of movement: The trapezoidal illusion among Zulus, *J. Abnorm. Soc. Psychol.*, 1957, *55*, 104–113.

Allport, G. W., Perception and public health, *Hlth Educ. Monogr.* (Oakland, Cal., Society of Health Educators), 1958, No. 2, pp. 2–15.

Allport, G. W., Personality: Normal and abnormal, *Sociol. Rev.*, 1958, 6, 167–180.

Allport, G. W., T. F. Pettigrew, and E. O. Barnett, Binocular resolution and perception of race in South Africa, *Brit. J. Psychol.*, 1958, 49, 265–278, Pt. IV.

Allport, G. W., Religion and prejudice, *Crane Rev.*, 1959, 2, 1–10.

Allport, G. W., The open system in personality theory, *J. Abnorm. Soc. Psychol.*, 1960, 60, No. 5.

Allport, G. W., Values and our youth, *Teachers Coll. Rec.*, 1961, 63, 211–219.

Allport, G. W., The general and the unique in psychological science, *J. Pers.*, 1962, 30, 405–422.

> Also in E. A. Southwell and M. Merbaum (eds.), *Personality: Readings in Theory and Research.* Belmont, Cal.: Wadsworth, 1964, pp. 244–258. Also in G. Lindzey and C. S. Hall (eds.), *Theories of Personality: Primary Sources and Research.* New York: Wiley, 1965, pp. 240–249.

Allport, G. W., Prejudice: Is it societal or personal? *J. Soc. Issues*, 1962, 18, 120–134.

Allport, G. W., Psychological models for guidance, *Harvard Educ. Rev.*, 1962, 32, 373–381.

Allport, G. W., Mental health: A generic attitude, *J. Relig. Hlth*, 1964a, 4, 7–21.

Allport, G. W., Crises in normal personality development, *Teachers Coll. Rec.*, 1964b, 66, 235–241.

Allport, G. W., The fruits of eclecticism: Bitter or sweet? *Acta Psychol.* (Amst.), 1964c, 23, 27–44.

Allport, G. W., Prejudice: Is it societal or personal? *Relig. Educ.*, 1964d, 59, 20–29.

Allport, G. W., The religious context of prejudice, *J. Sci. Stud. Relig.*, 1966, 5, 448–451.

Allport, G. W., Traits revisited, *Amer. Psychologist*, 1966, 21, 1–10.

Allport, G. W., William James and the behavioral sciences, *J. Hist. Behav. Sci.*, 1966, 2, 145–147.

Allport, G. W., and J. M. Ross, Personal religions orientation and prejudice, *J. Pers. Soc. Psychol.*, 1967, 5, 432–443.

TAPE RECORDINGS

Allport, G. W., *Motivation Theory and Psychodynamics* (G. W. Kisker, ed.), Sound Seminars, No. 132, Cincinnati, Ohio.

SUGGESTED READINGS

BOOKS

Allport, F. H., *Theories of Perception and the Concept of Structure.* New York: Wiley, 1955.

Angyal, A., *Neurosis and Treatment: A Holistic Theory*. New York: Wiley, 1965
Bischof, L. J., *Adult Psychology*. New York: Harper & Row, 1969.

> The development of the normal adult.

Hall, C. S., and G. Lindzey, *Theories of Personality*. New York: Wiley, 1957, pp.
257–295.
Lindzey, G., and C. S. Hall (eds.), *Theories of Personality: Primary Sources and
Research*. New York: Wiley, 1965, pp. 231–272.

> Reprints of four papers by Allport.

Maddi, S. R., Humanistic psychology: Allport and Murray, in J. M. Wepman and
R. W. Heine (eds.), *Concepts of Personality*. Chicago: Aldine, 1963.

> How usable is Allport's theory for research? Not very, but the future
> will tell.

Maddi, S. R., *Personality Theories: A Comparative Analysis*. Homewood, Ill.:
Dorsey, 1968, pp. 412–415.

> Allport and peripheral research.

Mednick, M. T., and S. A. Mednick (eds.), *Research in Personality*. New York:
Holt, Rinehart & Winston, 1963, pp. 63–73.
Wolff, W., *The Expression of Personality*. New York: Harper & Row, 1943.

PERIODICALS

Baldwin, A. L., Personal structure analysis: A statistical method for investigating
the single personality, *J. Abnorm. Soc. Psychol.*, 1942, 37, 163–183.
Baldwin, A. L., Statistical problems in the treatment of case histories, *J. Clin.
Psychol.*, 1950, 6, 6–12.
Benito, S. S., A proposed philosophy of guidance based on an analysis of Gordon
W. Allport's and Edgar S. Brightman's writings relative to personality, *Dis-
sert. Abstr.*, 1967, 27, 3299.
Bertocci, P. A., Critique of Gordon W. Allport's theory of motivation, *Psychol.
Rev.*, 1940, 47, 501–532.
Crijns, A. G., African personality structure: A critical review of bibliographical
sources and of principle findings, *Gawein*, 1966, 14, 239–248.

> Uses Allport's "functional autonomy of motives" and Lewin's "principle
> of contemporaneity."

Dukes, W. F., N = 1, *Psychol. Bull.*, 1965, 64, 74–79.

> Review of 246 single case studies used in research over the past twenty-
> five years.

Ford, J., D. Young, and S. Box, Functional autonomy, role distance and social
class, *Brit. J. Sociol.*, 1967, 18, 370–381.
Franck, I., The concept of human nature: A philosophical analysis of the concept
of human nature in the writings of G. W. Allport, S. E. Asch, Erich Fromm,
A. H. Maslow, and C. R. Rogers, *Dissert. Abstr.*, 1966, 27, 1079.

Hater, R. J., Psycho-philosophy of the human person: Gordon W. Allport's dynamic theory of human personality, with special emphasis on the philosophical implications derived from the study of his approach to man, *Dissert. Abstr.*, 1968, 28, 3712–3713.

Holt, R. R., Individuality and generalization in the psychology of personality, *J. Pers.*, 1962, 3, 377–404.

    Objects to Allport's use of idiographic terminology.

Kaul, J. H., How autonomous is functional autonomy? *J. Educ. Psychol., Baroda,* 1959, 16, 481–491.

    Allport is a good writer but theory is premature—evidence is anecdotal.

King, W. A., Communication theory ₂and the Allport concept of structure, *Audiovis. Commun. Rev.*, 1961, 9, 119–128.

Long, L. M. K., Alfred Adler and Gordon Allport: A comparison on certain topics in personality theory, *Amer. J. Indiv. Psychol.*, 1952–1953, 10, 43–53.

Lundy, R. M., Assimilative projection and accuracy of prediction in interpersonal perceptions, *J. Abnorm. Soc. Psychol.*, 1956, 52, 33–38.

McCreary, J. K., The problem of personality definition, *J. Gen. Psychol.*, 1960, 63, 107–111.

    Reviews definitions by Allport, Lewin, Murray, and Murphy.

O'Connell, D. C., Idiographic knowledge, *J. Gen. Psychol.*, 1958, 59, 21–33.

    A critique of Allport's idiographic approach.

Oppenheimer, O., A behavioral theory of traits, *Educ. Theor.*, 1957, 7, 112–121.

    In contrast to Allport, the author contends traits exist. Action is not inferred from personality.

Seward, J. P., The sign of a symbol: A reply to Professor Allport, *Psychol. Rev.*, 1948, 55, 277–296.

Seward, J. P., The structure of functional autonomy, *Amer. Psychologist*, 1963, 18, 703–710.

    Implications for functional autonomy are discussed. Functional autonomy becomes superfluous.

Shulman, B. H., A comparison of Allport's and the Adlerian concepts of life style: Contributions to a psychology of the self, *Indiv. Psychol.*, 1965, 3, 14–21.

    "Adler's 'life style' and Allport's 'proprium' are compared with regard to aspects of bodily sense, self-identity, ego enhancement, ego-extension, rational agent, self-image, propriate striving, and the knower."

Skaggs, E. B., Personalistic psychology as science, *Psychol. Rev.*, 1945, 52, 234–238.

Steer, H. O., Allport's concept of structure, *Canad. J. Psychol.*, 1957, 11, 75–78.

    Use of Allport's theories in conducting research.

Steward, N. S., Attitudes toward literary characters as related to factors in per-
    sonality, *Dissert. Abstr.*, 1955, *15*, 2301.
Turner, W. S., Correlation between test scores, life data, and behavior during
    testing, unpublished Ph.D. dissertation, University of California, 1963.
Wallace, J., What units shall we employ? Allport's question revisited, *J. Consult.
    Psychol.*, 1967, *31*, 56–64.
White, W. F., H. E. Anderson, and H. Cryder, Allport's theory of the emerging
    self-concept applied to secondary school students, *Proc. Amer. Psychol. Assoc.*,
    1966, 277–278.

The use of modification of self-concept through the high school years.

9

ROGERS

To hold as 'twere, the mirror up to nature.

SHAKESPEARE
Hamlet, III, 2

SOME BIOGRAPHICAL DATA

Carl Ransom Rogers was born in Oak Park, Illinois, on January 8, 1902, the son of Walter and Julia (Cushing) Rogers. His family was regarded as conservative Protestant. Rogers attended the University of Wisconsin, where he started in agriculture and finished up majoring in history. In 1924 he was graduated from Wisconsin, and in the same year, on August 28, married Helen Elliott. They have two children, David and Natalie. He attended Union Seminary in New York City from 1924 to 1926 and transferred to Columbia University in 1928, where he received his M.A. that year. At

Columbia, Rogers studied with W. H. Kilpatrick and Leta Hollingworth. He was awarded the Ph.D. degree in educational and clinical psychology at Columbia in 1931. During the years 1927 and 1928 Rogers obtained his first practical experience in clinical psychology as a fellow at the Institute of Child Guidance. From 1928 to 1930 he served as a clinical psychologist in the Child Study Department at the Society for the Prevention of Cruelty to Children in Rochester, New York. He was director of the society's Child Study Depart ment from 1930 to 1938. In 1939 the department was reorganized into a separate agency, the Rochester Guidance Center, with Rogers as the director Moving to Ohio State University in 1940, he became Professor of Clinical Psychology in 1945. Rogers was the director of the counseling service of the USO during 1944–1945. He then became a professor of psychology at the University of Chicago, having established the Counseling Center and served as its first executive secretary. In the fall of 1957, he accepted a dual position as Professor of Psychology and Psychiatry at the University of Wisconsin.

Rogers has received various awards, among them, in 1956, the American Psychological Association's Distinguished Scientific Contribution Award. He is a member of the APA and served as president in 1946–1947. Also, he is a member of the American Academy of Psychotherapists (president, 1956–1957), the Orthopsychiatric Association (vice-president, 1944–1945), and the American Association for Applied Psychologists (president, 1944–1945). In 1963 he joined the Western Behavioral Sciences Institute at La Jolla, California. He is a member of Phi Beta Kappa and has written several books on psychotherapy.

Carl Rogers exhibits a refreshing insight into his own personality. In a forthright autobiography he reveals the dynamics of his own personal and professional life. It is a delight to read (Boring and Lindzey, 1967).

INTRODUCTION

Carl Rogers has a tremendous empathy for all of mankind. This deep concern for the welfare of man is the reason he has confined the major part of his psychological effort to the practice of psychotherapy. Because of this passion ate feeling toward his fellow beings, because he has been extremely successful in therapy, and because he has through his professional work influenced many others, he is internationally known in the world of psychology.

The sincerity and success of Rogers have been so pronounced that he has acquired almost a cult of followers. During his tenure at the University of Chicago and at the University of Wisconsin, he has attracted psychologists from throughout the world.

Rogers has not always been popular. Shortly after the appearance of his 1942 book, *Counseling and Psychotherapy*, Rogers' work, especially in psychotherapy, was considered extremely heuristic. Actual rebuttal was delayed until the end of World War II in 1945, when, from approximately 1946 to 1950, many articles and speakers and books contradicted his theory of client-centered therapy. In the post-World War II period most of the arguments were centered on "directive *vs.* nondirective" counseling. However, Rogers has continued to ride out the storm evoked at one time by his theory.

Rogers' interests and talents have a wide scope. He has written for and worked with industry, religion, teaching (see chap. 9, "Student Centered Teaching," in *Client-Centered Therapy*), and, of course, the field in which he is most noted, psychotherapy. Like Moreno, he has also extended his talents to motion pictures (see the Bibliography).

Although Carl Rogers is primarily known as a therapist, he has not ignored theories of personality. His 1951 book, *Client-Centered Therapy*, culminates at chap. 11 in "A Theory of Personality and Behavior." Rogers wrote the chapter partially to answer charges that his psychotherapeutic methods were not based on any clear-cut theory of personality.

Rogers' psychotherapeutic work and theories have never been static; he continues to improve and expand both. One indication of the movement of his work is the change in titles given to his therapy: nondirective to client-centered to relationship-centered to "experiencing." Although Rogers is not totally responsible for the change from title to title, it does indicate the current of his thinking. Whatever the world considers him, Rogers feels that he is, in his practicing of psychotherapy, a "midwife to a new personality."

One of the refreshing things to come out of Rogers' work is his throwing open the door of the therapist's room to allow others to look and listen. Through the use of films and especially through the extensive use of taped interviews, Rogers has enabled his students and all those interested to see just what he is doing. He feels that it is necessary to "take a square look at the facts." Until the arrival of Rogers' tape-recorded interviews, the process of therapy was frequently hidden. Only by reading what the therapist chose to write was one able to discover or infer what actually went on in a counseling or clinical situation. No one knows, for example, exactly what and how Freud spoke, or Jung, or Adler, or any of the early therapists.

In some of his recent work Rogers has been leaning toward existentialism. He sees certain parallels between the emphasis on existentialism in European psychiatry and the philosophical basis of client-centered therapy. His extremely personal article in 1955 in the *American Psychologist*, "Persons or Science: A Philosophical Question," his dialogue with Martin Buber at Ann Arbor in 1957, and his position on the editorial board of the *Journal of Existential Psychiatry* and the *Review of Existential Psychology and Psychiatry* are indications of this trend.

For a dozen years Rogers had been working out his method of therapy in his work with children. About 1940 he began to present his point of view as "being different from the approaches carried on by others," he has stated.

Throughout the years since then, he has felt the need to mold a theory of personality or a theory of behavior which would come out of and be compatible with his therapeutic system. Rogers insists that theory grows out of therapy, much as Freud believed that his therapy emerged in a theory. Thus we find Rogers stating in *Client-Centered Therapy* (p. 17), "the fragile flower of theory has grown out of the solid soil of experience." Rogers is strongly opposed to theory building which precedes therapy or what he would refer to as research. Loose theory building not preceded by sound research, he feels, is extremely hazardous, time consuming, and almost worthless.

Hence, it is almost impossible for anyone to separate the therapeutic aspects from the dynamics of personality which were involved in Rogers' therapeutic program. Theory and therapy are so inextricably interwoven that separating them is like pulling out the warp from the woof in woven cloth. One is likely to make the theory disintegrate, just as one would cause the cloth to disintegrate into tangled skeins. It is also like trying to make a two-handed person wash only one hand. It can be done but it's most difficult and unnatural. However, as we shall see, there are enough identifiable threads of personality theory running through Rogers' work to make the effort well worthwhile for purposes of this text.

There is an additional difficulty in separating the man Rogers from his total work. There is so much of a highly personal nature in his contributions that at times one hardly knows where the personality of the man Rogers ends and Rogers' personality of man begins. In a beautifully moving first chapter ("This Is Me") of his book. *On Becoming a Person* (1961) the reader wonders whether the "becoming" refers to Rogers or to humanity. No other theorist puts his own personality "on the line" so poignantly. He is truly his own theory of personality come to life.

Actually, it is almost too soon to write Rogers' personality theory; he is the first to admit that it is still being formulated and that whatever is said now will be sure to change and be behind the times in the near future. At present his theory formulation is "full steam ahead."

ROGERS' DESCRIPTION OF HUMAN PERSONALITY

One of Carl Rogers' first efforts to delineate a personality theory or a theory of behavior was made in 1947 (*The American Psychologist*, 2, 358–368), one of his latest in the book edited by Koch, *Psychology: A Study of a Science*, Volume III: *Formulations of the Person in the Social Context*. In this book, Rogers' chapter is titled "A Theory of Therapy, Personality, and Interpersonal Relationships as Developed in the Client-Centered Framework." It must be reemphasized that Rogers himself does not consider that he has evolved a definitive theory of personality. Whatever theory he has created hus far he feels has been stated in the above chapter of Koch's *Psychology* (1959). (See footnote, page x of the Preface, in *On Becoming a Person*.)

Although the present book is not concerned with therapy but with theories of personality, a few words should be said in regard to Rogers' concept of the client-centered therapy. In line with this is the pertinent observation by a major writer in the personality theory area, "But a theory of personality is not a theory of psychotherapy" (Maddi, 1968, p. 71). Is the reverse then true? Rogers readily admits that we do not know exactly what the essential process of therapy is. He does feel that therapy is not built upon diagnosis. Psychotherapy, he believes, is the essence of life and should be so understood. In short, to him life itself is a therapeutic situation. Whether the individual is in the hands of a clinical psychologist or is pursuing the ordinary course of his life, therapeutic incidents are a natural consequence of living. The following, in an abbreviated form, are some of Rogers' thoughts on therapy: Therapy is internal revolution; client-centered therapy is not a technique, nor is the therapist to be considered a "method" actor; the client-centered therapist is probably best described as the subject's "alter ego." Finally, in client-centered therapy the therapist helps the client to experience and live through his problems so that the client controls and solves them himself. When Rogers says that client-centered therapy is not a technique, he means that client-centered therapy is a philosophy, a frame of reference, or a belief, dedicated to the idea that the client himself is the main actor who will eventually, with help, speak, write, and act out his own lines.

It has seemed feasible to include the above, although it is incomplete, because of the strong reputation that Rogers has and will continue to have as a successful, seeking, researching, dynamic believer in the process of psychotherapy as an ongoing necessary part of all human living. One last word should be added. In his early professional life, especially at the Rochester Clinic and prior to that in his training with Leta Hollingworth, Rogers held a view almost opposite to the one he now takes.

In describing man's behavior, Rogers, in contrast to Freud, is an optimist; humanity is positive, forward-moving, constructive, realistic, and quite trustworthy. Freud's belief is that man may be hostile, antisocial, destructive, or even evil, or in pursuit of a life which actually has no solutions ("A Note on the Nature of Man," *J. Counsel. Psychol.*, 1957, 4, 199–203).

Despite the fact that it may be too soon to write a theory of personality from the work of Carl Rogers, there do seem to be four significant trends in his formulation of a theory of behavior or a theory of personality. The trends, principles, or major themes are these: the self as an experiencing mechanism, and the three subsidiary themes of self-actualization, self-maintenance, and self-enhancement. It is the belief of the writer that most of Rogers' major ideas concerning personality can be fitted into the framework of these four themes. In a note to the author, Dr. Rogers said that he hoped the student would read chap. 11, "A Theory of Personality and Behavior," of *Client Centered Therapy*, because the author's interpretation departs somewhat from Rogers' own work.

Self Theme

To Rogers, client-centered personality theory is a self-centered theory of personality. We can best examine Rogers' theory of personality by listing the twenty-two propositions presented in 1951, and in 1959 in the publication previously mentioned (Koch, *Psychology: A Study of a Science*, Volume III. *Formulations of the Person in the Social Context.* "A Theory of Therapy, Personality, and Interpersonal Relationships, as Developed in the Client-Centered Framework"). The first nineteen propositions were formulated in 1951, the last three in 1959. Because the self is central to the theme of each proposition, it can be readily seen that Rogers' theory of personality revolves about the concept of self. All of the propositions discuss either the individual, the person, or the self. They are not abstractions about society as a whole or theoretical statements about life itself but somewhat like Gordon Allport's theory, in that each places a primary importance upon the uniqueness of a single human being.

Carl Rogers' Twenty-two Propositions Concerning Personality

Although each of Roger's propositions stands on its own feet, the writer will add statements wherever it is felt they will clarify the meaning for the student.

Proposition 1. *"Every individual exists in a continually changing world of experience of which he is the center."* We all live in our own private world of experience, in a world that is never the same from one day to the next. This viewpoint, of course, stresses introspection. It is called, by some, phenomenology. The experience may be conscious or subconscious. When the experience is conscious, it concerns the world of symbols. The individual's private world can be known only to himself.

Proposition 2. *"The organism reacts to the field as it is experienced and perceived."* This perceptual field is, for the individual, "reality." Reality may be abstract to the philosopher or the metaphysician, but to the individual experiencing it, reality is tested and accepted by his own perceptual system. When the individual has a perceptual system which is consistent for himself, he has a certain degree of predictability upon which he can depend.

Proposition 3. *"The organism reacts as an organized whole to this phenomenal field."* Rogers feels that a basic characteristic of an individual's life is his tendency toward total or organized goal-directed responses. Rogers cannot accept any simple S–R type of behavior explanation.

Proposition 4. "*The organism has one basic tendency and striving—to ctualize, maintain, and enhance the experiencing organism.*" Rogers credits nygg and Combs for this trichotomized phrasing. We shall have much more o say concerning actualizing, maintaining, and enhancing the self in the ollowing sections, which treat the subsidiary principles of Rogers.

Proposition 5. "*Behavior is basically the goal directed attempt of the rganism to satisfy its needs as experienced, in the field as perceived.*" All needs are basically related. Further, reactions are not to reality as others may ee them but to the individual's perception of reality. Rogers feels, as does Allport, that motivation exists primarily in the present. There is no behavior xcept to meet a present need.

Proposition 6. "*Emotion accompanies and in general facilitates such goal directed behavior, the kind of emotion being related to the seeking vs. the onsummatory aspects of the behavior, and the intensity of the emotion being elated to the perceived significance of the behavior for the maintenance and nhancement of the organism.*" Personality tries to integrate the two kinds of emotions, unpleasant or excited feelings, and calm or satisfied emotions. Perception determines the intensity of the emotional reaction.

Proposition 7. "*The best vantage point for understanding behavior is rom the internal frame of reference of the individual himself.*" What may eem to be meaningless and strange behavior to an observer is perhaps very purposeful behavior to the individual. There are many drawbacks and immense difficulties in getting at the introspective feeling of any particular person. Because there are counterparts in our own life to the life of another individual, we may become able to infer introspective behavior. Preconceptions on our part, however, may destroy the ability to see through the skin of another human.

Proposition 8. "*A portion of the total perceptual field gradually becomes differentiated as the self.*" Rogers agrees that how the self develops is extremely hard to study. We have made, he feels, not too much progress in this area.

Proposition 9. "*As a result of interaction with the environment and particularly as a result of evaluational interaction with others, the structure of self is formed—an organized, fluid, but consistent conceptual pattern of perceptions of characteristics and relationships of the 'I' or the 'me,' together with values attached to these concepts.*" Experience with others helps to develop a sense of self. Parental influence is essential at this stage of structuring the self.

Proposition 10. "*The values attached to experiences, and the values which are part of the self structure, in some instances are values experienced directly by the organism, and in some instances are values introjected or taken over from others, but perceived in distorted fashion, as if they had been experienced directly.*" Experiences have values. These values may be directly perceived, gained from others, distorted, but, whatever their source, they grow out of experiences.

Proposition 11. "*As experiences occur in the life of the individual, they are either (a) symbolized, perceived, and organized into some relationship to the self, (b) ignored because there is not perceived relationship to the self structure, (c) denied symbolization or given a distorted symbolization because the experience is inconsistent with the structure of the self.*" Again, the self is the keystone to open perception or to perception which is below the level of consciousness.

Proposition 12. "*Most of the ways of behaving which are adopted by the organism are those which are consistent with the concept of self.*" The self hopes to maintain behavior which is consistent with the picture it has of the self.

Proposition 13. "*Behavior may, in some instances, be brought about by organic experiences and needs which have not been symbolized.*" Such behavior may be inconsistent with the structure of the self, but in such cases the behavior is not "owned" by the individual. When behavior is not controlled, it is regarded as not belonging to the self.

Proposition 14. "*Psychological maladjustment exists when the organism denies to awareness significant sensory and visceral experiences, which consequently are not symbolized and organized into the gestalt of the self-structure. When this situation exists, there is a basic or potential psychological tension.*" The personality cannot actualize itself if the experiences are not true to the real self.

Proposition 15. "*Psychological adjustment exists when the concept of the self is such that all the sensory and visceral experiences of the organism are, or may be, assimilated on a symbolic level into a consistent relationship with the concept of self.*" Inner tension is reduced when the personality has a new feeling about itself.

Proposition 16. "*Any experience which is inconsistent with the organization or structure of the self may be perceived as a threat, and the more of these perceptions there are, the more rigidly the self structure is organized to maintain itself.*" Events which threaten the personality frequently make the personality stiff and rigid.

Proposition 17. "*Under certain conditions involving primarily complete absence of any threat to the self-structure, experiences which are inconsistent with it may be perceived, and examined, and the structure of self revised to assimilate and include such experiences.*" Change in a personality comes about when the personality can accept a new facet of itself.

Proposition 18. "*When the individual perceives and accepts into one consistent and integrated system all his sensory and visceral experiences, then he is necessarily more understanding of others and is more accepting of others as separate individuals."* When the personality can develop a consistent self-concept, it develops a good interpersonal relationship as a natural result.

Proposition 19. *"As the individual perceives and accepts into his self-structure more of his organic experiences, he finds that he is replacing his present value system—based so largely upon introjections which have been distortedly symbolized—with a continuing organismic valuing process."* As the individual gains confidence in the valuing process, he finds the old systems unnecessary and no longer threatening.

(The next three propositions are from S. Koch's *Psychology: A Study of a Science,* wherein Rogers presents the latest elements in his developing theory of personality. These three positions are not as neatly stated as the nineteen formulated in 1951.)

Proposition 20. This concerns the personality's desire for social esteem. At times, the desire to be right and praised and esteemed worthy by others in one's society overtakes the values that the self-organism desires. When it is important for the personality to be considered worthwhile by others, it may overrule the inner functions and inner dynamics of the organismic self.

Proposition 21. Rogers also finds an extremely strong desire for *self-esteem,* parallel with the desire for social esteem. Because this need for self-esteem grows out of experience, it is possible for the personality to ignore the pressures of society which gave him the desire for social esteem.

Proposition 22. Because of the forces, desires, and demands of social esteem and self-esteem, there develops an attitude of self-worthiness which helps the individual in the hurly-burly of everyday life. Therefore, the feeling that he is worthy of something helps one to buttress his desire for self-esteem and his capacity to obtain the feeling of social esteem.

Even a cursory examination of Rogers' original nineteen propositions and the latest three propositions will give the reader a strong feeling of the value that Rogers places upon the self. The term *self* (or its synonyms, *individual* or *person* or *organism*) is inherent in each of the twenty-two propositions. Several other terms are involved in the formulations of Rogers' theory; indeed it would be impossible to write the propositions without their use: *experienced, perceived, phenomenal, field* or *gestalt, structure of self,* and *symbolized* or *inner values.* These words are highly important to Rogers' theory of personality or human dynamics. Without them, it appears, Rogers would not be able to construct such a theory.

DEFINITION

At this point a definition of the word *self* is in order. This is not an easy assignment because Rogers at no point makes a definitive statement in regard to self or defines self in the way that Allport made a definitive statement about the term *personality.* Probably the best definitions of the term *self,* as

Rogers uses it, are the entire twenty-two statements mentioned above; th
shortest definition is "the awareness of being, of functioning" (*Client
Centered Therapy*, p. 498). Expanding this truncated definition we ma
consider *self* as "being the strivings, emotional feeling, and ideas that th
individual recognizes, interprets, and values as his very own."

GENERAL CONSIDERATIONS

1. One of the greatest strivings of the personality is for self-consistency

2. The personality or self, as Rogers considers it in its perceptua
dynamics, attempts to seek independence, greater spontaneity, and an inte
gration of all the life forces that impinge upon it.

3. When the self attempts to change its behavior, the change results no
only from learning; changes in the individual's picture of himself are highl
involved. In short, the personality is more than a learning mechanism. I
looks under the skin to determine that whatever it is learning is worthwhile
follows its own value system, and can be integrated into the self-picture.

4. Personalities which wish to examine what they are can best "explor
within" rather than coldly or objectively "observe the self."

It is obvious that Rogers' theory of personality is pointed toward on
goal: an examination or consideration of the self. We shall now look at th
three secondary principles by which the self operates in the world of livin
things. They are self-actualization, self-maintenance, and self-enhancement.

Self-Actualization Theme

Rogers finds the term *self-actualization* a convenient one, though not neces
sarily all-inclusive, for the dynamics which describe man as starting as an
infant and growing into adulthood. He further includes in self-actualizatio
all the processes by which man differentiates himself from others and hi
organic functions from his social functions, and moves in the direction of self
responsibility. Before the personality can do anything at all, it must actuall
begin. In a sense, this is what Rogers is talking about by self-actualization
Self-actualization goes from the simple to the complex. It starts at conceptio
and continues throughout maturity. In his 1958 paper, "Becoming a Person,"
Rogers characterizes the process as follows: "The goal the individual mos
wishes to achieve, the end which he knowingly or unknowingly pursues, is t
become himself."

The urge to create seems to be innate or inform. It follows, then, tha
the greatest thing man can create in his entire life-span is himself. The self i
the epitome of creativity. Out of the self that is created from childhoo
emerge all the other things that are normally considered creative: artisti
works, inventions, social systems. But man has to create a self before he ca
create anything else.

EXPERIENCING

One of the ways of actualizing a self is to undergo as many experiences as possible. Only by experiencing activities and knowing what it is experiencing can the self be actualized. Rogers considers that some of the experiencing the personality goes through may not be at the fully conscious level. But there is a difference between conscious and unconscious levels of experiencing. One of the prime factors in experiencing which leads to a true self-actualization is *congruence:* "being aware of and being open to all of the experiences which are integrated by the self." Rogers feels it is not enough, however, simply to experience things in a haphazard fashion with no other dynamics involved; experience must tell one its own meaning. Rogers gives credit to Snygg and Combs for the concept of self-actualization.

Self-Maintenance Theme

Once the personality has actualized himself to the fullest extent possible, he must continue to maintain himself. It is not enough to be something; one must keep being something.

It is generally considered that at the self-maintenance level one achieves self-understanding at its fullest. The self-maintenance level brings out the richness, maturity, and ramifications of the total personality.

Self-maintenance dynamics operate from current pressures or tensions. In contradistinction to Freud, Rogers feels that behavior is not directly caused by things which happened in the past. ". . . there is no behavior except to meet a present need" (*Client-Centered Therapy*, p. 492).[1]

He warns, however, that self-maintenance is not to be confused with homeostasis. Individuals move; there is a "flow" in the continuum of life. To put it briefly, life is a process, not a position.

As part of the process of maintaining one's self, the personality should have an "openness to experience." Only as the human is willing to try new things can there be a constructive feedback to the self. If the personality ignores the richness of the process of experiencing for self, he is likely to create an extremely faulty frame of reference.

Self-Enhancement Theme

As much as the human being wishes to get started in self-actualization and then keep and enrich what he was in going beyond dead center by self-maintenance, he also wishes to enhance himself. Life is more than getting

[1] Rogers has this to say of the author's explanation: "I feel you do not understand my point of view. I certainly do not deny that behavior is caused by past events. It is that we can never accurately know those causes, which are too complex and remote. The best way of understanding behavior is in terms of the function it serves in the present."

and preserving; one wishes to transcend the status quo. Rogers credits Angya
for the term *self-enhancement.*

Self-enhancement does not flow smoothly but consists of struggle and
pain. It is a process of going backward and forward, the losing and gaining of
goal structures.

Rogers feels strongly that it is man's privilege to enhance himself. Man
should be more than a robot or a controlled ploy of another individual. In a
timely article appearing in the *Personnel and Guidance Journal,* 1961, 39
"The Place of the Person in the New World of the Behavioral Sciences," h
takes issue with the goals of behavioral technology as stated by B. F. Skinner
Rogers makes a plea for freedom of the individual to enhance his own
personality. He sees as dangerous the possibilities of prediction and control of
human personalities in the future. The subjective value choice of any given
personality must never be threatened. In his conclusions, Carl Rogers say
that "we can choose to use the behavioral sciences in ways which will be free
not control; which will bring about constructive variability, not conformity
which will develop creativity, not contentment; which will facilitate each
person in his self-directed process of becoming; which will aid individuals
groups, and even the concept of science to become self-transcending in freshly
adaptive ways of meeting life and its problems" (p. 451).

Conclusions

It is obvious at this point that there can be no conclusions concerning Rogers
theory of personality. At present he is working extremely hard on the
problems of psychotherapy and a theory of personality. Whatever we say at
the moment concerns only the current status of an influential figure and hi
formulation of a theory regarding the dynamics of man's behavior.

As stated previously, Carl Rogers, in the way he lives and openly write
about himself, is his own best example of his theory of personality. Witness
the following quotations (numbers are mine) from "This Is Me," the firs
chapter in *On Becoming a Person* (pp. 16–27).

1. In my relationships with persons I have found that it does not help, in
   the long run, to act as though I were something that I am not.
2. I find I am more effective when I can listen acceptantly to myself, and
   can be myself . . . *the curious paradox is when I accept myself as I am,
   then I change.*
3. I have found it of enormous value when I can permit myself to under
   stand another person.
4. I have found it enriching to open channels whereby others can communi
   cate their feelings, their private perceptual worlds, to me.
5. I have found it highly rewarding when I can accept another person.
6. The more I am open to the realities in me and in the other person, the
   less do I find myself wishing to rush in to "fix things."

7. I can trust my experience.
8. . . . evaluation by others is not a guide for me.
9. Experience is, for me, the highest authority.
10. I enjoy the discovering of order in experience. [Research is a persistent disciplining effort and also highly rewarding.]
11. The facts are friendly. [Scientific evidence can only help, not harm; truth guides one to more truth.]
12. What is most personal is most general. [Others feel as I do.]
13. It has been my experience that persons have a basically positive direction. [Not Pollyanna-ish, but given the chance man moves up.]
14. Life, at its best, is a flowing, changing process in which nothing is fixed.

In a summary statement to the chapter, Roger says this:

> I trust it is clear now why there is no philosophy or belief or set of principles which I could encourage or persuade others to have or hold. I can only try to live by *my* interpretation of the current meaning of *my* experience, and try to give others the permission and freedom to develop their own inward freedom and thus their own meaningful interpretation of their own experience.

EXPLAINING HUMAN BEHAVIOR VIA ROGERS' SELF THEORY

All explanations are highly hypothetical and heavily loaded with inference. This is especially the case with the theory of personality presented by Carl Rogers. Actually, in Rogers' system no one can give an explanation for another because only the introspective self can validly explain an inner mechanism or an inner feeling. The best we can hope to do is to infer an explanation from what another human being shows us of himself. According to Rogers, all stems from an internal frame of reference. In a sense, in this section, the only explanation that is possible is for each of us to explain the nine behavioral phenomena for ourselves. Rogers himself says, "From my own phenomenological point of view, the best explanation of a given behavior comes from permitting the individual to explore his behavior in a safe climate and thus to learn its basis and its explanation."

PREDICTING HUMAN BEHAVIOR VIA ROGERS' SELF THEORY

Personal Prediction

In February, 1961, Carl Rogers published a strongly written paper which has some bearing upon personal prediction (*Personal Guid. J.*, 1961, 39, 442–451). In his ten-page article he is most concerned with a rebuttal to B. F. Skinner's thesis regarding prediction and control of human behavior

(Skinner, 1955–1956). The following lengthy quotations best represent Rogers' point of view.

In any scientific endeavor—whether "pure or applied science—there is a prior personal subjective choice of the purpose or the value which that scientific work is perceived as serving."

This subjective value choice, which brings the scientific endeavor into being, must always lie outside of that endeavor and can never become a part of the science involved in the endeavor.

> Science, to be sure, rests on the assumption that behavior is caused—that a specified event is followed by a consequent event. Hence, all is determined, nothing is free, choice is impossible. But, we must recall that science itself in each specific scientific endeavor, each change of course in a scientific research, each interpretation of the meaning of the scientific finding, and each decision as to how the finding shall be applied, rests upon a personal, subjective choice. Thus, science in general exists in the same paradoxical situation as does Dr. Skinner. A personal subjective choice made by man sets in motion the operations of science, which in time proclaims that there can be no such thing as a personal subjective choice.

Thus, Rogers is saying, science cannot investigate science (itself); science cannot erect its own goals; science cannot interpret its own findings; only man can do this, and he does so subjectively from his own frame of reference. "Science has its meaning as the objective pursuit of a purpose which has been subjectively chosen by a person or persons."

We find encouragement when such an eminent scientist and psychologist as Dr. Carl Rogers says that, no matter what theory of personality is under consideration, it is always considered from a subjective frame of reference. Rogers espouses the one-sided presentation or single school of thought as a necessary step in scientific formulation. We find the following in *Client-Centered Therapy* (p. 8):

> It appears to the writer that the somewhat critical attitude which is usually held toward anything which may be defined as a "school of thought" grows out of a lack of appreciation of the way in which science grows. In a new field of investigation which is being opened up to objective study, the school of thought is a necessary cultural step. Where objective evidence is limited, it is almost inevitable that markedly different hypotheses will be developed and offered to explain the phenomena which are observed. The corollaries and ramifications of any such hypotheses constitute a system which is a school of thought. These schools of thought will not be abolished by wishful thinking. The person who attempts to reconcile them by compromise will find himself left with a superficial eclecticism which does not increase objectivity, and which leads nowhere. Truth is not arrived at by concessions from differing schools of thought. The eventual disappearance of such rival formulations comes about either when the issues are settled by research evi-

dence, or when both types of hypotheses are absorbed into some new more penetrating view which sees the problems from a new vantage point, thus, re-defining the issues in a way not hitherto perceived.

It is now the task of the student of the theory of personality to evolve a personality theory of his own. He must base the decision upon a single source of theory, a multiple source, or a "homemade" theory of personality gained from his own experience. If one follows the Rogerian line of thought, he may defensibly evolve his own theory of personality. It may be eclectic and gathered from others. Rogers would insist that it is always formulated from a subjective frame of reference.

Scientific or Laboratory Prediction

Prediction actually is an unobtainable goal because we cannot get into another person's full frame of reference (*Client-Centered Therapy*, p. 495).

However, there is a certain efficiency of prediction in regard to psychotherapy. Thus, we find in a 1956 article (*Teachers Coll. Rec.*, 1956, 57, 316–322), "Implications of Recent Advances in the Prediction and Control of Behavior," some optimism toward predicting human behavior, at least in the psychotherapeutic situation. The key to predictability seems to lie in the degree of self-insight that the client is able to achieve through the therapeutic sessions. The more self-insight, the better the prognostication for a good adjustment. Toward this end, Rogers has been working upon a process scale. "It is . . . a possible tool for prediction of success in therapy" (Rogers, 1960, in Brower and Abt [eds.], *Progress in Clinical Psychology*, Vol. IV, p. 94).

In another sense, Rogers finds prediction of success as a therapist to depend primarily on the assimilation of attitudes and procedures rather than on the use of techniques or tools (*Client-Centered Therapy*, p. 458).

However, the strongest and most generalized feelings in regard to predicting human behavior from laboratory or scientific endeavors appear in the aforementioned article in which Dr. Rogers makes a rebuttal to Dr. Skinner's thesis on the prediction and control of human behavior. Rogers finds six areas in which prediction is possible.

1. We know how to set up the conditions under which many individuals will report as true, judgments which are contrary to the evidence of their senses.
2. We know how to change the opinions of an individual in a selected direction, without his ever becoming aware of the stimuli which changed his opinion.
3. We can predict, from the way individuals perceive the movement of a spot of light in a dark room, whether they tend to be prejudiced or unprejudiced.

4. We know the attitudes which, if provided by a counselor or therapist, will be predictably followed by a certain constructive personality and behavior changes in the client.

5. We know how to provide animals with a most satisfying experience consisting entirely of an electrical stimulation.

6. We know how to provide psychological conditions which will produce vivid hallucinations and other abnormal reactions in the thoroughly normal individual in the waking state.

Rogers finds the above six possibilities of prediction frightening. He further feels that most psychologists and social scientists have given little thought to what it means to predict and control human behavior. There are four steps by which man may control other men, steps which grow out of a background of the ability to predict human behavior. These steps are: first, the selection of goals; second, the use of the method of science of controlled experimentation; third, obtaining the power to establish the conditions or use the methods; and fourth, the exposure of the individuals to the previous three steps.

Since his joining the Western Behavioral Sciences Institute in La Jolla, California, Rogers has been intensively engaged in such group experiences as T groups, sensitivity training, marathons, and similar impact workshops. He is enthusiastic about these endeavors and yet realizes a need for a "study of the process in such basic encounter groups that I hope may eventuate in theoretical propositions which can be tested empirically." If Rogers' past is a valid indicator, it can be expected that he will achieve his goal of researching the dynamics of the "basic encounter groups" (Rogers, 1967b). There has been a diminution in recent years of publications by Rogers as compared at least to his previous work in the forties and fifties.

Meantime, psychologists continue to investigate the self-concept as it relates to Rogers' theory of personality. The studies here cited are intended to be representative of work in this field and not an exhaustive report.

Research on self-concept per se appears to cover the bulk of the reported studies, which range from factor analysis (Baker, 1968; Riley, 1962) to the validity of the tests used to measure self-concepts (Crowne *et al.*, 1961, Morgenstern, 1967) and analysis of the basic structure of self theories themselves (Akeret, 1959; Krause, 1964).

Schizophrenic self-images are involved in other research projects in which one indicates the difficulties of evaluating therapy with schizoids (Gendlin, 1962) while another finds that self-image is not a simple function of maladjustment (Achenbach and Zigler, 1963). The results of the six-year study of schizophrenics at the University of Wisconsin under Rogers' leadership have, after many complications, finally been published (Rogers, 1967c).

A representative listing of research studies reported since 1960 is as follows:

Rogers and Skinner (Vance, 1962).
Rogers and Eysenck (Vingoe, 1968).
Students and parents (Hollenbeck, 1965; Medinnus and Curtis, 1963).
Cognitive studies (Boshier and Hamid, 1968; Suinn, 1962; Suinn *et al.*, 1963).
Repression/sensitization (Byrne *et al.*, 1963; Lucky and Grigg, 1964).
Religion/theology (Walberg, 1967; Wilson, 1967).
Vocations (Wheeler and Carnes, 1968).
Prejudice (Tabachnick, 1962).

In conclusion, it is interesting to note that Rogers feels research, particularly in the field of psychotherapy (which almost translates as personality), is a "young man's field."

DELIMITATIONS

As can be seen from the long bibliography at the end of this chapter, there are many things concerning Rogers' theories which have not been covered by the author.

This chapter on the self theory of personality of Carl Rogers does not take up the methods of therapy, rich as his work is in this area. The Process Scale is barely mentioned. Other limitations are as follows: Rogers' work at the University of Wisconsin on autonomic responses in therapy is not covered; what he considers "necessary and sufficient conditions for therapeutic personality change" are omitted; and we have not included the many contributions toward pastoral psychology and industry, the vast contributions toward educational theory and practice, and Rogers' concern with the training of therapists.

■ SUMMARY

Probably the most conclusive statement one can make about Rogers' theory of personality is that it is not yet in final shape. It is changing and incomplete.

Throughout his work we find one central theme—the self. Whatever Rogers is discussing is always from the self frame of reference. All the ramifications of his work revolve around this concept.

Highly involved in the theory are the terms *self-structure, self-actualization, self-maintenance, self-enhancement, experiencing, phenomenological field,* and *congruence* (bringing together of the self-structure and experiencing as perceived by the self).

Interpreting Personality Theories

BIBLIOGRAPHY

PRIMARY SOURCES

BOOKS

Rogers, C. R., *Measuring Personality Adjustment in Children Nine to Thirteen.* New York: Teachers College, Columbia University, Bureau of Publications, 1931.

Rogers, C. R., *A Test of Personality Adjustment.* New York: Association Press, 1931.

Rogers, C. R., *The Clinical Treatment of the Problem Child.* Boston: Houghton Mifflin, 1939.

Rogers, C. R., *Counseling and Psychotherapy.* Boston: Houghton Mifflin, 1942.

Rogers, C. R., and J. L. Wallen, *Counseling with Returned Servicemen.* New York: McGraw-Hill, 1946.

Rogers, C. R., Current trends in psychotherapy, in W. Dennis (ed.), *Current Trends in Psychology.* University of Pittsburgh Press, 1947, pp. 109–137.

Rogers, C. R., The case of Mary Jane Tilden, in W. U. Snyder (ed.), *Casebook of Nondirective Counseling.* Boston: Houghton Mifflin, 1947, pp. 129–203.

Rogers, C. R., *Dealing with Social Tensions: A Presentation of Client-Centered Counseling as a Means of Handling Interpersonal Conflict.* New York: Hinds, Hayden & Eldredge, 1948.

> Also published in *Pastoral Psychol.*, 1952, 3 (28), 14–20; 3 (29), 37–44.

Rogers, C. R., Significance of the self-regarding attitudes and perceptions, in M. L. Reymert (ed.), *Feelings and Emotions.* New York: McGraw-Hill, 1950, pp. 374–382.

> Also published in L. Gorlow and W. Katkovsky (eds.), *Readings in the Psychology of Adjustment.* New York: McGraw-Hill, 1959.

Rogers, C. R., *Client-Centered Therapy: Its Current Practice, Implications, and Theory.* Boston: Houghton Mifflin, 1951.

Rogers, C. R., Perceptual reorganization in client-centered therapy, in R. R. Blake and G. V. Ramsey (eds.), *Perception: An Approach to Personality.* New York: Ronald Press, 1951, pp. 307–327.

Rogers, C. R., Some directions and the end points in therapy, in O. H. Mowrer (ed.), *Psychotherapy: Theory and Research.* New York: Ronald Press, 1953, pp. 44–68.

Rogers, C. R., and R. F. Dymond, *Psychotherapy and Personality Change.* Chicago: University of Chicago Press, 1954.

Rogers, C. R., Becoming a person, Oberlin College Lecture Series. Oberlin: Oberlin Printing Co., 1954. Reprinted by the Hogg Foundation for Mental Hygiene, University of Texas, 1956; also in *Pastoral Psychol.*, 1956, 7 (61), 9–13; and 1956, 7 (63), 16–26.

> Also published in S. Doniger (ed.), *Healing, Human and Divine.* New York: Association Press, 1957, pp. 57–67.

Rogers, C. R., Client-centered therapy: A current view, in F. Fromm-Reichmann and J. L. Moreno (eds.), *Progress in Psychotherapy.* New York: Grune & Stratton, 1956, pp. 199–209.

Rogers, C. R., What it means to become a person, in C. E. Moustakas (ed.), *The Self.* New York: Harper & Row, 1956, pp. 195–211.

Rogers, C. R., Training individuals to engage in the therapeutic process, in C. R. Strother (ed.), *Psychology and Mental Health.* Washington: American Psychological Association, 957, pp. 76–92.

Rogers, C. R., Case study, in *Great Cases in Psychoanalysis.* New York: Ballantine Books, 1959.

Rogers, C. R., A theory of therapy, personality, and interpersonal relationships as developed in the client-centered framework, in S. Koch (ed.), *Psychology: A Study of a Science*, Vol. III, *Formulations of the Person in the Social Context.* New York: McGraw-Hill, 1959, pp. 184–256.

Rogers, C. R., A tentative scale for the measurement of process in psychotherapy, in E. Rubinstein (ed.), *Research in Psychotherapy.* Washington: American Psychological Association, 1959, pp. 96–107.

Rogers, C. R., Comments on cases, in S. Standal and R. Corsini (eds.), *Critical Incidents in Psychotherapy.* Englewood Cliffs, N.J.: Prentice-Hall, 1959.

Rogers, C. R., M. Lewis, and J. Shlien, Two cases of time-limited client-centered psychotherapy, in A. Burton (ed.), *Case Studies of Counseling and Psychotherapy.* Englewood Cliffs, N.J.: Prentice-Hall, 1959, pp. 309–352.

Rogers, C. R., Significant trends in the client-centered orientation, in D. Brower and L. E. Abt (eds.), *Progress in Clinical Psychology*, Vol. IV. New York: Grune & Stratton, 1960, pp. 85–99.

Rogers, C. R., *On Becoming a Person: A Therapist's View of Psychotherapy.* Boston: Houghton Mifflin, 1961.

Rogers, C. R., A theory of psychotherapy with schizophrenics and a proposal for its empirical investigation, in J. G. Dawson, H. K. Stone, and N. P. Dellis (eds.), *Psychotherapy with Schizophrenics.* Baton Rouge: Louisiana State University Press, 1961, pp. 3–19.

Rogers, C. R., The meaning of the good life, in A. E. Kuenzli (ed.), *Reconstruction in Religion: A Symposium.* Boston: Beacon Press, 1961.

Rogers, C. R., Two divergent trends, in R. May (ed.), *Existential Psychology.* New York: Random House, 1961, pp. 85–93.

Rogers, C. R., Toward becoming a fully functioning person, in A. W. Combs (ed.), *Yearbook of the American Society for Curriculum Development.* Washington: The Society, 1962.

Rogers, C. R., Actualizing tendency in relation to motives and to consciousness, in M. R. Jones (ed.), *Nebraska Symposium on Motivation,* 1963. Lincoln: University of Nebraska Press, 1963.

Rogers, C. R., Toward a science of the person, in T. W. Wann (ed.), *Behaviorism and Phenomenology.* Chicago: University of Chicago Press, 1964, pp. 109–140.

Rogers, C. R., Psychotherapy today, or where do we go from here? in Walter D. Nunokowa (ed.), *Readings in Abnormal Psychology: Human Values and Abnormal Behavior.* Chicago: Scott, Foresman, 1965.

Rogers, C. R., A humanistic conception of man, in R. E. Farson (ed.), *Science and Human Affairs.* Palo Alto, Cal.: Science and Behavior Books, 1966, pp. 18–31.

Rogers, C. R., and Barry Stevers, *Person to Person: The Problem of Being Human: A New Trend in Psychology,* Walnut Creek, Cal.: Real People Press, 1967a.

Rogers, C. R., Autobiography, in E. G. Boring and G. Lindzey, *A History of Psychology in Autobiography,* Vol. V. New York: Appleton-Century-Crofts, 1967b, pp. 341–384.

Rogers, C. R. (ed.), *The Therapeutic Relationship and Its Impact: A Study of Psychotherapy with Schizophrenics.* Madison: University of Wisconsin Press, 1967c.

The *magnum opus* of a six-year study.

Rogers, C. R., Personal thoughts on teaching and learning (pp. 216–218), Implications of recent advances in prediction and control of behavior (pp. 540–548), The organization of personality (pp. 598–616), To be that self which one truly is: A therapist's view of personal goals (pp. 650–664), in D. E. Hamachek (ed.), *Human Dynamics in Psychology and Education: Selected Readings.* Boson: Allyn and Bacon, 1968.

Coulson, W. R., and C. R. Rogers (eds.), *Man and the Science of Man.* Columbus, Ohio: Merrill, 1968.

PERIODICALS

Rogers, C. R., and C. W. Carson, Intelligence as a factor in camping activities, *Camping Magazine,* 1930, 3, 8–11.

Rogers, C. R., A good foster home: Its achievements and limitations, *Ment. Hyg.,* 1933, 17, 21–40.

Also published in F. Lowry (ed.), *Readings in Social Case Work.* New York: Columbia University Press, 1939.

Rogers, C. R., The clinical psychologist's approach to personality problems, *Family,* 1937, 18, 133–143.

Rogers, C. R., Three surveys of treatment measures used with children, *Amer. J Orthopsychiat.,* 1937, 7, 48–57.

Rogers, C. R., Needed emphases in the training of clinical psychologists, *J. Consult. Psychol.*, 1939, 3, 141–143.

Rogers, C. R., and C. C. Bennett, The clinical significance of problem syndromes, *Amer. J. Orthopsychiat.*, 1941, 11, 222–229.

Rogers, C. R., Mental health problems in three elementary schools, *Educ. Res. Bull.*, 1942, 21, 69–79.

Rogers, C. R., The psychologist's contributions to parent, child, and community problems, *J. Consult. Psychol.*, 1942, 6, 8–18.

Rogers, C. R., A study of the mental health problems in three representative elementary schools, in T. C. Holy *et al.*, *A Study of Health and Physical Education in Columbus Public Schools*, Ohio State University Bureau of Education Research Monograph, No. 25, 1942, pp. 130–161.

Rogers, C. R., The use of electrically recorded interviews in improving psychotherapeutic techniques, *Amer. J. Orthopsychiat.*, 1942, 12, 429–434.

Rogers, C. R., Therapy in guidance clinics, *J. Abnorm. Soc. Psychol.*, 1943, 38, 284–289.

> Also published in R. Watson (ed.), *Readings in Clinical Psychology*. New York: Harper & Row, 1949, pp. 519–527.

Rogers, C. R., The development of insight in a counseling relationship, *J. Consult. Psychol.*, 1944, 8, 331–341.

> Also published in A. H. Brayfield (ed.), *Readings on Modern Methods of Counseling*. New York: Appleton-Century-Crofts, 1950, pp. 119–132.

Rogers, C. R., The psychological adjustments of discharged service personnel, *Psychol. Bull.*, 1944, 41, 689–696.

Rogers, C. R., Counseling, *Rev. Educ. Res.*, 1945, 15, 155–163.

Rogers, C. R., The nondirective method as a technique for social research, *Amer. J. Sociol.*, 1945, 50, 279–283.

Rogers, C. R., and V. M. Axline, A teacher-therapist deals with a handicapped child, *J. Abnorm. Soc. Psychol.*, 1945, 40, 119–142.

Rogers, C. R., R. Dicks, and S. B. Wortis, Current trends in counseling, a symposium, *Marriage Fam. Living*, 1945, 7.

Rogers, C. R., Psychometric tests and client-centered counseling, *Educ. Psychol. Measmt*, 1946, 6, 139–144.

Rogers, C. R., Recent research in nondirective therapy and its implications, *Amer. J. Abnorm. Soc. Psychol.*, 1946, 41, 207–216.

Rogers, C. R., Significant aspects of client-centered therapy, *Amer. Psychologist*, 1946, 1, 415–422.

Muench, G. A., and C. R. Rogers, Counseling of emotional blocking in an aviator, *J. Abnorm. Soc. Psychol.*, 1946, 41, 207–216.

Rogers, C. R., Effective principles for dealing with individual and group tensions and dissatisfactions, *Executive Seminar Series on Industrial Relations*, Session 10. Chicago: University of Chicago Press, 1947.

Rogers, C. R., Some observations on the organization of personality, *Amer. Psychologist*, 1947, 2, 358–368.

> Also published in A. Kuenzli (ed.), *The Phenomenological Problem*. New York: Harper & Row, 1959, pp. 49–75.

Rogers, C. R., Divergent trends in methods of improving adjustment, *Harvard Educ. Rev.*, 1948, *18*, 209–219.

> Also in *Pastoral Psychol.*, 1950, *1*, 11–18.

Rogers, C. R., Research in psychotherapy: Round table, *Amer. J. Orthopsychiat.*, 1948, *18*, 96–100.

Rogers, C. R., Some implications of client-centered counseling for college personnel work, *Educ. Psychol. Measmt*, 1948, 8, 540–549.

> Also published in *College and University*, 1948, and in *Registrar's Journal*, 1948.

Rogers, C. R., B. L. Kell, and H. McNeil, The role of self-understanding in the prediction of behavior, *J. Consult. Psychol.*, 1948, *12*, 174–186.

Rogers, C. R., The attitude and orientation of the counselor in client-centered therapy, *J. Consult. Psychol.*, 1949, *13*, 82–94.

Rogers, C. R., A coordinated research in psychotherapy: A nonobjective introduction, *J. Consult. Psychol.*, 1949, *13*, 149–153.

Rogers, C. R., A current formulation of client-centered therapy, *Soc. Serv. Rev.*, 1950, *24*, 442–450.

Rogers, C. R., What is to be our basic professional relationship? *Ann. Allergy*, 1950, *8*, 234–239.

> Also published in M. H. Krout (ed.), *Psychology, Psychiatry, and the Public Interest*. Minneapolis: University of Minnesota Press, 1956, pp. 135–145.

Rogers, C. R., and R. Becker, A basic orientation for counseling, *Pastoral Psychol.*, 1950, *1*, 26–34.

Rogers, C. R., D. G. Marquis, and E. R. Hilgard, ABEPP policies and procedures, *Amer. Psychologist*, 1950, *5*, 407–408.

Rogers, C. R., Studies in client-centered psychotherapy: III. The case of Mrs. Oak, a research analysis, *Psychol. Serv. Center J.*, 1951, *3*, 47–165.

> Also published in C. R. Rogers and R. F. Dymond (eds.), *Psychotherapy and Personality Change*. Chicago: University of Chicago Press, 1954, pp. 259–348.

Rogers, C. R., Through the eyes of a client, *Pastoral Psychol.*, 1951, *2* (16), 32–40; (17), 45–50; (18), 26–32.

Rogers, C. R., Where are we going in clinical psychology? *J. Consult. Psychol.*, 1951, *15*, 171–177.

Rogers, C. R., T. Gordon, D. L. Grummon, and J. Seeman, Studies in client-centered psychotherapy: I. Developing a program of research in psychotherapy, *Psychol. Serv. Center J.*, 1951, *3*, 3–28.

> Also published in C. R. Rogers and R. F. Dymond (eds.), *Psychotherapy and Personality Change*. Chicago: University of Chicago Press, 1954, pp. 12–34.

Rogers, C. R., Client-centered psychotherapy, *Sci. Amer.*, 1952, *187*, 66–74.

Rogers, C. R., Communication: Its blocking and facilitation, *Northwestern Univer. Information*, 1952, *20*, 9–15. Reprinted in *ETC*, 1952, *9*, 83–88; in *Harvard Bus. Rev.*, 1952, *30*, 46–50; and in C. E. Bursk (ed.), *Human Relations for Management* (New York: Harper & Row, 1956), pp. 150–158.

Rogers, C. R., A personal formulation of client-centered therapy, *Marriage Fam. Living*, 1952, *14*, 341–361.

> Also published in C. E. Vincent (ed.), *Readings in Marriage Counseling.* New York: Crowell, 1957, pp. 392–423.

Rogers, C. R., The interest in the practice of psychotherapy, *Amer. Psychologist*, 1953, *8*, 48–50.

Rogers, C. R., A research program in client-centered therapy, *Res. Publ. Assoc. Res. Nerv. Ment. Dis.*, 1953, *31*, 106–113.

Rogers, C. R., G. W. Brooks, R. S. Driver, W. V. Merrihue, P. Pigors, and A. J. Rinella, Removing the obstacles to good employee communications, *Mgmt Rec.*, 1953, *15*, 9–11, 32–40.

Rogers, C. R., Towards a theory of creativity, *ETC: A Review of General Semantics*, 1954, *11*, 249–260.

> Also published in H. H. Anderson (ed.), *Creativity and Its Cultivation.* New York: Harper & Row, 1959, pp. 69–82.

Rogers, C. R., A personal view of some issues facing psychologists, *Amer. Psychologist*, 1955, *10*, 247–249.

Rogers, C. R., Personality change in psychotherapy, *Int. J. Soc. Psychiat.*, 1955, *1*, 31–41.

Rogers, C. R., Persons or science? A philosophical question, *Amer. Psychologist*, 1955, *10*, 267–278.

> Also published in *Pastoral Psychol.*, 1959, *10* (nos. 92, 93).

Rogers, C. R., A counseling approach to human problems, *Amer. J. Nurs.*, 1956, *56*, 994–997.

Rogers, C. R., Implications of recent advances in the prediction and control of behavior, *Teachers Coll. Rec.*, 1956, *57*, 316–322.

> Also published in E. L. Hartley and R. E. Hartley (eds.), *Outside Readings in Psychology.* New York: Crowell, 1957, pp. 3–10.
> Also published in R. S. Daniel (ed.), *Contemporary Readings in General Psychology.* Boston: Houghton Mifflin, 1960.

Rogers, C. R., Some issues concerning the control of human behavior (Symposium with B. F. Skinner), *Science*, 1956, *124*, 1057–1066.

> Also published in L. Gorlow and W. Katkovsky (eds.), *Readings in the Psychology of Adjustment.* New York: McGraw-Hill, 1959, pp. 500–522.

Rogers, C. R., E. J. Shoben, O. H. Mowrer, B. A. Kimble, and J. G. Miller, Behavior theories and a counseling case, *J. Counsel. Psychol.*, 1956, *3*, 107–124.

Rogers, C. R., The necessary and sufficient conditions of therapeutic personality
   change, *J. Consult. Psychol.,* 1957, 21, 95–103.
Rogers, C. R., A note on the nature of man, *J. Counsel. Psychol.,* 1957, 4,
   199–203.

   Also published in *Pastoral Psychol.,* 1960, 11, pp. 23–26.

Rogers, C. R., Personal thoughts on teaching and learning, *Merrill-Palmer Quart.,*
   1957, 3, 241–243.

   Also published in *Improving College and University Teaching,* 1958, 6,
   4–5.

Rogers, C. R., A therapist's view of the good life, *Humanist,* 1957, 17, 291–300.
Rogers, C. R., The characteristics of a helping relationship, *Personnel Guid. J.,*
   1958, 37, 6–16.
Rogers, C. R., A process conception of psychotherapy, *Amer. Psychologist,* 1958,
   13, 142–149.
Rogers, C. R., The essence of psychotherapy: A client-centered view, *Ann.
   Psychother.,* 1959, 1, 51–57.
Rogers, C. R., Significant learning: In therapy and in education, *Educ. Leader.,*
   1959, 16, 232–242.
Rogers, C. R., A. Walker, and R. Rablen, Development of a scale to measure
   process changes in psychotherapy, *J. Clin. Psychol.,* 1960, 16, 79–85.
Rogers, C. R., The place of the person in the new world of the behavioral sciences,
   Personnel Guid. J., 1961, 39, 442–451.
Rogers, C. R., The process equation of psychotherapy, *Amer. J. Psychother.,* 1961,
   15, 27–45.
Rogers, C. R., The interpersonal relationship: The core of guidance, *Harvard
   Educ. Rev.,* 1962, 32, 416–429.
Rogers, C. R., The concept of the fully functioning person, *Psychother.: Theor.
   Res. Pract.,* 1963, 1, 17–26.
Rogers, C. R., Psychotherapy today, or where do we go from here? *Amer. J.
   Psychother.,* 1963, 17, 5–16.

   We need facts gained from naturalistic observations.

Rogers, C. R., Toward a science of the person, *J. Humanist. Psychol.,* 1963, 3,
   72–92.
Rogers, C. R., Toward a modern approach to values: The valuing process in the
   mature person, *J. Abnorm. Soc. Psychol.,* 1964, 68, 160–167.
Rogers, C. R., Some questions and challenges facing humanistic psychology, *J.
   Humanist. Psychol.,* 1965, 5, 1–5.
Rogers, C. R., Some thoughts regarding the current philosophy of the behavioral
   sciences, *J. Humanist. Psychol.,* 1965, 5, 182–194.
Rogers, C. R., The therapeutic relationship: Recent theory and research, *Aust. J.
   Psychol.,* 1965, 17, 95–108.

FILMS

Rogers, C. R., and R. H. Segel, *Client-Centered Therapy: Part I and II*, 16 mm., sound. State College: Pennsylvania State, Psychological Cinema Register, 1952.

Rogers, C. R., and R. H. Segel, *Psychotherapy Begins: The Case of Mr. Lin*, 16 mm., sound. State College: Pennsylvania State, Psychological Cinema Register, 1955.

Rogers, C. R., and R. H. Segel, *Psychotherapy in Process: The Case of Miss Mun*, 16 mm., sound. State College: Pennsylvania State, Psychological Cinema Register, 1955.

Rogers, C. R., *Psychotherapy: The Counselor*, and *Psychotherapy: The Client*, 16 mm., sound, distributed by Bureau of Audio-Visual Aids, Madison, University of Wisconsin, 1960.

SUGGESTED READINGS

BOOKS

Ard, B. N. (ed.), *Counseling and Psychotherapy; Classics on Theories and Issues.* Palo Alto, Cal.: Science and Behavior Books, 1966.

Boring, E. G., and G. Lindzey (eds.), *A History of Psychology in Autobiography.* New York: Appleton-Century-Crofts, 1967.

Byrne, D., *An Introduction to Personality: A Research Approach.* Englewood Cliffs, N.J.: Prentice-Hall, 1966, pp. 434–477.

Excellent presentation of self-as-object, self-as-process, and Rogers.

Chaplin, J. P., and T. S. Krawiec, *Systems and Theories of Psychology.* New York: Holt, Rinehart & Winston, 1968.

Hall, C. S., and G. Lindzey, *Theories of Personality.* New York: Wiley, 1957, pp. 257–295.

Rogers and others on the self theory.

Lecky, P., *Self-Consistency.* New York: Island Press, 1945.

Lindzey, G., and C. S. Hall, *Theories of Personality: Primary Sources and Research.* New York: Wiley, 1965, pp. 467–509.

Maddi, S. R., *Personality Theories: A Comparative Analysis.* Homewood, Ill.: Dorsey, 1968.

Rogers' theory as a fulfillment model.

Mead, G. H., *Mind, Self, and Society.* Chicago: University of Chicago Press, 1934.

Mehrabian, A., *An Analysis of Personality Theories.* Englewood Cliffs, N.J.: Prentice-Hall, 1968.

Chap. 2 attempts to simplify and modify the Rogers theory.

Perez, J. F., *Counseling: Theory and Practice*. Reading, Mass.: Addison-Wesley, 1963.

Rychlak, J. F., *A Philosophy of Science for Personality Theory*. Boston: Houghton Mifflin, 1968.

> Rogers as an ethical therapist—does he get at the "core" or merely adjust the client?

Seeman, J., Client-centered therapy, in D. Brower and L. E. Abt (eds.), *Progress in Clinical Psychology II*. New York: Grune & Stratton, 1956, pp. 98–113.

Sherif, M., and H. Cantril, *The Psychology of Ego-Involvements*. New York: Wiley, 1947.

Shlien, J. M., Phenomenology and personality, in J. M. Wepman and R. W. Heine (eds.), *Concepts of Personality*. Chicago: Aldine, 1963.

Skinner, B. F., *Science and Human Behavior*. New York: Macmillan, 1953, p. 447.

Snygg, D., and A. W. Combs, *Individual Behavior*. New York: Harper & Row, 1949.

Stephenson, W., *The Study of Behavior*. Chicago: University of Chicago Press, 1953.

Symonds, P. M., *The Ego and the Self*. New York: Appleton-Century-Crofts, 1951.

Taylor, J. F. A., and F. C. Thorne (eds.), *Self-Consistency: A Theory of Personality*. New York: Doubleday, 1969.

Wann, T. W. (ed.), *Behaviorism and Phenomenology: Contrasting Base for Modern Psychology*. Chicago: University of Chicago Press, 1964.

PERIODICALS

Achenbach, T., and E. Zigler, Social competence and self-image disparity in psychiatric and nonpsychiatric patients, *J. Abnorm. Soc. Psychol.*, 1963, 67, 197–205.

> Counter to Rogers, self-image disparity is not a simple function of maladjustment.

Akeret, R. V., Interrelationships among various dimensions of the self concept, *J. Counsel. Psychol.*, 1959, 6, 199–201.

> Self-concept is not unitary but has many kinds of self-feelings.

Baker, S. R., Factor analytic study of self-perception of graduate and undergraduate students, *Percept. Mot. Skills*, 1968, 26, 1073–1074.

> Graduate students vary more in describing self-concepts.

Bertocci, P. A., The psychological self, the ego and personality, *Psychol. Rev.*, 1945, 52, 91–99.

Boshier, R., and P. Hamid, Academic success and self-concept, *Psychol. Rep.*, 1968, 22, 1191–1192.

> No significant difference in self-concept between high passing and failing students in New Zealand.

Byrne, D., J. Barry, and D. Nelson, Relation of the revised Repression-Sensitization Scale to measures of self-description, *Psychol. Rep.*, 1963, *13*, 323–334.

> Repressives positive on self-concept measures; sensitizers negative.

Chein, I., The awareness of self and the structure of the ego, *Psychol. Rev.*, 1944, *51*, 304–314.

Chodorkoff, B., Self-perception, perceptual defense, and adjustment, *J. Abnorm. Soc. Psychol.*, 1954, *49*, 508–512.

Corsini, R., Freud, Rogers, and Moreno: An inquiry into the possible relationship between manifest personality, theory, and method of some eminent psychotherapists, *Group Psychother.*, 1956, *9*, 274–281.

> Calls Freud a man of intellect. Calls Rogers a gentle and friendly person. Calls Moreno a man who has the capacity for immediate action.

Crowne, D. P., W. Stephens, and R. Kelly, The validity and equivalence of tests of self-acceptance, *J. Psychol.*, 1961, *51*, 101–112.

Gendlin, E. T., Client-centered developments and work with schizophrenics, *J. Counsel. Psychol.*, 1962, *9*, 205–211.

Gettering, R. W., Philosophic idealism in Rogerian psychology, *Educ. Theor.*, 1955, *5*, 206–214.

Hilgard, E. R., Human motives and the concept of self, *Amer. Psychologist*, 1949, *4*, 374–382.

> Also in H. Brand (ed.), *The Study of Personality*. New York: Wiley, 1954, pp. 347–361.

Hollenbeck, B. P., Conditions and outcomes in the student-parent relationships, *J. Consult. Psychol.*, 1965, *29*, 237–241.

> Adjustment was related; achievement was not.

Jessor, R., Phenomenological personality theories and the data language of psychology, *Psychol. Rev.*, 1956, *15*, 173–180.

Krause, M. S., An analysis of Carl R. Rogers' theory of personality, *Genet. Psychol. Monogr.*, 1964, *69*, 49–99.

Lebo, D., The development of client-centered therapy in the writings of Carl Rogers, *Amer. J. Psychiat.*, 1953, *110*, 104–109.

Lucky, A. W., and A. E. Grigg, Repression-sensitization as a variable in deviant responding, *J. Clin. Psychol.*, 1964, *20*, 92–93.

> Repressives positive on self-concept measures; sensitizers negative.

Lundholm, H., Reflections upon the nature of the psychological self, *Psychol. Rev.*, 1940, *47*, 110–127.

Maslow, A. H., Critique of self-actualization: I. Some dangers of being-cognition, *J. Indiv. Psychol.*, 1959, *15*, 24–32.

Medinnus, G. R., and F. J. Curtis, The relation between maternal self-acceptance and child acceptance. *J. Consult. Psychol.*, 1963, *27*, 542–544.

> Easier to accept child when mother accepts self.

Morgenstern, D. P., An investigation of Rogers' theory of congruence through measures of self—and other—perception, *Dissert. Abstr.*, 1967, 28, 1171–1172.

Nameche, G. F., Two pictures of man, *J. Humanist. Psychol.*, 1961, *1*, 70–88.

Riley, R. C., Factor analysis of Rogers' theory of "regard," *Dissert. Abstr.*, 1962, *23*, 326–327.

Sarbin, T. R., A preface to the psychological analysis of self, *Psychol. Rev.*, 1952, *59*, 11–22.

Schultz, K. V., The psychologically healthy person: A study in identification and prediction, *J. Clin. Psychol.*, 1958, *14*, 112–117.

> Theology students self-actualization ratings correlate low but positive.

Skinner, B. F., Freedom and the control of men, *Amer. Scholar*, 1955–1956, *25*, 47–65.

Smith, D. E. P., Interdisciplinary approach to the genesis of anxiety, *Educ. Theor.*, 1956, *6*, 222–231.

> Compares Freud, Rank, Mowrer, Angyal, Goldstein, Lewin, Rogers, Kierkegaard, and Sullivan on theories of anxiety.

Smith, M. B., The phenomenological approach in personality theory: Some critical remarks, *J. Abnorm. Soc. Psychol.*, 1950, *45*, 516–522.

Stock, D., An investigation into the interrelations between self-concept and feelings directed toward other persons and groups, *J. Consult. Psychol.*, 1949, *13*, 176–180.

Strupp, H. H., An objective comparison of Rogerian and psychoanalytic techniques, *J. Consult. Psychol.* 1955, *19*, 1–7.

Suinn, R. M., The relationship between self-acceptance and acceptance of others: A learning theory analysis, *J. Abnorm. Soc. Psychol.*, 1962, *63*, 37–42.

> Learning theory and how self-acceptance aids in accepting others (fathers and teachers).

Suinn, R. M., D. Osborne, and P. Winfree, The self-concept and accuracy of recall of inconsistent self-related information. *J. Clin. Psychol.*, 1963, *18*, 473–474.

> Memory is better when consistent with self-concept.

Tabachnick, B. R., Some correlates of prejudice toward Negroes in elementary age children, *J. Genet. Psychol.*, 1962, *100*, 193–203.

> High satisfaction with self correlates with low prejudice.

Vance, L., Methodology versus ideology in psychological research, *J. Counsel. Psychol.*, 1962, *9*, 12–17.

Vingoe, F. J., Rogers' self theory and Eysenck's extraversion and neuroticism. *J. Consult. Clin. Psychol.*, 1968, *32*, 618–620.

> Study supports Rogers' self theory.

Walberg, H. M., Religious differences in cognitive associations and self-concept in prospective teachers, *J. Soc. Psychol.*, 1967, 73, 89–96.

> Among Jewish women self-concept rated higher than among Protestant and Catholic women.

Walker, W. E., Carl Rogers and the nature of man, *J. Consult. Psychol.*, 1956, 3, 89–91.

Wheeler, C. L., and E. R. Carnes, Relationships among self-concepts, ideal self-concepts, and stereotypes of probable and ideal vocational choices, *J. Counsel. Psychol.*, 1968, 15, 530–535.

> Job choice an attempt to enhance self-concept.

Wilson, T. J., Theological assimilation of Rogerian therapy, *Insight: Quart. Rev. Relig. Ment. Hlth*, 1967, 5, 18–30.

10

MURPHY

Every habit and faculty is preserved and increased by corresponding actions,—as the habit of walking, by walking; or running, by running.

EPICTETUS
How the Semblances of Things Are to be Combated

SOME BIOGRAPHICAL DATA

Gardner Murphy was born in Chillicothe, Ohio, on July 8, 1895. He was the son of Edgar Gardner Murphy, an Episcopal minister, and Maud (King) Murphy. He attended Hotchkiss School in Lakeville, Connecticut, from 1910 to 1912, received his B.A. from Yale in 1916, his M.A. from Harvard in 1917, and his Ph.D. from Columbia in 1923. During World War I he served with the American Expeditionary Forces in France. In 1921 Murphy began his teaching career at Columbia, where he taught in the capacity of a lecturer from 1921 to 1925, as an instructor from 1925 to 1929, and as an assistant professor from 1929 to 1940. He then left Columbia to accept the position of professor of psychology at City College of New York where he remained until accepting his present position, Director of Research at the Menninger Foundation in Topeka, Kansas. Murphy was married to the former Lois Barclay on November 27, 1926, and has two children, Alpen Gardner and Margaret. In 1932, for his studies in the field of experimental social psychology, Columbia University awarded Murphy the Butler Medal. He is a member of the American Psychological Association and a past member of the Eastern Psychological Association, serving as president of the former in 1943–1944 and of the latter in 1941–1942. Also he is a member of the American Association for the Advancement of Science and of the Society for the Psychological Study of Social Issues, of which he was president in 1938. In 1950 Murphy and his wife visited India on a UNESCO mission to study the cause of social tensions. From this resulted the book *In the Minds of Men* (1953), a nontechnical interpretation of his impressions and of the research reports of eight Indian social scientists. Since Murphy has not sought to popularize psychology, his largest portion of writing is a matter of serious scholarship. He is a specialist in personality theory and is also interested in social psychology. In addition, Murphy has been interested in the field of parapsychology, which considers the phenomena of clairvoyance and telepathy, and he has served as president of the London Society for Psychical Research. Murphy continues to be a prolific contributor to the psychological world.

INTRODUCTION

Murphy invents, but he also picks, chooses, interprets, and reemphasizes the work of many others. His interests are catholic; his interpretations are concise, his integrations of theories are comprehensive.

Murphy has an inheritance of ideas from the works of William James, McDougall, Allport, Woodworth, and others. Perhaps the strongest influence of another theorist upon Murphy has been the field theory emphasis of the late Kurt Lewin.

Murphy is a widely read and influential scholar of man's behavior. At many times in his career he has appeared to be out of the mainstream of psychological thought. Possibly one reason for his wide range of psychological interests has been his increasing desire for interaction among all fields of human endeavor. Parapsychology, for example, is not popular in current psychological thinking. Gardner Murphy dares to write what he thinks about a psychological field that the majority of psychologists are inclined to back away from in favor of more tried and true research areas and publishable fields. He is equally at home with the older psychologists such as James, McDougall, Thorndike, and Woodworth, who are inclined to be neglected because their dates of publishing predate the second world war. The older names not only are psychological history to Murphy but still hold his interest.

The following list of some of his major publications is an indication of the wide talents this psychologist displays.

General psychology
> *General Psychology*, 1933
> *Introduction to Psychology*, 1951
> *Encounter with Reality*, 1968

History of psychology
> *Historical Introduction to Modern Psychology*, 1929, revised 1949

Applied psychology
> *Public Opinion and the Individual*, 1938 (with Rensis Likert)
> *Human Nature and Enduring Peace*, 1945 (edited for the Society for the Psychological Study of Social Issues)
> *In the Minds of Men: The Study of Human Behavior and Social Tensions in India*, 1953

Social psychology
> *Experimental Social Psychology*, 1931 (with his wife Lois Barclay Murphy), 1937 (revised edition with another author, Theodore Newcomb)

Parapsychology
> *William James on Psychical Research*, edited by Gardner Murphy and Robert O. Ballou, 1960
> *Challenge of Psychical Research: A Primer of Parapsychology*, in collaboration with Laura A. Dale, 1961

Personality
> *Approaches to Personality*, 1932 (with Friedrich Jensen)
> *Personality: A Biosocial Approach to Origins and Structure*, 1947, 1966
> *Human Potentialities*, 1958

Education
> *Freeing Intelligence Through Teaching*, 1961

International
> *Asian Psychology*, edited by Gardner Murphy and Lois Barclay Murphy 1968

The ever present main theme of Gardner Murphy's personality theory is that man is both a biological phenomenon and a social phenomenon, and that these two aspects must be brought together in a third phenomenon, that of integration. Thus, when he states that "your hunger is different from my hunger" (*Personality*, p. 143), he means that man branches from a basic need for food toward the multiple kinds of aversions and appetites which he learns through the social order he lives in. Beyond that, however, is the highly important aspect of integrating the biological and social sides of man. Two further quotations are necessary to advance the major theme of integration. I is apparent that, although eleven years separate the quoted materials, Murphy has maintained the same idea. From his definitive work of 1947, *Personality*, we find, "But personality study is an art and an engineering enterprise as well as a science, and at the present stage in its development the three often flow together and refuse to be separated" (p. 14). In the philosophically and ethically oriented book of 1958, *Human Potentialities*, we find, "But I have believed for a long time that human nature is a reciprocity of what is inside the skin and what is outside; that it is definitely not 'rolled up inside us' but our way of being one with our fellows and our world. I call this field theory . . ." (p. viii).

Murphy has a strong tendency to think in characteristics of three. By no means, however, does he confine thoughts within a triadic framework. Nonetheless, so strong and clear is his penchant for threeness that the following list is offered. Two purposes may be served by the thirty-three examples of ideas in threes: The list itself approximates a summary of many of Murphy's theories and it surprises one with the scope of concepts which can be phrased in triadic form.

The first nineteen examples in abbreviated form are taken from *Personality: A Biosocial Approach to Origins and Structure* (1947). The remaining fourteen examples are from *Human Potentialities* (1958).

1. The "threads" from three fields, biology, clinical experience, and the social sciences, should be brought together in an attempt to define how personality grows (p. 26).

2. There are three levels of complexity in studying personality problems: personality as an object, a chrysalis, and a continuously changing field view (pp. 3–5).

3. There are three ways in which man refuses to cooperate in studying the whole man: Traits express intangibles, "some of the phases of this innner structure are hidden, pocketed off . . .," and he reacts in the present to situations which we do not understand (pp. 5–6).

4. Three major research tools are suggested: genetic—in both the developmental and the longitudinal sense—comparative, and experimental (pp. 15 ff.).

5. Murphy suggests at least three types of evolutionary forces in process these days: recombinations of germinal tendencies, differential birth rates, and cultural forces which redefine the significance of biological traits (pp. 45–46).

6. There are three ways in which the endocrine system relates to personality syndromes: Endocrine products in the bloodstream may lower the thresholds for muscular reaction patterns, endocrine products may intensify muscular reaction patterns, and endocrine products may stabilize and coordinate patterns already at work (p. 77).

7. Individual differences in motivation may be studied in three ways:

directly through organic processes, indirectly by inference of verbal and ges-
tural external behavior, and still more indirectly through inferential testimony
of observers (p. 118).

8. Organic traits may be of three types: broad characteristics of tissue
response, persistency in modes of reaction of individual tissues, and persistent
interaction between tissues (p. 133).

9. Anatomical clues, such as Sheldon uses to study personality, indirectly
may be valuable in three ways: Anatomical traits may limit or control
conduct, longtime trait effects may produce expressive behavior or may affect
appearance, and physical appearance may have an effect upon others (p.
150).

10. Murphy suggests three ways of measuring laboratory conditioning
situations: measuring the number of stimulations, the intensity of established
responses, or the number of repetitions needed for extinction (p. 194).

11. ". . . we may say that genuine individuality or personality in verbal
expression depends first upon the asocial physiognomic response of the child;
second, upon its antithesis, the stereotyping and freezing of formal linguistic
structure; third, synthetically, upon the capacity to transcend both asociality
and sociality in individual expression" (p. 268).

12. Most of the previous trichotomized ideas are an outgrowth of the
major theses of "three principles" which govern much of what personality is:
the original constitution, the early canalizations and conditioning, and the
field of organism-environoment interaction (p. 294).

13. There are three levels at which graphologists work: global, characteristics, and integrative (p. 692).

14. Usually there are three forms of response to frustration although a
fourth may be involved: aggression, resignation, reality distortion, and displaced aggression (p. 322).

15. Perceptual development proceeds in three stages: the "blur" stage,
the differentiation stage, and the integration stage (p. 342).

16. Capital punishment has three aspects: expiation, protection, and
reassertion of the conscience against hostile impulses (p. 388).

17. At least three factors contribute to genius: affective, intellectual, and
motor (p. 457).

18. Loss of selfhood may be induced in three ways: by organic changes,
by self-obliteration, and by reconstituting the self to find a new person (pp.
519–521).

19. ". . . economic determinism is valuable as an avenue of approach to
personality. Three points must be stressed:

> (1) The economic situation can limit the possibilities of personality
> growth in particular directions. . . .
> (2) . . . The economic situation will indicate the likely directions in
> which the various social patterns will evolve. . . .

(3) In defining the role of the economic arts, we shall use a principle well described by Margaret Mead: the same geographic problems may take entirely different forms by virtue of different social attitudes, different ways of 'phrasing the situation.' . . . If, then, we look closely at economic determinism, we find that it is not a question of the economic *situation*, but a question of the economic *behavior* of the group. Economic behavior does not result solely from the economic situation, but from a complex which includes non-economic factors. It would consequently be meaningless to say that the economic *situation* alone determines the personality pattern; the economic situation is one of several factors that shape the personalities who express and are expressed in the culture . . ." (pp. 775–776).

(NOTE: Eleven years later Gardner Murphy continued in his *Human Potentialities* [1958] to trichotomize his material.)

20. Gardner Murphy organizes the seventeen chapters of *Human Potentialities* around the concept of three kinds of human nature as follows (p. 5):

1st Human Nature: modifiable biological individuality;
2nd Human Nature: cultural forces;
3rd Human Nature: creative thrust to understand.

21. There are three specifications our animal ancestors were equipped to meet: physical warmth, response to others for interdependent living, and specific responses to the opposite sex (p. 27).

22. The three core qualities of humanness are the intense or slightly diffuse needs that are met biologically, the diffuse demands for activity such as rhythm, manipulation of objects or exercise, and the need and capacity to learn (p. 37).

23. How does human individuality come about? In approximately three different ways: (1) cognitive experiences—exploring the world; (2) affective experiences—feeling about the world; (3) impulse experiences—acting toward the world (p. 58).

24. The "great periods" of creativity in art depend upon three things: rationalizations, ego-involvement, and reciprocity between master and pupil (p. 48).

(NOTE: Lest the reader at this point become convinced that Murphy phrases all of his ideas in three, the following brief list may add perspective to the thirty-three triadic concepts. All of them are taken from *Human Potentialities*. The list in no way exhausts the nontrichotomized concepts.)

Four human needs (p. 61).
Six common kinds of learning (p. 64).
Two types of studies in sociology (p. 105).
"Thought, like perception, is bipolar" (p. 117).

Four specific steps to how wishes guide perceiving, remembering, an
thinking (p. 116).

Four stages in creative thinking (p. 129).

25. Creativeness is encouraged or freed by three steps: increasing sens
tiveness, building strong canalizations especially of the self as a creator, an
allowing freedom to move from fantasy to controlled thinking (p. 164).

26. Murphy speaks of the "three-fold basis for craving to know an
understand": visceral drives (instinctual), love of order (formal), and res
nance to the nature and structure of that which surrounds us—excitemen
about reality and the capacity to respond to it (sensory) (p. 179).

27. Human potentialities are withheld from fulfillment by three curren
crises: Huge power systems are in conflict, the systems we have evolved suc
as governments, industries, and social rules now control us more than v
control them, and biological changes in man through nuclear accidents ma
make man unfit for his environment (p. 198).

28. There are three factors in the biological changes in man: rapi
changes of a physical type, the increase and decrease of certain diseases, an
the fact that evolution is still going on (pp. 218–221).

29. Homogamy, or developing similar traits, is sensitive to three soci
factors: vertical mobility, horizontal mobility, and change of habitat (pp. 231
232).

30. The boundaries between the person and the world are the physic
and/or biological, the psychological, and the social (p. 288).

31. Out of the psychological boundaries just mentioned come thre
possible approaches to studying the relationships of man to his world: tl
Gestalt concept, the concept of Functional Interdependence, and the Lewi
ian Field Theory concept (p. 290).

32. Murphy feels that there are three directions toward which new r
search should be pushed: greater understanding of the physical world throug
astronomy, greater understanding of man through social psychology an
greater understanding of the immediate environment through organic chen
istry (p. 269).

33. The last of the triads to be outlined here is actually a triad upon
triad. After discussing the world that might be in the future, Murphy assum
"there will soon be a world scientific–technical–political system (a triad) i
which the question of the independence of sovereign states is less importai
than it seems today." If this system is to be created and is to survive chao
three higher components must come into interaction with one another. Tl
first is curiosity about man and his environment in which scientists ma
become a group apart in the service of humanity as a whole. The second is tl
development of something like "super-executives" or a "power elite" who:
job it will be to use the inventions and social interactions that are developin
The third and, in a sense, the most important component is a genuine vertic

communication system among all of the integrated parts of the scientific–technical–political world system (p. 264).

The strong passion for humanistic interpretations of man's foibles that runs through all the works of Murphy is probably best indicated by his statement "The castigation of one's fellows for their limited or warped outlook is comparable with the castigation of the heart for beating" (*Human Potentialities*, p. 57).

Somewhat like Gordon Allport, Murphy feels that the study of personality dynamics has been neglected by the psychologists of today; that psychology fails to appreciate personality because it lacks the rigors of the so-called scientific approach. As previously stated, personality study is more than a science or an engineering project; it is also an art.

A unique eulogy of Gardner Murphy was prepared by his former students and coworkers. It is in the form of a book entitled *Festschrift for Gardner Murphy*, published in 1960 and edited by Eugene L. Hartley and John G. Peatman, and avoids the cultism frequently found in such works although a play on the initials of Gardner Murphy as "Great Man" is apparent. With the exception of the first two chapters the book deals solidly with psychological material and research findings.

MURPHY'S DESCRIPTION OF HUMAN BEHAVIOR

Because Murphy writes extensively on varied topics, it is not possible to treat his work within the framework of principles, as has been done with the previous theorists. The author has chosen to present Gardner Murphy's ideas as four major themes rather than as principles. Murphy himself feels that the study of personality is a particular kind of "general psychology." The four major themes are the following: the biological personality, the emerging, integrating personality, the socialized personality, and human potentialities or new perspectives.

An indication of the vastness of Gardner Murphy's treatment of the dynamics of personality is best shown by a listing of the forty-one chapter titles in his major work, *Personality* (1947):

1. The Approach
2. The Organism
3. Heredity and Individual Growth
4. The Individual Constitution
5. The Elementary Biology of Motivation
6. The Biology of Motive Patterns
7. Organic Traits and Their Measurement
8. Canalization
9. Conditioning
10. The Hierarchy of Conditionings
11. The World of Symbols
12. The World of Values
13. Conflict
14. The Perceiver
15. Autism
16. Imagination and Thought
17. The Dreamer

What follows, then, approximates a book review. The wide dimensions and the total coverage of personality theory may all be found in the 1947 treatise. The strong eclectic approach of Murphy is no better illustrated than in the above listing of chapters.

Murphy does not sit in judgment on the material he uses from the research and work of others. Rather it is his desire to describe personality. However, he feels there is no "danger in this century" of anyone's completely describing or understanding the human personality.

To Murphy personality theory is synonymous with motivation theory. His primary purpose is to answer the question "Why does man do the things he does?" To him "every aspect of personality is conceived of in terms of motives."

To Hall and Lindzey, whose 1957 book added so much to personality theory, "The dimensions of his [Murphy's] theory are practically the same as those of the whole science of psychology." The techniques of outlining will be employed in presenting the theory of Gardner Murphy since a discursive treatment would only do poorly what Murphy does well. As with all the theorists discussed herein, one must read the theorist in the original if a full understanding is what the reader desires. The present work only hopes to sketch out the primary features for the beginning student of personality theory and then pass him on to the masters themselves.

The Biological Personality Theme

GENERAL CONCEPTS

"The first definition of personality is therefore in terms of a biochemical system" (*Personality*, p. 31). With these words we may begin to describe man's personality as Murphy sees it.

One of the difficulties in dealing with the human personality is the biological nature of the physical and chemical properties which are highly involved in man's behavior, since neither of these properties is amenable to adjusting to social pressures. Thus nature ignores our artificial distinctions between man and his environment.

The organic system is a tension system which operates in a complex hierarchy of interdependent parts. The biological personality is therefore to be considered as part of the field theory. A *field* in this case means "the distribution of energy in space and time." Because man is biological, the concept of homeostasis is important. But because he is also social and oper- ates in an uncontrollable and changing environment, homeostasis can render him incapable of changing to meet changing times. If he returns only to a state of equilibrium, he is forever going back, reactionary, to situations which no longer exist. This, Murphy feels, is a dilemma of human personality brought about by its biological basis. "It is the development, the differentia- tion, the integration [a triad again!] of these individual motive patterns that constitute the first great biological clue to personality" (*Personality*, p. 124).

Murphy feels strongly, as does the present author, the lack of value in pursuing the nature–nurture controversy. "There is no room, *ever*, for special pleading for heredity any more than for environment" (*ibid.*, p. 73).

The relationship of personality to anatomy may be studied in three ways. First, by studying indirectly the role the body plays in limiting and controlling conduct, we may obtain valuable information about an individual's person- ality. Second, an advantage may be gained by studying the continuing effect expressive behavior has upon body appearance, an effect illustrated by Abra- ham Lincoln's quip that a man is responsible for his face after the age of forty. Third, the effect of one's physical appearance on others may afford a valuable clue to the relationship of anatomy to personality.

ORGANIZATION

Four functions are involved in the organization of that part of man which is organic:

1. Energy is transmitted from one region of the body to another.
2. The transmission is simultaneous as energy flows in various directions and always in a highly interdependent fashion.
3. A degree of adjustment and regulation of each part to another is involved.
4. Each of the separate organic parts is responsive to "out of the skin" stimu- lation which in turn may create sympathetic responses of other organs.

INDIVIDUAL CONSTITUTION

The matter of individual differences springs, according to Murphy, from a constitutional fact which is indisputable. The fact that no two human bodies are exactly the same is hardly a new or startling revelation. All theorists acknowledge it. However, it is Murphy's use of individual differences which introduces an interesting aspect to personality theories. Only because a man has differing organic systems within himself and because his total organic system differs from all others is he able to fulfill a tremendously important function of integration. Integration, the functional interdependence of parts or the amalgamation of differing parts of any organism, is the crux of growth and development. If all the parts of a system were exactly alike, complete homeostasis would exist, and with complete homeostasis no action occurs. Action is essential to any kind of forward movement. Let us examine further this phenomenon of differences creating progress.

Keeping in mind that differences are extremely important because of the third factor, which involves the interdependence of parts, we may begin with a study of constitutional differences. The personality arises from the discontinuities of the tissue system: receptors and effectors, ducts and ductless glands, the central and autonomic nervous systems. The interplay and interdependence of these dual systems help to create a personality. To Murphy "nothing is more certain than discontinuities." There exist, therefore, not only differences of degree but differences of kind. An example is that certain species of animals cannot be mated to each other because of chromosomic differences. Even the mating of the horse with the donkey results in a sterile offspring, a mule. Murphy employs these illustrations to demonstrate that life and personality are more than points on a continuous scale.

Moving to the realm of social differences or discontinuities, he talks of quales and nodal points. A *quale* is "any characteristic which is distinct in an individual and which operates entirely independent of other forces." A *nodal point* (a term from the field of optics), as used by field theorists, is "an emanating point which has very complex and strong pervasive influence upon the field in which it operates." Murphy, following the tradition of the Gestaltists, denies that man's personality, both organic and social, has quale characteristics. He prefers to postulate a personality theory on the nodality of life forces, whether they be biological or sociological. Nodal points may have high or low energy concentration. Man is a nodal point in the field of society.

The above discussion reveals the importance of individual differences in constitution. They are the backbone of further differences in individual nodality in society, but both kinds of differences are unimportant in themselves. The main idea is that the third force brings these differences together to be played off against one another and then to be integrated. The individual's constitutional makeup merely serves as an original ingredient of an emerging personality.

DEVELOPMENT

The child begins to individualize his personality through the use of his five senses. These teach him through thresholds of receptivity to make affective judgments of hot–cold, sour–sweet, and so on. The sensory apparatus of velops unequally in time. Taste and touch may develop before sight and sound. The interplay of these senses may be important as an affective quality. Also, what the child does about the things which affect him brings about the effector qualities in developing his personality. The child initially evolves a personality from the organic senses which affect him and by the effect he has upon his own body in adjusting.

Murphy pays respect to Herbert Spencer and Heinz Werner in discussing the three developmental levels he feels are involved in the biological aspects of man and his personality. The first level is the global and undifferentiated mass activity of the new organism at birth. This may be traced back as far as the cellular division of the human in the embryonic stage. The second level concerns the organic parts as they begin to act individually in performing the duties for which they were formed. The third and most important level concerns the integrated action of each part with all the other organic parts and especially the interdependence of the parts. Thus, the heart, the visceral organs, the neural fibers, the skeletal structure, the musculature, and all the portions of the body must depend upon and act in concert with one another. To fail to do so is to fail to function properly, and death results.

NEEDS

Four inborn organic needs are assumed to be part of the biological nature of man's personality. They are as follows:

1. Visceral needs: food, water, air, etc.
2. Activity needs: exploration and manipulation.
3. Sensory needs: perceptual clarity in color, tone, rhythm, and orientation.
4. Preservation needs: avoidance of pain, death, threat, shocks, etc.

MOTIVATION

The theme of motivation runs through all Murphy's writings. It is treated here as it applies to the biological orientation of personality. The motivating theme will recur in later sections. For a fully adequate understanding of motivation in Murphy's work the reader is urged to study especially chaps. 5 and 6 of *Personality*. For the present we must content ourselves with an outline treatment in order to replicate the work without losing any of the essential features.

1. Every single cell in man's body has the capacity to initiate behavior.
2. "Motivation never 'starts' or 'stops,' " but there are tension gradients which produce degrees of motivation.
3. Because motivation depends upon the interdependence of outer and inner pressures of the organism, it is a fusion of parts and not a simple arithmetical addition of pressures.
4. Because "sheer readiness is the same thing as motivation," we may expect

to find that studying the human personality is the same thing as studying his preparatory responses. (For explanation of preparatory responses see "Canalization," below.)

5. The factor of discontinuity or individual differences also applies to motivation: "one man's motivation . . . can never be the duplicate of another's."

6. As seen from a motivational viewpoint, personality is as much a "way of becoming sensitive" as it is a "way of reacting upon the environment." Thus, man is as much inner directed as outer pushed.

7. It is only because there is a discontinuity in motivation that integration can possibly take place. In other words, with no discontinuity there is nothing to integrate, and with nothing to integrate there can be no motivation. As previously mentioned, it is the discontinuous parts of man which, because they must be integrated, lead to getting off dead center. A completely homeostatic, in-balance system is not prompted to do anything.

8. When motivation originates, it is not specifically aware of its goals. In the beginning, it more than less tries to integrate its bivariant parts. Only later in life does "purposivism" come into play. Then the personality knows what it is struggling for. Purposivism is a late-developing, derived, learned special experience. It is not essential to motivation as motivation originates.

9. There are three ways to study individual differences in motivation:
   (a) by measuring visceral or organic or physiological differences,
   (b) by measuring external behavior which is an indirect method of studying individual differences in motivation,
   (c) and, the most indirect study method of all, by the testimony of trained observers.

It is apparent that motivation begins with the biological aspects of man but that much more is involved, as we shall see in the sections on the emerging, integrating personality and on the socialized personality, below.

TRAITS

Murphy begins his discussion of traits in the consideration of the biological aspects of human personality. To him traits are only surface indicators of the highly dynamic interdependence of inner organic parts. Traits have their earliest beginnings as organic phenomena which consist of specific tissue tensions. These organic traits are frequently highly complex systems of functional relations between body tissues and the specific environment in which they operate. Out of this basic fabric of ideas Murphy finds his term: *biosocial.*

Man begins life with organic traits, which can be measured only in a very limited way. But organic traits help to explain the single person's unique self, different from all other selves on earth. Organic traits give him physiological strengths and weakness, drives, tendencies to relaxation or excitement, and the important factor of his proneness to success or failure in physiological interaction.

There are three kinds of organic traits: the broad characteristics of tissue response and needs, the persistent modes of individual reaction of tissues, and the persistent modes of interaction between tissues.

Eleven years after the above thesis was first developed, Murphy stated in *Human Potentialities*, "The more meaningful a trait is for social living, the further it is from simple determination through any single genetic factor" (p. 224). Thus, the more socially usable a trait is, the less directly traceable it is to a single organic factor. Social traits, therefore, are infinitely complex patterns of interdependent basic organic traits, consequently, they defy direct measurement. In this, Murphy is in contradiction to the trait theories of H. A. Murray. For example, Murphy feels that the primary mental abilities theory of Louis Thurstone embraces complicated, interwoven, primary organic traits which are most difficult to measure, if they can be measured at all.

The final word on traits can be found in the work cited above (p. 231) in which the degree of homogamy (inbreeding) of traits is sensitive to three social factors: vertical mobility, horizontal mobility, and acute changes in habitat.

FUTURE

Murphy asks the sensible question "What about the future of man as a biological specimen in the universe?" To this question he poses three possible points of view, not answers. The first consideration is the rapid changes one finds in physical types when they are compared with man of no more than a century ago. He cites the increased stature of the Japanese people or of American youth as an example which cannot be ignored. How far man will continue to change in physiological structure is a fair question to ask. These changes are, of course, not genetic.

Secondly, he finds a marked increase and also decrease in the prevalence of certain diseases. Cancer, for example, seems to be a more general problem in the present than it was in the past, even when one considers inadequate record systems in past centuries. Tuberculosis, on the other hand, seems to have a decreasing effect on the physical welfare of man.

In the third place, and most important, in what Murphy refers to as the "gene pool" that man has available, the changes have been extremely slow for thousands of years. Now, however, three considerations must be acknowledged. Using Sewell Wright's words, "Human evolution is still going on," Murphy notes that we seem to be manipulating and increasing changes in human evolution much more rapidly than they can be assimilated in the behavior of society. The first consideration is found in the field of genetic research. One illustration is the refined techniques which now bring us to the realization that man does not have forty-eight chromosomes but forty-six. Genetic research itself may show us means of rapidly changing human structure, just as it has in hybridizing corn. As a second illustration, he refers to the papal discussion of positive and negative eugenics which was pro-

claimed in 1953. To this we must add the non-Catholic emphasis upon birth
control, which may or may not change the relative numbers of racial groups.
One step beyond this is the consideration of amalgamating races through
interracial marriages. Will we finally in the centuries to come evolve a single
colored people throughout the world? But it is to the third consideration of
changes in man's biological makeup that Gardner Murphy directs most of his
pertinent thoughts: the transmutation of genetic structure by accident or
through atomic radiation. This, he feels, may change the human race beyond
all recognizable features. Being a realist, he does not automatically assume
that change will be all bad. It may be perfectly possible that man can
strengthen his biological structure through genetic manipulation via radiation.
Until we know much more about it, however, he joins most of the world in
fearing the evils which may come out of accidental radiation.

On this note, then, we leave the discussion of the biological personality
as one factor in man's makeup and take up the dynamics of man's personality
as it emerges through integration of its biological and social parts. To repeat,
personality study is almost the total field of psychological study in Gardner
Murphy's system.

The Emerging and Integrating Personality Theme

Once again we find that Murphy is capable of covering the entire panorama
of psychological concepts, using wisely, and choosing well, the ideas of other
as well as incorporating his own original thinking. Murphy uses the ideas of
the big three, Freud, Adler, and Jung, in his own personality theory formation. From Freud rises a vast discussion of the psychoanalytic mechanisms,
from Adler a discussion of inferiority and of positional psychology, and from
Jung a discussion of introversion and extraversion. Murphy devotes a chapter
to each in his 1947 book, *Personality*. There are also touches of Gordon
Allport's idea of *functional autonomy* as shown in the following sentence
from Murphy's *Human Potentialities*: "The very process of learning and
thinking may in themselves become satisfying." Also there are overtones of
Murray's personality theory in this quotation, also from *Human Potentialities*: "We have, then, a tremendous range of human motives which are
organized around the central nervous system and its processes." However, we
find some reluctance to speculate on the work of Sheldon in this section:
"We should prefer not to speculate much about the matter of body types"
(p. 41).

Another illustration of the range of Murphy's work is his treatment of
such concepts as feeling, willpower, autism, and the place of mood in personality formulation. In regard to feeling, which to Murphy connotes desire and
willpower, or the power to act in any given or desired direction, man can and
does change conditions. He may change them through canalizations, conflict,
his perceptual system, or symbols. In regard to autism, *"The best is the*

orm." Murphy very cleverly shows the duplicity of man by this quotation; all f us as we play golf, bowl, or participate in any kind of activity are inclined) think that our best golf shot or our strike in bowling is actually our average ame, and that all the other not so successful scores, number of fish caught, or ames are really below our usual performance. In regard to mood, "Personlity is first of all a drive system of which mood is a prominent aspect." We 1ay see from the three illustrations above the vast range of Murphy's eatment of man's personality.

Possibly the best illustration, however, of the strength, breadth, and omplication of the personality structure itself can be gained from the follow-ıg lengthy quotation (*Personality,* 1947 p. 641; italics as in the original).

> . . . *the ultimate elements in personality structure are the needs or tensions, and they are interrelated by means of the functional connections between regions which permit the spread of these tensions.* The result is a *tension system* whose lawful structure is expressed in terms of the relative strengths of tensions and the relative rigidity of barriers to their diffusion. Our hypothesis therefore claims that *the organism's tension system is organized,* in the sense that each event is limited and controlled by the relations between elements, as in homeostasis. There is organization at every moment in time, in the form of a "static" system. There is also temporal or dynamic organization, each tension or group of tensions initiating changes which eventually bring the organism to a new balance, or restore it to the first. Of special importance is Weiss' concept of the *development of a system that retains its organization.* This may be achieved through the gradual complication of individual parts, the overall relation between the parts remaining unchanged. Such phases of personality development as "kinetics," "style," "individual rhythm," etc., are of this type. The organism is a physiological gradient system. Jacobson's relaxation experiments indicate that muscular tension in one region spreads gradient-fashion to other muscle groups; similarly, the reduction of tension in one region spreads until the tension is reduced in the functionally correlated muscle groups, the process in all probability continuing until most or all of the muscle groups are involved. Considerable other evidence tends to the same direction; and the principle holds for neural and biochemical tensions as well.

We now consider in more detail those aspects of the personality which re attempting to integrate and emerge into the full stature of man as a living uman being. The following six terms, it is thought, adequately cover this econd theme. They are: canalization, conditioning, conflict, perception, mbols, and self.

ANALIZATION
'wo approaches may be taken in defining the term *canalization.* This term iardner Murphy has used extensively but it has not been generally adopted y the psychological world. The first definition, which is also the traditional efinition, is as follows: "Establishing and progressively strengthening a

preference for one among several potential ways of satisfying a drive or th
established preference itself" (English and English, *A Comprehensive Di
tionary of Psychological and Psychoanalytical Terms*, Longmans, 1958, p. 75
The second attempt to define the word is an excerpt from Gardner Murphy
Personality (p. 162).

> This process by which general motives (which are first rather no:
> specifically related to a class of stimuli) tend, upon repeated experience, t
> become more easily satisfied through the action of the specific satisfier than •
> others of the same general class, has been known so long that it would be in
> possible to name its discoverer. But good names are a great convenience, ar
> Janet's term *canalization* is a good name for this process. The energies awai
> ing an outlet break through the barrier at a given spot, are channeled •
> canalized in the process, and, as the barrier weakens, tend more and more t
> focus their pressure upon it.

Because the original treatment of canalization by Gardner Murphy
voluminous, the following outline may help the student to glimpse some •
the highlights of canalization and Murphy's use and emphasis of it.

1. The first canalizations center around the body itself in all the aspec
of bodily or organic growth. This, according to Murphy, is the first gre:
center for canalizations. Following the capacity of the body to individualiz
the differing sensations or senses, the first canalizations are upon specif
things, as far as a child can discriminate among specific things. However, sin(
the child first learns about the outside world through his body, it is th
canalizations of the body which are the initial ones. In this initial state th
intensity of the gratification that the object, the body, or the child receiv(
strengthens the individual response. As each response is strengthened, th
initial strength grows or gains in response as it receives further gratification
The process continues until a canalization or a strongly channeled respon:
results. In this developmental stage the frequency of certain responses whic
become canalized is of much importance.

2. Not all canalizations need be pleasant; some may be avoidant •
unpleasant. Hence, Murphy's theory is not a hedonistically oriented one.

3. Usually a canalization can be broken only by other more powerfi
canalizations or more powerful responses. It is possible to destroy one canal
zation if another more potent behavior or behavioral tendency competes wit
it in a manner powerful enough to prevent the original physiological expre
sion. However, it should be remembered that canalizations are in gener:
autonomous and free of interference from one another.

4. "Canalizations, then, are not, so far as we know, subject to extinctic
whether by disuse or by displacement of other canalizations" (*ibid.*, p. 169
It is not too far-fetched to use the analogy of a river as it wanders abou
channeling its course. If we can imagine a river as it flows, then meets
blockage and creates a new channel, but always remains with some vestige •

1e former channel, we can gain an idea of the effect of canalizations upon
1e behavior of man.

5. As long as some degree, even though small, of actual satisfaction of
1e drive occurs, a canalization of fixation will follow. In all major types of
1otivation, canalization occurs.

6. When there is a choice to be made in action and the contrast between
lternatives is great, canalized choices, it is assumed, will be made more
uickly.

7. Canalizations are dependent upon major interests, as well as upon
odily activity, as causal factors. The body may produce or the body may do
ertain things which it does not care to repeat, for example, a sneeze.

8. The rate of the canalization process depends to a degree upon the
scendance of one satisfaction over another. That is to say, the higher the
egree of satisfaction, the faster the rate of developing a canalization.

9. The process of the canalization formation is never ended but con-
inues throughout life.

10. One of the most important clues that the personologist may look for
r work toward is the concept of the canalization upon the self, or *self-
analization* (Murphy's terms). He feels that the closer one gets in experi-
1entation and research to discovering the roots of self-canalization, the closer
1e comes to discovering the inner structure of the human personality.

11. In the same light, self-love, or the love and respect of self, is probably
1e most powerful form of canalization. Although Murphy never ignores the
ffect of the environment upon the single human personality, he does feel
1at constitutional differences and especially the intensification of the needs
f each individual constitution or body may account for the individuality
mong people. Because there seems to him to be a quantitative difference in
analizations between one person and another, one individual may have few
analizations and these few may be deeply embedded, while another person
1ay have many canalizations, only some of which are deeply embedded.

12. The more complex a person has become, the more canalizations he is
kely to have. This does not necessarily mean that the older one is, the more
analizations he will have, but it does mean that the more experiences he
ndergoes, the more canalizations he will probably have. Consequently, the
1dividual living in a quiet rural environment is not likely to gain as many
analizations, although they may be deeper, as the individual who lives in a
omplicated, metropolitan area. Murphy feels that canalizations can be found
1 much of the language of modern man. In fact, he believes it is harder to
void references to canalizations than to find examples of them, like "Take
1e boy out of the country but not the country out of the boy," or the longing
or "My Old Kentucky Home." They abound in the literature and in the
anguage of all people.

13. Each society maintains a system of associated canalizations—i.e.,

stereotypes or similar canalizations within a society or ethnic group. As the society finds canalizations valuable, they are handed forward to the next generation. In a sense, then, there is a biological and cultural inheritance of canalizations, but not in the Jungian sense. Because society is reluctant to give up associated canalizations which have served it, we have such phenomena as the cultural lag, affecting, for example, the stability of the family unit.

Murphy makes a strong distinction between conditioning and canalization. For example, he feels that conditioning is subject to extinction, that the experimenter may extinguish any conditioned response, whereas a canalization, as far as he knows, is not capable of being extinguished but survives in some residual form throughout life. The major difference between conditioning and canalization responses in the human being is whether the stimulus itself, the thing that causes the action, starts a consummatory response or a preparatory response. By *consummatory response* is meant the thing achieved is achieved for itself alone and is then consumed for the value inherent in the activity itself. The *preparatory response*, as it is found in canalization, always assumes that the individual is preparing for another activity beyond the impact of the original stimulus. For example, a canalization which centers around thrift will be inclined, where money is the stimulus, to lead to the response of saving money in preparation for further use or further saving.

The following listing may help one to see the differences between Murphy's term *canalization* and the term generally accepted in psychology, *conditioning*.

CANALIZATION	CONDITIONING
1. Irreversible	1. Can be reversed
2. Stimulus is the satisfier	2. Symbol is the satisfier[1]
3. Nonextinctive	3. Can be extinguished
4. Consummatory response	4. Satisfying response

CONDITIONING

A second factor in how the human personality emerges from its organic and bodily conditions and integrates its inner and outer forces is found in Murphy's treatment of the word *conditioning*. He begins chap. 9 in *Personality* with the following words: "Most learning springs from struggle. The motivated individual strives, blindly or intelligently, to find the means of satisfaction. As he strives, he discovers things and activities that bring him into contact with the source of satisfaction. These things and activities come to elicit, in their own right, part (or sometimes all) of the responses made to the satisfier itself. In this very broad sense, the term conditioning will be used

[1] ". . . the second criterion of conditioning, 'symbol is the satisfier,' is quite likely to be misunderstood. Ordinarily the symbol would not be a satisfier but only a signal. The metronome beat, for example, does not satisfy the dog's hunger as the meat powder would. (Note to author.)

ut from the present point of view, conditioning occurs only because motiva-
on is present in the first place" (p. 192). Hence to Gardner Murphy,
Personality is grounded in the experience of satisfaction and frustration; it is
ot capriciously extensible in all directions" (p. 216).

It is now obvious that both canalizations and conditioning are absolutely
ssential to the emergence of any kind of human personality, and, although
onditioning is commonplace and essential to human behavior, the failure to
e conditioned is also commonplace. This factor, Murphy feels, is often
gnored or forgotten in the psychological work concerning personality and
ersonality theory research. It is too often assumed that conditioning is
utomatic because it happens to be so commonplace.

Emerging out of the concept of conditioning of the human personality
re a number of factors, such as that of individual difference. In *Personality*
p. 193) Murphy states,

> As a simple physiological principle, then, it is permissible to say that a
> given response originally aroused by one or only a few stimuli can in time, as
> a result of experience, be aroused by a wide range of stimuli, many of which
> bear no similarity whatever to the original stimulus and are connected with
> it only by close association with it. Since each individual encounters different
> patterns of stimulation and acquires different conditioned responses, person-
> ality may be conceived to consist in the system of conditionings which dis-
> tinguishes one man from another.

Murphy pays a great deal of attention to the principle of *dominance*,
hich he feels is sufficient to explain the acquisition and the loss of any
onditioned responses. Certain conditioned responses are far more dominant
an others. We have, then, a sort of hierarchy or "pecking order" of condi-
oned, dominant, and less dominant responses within the individual. Thus,
hen any dominant conditioned response is brought into activation, it in-
ibits numbers of other conditioned responses, putting the less dominant
onditioned responses in a lower order in controlling human behavior. In like
anner, the spontaneous recovery of a conditioned response is due to its
ominance over other less conditioned responses. Dominance and submission
conditioning, therefore, are of vital importance to the emerging personality
it attempts to integrate the numerous forces that are "in the skin and out
f the skin," one of Murphy's favorite terms.

As we have seen before, the problem of transfer or generalization of
imuli comes from established conditionings, which occur when there are
milarities between the stimulus situations. Since "All conditionings, as far as
e know, are subject to transfer," the problem of transfer or generalization
etween established conditioned responses is crucial in the study of human
ersonality. In addition, and on the assumption that all conditioning leads to
ansfer, when stimuli vary we may expect all conditionings to lead to differ-
ntiation between responses. In a sense, intellectual processes are due to the

value of, and the ability to make, differentiations; as differentiations are made, they become further compartmentalized. The inability to compartmentalize differentiations, it would seem, is the problem of the less intelligent human being. The greater the intelligence, we may then assume, the greater the ability to differentiate and compartmentalize conditioned responses.

There are three mechanisms which, under the rubric of conditioning, especially conditioning around cultural norms, have an important role in the early stylizing of behavior. They are *suggestibility, imitation,* and *sympathy.* Out of these three mechanisms a fourth factor emerges, that of *attitudes,* which are in themselves, according to Murphy, also conditioned responses. Attitudes help to determine what responses, especially cultural norm responses, may later be conditioned. Conditionings of those aspects involving the culture in the emerging and integrating personality are to patterns and not to isolated stimuli. This, of course, is much in the tradition of Kurt Lewin.

CONFLICT

In Murphy's treatment of conflict in human behavior, one is reminded somewhat of Adler's work on inferiority to superiority as a goal, or pathway, of emerging human behavior. Murphy gives a large place to the contribution that conflict can make to the individual. He feels, for example, that most learning actually springs out of struggle, or, to put it in other words, "Choice means conflict" (*Human Potentialities,* p. 79). Without getting into the question of whether man has free will, Murphy finds that because man does have some choices in life he must be cognizant that these choices will lead to conflict. Without choice there can be no conflict; everything is automatic. In short, choice begets conflict. This phenomenon begins with the earliest emergence of the human being as a living organism in which physiological balance and imbalance are to be considered normal and commonplace. However, physiological conflict is not true conflict because it can resolve itself. In other words, the imbalance between eating and starving to death, although not normal and commonplace, is not a true conflict since the body either is fed and survives or is not fed and dies. True conflict comes, for example, when one has to choose among a number of items on a menu or in the cafeteria line. Although death obviously is not imminent in this case, true conflict may come about through the inability to decide what one wants to eat at that particular moment.

Psychological conflict, in contrast to physiological conflict, is genuine especially when the signals given to the integrating self are ambiguous. Ambiguous signals are those for things which have varying values or about which we must make decisions or in which the pathways are obscure. For example, Pavlov's dogs were unable to distinguish between circles and ellipses. It was not starvation that caused the conflict, of a genuine psychological nature, in Pavlov's dogs; it was their inability to identify an ellipse, which is very like a circle.

Frustration comes from any blocking of an outlet. When the outlet is blocked, the energy is dammed up and seeks release through canalized drives. Following the exposition previously given of the biological personality, one can see that a high degree of individualization is always present in frustration. Tolerance to frustration is intrahuman and interhuman. That is, within the single human, it may vary from time to time, being higher in the morning, perhaps, than in the evening after a tiring day. There are also differences between two people, or interhuman toleration. Murphy feels that conflict is not the result of organic vs. functional, or body vs. mind, dichotomies; the process of conflict is far more involved than conflict between two opposing forces. It has to do with integration and hierarchy of dominance traits. Many factors enter into true psychological conflict, and, as we recall, psychological conflict is the only true conflict. One does not lead a life of struggle, therefore, between the mind and the body, both wanting to do different things. It is the integration of the mind and the body in relationship to the outside or cultural world, plus degrees in canalizations and dominance in conditionings, which is involved.

Murphy finds three forms of response to Freud's frustration, which comes out of psychological conflict: (1) aggression, (2) resignation, and (3) self-deception. An example of aggression is any direct or frontal attack upon the person or situation which causes the frustration. The "death feint" is an example of a resignation form of response to frustration. Self-deception as a form of response is of three different types. The first is distant self-image, a self with tremendous gifts and powers which can overcome any frustration. The second is fantasy, which provides a conflict-free life. The third is the concept of oneself as a superior being, above any kind of threat, a somewhat psychotic withdrawal syndrome. Murphy also sees a place for a fourth form of response to frustration in the activity of displaced aggression.

It can be seen, then, that Murphy considers conflict as essential not only to the existence of man but also to the progression of man beyond his simple biological organic self. It is, therefore, within the framework of the emerging and integrating personality, the second of the four major themes, that we are treating the work of Gardner Murphy.

PERCEPTION

Murphy feels that we do not really "see" with our eyes or "hear" with our ears. The sound of an automobile horn is perceived differently by all of us; even though the sound, the decibel content, the intensity, the timbre of the automobile horn remain the same, each person has a different way of hearing it. To some it is annoying; to others it heralds a future activity; to still others it means that an awaited friend has arrived and an enjoyable social engagement is soon to begin. Similarly, a mountain may mean to some of us a thing to be climbed or an obstacle which lies in our path or simply a spectacle of grandeur and beauty. Thus, all depends upon the perceptual system of the individual. This is, of course, not unlike the concept of perception within the general world of psychology.

Perception first begins in the human animal by self-reference; in the Piaget sense, it is egocentric. Continuing from this, Murphy finds the process of perceptual development involving three activities: identification, reaction, and differentiation. First, we must identify through our past experience any phenomenon which occurs to us. Upon identifying the phenomenon as pleasant or unpleasant, we respond to it with a favorable or unfavorable reaction. After having identified and reacted to the phenomenon, we then differentiate it further. The fourth step in integrating the stimulus or phenomenon lags far behind the first three processes of identification, reaction, and differentiation. Murphy feels that perception, like motor learning and maturation, develops in three stages. The first is the blur stage, the second is the differentiation stage, and the third is the integration stage. Only after these three stages have been reached in that order does one develop a fully successful or efficient perceptual system.

One of the valuable aspects of a perceptual system is that it solidifies human behavior and helps to resist change through the activity of canalization. It is canalization that keeps man from floating about like a leaf or a loose feather in the air. There is, of course, the difficulty in changing human behavior as perceptual systems canalize and resist change; however, Murphy feels that this is a saving grace in man's behavior. Man does not have to learn new methods of canalizing his behavior each morning as he arises to begin a new day.

Other factors in perception interest Murphy. He feels, for example, that much perception is intuitive or, using the Freudian term, is in the unconscious. Perception is not directly identifiable in the conscious processes, either by the person who perceives something or by the individual who studies a person who is perceiving. Murphy finds, also, that perception is quite satisfying to the self-system in that it is a tension-reducing process. The ability to achieve adequate perception for living is fundamental.

"NEEDS KEEP AHEAD OF PERCEPTS"

This often quoted statement of Murphy's from his book *Personality* (p. 378) means essentially that needs control the perceptual systems, or that, in a sense, they give the orders to the perceptual systems. We see what we want to see and not what actually exists. Thus, the things we need, the things we want, the things that motivate us, are always ahead of our perceptual systems and the perceptual system is guided by the need system in each human being.

According to Murphy, there are two principles under which perception is organized. The first is the regularity of the experience, which arouses an expectation. The second is the relevance or meaningfulness of the object to our desires or fears. Following these two principles of regularity of experience and relevance of the object, our perceptual system is organized.

LEARNING

In Murphy's view, the ability to learn entails five processes in the following order: (1) the capacity to form simple associations; (2) the ability to develop sound and gestures which enable one to communicate with himself and with other humans; (3) the ability to use symbols and in using symbols to think abstractly; (4) the capacity to invest personal feelings in stable and in specific objects; (5) the capacity to systematize and classify objects, feelings, and symbols so that one is able to share them socially with the world.

All five processes result in a consolidation of ways of perceiving. One cannot learn unless one is able to perceive. Murphy also feels that learning, and, in a sense, thinking, can be done only under the pressure of wants. In short, one does not learn, nor does one think, unless he has a desire or a pressure which creates or helps to create that capacity within his neurological system.

In *Human Potentialities*, Murphy speaks of six kinds (or six common kinds) of learning, as follows:

1. Pavlovian: classical conditioning (stimulus–response behavior).
2. Skinnerian: operant conditioning (rewarding and reinforcing correct responses).
3. Associative linkage: correlations (such as the natural phenomenon of thunder which occurs with lightning).
4. Reorganization of perception: insight (sudden resolution of a problem).
5. Reorganization of totality: Gestalt (use of all facilities—physical and mental—to reorient by way of feeling, cognition, emotions, etc.).
6. Canalization: channeling consummatory behavior habits (nonextinguishable direct satisfaction of a need by a specific want if no symbols necessarily involved).

Thus, canalization, conditioning, perception, and learning all have integral places in the emerging and integrating personality.

SYMBOLS

Symbol, to Gardner Murphy, has a wide range of meaning. It means essentially any stimulus which can stand for another stimulus. One word can stand for another word, one gesture can stand for or mean another gesture, and so on. The following outline will highlight the importance of symbols in the personality theory of Gardner Murphy.

1. Differences in personality are due in large measure to differing re sponses to the world of symbols. In other words, the way man responds to symbolic world is what makes individual differences possible.

2. As a human being acquires a language, it is completely socially con trolled and has no relationship (other than speech pathology) to any organi condition. This Murphy feels is the case in every stage of language acquisitio or, in other words, in the learning of symbols.

3. Frequently, in the field of research, what often passes as higher orde conditioning is nothing more than first order verbal conditioning or symboli manipulation.

4. Although man has language and uses language to conceal hi thoughts, the fact of having language and symbols also helps him to liberat his thoughts and to turn thoughts into actions.

5. The world of symbols actually comes from the world of action an returns constantly to a world of action in which man frequently does some thing physically because of his use or others' use of symbols.

6. Harking back to William James's phrase "stream of thought," Murphy feels that this inner speech is a method by which man is foreve signaling to himself. If only the researcher could know what the stream o thought is and could understand it, he would know everything that need b known about any given personality.

7. Man lives, dreams, hopes, and plans in a purely symbolic world.

8. Because symbols are inner cues to action, one may study the tensio systems of any human personality by studying the symbol content of tha personality.

9. An important factor in the shaping of any human personality and it organization for the future can be action which is solely symbolic. Thus, i counseling, in clinical work, in psychotherapy, much of what is done is don to the symbolic actions of the client. In short, we do not feed him differently clothe him differently, or treat him differently, physically, in this realm o therapy, but simply use symbols or words.

10. It is possible that a symbolic cue can set the stage or create a kind o behavior that will persist long after the particular symbols have been re moved. For example, someone may use a word which angers us very much Long after the word has been used, we continue to be angry. The symbol ha been removed, but the behavior caused by it persists, sometimes for a lon time.

11. As stated previously, Murphy does not believe that symbols ar restricted to language alone. Clothing, gestures, pictorial forms of art, all ma be classified as symbols. However, language is one of the richest clues to a individual's personality that a researcher may work with.

12. As the human being develops, the individual characteristics of hi speech patterns become highly stable. This is a form, of course, in the

Murphy terminology, of canalization. The speech patterns are quite set and firm regardless of outer pressures. Any speech pathologist or speech correctionist is certainly aware of the difficulties of altering a stuttering pattern of speech.

13. Murphy sees a valuable area of research in the relationship between symbols and value systems. When canalizations in the symbolic world become fully established, they may be called *values;* "the central fact about values is that they arise from definite wants, of all types . . ." (*Personality,* p. 272). Most values of the individual are "anchored deep within the skin." This is, in a sense, Murphy's way of dealing with the unconscious. Murphy sees a value in long periods of immaturity because the longer the period of immaturity, the more plastic or fluid is the organism. The more fluid the organism, the greater the number of values it can form. Organisms which are "set" at an early age are unable to gather many more values. The individual who keeps an open mind is likely to gain great breadth or depth in his value system. The long period of plasticity or immaturity has benefit to both the individual and society. It would be difficult to build a value system in a human being, or for that human being to experiment with the value system, were he to reach a level of maturity which would close off feeding in any further values. "There are many values partly because it takes so long to grow up" (*ibid.,* p. 284).

14. The world of symbols and the world of attitudes are also involved in the personality theory of Murphy. Whereas values arise from definite wants within and without the system and are integrated by the personality, attitudes are present dispositions toward action or toward setting up values. The relationship between symbols and attitudes is the result of a long and complex process. Equally involved is the relationship between attitudes and values. Attitudes are motivated. They are adjustments to present situations and remind us of values. The more closely we look at attitudes, the more difficult it is to find any essential differences between attitudes and values. Attitudes are defined by some as a value expression. Whereas Murphy feels value is inner or inner-centered, an attitude expresses a value via verbal symbols. "Value and attitude can be distinguished only by a convenient surgical separation whose utility is subject to doubt" (*ibid.,* p. 286). Social attitudes in the main are triggered by symbolic stimuli. These social attitudes are then expressed in symbolic form. In Murphy's view the human personality never has an entirely specific attitude and on the other hand never has an entirely general attitude.

15. Each personality has a symbol system integrated within itself. It is therefore not possible for an individual to make any integrated response to the symbol system of another human being prior to that person's integration of his own symbol system. In other words, it is not possible for an adult to respond to a child's symbolic value system of honesty or fair play before the child has created or integrated within himself such a system.

16. Much of personality as we know it is organized through the symbol that the personality acknowledges and has integrated within itself. However no system of symbols overrides the wisdom of the body; it is the integration of a symbolic world and an organic world within the human being that set the limits to which symbols can aspire.

17. Despite the implications of the above statement, it is possible for a neurotic or psychotic personality to live almost absolutely in a symbolic world ignoring demands for food, clothing, shelter, and any organic needs.

SELF

The preceding discussion regarding canalization, conditioning, conflict, perception, and symbols culminates in the emerging and integration of a self for each human personality. We may divide the material concerning the concept of self into three categories: the canalization of self, the enhancement of self and the defense of self. This approach is reminiscent of the work of Carl Rogers. The concept of self plays such a large part in Murphy's theory that he believes that much of what is personality, as it behaves in everyday living, is self-oriented or self-determined.

The canalization of self begins at a very early age, when it centers on the body and the mouth. In the beginning, then, the self grows out of a complex of indefinite feelings which exist at the first perceptual level. The feelings we have about ourselves from infancy on gradually come into being as the result of a process of differentiation which goes on within the perceptual field. "Our thesis is, then, the perceptual activities and motor activities are at first utterly selfless; that as one perceptual object, the body, becomes defined, other objects are related to it in context; and, similarly, that motor responses which are at first rather independent activities become activities oriented to or serving the self. Unconscious dispositions maintain the self-reference of our activities, and these dispositions have become associated with selfhood through a nexus of associative processes similar to those in operation elsewhere" (*ibid.*, p. 502).

The second of the considerations concerning self is self-enhancement. Because the self is a perceived object, it follows all the laws of perception. In its efforts to enhance itself, the self depends upon the process of identification in a truly active way. This process includes strong feelings of autism. Also involved in the emerging self-concept are the activities of projection and introjection. Murphy feels that whatever the self is, it becomes the center, the focal point, and a standard of comparison to ultimate reality. This leads inevitably to having the self take its place as a supreme value for any human personality. Thus, the self moves from a feeling of body awareness to one of prestige and power. All this is designed to enhance the self. As the self tries to enhance itself, it becomes less and less a purely perceptual object and moves more and more toward being a conceptual trait system.

Eventually the self, through trying to enhance its value system, achieves the level of ego-structure. However, the self depends not so much upon who a person is as what he is, and what value he has in life. Whether the self is a direct physical object, such as the body, or a type of abstraction; whether the self is loosely organized or well structured, the thing of primary importance is the ego. Murphy advances four hypotheses which are individual factors in determining selfhood. The first is that education seems to have a bearing upon whether one considers himself a physical object or a system of high abstraction. The second hypothesis is that one tends to use verbal symbols extensively in attempting to integrate one's picture of the self. The third hypothesis is that one evaluates or esteems himself to the degree that the culture in which he lives promotes respect for the self. The fourth hypothesis depends upon parental approval; we are inclined to value or undervalue ourselves in line with the amount of parental approval we receive. The more approval from parents, the higher the value upon the self. Murphy is careful to point out that these hypotheses could lend themselves quite readily to clinical research.

After the self has evolved from a disorganized, unintegrated beginning and is attempting to enhance its position, self-defending tendencies appear. Murphy thinks it is not possible to enhance or defend oneself without encroaching on the self-defense and self-enhancement of others. Defense self, he maintains, is a primary concept in the study of human personality. Man cannot but feel that he is, like the spider at the center of a web, the being in which all things of value begin and end. In short, instead of all roads leading to Rome, all things lead to the self. This self-centeredness not only enhances man but helps him to defend himself. Man has the ability to canalize his feelings, and the canalization tends to increase the rigidity in which he conceives of himself and the rigidity of the self in a place in society. Thus, egocentrism and sociocentrism are natural, parallel developments.

However, man has some difficulties in delineating where the self begins and where it ends as he tries to enhance and defend himself. Consequently, where the human personality is attempting to identify with two individuals, the canalizations that result are inclined to create for one human personality two or more incomplete, diverging selves. Such divergences can, and in a sense almost must, lead to neurotic or psychotic involvement. Somewhat similar to this development, Murphy feels, are the degrees of independence of the self from the nonself. Although in the early organic stages the child has some difficulty with this concept, he is on fairly safe ground. The self either ends with the skin or does not end with the skin. However, after a time, *symbolization* and *canalization* by *identification* with others (parents and other ego objects) become blurred. The delineation between self and nonself becomes indistinct. Murphy thinks that this particular area of study between self and nonself can be a rich and rewarding one for the research-oriented psychologist. Murphy tentatively states that the study of telepathy may provide new clues.

In summary, then, Murphy feels that as we learn to accept our place in the world and the way our self, or self-system, fits this complex, we may better realize the nature of our own self-system.

The Socialized Personality Theme

The socialized personality is the third of the four major themes in the present author's treatment of the work of Gardner Murphy. Man begins as a biological being and, as he later integrates his biological and cultural milieu, reaches the third level of a socialized human being, that in which he is capable of living in harmony with other human beings. Whether this is called culture, society, or family, it is a necessary step in the total concept of human personality.

According to Murphy it is impossible to consider a human personality without considering the social process in which that personality operates, for even among the protozoa one individual is sensitized to another. Again, because Murphy's work is voluminous and all-inclusive, we find it profitable to enumerate some of the factors which he regards as components of the socialized personality.

1. All personalities are interdependent. It is not possible to look on personalities as independent building stones in a social world.

2. Personalities, however, are not the sole components of a group or social life. One must consider weather, climate, the fertility of the soil, and economic life, which also help to make up the totality of what we call a culture.

3. Man is not entirely passive in his relationship to the pressures of a group life. He may accept, reject, compromise, or integrate those pressures. For example, a child, we believe at times, is unable to manipulate his environment. Murphy feels, however, that the child does influence his environment, and in his own individual way. The mother or father may be much manipulated by the child.

4. It is important to keep in mind that any individual reacts, not to the culture at large, but to specific aspects of the culture which his perceptual system recognizes. Much as the soldier in Stephen Crane's *The Red Badge of Courage* could know only that part of the battle which he could see, so man can know only that part of the world which he can feel or perceive. Even though he may read in newsmagazines and newspapers of international events, it is not possible for him to be too greatly moved by what is not a specific aspect of his social world.

5. Murphy makes good use of the research of Linton, Mead, Ruth Benedict, Kardiner, Bateson, Fromm, Horney, the Lynds, the Gluecks, and

Moreno in his treatment of the social world of man. In regard to economic determinism (any system of thought in which main outlines of social life are derived from economic organization of the group) Murphy feels that this is too often a neglected area of study as it pertains to personalities. There are three ways in which economic determinism may be used as an approach to personality study. First, man's economic life may restrict his activities, as is certainly evident in the experience of Karen Horney or in the writings of Fromm. Second, economic determinism may so strongly direct human behavior as to highly affect the individual and his personality. Third, economic determinism is a part of the total economic environment in which one's employment, his chances of success, and his chances for gaining superiority over others are influenced or even controlled. Economic determinism means both situation, that is, the resources that are available, and institutions, such as banks, guilds, and unions.

6. Murphy feels that the values of mores has been underestimated in personality study. Mores add vitality and love to social institutions. These institutions play an important part in the formation of individual and collective personalities. Murphy divides them into four valuable kinds of groups: (1) self-maintenance—farming, manufacturing, forestry; (2) self-perpetuation—marriage, family, courtship; (3) self-gratification—amusements, culinary arts, painting, literature, and music; and (4) self-regulation—police, courts of law, the Constitution, etc. These four groups of institutions aid the flow of the history of man.

7. Murphy does not deemphasize or ignore the value of social roles in the formation of a personality; roles shape personality. The two most clearly defined bases for roles are age and sex. Resemblances between parents and children are partially due to the child's carrying forward the roles learned from parents. Much in the same tradition as influenced Karen Horney, Murphy feels that economic factors strongly influence personal outlook, which, in turn, determines role acceptance or role rejection by any given person. Murphy rejects the rigid adherence to cultural relativism. (All cultures are equally well adapted to human nature, or human nature can take on any shape with equal ease.) He believes that cultural relativism denies and even ignores the strong, common biological bases of human adaptation although there are many deviates or nonconformists in any culture.

> In summary of our thesis regarding roles, we have attempted to show (1) that society, with its system of mores, and with the self maintenance mores more or less central in the pattern, does not merely "mold" people, but requires from them the enactment of specific roles in accordance with their place in the system; (2) that not all roles are easily accepted, but that many require effort, and indeed frequently put a strain upon the individual; (3) that a given person must enact several different roles (sex, class, etc.) at once, and that their integration is no obvious or mechanical matter; (4) that roles

derive not merely from primary obligations, but also in response to the roles of others (there is not only melody but counterpoint); (5) that in consequence of all this the individual develops balancing or complementary roles, so that he is a complement both to others and to himself; and (6) that it is thus a long way from the simplest economic determinism to a realistic role psychology based ultimately upon the recognition of self-maintenance factors (*Personality*, p. 794).

8. The family, as an agent of personality formation, acts as the mediator and as the canalization agent of culture, for it is through the parents that the personality socializes itself and learns the standards by which it must operate. Moreover, the family as a unit acts as a small society or unique culture in which it is less expensive for the emerging socializing personality to use trial and error in its own formulation.

9. Given a changed situation which is total and powerful, it is quite likely that one may change roles and that consequently a changed personality, in the social sense, may emerge. Situationism may further determine differences between persons which are fundamentally those of the roles they must enact. For example, from the work of Hartshorne and May, *Character Education Inquiry*, it appears that honesty consists of what others are doing, not that it is necessarily an integral part of a human being. That is to say, we act honestly or dishonestly at a gradient level that is affected by the others who are around us. If others are highly honest, we are inclined to be highly honest; if others are somewhat dishonest, we follow that pattern. Thus, situationism has a strong effect upon the socialized personality. Situationism applies mainly to everyday personality changes. Personality must be free to select its own environment and its own situational content. Only in this way can it truly unfold. In the final analysis, situationism becomes actually a field theory in the traditional sense of the Lewinian Gestalt approach.

10. When attitudes affect behavior, they may do so in dichotomized ways. We can expect a normal distribution of attitudes when they are viewed impersonally or in a quantified way. However, from a personal viewpoint attitudes involving stress or decisions take a bimodal distribution. By this Murphy means that we are forced through attitudinal sets to be either for or against something. On the other hand, in measuring a group and its attitudes, we can create a continuum from very high to very low attitudinal sets regarding any phenomenon.

11. Murphy finds that society molds personality through social pressure in four different ways. (1) The individual is sensitized to the symbols which the society values. Even though he is not aware of these symbols they do determine his behavior. (2) Because of canalizations of a social nature and a stereotyped structure, the individual is molded by that which society considers to be satisfactory. Thus, his satisfactions are reinforced and deepened by competitive exposure. Science, art, and music are all examples of this phenomenon.

(3) Drives and needs such as food preferences may actually determine the level, amount, and direction of hunger in a human being. (4) The predominant feeling tone of an individual—the ethos—is highly dependent upon the cultural process through which he goes as he develops into a socialized creature. However, "the cultural relativists" do not accept the wide patterns of human conduct, and man is not merely the product of his environment.

Murphy makes an interesting comparison between the assets and liabilities of our Western culture and those of the Soviet culture. The assets of the Western culture are these: (1) We have a high level of moral and legal recognition of the importance of the individual. (2) We have a deep recognition and acceptance of individual differences both in our educational systems and in our social customs. (3) We have had, since the Bill of Rights, a continuing sense of freedom to think, talk, and read what we want. (4) We have an abiding faith in the continuity of progress.

The liabilities of our Western culture are these: (1) Because our ego needs become frustrated and our needs for status and prestige are difficult to fulfill in a complex society, there is an accompanying feeling of pathological insecurity among most people. (2) Because family ties are becoming looser and there is great mobility both geographically and socially, there is a pronounced loss of group identification. (3) Because of the multiple conflicts between our own and others' value systems, there is an overriding feeling of conflict with our culture. (4) Because of the impersonality of much that happens to us, we often feel a lack of support and a loneliness despite the crowded conditions that frequently surround the metropolitan citizen.

Murphy finds three assets of the Soviet Union's style of life. The first is a strong feeling of identification with the group; citizens of the Soviet Union have little doubt in their mind that they belong to that particular type of society which we call Communist. Second, there is freedom from the insecurity of joblessness. Despite the Russian claims that all people are equal within their system of government, there is wide latitude and much structuring of each person's role in that society. Third, with security needs met, the citizen may turn his thoughts toward art, music, and the drama, as witness the strong interest of Russians in the Bolshoi Ballet.

Murphy feels that from the standpoint of personality needs there are also liabilities in the Soviet system. The first is coercion. The individual personality has little freedom in the highly structured, tightly administered plan of life which is laid out for him and which he must accept regardless of his feeling about it. Another liability is the difficulty in knowing with whom to identify. In the history of the Soviet system, citizens have had an identification with Lenin or Trotsky, then Stalin, who was followed by Malenkov, then Khrushchev, and now, of course, Kosygin. A third negative factor is the complete lack of recognition of individual differences. In general, the Soviet system follows Lysenko, in whose viewpoint heredity is equal for all peoples, while the environmental factors help determine how an individual personality will succeed or fail. The Russian system considers, then, that it can make "a silk purse out of a sow's ear."

In the long run it would seem that the Soviet style of life is bound to fail because it ignores the fundamental, psychological dynamics of human personality. On the other hand, our own society must attempt to alleviate or correct some of its liabilities. Although both are Occidental systems, we must assume that there will be a deep assimilation from the Oriental cultures.

Murphy thinks that if a society is destroyed, and such possibility does not seem remote, it may not mean the complete cessation of a special form of life. A phenomenally strong, overriding personality will perhaps be able to reorganize and reorient and restructure a society to meet the new demands with a new image. In the history of man there have always been immense figures or "men of destiny" who were capable of meeting the needs of a new order.

With the publication of *Human Potentialities* in 1958 Murphy continued a discussion of the future of man. The main rationale is that man always has had a changing body and always has been a changing social animal trying to avoid annihilation. It is, therefore, important that we seek new insights into the future.

Individual differences which are caused by culture are of three types:

1. Cognitive differences: these are differences caused by ways of exploring the world.
2. Affective differences: these are ways in which each individual begins to feel about his world.
3. Impulse differences: these are ways in which each individual is taught how to act toward the world about him in its biological, organic, geographical, climatic, and social aspects.

Human Potentialities or New Perspectives Theme

The fourth major theme of Gardner Murphy's theory of personality is obtained almost entirely from *Human Potentialities*. Murphy outlines three human natures: biological (man meets intense and diffuse organic needs); cultural (man becomes fixed and standardized); and creative thrust (man attempts the creative thrust to understand himself, the world in which he lives, and, from a philosophical frame of reference, why he is in the world).

Inherent in this book is a decided touch of Jungianism. Murphy broadens his perspective and is willing to admit that "man is a part of the sweep of the cosmos."

BARRIERS TO FULFILLMENT

If man tries to reach the fullest potentialities of the good life, he will find many barriers to this achievement. In a sense the entire book is about one of life's problems: the gaining of new horizons to combat the rigidity of present society. At the present time, because the Russians have the more rigid society and our society is the less rigid, we are made to look the weaker. This weakness may in the long run be our strongest asset because we may be better able to adapt to changing conditions.

Industrialization with its emphasis on automation and synchronized parts vastly increases the rigidity within our own society.

Following the work of David Riesman, Murphy finds another barrier to fulfilling the huge potential of mankind: too much outer-directed instead of inner-directed behavior. Although rigidity and ossification seem to characterize the twentieth century more and more, historically and personally we have always been a flexible and creative nation. In trying to break the hold of outer-directed behavior, our culture must be stimulated to strive for greater flexibility and creativeness, for "Creation is in itself satisfying" beyond the actual benefits of any created object or social system.

It is necessary that all of us realize there has been almost a geometrical increase in social change and creativeness. We now invent in ten years what formerly may have taken as much as one hundred years.

Still another barrier to the fulfillment of man's potential is unwillingness to accept new dimensions in society and in science as additional factors toward a better life. It is our inclination to force the newer dimensions into the forms of the old culture. In no way, however, does Murphy ignore the strength of a conservative position; after all, his concept of canalization indicates its benefits. However, complete adherence to a stylized, conservative frame of reference, he feels, is destructive because it does not allow for meeting the challenges of change, and change is inevitable.

One of the greatest problems in releasing human potential is the transfer of the "fire" of an infant's enthusiasm into structured and disciplined creativeness. All too frequently this "precious freshness" of response is stifled or distorted in further development.

It is one of the tragedies in attempts to fulfill the human potential in mankind that no political or social system has a true long-range method of development. The Soviet Republics do seem to have a long-range plan for conquering the world which makes them appear stronger and more directed in their efforts than the other cultures, ethnic groups, or political organizations. It affects other social systems as they bend to the varying pressures. The dilemma is difficult to resolve. On the one hand, necessary adjustments must be made in order not to be too rigid in policy. On the other hand, excessive rigidity of thought which makes one appear strong and oriented toward direct goals denies the flexibility and creativity that appear to be necessary in any social order.

At the present time, there seems to be a threefold crisis in fulfilling the human potentiality. In the first place, huge power systems are locked in a struggle to gain superiority or at least a favorable position. Russia and the United States are current examples. In the second place, as shown in the thinking of Erich Fromm, man has evolved and created social systems, political systems, and economic systems which control man more than he controls them. In the third place, there is a biological unfitness in the organic structure of man to meet future changes in environment. Medical science has made huge advances which have caused man to live longer but not necessarily to adjust to differing environments, as may be necessary for interplanetary existence, for example.

Despite this rather dismal situation, Murphy sees possibilities for alleviating or eliminating the current crisis of failure to fulfill the potentialities of mankind. Four short-range ones are as follows:

1. The crisis may be ended in short order through technical advances, brought about either in the U.S.A. or the U.S.S.R. Whichever social order or political system makes the most technical advances can win the power struggle.

2. A total, annihilating war could, obviously, end the crisis.

3. The third possibility is the one espoused by the United Nations: a disarmament program, which may begin by short steps but eventuate in a reduction or elimination of machines and power to make total war. This step may be taken by all nations, either by achieving an atomic method of waging war or by going in the opposite direction: creating a device to make atomic war impossible.

4. Closer to the present situation in the world today is the possibility of a long period of garrison life. This would be somewhat like the situation in medieval times, in which small groups lived a garrison existence in fortified castles. Murphy considers this kind of existence, one nation walling itself off from others, quite unlikely to endure for long because men are so interrelated in economic and social systems.

The long range possibilities for ending the current crisis are quite interesting as Murphy presents them.

1. He admits that it may take a very long time to create an international authoritarian system with full police powers. This would be a possibility for not only ending the crisis but maintaining some sort of peace.

2. In addition to an international state which might grow out of the United Nations organization, Murphy feels that an extremely high degree of centralization of scientific investigation, with immediate feedback of research findings, could mean that no nation would be superior to any other. Whatever was created or invented would be immediately available to all the peoples of the world.

3. It is unlikely, but possible, that a world society under a very loose political unity, something like the United Nations, might be based on a competition of ideas. Information would have to be readily available, but the ideas would extend beyond the scientific fields and include art, music, educational systems, literature, etc.

4. The fourth possibility is dismal but cannot be ignored in the present

state of chaos. If all political systems disintegrate or break down, man may end the current crisis in the long-range view of things by existing in an anthill or leaderless, machine-like system. This would approximate the type of tribal organization of world civilization in the distant past.

In considering the short- and long-range possibilities of ending the current crisis and bringing about a richer fulfillment of mankind, Murphy sees three kinds of social order. In the first place, he has strong convictions that "a world system, there must be." His second point is that there should be "a loose-jointed Authoritaria." The third suggestion is for democratic group planning in most areas of the world, controlled by those who were to be influenced by the plans. This, of course, is very much in the democratic tradition of the United States.

Murphy asks the pertinent question "Can the three human natures . . . be entirely fulfilled?" He admits that the three human natures are and will be in conflict at most times. In answer to his question, Murphy gives a qualified affirmative with four reasons. (It will be remembered that the three human natures mentioned are the biological, the cultural, and the creative thrust to understand.)

1. Heredity or environment alone is impotent. Consequently, interdependence of these two factors may lead to a fulfillment of all three human natures.

2. Mann has always been a beautiful example of "adaptive radiation." No matter what he came from in the past, he has always been able to change in response to new environments. Murphy sees no reason why man, given enough time, cannot continue to change and adjust to his environmental differences.

3. Another favorable aspect of the fulfillment of the three natures of a human being is that both extrapolation (projection into the future) and especially the emergence of new skills can work toward the fulfillment of man. However, the underlying structure of human behavior must be better known than it is at present.

4. The last condition that gives hope for the fulfillment of man is a decentralization of democratic procedures for better control of new scientific data. This is Murphy's way of saying that scientific research should be allowed a free hand and not be controlled by a central authority.

The last of the barriers to fulfilling the three basic human natures of man is the boundaries that lie between the individual and his world. There are three such boundaries according to Murphy.

1. There has been, is now, and always will be a definite barrier between the inner skin and the outer skin, that is, between the physical or biological self and all that surrounds it.

2. The psychological boundary between one human being and another is inevitable, though it may not always be so. Despite the deep and intense knowledge one human being may have of another, it is never possible to have

a total exchange of personalities. It is not possible to be completely within the psychological framework of another human.

3. The social boundary between the person and his world is not easily defined and is more nebulous than the boundaries of the physical or the psychological nature.

FUTURE

Murphy says that "we cannot set limits upon human potentials or tell what can or cannot come into existence. . . ." The predispositions within the cosmic structure are unpredictable. However, "the potential self-fulfillments lie scattered there beyond the horizon; and man, with all the wisdom he can marshal, must strive to define them—and then to choose among them" (*Human Potentialities*, p. 301).

Later on, in "Human Natures of the Future," which began as a lecture for the Lewin Memorial address given to the Society for the Psychological Study of Social Issues in 1953, Murphy again introduces the keystone of much of his theoretical position on the personality: interaction.

> Let us begin with the fact, already noted, that nothing is inherited, nothing acquired; everything is the realization through the environment of a specific potentiality permitted by the genes; or, if you prefer, the realization by the genes of a potentiality permitted by the environment.
>
> Let us go on from this to the self-evident, yet shocking fact that in my experience nothing springs from *me* and nothing from my environment, but everything from the interaction, the "life space" in which I, as a person, navigate (*ibid.*, p. 303).

SCIENCE OF HUMAN POTENTIALITIES

Murphy suggests four steps in the fulfillment of the field science of human potentialities: (1) quantitative (the measurable attributes of personality); (2) qualitative (changes in richness and new dimensions as the personality grows), (3) addition-in-fusion (recognition of new elements), and (4) configurational (recombining and reorganizing the familiar and the newly known into new forms).

FIVE THEORETICAL PRINCIPLES TO EVOLVING INDIVIDUAL POTENTIALITIES

Murphy considers two negative and three positive principles that are involved in discovering the individual potentialities in the total fulfillment of human nature.

1. The first principle is not to provide easy conflict resolution for any human being. On the ground that a homeostatic existence leads to nothing or leads to no future growth, Murphy feels, as does Adler, that the pampered existence is to be avoided.

2. A second principle is to avoid overemphasis on competition. Competi

tion may lead to deep ego-involvement and consequently may ignore the best avenues of fulfillment through overemphasis on victory at all costs.

3. The third principle is the need for studying progressively richer human experiences rather than a repetitive study of the past.

4. The only avenue to self-fulfillment is active effort on the part of all concerned. Although there is room for passive, reflective efforts, they will not fulfill the human natures of man until some active participation is attempted, even though it may be of a trial and error nature.

5. Murphy concludes with a plea to "express the humaneness of the movement in the direction of integration—fluid, sensitive, ever-changing integration as a step toward further integration" (*ibid.*, p. 322).

Murphy ends on a note of optimism, for he feels that fulfillment is never ending, that the entire history of the world and of the cosmos is one of being more and more fulfilled and less destructive. There almost seems to be built into the natural order of things a progressive desire for fulfillment beyond the present state.

Summary

We have now examined the four major themes involved, as this author sees them, in the personality theory of Gardner Murphy: the biological personality, the emerging–integrating personality, the socialized personality, and the potentialities that the human has for full, integrated fulfillment. Probably the most outstanding strain is that of the interaction among the three kinds of human nature. The word *interaction* is very valuable to Murphy's theoretical position on personality. Much of the richness of his theory is necessarily lost in any attempt to summarize his work. The student of personality theory, therefore, is urged to make reading excursions into the work of this well-known and beloved personality theorist.

EXPLAINING HUMAN BEHAVIOR VIA MURPHY'S THEORY

Once again, you may put each theory to the test in an attempt to see if it can explain why man does certain things. The difficulty with Murphy's theory lies not in its failure to explain the dynamics of human behavior but in one's choice of the many, many possible answers. The nine behavioral phenomena used in all the chapters are as follows: marriage, perversions, suicide, lawbreaking, supranatural being, humor, smoking, play and recreation, and psychoses and neuroses.

Although it does not do justice to the theory of Murphy, it is possible to explain human behavior by using only six or seven of the principal points in his theory. For example, we may explain lawbreaking, marriage, or smoking, or any of the other nine behavior patterns, by stating that an individual fails to pursue life and ends in suicide, or fails to reach emotional stability through psychoses or neuroses, because he has failed to integrate the three characteristics of his personality. Another all-inclusive explanation may be gained from nodal behavior or perseveration or projection. Finally, we may turn to the four human needs, visceral needs, activity needs, sensory needs, and the need to avoid or escape attack, injury, or threat, to explain why man does the things he does.

PREDICTING HUMAN BEHAVIOR VIA MURPHY'S THEORY

Personal Prediction

It is now the privilege of the reader to decide how valuable Gardner Murphy's theory is in predicting his own behavior.

Some of the factors involved in this personal prediction are as follows:

1. Psychology as we know it continues to change and will be changing. Psychology is a new science, a thrilling science, and a changing science. The individual may find it difficult, therefore, to extract material from the field of psychology that will help him to make a prediction for himself.

2. Much of Murphy's book *Human Potentialities* concerns itself with the future of mankind. The title itself indicates that. Consequently, in striving for a prediction of personal self, one must read and digest practically all of this work.

3. Whatever psychology has to say, Murphy has used. One of his greatest strengths lies in his capacity to fortify his position with good research.

Scientific or Laboratory Prediction

How much stimulation for research on personality theory does Murphy's position currently exert, whether on his own or other theories? If we examine one type of information, the answer is none. However, the literature on personality theories does reveal direct and pertinent effects upon research from Murphy's biosocial approach.

In the first instance, Murphy's name is not mentioned even once in either of two leading books on personality: Byrne's *An Introduction to Personality: A Research Approach* (1966) and Maddi's *Personality Theories: A Comparative Analysis* (1968). Bibliographical citations of his name are also sparse in a majority of the personality books published since 1960. Yet is this a fair criterion?

It does not appear to be when we consider all the other evidence. First is Murphy's own persistent efforts to refine his theoretical stance both in research and in further publication, e.g., the 1966 revised edition of the 1947 *Personality: A Biosocial Approach to Origins and Structure*, which is just as sound and fruitful as it was when first issued. Lindzey and Hall see him in proper perspective in their 1965 *Theories of Personality: Primary Sources and Research:* "Gardner Murphy, like so many other major personality theorists, is still very active in elaborating and expanding his biosocial theory, and in applying it to a number of critical human problems. Nor has he been inactive in pursuing empirical support for his theory. The Menninger Foundation program of studies on perceptual learning, which Murphy heads, is well known to psychologists" (p. 511).

On the other hand, Lindzey and Hall find that Hartley and Perelman's study "is one of the few investigations of the canalization process." Incidentally, this study comments, "Clearly, Murphy's canalization process with respect to the increase in liking for one among several potential ways of satisfying a need is supported" (Hartley and Perelman, 1963).

Consequently, the language of Murphy's biosocial theory may not instigate research, but the ramifications of his eclectic approach appear in great amounts of research. A case in point, of course, is his leadership in the field of perceptual learning, as Lindzey and Hall have stated above.

At this juncture we must deal with Murphy's abiding interest in extrasensory perception, which interest dates all the way back to about 1916. Perhaps not many would support Murphy's contention "that the paranormal dimensions of personality obey the same laws as the normal dimensions." If this be true, "Murphy's work in this area and his stimulation of such research . . . will turn out to be the most significant contribution that he has made to psychology," according to Lindzey and Hall's 1965 text. Parapsychology has never been popular on the psychological scene. But Gardner Murphy feels that popularity is not the way to solve human problems. In fact, he begins his autobiography by stating he has always been on the side of "mavericks," "minorities," and the "underdog." "They are my kind of people" (Murphy, 1967a).

Like Murray, and particularly like Allport, Fromm, Moreno, and Mowrer, Murphy is interested in the religious life of man. Again, this does not appeal to investigative-minded psychologists. Murphy's effect, then, is with those outside of academic psychology. It must be remembered that academic psychologists are the most welcome contributors to the professional journals. Few others are accepted.

In conclusion, Murphy himself recognizes—and always has—the need for research and experimentation even though the "hard" and the "soft" approaches may produce a false dichotomy (what is "hard" to one centripetal group of investigators may be "soft" to another, and the reverse equally holds true).

In the hard approach he finds such factors as these:

The scientific effort to study personality has proved to be extraordinarily difficult. . . . The trouble lies partly in the fact that personality is far more complex than most of the phenomena of the life sciences . . . that science is made chiefly not by advance in content, but by advance in method . . . method predetermines the subject matter of the special disciplines . . . experimentalists usually consider themselves the aristocracy, the elite among psychological invstigators. . . . The experimental method has been bringing into psychology, particularly into personality study, a number of things which we do not like at all . . . personality has been fractionated by the narrowness of method . . . there are the growing pains and the acute frustrations engendered by concepts bigger than the imagination of the methodologists . . . [and] . . . it is interesting that none of the five new revolutionary methods of today was devised by a professional psychologist. Most of the methods which have proved most novel and successful for personality study have come to us from biology, medicine, physiology, psychoanalysis, and mathematics (Murphy, 1967a).

Now to the soft approach. It needs less "ossification" in training psychologists, more and more "outrageous hypotheses," and major opportunities "for intellctual risk-taking." "Lack of knowledge about human beings is not a trivial, but a major threat to life. Lack of knowledge about personality is perhaps the central core of the issue that is most relevant for us today . . ." (Murphy, 1967).

Does Murphy suggest what to do about research in personality theory? He does in at least two selections: "How can the young psychologist select significant problems for his Ph.D. dissertation research?" *Psychologia*, 1967, *10* 217–222, and in chap. 7–10 of his 1968 book with Spohn, *Encounter with Reality: New Forms for an Old Quest.*

We end this section on scientific prediction which should come from research with the words Gardner Murphy used to end his autobiography, ". . . *that all kinds of people, all kinds of methods, all kinds of ideas be winnowed, screened, and studied; none arbitrarily rejected, and none arbitrarily accepted, but all brought humbly yet systematically before the reviewing stand of determined reality seeking*" (Murphy, 1967a; italics added).

■ SUMMARY

Gardner Murphy's theory of personality is the result of long years of labor. Into it he has put all the richness and depth of his own research and that of many others. Murphy is an eclectic in his approach to personality theory. He does not neglect a contribution to a more thorough understanding of man regardless of the source of the contribution. He uses, and knows how to use, the endeavors of biologists, psychologists, and sociologists in building a theory about personality dynamics.

This chapter highlights some of the major themes of personality theory as found in his published works. We are using four themes: the biological personality, the emerging and integrating personality, the socialized personality, and human potentialities or new perspectives. They by no means exhaust the material in his theory.

In the biological personality theme we have indicated that man is first of all a biological creature and from this basic nature stems much of the magic with which his personality will be constructed. Essential to man's biological self is the fundamental interdependence of the inner organic parts. Nothing in man's body functions by and for itself. Each part is important because it is different from other parts, and because of this difference it can function with other organic parts.

The second theme concerns itself with the emergence of physiological, psychological, and sociological aspects of behavior and how these three aspects emerge into a human personality. Included in this section are discussions of canalization, conditioning, conflict, perception, learning, symbols, and self.

Man begins life as a biological being, and as he later integrates his biological and cultural forces, he achieves a third level—the socialized personality. This is the third theme in this chapter.

In the final and fourth theme we have summarized the concepts of Murphy's *Human Potentialities* (1958). Murphy outlines three human natures: biological (man meets intense and diffuse organic needs), cultural (man becomes fixed and standardized), and creative thrust (man attempts the creative thrust to understand himself, the world in which he lives, and, from a philosophical frame of reference, why he is in the world and what to do about his future).

Throughout Gardner Murphy's theory of personality there seems to be a binding pivotal idea: The universe is comprised of differing objects, and they *must* interact, *must* be interdependent, *must* be integrated.

The author has found many ideas of Murphy's to be expressed in triadic form. This three-ness has been used as a device to present some of his theoretical considerations.

Finally, to study Murphy's work is to study the field of psychology as we know it today. It is exciting, challenging, and worthwhile.

BIBLIOGRAPHY

PRIMARY SOURCES

BOOKS

Murphy, G., Telepathy as an experimental problem, in C. Murchison (ed.), *Case for and Against Psychical Belief*. Worcester, Mass.: Clark University Press, 1927.

Murphy, G., *Historical Introduction to Modern Psychology*. New York: Harcourt, Brace & World, 1929. Revised 1949.

Murphy, G., and L. B. Murphy, *Experimental Social Psychology*. New York: Harper & Row, 1931.

Murphy, G., and F. Jensen, *Approaches to Personality*. New York: Coward-McCann, 1932.

Murphy, G., *General Psychology*. New York: Harper & Row, 1933.

Murphy, G., *A Briefer General Psychology*. New York: Harper & Row, 1935.

Murphy, G., and T. M. Newcomb, *Experimental Social Psychology* (1931), rev. 2nd ed. New York: Harper & Row, 1937.

Murphy, G., and R. Likert, *Public Opinion and the Individual*. New York: Harper & Row, 1938.

Murphy, G. (ed.), *Human Nature and Enduring Peace*. Boston: Houghton Mifflin, 1945.

Murphy, G., Parapsychology, in P. L. Harriman (ed.), *Encyclopedia of Psychology*. New York: Philosophical Library, 1947.

Murphy, G., *Personality: A Biosocial Approach to Origins and Structure*. New York: Harper & Row, 1947.

Also Basic Books, rev. ed., 1966, paper.

Murphy, G., *Historical Introduction to Modern Psychology*, 2nd ed. New York: Harcourt, Brace & World, 1949.

Murphy, G., The relationships of culture and personality, in S. S. Sargent (ed.) *Culture and Personality*. New York: Viking Fund, 1949.

Murphy, G., *Introduction to Psychology*. New York: Harper & Row, 1951.

Murphy, G., *In the Minds of Men: The Study of Human Behavior and Social Tensions in India*. New York: Basic Books, 1953.

Murphy, G., The internalization of social controls, in M. Berger, T. Abel, and C

Page (eds.), *Social Control, the Group and the Individual*. Princeton, N.J.: Van Nostrand, 1954.

Murphy, G., Social motivation, in G. Lindzey (ed.), *Handbook of Social Psychology*. Cambridge, Mass.: Addison-Wesley, 1954.

Murphy, G., and A. J. Bachrach (eds.), *An Outline of Abnormal Psychology*. New York: Modern Library, 1954.

Murphy, G., Psychology and the knowledge of man, in L. Leary (ed.), *The Unity of Knowledge*, Columbia University Bicentennial Conference Series. Garden City, N.Y.: Doubleday, 1955.

Murphy, G., Concepts of personality—then and now, in *Proceedings of the 1956 Invitational Conference on Testing Problems*. Princeton, N.J.: Educational Testing Service, 1956.

Murphy, G., Psychology: New ways to self-discovery, in L. White, Jr. (ed.), *The Frontiers of Knowledge*. New York: Harper & Row, 1956.

Murphy, G., *Human Potentialities*. New York: Basic Books, 1958.

Murphy, G., Some relations of perception to motivation, in G. H. Seward and J. P. Seward (eds.), *Current Psychological Issues: Essays in Honor of Robert S. Woodworth*. New York: Holt, Rinehart & Winston, 1958.

Murphy, G., Social psychology, in S. Arieti (ed.), *American Handbook of Psychiatry*. New York: Basic Books, 1959.

Murphy, G., Organism and quantity: A study of organic structure as a quantitative problem, in S. Wapner and B. Kaplan (eds.), *Perspectives in Psychological Theory*. New York: International Uiversities Press, 1960.

Murphy, G., Psychoanalysis as a Unified theory of social behavior, in J. Masserman (ed.), *Psychoanalysis and Human Values*. New York: Grune & Stratton, 1960.

> Also in *Psychiatry*, 1960, 23, 341–346.

Murphy, G., and R. O. Ballou (eds.), *William James on Psychical Research*. New York: Viking, 1960.

Murphy, G., and L. B. Murphy, The child as potential, in *The Nation's Children*, Vol. II, *Development and Education*, Golden Anniversary White House Conference on Children and Youth. New York: Columbia University Press, 1960.

Murphy, G., and L. B. Murphy, Hermann Rorschach and personality research, in M. Rickers-Ovsiankina (ed.), *Rorschach Psychology*. New York: Wiley, 1960.

Solley, C. M., and G. Murphy, *Development of the Perceptual World*. New York: Basic Books, 1960.

Murphy, G. (with collaboration of Laura A. Dale), *Challenge of Psychical Research: A Primer of Parapsychology*, Vol. XXVI in the World Perspectives Series. New York: Harper & Row, 1961.

Murphy, G., *Freeing Intelligence Through Teaching*. New York: Harper & Row, 1961.

Murphy, G., Group psychotherapy in our society, in M. Rosenbaum and M. Berger (eds.), *Group Psychotherapy and Group Function*. New York: Basic Books, 1963.

Murphy, G., Parapsychology, in N. L. Farberow (ed.), *Taboo Topics*. New York: Atherton Press, 1963.

Murphy, G., The biosocial theory of personality, in W. S. Sahakian (ed.), *Psychology of Personality: Readings in Theory*. Chicago: Rand McNally, 1965, pp. 188–209.

Murphy, G., Discussion, in S. Tomkins and C. Izard (eds.), *Affect, Cognition, and Personality*. New York: Springer, 1965.

Murphy, G., The future of social psychology in historical perspective, in O. Klineberg and B. Christie (eds.), *Perspectives in Social Psychology*. New York: Holt, Rinehart & Winston, 1965.

Murphy, G., Murphy's biosocial theory, in G. Lindzey and C. S. Hall, *Theories of Personality: Primary Sources and Research*. New York: Wiley, 1965, pp. 511–543.

> A small collection of Murphy's general writing and also on ESP.

Murphy, G., The nature of man, in C. Banks and P. L. Broadhurst (eds.), *Stephanos: Studies in Psychology Presented to Cyril Burt*. London: University of London Press, 1965.

Murphy, G., Political invention as a strategy against war, in G. Sperrazzo (ed.), *Psychology and International Relations*. Washington: Georgetown University Press, 1965.

Murphy, G., In E. G. Boring and G. Lindzey (eds.), *A History of Psychology in Autobiography*, Vol. V. New York: Appleton-Century-Crofts, 1967a.

Murphy, G., The communications continuum, in L. Thayer (ed.), *Communication: Concepts and Perspectives*. Washington: Spartan Books, 1967b.

Murphy, G., Personal impressions of Kurt Goldstein, in M. Simmel (ed.), *The Reach of Mind: Essays in Memory of Kurt Goldstein*. New York: Springer, 1968.

Murphy, G., *Psychological Thought from Pythagoras to Freud: An Informal Introduction*. New York: Harcourt, Brace, & World, 1968.

Murphy, G., Psychological views of personality and contributions to its study, in E. Norbeck, D. Price-Williams, and W. M. McCord (eds.), *The Study of Personality: An Interdisciplinary Appraisal*. New York: Holt, Rinehart & Winston, 1968.

Murphy, G., and L. B. Murphy (eds.), *Asian Psychology*. New York: Basic Books, 1968.

Murphy, G., and H. E. Spohn, *Encounter with Reality: New Forms for an Old Quest*. Boston: Houghton Mifflin, 1968.

> Using experimental, clinical, and developmental research "there are limit to what we can claim really to know."

PERIODICALS

Murphy, G., An experimental study of literary vs. scientific types, *Amer. Psychol.*, 1917, 28, 238–262.

Murphy, G., Types of word-association in dementia praecox, manic-depressives, and normal persons, *Amer. J. Psychiat.*, 1923, *11*, 1–33.

Murphy, G., Extra-sensory perception: A review, *J. Gen. Psychol.*, 1934, *2*, 454–458.

Murphy, G., Personality and social adjustments, *Soc. Forces*, 1937, *15*, 472–476.

Murphy, G., Dr. Rhine and the mind's eye, *Amer. Scholar*, 1938, *1*, 189–200.

Murphy, G., On limits of recording errors, *J. Parapsychol.*, 1938, *2*, 262–266.

Murphy, G., Research task of social psychology, *J. Soc. Psychol.*, 1939, *10*, 107–120.

Murphy, G., and E. Taves, Convariance methods in the comparison of extra-sensory tasks, *J. Parapsychol.*, 1939, *3*, 38–78.

Murphy, G., Some obscure relations of organism and environment, *Sci. Mon.*, 1941, *53*, 267–272.

Murphy, G., and L. A. Dale, Some present-day trends in psychical research, *J. Amer. Soc. Psychical Res.*, 1941, *35*, 118–132.

Levine, R., I. Chein, and G. Murphy, The relation of the intensity of a need to the amount of perceptual distortion: A preliminary report, *J. Psychol.*, 1942, *13*, 283–293.

Murphy, G., Psychology and the post-war world, *Psychol. Rev.*, 1942, *49*, 298–318.

Proshansky, H., and G. Murphy, The effects of reward and punishment on perception, *J. Psychol.*, 1942, *13*, 295–305.

Levine, J. M., and G. Murphy, The learning and forgetting of controversial material, *J. Abnorm. Soc. Psychol.*, 1943, *38*, 506–517.

Murphy, G., Psychical phenomena and human needs, *J. Amer. Soc. Psychical Res.*, 1943, *37*, 163–191.

Murphy, G., Spontaneous telepathy and the problem of survival, *J. Parapsychol.*, 1943, *7*, 50–60.

Postman, L., and G. Murphy, The factor of attitude in associative memory, *J. Exp. Psychol.*, 1943, *33*, 228–238.

Murphy, G., and L. A. Dale, Concentration versus relaxation in relation to telepathy, *J. Amer. Soc. Psychical Res.*, 1943, *37*, 2–15.

Murphy, G., E. Taves, and L. A. Dale, A further report on the Midas Touch, *J. Amer. Soc. Psychical Res.*, 1943, *37*, 111–118.

Murphy, G., and J. L. Woodruff, Effect of incentives on ESP and visual perception, *J. Parapsychol.*, 1943, *7*, 144–157.

Schafer, R., and G. Murphy, The role of autism in a visual figure-ground relationship, *J. Exp. Psychol.*, 1943, *32*, 335–343.

Murphy, G., Removal of impediments to the paranormal, *J. Amer. Soc. Psychical Res.*, 1944, *38*, 2–23.

Murphy, G., Field theory and survival, *J. Amer. Soc. Psychical Res.*, 1945, *39*, 181–209.

Murphy, G., The freeing of intelligence, *Psychol. Bull.*, 1945, *42*, 1–19.

Murphy, G., E. Taves, and L. A. Dale, American experiments on the paranormal cognition of drawings, *J. Amer. Soc. Psychical Res.*, 1945, *39*, 144–150.

Murphy, G., Psychical research and the mind-body relation, *J. Amer. Soc. Psychical Res.*, 1946, 40, 189–207.

Schmeidler, G. R., and G. Murphy, The influence of belief and disbelief in ESP upon individual scoring levels, *J. Exp. Psychol.*, 1946, 36, 271–276.

Murphy, G., A review of relevant research on the inheritance of mental traits, *Milbank Fund Quart.*, 1947, 25, 359–382.

Murphy, G., W. Whateley Carington: In memoriam, *J. Amer. Soc. Psychical Res.*, 1947, 41, 123–135.

Murphy, G., An approach to precognition, *J. Amer. Soc. Psychical Res.*, 1948, 43, 3–14.

Murphy, G., Psychology serving society, *Survey Graphic*, 1948, 37, 12–15.

Murphy, G., What needs to be done in parapsychology, in Symposium: A Program for the Next Ten Years of Research in Parapsychology, *J. Parapsychol.*, 194, 12, 15–19.

Murphy, G., Interrelationships between perception and personality: A symposium, Part I, *J. Pers.*, 1949, 18, 51–55.

Murphy, G., The place of parapsychology among the sciences, in Symposium (1948) of the (Washington) Society for Parapsychology, *J. Parapsychol.*, 1949, 13, 62–71.

Murphy, G., Psychical research and personality, *Proc. Soc. Psychical Res.* (London), 1949, 49, 1–15.

Murphy, G., A visit to the S.R.R. in London, *J. Amer. Soc. Psychical Res.*, 1949, 43, 137–142.

Murphy, G., William James and psychical research, *J. Amer. Soc. Psychical Res.*, 1949, 43, 85–93.

Murphy, G., Nuclear dementia, *Nation*, 1950, pp. 484–485.

Chein, I., R. Levine, G. Murphy, H. Proshansky, and R. Schafer, Need as a determinant of perception: A reply to Pastore, *J. Psychol.*, 1951, 31, 129–136.

Murphy, G., *et al.*, Dowsing: A field experiment in water divining, *J. Amer. Soc Psychical Res.*, 1951, 45, 3–16.

Murphy, G., and J. Hochberg, Perceptual development: Some tentative hypotheses, *Psychol. Rev.*, 1951, 58, 332–349.

Murphy, G., The American eugenics movement, *Eugen. Rev.*, 1952, 37, 35–37.

Murphy, G., Current developments in psychical research, *J. Amer. Soc. Psychical Res.*, 1952, 46, 47–61.

Murphy, G., The natural, the mystical, and the paranormal, *J. Amer. Soc. Psychical Res.*, 1952, 46, 125–142.

Murphy, G., What should be the relation of morals to law? A round table. Part V: The psychologist, the theologian, *J. Publ. Law*, 1952, 1, 313–316.

Murphy, G., A. O. Ross, and G. R. Schmeidler, The spontaneity factor in extrasensory perception, *J. Amer. Psychical Res.*, 1952, 46, 14–16.

Murphy, G., The patient's psychological resources in fighting diseases, *Neuropsychiatry*, 1952–1953, 2, 121–140.

Murphy, G., Human potentialities, *J. Soc. Issues*, Suppl. Series, No. 7, Kurt Lewin Memorial Award Issue, 1953.

Murphy, G., The importance of spontaneous cases, *J. Amer. Soc. Psychical Res.*, 1953, *47*, 89–103.

Murphy, G., Psychology and psychical research, *Proc. Soc. Psychical Res.* (London), 1953, *50*, 26–49.

Murphy, G., International collaboration in psychical research: Some reflections on the Utrecht Conference, *J. Amer. Soc. Psychical Res.*, 1954, *48*, 81–95.

Murphy, G., The life work of Frederic W. H. Myers, *Tomorrow*, 1954, *2*, 33–39.

Murphy, G., Professional progress through personal growth, *Amer. J. Nurs.*, 1954, *54*, 1464–1467.

Murphy, G., and R. S. Wallerstein, Perspectives of the research department of the Menninger Foundation, *Bull. Menninger Clin.*, 1954, *18*, 223–231.

Murphy, G., The cultural context of guidance, *Personnel Guid. J.*, 1955, *34*, 4–9.

Murphy, G., New evaluation of sociometry, *Sociometry Sci. Man*, 1955, *18*, 37–38.

Murphy, G., Plans for research on spontaneous cases, *J. Amer. Soc. Psychical Res.*, 1955, *49*, 85–98.

Murphy, G., What constitutes a well-integrated individual? *J. Home Economics*, 1955, *47*, 581–588.

Murphy, G., Affect and perceptual learning, *Psychol. Rev.*, 1956, *63*, 1–15.

Murphy, G., The boundaries between the person and the world, *Brit. J. Psychol.*, 1956, *47*, 88–94.

Murphy, G., The current impact of Freud upon psychology, *Amer. Psychologist*, 1956, *11*, 663–672.

Murphy, G., The enigma of human nature, *Main Currents in Modern Thought*, 1956, *13*, 3–7.

Murphy, G., Integration of experimental research with investigation of spontaneous cases, *J. Amer. Soc. Psychical Res.*, 1956, *50*, 147–150.

Murphy, G., Planning for the future, *Neuropsychiatry*, 1956, *4*, 10–26.

Murphy, G., The process of creative thinking, *Educ. Leader.*, 1956, *14*, 11–15.

Murphy, G., Professional growth and personal fulfillment, *Amer. J. Nurs.*, November, 1956, 1426–1429.

Murphy, G., Toward a dynamic trace theory, *Bull. Menninger Clin.*, 1956, *20*, 125–134.

Murphy, G., The third human nature, *J. Indiv. Psychol.*, 1957, *13*, 125–133.

Murphy, G., Triumphs and defeats in the study of mediumship, *J. Amer. Soc. Psychical Res.*, 1957, *51*, 125–135.

Murphy, G., and C. M. Solley, Learning to perceive as we wish to perceive, *Bull. Menninger Clin.*, 1957, *21*, 225–237.

Murphy, G., A cosmic Christmas carol, *Sat. Rev.*, 1958, *41*, 45–48.

Murphy, G., Face those atomic fears, *Christian Century*, 1958, *75*, 250–251.

Murphy, G., Our pioneers: III. William James, *J. Amer. Soc. Psychical Res.*, 1958, *52*, 309–313.

Murphy, G., Progress in parapsychology, *J. Parapsychol.*, 1958, *22*, 229–236.

Murphy, G., Trends in the study of extrasensory perception, *Amer. Psychologist*, 1958, *13*, 69–75.

Murphy, G., A comparison of India and the West in viewpoints regarding psychcal phenomena, *J. Amer. Soc. Psychical Res.*, 1959, 53, 43–49.

Murphy, G., Is bigger better? *Contemp. Psychol.*, 1959, 4, 204.

Murphy, G., New knowledge about family dynamics, *Soc. Casewk*, 1959, 4(363–370.

Murphy, G., Self-realization and mental health, *Bull. Menninger Clin.*, 1959, 2. 81–84.

Murphy, G., Self-realization and social responsibility, *Intercollegian*, 1959, 7(6–7.

Murphy, G., Experimental and other methods in parapsychology, *Indian Parapsychol.*, 1960, 2, 41–47.

Murphy, G., Future research in precognition, *Int. J. Parapsychol.*, 1960, 2, 5–2(

Murphy, G., The prevention of mental disorder: Some research suggestions, *Hillside Hosp.*, 1960, 9, 131–146.

Murphy, G., Psychoanalysis as a unified theory of human behavior, *Psychiatr* 1960, 23, 341, 346.

Murphy, G., The psychology of freedom, *Challenge*, January, 1960, pp. 27–33.

Santos, J. F., and G. Murphy, An odyssey in perceptual learning, *Bull. Menninge Clin.*, 1960, 24, 6–17.

Murphy, G., Four conceptions of research in clinical psychology, *Bull. Menninge Clin.*, 1961, 25, 290–295.

Murphy, G., Hornell Hart's analysis of the evidence for survival, *J. Amer. Soc Psychical Res.*, 1961, 55, 3–18.

Murphy, G., New vistas in personality research, *Personnel Guid. J.*, 1961, 4(114–122.

Murphy, G., Some reflections on John Dewey's psychology, *Univer. Colorad Stud. Ser. Phil.*, Aug., 1961, No. 2, pp. 26–34.

Murphy, G., Testing the limits of man, *J. Soc. Issues*, 1961, 17, 5–14.

Murphy, G., Where is the human race going? Report No. 2, Western Behaviora Sciences Institute, La Jolla, Cal., 1961, 22 pp. Reprinted in *Science an Human Affairs*, The Lucile P. Morrison Lectures, Western Behavioral Sc ences Institute, Richard E. Farson (ed.). Palo Alto, Cal.: Science and Behav ior Books, 1966, pp. 7–17.

Murphy, G., and J. Santos, Perceptual learning and reality testing, *Percept. Mot Skills*, 1961, 13, 130.

Murphy, G., Creativeness and extrasensory perception, *Menninger Quart.*, 1962 16, 16–19.

Murphy, G., Professor Piaget's visit, *Bull. Menninger Clin.*, 1962, 26, 113–114.

Murphy, G., A qualitative study of telepathic phenomena, *J. Amer. Soc. Psychica Res.*, 1962, 56, 63–79.

Murphy, G., Report on paper by Edward Girden on psychokinesis, *Psychol. Bull* 1962, 59, 520–528.

Murphy, G., L. A. Dale, and R. White, A selection of cases from a recent surve of spontaneous ESP phenomena, *J. Amer. Soc. Psychical Res.*, 1962, 56 3–47.

Murphy, G., and L. B. Murphy, The urge toward discovery, *AAUW J.*, 1962, 55, 248–250.

Murphy, G., Creativity and its relation to extrasensory perception, *J. Amer. Soc. Psychical Res.*, 1963, 57, 203–214.

Murphy, G., Freeing intelligence, *Childh. Educ.*, 1963, 39, 363.

Murphy, G., Learning to live, *New Outlook*, 1963, 16, 23–24.

Murphy, G., The psychology of 1975: An extrapolation, *Amer. Psychologist*, 1963, 18, 689–695.

Murphy, G., Science and world order, *Amer. J. Orthopsychiat.*, 1963, 33, 8–14.

Murphy, G., The statue with a sense of smell, *J. Psychol. Res.*, 1963, 7, 1–3.

Murphy, G., Studies of creativeness with special reference to extrasensory perception, *Parapsychol. Yoga*, 1963, 1, 132–137.

Murphy, G., Communication and mental health, *Psychiatry*, 1964, 27, 100–106.

Murphy, G., Lawfulness versus caprice: Is there a law of psychic phenomena? *J. Amer. Soc. Psychical Res.*, 1964, 58, 238–249.

Murphy, G., Shall we ever really understand personality? *J. Proj. Tech.*, 1964, 28, 140–143.

Murphy, G., Studies of creativeness with special reference to extrasensory perception, *Res. J. Phil. Soc. Sci.*, 1964, 1, 132–137.

Murphy, G., S. N. Harrell, and H. J. McNamara, Curiosity and reality contact: A preliminary report, *Percept. Mot. Skills*, 1964, 18, 976.

Murphy, G., Body-mind theory as a factor guiding survival research, *J. Amer. Soc. Psychical Res.*, 1965, 59, 148–156.

Murphy, G., A cross-cultural view of ego dynamics, *Bull. N.Y. Acad. Med.*, 1965, 41, 268–285, 335–346.

Murphy, G., Education of the will, *Quest* (Monogr. IV), Apr., 1965, pp. 1–9.

Murphy, G., Human psychology in the context of the new knowledge, *Main Currents in Modern Thought*, 1965, 21, 75–81.

Murphy, G., and S. Cohen, The search for person-world isomorphism, *Main Currents in Modern Thought*, 1965, 22, 31–34.

Murphy, G., Advancement of parapsychology as a science, *J. Amer. Soc. Psychical Res.*, 1966, 60, 212–213.

Murphy, G., Karl Buhler and the psychology of thought, *J. Gen. Psychol.*, 1966, 75, 188–195.

Murphy, G., Kurt Lewin and field theory, *Bull. Menninger Clin.*, 1966, 30, 358–367.

Murphy, G., Perspective—roaming the behavioral sciences, *Psychiat. News*, 1966, 1, 6.

Murphy, G., Psychical research in 1965, *J. Amer. Soc. Psychical Res.*, 1966, 60, 198–201.

Murphy, G., Psychical research today, *Int. J. Neuropsychiat.*, 1966, 2, 357–362.

Murphy, G., Research in creativeness: What can it tell us about extrasensory perception? *Amer. J. Soc. Psychical Res.*, 1966, 60, 8–22.

Murphy, G., Sensory enrichment and social therapy, *Correct. Psychiat. J. Soc. Ther.*, 1966, 12, 83–95.

Murphy, G., and H. L. Klemme, Unfinished business, *J. Amer. Soc. Psychical Res.*, 1966, 60, 306–320.

Murphy, G., What can youth tell us about its potentialities? *Natl., Assoc. Sec. Schl. Prin. Bull.*, May, 1966, pp. 10–43.

Murphy, G., Direct contacts with past and future: Retrocognition and precognition, *J. Amer. Soc. Psychical Res.*, 1967, *61*, 3–23.

Murphy, G., How can the young psychologist select significant problems for his Ph.D. dissertation research? *Psychologia*, 1967, *10*, 217–222.

Murphy, G., Introductory aspects of modern parapsychological research, *Trans. N.Y. Acad. Sci.* (Ser. II'), 1967, *30*, 256–260.

Murphy, G., Methods in parapsychology, *Science*, 1967, *155*, 951–952.

Murphy, G., Pythagorean number theory and its implications for psychology, *Amer. Psychologist*, 1967, *22*, 423–431.

Murphy, G., The viewpoint of a contemporary psychologist, *Main Currents*, 1967, *24*, 48–49.

Murphy, G., and A. E. Moriarty, An experimental study of ESP potential and its relationship to creativity, *J. Amer. Soc. Psychical Res.*, 1967, *61*, 326–338.

Murphy, G., and A. E. Moriarty, Some thoughts about prerequisite conditions or states in creativity and paranormal experience, *J. Amer. Soc. Psychical Res.*, 1967, *61*, 203–218.

Murphy, G., Evolution: Charles Darwin, *Bull. Menninger Clin.*, 1968, *32*, 86–101.

Murphy, G., Parapsychology: New neighbor or unwelcome guest?, *Psychol. Today*, 1968, *1*, 52–55, 65.

Murphy, G., Reflections on the field of clinical psychology, *Clin. Psychologist*, 1968, *21*, 117–120.

Murphy, G., J. F. Santos, and C. M. Solley, Development and transfer of attentional habits, *Percept. Mot. Skills*, 1968, *26*, 515–519.

TAPE RECORDINGS

Murphy, G., *Introduction to Parapsychology* (G. W. Kisker, ed.), Sound Seminars, No. 124, Cincinnati, Ohio.

Murphy, G., *The Boundaries Between the Individual and His World* (G. W. Kisker, ed.), Sound Seminars, No. 174, Cincinnati, Ohio.

SUGGESTED READINGS

BOOKS

Blake, R. R., and G. V. Ramsey (eds.), *Perception: An Approach to Personality* New York: Ronald Press, 1951.

Bruner, J. S., and D. Krech (eds.), *Perception and Personality*. Durham, N.C. Duke University Press, 1950.

Hall, C. S., and G. Lindzey, *Theories of Personality*. New York: Wiley, 1957, pp 503–537.

Hartshorne, H., and M. May, *Studies in Deceit*. New York: Macmillan, 1928.

Lindzey, G., and C. S. Hall (eds.), *Theories of Personality: Primary Sources and Research*. New York: Wiley, 1965, pp. 511–543.

Peatman, J. G., and E. L. Hartley (eds.), *Festschrift for Gardner Murphy*. New York: Harper & Row, 1960.

Articles in honor of Murphy's sixty-fifth birthday.

Sherif, M., *The Psychology of Social Norms*. New York: Harper & Row, 1936.

PERIODICALS

Collier, R. M., Independence: An overlooked implication of the open system concept, *J. Indiv. Psychol.*, 1962, *18*, 103–113.

Living tissue integrates but is also independent.

Hartley, E. L., and M. A. Perelman, Deprivation and the canalization of responses to food, *Psychol. Rep.*, 1963, *13*, 647–650.

Murphy's hypothesis is supported.

McCreary, J. K., The problem of personality definition, *J. Gen. Psychol.*, 1960, *63*, 107–111.

Reviews definitions by Allport, Lewin, Murray, and Murphy.

Smith, M. B., Murphy's *Novum Organum*, *Contemp. Psychol.*, 1959, *4*, 161–164.

An ambivalent review of Murphy's *Human Potentialities*.

Williams, R. J. Biochemical approach to the study of personality, *Psychiat. Res. Rep.*, 1955, No. 2, pp. 31–33.

Part

V

Psychobiological

NO PERSONALITY THEORY now known quite parallels that of William
H. Sheldon. Its antecedents probably have deeper roots in history than do
those of any other theory. Obviously, Jung's theory goes back to the earliest
history of man, but Jung seems to *use* history for his data whereas Sheldon
comes *out* of history. We have placed Sheldon's somatotypic theory in a
separate section for two reasons: its uniqueness concerning the relationships
between body and behavior and, particularly, the wisps of evidence concerning the future of personality theory. It may be that research on the body and
its neural systems is the future of personality theory. Quite possibly future

413

editions of this book will need a section on body chemistry, neurological components of behavior, and whatever comes of the combined efforts of teams of physiologists, psychologists, biochemists, and neurologists.

If so, we are ready, and Sheldon's work may be a tangential beginning.

11

SHELDON

*. . . the state of the body inevitably
affected the action of the mind . . .*

HIPPOLYTE TAINE
The Origins of Contemporary France

*It is native personality, and that alone,
that endows a man . . .*

WALT WHITMAN
Democratic Vistas

SOME BIOGRAPHICAL DATA

William H. Sheldon is a highly trained investigator with a wide background
and interests although his work may give the impression that he is a scientist
with a narrow field. He was born in Warwick, Rhode Island, in 1899. His
Bachelor of Arts degree was granted in 1919 by Brown University. Later he
received his M.A. from the University of Colorado and in 1926, his Ph.D.
from the University of Chicago, where he majored in psychology. He continued to study at Chicago and obtained an M.D. in 1933. During his training

he also taught for two years in the Psychology Department of Chicago (1924–1926) and later at Northwestern University and the University of Wisconsin.

He served too on the medical staff of the Children's Hospital in Chicago before becoming interested in psychiatry. As a result of this new interest, Sheldon spent the years 1935 and 1936 studying and traveling in Europe. He was particularly interested in the work of Carl Jung in Switzerland and also spent some time with Freud and Kretschmer during his foreign study. When he returned, he went again to the University of Chicago as a full professor of psychology and after two years transferred to Harvard University. In World War II Sheldon served as a flight surgeon in the Army Air Force.

Upon his return from service, Sheldon became the Director of the Constitution Laboratory, in the College of Physicians and Surgeons at Columbia University. He is now continuing his work with the Atlas of Women and the Atlas of Children at Columbia as well as retaining interest in clinical disease and the relationship of human constitutional variation to psychiatry.

We are studying, then, the theory of a man who is extremely well trained, with a wide background of teaching and research in leading universities, and who now commands the full resources of an excellent laboratory designed to further the aspects of constitutional psychology.

Demonstrating the breadth of his mind, Sheldon has written two interesting nonprofessional pieces, one an essay and the other a technical work. The essay, written in 1936, concerns the value of religion in modern society and is entitled *Psychology and the Promethean Will*. His technical work, called *Early American Cents, 1793–1814*, was written in 1949. Sheldon has by no means a one-track mind.

INTRODUCTION

Let us suppose that a theory were constructed, based on research of a quantitative nature, which not only helped to predict man's nature, both as an individual and in groups, but also gave us a checklist so that the untrained observer could make approximations of a person's personality. This would be a long step in the advancement of personality theory. To some students of personality theory such is the nature of William Sheldon's somatotypic theory.

Sheldon's description of man's behavior is probably the neatest and most compact of all the theories covered in the present text. It has one central theme, a direct approach to the problem, relatively simple language and concepts that come from our everyday life, a degree of repeatability which makes possible further examination by others, and a very high degree of consistency within itself; it permits for continua in human behavior and i practical for studying such deviant groups as psychotics and juvenile delinquents.

In 1934–1935 Sheldon visited Freud, who at that time was still living in Vienna, and, although Sheldon was primarily interested in working with Jung, he undoubtedly felt some of the impact of Freud's ideas upon his own emerging theories. Sheldon still believes that the psychoanalyst is fumbling with language in trying to describe and understand the unconscious. For example, in his view there is no difference between the unconscious and the body—they are the same. The Freudians are wasting their time in inexact approaches because they ignore this fact. What the analyst should do, according to Sheldon, is follow a definitive, morphological measuring system which would bring the concept of the unconscious out of the realm of darkness into the light where it could be examined with much more meaning.

William Sheldon is known as a constitutional psychologist. He is interested in studying the "psychological aspects of human behavior as they are related to the morphology [science of bodily form, structure, anatomy] and physiology of the body" (Sheldon, Stevens, and Tucker, 1940). In other words, Sheldon maintains that a relationship exists between the kind of body man has and his behavior as a human being, and that each has an effect upon the other.

SHELDON'S DESCRIPTION
OF HUMAN BEHAVIOR

Body–Temperament Principle

Starting about 1938 and continuing to the present day, Sheldon has espoused a theory which, in its most elementary form, states that there are three primary components of body form and three primary components of temperament to go with the body form. In the following pages we shall examine the derivation of his theory; now we shall look at the kinds of people he defined.

Table 11.1 shows the body types and the corresponding behavior that accompanies each one. The names (body type and behavioral characteristic) have been conjoined for ease in remembering and reference, and may be said to describe special personality types.

We must now examine these types of people and describe their behavior, especially the predominant characteristics. For purposes of drawing a clearer picture each type will be described as a *pure* type although it is to be understood that such cases are so exceptional in Sheldon's system as to be practically nonexistent. Almost all people are a combination of all three, as we shall see in the subsequent section dealing with continuous variables. It is important not to judge Sheldon until one understands that practically all of us are combinations of the three types mentioned in Table 11.1.

TABLE 11.1. *Sheldon's relationship of body type to behavior–personality*

BODY TYPE	BEHAVIOR	PERSONALITY
Endomorph (tends to be fat)	Viscerotonia (tends to be relaxed)	Endo/viscerotone
Mesomorph (tends to be muscular)	Somatotonia (tends to be assertive)	Meso/somatoton
Ectomorph (tends to be thin)	Cerebrotonia (tends to be restrained)	Ecto/cerebrotone

Endomorph–viscerotonia—Does the reader know anyone who is inclined toward fatness, especially if he does not watch his diet very well? This person has the kind of body which floats high in the water, is likely to be spherical although most babies are fat and soft, this individual retains a softness and baby-like quality of the skin and flesh. The lips may be thicker than those of most people.

The endomorph body and the individual with a viscerotonia temperament, henceforth to be called the endo/viscerotone, is inclined to behave according to the following twenty criteria. (Not all of the behavioral characteristics must be present for one to be classified as an endo/viscerotone, but certainly if one has at least ten of the twenty behavioral characteristics he should be included in this category.)[1]

1. Relaxation in posture and movement. The endo/viscerotone walks with an easy gait. Sometimes he shuffles; most of the time he ambles. He is the kind of soldier who is often hard to train and very hard to keep in step with the marching troops. He opens doors and closes doors sloppily. His lighting a cigarette is a casual kind of maneuver, and he is quite sure to sprinkle ashes around himself and the rug and will not always hit the ashtray even when he tries to use it. The endo/viscerotone is a relaxed guy! When he stands, it is usually to lean against a post, door, or anything that affords support, because he would rather be sitting.

2. Love of physical comfort. Not only does the endo/viscerotone like to sit down; he slouches. If he can do so, he will put his feet up on some convenient object or throw his arm around the back of the chair, sit sideways—anything that makes life easier. His clothes are chosen for comfort. If his wife or friend helps him and wishes him to appear more "smart and well-pressed," it isn't too long until he has the unpressed, slept-in look and is back in his old comfortable clothes.

[1] The list of twenty characteristics is adapted from Sheldon's *The Varieties of Temperament: A Psychology of Constitutional Differences*, 1942, p. 26, although the author has extended some of the descriptions to afford the student a clearer understanding.

3. Slow reaction. The endo/viscerotone is the bane of his roommate because it takes him forever to wake up, get washed, get dressed, or get anywhere. He is inclined to be perpetually late because he does things so deliberately. In playing games he is the slowest of the slow. Tennis is not his game, nor is table tennis, because these games require quick reactive movements, something of which he is incapable. He even plays bridge so slowly that his opponents are likely to complain. In general, he rather irritates others because he must be waited for, no matter the occasion. He shaves slowly, he walks slowly, he lives slowly.

4. Love of eating. Eating is almost a ritual with the endo/viscerotone. He will eat all day long but not in a refined manner. Crumbs fall while food disappears. Thus eating is more of a vocation than a ritual. He loves to hunt out exotic dining places and will remember enjoyable meals, the place, the menu, and all the trimmings, for months and even years.

5. Socialization of eating. Have you ever sat at a restaurant counter with no one else present when an individual came in and sat right next to you? With all that room, this person sat right next to you! That was an endo/viscerotone, for he intensely dislikes eating alone. In fact, he will postpone or forgo a meal if it must be eaten in solitude.

6. Pleasure in digestion. The endo/viscerotone likes to pat his stomach after a meal and declare how nice it all was. The satiated feeling is one he likes and cultivates whenever possible. One of his favorite days of the year is Thanksgiving Day, especially after the meal.

7. Love of polite ceremony. Introductions all around at a social gathering are his meat. The ritual of lighting candles and the memorizing part of the fraternity initiation make sense to the endo/viscerotone, and he participates with quiet enthusiasm. The church service, the wedding, the reception—all are part of his repertoire, and he doesn't mind spending time and energy in arranging them properly.

8. Sociophilia. People are the staff of life to the endo/viscerotone. He loves people. This is the individual about whom it was once said, "There are no strangers in his life." He almost feels that it is a challenge to have someone in the group whom he does not know. This is one of his predominant characteristics.

9. Indiscriminate amiability. At a party, Caribbean cruise, social tea, or reception the endo/viscerotone is an inveterate and amiable "table-hopper." It is almost impossible to cut him off or be rude, because he fails to accept the snub. He may be hurt for the moment, but within seconds he's trying with renewed vigor to "win friends and influence people" to the joys of living. Rich or poor, friend or foe, they are all grist for his mill.

10. Greed for affection and approval. (See Horney's "moving toward people.") This kind of person, when approaching pure viscerotonia, is

miserable if he feels you do not like him. He worries about it, mulls it over, and comes to the conclusion that he hasn't tried hard enough to make you like him, because like him you must.

11. Orientation to people. When he visits a scientific exhibit, he is interested in the man who built the machine or the man who operates and demonstrates it, but not the machine. Technical, mechanical, and scientific phenomena bore him or frustrate him because he cannot understand them. If he reads (he is rather disinterested in reading), he will choose biographies or fast-moving fiction.

12. Evenness of emotional flow. He is often the envy of his acquaintances. Nothing much seems to bother him as he whistles his way through life. Procrastination comes easy, for there is always another day, and worry solves nothing.

13. Tolerance. He is quite willing to forgive you your errors of omission and commission and will feel grateful to be forgiven his. In the fraternity or sorority meeting, he can be trusted to introduce the conciliatory motion that is designed to calm ruffled feelings and soothe irritation.

14. Complacency. Every cloud has a silver lining, and the endo/viscerotone knows this better than anyone else.

15. Deep sleep. This is the roommate who can sleep through anything. Neither storm, voices, nor the blaring radio can disturb his sleep. And in the morning, if an exciting event took place in the dormitory during the night, he will plaintively complain the next morning, "Why didn't you guys wake me up?" For after all there was excitement and people, and he was not of it. The endo/viscerotone sleeps like an exhausted baby, all relaxed and played out.

16. The untempered characteristic. He is malleable. He feels there are good points to both sides. Any dilemma he wants to resolve by finding out what the others think. With the collaboration of the majority will, he knows that he has made the best decision under the circumstances.

17. Smooth, easy communication of feeling. This person loves to talk and he is good at it. Writing is painful, partially because one must be alone to write, but also because talking is more direct—and he can do it with ease.

18. Relaxation and sociophilia under alcohol (key characteristic). This is the happy, talkative, singing drunk. While the party continues and the liquor holds out, he is a very happy inebriate. Possibly this feature and the one following (number 19) delineate his personality more accurately than do any others, especially when many of the preceding characteristics are not apparent, or when there is scant time to observe all of them.

19. Need of people when troubled (key characteristic). Do you have someone living in the dormitory whose every problem is known by all the residents of the hall? This is the endo/viscerotone. The "Dear John" letter, the failing grade, the sickness at home—the endo/viscerotone is ready and eager to communicate them all. He must do so, for there are no secrets or

silent sorrows in his existence. Like a child, he cannot hold the secret but must tell. It does not matter whether help comes from the listener; to share one's problems with one's fellow man is enough to ease the burden.

20. Orientation toward childhood and family relationships. With all the lovableness, charm, disarming frankness, and zest for living of childhood, the endo/viscerotone lives his life whatever his chronological age. He loves life and wants to help you enjoy it too. He is not a fool but a sensitive human being with a vast capacity to see, hear, love, and live with clarity and simplicity. He harbors no grudge and wears his heart on his sleeve.

If any true unadulterated endo/viscerotone lives, the reader must decide. As we shall see, Sheldon believes in the continuous variable, which means that all of us have some of these characteristics in conjunction with those of the next two types. It must be emphasized, however, that some of us are overwhelmingly oriented toward the endo/viscerotonic personality and will be so for the major portion of our lives. Sheldon's theory subsumes a genetic influence and disposition toward being more of one type than another. The personality with exactly even portions of all three types (endo/viscerotone, meso/somatotone, ecto/cerebrotone) is possibly even more rare than the pure type. In the case of this trichotomized personality, the problems of trivalency may be so overpowering as to eliminate him from the life scene. He must so continuously balance three primary modes of behavior as eventually to break down and reach neurotic or psychotic levels of behavior. The trichotomized type is an interesting subject of conjecture.

Mesomorph–somatotonia—The meso/somatotone is all muscle, bone, and sinews. He is strong of body, much like the professional football player. He has the kind of body that can absorb and administer great physical punishment. His muscles are hard, and his frame is usually big and always powerful. Though he may not be overly tall, he has a look of brute strength. Whereas the first type, the endo/viscerotone, had a physique developing primarily out of the endodermal layers of the body, the meso/somatotone is named for the mesodermal or middle layer of the human structure. This individual takes pride in his body, for therein lies his mode of operation. He thinks physically, he acts physically, and he is dominated by his physical existence. To him, all else is soft living or highbrow. He is characterized, then, by the following manifestations of behavior, twenty in number, as was true for the previous type.

1. Assertiveness of posture and movement. Whereas the endo/viscerotone went through a door by casually opening and closing it, the meso/somatotone explodes through. He doesn't open doors; he attacks them. He does not walk or amble; he strides. Lighting a cigarette is an act of physical exertion which often causes the match to break. He smokes vigorously with excited inhalation and expulsion of smoke until the cigarette end glows

furiously. If he is standing about, it is nearly impossible for him to be immobile. The meso/somatotone jiggles on his toes, works his fingers, or simply bounces without moving. To be still, unless in a physically challenging soldier's "attention" stance, is most distressing to this type of personality. He wants action.

2. Love of physical adventure. Instead of wanting to sit after a heavy meal and nod off to sleep as the endo/viscerotone loves to do, this human being gets fretful and restless. He much prefers taking a walk, throwing a ball or football, doing anything rather than just stagnating in inactivity.

3. Energetic characteristic. Throughout the ages the game of follow-the-leader has been perpetuated by the meso/somatotone. Whatever he does, he does with the full energy and capacity of his body, from playing cards (all tricks are taken by smashing the card onto the table) to dancing (the rhythm is followed with hand-pumping energy, and waltzes are always too slow).

4. Need for, and enjoyment of, exercise. The meso/somatotone is a miserable patient at home or in the hospital. To be bedridden is the worst of all possible states. To lie in bed on a morning makes him restless to be about the business of the day. He most enjoys games and recreations in which an opponent is involved and the reciprocity of the game is paramount, as in tennis, football, or wrestling, rather than golf or bowling. If he does bowl, he throws the ball down the alley with all his might. He is probably happiest after a hard workout in athletics followed by a shower with a vigorous, cold, stinging spray. Sedentary activities bore him, and thus he finds reading somewhat painful, not for intellectual reasons but because it necessitates keeping in one place. He almost always scans rather than reads.

5. Love of dominating, lust for power. (See Horney's "moving against people.") In addition to liking reciprocal sports because action is involved, he likes them because they are competitive. It is almost impossible for the meso/somatotone to play anything without a struggle for superiority, even with small children. When chastised for not allowing the little one to win occasionally, he retorts that he is just "teaching him the game, and you don't want the kid to be a baby all his life, do you?"

6. Love of risk and chance. Along with follow-the-leader, which gives him exercise and a chance to dominate, the meso/somatotone has an abiding interest in roller-coaster rides and all manner of whirly rides at the amusement park, as well as in driving cars extremely fast in all kinds of traffic. Water skiing, snow skiing, any type of activity in which danger and possible injury are components, attract him. It is an exhilaration to skirt potential injury and emerge safely, demonstrating that he has conquered another facet of life and emerged triumphant. If another individual duplicates his performance, he must try again and again to win the victory of superior performance. Parroting the musical comedy line, he would say, "Anything you can do, I can do better."

7. Bold directness of manner. Most of his conversation expresses the frontal attack. He approaches his acquaintances with a gibe or critical remark, thus putting them on the immediate defensive and giving himself the upper hand. The first type (endo/viscerotone) makes every effort to have you like him; this type makes every effort to have you notice him and respect his power. His handshake is a bone crusher, designed to make you at once aware of his superior strength.

8. Physical courage for combat. He makes the ideal soldier in combat, for to attain superiority over his fellow man is a natural goal.

9. Competitive aggressiveness. The smashing volley in table tennis or outdoor tennis, the bone-rattling tackle in football, the vociferous trumping of an opponent's ace, the powerfully smashed golf ball are what the meso/somatotone lives for in his recreational pursuits.

10. Psychological callousness. When his fiancée wishes to indulge in love play and his own sexual appetites are not engaged, he roughly rejects the advances and declares, "It's too hot to be mushy." Sex play for him is for self-gratification and not for demonstration of affection. Poignant death scenes are almost always met with a grimace or unveiled laugh. Sentimentality indicates to the meso/somatotone a weakness in character.

11. Claustrophobia. He never makes a telephone call from a booth with the door closed. He intensely hates to feel "cooped up." He wants the wide open spaces. Small rooms, tight clothing, intimate gatherings are anathema to him.

12. Ruthlessness, freedom from squeamishness. Violent scenes of death do not disturb him. He is more interested in how it happened than in the fact that a victim resulted. Exhibits of medieval tortures fascinate him to the point that he cannot pass one up and lingers over the more macabre ones.

13. Unrestrained voice. It is loud, clear, stentorian, with no attempt at modulation. Statements are declared, not uttered, by the meso/somatotone. He finds whispering in the movie theater or library an obnoxious restraint on his freedom. "A man should stand up and be heard" is his vocal credo.

14. Spartan indifference to pain. The last thing in the world he wants to admit is that the injury hurts; only weaklings admit pain, and he is not a weakling. Only sissies cry.

15. General noisiness. His deportment in the theater or library is matched by the loud muffler on his car and the loud guffaw at anything he considers humorous. (Humor, incidentally, for the meso/somatotone is largely based on man's inhumanity to man.) You can hear him come into the house, close doors, open drawers, and go about the business of the day, for his vigor begets collisions of objects as the lightning begets thunder.

16. Overmaturity of appearance. As a youth, he needs to shave long before his peers. His face and general demeanor frequently make him look older than his years. He uses his body vigorously, and it shows the strain.

17. Horizontal mental cleavage. His mind operates in an across-the-board manner which accepts an idea or rejects it but is not interested in delving into the background or tangential reasons. This characteristic leads to stereotyped thinking, for the meso/somatotone asks only for decisions and not for the philosophy underlying a position. A thing is either true or not true, and to entertain too many doubts is to admit that one does not know what he believes in. The meso/somatotone knows what he believes in, and he dislikes contrary evidence.

18. Assertiveness and aggression under alcohol (key characteristic). This is the drunk who likes to fight, pick quarrels, and declare himself "the best man in the house." Alcohol appears to release pent-up aggressive feelings. Although no actual physical violence may take place, the meso/somatotone under the influence of alcohol will appear loud and boastful. His statements will all be made as a challenge. He defies anyone present to contradict him. Should he meet a like-minded person, there is the challenge to "go outside and settle this thing." He most often, however, selects the "Milquetoast" figure at the bar, walks up to him and states, "I don't like you," possibly, of course, never having seen the meek one before in his life.

As in the case of the previous type, the endo/viscerotone, the meso/somatotone reveals more of his basic personality via alcohol than at other times. During the normal course of each day, he may socialize or minimize his other attributes, but when drinking gets beyond his control he is not able to conceal much of what he really is.

19. Need of action when troubled (key characteristic). Perhaps the reader knows someone on the college scene who received a lower grade in a course than he thought he was going to get. The endo/viscerotone would tell his friends, write his parents, and seek out other people to commiserate with him in his bad fortune. Not so with the meso/somatotone. He appeals strongly and forcefully to the instructor; failing to get the grade changed, he proceeds to the departmental chairman, the dean, the president of the university, and to any figure of authority who he feels may redress his wrong. In each case his appeal is made vehemently. He wants action.

20. Orientation toward goals and activities of youth. The muscular individual with the assertive behavior must, when he engages in recreational activities, do so with a purpose. He finds it almost impossible to participate in a game without scoring more points, hitting the ball farther, collecting more specimens than others in like pursuits. His life is goal-directed, usually with the purpose of being the first to reach the goal.

His behavior reminds one of the boastful adolescent who loves activity, who loves to indicate his strength and emergence toward manhood, who directs his energies toward winning. This is the pure type of meso/somatotone.

Ectomorph–cerebrotonia—The ecto/cerebrotone is usually thin, ascetic appearing, meticulous in dress, and most of the time a lonely "thinker." He finds that the best of all possible worlds lies in the self, his own self. He is rarely heavily muscled, though he may become so through dedicated and solitary, muscle-building exercise in which he engages solely for health reasons. He is inclined toward frailty and angularity of structure, though he is not necessarily tall. He has nervous quick movements.

Again, the reader should keep in mind that the following descriptions are perhaps grossly overdrawn but do serve to delineate the pure type of ecto/cerebrotone.

1. Restraint in posture and movement. The endo/viscerotone shrugs into a coat, the meso/somatotone muscles his way into a coat, but the ecto/cerebrotone is a symphony of delicate and refined movement as he carefully places each arm in the sleeves of his coat, slowly draws it around his body, and possibly ends with an additional check of his entire attire to see that nothing is out of place. He opens doors with military precision. His every physical act is a discipline of motion. He stands erect, sits erect, sleeps rigidly, and never seems to relax in body.

2. Physiological overresponse. The thin man of the cerebrotonic personality treats his body like a machine. It must always be "at the ready." He drives an automobile with quick birdlike movements which respond immediately to any suspected danger on the road ahead. He considers the automobile to be an extension of his body, and therefore he must be in possession of its movements at all times. When a nonroutine condition occurs on the road, he immediately decreases speed, applies the brakes, and is alert for an accident.

3. Overly fast reactions. Neurologically the ecto/cerebrotone is like a taut violin string. Whatever physical response he makes is made immediately and with predictable precision. In playing tennis he is light, fast, and accurate, but never powerful. If something spills, he is on his feet instantly. Whereas the endo/viscerotone stumbles up to avoid the spilled soup, and the meso/somatotone roars up, the ecto/cerebrotone dances up lightly and graciously, having sensed the danger of hot soup almost before it landed. Incidentally, the first type would be apologetic and would assume some responsibility for having caused the mishap; he would try to keep the waitress his friend and not have hurt feelings. The second type would demand apologies from the waitress and require redress of some kind for the soiled garments. The third type would brood about the accident, go home immediately to change the garment, and spend the rest of the day wondering, "Why does it always happen to me?"

4. Love of privacy. The ecto/cerebrotone is a loner. He must have some time to himself each day. He enjoys eating alone, listening to records alone,

attending the theater alone, and studying alone. Solitude is the staff of life. He is miserable with a roommate. As a college student, he makes every effort to live in a single room, where he can control his things and his life even if it means living off campus and traveling inconvenient distances to and from classes. He regularly plans for a solitary walk in the dark of the night. To be alone for him is to have control of one's environment.

5. Mental overintensity, hyperattention. The ecto/cerebrotone knows how many steps there are up to the library door; he has counted them. During a dull lecture his mind cannot lapse off into reverie or sleep. He continuously must be mentally alert and active. He counts the number of students in the room, the light bulbs in the overhead fixtures, and the number of "uh's" the instructor utters.

6. Secretiveness of feeling, emotional restraint. This type of personality feels that to reveal an emotion is a sign of weakness in control and character. His response to love play is made primarily to satisfy an organic sexual appetite and does not indicate an emotional feeling on his part. This is the person you may be acquainted with for years as a working mate or a neighbor and yet feel in twenty years of friendship that you really know nothing about him. A death in his immediate family may not be revealed for months, while the first Sheldonian type will reveal all the details, even the deathbed scene.

7. Self-conscious mobility of the eyes and face. When the ecto/cerebrotone talks to you, he avoids looking directly at you. When he laughs, he does so self-consciously and probably with his hand over his mouth. There appears to be almost a furtiveness about any direct conversational contact with another human being.

8. Sociophobia. Essentially he dislikes people—especially when he meets them in large groups. He most emphatically dislikes and probably never will give large parties. He prefers small intimate groups whose entertainment centers on passive activities such as listening to symphonic recordings, with talk at a minimum. He avoids to the point of ridicule the meso/somatatone and tolerates only for brief periods of time the happy-go-lucky endo/viscerotone. He literally fears large crowds. He is most uncomfortable sitting in the middle of a mass of people, especially at vociferous gatherings like football games. Such activities seem inane and threatening to him. He much prefers small musicals, art museums, and any type of group activity where the participants are orderly and quietly reserved.

9. Inhibited social address. It would be interesting to study the three types as they walk from class to class on a college campus. The first type looks at all the eyes and seeks recognition of any friendly face or gesture. Whether the second type says "Hello" or not depends upon his mood at the moment and the status of the recipient of his potential greeting. The third and present type under discussion looks at the ground, or away, or is deeply involved in thought with no concern for the passing students. The first type loves to see

that all are introduced around the gathering, the second type uses introductions to gain a status position, while the ecto/cerebrotone avoids, to the point of rudeness, introducing people.

10. Resistance to habit and poor routinizing. With the ecto/cerebrotone there is a tendency to do things differently from day to day and thus resist the monotony of habitual conduct.

11. Agoraphobia. The ecto/cerebrotone dislikes wide open spaces. He much prefers the rainy day, the in-front-of-the-fireplace feeling with a good book and solitude, to the wide open spaces of the beach and surf boarding. He likes to feel snug, warm, and cozy no matter the weather. Whereas the meso/somatotone dislikes telephoning from a booth with the door closed, the ecto/cerebrotone always closes the door tightly for reasons of personal privacy as well as for a cozy feeling. He likes clothing to envelop him, eschews shorts and open-throated sports attire, and is inclined to choose apparel that fits tightly.

12. Unpredictability of attitude. Because the ecto/cerebrotone does not reveal the thought processes behind his decisions, he is hard to predict.

13. Vocal restraint and general restraint of noise. He is a quiet person with a well-modulated voice, usually with excellent diction. He does not, however, speak a great deal. In all his actions he is carefully considerate, with the result that doors close quietly, music is muted, automobile gears are engaged smoothly, and life is lived in a low register of sound.

14. Hypersensitivity to pain. Things seem to hurt the ecto/cerebrotone more than they hurt other types. A pain is a deep-seated, shocking, horrible experience to him with lasting effects, while to the muscular meso/somatotone pain is an enemy to be conquered, and to the roly-poly endo/viscerotone pain is quickly forgotten and rather easily endured. The lingering sting of a severe burn is constantly on the mind of the ecto/cerebrotone. The other two types either become so involved with the outside world as to momentarily forget the burn or accept its nagging pain as a challenge to manhood.

15. Poor sleep habits, chronic fatigue. Because the ecto/cerebrotone never really quite relaxes his mental activities, sleep is a difficult state for him to enter. To relax is to lower one's control of self, yet to relax is the *sine qua non* of sleep. Consequently, unable to lose himself, he tosses at night, thinking through the day's activities, reconstructing the problems of the day, and getting farther and farther from sleep. The entire mental tightrope that he walks keeps him chronically fatigued.

16. Youthful intentness and manner of appearance. This is the person whose age is very difficult to guess from appearance. While the endo/viscerotone is the St. Bernard dog of the species, being easygoing, ambling, friendly, hard to arouse to anger, and the meso/somatotone is the boxer or aggressive German shepherd police dog who bristles with muscle and snarls at threatening overtures, the ecto/cerebrotone is a cross between the dandified French

poodle with high intelligence and the fox terrier with sleek coat and quick movements. The ecto/cerebrotone dresses well, looks young, and stays that way even into advanced age.

17. Vertical mental cleavage, introversion. The third of Sheldon's types likes to think things through to their ultimate sources. Rather than follow the crowd in his avocational pursuits like the endo/viscerotone, he prefers, for example, to become an expert on fourteenth-century tapestries. He would like most to specialize, perhaps, in the tapestries of a particular country, or a particular group of weavers. To go deep, to be thorough, and by all means to be exhaustive is his way, whether it be his vocation or avocation. For this reason he often becomes a dedicated researcher or scientist, working away from the mainstream of life, devoting himself to studying the mating habits of the Galapagos turtle or the use of the pronoun in early hieroglyphic tablets. In so doing he can avoid people, people being unpredictable, demanding, and confusing.

18. Resistance to alcohol (key characteristic). The thin man of the ecto/cerebrotonic personality does not like alcohol, and if he does imbibe, it is only to make a ritual of collecting wines or exotic liquors but hardly for the effect they produce. For to the ecto/cerebrotone, to be drunk is to lose possession of one's faculties, and to lose control of oneself is the worst of all possible living states. He rejects, resists, and abstains from alcohol, not on moral grounds, but on personal fear of being incapable of controlling his own actions. A "small adequate red wine" is much to be preferred to the grossness of drinks that are usually consumed in quantities. Beer, unless it is a very special imported foreign variety, is vulgar. The delicate aperitif is much to be preferred.

19. Need of solitude when troubled (key characteristic). Perhaps the reader will recall that the endo/viscerotone turned to people when he had problems, and the meso/somatotone turned to action when he had problems. The ecto/cerebrotone just turns away, to be by himself, when he has problems. The outside world of acquaintances never knows how deeply or how often the ecto/cerebrotonic personality with the ectomorphic body suffers. He suffers alone. He considers having problems a sign of weakness. He does not wish to appear weak in front of his fellow man. Since he does not possess the aggressive strength of the meso/somatotone, he withdraws within himself. Such withdrawal obviously removes him from professional counseling help. Thus, he may accentuate his problem as it becomes more and more centripetally directed into himself until complete withdrawal from society results.

20. Orientation toward the later periods of life. Even as an adolescent, the ecto/cerebrotone acts older than his contemporaries. He is sedate, they are boisterous; he is polite, they are rough and crude; he appears well dressed, they are sloppy; he likes and prefers to be alone much of the time, they make

cult of doing what the gang does. The ecto/cerebrotone is "old before his ime" in the opinion of family and friends.

Those things which elderly people most prefer and enjoy can be said to escribe the true ectomorphic body with the ecto/cerebrotonic behavior.

PHYSIQUE OR BODY STRUCTURE

Having put together the two primary components of Sheldon's theory, body type and behavior, and discussed them at some length as they would appear in perfect types, we need to describe the development of Sheldon's work as he outlined the three basic types of body, the refinements of his work, and the primary and secondary characteristics of the body types.

Morphogenotype—Fundamentally what Sheldon is interested in is the morphogenotype as it is correlated to man's behavioral self. But the morphogenotype, which is man considered at the earliest beginning, and on through all ages of his development as an organic structure, is obviously denied as an avenue of research. Implied in such a study are multitudes of variables for each single human being. Further implied in the morphogenotypic type of study are the ramifications of Darwin's work, Mendel's work, and the entire history of man from whatever he once was to his present state of existence physiologically. To study a single human being, then, from this approach, is to trace his ancestry from the beginning, a manifestly impossible task.

Phenotype—The phenotype is man's body as we see it at the moment. In some degree it is like a photograph. The photograph shows what it is, how it looks, the size, the conformation, the present moment of fact. It does not, however, reveal the history of the picture. We do not know what went on in the past other than what we can infer from the present picture, and we are completely unable to predict any of the future, again except by highly conjectural inference.

Therefore, Sheldon felt it was mandatory to construct a third measure of man which would bring together the two ends of the continuous morphogenotype–phenotype.

Somatotype—This is Sheldon's answer to bringing continuity into a consideration of the two aspects of man's organic life: the morphogenotype and the phenotype. The somatotype is man's body in regard to its past, and all the ramifications which that can entail, and an attempt to bring this information together with what we can see of his body in the precise present moment as well as to amalgamate these two factors into what we may expect of the organism in the future. Sheldon cautions that this may be done only if the organism has not undergone violent injury or disturbing conditions of nutrition; that is to say, that a fairly normal kind of life is being, and will be, led by the organism. He feels that somatotyping as a method is creating a "pathway" which the body will travel "under standard conditions" of existence. The interesting and involved method by which somatotyping is done by Sheldon and his coworkers will be considered in the section following, wherein his objective measurement principle is discussed.

PRIMARY BODY SOMATOTYPES

The endomorph—As we have previously seen, this is the human being who is inclined to be rounded in figure and soft of muscle. Sheldon used the term *endomorph* because the functional characteristics of the endodermal layers of the body most closely describe this type: visceral, digestive, etc. In appearance, the endomorph looks most like the caricaturist's drawing of the roly-poly clown. The fat tends to distribute around the trunk of the body. The breasts are inclined to be heavy and somewhat pendulous. The lips are usually thick. The neck is short. The legs and arms are shorter in ratio to the trunk than they are for the other two types.[2]

The mesomorph—The mesodermal layer of the embryo, the middle layer, eventually gives rise to the muscles that man develops in postnatal life. Sheldon therefore gave the name *mesomorph* to the second type he defined, the muscular, athletic person with strong bone structure. The mesomorph usually has wide shoulders, a tapering figure, and wide chest expansion, and he is likely to be average-to-tall in height. He is rarely inclined to flabbiness, and his stomach is flat and well held by superb, striated muscles.

The ectomorph—The brain and central nervous system emanate from the ectodermal layers of the embryo. Sheldon used the term *ectomorph* for the third type of body build in his somatotypic system. The ectomorph has, for his size, the largest central nervous system and brain of all three types. He is deficient in thickness of the arms, hands, trunk, legs and neck. He is linear and thin, and his skull is angular. He gives the impression of being delicate however, his strength may be surprising, for all his wiriness. The ratio of surface to mass of his body is in favor of the surface of his body, the mass being proportionately much less than the skin surface. In short, he has much more skin in relation to his body mass than does the endomorph (who is just the opposite) or the mesomorph (whose balance is about normal). Having more skin and thus more afferent nerve receptors in relation to the remainder of his interior mass, the ectomorph is more acutely stimulated by externally

2 This short description in no way takes the place of Sheldon's exactitude in measuring body types. All that is intended is to give the reader some clues to what Sheldon measures Anyone interested in this technique is urged to consult Sheldon's *Atlas of Men*, 1954.

erived pain. A sharp blow falls upon less body to absorb shock than it does
or the muscular mesomorph or the fatty-tissued endomorph.

ECONDARY BODY SOMATOTYPES

heldon was well aware that there could be and is wide variation within the
omatotyping of a single individual. For example, as was stated in describing
ie "pure" types, it is almost impossible to find a pure endomorphic body or
ie pure viscerotonic temperament that would correlate with this body type.
ll of Sheldon's work is based on the relativity of body to temperament for
roups. He would submit that there are always individual variations from the
verage, but as he found in his work, the individual variations are very few
hen all the data are considered. We now turn our attention to the indi-
idual variations that occur only in body type without correlating the body to
 temperament type. The body–temperament variations will be dealt with
nder the heading "Continuous Variables Principle."

Dysplasia—Sheldon discovered inconsistencies, but not many, among the
iree previous somatotypes as represented in one person's body. That is, a
erson may have the fleshy trunk of an endomorph and the muscular legs and
rms of a mesomorph. He discovered a few uneven physiques, for example,
ith the angular skull and skin structure of the ectomorph but the remainder
f the physique quite in harmony with the rounded endomorph. Other
ombinations were also possible. These inconsistencies were termed *dysplasia*
r the "d" index in somatotyping. It should be emphasized that there were
ery few types of combinations. The term *dysplasia* comes from the work of
retschmer, an early exponent of the relationship of behavior to physique.

In his initial work Sheldon found that the ectomorphic body type was
iore dysplasia prone than were the endomorph or mesomorph, who were
clined to be purer types. He also found in another small study in 1940 that
ollege students seemed to have more coherent patterns of physique than a
sychotic population. Although it is considered a secondary component in his
lassification system, the "d" index is fundamental to Sheldon's somatotypes.

Pyknic practical joke (PPJ)—Though we shall discuss the constancy of the
omatotypes later in this chapter, the PPJ type refers to a person who has a
iuscular mesomorphic body in adolescence but in later life balloons out into
besity to become an endomorph. This type does not have to have eaten large
mounts of food in order to change types. The basic type was endomorph in
ie beginning, but maturity was needed to reveal its true manifestations.
hus, a secondary factor of somatotyping is sufficient age to get a more
ccurate picture of the physique. It is not a question of constancy but a
uestion of delayed development. Sheldon feels that at about the age of thirty
ie true type of body form will emerge regardless of amounts of food

consumed. Gross nutritional deficiencies will, of course, alter the physiqu
but the major relationships of head to trunk, trunk to limbs, and so on, th
are used as indexes will remain constant even in the face of stringent nutr
tional difficulties.

Textural aspect—The secondary component, called *textural aspect* or "t
index, is Sheldon's acknowledgment that some people are more pleasing i
appearance to their fellow men than are others. In some sense, then, it refe
to beauty or handsomeness as any culture would define it. Given identic:
ectomorphic types whose bodies measure similarly, one of them may appe:
much more handsome to us than the other. One mesomorph may appe:
gross, the other Adonis-like; one endomorph sleek and well-rounded, th
other blubbery, though all would be identical in measurements to the oth
within their somatotypes. This quality of aesthetic pleasingness Sheldon fe
should be acknowledged, even though it is of secondary importance in th
immediate phenotype. The "t" index does, of course, influence how societ
will react toward the individual, especially if female. The woman with a lo
"t" index may be called "healthy," while the woman with a high "t" inde
may be called "beautiful," yet each carries the same bodily proportions.

Gynandromorphy—The "g" index refers to the degree of hermaphroditis:
that the body possesses. Hermaphroditism is the condition, in this case, c
having both kinds of sexual characteristics, not necessarily both kinds c
sexual organs. Consequently, a male having a high "g" index is very feminir
in appearance though he may not have organically a hermaphroditic structur
The body is soft, the hips wide, the breasts rather fully developed, and the
is a fine, feminine texture to the facial skin. This characteristic is, again,
secondary one in Sheldon's system. It does indicate his willingness to broade
the system beyond only three body types. Also, as in the case of the "t" inde:
this characteristic would have an immediate effect upon society, and th
individual's society would in turn affect the individual. The degree woul
depend upon the societal mores.

Male–female aspects—It must be apparent by now even to the most casu:
reader that Sheldon's theory is essentially a male one, concerned with th
study of male physique and its relationship to behavior. This emphasis
accidental on Sheldon's part, nor does he conclude that female somatotypir
will necessarily parallel male somatotyping. As we shall see, he found som
fundamental differences. Why then did he specialize in typing men's bodi
and build up such a formidable array of statistics on only men? The reason
very practical. Somatotyping (as we shall later discuss) requires studyir
photographs and making measurements of the nude body. Society will hard
tolerate such research on female subjects, but anyone familiar with milita:
procedures will recognize that the nude male is an acceptable phenomeno

or study, providing the research is conducted with discretion. Sheldon is well
aware of the one-sidedness of his approach, and he can scarcely be con-
demned for the slant of his work. Lest the reader feel that his theory is to be
limited forever to maleness, recent reports indicate that through screening,
masking silhouette techniques, and sensible controls some preliminary somatotyping has been done with females, although the research is not of the
scope achieved with male populations.

What, then, do the data indicate in comparing somatotyping of women
and men? (This has nothing to do with gynandromorphy, which is concerned
with the feminine characteristics of men and masculine characteristics of
women; here we are comparing men vis-à-vis women.) Sheldon is at present
working on a companion book to his *Atlas of Men*, to be entitled *Atlas of
Women*, in which he will report his ongoing research with somatotyping
females. One wonders if a third work will emerge in which the picture will be
drawn for the total population.

To date, Sheldon reports that women are more prone to the mixing of
endomorphic–ectomorphic body types than are men. A consideration of the
total population shows women also more inclined toward endomorphy than
are men. There is further a smaller range in body types of women than there is
in men. Dysplasia is more prevalent among women than men. Despite these
differences, Sheldon believes that his original theory for men will and does
hold true for women. In short, there is a unique relationship between a
woman's body type and her corresponding behavioral pattern, just as there is
for the men he studied. He feels the basis of his theoretical foundation is
sound and scientific.

Continuous Variable Principle

In the process of his work, Sheldon felt that a fundamental principle concerning the typing of human bodies was that practically no body is a pure type but
always has features of the other two types connected with it. He further
maintained that this condition of continuity of bodies holds equally true for
temperament. No one appears to be exclusively one kind of body and/or
temperament but has within him the physique and behavioral characteristics
of all three. He is part endo/viscerone, meso/somatotone, ecto/cerebrotone.
But he is always more of one type than he is of the other two. To handle this
continuous variable of body–body to behavior–behavior, Sheldon constructed
a numbering system that is both unique and also a tremendous refinement
over the work of his predecessors, both of whom we shall read more about
later on.

Sheldon uses a numerical system to indicate the amounts of variation
there are in body–behavior types. The numbers range from an absolute
minimum, which would be 1, to an absolute maximum, which would be 7.
The range of 1 to 7 applies for body types as well as behavioral patterns. (As

we shall see later in studying his principle that personality can be measured
objectively, the body is measured on a 1 to 7 scale, as are the behavior
patterns, and the total of these is also derived on a 1 to 7 scale.) One can see
now by consulting Table 11.2 that a tremendous number of variations in
personality can result from using Sheldon's methods. Theoretically, it should
be possible to have 343 different somatotypes, but Sheldon found in two
studies, one with 4000 college students and the other with 40,000 males, that
he was able to define distinctly only 76 in the first study and 88 in the
second.

In the numbering system, the endo/viscerotone figure is always given
first, the meso/somatotone figure is always given second, and the ecto/
cerebrotone figure is always given last. Thus, the numbers 1–1–7 indicate a
person who is very low in endo/viscerotonia, very low in meso/somatotonia,
and extremely high in ecto/cerebrontonia. To explore further the possibilities
we offer three examples:

(A) 7–1–7: An individual who has equal amounts of endo/viscerotonia
and ecto/cerebrotonic characteristics but who is extremely low in meso/
somatotonic characteristics. We may suppose that this is an ambivalent
person who is torn between liking people and wanting to be alone. He
supposedly vacillates between the two extremes and will be inclined to be
somewhat unhappy about resolving the ambivalency of his life.

(B) 7–3–1: A person who is high in endo/viscerotonia with some overtone
of the meso/somatotone but almost no feeling of the ecto/cerebrotone.
He acts like the ebullient viscerotone, but we may assume that when
pushed too far in certain circumstances he will exhibit the aggressiveness
of the meso/somatotone. One thing he apparently never does is go off
by himself. He either wants people to like him or failing that will consider controlling them.

(C) 1–7–1: The nearly pure meso/somatotone, who has all the capacities
physically and temperamentally of the "pure" type we talked about in
the beginning of the chapter.

This analysis of people can become a fascinating game, but the point
being made here is that Sheldon's system is highly flexible and does not mold
people because of a body type. No one, apparently, fits into any kind of set
pattern of behavior. This fact is such an integral part of Sheldon's scheme
that the writer has chosen to consider it a fundamental principle of the
theory.

Inductive–Empirical Principle

Sheldon came upon his theory not by philosophizing or by any armchair
techniques but through prodigious numbers of hours dedicated to the exploration of man and the relationship of his body to his behavior, using the

chnique he called somatotyping. Sheldon patiently built up his theory,
udy by study, within a laboratory setting and with full acknowledgment of
search controls. In trying to prove that man's genetic past and biological
akeup play a crucial part in the development of his personality (morpho-
nesis) and in being restricted to phenotypic methods, he evolved and is still
rsistently accruing, via his somatotypic methods, a vast fund of information
uch clearer and more defensible than that of his predecessors. Sheldon
ilds up his data in current research form and then draws his conclusions.
his is his principle *modus operandi* for all his work. Actually, Sheldon has
ot himself indicated a theory, nor has he purported to claim one. His main
forts have been to explore the empirically derived data he has, with the
sumption that there is strong enough evidence to indicate a continuity
tween body and behavior. Although he states no theory as such, he
bsumes, as he must, a theoretical rationale; otherwise he would have
rminated his work long ago.

Many students are familiar with or will recognize the progenitor of
nstitutional psychology in the name of Hippocrates. Thus, Sheldon, like
any other investigators of man's behavior, has roots that go deeply into the
ist. Although Sheldon's work owes no direct obeisance to that of Hippoc-
tes (which was more oriented to an endocrine system), there are unique
rallels between them. Hippocrates also created a typology of body and a
pology of behavior—his being, however, more discrete and with no provi-
on for variable types. Sheldon's interest in constitutional medicine reflects
e early belief of Hippocrates that certain types of body were disposed
ward certain types of diseases. Hippocrates suggested that there were two
nds of bodies, the first roughly corresponding with Sheldon's ectomorph
id the second being something of a combination of Sheldon's endomorph
id mesomorph, with emphasis on endomorphy. Their behavior would also
ughly correspond to the Sheldonian descriptions. In addition to the di-
otomized types of men, Hippocrates believed that all men could be divided
to four behavior patterns, or, as he called them, four humors. The humors,
tterned after the fluids of the body, were black bile, yellow bile, red bile,
id white bile. Each person was assumed to be predominant in one of the
les and consequently had a temperament that corresponded to that bile.

Later, a French scientist named Rostan began the actual measurement of
dy–personality types and became the forerunner of much of the work now
ing done by the constitutional psychologists. Publishing in 1824, he stated
at there were four types of bodies with correlated personalities, which he
med the *digestive, muscular, cerebral,* and *respiratory.* One can see the
ose affinity in results between Rostan's first three types and Sheldon's
domorph, mesomorph, and ectomorph.

In 1909 an Italian anthropologist, Viola, refined the techniques of
easurement with much more detailed procedures. He also became con-

vinced that there were three types of bodies, with some secondary qualities t
be considered. Viola actually had two separate types called the *microsplancí
nic* (small body with long legs and arms) and the *macrosplanchnic* (larg
body with short legs and arms). His third type, the *normosplanchnic*, was
combination of the other two types. Viola, however, did little ascribing o
behavioral characteristics to the three types. His contribution lay in tl
refinement of measuring techniques, which were remarkably good for h
day.

Many others come into the picture of constitutional psychology, bu
perhaps the most advanced theory prior to Sheldon's was the work o
Kretschmer, who was a German psychiatrist and whose nomenclature fo
psychoses will be familiar to students of abnormal psychology. Kretschme
also evolved a trichotomized typology. His three body types were called tl
pyknic (short and plump: Sheldon's endomorph and Rostan's digestiv
type), the *athletic* (strong and aggressive: Sheldon's mesomorph an
Rostan's muscular type), and the *asthenic* (thin and lonely: Sheldon's ect
morph and Rostan's cerebral type). If the reader is enchanted by tl
discovery that personality types seem to come in threes, he will recall the eve
more trichotomized approach in the work of Karen Horney. Kretschmer
interest, gained through work with mentally disturbed people, was primari
directed toward studying the propensity of certain body types to succumb t
certain kinds of mental disorders, especially in regard to schizophrenics. F
was a meticulous researcher, and his work is still worth reading as an approac
to the study of body–behavior dynamics in man.

In 1934–1935 Sheldon visited Kretschmer, and he has since paid tribu
to the man who advanced the field of constitutional typology prior to his ow
investigations. Though Sheldon was undoubtedly influenced and certain
interested in Kretschmer's work, he began afresh to gather his own dat
perfect his own techniques, and draw his own conclusions independent o
Kretschmer. Sheldon did not copy Kretschmer; he simply noted with dee
interest what Kretschmer had done and then proceeded to conduct researc
along his own lines.

Sheldon proved, he felt, that certain body types have an affinity fo
specific kinds of mental disorders. He was further convinced that psychosis
but a continuum of normal behavior and *not* as difference in kind o
behavior. This was a revolutionary idea for his time for psychotics were co
sidered to be of the devil and not human at all.

So we find that Sheldon pays a great deal of attention to the uniquene
of each individual, or what we have chosen to call the continuous variable
man's personality. The pattern of relationships, such as 1–1–7, or 3–4–1,
2–5–7, or any combination of these as previously discussed, is of much great
interest to Sheldon than is the so-called pure type. To Sheldon, man is
complex creature, and possibly the key to his dynamics lies in the relationsh
of the body to behavior.

Objective Measurement Principle

There are times in Sheldon's writings when he seems almost obsessed with the objectivity of measurement. He continually cautions against premature judgments concerning typing bodies and behavior and has in his later writings extended the periods of observation almost to the point of utilizing a life-study technique prior to diagnosis. As his work has progressed, the time interval he feels in adequate to study an individual has lengthened.

Interestingly enough, Sheldon and his coworkers approached the problem in two separate but parallel ways: One task group studied the measurement of man's body (the taxonomic approach) while another force of workers initiated and carried on the study of man as he behaves in his everyday life. Thus, two groups, each doing a different thing, progressed almost simultaneously and eventually were brought together so that their separate work was matched. The results for Sheldon upheld his original hypothesis of a unique relationship between body and behavior, even though he was unable to explore the morphogenetic influences, his primary thesis.

First we shall very briefly cover some of the interesting approaches he took to studying man's bodily structure.

BODY

In a beginning study 4000 male college students were photographed, front, back, and side, each standing in front of the same background. Using many judges to examine all the variant body forms, and through quite complicated but controlled methods, Sheldon finally satisfied himself that there were three basic body forms: the now familiar endo, ecto, and meso morphs. In addition, he instituted a tremendous variety of physical measurements which were tried on the same 4000 male college students. Through involved analysis, he reduced these measurements to seventeen. All physical measurements were in relationship to the height of the student-subject. A coworker, S. S. Stevens, invented a machine which, with a relatively untrained operator, could make the same seventeen measurements, but it was eventually discarded since, in further work, Sheldon discovered that the photographs were as accurate as the actual physical measurement.

As many as 40,000 males have been somatotyped by Sheldon and his coworkers in refining the technique. As his work has progressed, he has strongly advocated a set of photographs taken over a prolonged period (the optimal length of time is not stated because of individual differences) along with as complete a medical hostory as is possible and as many biological tests as are practical to administer. Failing these optimal conditions, however, one may still utilize his system of somatotyping through the photographic technique.

It is hoped that the reader's curiosity has been sufficiently whetted so

that he will examine Sheldon's *Atlas of Men,* in which the entire procedure
discussed and illustrated with many photographs for reference and tables
eliminate computation. The measurement method is called the Somatoty
Performance Test.

BEHAVIOR

Next, Sheldon turned his attention to the measurement of behavior with th
same inductive approach. A list of 650 behavioral traits was culled from
study of the vast literature concerning personality, behavior, and any type o
work which seemed to describe man's behavior. After scrutinizing the 65
items, Sheldon and his collaborators reduced the number to 50 by eliminatir
terms that overlapped, terms that were so nebulous as to defy definition, ar
those that seemed so insignificant as not to describe behavior at all. Thirt
three males were selected as subjects for validating the list of 50 items. Eac
subject was observed and studied through intensive interviews for approx
mately twelve months. The results of the ratings which Sheldon and h
coworkers made (using again a seven-point scale just as they had for studyir
body types) were correlated, and certain ratings seemed to group themselve
in clusters of commonality. These clusters were considered to represent th
same kind of behavior pattern. For a rating to be included within a cluster,
had to correlate positively a +.60 or higher and negatively with the oth
clusters at —.30. From these data Sheldon discovered that only 22 of th
originally culled 50 items were meaningful, and that these 22 items of beha
ioral description clustered statistically *into three groups.* So once again th
three-ness of things emerged from Sheldon's work just as it had for the boc
types. Both procedures, of course, were conducted by statistical analysis. Th
three clusters describing behavior were the aforementioned *viscerotoni
somatotonia,* and *cerebrotonia* with the meanings previously described.

Sheldon continued to refine his preliminary results by conducting eigh
more trial studies. He added, subtracted, and changed the trait descriptio
and their combinations, always using his preliminary study criteria: i.e., tra
descriptions to be included in a cluster must correlate with each other a
+.60 and be mutually exclusive to other clusters at —.30.

By a ninth and final study he had refined his method sufficiently so tha
with a group of 100 subjects, measured on 78 behavioral trait descriptions, I
was able to select 20 traits (all meeting the criteria) for each type (viscer
tonia, somatotonia, cerebrotonia) for a total of 60 descriptive terms wit
which he felt behavior could be sensibly measured. These 60 terms compri
his *Scale for Temperament,* the scale which was used in extended form t
begin the present chapter. He has continued to use this temperament scal
virtually unchanged, in all of his subsequent work.

The next logical step, of course, was to select a group of subjects and t

vestigate the degree of relationship between their behavior and their bodies
᾿ measuring both and comparing the results.

)DY–BEHAVIOR RELATIONSHIPS

ɔr the study of the statistical relationship between body and behavior, which
ok over five years, Sheldon and his staff selected 200 white male subjects
ho would be willing and able to participate over so long a period. The
bjects were by and large college students (who, of course, are generally
᾿ailable for four years) and professional personnel who would be inclined to
aintain rapport with the study. Over an extended period of time the sub-
cts were observed and interviewed with care through use of the Scale of
ɛmperament. Only after they had been classified by the scale were they
ɛasured for bodily characteristics again by use of the seven-point scale that
ɹeldon had created.

The denouement of Sheldon's work was even more satisfactory than he
ιd hoped, for the relationships between body and behavior were startlingly
gh. Table 11.2 reveals the basic findings of this study. In Sheldon's words,
These are higher correlations than we expected to find. . . ."

A study of Table 11.2 indicates that viscerotonic behavior correlates with
ɛ endomorphic body at .79, somatotonic behavior correlates with the
ɛsomorphic body at .82, and the cerebrotonic behavior pattern correlates
th the ectomorphic body type at .83. All three correlations are significantly
gh in a statistical sense. Equally of interest is the amount of relationship
at does *not* exist among the six components of the matrix.

BLE 11.2. *Correlations between body
and behavior*

	BODY TYPES		
HAVIOR TYPES	ENDOMORPH (fat)	MESOMORPH (muscular)	ECTOMORPH (thin)
scerotonia (likes people)	.79		
matotonia (controls people)	−.29	.82	
ɛrebrotonia (avoids people)	−.32	−.58	.83

Sheldon felt that because of the high correlations resulting from this
ιdy it was possible that he was measuring "the same thing at different levels
. . . expression." Putting the proposition another way, would it not be
᾿ssible to measure temperament alone or measure body type alone and thus
᾿ able to predict the opposite characteristic without having to measure it?

He would, of course, admit that this technique is primarily a group assumption and that any single individual would vary from the mean data. Nevertheless, it appears that Sheldon may have put an extremely valuable tool into the hands of the student of personality.

And so the objective measurement technique of Sheldon, which he so faithfully followed as a principal guide to his work, was for him successful beyond his expectations.

Constancy of Somatotype Principle

Although Sheldon has advocated more and more in his recent writings that the researcher take repeated "readings" of the subject's body and conduct exhaustive interviews and observations in somatotyping, he is not suggesting this procedure because the somatotype is likely to change, but because one must arrive at an *accurate* somatotype. The type does not change, but the investigator may be misled by fragments of information in typing the body and/or behavior. (See, for example, the Pyknic Practical Joke type mentioned previously.)

Sheldon admits that people do grow fatter if they eat too much and that in senility the skeletal structure does decrease slightly, but he stoutly maintains that the *ratio* between the various parts of the body remains constant. In some of the cases which he has studied over a ten-year period the weights of the subjects increased or decreased as much as a hundred pounds without altering the basic characteristics of the somatotype. Apparently the ectomorph may gain weight, but this change does not make him want to be with people any more than he did in the past. He remains a cerebrotone in an ectomorphic body despite his nutritional digressions. Likewise one may starve an endomorph, but he is still inclined to seek people when in trouble and be happy when drunk. As Hall and Lindzey in their classic text state, "Sheldon suggests that as a starved mastiff does not become a poodle, so a starved mesomorph does not become an ectomorph."

What particularly interests Sheldon in his measurements is the ratios of head–neck, chest–trunk, arms, stomach–trunk, and legs, and all in relation to the entire skeletal structure. These, he maintains, are constant. What is not constant is the distribution of fatty tissue and, most obviously, the inaccuracies of measurement.

Behavioral Environment Principle

Oddly enough for an investigator who is called a constitutional psychologist and whose efforts have been directed along organic measurement lines Sheldon is not at all unaware of the environmental influences upon the dividual. He does not eschew them as much as he pleads that one always vestigate the total field in which the organism operates before making even tentative diagnosis of type. It is important to note, however, that it is *havior* that Sheldon is talking about primarily; hence his fervent admoni- >n, which has grown more frequent as his work has continued, that the searcher-classifier must take into account all the aspects of the human's *havior via depth interviews and direct observations to be conducted over tended periods of time.

Thus, we have dealt with man's personality as Sheldon, the constitu- >nal psychologist, describes it and as we have interpreted that description. 'e shall see how the Sheldonian approach deals with the problem of plaining why man does the things he does, using the same rubric as in the apter on Freud.

ELIMITATIONS

he author has in no way attempted to be exhaustive in the treatment of eldon's work but only tried to interpret the major aspects of his constitu- >nal psychology.

To get the true flavor of his work, one should read especially Sheldon's cond major work, *The Varieties of Temperament: A Psychology of Consti- tional Differences* (1942) or his *Atlas of Men, A Guide for Somatotyping e Adult Male at All Ages.* The latter is absolutely necessary for any gnificant use of his technique.

XPLAINING HUMAN BEHAVIOR VIA HELDON'S CONSTITUTIONAL PSYCHOLOGY

may appear that using Sheldon's theory to explain man's behavior would oduce a pronounced, singular explanation: The morphogenesis of the body fluences man's behavior. Although this may be true to some extent, there e further considerations. For example, which kind of body form typically akes which kind of response to marriage, perversions, and the other seven e situations being used to explain man's behavior? Keeping in mind again at no pure types exist in Sheldon's system, one may proceed as though each dy type were involved individually. Thus, why does the endo/viscerotone, e meso/somatotone, the ecto/cerebrotone get married, and so on?

The reader is now invited to try his hand at explaining human behavior ing Sheldon's theory. An example of this may be found in Chapter 2 in nnection with Freud's theory. The criteria are also set forth there.

The suggested seven behavioral phenomena are as follows: marriage, rversions, suicide, lawbreaking, supranatural being, humor, smoking, recrea- >n, and psychoses–neuroses.

PREDICTING HUMAN BEHAVIOR VIA
SHELDON'S CONSTITUTIONAL THEORY

Sheldon, perhaps more than most of the other theorists, is very concern
about the predictability of man's behavior. Although his interest is mainly
predicting the results he will get from his research, the connection betwe
this and a general prediction of man's behavior is quite direct, for he de
with man as a behaving animal in the total life scene, not with just o
aspect of his behavior, such as eye-blink response.

Personal Prediction

Let us first turn to predicting human behavior from the reader's own fran
of reference. In order to give this some structure, the reader is referred to t
list of behavioral characteristics near the beginning of the chapter. A stro
note of caution: This estimation in no way substitutes for Sheldon's Scale
Temperament although the sixty items he used are involved. It is likewi
pure nonsense for the reader to attempt to diagnose his friends for the
edification with such a crude instrument in the hands of an untrain
diagnostician. The method simply adds some grains of objectivity in t
evaluation of Sheldon's theory when practiced by the reader.

    After the list has been used, the reader may be more objective
deciding the predictability of Sheldon's work strictly from his own experien
with the system.

Instructions for Estimating the Somatotypes

    1. Select a person for study who has been well known to you for yea
such as a friend or member of the family.

    2. Start with the endo/viscerotone and consider each item carefully as
whether it applies *most of the time* to the selected subject. If it seems
describe him fairly accurately, make a checkmark for that item. Do not
concerned if it seems to contradict another item at the moment. If t
activity is one which you are unable to observe or judge for the subject, do n
mark it.

    3. After you have carefully considered and marked the items for all thr
descriptions, add each in a column separately (one for the endo/visceroton
one for the meso/somatotone, and one for the ecto/cerebrotone) and wri
the total at the bottom of the column. The totals give a *rough approximatic*
of the endo/viscerotonic, meso/somatotonic, and ecto/cerebrotonic chara
teristics of the subject.

4. To check the accuracy of his rating, the reader may do one of the following (these do not necessarily evaluate Sheldon's work but rather his method as a predicting agency):

a. Put the rating aside and attempt another one some months later; compare the results.

b. Have the subject rate himself or herself and then compare the ratings with yours.

c. Reverse the process by having someone rate you; then rate yourself and compare the results.

d. Select a subject well known to you and a group of your acquaintances; have each one rate the person separately; compare your results as to typology.

e. Select a subject sufficiently well known in history and biography, such as Lincoln, Napoleon; rate this person, and compare your rating with the general opinion of historians or others who have rated the personage.

f. (This method comes closer to the task of prediction.) Have your parents rate you as they knew you ten years ago. Does the rating still describe you? Do the same thing yourself by rating a friend or family member as you knew him some years back; does he still behave in this manner?

None of the above procedures prove that Sheldon's method can predict human behavior, but they do help the student of personality to apply this theory directly to a life situation and thus to draw some empirical conclusions about it. In this respect a degree of prediction evolves out of agreement with one's own acceptance of the theory. In short, should the ratings equate to one's living experience of another human being, one might further assume that the system has enough merit when applied to others to lead toward prediction.

Scientific or Laboratory Prediction

How shall we judge the scientific predictability of Sheldon's work? What is the evidence both for and against constitutional psychology? This theory is an example of the rise and fall of a theory in affecting research.

It is almost traditional in introductory psychology courses to use Sheldon's findings as an example of biased research: It could not possibly come out that neatly, the statistics were inadequate, and the experimenter bias of rating both sets of ratings is evident. Where were the traditional control groups (one might also ask the same question of Piaget)? How can one manipulate the data to test for significant differences? These criticisms and many more have been advanced by genuinely concerned psychologists and a few overly righteous experimenters whose own work may suffer some from crystal purity. In psychological research it is always easier to attack another's research than to defend one's own. To do the former connotes rigorous intellectual scientism. To attempt the latter brings about a bashful modesty, some question begging, and an implied plea that truth cannot be discovered overnight. Sheldon appears to have stated his findings unequivocably and lets them speak for themselves. He has attempted almost no rebuttals, which is irritating to his critics, and he has produced almost no follow-up research.

Why then has Sheldon's work not dried up and shriveled away? (Almost all introductory psychology texts continue to discuss somatotyping.) There are at least three reasons. (1) Somatotyping has a long history, as we have seen in the efforts of Hippocrates, Rostan, Viola, and particularly Kretschmer. (2) At times one gets the feeling that Sheldon's work lingers in the textbooks as a convenient object for attack. (3) Finally, the general populace uses it in daily descriptions ("He's fat and jolly"; "sort of a big brute of a guy"—brutes are rarely described as skinny or short), and body–behavior descriptions are used generously in drama and literature ("Methinks yon Cassius hath a lean and hungry look"; "Falstaff, thy bloated fool"). In addition to description it is not easy for a petite person to be aggressive in society with anything other than verbal insult.

However, none of the above directly relates to scientific research although it may be influential. What is the status of Sheldon's work? It may be changing.

Shortly after Sheldon's 1942 book, *The Varieties of Temperament,* and his 1954 *Atlas of Men,* a degree of interest was shown in replicating his work. The results were mixed. Some research appeared to support his findings (Child, 1950; Glueck and Glueck, 1956; Glueck, 1959; Wittman et al., 1948). Other investigators found no support for Sheldon's theory that body and behavior were uniquely correlated, and in some instances the rebuttals were openly hostile (Eysenck, 1947; Howells, 1952; Lasker, 1947; Newman, 1952; Thurstone, 1946). One newer rebuttal has also been reported (Pivnicki, 1964).

Now we have one of the most knowledgeable students of personality theory, Gardner Lindzey, taking a clear and astute look at the status and value of "morphology and behavior." His rational exposition generalizes that "it appears altogether reasonable for one to expect to observe *important associations* between morphology and behavior," and ". . . the most firmly based evidence we now possess suggests the existence of *important associations* between morphology and behavior (just as reason would assert) while the magnitude of this relation . . . remains to be determined precisely" (Lindzey and Hall, 1965; italics added).

On what basis does Lindzey reexamine the relationships between body and behavior—not always, however, from a strictly Sheldonian approach? Supportive studies range from England's Borstal system (Gibbons, 1963) to Cortes' 1961 doctoral dissertation, "Physique, Need for Achievement and Delinquency," on 100 American delinquent boys, wherein we find, "these results almost exactly parallel the findings of the Gluecks and provide further confirmation for the original association reported by Sheldon." An additional study from England of delinquent females found them to be "shorter and heavier in build, more muscular and fat" than a control group of female college students (Epps and Parnell, 1952). Moreover, ". . . it is now carefully documented for women that linearity (ectomorphy) is negatively associated with rate of physical and biological maturation" (McNeil and Levison, 1963). And finally, Walker's study concerning body build and behavior components in 125 nursery school boys and girls concluded "that in this group of preschool children *important associations* do exist between individuals' physiques and particular behavior characteristics. Further, these associations show considerable similarity to those described by Sheldon for college-aged men, though the strength of association is not as strong as he reports" (Walker, 1962; italics added).

It should be most significant in the previous supportive studies that "important associations" are stressed and not causality.

In reviewing all this literature one is cognizant of the fact that techniques other than Sheldon's were at times used. It may be pertinent to question older studies confronting Sheldon's findings particularly when they were not true replications but used different methods. Understandably the results might very well be different.

◼ SUMMARY

Sheldon searches for a relationship between the genetic–biological aspects of man, which he calls the *morphogenotypes,* and the behavior of man, which he calls *temperament.* Knowing that morphogenotype research is not possible, he advocates the use of phenotyping. Phenotyping is done through measurement and photographs and leads to somatotyping, which is the method of evaluating body types and behavioral patterns.

From his data, Sheldon has constructed a theory which indicates to him a direct and positive correlation between man's body and his behavior. Certain body types seem to behave in certain ways. Primary body somatotypes with their corresponding behavioral characteristics he named as follows:

Endomorph—Viscerotonia
Mesomorph—Somatotonia
Ectomorph—Cerebrotonia

Secondary body somatotypes he classified as (1) dysplasia—or the "d" index, referring to inconsistencies in the primary types; (2) Pyknic Practical oke (PPJ)—the late developer who looks like a mesomorph in his youth but turns out to be an endomorph in later years; (3) textural aspect—the "t" index which referred to handsomeness or beauty of the body; and (4) gynandromorphy—the so-called "g" index measuring female characteristics in the male and vice versa.

Figure 9 highlights the main features of Sheldon's constitutional psychology. Starting at the center and reading outward with the endomorph, we find he has a body inclined to fleshiness which correlates +.79 with the viscerotonic temperament. The viscerotonic enjoys being with people, he likes such things as beer and food, and he correlates negatively at —.32 with the cerebrotonic and at —.29 with the somatotonic.

FIGURE 9. *Diagrammatic summary of Sheldon's theory.*

Going clockwise, we come to the muscular mesomorph, who correlates with the somatotonic temperament at +.82. Somatotonia describes the person who prefers to control people, play contact sports like football or boxing. Being very dissimilar to the cerebrotonic, he correlates at —.58 with him.

The thin, asthenic ectomorph correlates +.83 with the counterpart mperament of cerebrotonia. His pleasures are exemplified by Bach and ooks, while he continues his solitary way in life *sans* people.

The outstanding features of Figure 9 are not the types, however; the ndamental fact, according to Sheldon, is that all of us have these components in varying degrees within our personalities. Consequently the entire gure is surrounded by the term *personality*. We may suppose that in the gure the equal portions of the three types indicate a 4–4–4 distribution; ieldon used a numerical system to describe the total personality pattern ter having measured the body and behavior of an individual. Thus, the ree lower figures indicate more or less pure types of endo/viscerotone, eso/somatotone and ecto/cerebrotone.

In final summary, then, Sheldon does not state directly that the body ntrols behavior but says that by studying the body one may receive valuable ues to the underlying factors which determine behavior.

BIBLIOGRAPHY

RIMARY SOURCES

OOKS

eldon, W. H., *Psychology and the Promethean Will*. New York: Harper & Row, 1936.
eldon, W. H., S. S. Stevens, and W. B. Tucker, *The Varieties of Human Physique: An Introduction to Constitutional Psychology*. New York: Harper & Row, 1940.

> His introductory book which spells out in detail his methods of measuring the body. Stevens, a Harvard experimental psychologist of considerable talent, has contributed much to this.

eldon, W. H., and S. S. Stevens, *The Varieties of Temperament: A Psychology of Constitutional Differences*. New York: Harper & Row, 1942.

> Probably one of his most interesting books to read as he develops the measurement technique for behavior.

Sheldon, W. H., Constitutional factors in personality, in J. McV. Hunt (ed.
Personality and the Behavior Disorders. New York: Ronald Press, 1944, p
526–549.

> Concise exposition of his work to this date. The volume itself is we
> worth reading for the serious student of personality.

Sheldon, W. H., *Early American Cents, 1793–1814.* New York: Harper & Rov
1949.

Sheldon, W. H., E. M. Hartl, and E. McDermott, *Varieties of Delinquent Youtl
An Introduction to Constitutional Psychiatry.* New York: Harper & Rov
1949.

> Longitudinal study started in 1939 comparing college students with i
> mates of a rehabilitation home. Consists of many biological sketches.

Sheldon, W. H., C. W. Dupertuis, and E. McDermott, *Atlas of Men: A Guie
for Somatotyping the Adult Male of All Ages.* New York: Harper & Rov
1954.

> Sheldon's *magnum opus* to date. Some of his earlier positions have bee
> modified or refined. If only one source is to be used to study Sheldon, th
> is the best.

PERIODICALS

Child, I. L., and W. H. Sheldon, The correlation between components
physique and scores on certain psychological tests, *Charact. & Pers.*, 1941, 1
23–24.

Wittman, P., W. H. Sheldon, and C. J. Katz, A study of the relationship betwee
constitutional variations and fundamental psychotic behavior reactions,
Nerv. Ment. Dis., 1948, *108,* 470–476.

Sheldon, W. H., Mesomorphs in mischief, *Contemp. Psychol.*, 1957, 2, 125–12

SUGGESTED READINGS

BOOKS

Eysenck, H. J., *Dimensions of Personality.* London: Routledge, 1947.

Gibbons, T. C. N., *Psychiatric Studies of Borstal Lads.* London: Oxford Unive
sity Press, 1963.

Glueck, S. (ed.), *The Problem of Delinquency.* Boston: Houghton Mifflin, 195

> See section on body types and delinquency.

Glueck, S., and E. Glueck, *Physique and Delinquency.* New York: Harper & Rov
1956.

Hall, C. S., and G. Lindzey, *Theories of Personality.* New York: Wiley, 1957.

Kretschmer, E., *Physique and Character.* New York: Harcourt, Brace & Worl
1925.

Translation of a 1921 work by W. J. H. Sprott. Kretschmer published in German the twentieth edition of this work in 1951.

Lindzey, G., and C. Hall, *Theories of Personality: Primary Sources and Research.* New York: Wiley, 1965.

Palthe, P. M. W., In NATO: *Agardograph,* No. 5, *Anthropometry and Human Engineering.* New York: Wiley (Interscience), 1955.

Use of Sheldon's methods to measure candidates for pilot training.

Parnell, R. W., *Behavior and Physique: An Introduction to Practical and Applied Somatometry.* Baltimore: Williams & Wilkins, 1958.

Worth reading to compare with Sheldon's methods.

Paterson, D. G., *Physique and Intellect.* New York: Appleton-Century-Crofts, 1930.

PERIODICALS

Bernstein, M. E., and G. M. Gustin, Physical and psychological variation and the sex ratio, *J. Hered.,* 1961, *52,* 109–112.

Sheldon's somatotypes and genetic mechanisms.

Brodsky, C. M., A study of norms for body form–behavior relationships, *Anthrop. Quart.,* 1954, *27,* 91–101.

Child, I. L., The relationship of somatotype to self-ratings on Sheldon's temperamental traits, *J. Pers.,* 1950, *18,* 440–453.

Four hundred male college students previously somatotyped answered a revised questionnaire. Sheldon's findings were on the whole confirmed.

Cortes, J. B., Physique, need for achievement and delinquency, unpublished doctoral dissertation, Harvard University, 1961.

Damon, A., Constitution and smoking, *Science,* 1961, *134,* 339–340.

Epps, P., and R. W. Parnell, Physique and temperament of women delinquents compared with women undergraduates, *Brit. J. Med. Psychol.,* 1952, *25,* 249–255.

Eysenck, H. J., The Rees-Eysenck body index and Sheldon's somatotype system, *J. Ment. Sci.,* 1959, *105,* 1053–1058.

Fiske, D. W., A study of relationships to somatotype, *J. Appl. Psychol.,* 1944, *28,* 504–519.

Funk, I. C., I. Shatin, E. X. Freed, and L. Rockmore, Somatopsychotherapeutic approach to long-term schizophrenic patients, *J. Nerv. Ment. Dis.,* 1955, *121,* 423–437.

Glueck, E. T., Body build and the prediction of delinquency, *J. Crim. Law Criminol.,* 1958, *48,* 577–579.

Hood, A. B., A study of the relationship between physique and personality variables as measured by the MMPI, *J. Pers.,* 1963, *31,* 97–107.

Howells, W. W., A factorial study of constitutional type, *Amer. J. Phys. Anthrop.,* 1952, *10,* 91–118.

Humphreys, L. G., Characteristics of type concepts with special reference to Sheldon's typology, *Psychol. Bull.*, 1957, *54*, 218–228.

Several limitations in Sheldon's typology.

Janoff, I. Z., L. H. Beck, and I. L. Child, The relation of somatotype to reaction time, resistance to pain, and expressive movement, *J. Pers.*, 1950, *18*, 454–460.

Kline, N. S., Constitutional factors in the prognosis of schizophrenia: Further observations, *Amer. J. Psychiat.*, 1952, *108*, 909–911.

Kline, N. S., and A. M. Tenny, Constitutional factors in prognosis of schizophrenia, *Amer. J. Psychiat.*, 1950, *107*, 432–441.

Klineberg, O., S. E. Asch, and H. Block, An experimental study of constitutional types, *Genet. Psychol. Monogr.*, 1934, *16*, 139–221.

Lasker, G., The effects of partial starvation on somatotype, *Amer. J. Phys. Anthrop.*, 1947, *5*, 323–341.

McNeil, E., and N. Levison, Maturation rate and body build in women, *Child Developm.*, 1963, *34*, 25–32.

Ectomorphy negatively related to rate of biological maturation.

Matte-Blanco, I., The constitutional approach to the study of human personality, *Psychiat. Res. Rep.*, 1955, No. 2, pp. 132–154.

Psychoanalytic concepts related to body constitution, clinically illustrated.

Naccarati, S., The morphologic aspect of intelligence, *Arch. Psychol.*, 1921, No. 45.

Newman, R. W., Age changes in body build, *Amer. J. Phys. Anthrop.*, 1952, *10*, 75–90.

Parnell, R. W., Simplified somatotypes, *J. Psychosom. Res.*, 1964, *8*, 311–315.

Rationale and conversion tables are presented for calculating Sheldon's fat and muscularity indexes from height, weight, and three skinfold measures.

Perbix, S. A., Relationships between somatotype and motor fitness, *Res. Quart. Amer. Assoc. Hlth Phys. Educ.*, 1954, *25*, 84–90.

Physical education majors slightly more mesomorphic.

Pivnicki, D., A consideration of constitutional concepts, *Psychiat. Quart.*, 1964, *38*, 679–688.

No rigorous scientific proof of a correlation between body build and character structure.

Robbins, L. M., Personality, race and physique in college women, *Proc. Indian Acad. Sci.*, 1962, *72*, 63–66.

Seltzer, C. C., The relationship between the masculine component and personality, *Amer. J. Phys. Anthrop.*, 1943, *3*, 33–47.

Seltzer, C. C., F. L. Wells, and E. B. McTernon, A relationship between Sheldonian somatotype and psychotype, *J. Pers.*, 1948, *16*, 431–436.

Smith, H. C., Psychometric checks on hypotheses derived from Sheldon's work on physique and temperament, *J. Pers.*, 1949, *17*, 310–320.

Smith, H. C., and S. Boyarsky, The relationship between physique and simple reaction time, *Charact. & Pers.*, 1943, *12*, 46–53.

Sutherland, E. H., Critique of Sheldon's *Varieties of Delinquent Youth*, *Amer. Sociol. Rev.*, 1951, *16*, 10–13.

Thurstone, L. L., Factor analysis and body types, *Psychometrika*, 1946, *11*, 15–21.

Walker, R. N., Body build and behavior in young children: Body build and nursery school teachers' ratings, *Child Develpm. Monogr.*, 1962, pp. 75–79.

Winthrop, H., The consistency of attitude patterns as a function of body type, *J. Pers.*, 1957, *25*, 372–383.

VI

Psychostatistical

RAYMOND B. CATTELL and Hans J. Eysenck have been accorded full chapters in this issue. The reasons, at this point in time, seem obvious even though their work is not evenly accepted by many personologists.

In reviewing their vast contributions, one gets the impression that the psychological world doesn't quite know what to do with these two men. In some ways psychologists are still trying to catch their breath and keep up with the sheer volume of work both Cattell and Eysenck have produced in the past ten years. At times it is almost a factorial analysis factory in output (the computer has created an ocean of data). Some young psychologist may carve out a career for himself just reordering this vast amount of research. One also gets the impression that there is almost a friendly rivalry between Eysenck and Cattell as to which can produce the most research. This is not the case, but there are parallels: both were trained in England, they are personally acquainted, and both employ factor analysis as a primary tool although they differ somewhat in the factoring technique.

Maybe the psychological guild is confused about the value, status, and bulk of their worth, but it cannot ignore them.

12

CATTELL

Science moves but slowly, slowly,
creeping on from point to point.[1]

TENNYSON
Locksley Hall, Line 134

SOME BIOGRAPHICAL DATA

Raymond B. Cattell was born in Staffordshire, England, in 1905. He received his B.S., M.A., Ph.D., and D.Sc. at Kings College, University of London. He married Monica Rogers on December 1, 1930, and they have one son, Hereward Seagrieve, a surgeon. He was married again on April 2, 1946, to Alberta Karen Schuettler, and they have four children: Mary, Heather, Roderic, and Elaine. Cattell was lecturer at the University of Exeter, 1927–

[1] The author is most grateful to Dr. Cattell for suggesting this couplet from Tennyson.

1932; director at the City of Leicester Child Guidance Clinic, 1932–1937; Research Associate to E. L. Thorndike, 1937–1938; and G. Stanley Hall Professor of Genetic Psychology, 1938–1941. In 1941 he went to Harvard, where he served in the capacity of lecturer in psychology until 1944, and, after war service, left for the University of Illinois, where he has been research professor in psychology ever since. Cattell was awarded the Darwin Research Fellowship in 1935 and he wrote the Wenner-Gren Prize Essay on Research in 1953. He is a fellow of the British Psychological Society and a member of the American Psychological Association. Furthermore, he is a member of the Eugenics Society and of the Human Genetics Society. He is a member of Sigma Xi. Cattell also serves as a civilian consultant on personal research at the Adjutant General's Office of the War Department.

INTRODUCTION

It should be understood right from the beginning that the following expository material on Raymond Cattell's work can only touch the high spots. In the present book, considering its size and the task of covering to some degree nineteen theorists, it is not possible to do more than a suggestive outline of what Cattell has been doing for at least the past twenty years. Thus, all we can do is acknowledge the work that this man has produced and hope to introduce to the student interested in personology some of its main features. Cattell's reputation is truly international. He has published in American, British, Australian, Japanese, Indian, and African journals. Whatever effect he has had upon the world of personality theory, it has been international.

Since we have chosen to consider Cattell a major theorist, in contrast to the first edition, the question should be asked, How important has Cattell's work been, particularly in the last ten years? Possibly the most meaningful answer can be found in his evaluation by others who are acknowledged as being sophisticated in the field of personality and personality theory. We turn now to three volumes of the *Annual Review of Psychology*, 1965, 1967, and 1968. It is interesting to note the impact of Cattell as we peruse these three volumes. Wayne Holtzman, a sophisticated student of personality, spends three and a half pages of his concise summary of personalities study on Cattell's work alone. Although he feels that many have paid little attention to Cattell, and in return Cattell has paid little attention to others' work, Holtzman states that

> In spite of the many inconsistencies and questionable interpretations that can be uncovered in Cattell's work, the sheer magnitude and scope of his empirical studies which have been systematically presented in clear detail with the help of Hundleby and Pawlik, and the frequently Promethean char-

acter of Cattell's inventiveness in thinking up new ways of measuring personality make it essential for others concerned with personality structure to master the empirical findings he has presented. At the very least, this new contribution from Cattell's laboratory should spur others into expanded multi-variate research aimed at improving the identification of basic personality dimensions (Holtzman, 1965).

Two years later, in 1967, Klein, Barr, and Wolitzky, responsible for reviewing research on personality, evaluated Cattell as follows: "How, then, to evaluate Cattell's contributions? Many researchers in personality (including the present reviewers before they began this review) have been unaware of the scope and sophistication of Cattell's conceptions, the amount of evidence he amassed, and its potential relevance to their theorizing." The authors then point out the difficulties in factorial methods and the criticisms which have been leveled at Cattell, but they conclude with, "It seems to us that, with all its limitations, Cattell's work has gone farther than many personality theorists are aware in pursuing this goal. . . . In summary, we feel that Cattell's work has created important tools largely unutilized by many of those to whom they might be most useful. In particular the ways of using the products of his work in the service of other problems have not been sufficiently explored" (Klein *et al.*, 1967).

And in the 1968 issue of *Annual Review of Psychology* Wiggins devotes a special section to Raymond B. Cattell's name and work.

Cattell occupies such a unique position in the field of personality structure that his work demands separate consideration. (3 years, May 1964–May 1967) Cattell has published 4 books, 12 chapters, and 40 articles, a total of almost 4 thousand pages that must somehow be summarized. In addition, he has found time to launch a new journal (*Multivariate Behavioral Research*) and edit a massive handbook (*Handbook of Multivariate Experimental Psychology*). This alone would warrant separate consideration but there is more. The appearance of so many major works and especially the publication of his collected papers (*Personality and Social Psychology*) has once again forced an evaluation of a body of literature so vast, uneven, and demanding that many American workers have simply tended to ignore it.

As we have stated in the introduction to Part VI, perhaps the psychological guild is confused about the value, status, and bulk of Cattell's work but it certainly cannot ignore him.

The responses, both pro and con, of the psychologists we shall deal with in the last part of this chapter called "Scientific or Laboratory Prediction."

Cattell has published six books since 1964, none of which are easy reading and all of which are fantastically full of his various research efforts. They are as follows: *Personality and Social Psychology*, 1964; *The Scientific*

Analysis of Personality, 1965; *Personality Factors in Objective Test Devices: A Critical Integration of a Quarter of a Century's Research*, 1965; *Handbook of Multivariate Experimental Psychology*, 1966; *Objective Personality and Motivation Tests: A Theoretical and Practical Compendium*, 1967; and *The Prediction of Achievement and Creativity*, 1967. The reader may also note from the bibliography at the end of this chapter that Cattell has averaged about one article per month for almost the last twenty years.

Cattell's feelings about the current status of personality theory are in some ways amusing and in some ways are cuttingly critical: ". . . For theories are all things to all men; . . . a wide-spread human tendency has been to believe that *because there is one word there must be one thing*, and the bivariate experimenter has, typically, blindly made this assumption." And ". . . the main difference between the clinical inheritance of theory and that now growing from multivariate experiment is seen obviously at first in the introduction of precise measurement and complex calculation into the latter. But this brings with it a still more striking difference in terms of exactness with regard to *the stage of observation at which it is considered profitable to develop theories* in the experimenter's view the clinician developed elaborate theories all too soon and they have plagued and misled him." ". . . Of course, there must be theorizing, but it is a question of *when*." And finally, "The definition of personality developed by workers in the field cannot be made more concise in words than it has already been made in mathematical formulae" (Cattell, 1963a).

Lindzey and Hall, longtime leaders in the field of personality, agree that Cattell has had an impressive productivity and an absolutely amazing array of books and articles that make it difficult to capsulate. If nothing else, Cattell's work has made enormous strides in the fundamental problems of classification and taxonomy (Lindzey and Hall, 1965).

Cattell has a wide variety of talents which he puts to use in many fields. Even a cursory examination of the voluminous bibliography for Cattell brings out his interest in music, his interest in national differences, his interest in organic tests, the culture-free intelligence test he has worked on, and, of course, his extremely sophisticated work as a statistician.

As one might expect, because of his earlier training in English universities and abroad and his abiding interest in the international scene, Cattell is both a personal and a professional friend of Eysenck and Sir Cyril Burt.

For the purposes of further delineating, briefly at least, Cattell's work, we have chosen to divide his psychostatistical efforts into four principles: methods, dynamic structure, developmental, and social principles. It must be admitted that these rubics are but a skeletal arrangement for Cattell's work. As yet no one has been able to concisely present the essential features of this man's work.

CATTELL'S DESCRIPTION
OF HUMAN BEHAVIOR

According to Cattell, the goal of psychology and personality theory is to formulate laws which enable us to predict behavior under many conditions. His definition of personality is not surprising in that it is based on prediction. *"Personality is that which permits a prediction of what a person will do in a given situation"* (*Personality: A Systematic, Theoretical, and Factual Study*, 1950, p. 2). Cattell emphasizes that there are many motivation variables which must be carefully spelled out. His feeling is that personality theory is still in transition or being formed. He believes that current personologists have neglected the hereditary aspects of human personality. His emphasis is on the structure of personality in regard both to biological background and to social determiners. All of Cattell's interest in personality theory and the dynamics of personality have grown out of the findings of continuous research rather than in speculative writings.

Raymond Cattell feels very strongly that if personality cannot be demonstrated, measured, and quantified it should be called *philosophy or art and not personality theory in psychology*. However, he does not mean by experiment "only brass instrument laboratory experiments," as he explained in a letter to me. His feeling is best expressed in his remarks to the Kentucky Symposium, 1954 (p. 109): "We let events happen in life as they will and tease out with statistical finesse what cannot be handled by brute experimental control." In the same symposium Cattell argued that psychology must answer the small questions first before attempting the global answers. The clinic may be the best place to study personality but it may not be the best place to verify hypotheses that predict behavior change for its methods are weak until measurement control and subtle statistical analyses are introduced. There is a difference in personality theory between what is socially acceptable and a popular subject and what is scientifically respectable. Thus, change that may occur through therapy may be quite acceptable to society yet not be demonstrable with any scientific reliability. Feeling that personality theory in the present day has much "semantic nonsense," Cattell likens it to Oscar Wilde's definition of history: "An account of things that never should have happened." Cattell advocates a concentrated study of personality which should be done in the life situation. After the facts have been gathered, they should be treated statistically and not philosophically.

In a 1957 article, "A Universal Index for Psychological Factors," Cattell pleads for standardized symbols for describing psychological data while concepts are being developed. They could be set up by a committee to create standards for international research and to publish these standards so that all who work on the common factors of personality are doing so within the same framework. His desire for a common language has been irritating to some because of his penchant for using letters of the alphabet or neologisms for the factors he has found in his research. Confusion has mounted as Cattell has proceeded in the last twenty years to refine his concepts by giving them one name, changing to another name, and adopting a third name, as we shall see in discussing the dynamic structure principle.

Methods Principle

Cattell employs two types of factor analysis techniques, the P technique ("the factoring of the unique structure of the single person") and the R technique. The primary distinction between them is that the P technique is an ipsative technique which can reveal causal sequences while the R technique is a normative unit technique. He points out that clinical use of the P technique is at present unexplored. We further find that P technique factor analysis produces states of human behavior while the R technique reveals traits between people.

In measuring personality, Cattell employs two units: normative and ipsative. Normative units concern themselves with the amount an individual will vary from other individuals. The ipsative unit is the amount of variation within the individual himself—for example, in anxiety and other dynamic states.

Cattell has through the years been a devoted exponent of the multi-variate experimental technique, in contrast to the bivariate. The essentials of factor analysis are so complicated that entire volumes and series of lectures must be given to provide even a rudimentary grasp of their intricacies.

> Essentially, however, it may be said that multi-variate methods are distinguished from the bivariate methods first by treating many variables at once and taking care to look at the totality of manifestations simultaneously and holistically. Secondly, they differ by not requiring manipulative control, but allowing things to happen in nature as they normally happen. Thirdly, they develop refined statistics to tease out by analysis what they cannot separate by brute physical control. There are, of course, advantages and disadvantages to both approaches (Cattell, 1963, in Wepman and Heine).

In contrast to Eysenck, Guilford, and Zimmerman, who prefer to rotate the axis or orthogonal factors and thus remove only a few factors, Cattell prefers to take out as many factors as possible and then rotate for maximum simple structure with oblique factors. There has been much controversy over which is the more propitious and efficient factoral method. From essentially the same data Eysenck usually extracts two or three factors while Cattell feels it ecessary to extract at least sixteen to twenty-one factors and in some cases nore, depending upon the kind of data he is using. "Essentially, first order actors predict concrete criteria better while higher order ones contribute nore to theory." Also we find that second order factors are usually considered s broad descriptive categories which do not have the predictive power of first rder factors but continue nevertheless to contribute to the understanding of ersonality.

In general, Cattell gains his data by three methods. The first method is alled the life record (L-data). This deals with behavior in the everyday ifelike situation. Examples would be number of automobile accidents, frequency of social engagements, number of societies a person belongs to, cademic grades, and so forth. Such "hard data" are difficult to get and requently must come secondhand because they are rated by another person.

Cattell also seeks to get personality information through use of questionnaires (Q-data). As we shall see later on in the 16 PF tests, this is currently ne of his most popular modes.

A third methodology for getting evidence in regard to the personality tructure involves objective tests (T-data). An objective test is defined as "a est in which the subject's behavior is measured for inferring personality, vithout his being aware in what ways his behavior is likely to affect the nterpretation." Objectivity, therefore, is achieved when a test is resistant to listortion, to sensitivity toward the tester, and to any kind of faking by the ndividual taking the test.

In regard to methodology Cattell advocates a systematic attack on the tructure of personality in which five approaches are utilized: (1) the three ossible media of observation, L-data, Q-data, and T-data, with cross comparisons; (2) study across all age levels from the very young to the very old; (3) study of the relationships by the techniques of the P and R factor analytic states; (4) study of differing cultures for constant personality structure and dynamics, as in American, Australian, British, French, Italian, and apanese groups; and (5) the multivariate approach in which "all factors must e ultimately figured together," i.e., ability, temperament, and motivational actors.

How completely Cattell goes about getting personality measurements nay be found in a study which attempted to measure physiological processes s they are involved in emotionality. Emotionality in the subjects was measured by urine analysis, handwriting pressure, increase in pulse rate when an rm was plunged into ice water, and response to newspaper headlines. These hysiological responses were then compared to a paper and pencil inventory f emotionality. Cattell felt that "one can therefore use questionnaire and bjective tests according to circumstances." Part of the findings in this study vere contrary to popular opinion; most of the highly emotional people had very light or little handwriting pressure. The subjects had greater muscular

tension at the back of the neck and shoulder but far less tension in their fe
and hands (*The Scientific Analysis of Personality*).

Finally (it must be admitted that this section offers but a small samplir
of the total methodological approach of Cattell) we turn to the types of tes
that Cattell and his coworkers have produced in the last twenty-five yeaı
Each test has had a fantastic amount of factorial work and in some cas
represents many revisions. It is Cattell's contention that work in personali
dynamics and structure should eventuate in usable psychometric devic
which can be employed in clinic and school settings. We will mention on
fifteen of the tests that Cattell has produced through his work at the Institu
for Personality and Ability Testing (IPAT).

The tests are as follows: Personality—(1) the 16 Personality Fact
Questionnaires, (2) the Junior–Senior High School Personality Questio
naire, (3) the Children's Personality Questionnaire, (4) the Early Scho
Personality Questionnaire, (5) the Contact Personality Factor Test, (6) tl
Neuroticism Scale Questionnaire, (7) IPAT Anxiety Questionnaire, (8) tl
IPAT 8-Parallel-Form Anxiety Battery, (9) the Objective–Analytic Anxie
Battery, (10) the Objective–Analytic Personality Test Battery, (11) tl
IPAT Humor Test of Personality, (12) the IPTA Music Preference Test •
Personality; Motivation—(13) the Motivation Analysis Tests (MAT) aı
(14) the School Motivation Analysis Test (SMAT).

Cattell has also constructed a mental ability test which he has called tl
IPAT Culture Fair (or Culture Free) intelligence tests which have thrє
scales.

To any student of Cattell's work it is quite obvious that the abov
treatment is elementary and far from inclusive. One has to devote what mə
amount to hundreds of hours of reading and searching to ferret out tl
nuances that Cattell uses in studying the personalities of human beings.

Dynamic Structure Principle

In a historical sense it may be best to begin this section with Cattell's postı
lated seventeen laws of personality formation from his 1950 book, *Personalit
A Systematic, Theoretical, and Factual Study* (p. 664).

1. The Law of Innate Goal Tension Patterns
2. The Law of Satisfaction in Rigidity
3. The Law of Dispersion with Excitement and Deprivation
4. The Law of Dynamic Effect
5. The Law of Alternating Expression in Naive Conflict
6. The Law of Suppressive Mechanisms in Permanent Conflict
7. The Law of the Nature of Conditions of Repression in Permanent Coı
   flict
8. The Law of Consequences of Repression
9. The Law of Combined Expression

10. The Law of Deflection Strain
11. The Law of Cognitive–Dynamic Investment Strain
12. The Law of Short-Circuiting
13. The Law of Integration by the Contemplated Self
14. The Law of Persisting Dissociations from the Ego
15. The Law of Subsidiation and Integration of the Dual-Self Concepts in the Self-Sentiment
16. The Law of Ergic and General Regression
17. The Law of Superpersonal Contest and Limitation of Prediction

Since the foregoing discussion has centered on these laws, no attempt is made to follow Cattell's long discourse on his seventeen laws of personality formation. The interested reader who wishes to follow the evolution of Cattell's work is invited to reread the above section.

Another factor in the dynamic structure of the human personality may be found in the definition of personality: "Personality is that which permits a prediction of what a person will do in a given situation." As we shall see later, Cattell is interested in the group norm and in the ipsative qualities of the uniqueness of the self.

Cattell divides traits into three modalities: temperament, dynamics, and ability. Temperament traits are often allied with constitutional body characteristics. Dynamic traits concern themselves with initiating behavioral acts. Ability traits measure or express the efficiency of the personality in behavior directed at solving cognitive problems.

The manner in which one dynamic trait is linked with another in trying to achieve a goal is called subsidiation. The term *subsidiation* originated largely from the work of Murray, who felt that there should be more goal levels or a hierarchy of goals. Subsidiation has to do primarily with the innumerable interrelated and highly complex pathways that an individual may have to take to achieve a final goal. In other words, an individual may have to attain many minor goals or subgoals in order to arrive at the final goal state. The intermediate steps are frequently highly involved. Thus, Cattell feels that only by factor analysis can they be discovered.

Furthermore, there are two major kinds of traits: source traits and surface traits. Surface traits are clusters of observable behavioral events. They are less stable and descriptive and therefore less important in Cattell's viewpoint. On the other hand, source traits are the genuine influences that help determine and explain human behavior. Source traits are the underlying influences that help to determine surface traits. Source traits are stable and extremely important; they are the major material which the personality psychologist should be studying. Source traits may be divided into constitutional traits and environmental-mold traits. The former are internal or within the skin and have some basis in heredity. Environmental-mold traits come from the environment and are shaped by events which occur outside the skin.

We come now to one of the most difficult and complex, yet fruitful, contributions which Cattell has made to the field of personality theory. The following list of source traits is the result of an enormous amount of factoring over the last twenty-five years. One of the difficulties in dealing with this material is that in the beginning Cattell did not name the traits but simply identified them with alphabetical letters because, as we have stated before, he felt that language was a poor carrier of the psychological concepts he found in factoring human performance. Through the years, he did give names to the source traits, but frequently they were made-up names, as the reader can see in the following list. Some criticism and his own further refinements have led him gradually to give more stereotyped labels to these source traits.

Cattell does not rest upon his past performances but continues to extract new source traits by first, second, or third order factoring. Witness for example the last four source traits named F Q_1, F Q_2, F Q_3, and F Q_4, and then the simple Roman numerals I–IV. As we shall see, these also eventually received names. In his current work, Cattell calls the source traits Primary Personality Factors. With few exceptions, the Primary Personality Factors are bipolar or dichotomized. This situation is somewhat reminiscent of Freud' polarity or duality principle. It is interesting to note that many personality theorists create polar concepts. The exceptions are Sheldon and Horney, who deal with trichotomized concepts.

At times it is confusing in reading Cattell's literature to follow the Primary Personality Factors. He discusses them as neologisms (cyclothymia) by their popular names (intelligence), and sometimes by number (e.g., U.I. 16). When Cattell decided to number the factors in 1957, according to what he called the Universal Index, the first fifteen numbers had already been used by French in 1951. Therefore, Cattell proceeded to number his Primary Personality Factors from 16 on.

Trait Description in the IPAT 16 Factors Questionnaire

Factor A (U.I. 16)

| Cyclothymia | *vs.* | Schizothymia |
| Warmhearted, easygoing, participating | | Detached, critical, cool |

Factor B (U.I. 17)

| General Intelligence | *vs.* | Mental Defect |
| Abstract-thinking, bright | | Concrete-thinking |

Factor C (U.I. 18)

| Emotional Stability or Ego Strength | | Dissatisfied Emotionality |
| Stable, faces reality, calm, mature | | Emotionally less stable, easily upset |

Factor E (U.I. 19)

Dominance or Ascendance
Independent, aggressive,
  stubborn

vs.

Submission
Mild, accommodating, con-
  forming

Factor F (U.I. 20)

Surgency

Impulsively lively, gay, enthusiastic

vs.

Desurgency, or Depressive
  Anxiety
Sober, serious, taciturn

Factor G (U.I. 21)

Character or Super-ego
  Strength
Persevering, staid, rule-bound

vs.

Lack of Internal Standards

Evades rules, feels few obligations

Factor H (U.I. 22)

Parmia
Adventurous, Autonomic
  Resilience
Socially bold, uninhibited,
  spontaneous

vs.

Threctia
Inherent, Withdrawn,
  Schizothymia
Restrained, diffident, timid

Factor I (U.I. 23)

Premsia
Emotional Sensitivity
Dependent, overprotected,
  sensitive

vs.

Harria
Tough Maturity
Self-reliant, realistic, no-
  nonsense

Factor L (U.I. 24)

Protension
Paranoid Schizothymia
Self-opinionated, hard to fool

vs.

Inner Relaxation
Trustful Altruism
Adaptable, free of jealousy,
  easy to get on with

Factor M (U.I. 25)

Autia
Hysteric Unconcern (or
  "Bohemianism")
Wrapped up in inner urgen-
  cies, careless of practical
  matters, Bohemian

vs.

Praxernia
Practical Concernedness

Careful, conventional, proper

Factor N (U.I. 26)

Shrewdness
Sophistication
Calculating, worldly, pene-
  trating

vs.

Naiveté
Rough Simplicity
Natural, artless, sentimental

Factor O (U.I. 27)

Guilt Proneness	*vs.*	Confidence
Anxious Insecurity		Placid Self-Confidence
Worrying, depressive, troubled		Self-assured, confident, seren

Factor Q_1 (U.I. 28)

| Radicalism | *vs.* | Conservatism |
| Critical, liberal, analytical, free thinking | | Respecting established ideas |

Factor Q_2 (U.I. 29)

| Independent Self-Sufficiency | *vs.* | Lack of Resolution |
| Prefers own decisions, re-sourceful | | A "joiner" and sound follow |

Factor Q_3 (U.I. 30)

| Will Control | *vs.* | Character Stability |
| Socially precise, following self-image | | Careless of protocol |

Factor Q_4 (U.I. 31)

| Nervous Tension, frustrated, driven, overwrought | *vs.* | Tranquil, torpid, unfrustrate |

Factor I (U.I. 32)

| Invia or Introversion | *vs.* | (Extraversion) |

Factor II (U.I. 33)

Anxiety

Factor III (U.I. 34)

| Pathemia | *vs.* | Cortical alertness |

Factor IV (U.I. 35)

| Promethean will | *vs.* | Resignation |

Cattell acknowledges the primary position of motivational factors i human behavior and finds approximately five aspects or motivational con ponents in man's behavior, ranging from Alpha to Epsilon. In very abbrev ated form they are as follows:

UCs	Alpha "I want"	*id*
	Beta "I am interested"	*ego*
	Gamma "I ought to be interested"	*super-ego*
	Epsilon Physiological Reaction, i.e., GSR, poorness of memory, poor-ness of reminiscence	
UCS	Delta Physiological Processes, organic components	

In addition to the above structure, Cattell advocates a method of analyzing quantitatively the goals or the incentives which motivate the human personality in action in a natural setting. This he calls the Dynamic Calculus. Attitudes and responses of all kinds are considered to come from dynamic source traits of two kinds: the erg and the sentiment. The erg is almost like an instinct. The term *erg* comes from the field of physics and in its simplest definition is a unit of energy. An erg is also defined as "an innate psychophysical disposition which permits its possessors to acquire reactivity to a certain class of objects more readily than do others, to experience a specific emotion in regard to them, and to start on a course of action which ceases more completely at a specific goal activity than at any other." Cattell feels he has identified approximately nine ergs, including sex, fear, parental protectiveness, assertion, curiosity, etc. He uses the term *erg* to get away from what he calls the "semantic confusion" that is usually involved in the mixing of drive with instincts. A sentiment, on the other hand, is a motivational source trait which comes out of the environmental influences—religious sentiment, sentiment to home and family, sentiment to self, and so on.

"His investigation of dynamic structure has been possible only through advances in the objective measurement of motivation strength. By measuring attitudes, Cattell has been able to demonstrate, through these objective devices, the presence of basic motivational source factors. The atomic attitudes follow this pattern: 'Under these conditions I wish (so much) to do this with that,' and thus each contains the characteristics of the incentive or situational conditions, the organism, the intensity (which is to be measured), the goal-directed activity, and the goal objects.

"His objective motivation tests utilize experimental principles, many of which have been well studied by other investigators in the area of motivation, such as: differential information, selective memory, autism, projection, selective perception, and selective attention. A large number of new measurement devices have been demonstrated to be related to motivation measured in this way. Over sixty objective device methods have been established and studied intensely for directly measuring the manifested change within the organism which can be attributed to the introduction of incentive stimulation. The analysis of these measures has shown that basic patterns of motivational expression exist which are relatively uniform, regardless of the specific characteristics of the goal object. Seven factors of devices which measure the same way have been found. These can be considered to be made up of motivational behaviors and fall into the general patterns of the id, ego, superego and some other components of motivation not proposed by Freud. The value of having theoretical framework which permits measurement of motivation on different levels is of great importance, and sets his theory and experimental procedures on a different plane from the other monotonic measures being used.

"He refers to the motivational structures of related goal directions as 'dynamic factors,' as an acknowledgment of their sensitivity to environmental presses and incentive conditions. A list of these 'ergs' and 'sentimentals' would sound not too different from McDougall's 'instincts' or Murray's 'needs.' The real difference lies in the fact that these are dimensions which are empirically discovered and repeatedly measurable. For example, the pugnacity erg found in both adults and children contributes major variance to such attitudes as 'I want the United States to beat its enemies,' 'I want to beat up other kids who cause me trouble,' or 'I want to see more gangster movies.'

"By means of factor analysis, eighteen replicable ergs and sentiments have been found in children and thirteen in adults. The ergs seem to be more primary and to be more directly related to the actual goal activity such as eating, sleeping, fighting, and so forth. The sentiment structures are made up of attitudes having the same institution or goal object which has seemingly proved useful over a long period of time for the satisfaction of many varied primary motives. These primary motives include religion, patriotism, sweetheart, self, parents, and mass amusement. Thus, some have compared sentiments to instrumentalities and ergs to more basic needs.

"It is very easy to become involved in a morass of conflicting terminology in this area. This is a special reason that Cattell has purposely delineated his system from others seeking to systematize motivation. He feels that if his 'protective erg' measures the same variance found by Murray's 'nurturance need' then the path of science will be made easier, but that this is not necessary for the measurement of both concepts in their present systems.

"This fundamental work in motivation is now opening new vistas for measurement, central to the needs of clinical and industrial psychology. Areas of repression, motivational conflict, intrafamilial attitudes, as well as vocational motives, are all in various stages of systematization."[2]

Possibly one of the most interesting and fruitful endeavors for further research is Cattell's work on intelligence. After much research and factoring Cattell divided intelligence into two types: fluid and crystallized. Most of the time he prefers to call these general abilities rather than intelligence. In contrast to Spearman, who in his early work felt there was just one general ability, Cattell argues that there are two, and they are of major importance. Crystallized intelligence is more involved in learning such as that required in educational tasks, tests of vocabulary and numerical ability, and measures of the traditional intelligence tests. Crystallized intelligence depends upon the environment and is subject to fluctuation. It also depends upon the amount of exercise and the interest of the individual in factual data. Cattell feels that

[2] This section has been prepared almost exclusively by a close associate of Cattell's, Professor Arthur Sweney. I am obligated to both Professor Sweney and Dr. Cattell for permission to use it.

crystallized intelligence may increase up to about the age of twenty-five or thirty, at which time it levels off. Crystallized intelligence is less culture bound; it may also show a systematic increase as the individual ages.

On the other hand, fluid intelligence is that type of mental ability which is required in adapting to new situations. It is more of a hereditary factor than crystallized intelligence. It depends upon the general physiological state of the individual and usually levels off at about fifteen to sixteen years of age. Therefore, fluid intelligence is inclined to decrease as the individual grows older. The contribution of Cattell to the concepts of intelligence is another example of his ingenious interests. The basis for this work comes from the factor analysis of tests. The crystallized and fluid intelligence concepts were more from second order than from first order factor analysis.

As long ago as 1953 Cattell concerned himself with the effect of the nature–nurture paradigm in contrast to Eysenck's method of twin control studies, particularly between monozygotic and dizygotic twins. Cattell prefers multiple abstract variance analysis, in which he is working with continuous variables in the twin method. In this system, using analysis of variance Cattell looks for four components in studying twins: (1) differences of the environments between the families, (2) differences of heredity between the families, (3) differences of heredity of brothers and sisters within the same family, and (4) differences of environments for individuals within the same family. Thus, Cattell applies a statistical method in a highly sophisticated manner, somewhat in contrast to other personologists.

Like almost all contemporary personality theorists, Raymond Cattell puts the aspect of self in an important place. He speaks of the self sentiment, which gives stability and a high degree of organization to the source traits. He divides his consideration of the total self into three parts: self sentiment, real self, and ideal self. Self sentiment means "the concern which one has about his conceived self." Real self is, as one might expect, "actually the personality." The ideal self is what "one would like to be, granted all things and all power." For many of Cattell's research projects he hopes to study the unique personality when this personality meets a unique situation.

Cattell presents his concepts of role and role playing as a puzzle for psychology to solve. The question is "whether the change in perception which generates a change in action when this person steps into a role is due to change in the situational indices, or a change in the basic personality structure self." Thus he is saying, Does the individual actually see the situation differently or is the individual actually changed in the role situation? He tentatively concludes that both kinds of modification occur: Entering into a role does modify the individual, and the individual modifies the role in turn.

Finally, Pawlic and Cattell, in a study reported in the *British Journal of Psychology* (1964), by combining the data from three studies, came to the conclusion that there were three factors which come very close to Freud's concept of the id, ego, and superego. This is particularly interesting

since the two authors claim they had an a priori bias against the psychoanalytic theory.

Developmental Principle

It is obvious to anyone familiar with Cattell's work that the present author's
dividing his work into four principles is highly arbitrary. However, there does
seem to be enough material to incorporate into a developmental principle.

Cattell's concern with the influence of heredity and environment, or the
age-old nurture–nature controversy, is considerable. He has through the year
done a good deal of research on the problem. The total volume of his production is far too great to cover in this short chapter. However, "We still do not
know the detailed manner in which heredity and environment interact."
Despite this difficulty, Cattell believes there should not be a defeatist attitude
as he so often observes among others. In addition to finding that the influences of heredity are not always completely present at birth, but may emerge
later on in life, he has discovered that certain characteristics of intelligence
predominate in hereditary patterns. Such factors as tender-mindedness, nervous tension, and self-control appear to be mostly environmentally induced.
As we shall see in the chapter on Eysenck, there is some conflicting evidence
from other experimentalists. In concluding our summary of Cattell's work on
environment and heredity, we note that there is less a law than a reminder for
the proper "sorting out of environmental and hereditary effects." Thus, "the
effects of environment often determine the *area* in which a trait is displayed
whereas heredity more often governs its *amount*."

Somewhat in the same vein as the nature–nurture problem, in one study
reported in 1965 Cattell felt that some infants were born with a "thin skin."
They were physically inactive but physiologically overresponsive. Other children were born with a "thick skin." They were physically active, placid, and
cheerful. He conjectured that the thin-skinned children would be inclined to
become introverted while the thick-skinned children would be inclined to
become extraverted (*The Scientific Analysis of Personality*). (It must be
understood that in citing just a few cases from Cattell's work there is the
possibility of abusing the general trend of his research.)

Adolescents try to get economic, social, and sexual recognition. The
attempt may lead to frustration and internalized conflict with consequent
repression. There may be a rise in guilt feelings. Later on there is an increase
in the ego content as the adolescent reaches adulthood.

Cattell finds that the individual develops his personality through three
forms of learning. The first is simple conditioning or classic conditioning. The
second is means–end learning or what he later calls goal–path–reward learning
in which a new way toward an old goal is learned because the new way
more rewarding. The third mode of forming a personality is through integration learning, which also has its rewards system. In this type total satisfaction

1ust be achieved. Cattell feels that most of the present learning theorists
ave ignored integration learning. "There are several independent dynamic
oals and the organism has to learn to maximize its total satisfaction by
1hibiting some satisfactions in favor of others." An individual learns to have
 personality through "a multidimensional change in response to experience
f a multidimensional situation."

As previously mentioned, there is also a developmental aspect to fluid
nd crystallized intelligence. Fluid intelligence levels off at about sixteen years
f age; there is a slight decrease as the individual grows older. Crystallized
1telligence increases to about the age of thirty, particularly in the avenues of
erbal ability.

One short example of Cattell's work on emotionality and its develop-
1ental aspects indicates that emotionality varies in the life cycle. The peak
motional periods apparently are in the early twenties, usually when the
erson is involved in establishing a marital, social, and occupational position
1 society. Some evidence indicated that emotionality in housewives increased
s they approached middle age, most often when their active role as mother
·as considerably reduced. Approximately at the age of sixty Cattell felt that
1e emotionality levels for both men and women climb as compared to
revious years.

Finally, in regard to the psychoanalytic concept of the superego, Cattell
ound that it declined somewhat between the ages of nine and fifteen.
·eelings of guilt and undischarged drive tensions showed a marked increase in
dolescence and then a considerable decrease in the postadolescent years.

ocial Principle

'attell is vitally interested in the effect of the individual upon society and
ociety upon the individual, particularity in the realm of personality de-
elopment.

The following descriptions are but a few examples of his work in this
rea. In relating social groups and the family to individual personalities,
'attell has introduced the concept of group syntality. Briefly, syntality means
the relevant characteristics of an entire group which leads to consistent
ehavior by that group, thereby leading to possible prediction of group
erformance." It is the factor of syntality, or the sociocultural pressures as
1ey influence the behavior of the individual, that Cattell has examined at
ome length. He finds three ways in which social institutions may influence
1e behavior of an individual: by the deliberate inculcation of social values,
·y situations which are purely happenstance, and by the reaction of the
1dividual to these two factors. Family and/or cultural milieus are significant
or the personality formation of the individual. In the phenomena of
·ntality, one responds to pressures from inside and outside of the family and
f society.

In summary form, we offer other examples, albeit much too short, of Cattell's interest in the social dynamics of personality formation.

1. Differences appear to exist in variability of the crystallized and fluid intelligence. Crystallized intelligence is probably less variable in cultures with school systems such as our own.

2. In a study of Hawaiian children, approximately half of whom were of Japanese extraction, Cattell found a commonality or corresponding agreement of the Primary Personality Factors in both American and Japanese extraction children.

3. Other data indicate that citizens of the United States have lower emotional scores than other national groups. The averages for French citizens and Asiatic Indians were approximately twice as high in degrees of emotionality. Emotionality scores for British, Japanese, and Italian subjects fell, in the average, somewhere between the French and American emotionality measurements. Cattell tentatively concluded that people living in nations which bordered free enterprise and communist nations had the highest scores on emotionality.

4. In a comparison between American and British university undergraduate students, there was a significantly higher level of anxiety among the Americans. American university students seemed to be more extraverted than the British. The undergraduates in Britain indicated higher ego strength than the American group. The American group indicated a higher superego development than the British group. Further work with second order factors gave some indication that the American students were more emotionally sensitive and far more radical than their British counterparts. The British students also seemed to be less anxious and more conservative.

5. Cattell found that both large and small groups, when given the choice of working with or without a leader after some experience, always decided to elect a leader. Cattell's concern has been not with how or when they picked a leader but with the very poor method of leader selection that he found in the groups he studied. Most of the leaders were extremely inefficient and widely prone to making errors.

We repeat, the examples above only touch upon the vast work that Cattell has produced in the last twenty-five years. It is hoped that no injustice has been done to his work but rather that the individual may get a clearer idea of the global aspects of this particular personologist.

EXPLAINING HUMAN BEHAVIOR VIA CATTELL'S PSYCHOSTATISTICAL THEORY

The reader is faced once again with attempting to explain certain of man's behavioral problems using the work of Cattell. These behavioral problems, it may be remembered, are marriage, perversions, suicide, lawbreaking, supranatural being, humor, smoking, play and recreation, and psychoses–neuroses. This may be an almost impossible task since Cattell takes a statistical approach. All one can do is adapt from a highly complicated convoluted theoretical system.

PREDICTING HUMAN BEHAVIOR VIA CATTELL'S THEORY

Personal Prediction

Perhaps the most pragmatic method of comparing one's own personality to Cattell's system is to take any one of the fifteen IPAT personality tests. After scoring these tests, does the individual feel that they adequately represent his own personality dynamics?

Scientific or Laboratory Prediction

The present writer feels most inadequate to adjudicate and rank the research output of so prolific a producer of research data as Raymond Cattell has become. What to put in? What to highlight? At this point, the problem seems insoluble. Suggestions, therefore, are in order.

Perhaps the shortest and most efficient way to judge Cattell's research ability for scientific prediction is to read the following concise selections in the *Annual Review of Psychology*, Volumes 15, 16, 18, 19, and 20. The reviewers, both individuals and groups, have reduced an enormous amount of personality research data to compact reports. The reviewers were carefully chosen because of the expertise and in most cases had released time supported by financial grants. Here, then, may be the place to find objective evidence of the pros and cons of Cattell's work in personality testing and personality theory. As stated, all selections are from *Annual Review of Psychology*.

1. Perry London, "Personality Dynamics," 1964, *15*, 447–492 (223-item bibliography).
2. Wayne Holtzman, "Personality Structure," 1965, *16*, 119–156 (162-item bibliography).
3. George Klein, Harriet Barr, and David Wolitzky, "Personality," 1967, *18*, 467–560 (469-item bibliography).
4. Jerry Wiggins, "Personality Structure," 1968, *19*, 293–350 (555-item bibliography).
5. Joseph Adelson, "Personality," 1969, 20, 217–252 (210-item bibliography).

For the psychologically sophisticated and particularly statistically astute student, reading Cattell's six most recent books may help him judge the theory's capacity to support and stimulate research. The advice is: one book at a time and probably best read in the order they were written or the reader may get intellectual indigestion. Aside from that, the most elementary book is *The Scientific Analysis of Personality,* originally written for a British reading public.

1. *Personality and Social Psychology,* 1964.
2. *The Scientific Analysis of Personality,* 1965.
3. *Personality Factors in Objective Test Devices: A Critical Integration of a Quarter of a Century's Research,* 1965.
4. *Handbook of Multivariate Experimental Psychology,* 1966 (edited by Cattell).
5. *Objective Personality and Motivation Tests: A Theoretical and Practical Compendium,* 1967 (authored with F. W. Warburton).
6. *The Prediction of Achievement and Creativity,* 1967 (authored with H. J. Butcher).

What the future holds for the work of Cattell, whose personality theories grew out of multivariate statistics based on ipsative and normative objective data, we cannot tell. Currently, the guild of personality psychologists feels stunned by the sheer volume of computerized research but is beginning to show an increasing interest and respect for this lively, ever producing psychologist. The negative comments center around the feeling that you can computerize anything as long as it has a number and can be quantified. The positive comments seem to say, "Yes, but he has found things which many of us have missed." In any case, personality theory needs the energy of Raymond Bernard Cattell.

BIBLIOGRAPHY

PRIMARY SOURCES

BOOKS

Cattell, R. B., A *Guide to Mental Testing for Psychological Clinics, Schools, and Industrial Psychologists.* Bickly, Kent, Eng.: London Press, 1936; rev. ed. 1948.

    3rd rev. ed. London: University of London Press, 1953.

Cattell, R. B., *The Factors of the Mind.* New York: Macmillan, 1941.

Cattell, R. B., *General Psychology*. Cambridge, Mass.: Sci-Art, 1941.

Cattell, R. B., *The Culture Free Test of Intelligence*. Champaign, Ill.: Institute of Personality and Ability Testing, 1944.

Cattell, R. B., *Description and Measurement of Personality*. New York: Harcourt, Brace & World, 1946.

Cattell, R. B., *An Introduction to Personality Study*. London: Hutchinson, 1950.

Cattell, R. B., *Personality: A Systematic, Theoretical, and Factual Study*. New York: McGraw-Hill, 1950.

Cattell, R. B., D. R. Saunders, and G. F. Stice, *The 16 Personality Factor Questionnaire*. Champaign, Ill.: Institute of Personality and Ability Testing, 1950.

Cattell, R. B., *Factor Analysis: An Introduction and Manual for the Psychologist and Social Scientist*. New York: Harper & Row, 1952.

Cattell, R. B., Personality structure and personality measurement, in *ETS, 1951, Invitational Conference on Testing Problems*, Princeton, N.J.: Educational Testing Service, 1952, pp. 82–88.

Cattell, R. B., Personality structures as learning and motivation patterns—a theme for the integration of methodologies, in *Learning Theory, Personality Theory and Clinical Research: The Kentucky Symposium*. New York: Wiley, 1954, pp. 91–113.

Cattell, R. B., J. E. King, and A. K. Schuettler, *Personality Factor Series* (series of three tests) (the O–A Personality Test Battery). Champaign, Ill.: Institute of Personality and Ability Testing, 1954.

Cattell, R. B., Personality and motivation theory based on structural measurement in J. L. McCary (ed.), *Psychology of Personality: Six Modern Approaches*. New York: Logos Press, 1956.

Cattell, R. B., *Personality and Motivation Structure and Measurement*. New York: Harcourt, Brace & World, 1957.

Cattell, R. B., *The I.P.A.T. Anxiety Scale*. Champaign, Ill.: Institute of Personality and Ability Testing, 1958.

Cattell, R. B., H. Beloff, and R. Coan, *IPAT High School Personality Questionnaire* (HSPQ). Champaign, Ill.: Institute of Personality and Ability Testing, 1958.

Cattell, R. B., The dynamic calculus: Concepts and crucial experiments, in M. R. Jones (ed.), *Nebraska Symposium on Motivation*. Lincoln: University of Nebraska Press, 1959, pp. 84–134.

Cattell, R. B., Foundations of personality measurement theory in multivariate experiment, in B. M. Bass and I. A. Berg (eds.), *Objective Approaches to Personality Assessment*. Princeton, N.J.: Van Nostrand, 1959.

Cattell, R. B., Personality theory growing from multivariate quantitative research, in S. Koch (ed.), *Psychology: A Study of a Science*, Vol. III, *Formulations of the Person and the Social Context*. New York: McGraw-Hill, 1959.

Cattell, R. B., and I. H. Scheier, *The Meaning and Measurement of Neuroticism and Anxiety*. New York: Ronald Press, 1961.

Cattell, R. B., Group theory, personality and role: A model for experimental researches, in F. Geldard (ed.), *Defence Psychology*. London: Pergamon, 1962.

Cattell, R. B., Personality measurement functionally related to source trait structure, in S. Messick and J. Ross (eds.), Measurement in Personality and Cognition. New York: Wiley, 1962.

Cattell, R. B., Concepts of personality growing from multivariate experiment, in J. M. Wepman and R. W. Heine (eds.), Concepts of Personality. Chicago: Aldine, 1963a.

Cattell, R. B., The structuring of change by P-technique and incremental R-technique, in C. W. Harris (ed.), Problems of Measuring Change. Madison: University of Wisconsin Press, 1963b.

Cattell, R. B., Personality and Social Psychology. San Diego, Cal.: Knapp, 1964.

Cattell, R. B., What is "objective" in "objective personality tests"? in W. L. Barnette (ed.), Readings in Psychological Tests and Measurements. Homewood, Ill.: Dorsey Press, 1964.

Cattell, R. B., and H. W. Eber, Handbook for the Sixteen Personality Factor Questionnaire. Champaign, Ill.: Institute of Personality and Ability Testing, 1964.

Catttell, R. B., Factor theory psychology: A statistical approach to personality, in W. S. Sahakian (ed.), Psychology of Personality: Readings in Theory. Chicago: Rand McNally, 1965.

Cattell, R. B., Higher order factor structures and reticular versus hierarchical formula for their interpretation, in C. Banks and P. L. Broadhurst (eds.), Studies in Psychology Presented to Cyril Burt. London: University of London Press, 1965.

Cattell, R. B., Methodological and conceptual advances in evaluating hereditary and environmental influences and their interaction, in S. G. Vandenberg (ed.), Methods and Goals in Human Behavior Genetics. New York: Academic Press, 1965.

Cattell, R. B., The Scientific Analysis of Personality. Baltimore: Penguin Books, 1965.

Hundleby, J. D., K. Pawlik, and R. B. Cattell, Personality Factors in Objective Test Devices: A Critical Integration of a Quarter of a Century's Research. San Diego, Cal.: Knapp, 1965.

Results of over thirty independent multivariate studies.

Cattell, R. B., Anxiety and motivation: Theory and crucial experiments, in C. D. Spielberger (ed.), Anxiety and Behavior. New York: Academic Press, 1966.

Cattell, R. B. (ed.), Handbook of Multivariate Experimental Psychology. Chicago: Rand McNally, 1966.

Cattell, R. B., The meaning of clinical psychology, in I. A. Berg and L. A. Pennington (eds.), An Introduction to Clinical Psychology. New York: Ronald Press, 1966.

Cattell, R. B., Personality structure: The larger dimensions, in B. Semeonoff (ed.), Personality Assessment. Baltimore: Penguin Books, 1966.

Cattell, R. B., and H. J. Butcher, The Prediction of Achievement and Creativity. Indianapolis: Bobbs-Merrill, 1967.

Cattell, R. B., and F. W. Warburton, *Objective Personality and Motivation Tests: A Theoretical and Practical Compendium.* Urbana: University of Illinois Press, 1967.

Cattell is psychology's Linnaeus, the great taxonomist.

PERIODICALS

Cattell, R. B., and J. L. Willston, Contributions concerning mental inheritance: I. Of intelligence, *Brit. J. Educ. Psychol.*, 1938, 8, 129–149.

Cattell, R. B., and E. J. Molteno, Contributions concerning mental inheritance: II. Temperament, *J. Genet. Psychol.*, 1940, 57, 31–47.

Cattell, R. B., The description of personality: Basic traits resolved into clusters, *J. Abnorm. Soc. Psychol.*, 1943, 38, 476–506.

Cattell, R. B., Psychological measurement: normative, ipsative, interactive, *Psychol. Rev.*, 1944, 51, 292–303.

Cattell, R. B., The cultural functions of social stratification: I. Regarding the genetic basis of society, *J. Soc. Psychol.*, 1945, 21, 3–23.

Cattell, R. B., The riddle of perseveration, *J. Pers.*, 1946, 14, 229–267.

Cattell, R. B., Concepts and methods in the measurement of group syntality, *Psychol. Rev.*, 1948, 55, 48–63.

Cattell, R. B., and L. G. Wispe, The dimensions of syntality in small groups, *J. Soc. Psychol.*, 1948, 28, 57–78.

Cattell, R. B., The dimensions of culture patterns by factorization of national character, *J. Abnorm. Soc. Psychol.*, 1949, 44, 443–469.

Cattell, R. B., and L. G. Tiner, The varieties of structural rigidity, *J. Pers.*, 1949, 17, 321–341.

Cattell, R. B., The main personality factors in questionnaire, self-estimate material, *J. Soc. Psychol.*, 1950, 31, 3–38.

Cattell, R. B., and L. Luborsky, P-technique demonstrated as a new clinical method for determining personality and symptom structure, *J. Gen. Psychol.*, 1950, 42, 3–24.

Cattell, R. B., and D. R. Saunders, Interrelation and matching of personality factors from behavior rating, questionnaire, and objective test data, *J. Soc. Psychol.*, 1950, 31, 243–260.

Cattell, R. B., The three basic factor-analytic research designs—their interrelations and derivatives, *Psychol. Bull.*, 1952, 49, 499–520.

Cattell, R. B., H. Breul, and H. P. Hartman, An attempt at more refined definition of the cultural dimensions of syntality in modern nations, *Amer. Soc. Rev.*, 1952, 17, 408–421.

Cattell, R. B., and K. P. Cross, Comparison of ergic and self-sentiment structures found in synamic traits by R- and P- techniques, *J. Pers.*, 1952, 21, 250–271.

Cattell, R. B., The personality factor structuring of 11-year-old children in terms of behavior rating data, *J. Clin. Psychol.*, 1953, 9, 256–266.

Cattell, R. B., Research designs in psychological genetics with special reference to the multiple variance method, *Amer. J. Hum. Genet.*, 1953, 5, 76–93.

Cattell, R. B., and J. C. Anderson, The measurement of personality and behavior disorders by the IPAT Music Preference Test, *J. Appl. Psychol.*, 1953, 37, 446–454.

Cattell, R. B., and H. Beloff, Research origin and construction of the IPAT Junior Personality Quiz, *J. Consult. Psychol.*, 1953, 17, 436–442.

Cattell, R. B., Musical preferences and personality diagnosis, *J. Soc. Psychol.*, 1954, 39, 3–24.

Cattell, R. B., S. S. Dubin, and D. R. Saunders, Personality structure in psychotics by factorization of objective clinical tests, *J. Ment. Sci.*, 1954, 100, 154–176.

Cattell, R. B., and W. Gruen, The primary personality factors in the questionnaire medium for children 10–14 years old, *Educ. Psychol. Measmt*, 1954, 14, 50–76.

Cattell, R. B., and G. F. Stice, Four formulae for selecting leaders on the basis of personality, *Hum. Relat.*, 1954, 7, 493–507.

Cattell, R. B., The chief invariant psychological and psychophysical functional unities found by P-technique, *J. Clin. Psychol.*, 1955, 11, 319–343.

Cattell, R. B., The principle replicated factors discovered in objective personality tests, *J. Abnorm. Soc. Psychol.*, 1955, 50, 291–314.

Cattell, R. B., D. B. Blewett, and J. R. Beloff, The inheritance of personality: A multiple variance analysis determination of approximate nature–nurture ratio for primary personality factors in Q-data, *Amer. J. Hum. Genet.*, 1955, 7, 122–146.

Cattell, R. B., and J. E. Drevdahl, A comparison of the personality profile (16 P.F.) of eminent researchers with that of eminent teachers and administrators and of the general population, *Brit. J. Psychol.*, 1955, 46, 248–261.

Cattell, R. B., and W. Gruen, The primary personality factors in 11-year-old children, by objective tests, *J. Pers.*, 1955, 23, 460–748.

Cattell, R. B., Second-order personality factors in the questionnaire realm, *J. Consult. Psychol.*, 1956, 20, 411–418.

Cattell, R. B., A shortened "Basic English" version (Form C) of the 16 P.F. Questionnaire, *J. Soc. Psychol.*, 1956, 44, 257–278.

Cattell, R. B., Validation and intensification of the Sixteen Personality Factor Questionnaire, *J. Clin. Psychol.*, 1956, 12, 205–214.

Cattell, R. B., and A. R. Baggaley, The objective measurement of attitude motivation: Development and evaluation of principles and devices, *J. Pers.*, 1956, 24, 401–423.

Cattell, R. B., and R. W. Coan, Personality factors in middle childhood as revealed in parents' ratings, *Child Develpm.*, 1957, 28, 439–458.

Cattell, R. B., The conceptual and test distinction of neuroticism and anxiety, *Clin. Psychol.*, 1957, 13, 221–223.

Cattell, R. B., Formulae and table for obtaining validities and reliabilities of extended factor scales, *Educ. Psychol. Measmt.*, 1957, 17, 491–498.

Cattell, R. B., A universal index for psychological factors, *Psychologia*, 1957, 74–85.

Cattell, R. B., and R. W. Coan, Child personality structure as revealed teacher's behavior ratings, *J. Clin. Psychol.*, 1957, 13, 315–327.

Cattell, R. B., G. F. Stice, and N. F. Kristy, A first approximation to nature–nurture ratios for eleven primary personality factors in objective tests, *J. Abnorm. Soc. Psychol.*, 1957, 54, 143–159.

Cattell, R. B., Extracting the correct number of factors in factor analysis, *Educ. Psychol. Measmt*, 1958, 18, 791–838.

Cattell, R. B., A need for alertness to multivariate experimental findings in integrative surveys, *Psychol. Bull.*, 1958, 55, 253–256.

Cattell, R. B., What is "objective" in "Objective Personality Tests"? *J. Counsel. Psychol.*, 1958, 5, 285–289.

Cattell, R. B., and A. R. Baggaley, A confirmation of ergic and engram structures in attitudes objectively measured, *Aust. J. Psychol.*, 1958, 10, 289–318.

Cattell, R. B., and R. W. Coan, Personality dimensions in the questionnaire responses of six- and seven-year-olds, *Brit. J. Educ. Psychol.*, 1958, 28, 232–242.

Cattell, R. B., R. W. Coan, and H. Beloff, A reexamination of personality structure in late childhood, and development of the High School Personality Questionnaire, *J. Exp. Educ.*, 1958, 27, 73–88.

Cattell, R. B., and I. H. Scheier, Clinical validities by analyzing the psychiatrist exemplified in relation to anxiety diagnosis, *Amer. J. Orothopsychiat.*, 1958, 28, 699–713.

Cattell, R. B., and I. H. Scheier, The nature of anxiety: A review of thirteen multivariate analyses comprising 814 variables, *Psychol. Rep.*, 1958, 4, 351–388.

Coan, R. W., and R. B. Cattell, Reproducible personality factors in middle childhood, *J. Clin. Psychol.*, 1958, 14, 339–345.

Drevdahl, J. E., and R. B. Cattell, Personality and creativity in artists and writers, *J. Clin. Psychol.*, 1958, 14, 107–111.

Peterson, D. R., and R. B. Cattell, Personality factors in nursery school children as derived from parent ratings, *J. Clin. Psychol.*, 1958, 14, 346–355.

Scheier, I. H., and R. B. Cattell, Confirmation of objective test factors and assessment of their relation to questionnaire factors: A factor analysis of 113 ratings, questionnaire and objective test measurements of personality, *J. Ment. Sci.*, 1958, 104, 608–624.

Cattell, R. B., and R. W. Coan, Objective test assessment of the primary personality dimensions in middle childhood, *Brit. J. Psychol.*, 1959, 50, 235–252.

Cattell, R. B., and D. R. Peterson, Personality structure in four- and five-year-olds in terms of objective tests, *J. Clin. Psychol.*, 1959, 15, 355–369.

Cattell, R. B., and I. H. Scheier, Extension of meaning of objective test personality factors: Especially into anxiety neuroticism, questionnaire, and physical factors, *J. Gen. Psychol.*, 1959, 61, 287–315.

Coan, R. W., and R. B. Cattell, The development of the early school personality questionnaire, *J. Exp. Educ.*, 1959, 28, 143–152.

Peterson, D. R., and R. B. Cattell, Personality factors in nursery school children as derived from teacher's ratings, *J. Consult. Psychol.*, 1959, 23, 562.

Cattell, R. B., and A. R. Baggaley, The salient variable similarity index for factor matching, *Brit. J. Statist. Psychol.*, 1960, 13, 33–46.

Cattell, R. B., Evaluating interaction and non-linear relations by factor analysis, *Psychol. Rep.*, 1960, 7, 69–70.

Cattell, R. B., and R. B. McMichael, Clinical diagnosis by the IPAT music preference test, *J. Consult. Psychol.*, 1960, 24, 333–341.

Cattell, R. B., and J. L. Muerle, The "max plane" program for factor rotation to oblique simple structure, *Educ. Psychol. Measmt.*, 1960, 20, 569–590.

Cattell, R. B., and I. H. Scheier, Stimuli related to stress, neuroticism, excitation, and anxiety response patterns: Illustrating a new multivariate experimental design, *J. Abnorm. Soc. Psychol.*, 1960, 60, 195–204.

Cattell, R. B., A. B. Sweney, and J. A. Radcliffe, The objective measurement of motivation structure in children, *J. Clin. Psychol.*, 1960, 16, 227–232.

Scheier, I. H., R. B. Cattell, and J. L. Horn, Objective test factor V. I. 23: Its measurement and its relation to clinically-judged neuroticism, *J. Clin. Psychol.*, 1960, 16, 134–145.

Cattell, R. B., The theory of situational, instrument, second order, and refraction factors in personality structure research, *Psychol. Bull.*, 1961, 58, 160–174, 176.

A rebuttal to Becker's challenge (see *Psychol. Bull.*, 1960, 57, 201–212).

Cattell, R. B., R. R. Knapp, and I. H. Scheier, Second-order personality factor structure in the objective test realm, *J. Consult. Psychol.*, 1961, 25, 345–352.

Cattell, R. B., and F. W. Warburton, A cross cultural comparison of patterns of extraversion and anxiety, *Brit. J. Psychol.*, 1961, 52, 3–15.

Shotwell, A. M., J. R. Hurley, and R. B. Cattell, Motivational structure of an hospitalized mental defective, *J. Abnorm. Soc. Psychol.*, 1961, 62, 422–426.

Sweney, A. B., and R. B. Cattell, Dynamic factors in twelve-year-old children as revealed in measures of integrated motivation, *J. Clin. Psychol.*, 1961, 17, 360–369.

Cattell, R. B., Advances in the measurement of neuroticism and anxiety, in a conceptual framework of unitary-trait theory, *Ann. N.Y. Acad. Sci.*, 1962, 93 815–839.

Cattell, R. B., J. Horn, and H. J. Butcher, The dynamic structure of attitudes in adults, *Brit. J. Psychol.*, 1962, 53, 57–69.

Research on ergs, sentiments, and motivation.

Cattell, R. B., and E. Howarth, Hypotheses on the principal personality dimensions in children and tests constructed for them, *J. Genet. Psychol.*, 1962 101, 145–163.

Cattell, R. B., and E. D. Lawson, Sex differences in small group performance, *J. Soc. Psychol.*, 1962, 58, 141–145.

Cattell, R. B., and J. H. Morony, The use of the 16 PF in distinguishing homosexuals, normals, and general criminals, *J. Consult. Psychol.*, 1962, 26, 531–540.

Cattell, R. B., and J. A. Radcliffe, Reliabilities and validities of simple and extended weighted and buffered unifactor scales, *Brit. J. Statist. Psychol.*, 1962 15, 113–127.

Cattell, R. B., and W. Sullivan, The scientific nature of factors: A demonstration by cups of coffee, *Behav. Sci.* 1962, 7, 184–193.

Factor analysis and cups of coffee as the model.

Hurley, J. R., and R. B. Cattell, The Procrustes Program: Producing direct rotation to test a hypothesized factor structure, *Behav. Sci.*, 1962, 7, 258–262.

Sweney, A. B., and R. B. Cattell, Relationships between integrated and unintegrated motivation structure examined by objective tests, *J. Soc. Psychol.*, 1962, 57, 217–226.

Cattell, R. B., The interaction of hereditary and environmental influences, *Brit. J. Statist. Psychol.*, 1963, 16, 191–210.

Cattell, R. B., The meaning and measurement of neuroticism and anxiety: Supplement to a review, *Brit. J. Soc. Clin. Psychol.*, 1963, 2, 224–226.

Cattell, R. B., The nature and measurement of anxiety, *Sci. Amer.*, 1963, 208, 96–104.

Cattell, R. B., Personality, role, mood, and situation-perception: A unifying theory of modulators, *Psychol. Rev.*, 1963, 70, 1–18.

Cattell, R. B., Teachers' personality description of six-year-olds: A check on structure, *Brit. J. Educ. Psychol.*, 1963, 33, 219–235.

Cattell, R. B., Theory of fluid and crystallized intelligence: A critical experiment, *J. Educ. Psychol.*, 1963, 54, 1–22.

Cattell, R. B., and M. J. Foster, The Rotoplot program for multiple, single-plane, visually-guided rotation, *Behav. Sci.*, 1963, 8, 156–165.

Cattell, R. B., and R. L. Gorsuch, The uniqueness and significance of simple structure demonstrated by contrasting organic "natural structure" and "random structure" data, *Psychometrika*, 1963, 28, 55–67.

Cattell, R. B., J. A. Radcliffe, and A. B. Sweney. The nature and measurement of components of motivation, *Genet. Psychol. Monogr.*, 1963, 68, 49–211.

Cattell, R. B., Beyond validity and reliability: Some further concepts and coefficients for evaluating tests, *J. Exp. Educ.*, 1964, 33, 133–143.

Cattell, R. B., The definitions of anxiety, *J.A.M.A.*, 1964, 190, 859.

Cattell, R. B., Objective personality tests. A reply to Dr. Eysenck, *Occup. Psychol.*, 1964, 38, 69–86.

Cattell, R. B., The parental early repressiveness hypothesis for the authoritarian personality factor, U. I. 28, *J. Genet. Psychol.*, 1964, 106, 333–349.

Cattell, R. B., Psychological definition and measurement of anxiety. *J. Neuropsychiat.*, 1964, 5, 7, 396–402.

Cattell, R. B., Validity and reliability: A proposed more basic set of concepts, *J. Educ. Psychol.*, 1964, 55, 1–22.

Cattell, R. B., H. J. Boutourline, and J. D. Hundleby, Blood groups and personality traits, *Amer. J. Hum. Genet.*, 1964, 16, 397–402.

Cattell, R. B., and J. M. Digman, A theory of the structure of perturbations in observer ratings and questionnaire data in personality research, *Behav. Sci.*, 1964, 9, 4, 341–358.

Cattell, R. B., and E. Howarth, Verification of objective test personality factor patterns in middle childhood, *J. Genet. Psychol.*, 1964, 104, 331–349.

Cattell, R. B., and K. Rickels, Diagnostic power of IPAT Objective Anxiety Neuroticism tests, *Arch. Gen. Psychiat.*, 1964, 11, 459–465.

Cattell, R. B., and A. B. Sweney, Components measurable in manifestations of mental conflict, *J. Abnorm. Soc. Psychol.*, 1964, 68, 479–490.

Cattell, R. B., D. Tatro, and E. Komlos, The diagnosis and inferred structure of paranoid and non-paranoid schizophrenia from the 16 P. F. profile 3, *Indian J. Psychol.*, 1964, 1, 52–61.

Cattell, R. B., and B. Tsujioka, The importance of factor-trueness and validity versus homogeneity and orthogonality in test scales, *Educ. Psychol. Measmt.* 1964, 24, 3–30.

Cattell, R. B., H. B. Young, and J. D. Hundleby, Blood groups and personality traits, *Amer. J. Hum. Genet.*, 1964, 16, 397–402.

Pawlik, K., and R. B. Cattell, Third-order factors in objective personality tests *Brit. J. Psychol.*, 1964, 55, 1–18.

Cattell, R. B. The configurative method for surer identification of personality dimensions, notably in child study, *Psychol. Rep.*, 1965, 16, 269–270.

Cattell, R. B., A cross-cultural check on second stratum personality structure Notably of anxiety and exvia, *Aust. J. Psychol.*, 1965, 17, 12–23.

Cattell, R. B., Factor analysis: An introduction to essentials, *Biometrics*, 1965, 21 190–215.

Cattell, R. B., Factor analysis: An introduction to essentials: II. The role of factor analysis in research, *Biometrics*, 165, 21, 405–435.

Cattell, R. B., Some deeper significances of the computer for the practicing psychologist, *Personnel Guid. J.*, 1965, 44, 160–166.

Cattell, R. B., and R. L. Gorsuch, The definition and measurement of national morale and morality, *J. Soc. Psychol.*, 1965, 67, 77–96.

Cattell, R. B., D. Tatro, and E. Komlos, The diagnosis and inferred structure of paranoid and nonparanoid schizophrenia from the 16 P. F. profile 2, *Indian Psychol. Rev.*, 1965, 1, 108–115.

Horn, J. L., and R. B. Cattell, Vehicles, ipsatization, and the multiple-method measurement of motivation, *Canad. J. Psychol.*, 1965, 19, 265–279.

Rickels, K., and R. B. Cattell, The clinical factor validity and trueness of the IPAT verbal and objective batteries for anxiety and regression, *J. Clin Psychol.*, 1965, 21, 257–264.

Rickels, K., R. B. Cattell, A. MacAfee, and P. Hesbacher, Drug response and important external events in the patient's life, *Dis. Nerv. Syst.*; 1965, 26 782–786.

Tsujioka, B., and R. B. Cattell, Constancy and difference in personality structur and mean profile, in the questionnaire medium, from applying the 16 P. F. test in America and Japan, *Brit. J. Soc. Clin. Psychol.*, 1965, 4, 287–297.

Tsujioka, B., and R. B. Cattell, A cross-cultural comparison of second-statur (questionnaire) personality factor structures—anxiety and extraversion—i America and Japan, *J. Psychol.*, 1965, 65, 205–219.

Cattell, R. B., Evaluating therapy as total personality change: Theory and avail able instruments, *Amer. J. Psychother.*, 1966, 20, 69–88.

Cattell, R. B., Multivariate behavioral research and the integrative challenge, *Multivariate Behav. Res.*, 1966, *1*, 4–23.

Cattell, R. B., The scree test for the number of factors, *Multivariate Behav. Res.*, 1966, *1*, 245–276.

Cattell, R. B., and A. Bjerstedt, The structure of depression, by factoring Q-data, in relation to general personality source traits, in normal and pathological subjects, *Educ. Psychol. Interactions*, 1966, *16*, 13.

Cattell, R. B., and M. A. Coulter, Principles of behavioral taxonomy and the mathematical basis of the taxonome computer program, *Brit. J. Math. Statist. Psychol.*, 1966, *19*, 237–269.

Cattell, R. B., M. A. Coulter, and B. Tsujioka, The taxonometric recognition of types and functional emergents, *Brit. J. Math. Statist. Psychol.*, 1966, *19*, 288–329.

Cattell, R. B., A. P. Sealy, and A. B. Sweney, What can personality and motivation source trait measurements add to the prediction of school achievement? *Brit. J. Educ. Psychol.*, 1966, *36*, 280–295.

Cattell, R. B., and D. F. Tatro, The personality factors, objectively measured, which distinguish psychotics from normals, *Behav. Res. Ther.*, 1966, *4*, 39–51.

Horn, J. L., and R. B. Cattell, Age differences in primary mental ability factors, *J. Geront.*, 1966, *21*, 210–220.

Horn, J. L., and R. B. Cattell, Refinement and test of the theory of fluid and crystallized general intelligences, *J. Educ. Psychol.*, 1966, *57*, 253–270.

Pierson, G. R., R. B. Cattell, and J. Pierce, A demonstration by the HSPQ of the nature of the personality changes produced by institutionalization of delinquents, *J. Soc. Psychol*, 1966, *70*, 229–239.

Sealy, A. P., and R. B. Cattell, Adolescent personality trends in primary factors measured on the 16 PF and the HSPQ questionnaires through ages 11 to 23, *Brit. J. Soc. Clin. Psychol.*, 1966, *5*, 172–184.

Cattell, R. B., The theory of fluid and crystallized general intelligence checked at the 5–6 year-old level, *Brit. J. Educ. Psychol.*, 1967, *37*, 209–224.

Cattell, R. B., and A. Bjerstedt, The structure of depression, by factoring Q-data, in relation to general personality source traits, *Scand. J. Psychol.*, 1967, *8*, 17–24.

Cattell, R. B., and J. Jaspers, A General plasmode (No. 30–10–5–2) for factor analytic exercises and research, *Multivariate Behav. Res. Monogr.*, 1967, *67*, 211.

Cattell, R. B., and L. R. Killian, The pattern of objective test personality factor difference in schizophrenia and the character disorders, *J. Clin. Psychol.*, 1967, *23*, 342–348.

Cattell, R. B., and S. Krug, Personality factor profile peculiar to the student smoker, *J. Counsel. Psychol.*, 1967, *14*, 116–121.

Cattell, R. B., and J. R. Nesselroade, Likeness and completeness theories examined by Sixteen Personality Factor measures on stably and unstably married couples, *J. Pers. Soc. Psychol.*, 1967, *7*, 351–361.

Cross, P. G., R. B. Cattell, and H. J. Butcher, The personality pattern of creative artists, *Brit. J. Educ. Psychol*, 1967, 37, 292–299.

Gorsuch, R. L., and R. B. Cattell, Second Stratum personality factors defined in the questionnaire realm by the 16 P. F., *Multivariate Behav. Res.*, 1967, 2, 211–223.

Horn, J. L., and R. B. Cattell, Age differences in fluid and crystallized intelligence, *Acta Psychol.* (Amst.), 1967, 26, 107–129.

Cattell, R. B., Progress in clinical psychology through multivariate experimental designs, *Multivariate Behav. Res.*, 1968, Special Issue, pp. 4–8.

Cattell, R. B., Trait-view theory of perturbations in ratings and self ratings (L(BR)- and Q-data): Its application to obtaining pure trait score estimates in questionnaires, *Psychol. Rev.*, 1968, 75, 96–113.

Cattell, R. B., H. W. Eber, and K. H. Delhees, A large sample cross validation of the personality trait structure of the 16 P. F. with some clinical implications, *Multivariate Behav. Res.*, 1968, Special Issue, pp. 107–131.

Cattell, R. B., and B. D. Gibbons, Personality factor structure of the combined Guilford and Cattell personality questionnaires, *J. Pers. Soc. Psychol.*, 1968, 9, 107–120.

Cattell, R. B., and J. H. Hundleby, Conceptual and experimental requirements in relating independence (U. I. 19) and field independence in L- and Q-data media: A comment on Dr. Ohnmacht's research, *Percept. Mot. Skills*, 1968, 27, 733–734.

Cattell, R. B., E. Komlos, and D. F. Tatro, Significant differences of affect, paranoid, and non-paranoid schizophrenic psychotics on primary source traits in the 16 P. F., *Multivariate Behav. Res.*, 1968, Special Issue, pp. 33–54.

Cattell, R. B., and J. R. Nesselroade, Note on analyzing personality relations in married couples, *Psychol. Rep.*, 1968, 22, 381–382.

Cattell, R. B., and K. Rickels, The relationship of clinical symptoms and IPAT-factored tests of anxiety, regression and asthenia: A factor analytic study, *J. Nerv. Ment. Dis.*, 1968, 146, 147–160.

TAPE RECORDINGS

Cattell, R. B., *Theory and Method in Personality Research* (G. W. Kisker, ed.), Sound Seminars, No. 143, Cincinnati, Ohio.

Cattell, R. B., *Measuring Personality by Structurally Defined Factors* (G. W. Kisker, ed.), Sound Seminars, No. 144, Cincinnati, Ohio.

Cattell, R. B., *The Dynamic Calculus of Personality* (G. W. Kisker, ed.), Sound Seminars, No. 145, Cincinnati, Ohio.

Cattell, R. B. *Group Dynamics and the Measurement of Group Characters* (G. W. Kisker, ed.), Sound Seminars, No. 146, Cincinnati, Ohio.

Cattell, R. B., *The Psychological Measurement of Culture Patterns* (G. W. Kisker, ed.), Sound Seminars, No. 147, Cincinnati, Ohio.

SUGGESTED READINGS

BOOKS

Adcock, C. D., Review of the 16 P. F. questionnaire, in O. K. Buros (ed.), *Fifth Mental Measurements Yearbook*. Highland Park, N.J.: Gryphon Press, 1959, pp. 196–199.

Baughman, E. E., and G. S. Welsh, *Personality: A Behavioral Science*, Englewood Cliffs, N.J.: Prentice-Hall, 1962, pp. 327–330.

Good short explanation of factoring.

Chaplin, J. P., and T. S. Krawiec, *Systems and Theories of Psychology*. New York: Holt, Rinehart & Winston, 1960, pp. 424–431.

French, J. W., The description of personality measurements in terms of rotated factors, *E.T.S. Bull.* Princeton, N.J.: Educational Testing Service, 1963.

Hall, C. S., and G. Lindzey, *Theories of Personality*. New York: Wiley, 1957, pp. 393–417.

Harsh, C. M., and H. G. Schrickel, *Personality: Development and Assessment*, 2nd ed. New York: Ronald Press, 1959, pp. 456–466.

Holt, R. R., A clinical-experimental strategy for research in personality, in S. Messick and J. Ross (eds.), *Measurement in Personality and Cognition*. New York: Wiley, 1962, pp. 269–283.

Criticizes Cattell's factor analysis.

Holtzman, W. H., Personality structure, in *Annual Review of Psychology*, Vol. 16. Palo Alto, Cal.: Annual Reviews, Inc., 1965, pp. 119–156.

Horn, J. L., Motivation and dynamic calculus concepts from multivariate experiment, in R. B. Cattell (ed.), *Handbook of Multivariate Experimental Psychology*. Chicago: Rand McNally, 1966.

Klein, G. S., H. L. Barr, and D. L. Wolitzky, Personality, in *Annual Review of Psychology*, Vol. 18. Palo Alto, Cal.: Annual Reviews, Inc., 1967, pp. 467–560.

Lindzey, G., and C. S. Hall, *Theories of Personality*. New York: Wiley, 1965, pp. 355–382.

Lorr, M., Review of Cattell's 16 P. F. Questionnaire, in O. K. Buros (ed.), *Sixth Mental Measurements Yearbook*. Highland Park, N.J.: Gryphon Press, 1965.

Nesselroade, J. R., and K. H. Delhees, Methods and findings in experimentally based personality theory, in R. B. Cattell, *Handbook of Multivariate Experimental Psychology*. Chicago: Rand McNally, 1966, pp. 563–610.

Spearman, C., *Abilities of Man*. New York: Macmillan, 1927.

Thomson, G. H., *The Factorial Analysis of Human Ability*, 5th ed. Boston: Houghton Mifflin, 1951.

Thurstone, L. L., *Multiple Factor Analysis: A Development and Expansion of the Vectors of the Mind*. Chicago: University of Chicago Press, 1947.

Tomkins, S., A discussion of "personality structure and personality measurement" of R. B. Cattell, in *ETS, 1951, Invitational Conference on Testing Problems.* Princeton, N.J.: Educational Testing Service, 1952, pp. 97–107.

A sharp critique of Cattell's comments.

Varnon, P. E., *Personality Assessment: A Critical Survey*, London: Methuen, 1964.

Wiggins, J. S., Personality structure, in *Annual Review of Psychology*, Vol. 19. Palo Alto, Cal.: Annual Reviews, Inc., 1968, pp. 293–350.

PERIODICALS

Becker, W. C., The matching of behavior rating and questionnaire personality factors, *Psychol. Bull.*, 1960, 57, 201–212.

Bendig, A. W., Comparative reliability of Cattell's "covert" and "overt" items as measures of the anxiety factor, *J. Gen. Psychol.*, 1963, 69, 175–179.

Bensberg, G. J., and W. Sloan, The use of the Cattell Culture-Free Test with mental defectives, *Amer. J. Ment. Defic.*, 1955, 59, 499–503.

Fail to find evidence of culture-free aspects.

Cavanaugh, M. C., I. Cohen, D. Dunphy, E. A. Ringwell, and I. D. Goldberg, Prediction from the Cattell infant intelligence scale, *J. Consult. Psychol.*, 1957, 21, 33–37.

Crowne, D. P., Review of R. B. Cattell, *The Scientific Analysis of Personality*, *Contemp. Psychol.*, 1967, 12, 40–41.

Dowdy, C. D., An experimental test of Eysenck's and Cattell's theories of extroversion-introversion, *Dissert. Abstr.*, 1960, 20, 3376.

Eysenck, H. J., The nature of anxiety and the factorial method, *Psychol. Rep.*, 1958, 4, 453–454.

Cattell's work is a "landmark in the development of personality theory" but it has its statistical weaknesses.

Gordon, J. E., Review of R. B. Cattell, *Personality and Social Psychology*, *Contemp. Psychol.*, 1966, 11, 236–238.

Hypercritical analysis of Cattell the man rather than the theory or book.

Guilford, J. P., When not to factor analyze, *Psychol. Bull.*, 1952, 49, 26–37.

Holtzman, W. H., Methodological issues in P-technique, *Psychol. Bull.*, 1962, 59, 248–256.

Humphreys, L. G., The organization of human abilities, *Amer. Psychologist*, 1962, 17, 475–483.

Too many factors are too narrow, or artificial; need a hierarchy of abilities.

Humphreys, L. G., Critique of Cattell's "Theory of fluid and crystallized intelligence: A critical experiment," *J. Educ. Psychol.*, 1967, 58, 129–136.

Claims there are methodological weaknesses from start to finish.

Jain, K. S. P., Recent development in the theory of intelligence, *Manas*, 1963, *10*, 65–73.

Loevinger, J., The meaning and measurement of ego development, *Amer. Psychologist*, 1966, *21*, 195–206.

Factorial methods and "milestone sequences."

Marshall, I. N., Extraversion and libido in Jung and Cattell, *J. Anal. Psychol.*, 1967, *12*, 115–136.

Some correspondences are suggested between Jung's clinical descriptions of extraversion/introversion and Cattell's experimental studies of the same.

Mitchell, J. V., Jr., A comparison of the first and second order dimensions of the 16 P. F. and C. P. I. inventories, *J. Soc. Psychol.*, 1963, *61*, 151–166.

Overall, J. E., Note on the scientific status of factors, *Psychol. Bull.*, 1964, *61*, 270–276.

Results do not necessarily deal with primary characteristics or structures.

Peterson, D. R., Scope and generality of verbally defined personality factors, *Psychol. Rev.*, 1965, *72*, 48–59.

Factoring produces simple terms of broad semantic scope.

Sells, S. B., Structured measurement of personality and motivation: A review of contributions of Raymond B. Cattell, *J. Clin. Psychol.*, 1959, *15*, 3–21.

Broad critical review of Cattell's work.

Spearman, C., General intelligence objectively determined and measured, *Amer. J. Psychol.*, 1904, *15*, 201–293.

Thurstone, L. L. Psychological implications of factor analysis, *Amer. Psychologist*, 1948, *3*, 402–408.

13

EYSENCK

SOME BIOGRAPHICAL DATA

Hans Jurgen Eysenck was born in Germany on March 4, 1916, the son of Edward Anton and Ruth Eysenck. His parents were considered to be from an old liberal family in Berlin. Eysenck left Germany in 1934, when he was eighteen years old in protest against the Nazi regime. He was educated in schools in Germany, France, and England. For a while he studied at the Universities of Dijon and Exeter before obtaining his B.A. and Ph.D. degrees at University College, London, where he has also been awarded the Doctor o.

Science degree. Eysenck was first married in 1938 to Margaret Malcolm Davies, from which marriage was born one son, David. In 1950 Eysenck married Sybil Bianca Giuletta Rostal, and they have three sons and one daughter. Currently, Eysenck is doing considerable research and publication in periodicals and co-authoring textbooks with his wife Sybil. From 1942 to 1946 he served as senior research psychologist, Mill Hill Emergency Hospital. From 1950 to 1954 he was a Reader in Psychology, University of London (Institute of Psychiatry). Eysenck also has had experience in the United States. In 1949 through 1950 he served as visiting professor at the University of Pennsylvania and in 1954 as visiting professor at the University of California, Berkeley. At the present time, Eysenck is Professor of Psychology at the University of London in the Institute of Psychiatry, which position he has held since 1955. He has also been Director of the Psychological Department, Maudsley and Bethlehem Hospitals in London, since 1946. Hans Jurgen Eysenck is a very active man. He says his recreations are walking, tennis, chess, detective stories, and driving through the delightful English countryside. In addition, he is phenomenally active as a research psychologist, having published more than 200 articles in British, American, German, and French journals of psychology.

INTRODUCTION

The volume of work that Hans Jurgen Eysenck turns out is gigantic and ranges over a multitude of interests. At one time or another he has studied and written about body types, handwriting, psychotic–neurotic behavior, the effects of heredity in twin studies, tranquilizing drugs, and jokes and cartoons. Much of this breadth of interest can be seen in this partial list of his books: *The Structure of Human Personality* (1960, 2nd ed.), *The Dynamics of Anxiety and Hysteria* (1957), *Experiments in Personality* (ed.) (1959), *Behavior Therapy and the Neuroses* (ed.) (1960), *Handbook of Abnormal Psychology* (ed.) (1961), *Experiments with Drugs* (ed.) (1963), *Crime and Personality* (1964), *Experiments in Behavior Therapy* (ed.) (1964), *The Causes and Cures of Neuroses* (with S. Rachman) (1965), *The Biological Basis of Personality* (1967), and *The Structure and Measurement of Personality* (1969).

With the exception of Sigmund Freud, Hans Eysenck may be the most controversial figure to appear in this book. Eysenck is attacked and freely attacks in return. He scorns nonempirical research and invites controversy in his outspoken statements. However, as Gordon Allport has said, "controversy is the *sine qua non* of psychological progress."

At one time or another Eysenck has crossed swords with Beezhold,

Albino, Luborsky, Hamilton, Karon, Saunders, Rosenzweig, Mowrer, Sheldon, Rokeach, Christie, Wellek, Wyatt, and Else Frenkel-Brunswik. In most cases, Eysenck's rebuttal has been as sharp as the original attack upon him.

Eysenck's criticisms have centered primarily about projective tests, psychiatrists, Sheldon, nonscientific formulations, psychotherapy, and especially the entire procedure of psychoanalysis. For example, in his attack upon Sheldon (see *J. Ment. Sci.*, 1959, *105*, 1053–1058) he finds that Sheldon's system is "unnecessarily complicated, statistically inadequate, and theoretically not well founded." His strong criticism, with an almost passionate emotional appeal that psychotherapy needs methodology, has been repeated a number of times. He states categorically that psychotherapy is not a science but a loose art form. He feels that acceptable statements about personality must be scientifically established and that if they are not, they are to be relegated to the fields of literature, philosophy, or religion. His criticism of Freudian psychoanalysis is that, even if it were able to explain everything, it could predict nothing. In one of the rebuttals to Eysenck's comments, Wyatt (in David and von Bracken, *Perspectives in Personality Theory*, p. 350) accuses Eysenck of being against psychoanalysis but somehow quite dependent upon it for his original ideas.

Eysenck, like Cattell, publishes internationally, and his work has been translated for foreign psychological journals. At times one has the impression that Eysenck and Cattell are in a race to put articles into print. Eysenck has managed to publish approximately ten articles per year in the period from 1950 to 1960. The bibliography at the end of this chapter covers about half of his work. Eysenck has visited Cattell at the latter's laboratory at the University of Illinois. In some ways, because of their statistical interest, the two theorists may be considered to be somewhat alike.

Through his persistent efforts to create good replicable research, Eysenck has given a refreshing impetus to investigations in the field of personality study. There appears to be an emerging interest in his work, primarily from the statistically oriented psychologists of this country. To date, the primary effect is in the increase of citations found in texts on personality. With few exceptions, the newer references are highly favorable.

Eysenck considers himself a "cautious psychologist," unwilling and unable to make statements unless they are the results of replicable research, statistically controlled and openly reported.

There is some evidence of a diminution of publications by Eysenck. Previous issues of *Psychological Abstracts* at one time gave him a separate category in the index, as was accorded Freud. This has not been the case lately. Also, Adelson's article on personality, in *Annual Review of Psychology*, Vol. 20, 1969, with a bibliography of 210 items, makes no mention of Eysenck.

EYSENCK'S PSYCHOSTATISTICAL
DESCRIPTION OF HUMAN BEHAVIOR

Eysenck states that it is much too early to have a meaningful, sensible, testable, researchable theory of personality. In his own work he makes no claim to having a full-fledged theory of personality. He also feels that all other workers in this field are premature or faulty in their theory of personality formation since he considers the present state of personality theory formulation in general primarily descriptive more than concerned with the basic dynamics of human behavior. His own theory, therefore, is in the descriptive or classification stage.

However, Eysenck has recently become more and more concerned with the causal or dynamic aspects of behavior, as is especially evident in his 1957 book, *The Dynamics of Anxiety and Hysteria,* which contains his concepts of learning theory and its application to psychotherapy. As he wrote to me, ". . . [I] not only abjure Freud and all his works, but have tried to put a *rational* method of diagnosis and treatment in the place of psychoanalysis— i.e., Behavior Therapy. This is an important part of my system."

Eysenck has been influenced by Jung's typology of introversion and extraversion, and by the work of Kretschmer and body or constitutional dimensions. Eysenck is strongly against the proliferation of components in a personality theory. He much favors parsimonious practicality in theory construction. In any case, theory must always be buttressed by replicable research. To talk about the "whole man" is vague and overly philosophical. He is not against philosophy but does not believe philosophically couched terms should be called "psychology" or "scientific." There is a need, therefore, to find the dimensions of personality before a theory can be constructed. In working with these dimensions, one must use factor analysis, even though factor analysis may be weak, because no other method appears to be practicable. It is necessary to quantify fundamental facts in the behavioral sciences. Eysenck also wrote to me, "I think you make too much of the factor analytic method in our work; in recent years we have repeated it all using multiple discriminant functions. It has been very welcome to see that this much more respectable method gives very similar results."

In his own work with personality theory, Eysenck insists upon as many variables as it is possible to obtain. Variables such as ratings by self and others, body measurements, galvanometric measurements, biographical data, historical data, and observational reports are all quite necessary to fill out the picture of personality for any one being. In addition to including as many variables as possible in studying personality, Eysenck always tries to get a criterion or a control group that does not have these quantities, or differs in the amounts possessed to a measurable and discrete degree. Then, he feels one can do research. Consequently, Eysenck almost always works with two groups which are dichotomous in any category—honesty–dishonesty; cowardice–courage—which he happens to be studying.

From the above, it is easy to see that Eysenck favors the team approach to narrow down the data by the "hypothetico-deductive" method. He prefers to study personality founded on a hypothetical structure and then, through deductive testing and the use of statistical methods, to arrive at a defensible position with as few components as possible.

Eysenck's definition of personality revolves around four behavior patterns: the cognitive (intelligence), the conative (character), the affective (temperament), and the somatic (constitution). Thus, personality is "The sum total of the actual or potential behavior-patterns of the organism, as determined by heredity and environment; it originates and develops through the functional interaction of the forming sectors into which these behavior patterns are organized . . ." (*Dimensions of Personality*, p. 25). In the past Eysenck has also considered Allport's famous and oft-repeated definition which Eysenck accepted in his 1953 work, *Structure of Human Personality* and he has utilized Roback's definition of personality (1934): "The integrated organization of all the cognitive, affective, conative, and physical characteristics of an individual as it manifests itself in focal distinctness to others." Inherent in this definition of personality by Eysenck is his belief in the continuity of behavior.

In regard to the idiographic (individual) *vs.* the nomothetic (discovering general laws of behavior), Eysenck states that if personality study is to be a science, it must by its very nature be nomothetic.

Only for purposes of pedagogical clarity. Eysenck's theory is presented as four principles: biological, methodological, dynamic/structural, and learning/empirical. This rubric does not cover all of his work but does embrace the major components of his theoretical position.

Biological Principle

There is much evidence indicating that to Eysenck personality has very definite biological bases. Actually as one studies his work it almost amounts to a discussion of the acknowledgment of the fundamental principle of man's neural system.

For example, "I consider introversion–extraversion to be just as much constitutionally determined as neuroticism" (note to author). Much of Eysenck's consideration of the biological man concerns itself with the central nervous system and particularly the cortical inhibitions that he finds in his research data. Neuroticism and introversion–extraversion operate at the causal level in the neural system. Neuroticism is believed to come from the excitabil-

y of the autonomic nervous system. On the other hand, introversion–extra-
ersion is based on the properties of the central nervous system. In another
xample, ". . . depressant drugs increase cortical inhibition, decrease cortical
xcitation and thereby produce extraverted behavior patterns." Stimulant
rugs are seen to decrease cortical inhibition and increase cortical excitation
nd in that way produce an introverted individual.

Primarily through the study of identical twins Eysenck concluded that
euroticism may have a constitutional basis or may be based upon heredity.
Jsing self-devised instruments and tests for measuring neuroticism, he found
correlation of .85 between neurotic behavior and nonneurotic behavior in
lentical twins, while in fraternal twins the correlation was only .21. In some
ays he even goes so far as to present the argument that the relationships
etween parents and their children may be determined by heredity and not
ctually be represented as a total environmental influence.

To consolidate his thinking, in 1967 Eysenck presented an entire book
ntitled *The Biological Basis of Personality*, recapitulating his past work and
roposing that some laws of behavior have a complete biological basis. Two
imensions are involved. One embodies emotionality, neuroticism, and in-
tability. On the other hand, introversion–extraversion are also affected by the
uman biological heredity. In what may appear to be a deviant approach, he
lso includes the age-old classification system of Hippocrates and Galen,
eeling unable to reject the concepts of the melancholic type, the choleric
ype, the phlegmatic type, and the sanguine type of constitutional makeup.
hus we find there are biological causes which underlie the psychological
oncepts of emotion, excitation, and inhibition. There is a relationship
etween the organic structure of humans and their susceptibility to condition-
1g, the types of diseases to which they may be prone, and their responses to
arious drugs.

Methodological Principle

s we have previously seen, Eysenck is extremely inventive in the methods
vith which he studies human personalities. Whatever they are, and they are
umerous, all of his methods are directed to studying the relationship of
ehavior to introversion–extraversion and neuroticism and psychoticism.
hrough the years, he has used all of the following methods in his multi-
ariant approach: eyelid conditioning, galvanic stimulus response, self-ratings,
peech, salivating, smoking, mirror drawing, dark vision, pursuit-rotor tasks,
apacity for body sway, jokes and cartoons, graphology, hypnosis, and animals.
his is not a complete list but gives some idea of the breadth of his approach.

Eysenck's primary approach is the hypothetico-deductive method. He
ets up hypotheses and then tests them deductively.

Like Cattell and Guilford, Eysenck favors factoral analysis and lately the multivariant statistical method in treating the data he gathers. In contrast to Cattell but more in the framework of Guilford, Eysenck prefers to focus almost entirely upon higher levels of abstraction in which he ignores the first order factors that emerge. Cattell prefers second and in many cases third order factors. This means that Eysenck generally extracts two or three factors whereas, as we have seen, Cattell finds approximately twenty factors are necessary and in many cases more, depending upon the raw data he is using. There is a major difference between these two personality theorists, in that Cattell prefers the criteria of rotation to simple structure which almost always is in the oblique manner. Cattell then feels that he gets closer to the true nature of personality structure. Eysenck, on the other hand, depends more on rotation which is usually orthogonal to other external criteria. Thus,

> The consequence of the first difference explains the second; since rotation to simple structure usually yields correlated (oblique) first order factors, these can again be factored to give second order factors, and so on, until the higher order factors are reached that are either uncorrelated or too few to permit further factorization. Thus, the apparent difference in number of factors is merely one of level; Eysenck's two major factors are neuroticism and introversion–extraversion typically appear as second order factors in Cattell's analyses of verbal data, so that the two systems actually correspond (Klein et al., 1967).

As Eysenck has moved farther from the basic computations of factoral analysis he proposes work in multiple discriminant function analysis, which he prefers as a tool to arrive at his typologies.

Throughout the years Eysenck has continued to validate and collect data on a paper and pencil test which he has named the Maudsley Personality Inventory (MPI). The initial validation of this instrument originally covered the period from 1959 to 1962. The MPI is designed primarily to measure neuroticism and introversion–extraversion. Eysenck, with the help of his wife Sybil, introduced an American version in 1963 called the Eysenck Personality Inventory (EPI). This latest paper and pencil device consists of forty-eight items of which twenty-four are keyed to each of the factors of neuroticism and introversion–extraversion. Like Cattell, the Eysencks continue to modify and validate the laboratory findings in both instruments. The EPI differs somewhat from the original Maudsley Inventory in that it incorporates a Lie Scale. The authors of the test maintained that the only true criterion for evaluating both the MPI and the EPI is the "power to predict outside of the closed circle of factor analysis into the realm of laboratory experiment." Thus they do not feel that personality can be exclusively measured on a paper and pencil test. Both personality scales are similar to all such scales (phenotypic instruments); they describe but in themselves do not offer a theory about ausation. However, Eysenck emphasizes that one should try to understand ersonality at the genotypic level; the task is to develop and test causal eories for which the descriptive elements are then observable.

Dynamic/Structural Principle

Whereas Cattell emphasizes traits, Eysenck emphasizes types. Much of the oal of his work has been to identify types, and at times they have been efined by what we generally consider descriptions of traits.

THREE PRIMARY DIMENSIONS OF PERSONALITY

In his work so far, Hans Eysenck has identified three primary dimensions of ersonality:

Introversion (superego)	Extraversion (id)
Neuroticism	Non-neuroticism
Psychoticism	Non-psychoticism

In most personality systems which deal with deviant behavior the general oncept is that of the Gaussian curve or bell-shaped curve. By this device ormal subjects distribute themselves at the center with neurotics and sychotics being indicated at the opposite sides. Thus we have a situation as ollows.

Psychotics   Normals   Neurotics

Other attempts to delineate the differences between psychotics, neu-otics, and normals assume a dichotomy in which the normal individual eviates either as a psychotic *or* neurotic in the following manner.

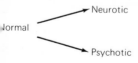

Normal ⟨ Neurotic / Psychotic

Out of his vast experience and experimentation, Eysenck suggests an riginal third method of viewing the differences among people who are ormal or neurotic or psychotic. The following is a schematic presentation omewhat adapted from the orthogonal concepts first proposed by Eysenck in his *Scientific Study of Personality* (1952) and later presented in his Maudsley Monograph Number Two, *Perceptual Processes in Mental Illness* (1957), with Granger and Brengelmann.

Thus the human personality can move from normal to neurotic, norma
to psychotic, and normal to a mixed psychotic–neurotic behavior pattern
Movement can also take place from neurotic through the mixed psychotic
neurotic area and then into straight psychotic behavior without entering the
area of normal behavior. The reverse of any of these movements is, of course
equally possible. Eysenck feels that mixed cases of psychoticism–neuroticism
are far more likely to occur than pure psychotic or neurotic behaviors. H

```
┌──────────────┬──────────────────┐
│ Psychotic    ┆ Mixed            │
│ Behavior     ┆ Psychotic and    │
│      (B)     ┆ Neurotic         │
│              ┆ Behavior         │
│              ┆ (C)              │
├┄┄┄┄┄┄┄┄┄┄┄┄┄┄┼┄┄┄┄┄┄┄┄┄┄┄┄┄┄┄┄┄┤
│              ┆                  │
│ Normal       ┆ Neurotic         │
│ Behavior     ┆ Behavior (D)     │
│      (A)     ┆                  │
│              ┆                  │
└──────────────┴──────────────────┘
```

believes, as do others, that the preponderance of mixed cases "agrees well
with clinical experience," and his data now indicate that the "either . . . or
classification method is passé. Rather, an individual is placed on the plane
which comes nearest to his true emotional self. Referring again to the
schematic presentation we can see that person (A) is normal, (B) is psy
chotic but close to the limits of being a mixed type, (C) is very much at the
borderline of being mixed psychotic–neurotic but also close to the outer
fringes of normalcy, while (D) is far to the right in the area of true neurot
cism. Admittedly the schema is only a device and not operationally a true
phenomenon. It does, however, closely approximate Eysenck's original orthog
onal relationships drawn from his factorial work. Eysenck also feels that the
above three dimensions of personality are certainly not the only possibilities
Further research will uncover more of them. He credits Cattell with the skill
to "prospect" for more dimensions.

It is hoped the following list will help the reader summarize in his own
mind some of the differences between the factors of introversion–extraver
sion, neuroticism, and psychoticism.

Introverts

1. Condition better than extraverts via Hullian and Pavlovian methods.
2. Based on properties of central nervous system.
3. Constitutionally predisposed to develop strong excitatory and weak inhib
   tory potentials.

4. (See Extraverts #4, as introverts exhibit opposite behavior in laboratory experiments.)
5. Faster at computational tasks when under slow conditional pressures but not when conditions change rapidly.
6. Reproduce drawings faster and remember drawings for longer period.
7. Secrete more saliva when stimulated with lemon juice.
8. Normally sleep less than psychiatric patients but sleep longer when sedated.
9. Probably more sensitive to certain medication.
0. More difficult to inhibit.
1. More affected by stimulants.
2. Underreact to small doses of depressant drugs.
3. Judge time intervals as longer than others.
4. Smoke less but prefer pipes.
5. Seem to avoid stimuli.
6. Prefer subtler shades and less highly colored pictures.
7. When faced with novel situations want more information.
8. Relatively cautious.
9. Less inclined to gamble.
0. Relate to Hippocrates' melancholic and phlegmatic types.

Extraverts

1. Condition more poorly than introverts via Hullian and Pavlovian methods.
2. Also based on properties of central nervous system.
3. Constitutionally predisposed to develop weak excitatory and strong inhibitory potentials.
4. In laboratories (a) condition more poorly, (b) dislike repetitive tasks, (c) extinguish learned behaviors more readily, (d) task satiation is greater, and (e) exhibit stronger reminiscence effects than do introverts.
5. Longer immediate memory for digits.
6. Could hold their breath longer.
7. Could keep one leg raised longer.
8. Easier to inhibit than others.
9. Little affected by stimulants.
0. Overreact to small doses of depressant drugs.
1. Judge time intervals as being shorter than do introverts.
2. Smoke more than introverts and prefer cigarettes.
3. Seem to seek out stimuli.
4. Prefer brighter and more highly colored pictures.
5. When faced with novel situations more inclined to focus on details.
6. Relatively compulsive.
7. Willing to take greater risks and gamble at larger odds.
8. Relate to Hippocrates' choleric and sanguine types.

Neurotics

1. Neuroticism a primary structure and not merely a syndrome.
2. Derived from excitation of autonomic system.
3. Behavior not as readily apparent to others as is extraversion.
4. Less able to see in the dark than normal subjects.
5. When blindfolded will sway forward more than normals.
6. Seem to have higher drive level than normals.

Psychotics

1. Less fluent.
2. Very poor performance on mirror drawings.
3. Dissipate inhibitions very slowly.
4. Unable to adjust readily to change in environment.
5. Extremely slow in intellectual, perceptual, and motor tasks.
6. Highly immobile.

Eysenck has also adapted some of his basic personality dynamics and structure to the work of Pavlov and Hull and formulated a *Postulate of Individual Differences.* This is based on the physical structures which are involved in making stimulus–response connections in the neural system. Thus he feels that individuals will differ in respect to three characteristics. The first is the speed or alacrity at which inhibition and excitation are produced in the neural system. The second also refers to the speed, this time at which inhibition is dissipated in the neural system. The third characteristic is the strength of the inhibition and excitation produced.

Eysenck also formulated a postulate of typologies, which states essentially the strong predisposition for introverted and extraverted behavioral patterns particularly when the individual is under stress or anxiety or faced by unsurmountable difficulties as interpreted by the individual. It should be carefully noted that Eysenck has stressed the word *predisposed* and not discussed the typologies as distinctly instinctive.

To any dedicated student of Eysenck's theory it is obvious that in the above summaries we have not included all of the Eysenck data but have to some degree included a few research findings of his coworkers and a few others.

It is interesting to relate particularly Eysenck's introversion–extraversion concepts with Sheldon's ectomorph as comparable to the introvert and Sheldon's endomorph/mesomorph (combined) in regard to the extravert. Many parallels should be evident. Perhaps some ambitious psychologist will enter this research area.

Not included in the above summaries is the work on sex difference, test anxiety, and cross-cultural effects, and the relationship of Eysenck's work to Janet Taylor Spence's work with the Manifest Anxiety Scale which was derived from items of the Minnesota Multiphasic Personality Inventory. W

ave saved some of the argument about eye-blink responses for the latter part
f this chapter under "Scientific or Laboratory Prediction."

We should also like to remind the reader that considerable research on
ntroversion and extraversion, as done by Eysenck and others, is taken up in
he Jung chapter ("Scientific or Laboratory Prediction" section).

At this point it should be evident that Eysenck's hypothetico-deductive
nethods have influenced his work a great deal. The research ranges from
alivating to body swaying to animal research and is designed to seek out
esearchable ideas prior to trying to formulate large categories other than, of
ourse, the big four: introversion–extraversion, neuroticism, and psychoticism.

The outline that follows is a summary of some of the factor analysis and
ype and trait work which Eysenck has been pursuing in the past ten to
fteen years.

YSENCK'S FACTORS	PERSONALITY FACTORS	POLITICAL CORRELATES
eneral factor (high importance)	Type (constellation of traits)	Ideology
roup factor	Traits (consistent habits)	Attitude
pecific factor	Habitual responses (reoccur in similar circumstances)	Habitual opinion
rror factor (low importance)	Specific responses (one single act)	Specific opinion

On the left side are Eysenck's categories, drawn from factor analysis and
mploying to some extent the work of C. L. Burt in *Factors of the Mind.*
ysenck has discovered four kinds of factors through his factor analysis work:
he general, the group, the specific, and the error factors. In the center of the
utline are the four comparable personality factors. The personality types
rew out of his general factors. It may be remembered that the personality
ypes were introversion–extraversion, neuroticism–non-neuroticism, and psy-
hoticism–non-psychoticism. Traits grew out of the group factors. Eysenck
nakes a strong point that traits must be operationally defined and capable of
eing measured. He finds that traits are approximate to consistent habits of
ehavior. Specific factors grow out of habitual responses which are behavioral
cts and which reoccur in similar circumstances. Error factors, which are the
west in importance, grow out of specific responses to any single act and
annot be used with a great degree of accuracy in the discussion of personality
r personality theory.

One of Eysenck's most recent interests is to link learning theory with
hat he has called *behavior therapy.* In *Behavior Therapy and the Neuroses*
1960), which he edited and supplied with two chapters, "Learning Theory

and Behavior Therapy" and "Modern Learning Theory," Eysenck interestingly enough dedicates the book, "To the memory of J. B. Watson." The gist
of Eysenck's position is that "neurotic symptoms are *learned patterns of
behavior*" which apparently become "*unadaptive*"; but it may be possible to
uncondition that which was once conditioned: neurotic symptoms. He feels
compelled to utilize learning theory in restructuring human behavior because
psychotherapeutic techniques, whether Freudian or neo-Freudian, have long
since entered a blind alley, despite fifty or more years of trial. Because
Freudianism is inconsistent, generates no testable deductions, he feels it is
time to examine human behavior and its derivations within the full framework of learning theory. As his theoretical models he uses the theories of
Pavlov, Thorndike, Tolman, Guthrie, and Hull. Eysenck also pays tribute to
the work of Miller and Mowrer, Spence, Wolpe, and especially Watson. In
summary, then, "Once we are agreed that learning and conditioning are
instrumental in determining the different kinds of reaction we may make to
environmental stimulation, we will find it very difficult to deny that neurotic
reactions, like all others, are *learned* reactions and must obey the laws of
learning" (*Behavior Therapy and the Neuroses*, p. 5; italics in the original).
And again at the end of this book, "We have, then, the beginnings of a
genuinely scientific system of learning theory from which we can deduce
certain methods of treatment for behavioral disorders" (*ibid.*, p. 466).

In *The Psychology of Politics* (1954) Eysenck stated that he had found
political correlates in the four kinds of factors growing out of his work. The
general factor seemed to him to be an ideology, the group factor an attitude,
the specific factor a habitual opinion, and the error factor any kind of specific
opinion, regarding a political situation.

Learning/Empirical Principle

Eysenck's work, particularly in the middle and late 1960's, has begun to lay a
great deal of stress on the learning processes and learning theory, particularly
from the Pavlovian and Hullian frames of reference. Thus Eysenck hopes to
find much better predictors and indicators of personality structure and
personality dynamics.

In some ways the key term for Eysenck is the *conditionability* of the
human organism. Although, as we have seen, it may have predispositions,
there is a strong and overpowering factor of learning in regard to human
personality. Not only does the individual learn to have a personality, but
when it is restructured, it follows the laws of learning, particularly as postulated by Hull and Pavlov.

Keeping abreast of the times, therefore, Eysenck has paid much attention to and done some replication of the work of Wolpe, which he finds

xtremely valuable. His interest in utilizing learning theory for restructuring ersonality is indicated by Eysenck's helping to create a new journal, *Behavor, Research, and Therapy,* begun in 1963 as an international multidiscipliary periodical. Both Mowrer and Wolpe are on the editorial board. Eysenck articularly is interested in Mowrer's two-factor theory of behavioral change. Eysenck's thesis is that the treatment of choice with such more overtly •chavioral conditions of this type should be a treatment based upon the rinciple of partial reinforcement and not classical extinction. This theoretical osition is an interesting current application of Mowrer's earlier two-factor heory of learning to psychotherapeutic treatment procedures" (Matarazzo, \nn. Rev. Psychol., 1965, 16, 185).

Thus, five years after Eysenck's first proposal of the term *behavior herapy* in 1960, he follows up with the publication of *The Causes and Cures f Neuroses.*

> In this book, Eysenck and Rachman make a serious attempt to translate experimental findings into clinical applications, leaning heavily on conditioning theory. The central focus is not how the person got that way but on how the behavior is presently functioning. They divide disorders into two groups, those in which faulty habits have been learned on the basis of conditioned fear, and those in which valuable habits have not been learned or faulty habits have been acquired instrumentally rather than as a fear avoidance. The first require extinction procedures, the second "the building up of missing stimulus-response connections." Treatment not only seeks to alter disordered behavior, but also to promote the development of effective alternate behavior patterns (Ford and Urban, *Ann. Rev. Psychol.,* 1967, *18,* 335).

As a result, Eysenck and Rachman feel that the psychotherapist should esign the therapy to fit each individual patient or client rather than to make ll the clients fit the overall aspects of one system of therapy. Despite the fact hat to some learning theory as expressed in behavior therapy is an overall ystem, Eysenck would hold that the general rubric of behavior therapy is a iighly individualistic one: Each client or patient requires, because he is an idividual, a highly individualistic paradigm in which to resolve his emotional •roblem.

)ELIMITATION

Ve have by no means exhaustively treated the fantastic amount of research hat Eysenck has done. Obviously, missing is the huge literature simply on iultivariate experimental procedures. Nor have we covered the ramifications f the Maudsley Medical Questionnaire, the Rees-Eysenck Body Index, and iany of the other tangential publications of Eysenck and, currently, his wife •ybil.

PREDICTING HUMAN BEHAVIOR
VIA EYSENCK'S THEORY

Personal Prediction

It is most difficult for this writer to recommend what the reader may do i
employing Eysenck's personality theory in connection with his own behavio
Perhaps, as suggested in the Cattell chapter, the individual may take some o
Eysenck's tests and apply them to his own phenomenological and exper
ential self. This procedure, of course, would not be highly approved t
Eysenck in principle. Thus, we are at a loss to suggest the personal predictio
for the individual. However, in good Rogerian framework, perhaps eac
reader of this text will have far more ingenuity and creativeness than th
present writer.

Scientific or Laboratory Prediction

Eysenck's prediction of human behavior is strictly.according to the nom
thetic approach he uses in the scientific or laboratory experiments he h
conducted since the mid-1940s. His experimental approach is therefore apt
suited to this section.

Rather than recapitulate the enormous amount of data accumulated t
Eysenck, we prefer to present the research of other experimenters whic
either substantiates some of his findings or disagrees, in some cases violentl
with his findings.

1. In a brief report of a study of personality and speech of extraverts an
introverts, Eysenck's theory was somewhat supported in that the exper
menter found extraverts using louder sounds and shorter silences in the
speech patterns (Ramsay, 1966).

2. Gottesman studied thirty-four identical and thirty-four fratern
twins. Although he did not apply Eysenck's measures but administered th
MMPI and Cattell's High School Personality Quiz, and also used a numb
of different measures such as fingerprint ridge counts, photographs, and bloo
types, he did manage to factor analyze a second order factor of introversion
extraversion which could be considered a substantiation of Eysenck's earli
conclusion in regard to inheritability of factors (Gottesman, 1963).

3. In another study, again not using Eysenck's Maudsley tests, a
attempt was made to cross-validate the California Psychological Invento
and Cattell's 16 Personality Factor Test along with behavior ratings. A
though the correlations among the thirty-four scales were not very high, th
second order factoring appeared to lend strong support to the contention th
introversion–extraversion and neuroticism are two valuable dimensions o
personality (Mitchell, 1963).

4. As we have stated previously in this chapter, Eysenck continues to
ndemn psychotherapy and any traditional therapeutic approaches as being
t much better than chance. Kiesler, in an effort to attack the myth of
ontaneous remission, comes very close to substantiating Eysenck's conclu-
ons in regard to what therapy is and how it fails in many of the traditional
pes of therapeutic processes (Kiesler, 1966).

5. Eysenck has stated that extraverts will have greater reminiscence after
ting and following a mass practice experience because of their higher level
inhibition. This prediction has been confirmed (Star, 1963).

6. Another study done by coworkers of Eysenck at the Maudsley Hospi-
l supports Eysenck's contention of a three-factor theory of reminiscence as
idied by a mirror-rotor task (Rachman and Grassi, 1965).

The above list, far from exhausting the corroborative research for
senck's work, is only meant as an indicator that Eysenck does not stand
ne in supporting his own theoretical position.

On the other hand, other evidence, equally dedicated to "Hard" re-
irch, refutes many of the studies which Eysenck has reported.

1. Anastasi in the second edition of her popular book *Psychological
sting* (1961) discusses criterion analyses. The general drift of the criticism
somewhat akin to Bakan's in that within the hypothetico-deductive system
e is inclined to find out what one set out to discover. Thus, if you already
ve a particular hypothesis in mind, you will plan the study in order to test
at hypothesis. Eysenck's original work began with the description of
urotic soldiers. However, in the final standardization of his testing device,
e Maudsley test and the Eysenck test, information about more than 10,000
her subjects has been added to the data. But Anastasi feels that to divide
ople into two factors alone is somewhat spurious. In final summation, it
ould not be too surprising that if you put small amounts of information into
e factor analysis you will get a small amount out of the factor analysis.

2. The work of Spence and Spence refutes Eysenck's contention that
traversion–introversion correlates at all with conditioning and extinction
pence and Spence, 1964).

3. Although the rebuttals to Eysenck's critical comments on therapy are
gion, probably the most noted is that of Rosenzweig. Despite the fact that
1960 or approximately ten years after Eysenck's original blast he found no
idence to change his mind, the Rosenzweig rebuttal is probably the best
ample that therapy does matter to human behavior (Rosenzweig, 1954).

4. Adams takes sixteen pages to rebut Eysenck's contention in regard to
otivation and the warm-up decrement in task response (Adams, 1961).

5. Although there is more than one attack on Eysenck's factoral and
ultivariate methods, probably the refutation by Lorr and coworkers is the
ost representative rebuttal (Lorr *et al.*, 1963).

6. Another rebuttal was an attempt to replicate an eye-blink condition-
g experiment using a rather small sample. It failed to confirm Eysenck's

measures, primarily finding that, or suggesting that, the questionnaire technique may be quite faulty in correlating with eye-blink conditioning (Franks,
1963).

7. Among the criticisms of Eysenck's work on drugs and the effects of
drugs on cortical inhibitions, probably one of the strongest is that of Joyce, in
Horizons in Psychology (Joyce, 1966).

Probably the best way to summarize the scientific and laboratory work of
Eysenck is to quote from the article by Klein, Barr, and Wolitsky, *Annual
Review of Psychology*, 1967, *18*, 503 (italics added):

> How, then, to assess Eysenck's theories and the considerable body of research
> they have stimulated? The theories represent a leap from higher to deeper
> levels of functioning, and many of the reported findings, especially by Ey-
> senck and his students, appear to support these theories. There are, however,
> many contradictory findings, which he often dismisses too glibly, and the most
> glaring lack is in physiological studies that might deal more directly with the
> issues. These may be forthcoming with increasing knowledge in that area, and
> the drug studies represent an attempt in that direction. An encouraging aspect
> to us, is the fact that contradictory findings *have often stimulated Eysenck
> not only to clarify his concepts, but to explore the relevant parameters of the
> laboratory tasks.*

■ SUMMARY

Eysenck, like Cattell, makes frequent use of the statistical technique of factor
analysis. However, he does not feel it is too strong a tool. He denies the
crucial significance of individuality in favor of a nomothetic approach. He
feels self should not be considered overly important in the study of personality. He also gives heavy emphasis to the role of heredity because of his study
of fraternal and identical twins. There are relatively few motivational concepts in Eysenck's theory because he prefers the parsimonious approach. In
the last analysis, Eysenck is a tremendous generator of research on his own
theory. He does not consider a theory of personality to have emerged yet from
his own work or the work of anyone else.

BIBLIOGRAPHY

RIMARY SOURCES

)OKS

ysenck, H. J., *Dimensions of Personality.* London: Routledge, 1947.
ysenck, H. J., *The Scientific Study of Personality.* New York: Macmillan, 1952.
  Sequel to *Dimensions of Personality,* 1947.
ysenck, H. J., *The Structure of Human Personality.* New York: Wiley, 1953.
ysenck, H. J., *Uses and Abuses of Psychology.* Baltimore: Penguin Books, 1953.
ysenck, H. J., *The Psychology of Politics.* London: Routledge, 1954.
  Also published by Praeger, New York, 1955.
ysenck, H. J., *Psychology and the Foundations of Psychiatry.* London: Lewis, 1955.
ysenck, H. J., Characterology, stratification theory and psychotherapy: An evaluation, in H. P. David and H. von Bracken (eds.), *Perspectives in Personality Theory.* New York: Basic Books, 1957, pp. 323–335.
ysenck, H. J., *The Dynamics of Anxiety and Hysteria: An Experimental Application of Modern Learning Theory to Psychiatry.* New York: Praeger, 1957.
ysenck, H. J., *Sense and Nonsense in Psychology.* Baltimore: Penguin Books, 1957.
ysenck, H. J., E. W. Granger, and J. C. Brengelmann, *Perceptual Processes in Mental Illness.* New York: Basic Books, 1957.
ynseck, H. J. (ed.), *Experiments in Personality,* 2 vols. London-Routledge, 1959.
ysenck, H. J., *Maudsley Personality Inventory.* London: University of London Press, 1959.
ysenck, H. J., Personality Tests: 1950–1959, in G. W: T. H. Fleming and A. Walk (eds.), *Recent Progress in Psychiatry,* Vol. III. New York: Grove Press, 1959.
ysenck, H. J. (ed.), *Behavior Therapy and the Neuroses.* London: Pergamon, 1960.
ysenck, H. J., Drug postulates, theoretical deductions, and methodological considerations, in L. Uhr and J. G. Miller (eds.), *Drugs and Behavior.* New York: Wiley, 1960.

Eysenck, H. J., A rational system of diagnosis and therapy in mental illness,
    L. E. Abt and B. F. Riess (eds.), *Progress in Clinical Psychology*, Vol. I
    New York: Grune & Stratton, 1960.
Eysenck, H. J., *The Structure of Human Personality*. London: Methuen, 1960.
Eysenck, H. J. (ed.), *Handbook of Abnormal Psychology: An Experimen*
    Approach. New York: Basic Books, 1961.
Eysenck, H. J. (ed.), *Experiments with Drugs: Studies in the Relation Betwe*
    Personality, Learning Theory and Drug Action. New York: Macmillan, 19(

    Also as a Pergamon Press book.

Eysenck, H. J., and S. B. G. Eysenck, *Eysenck Personality Inventory*. Londc
    University of London Press, 1963.
Eysenck, H. J., *Crime and Personality*. Boston: Houghton Mifflin, 1964.
Eysenck, H. J. (ed.), *Experiments in Behavior Therapy*. New York: Macmill.
    1964.

    Forty or more papers (American and British) about the value of I
    havior therapy.

Eysenck, H. J. (ed.), *Experiments in Motivation*. New York: Macmillan, 1964.
Eysenck, H. J., and S. B. G. Eysenck, *Manual of the Eysenck Personality Inve*
    tory. London: University of London Press, 1964.
Eysenck, H. J., *Fact and Fiction in Psychology*. Baltimore: Penguin Books, 19(
Eysenck, H. J., Factor theory psychology: A dimensional approach to personali
    in W. S. Sahakian (ed.), *Psychology of Personality: Readings in Theo*
    Chicago: Rand McNally, 1965, pp. 415–436.
Eysenck, H. J., Review of the Holtzman Inkblot Technique, in O. K. Buros (ed
    Sixth Mental Measurements Yearbook. Highland Park, N.J.: Gryphon Pre
    1965, pp. 440–441.
Eysenck, H. J., *Smoking, Health and Personality*. New York: Basic Books, 19(
Eysenck, H. J., and S. Rachman, *The Causes and Cures of Neuroses: An Int*
    duction to Modern Behavior Therapy Based on Learning Theory and t
    Principles of Conditioning. San Diego, Cal.: Knapp, 1965.

    Summary of Togears' research.

Eysenck, H. J., *The Biological Basis of Personality*. Springfield, Ill.: Thom:
    1967.
Eysenck, H. J., and S. B. G. Eysenck, *The Structure and Measurement of Perso*
    ality. London: Routledge, 1969.

PERIODICALS

Eysenck, H. J., Some factors in the appreciation of poetry and their relation
    temperamental qualities, *Charact. & Pers.*, 1941, 9, 160–167.
Eysenck, H. J., Type-factors in aesthetic judgment, *Brit. J. Psychol.*, 1941, 3
    262–270.
Eysenck, H. J., Suggestibility and hypnosis—an experimental analysis, *Proc. Rc*
    Soc. Med., 1943, 36, 349–354.

ysenck, H. J., Suggestibility and hysteria, *J. Neurol. Psychiat.*, 1943, 6, 22–31.

ysenck, H. J., States of high suggestibility and the neuroses, *Amer. J. Psychol.*, 1944, 57, 406–411.

ysenck, H. J., Graphological analysis and psychiatry: An experimental study, *Brit. J. Psychol.*, 1945, 35, 70–81.

ysenck, H. J., and W. D. Furneaux, Primary and secondary suggestibility: An experimental and statistical study, *J. Exp. Psychol.*, 1945, 35, 485–502.

ysenck, H. J., and W. L. Rees, States of heightened suggestibility: Narcosis, *J. Ment. Sci.*, 1945, 91, 301–310.

immelweit, H. T., and H. J. Eysenck, An experimental analysis of the mosaic projection test, *Brit. J. Med. Psychol.*, 1945, 20, 283–294.

ysenck, H. J., Primary social attitudes: I. The organization and measurement of social attitudes, *Int. J. Opin. Attitude Res.*, 1947, 1, 49–84.

ysenck, H. H., "Neuroticism" and handwriting, *J. Abnorm. Soc. Psychol.*, 1948, 43, 94–96.

ysenck, H. J., Criterion analysis: An application of the hypothetico-deductive method to factor analysis, *Psychol. Rev.*, 1950, 57, 38–53.

ysenck, H. J., Schizothymia–cyclothymia as a dimension of personality: I. Historical, *J. Pers.*, 1950, 19, 123–152.

ysenck, H. J., Neuroticism in twins, *Eugen. Rev.*, 1951, 43, 79–82.

ysenck, H. J., Psychology Department, Institute of Psychiatry (Maudsley Hospital), University of London, *Acta Psychol.*, 1951, 8, 63–68.

ysenck, H. J., and D. B. Prell, The inheritance of neuroticism: An experimental study, *J. Ment. Sci.*, 1951, 97, 441–465.

ysenck, H. J., The effects of psychotherapy: An evaluation, *J. Consult. Psychol.*, 1952, 16, 319–324.

ysenck, H. J., The organization of personality, *J. Pers.*, 1952, 20, 101–118.

ysenck, H. J., Personality, *Ann. Rev. Psychol.*, 1952, 3, 151–174.

ysenck, H. J., Schizothymia–cyclothymia as a dimension of personality: II. Experimental, *J. Pers.*, 1952, 20, 345–384.

ysenck, H. J., The application of factor analysis to the study of personality: A reply, *Brit. J. Psychol.*, 1953, 44, 169–172.

ysenck, H. J., The logical basis of factor analysis, *Amer. Psychologist*, 1953, 8, 105–114.

ysenck, H. J., A reply to Luborsky's note, *Brit. J. Psychol.*, 1954, 45, 132–133.

ysenck, H. J., The science of personality: Nomothetic! *Psychol. Rev.*, 1954, 61, 339–342.

ysenck, H. J., Cortical inhibition, figural after-effect, and theory of personality, *J. Abnorm. Soc. Psychol.*, 1955, 51, 94–106.

ysenck, H. J., A dynamic theory of anxiety and hysteria, *J. Ment. Sci.*, 1955, 101, 28–51.

ysenck, H. J., The effects of psychotherapy: A reply, *J. Abnorm. Soc. Psychol.*, 1955, 50, 147–148.

ysenck, H. J., Psychiatric diagnosis as a psychological and statistical problem, *Psychol. Rep.*, 1955, 1, 3–17.

Eysenck, H. J., Psychology, philosophy, and psychoanalysis, *Manasi*, 1955, 2, 1–6.

Eysenck, H. J., Diagnosis and measurement: A reply to Loevinger, *Psychol. Rep.*, 1956, 2, 117–118.

Eysenck, H. J., The inheritance of extraversion–introversion, *Acta Psychol.*, 1956, 12, 95–110.

Eysenck, H. J., The inheritance and nature of extraversion, *Eugen. Rev.*, 1956, 48, 23–30.

Eysenck, H. J., The psychology of politics: A reply, *Psychol. Bull.*, 1956, 53, 177–182.

Eysenck, H. J., The psychology of Politics and personality: Similarities between fascists and communists, *Psychol. Bull.*, 1956, 53, 431–438.

Eysenck, H. J., Reminiscence, drive, and personality theory, *J. Abnorm. Soc. Psychol.*, 1956, 53, 328–333.

Eysenck, H. J., Drugs and personality: I. Theory and methodology, *J. Ment. Sci.*, 1957, 103, 119–131.

Eysenck, H. J., S. Casey, and D. S. Trouton, Drugs and personality: II. The effect of stimulant and depressant drugs on continuous work, *J. Ment. Sci.*, 1957, 103, 645–649.

Eysenck, H. J., H. Holland, and D. S. Trouton, Drugs and personality: III. The effects of depressant and stimulant drugs on visual aftereffects, *J. Ment. Sci.* 1957, 103, 650–655.

Eysenck, H. J., H. Holland, and D. S. Trouton, Drugs and personality: IV. The effects of stimulant and depressant drugs on the rate of fluctuation of a reversible perspective figure, *J. Ment. Sci.*, 1957, 103, 656–660.

Eysenck, H. J., and S. Aiba, Drugs and personality: V. The effects of stimulant and depressant drugs on the suppression of the primary visual stimulus, *J. Ment. Sci.*, 1957, 103, 661–665.

Eysenck, H. J., The continuity of abnormal and normal behavior, *Psychol. Bull.* 1958, 55, 429–432.

Eysenck, H. J., Hysterics and dysthymics as criterion groups in the study of introversion–extraversion: A reply, *J. Abnorm. Soc. Psychol.*, 1958, 57, 250–252.

Eysenck, H. J., The nature of anxiety and the factorial method, *Psychol. Rep.* 1958, 4, 453–454.

Eysenck, H. J., A short questionnaire for the measurement of two dimensions of personality, *J. Appl. Psychol.*, 1958, 42, 14–17.

Eysenck, H. J., and P. Slater, Effects of practice and rest on fluctuations in the Müller-Lyer illusion, *Brit. J. Psychol.*, 1958, 49, 246–256.

Eysenck, H. J., Anxiety and hysteria: A reply to Vernon Hamilton, *Brit. J. Psychol.*, 1959, 50, 64–69.

Eysenck, H. J., Comments on a test of the personality–satiation–inhibition theory, *Psychol. Rep.*, 1959, 5, 395–396.

Eysenck, H. J., The differentiation between normal and various neurotic groups on the Maudsley Personality Inventory, *Brit. J. Psychol.*, 1959, 50, 176–177.

Eysenck, H. J., The inheritance of neuroticism: A reply, *J. Ment. Sci.*, 1959, 105, 76–80.

Eysenck, H. J., Learning theory and behavior therapy, *J. Ment. Sci.*, 1959, *105*, 61–75.

Eysenck, H. J., Personality and the dimension of time, *Percept. Mot. Skills*, 1959, *9*, 405–406.

Eysenck, H. J, Personality and problem solving, *Psychol. Rep.*, 1959, *5*, 592.

Eysenck, H. J., Personality and verbal conditioning, *Psychol. Rep.*, 1959, *5*, 570.

Eysenck, H. J., The Rees-Eysenck body index and Sheldon's somatotype system, *J. Ment. Sci.*, 1959, *105*, 1053–1058.

Eysenck, H. J., Serial position effects in nonsense syllable learning as a function of interlist rest pauses, *Brit. J. Psychol.*, 1959, *50*, 360–362.

Eysenck, H. J., Some recent criticisms of the dimensional analysis of personality, *J. Ment. Sci.*, 1959, *105*, 220–223.

Eysenck, H. J., The concept of statistical significance and the controversy about one-tailed tests, *Psychol. Rev.*, 1960, *67*, 269–271.

Eysenck, H. J., Levels of personality, constitutional factors, and social influences: An experimental approach, *Int. J. Soc. Psychiat.*, 1960, *6*, 12–24.

Eysenck, H. J., Reminiscence, extraversion, and neuroticism, *Percept. Mot. Skills*, 1960, *11*, 21–22.

Eysenck, H. J., Reminiscence as a function of rest, practice and personality, *Percept. Mot. Skills*, 1960, *11*, 91–94.

Eysenck, H. J., Reminiscence and post-rest increment after massed practice, *Percept. Mot. Skills*, 1960, *11*, 221–222.

Eysenck, H. J. and J. A. Easterbrook, Drugs and personality: VI–XI, *J. Ment. Sci.*, 1960, *106*, 831–857.

Eysenck, H. J., and H. Holland, Length of spiral after-effect as a function of drive, *Percept. Mot. Skills*, 1960, *11*, 129–130.

Eysenck, H. J., M. Tarrant, and L. England, Smoking and personality, *Brit. Med. J.*, 1960, *1*, 1456–1460.

Eysenck, S. B. G., H. J. Eysenck, and G. Claridge, Dimensions of personality, psychiatric syndromes, and mathematical models, *J. Ment. Sci.*, 1960, *106*, 581–589.

Holland, H., and H. J. Eysenck, Spiral after-effects as a function of length of stimulation, *Percept. Mot. Skills*, 1960, *11*, 228.

Singh, S. D., and H. J. Eysenck, Conditioned emotional response in the rat: III. Drug antagonism, *J. Gen. Psychol.*, 1960, *63*, 275–285.

Eysenck, H. J., The concept of mind: A behavioristic approach, *J. Psychol. Res.*, 1961, *5*, 37–47.

Eysenck, H. J., The measurement of motivation through the use of objective indices, *J. Ment. Sci.*, 1961, *107*, 961–968.

Eysenck, H. J., A note on "Impulse Repression and Emotional Adjustment," *J. Consult. Psychol.*, 1961, *25*, 362–363.

     Critique of Grater's work with morals and the MMPI in 1960 (see *Psychol. Abstr.*, 1960, *34*, 8202).

Eysenck, H. J., Personality and social attitudes, *J. Soc. Psychol.*, 1961, *53*, 243–248.

Eysenck, H. J., Psychosis, drive and inhibition: A theoretical and experimental account, *Amer. J. Psychiat.*, 1961, *118*, 198–204.

Eysenck, H. J., Review of R. B. Cattell and I. H. Scheier, *The Meaning and Measurement of Neuroticism and Anxiety, Occup. Psychol.*, 1961, *35*, 253–256.

Eysenck, H. J., and A. E. Maxwell, Reminiscence as a function drive, *Brit. J. Psychol.*, 1961, *52*, 43–52.

Costello, C. G., and H. J. Eysenck, Persistence, personality, and motivation, *Percept. Mot. Skills*, 1961, *12*, 169–170.

Lynn, R., and H. J. Eysenck, Tolerance for pain, extraversion, and neuroticism, *Percept. Mot. Skills*, 1961, *12*, 161–162.

Eysenck, H. J., Conditioning and personality, *Brit. J. Psychol.*, 1962, *53*, 299–305.

Defends self against criticisms by Champion.

Eysenck, H. J., Figural aftereffects, personality, and intersensory comparisons, *Percept. Mot. Skills*, 1962, *15*, 405–406.

Eysenck, H. J., Reminiscence, drive and personality: Revision and extension of a theory, *Brit. J. Soc. Clin. Psychol.*, 1962, *1*, 127–140.

Summary of twenty studies on extraversion and introversion.

Eysenck, H. J., Response set, authoritarianism and personality questionnaires, *Brit J. Soc. Clin. Psychol.*, 1962, *1*, 20–24.

Eysenck, H. J., and G. Claridge, The position of hysterics and dysthymics in a two dimensional framework of personality description, *J. Abnorm. Soc. Psychol.* 1962, *64*, 46–55.

Statistical proof of his theory.

Eysenck, H. J., and S. B. G. Eysenck, A factorial study of interview-questionnaire *J. Clin. Psychol.*, 1962, *18*, 286–290.

Eysenck, H.. J., and R. A. Willett, Performance and reminiscence on a symbo substitution task as a function of drive, *Percept. Mot. Skills*, 1962, *15* 389–390.

Eysenck, S. B. G., and H. J. Eysenck, Rigidity as a function of introversion and neuroticism: A study of unmarried mothers, *Int. J. Soc. Psychiat.*, 1962, *8* 180–184.

Willett, R. A., and H. J. Eysenck, Experimentally induced drive and difficulty level in serial rote learning, *Brit. J. Psychol.*, 1962, *53*, 35–39.

Eysenck, H. J., Behavior therapy, extinction, and relapse in neurosis, *Brit. J Psychiat.*, 1963, *109*, 12–18.

Eysenck, H. J., Behavior therapy, spontaneous remission, and transference in neurotics, *Amer. J. Psychiat.*, 1963, *119*, 867–871.

Mowrer's early two-factor learning theory and psychotherapy.

Eysenck, H. J., The biological basis of criminal behavior, *Advanc. Sci.*, 1963–1964 *20*, 1–11.

Eysenck, H. J., Biological basis of personality, *Nature* (London), 1963, *199*, 1031–1034.

Also in G. Lindzey and C. S. Hall (eds.), *Theories of Personality: Primary Sources and Research*. New York: Wiley, 1965.

Eysenck, H. J., The measurement of motivation, *Sci. Amer.*, 1963, *208*, 130–140.

Eysenck, H. J., Psychoticism or ten psychotic syndromes? *J. Consult. Psychol.*, 1963, *27*, 179.

Eysenck, H. J., Smoking, personality and psychosomatic disorders, *J. Psychosom. Res.*, 1963, *7*, 107–130.

Eysenck, S. B. G., and H. J. Eysenck, Acquiescent response set in personality questionnaires, *Life Sci.*, 1963, *2*, 144–147.

Eysenck, S. B. G., and H. J. Eysenck, On the dual nature of extraversion, *Brit. J. Soc. Clin. Psychol.*, 1963, *2*, 46–55.

Eysenck, S. B. G., and H. J. Eysenck, An experimental investigation of "desirability" response set in a personality questionnaire, *Life Sci.*, 1963, *5*, 343–355.

Eysenck, S. B. G., and H. J. Eysenck, The validity of questionnaire and rating assessments of extraversion and neuroticism, and their factorial stability, *Brit. J. Psychol.*, 1963, *54*, 51–62.

Warwick, K. M., and H. J. Eysenck, The effects of smoking on the CFF threshold, *Life Sci.*, 1963, *4*, 219–225.

Eysenck, H. J., An experimental test of the "inhibition" and "consolidation" theories of reminiscence, *Life Sci.*, 1964, *3*, 175–188.

Eysenck, H. J., Involuntary rest pauses in tapping as a function of drive and personality, *Percept. Mot. Skills*, 1964, *18*, 173–174.

Eysenck, H. J., The measurement of personality: A new inventory, *J. Indian Acad. Appl. Psychol.*, 1964, *1*, 1–11.

Eysenck, H. J., The outcome problem in psychotherapy: A reply, *Psychother. Theor. Res. Pract.*, 1964, *1*, 97–100.

Eysenck, H. J., Personality and cigarette smoking, *Life Sci.*, 1964, *3*, 777–790.

Eysenck, H. J., Personality and reminiscence: An experimental study of the "reactive inhibition" and the "conditional inhibition theories," *Life Sci.*, 1964, *3*, 189–198.

Eysenck, H. J., Principles and methods of personality description, classification and diagnosis, *Brit. J. Psychol.*, 1964, *55*, 284–294.

Eysenck, H. J., Psychotherapy or behavior therapy, *Indian Psychol. Rev.*, 1964, *1*, 33–41.

Eysenck, S. B. G., and H. J. Eysenck, "Acquiescence" response set in personality inventory items, *Psychol. Rep.*, 1964, *14*, 513–514.

Eysenck, S. B. G., and H. J. Eysenck, An improved short questionnaire for the measurement of extraversion and neuroticism, *Life Sci.*, 1964, *3*, 1103–1109.

Eysenck, S. B. G., and H. J. Eysenck, Personality of judges as a factor in the validity of their judgments of extraversion–introversion, *Brit. J. Soc. Clin. Psychol.*, 1964, *3*, 141–148.

Eysenck, H. J., and P. O. White, Personality and the measurement of intelligence, *Brit. J. Educ. Psychol.*, 1964, *34*, 197–202.

Eysenck, H. J., The effects of psychotherapy, *Int. J. Psychiat.*, 1965, *1*, 97–144.

Eysenck, H. J., Extraversion and the acquisition of eyeblink and GSR conditioned responses, *Psychol. Bull.*, 1965, *63*, 258–270.

Eysenck, H. J., A note on some criticisms of the Mowrer/Eysenck conditioning theory of conscience, *Brit. J. Psychol.*, 1965, *56*, 305–307.

Eysenck, H. J., A three-factor theory of reminiscence, *Brit. J. Psychol.*, 1965, *56*, 163–181.

Eysenck, H. J., and A. Levey, Alternation in choice behavior and extraversion, *Life Sci.*, 1965, *4*, 115–119.

Kerstein, S., and H. J. Eysenck, Pursuit rotor performance as a function of different degrees of distraction, *Life Sci.*, 1965, *4*, 889–897.

Eysenck, H. J., On the dual function of consolidation, *Percept. Mot. Skills*, 1966, *22*, 273–274.

Eysenck, H. J., On the other hand, *Contemp. Psychol.*, 1966, *11*, 508.

Eysenck, H. J., Personality and experimental psychology, *Bull. Brit. Psychol. Soc.*, 1966, *19*, 1–28.

Eysenck, H. J., A reply to McPherson's comments on the Aberdeen conditioning studies, *Brit. J. Psychol.*, 1966, *57*, 419–421.

Eysenck, H. J., and W. Thompson, The effects of distraction on pursuit rotor learning, performance and reminiscence, *Brit. J. Psychol.*, 1966, *57*, 99–106.

Eysenck, H. J., and R. A. Willett, The effect of drive on performance and reminiscence in a complex tracing task, *Brit. J. Psychol.*, 1966, *57*, 107–112.

Eysenck, S. B. G., I. A. Syed, and H. J. Eysenck, Desirability response set in children, *Brit. J. Educ. Psychol.*, 1966, *36*, 87–90.

McLaughlin, R. J., and H. J. Eysenck, Visual masking as a function of personality, *Brit. J. Psychol.*, 1966, *57*, 393–396.

Extraverts have a higher masking threshold than introverts.

Rachman, S., and H. J. Eysenck, Reply to a "critique and reformulation" of behavior therapy, *Psychol. Bull.*, 1966, *65*, 165–169.

Eysenck, H. J., Epiphenomenalism and the contradictions of its critics, *Brit. J Psychol.*, 1967, *58*, 451–453.

Eysenck, H. J., Factor-analytic study of the Maitland Graves design judgment test *Percept. Mot. Skills*, 1967, *24*, 73–74.

Eysenck, H. J., New waves in psychotherapy, *Psychol. Today*, 1967, *1*, 39–47.

Eysenck, H. J., New ways of curing the neurotic, *Psychol. Scene*, 1967, *1*, 2–8.

Eysenck, H. J., Personality and extra-sensory perception, *J. Amer. Soc. Psychical Res.*, 1967, *44*, 55–71.

Eysenck, H. J., Single-trial conditioning, neurosis, and the Napalkov phenomenon *Behaviour Res. Ther.*, 1967, *5*, 63–65.

Eysenck, H. J., and S. B. G. Eysenck, On the unitary nature of extraversion, *Act Psychologica* (Amst.), 1967, *26*, 383–390.

Eysenck, S. B. G., and H. J. Eysenck, Physiological reactivity to sensory stimula tion as a measure of personality, *Psychol. Rep.*, 1967, *20*, 45–46.

Eysenck, S. B. G., and H. J. Eysenck, Salivary response to lemon juice as measure of introversion, *Percept. Mot. Skills*, 1967, *24*, 1047–1053.

McLaughlin, R. J., and H. J. Eysenck, Extraversion, neuroticism and paired-associates learning, *J. Exp. Res. Pers.*, 1967, 2, 128–132.

Moderate anxiety facilitates learning an easy list; low anxiety facilitates learning a difficult list.

Eysenck, H. J., An experimental study of aesthetic preference for polygonal figures, *J. Gen. Psychol.*, 1968, 79, 3–17.

Eysenck, H. J., and S. B. G. Eysenck, A factorial study of psychoticism as a dimension of personality, *Multivariate Behav. Res.*, 1968, Special Issue, pp. 15–31.

SUGGESTED READINGS

BOOKS

Anastasi, A., *Psychological Testing*, 2nd ed. New York: Macmillan, 1961.

Atkinson, J. W., *An Introduction to Motivation*. Princeton, N.J.: Van Nostrand, 1964.

Reviewed by H. J. Eysenck.

Berlyne, D. E., Behavior theory as personality theory, in E. F. Borgatta and W. W. Lambert (eds.), *Handbook of Personality Theory and Research*. Chicago: Rand McNally, 1968, pp. 651–662.

Excellent chronology of Eysenck and his work.

Bonner, H., *Psychology of Personality*. New York: Ronald Press, 1961.

Burt, C. L., *Factors of the Mind*. New York: Macmillan, 1941.

David, H. P., and H. von Bracken (eds.), *Perspectives in Personality Theory*. New York: Basic Books, 1957.

Ford, D. H., and H. B. Urban, Psychotherapy, in *Annual Review of Psychology*, Vol. 18. Palo Alto, Cal.: Annual Reviews, Inc., 1967, pp. 333–372.

Gray, J. A., *Pavlov's Typology: Recent Theoretical and Experimental Developments from the Laboratory of B. M. Teplov*. New York: Pergamon, 1964.

Editorial introduction by H. J. Eysenck.

Guiford, J. P., *Personality*. New York: McGraw-Hill, 1959.

The factor analytic approach to personality.

Hall, C. S., and Lindzey, G., *Theories of Personality*. New York: Wiley, 1957, pp. 381–393.

Holtzman, W. H., Personality structure, in *Annual Review of Psychology*, Vol. 16. Palo Alto, Cal.: Annual Reviews, Inc., 1965, pp. 119–156.

Joyce, C. R. B., Drugs and personality, in B. M. Foss (ed.), *Horizons in Psychology*. Baltimore: Penguin Books, 1966.

Klein, G. S., H. L. Barr, and D. L. Wolitzky, Personality, in *Annual Review of Psychology*, Vol. 18. Palo Alto, Cal.: Annual Reviews, Inc., 1967, pp. 467–560.

Matarazzo, J. D., Psychotherapeutic processes, in *Annual Review of Psychology,* Vol. 16, Palo Alto, Cal.: Annual Reviews, Inc., 1965, pp. 181–224.

Rachman, S. (ed.), *Critical Essays on Psychoanalysis.* New York: Macmillan, 1963.

Spence, J. T., Learning theory and personality, in J. M. Wepman and R. W. Heine (eds.), *Concepts of Personality.* Chicago: Aldine, 1963, pp. 3–30.

PERIODICALS

Adams, J. A., The second facet of forgetting: A review of warm-up decrement, *Psychol. Bull.*, 1961, 58, 257–273.

    A long rebuttal on Eysenck's inadequacies.

Albino, R. C., Some criteria of the application of factor analysis to the study of personality, *Brit. J. Psychol.*, 1953, 44, 164–168.

Al-Issa, I., The effect of Hitudinal Factors on the relationship between conditioning and personality, *Brit. J. Soc. Clin. Psychol.*, 1964, 3, 113–119.

    Tested Eysenck's hypothesis that eye-blink conditioning is negatively correlated with extraversion, and Spence-Hull hypothesis that there is positive correlation between eye-blink conditioning and neuroticism and anxiety. Results were inconsistent.

Bergin, A. E., Some implications of psychotherapy research for therapeutic practice, *Int. J. Psychol.*, 1967, 3, 136–160.

Biggs, J. B., The relation of neuroticism and extraversion to intelligence and educational attainment, *Brit. J. Educ. Psychol.*, 1962, 32, 188–195.

    Criticizes Eysenck's theory of conditionability.

Carrigan, P. M., Extraversion–introversion as a dimension of personality: A re appraisal, *Psychol. Bull.*, 1960, 57, 329–360.

Christie, R., Eysenck's treatment of the personality of communists, *Psychol. Bull.* 1956, 53, 411–430.

Christie, R., Some abuses of psychology, *Psychol. Bull.*, 1956, 53, 439–451.

    Eysenck is guilty.

Dowdy, C. D., An experimental test of Eysenck's and Cattell's theories of extra version–introversion, *Dissert. Abstr.*, 1960, 20, 3376 (abstract).

DuPreez, P. D., Judgment of time and aspects of personality, *J. Abnorm. Soc. Psychol.*, 1964, 69, 228–233.

    Refuted several of Eysenck's hypotheses on extraversion and judgment of time.

Eysenck, S. B. G., The validity of a personality questionnaire as determined by the method of nominated groups, *Life Sci.*, 1962, 1, 13–18.

Farley, F., and S. V. Farley, Extraversion and stimulus-seeking motivation, *Consult. Psychol.*, 1967, 31, 215–216.

Substantiates that part of Eysenck's personality theory which predicts that extraversion correlates with stimulus-seeking.

'ranks, C. M., Personality and eye-blink conditioning seven years later, *Acta Psychol.*, 1963, *21*, 295–312.

Agrees and disagrees with Eysenck.

'ranks, C. M., E. A. Holden, and M. Phillips, Eysenck's "stratification" theory and the questionnaire method of measuring personality, *J. Clin. Psychol.*, 1961, *17*, 248–253.

;ard, J. G., and A. W. Bendig, A factor analytic study of Eysenck's and Schutz's personality dimensions among psychiatric groups, *J. Consult. Psychol.*, 1964, *28*, 252–258.

;ottesman, I. I., Heritability of personality: A demonstration, *Psychol. Monogr.*, 1963, *77*, No. 572.

Identical and fraternal twins indicate introversion–extraversion à la Eysenck.

;ranger, E. W., Eysenck's theory of anxiety and hysteria and the results of visual adaptation experiments, *Acta Psychol.*, 1957, *3*, 98–126.

;uilford, J. P., When not to factor analyze, *Psychol. Bull.*, 1952, *49*, 26–37.

Ionigfeld, G., Cortical inhibition, perceptual satiation, and introversion–extraversion, *J. Abnorm. Soc. Psychol.*, 1962, *65*, 278–280.

Iowarth, E., Differences between extraverts and intraverts on a button pressing test, *Psychol. Rep.*, 1964, *14*, 949–950.

Finding didn't agree with Eysenck's theory, but Eysenck suggests an explanation to the author.

∍nsen, A. R., The Maudsley Personality Inventory, *Acta Psychol.*, 1958, *4*, 314–325.

Good questionnaire for intro-extraversion and neuroticism.

∍nes, H. G., Inhibition: A symposium: IV. Individual differences in inhibitory potential, *Brit. J. Psychol.*, 1960, *51*, 220–225.

Eysenck's theory may have to be modified.

'iesler, D. J., Some myths of psychotherapy research and the search for a paradigm, *Psychol. Bull.*, 1966, *65*, 110–136.

Fair agreement with Eysenck's concepts of therapy.

ittle, A., Professor Eysenck's theory of crime: An empirical test on adolescent offenders, *Brit. J. Criminol.*, 1963, *4*, 152–163.

∍rr, M., D. M. McNair, C. J. Klett, and J. J. Lasky, Canonical variates and second-order factors: A reply, *J. Consult. Psychol.*, 1963, *27*, 180–181.

uborsky, L., A note on Eysenck's article, "The effects of psychotherapy: An evaluation," *Brit. J. Psychol.*, 1954, *45*, 129–131.

Lynn, R., Comments on the article by J. B. Biggs, *Brit. J. Educ. Psychol.*, 1962, 32, 196–199.

States that Biggs misunderstands Eysenck's theory.

Lynn, R., and J. Butler, Introversion and the arousal jag, *Brit. J. Soc. Clin. Psychol.*, 1962, 1, 150–151.

Supports Eysenck's theory.

Lynn, R., and I. E. Gordon, The relation of neuroticism and extraversion to intelligence and educational attainment, *Brit. J. Educ. Psychol.*, 1961, 31, 194–203.

Five of Eysenck's predictions statistically significant.

McDonell, C. R., and J. Inglis, Verbal conditioning and personality, *Psychol. Rep.*, 1962, 10, 374.

Fails to support Eysenck's theory.

Mitchell, J. V., A comparison of the first and second order dimensions of the 16 PF and CPI inventories, *J. Soc. Psychol.*, 1963, 60, 151–166.

Mohan, J., and V. Mohan, Personality and variability in aesthetic evaluation, *Psychologia: An Int. J. Psychol. in the Orient*, 1965, 8, 218–219.

Uses aesthetic preferences for paintings. Extraverts vary more because of higher level of suggestibility. Supports Eysenck's theory of personality.

Okamoto, E., Personality trait deduced from behavior: Theory I. Mirror drawing measures on the vertivity axis, *Japan Psychol. Res.*, 1964, 6, 99–107.

Parnell, R. W., The Rees-Eysenck body index of individual somatotypes, *J. Ment. Sci.*, 1957, 103, 209–213.

Rachman, S., and J. Grassi, Reminiscence, inhibition, and consolidation, *Brit. J. Psychol.*, 1965, 56, 157–162.

Support Eysenck on pursuit rotor data.

Ramsay, R. W., Personality and speech, *J. Pers. Soc. Psychol.*, 1966, 4, 116–118

Extraverts make more sounds and have less silences.

Richardson, J. F., Correlations between the extraversion and neuroticism scales of the Eysenck Personality Inventory under Australian conditions, *Aust. Milit. Forces Res. Rep.*, 1967, No. 12, p. 67.

Rohrs, F. W., The relationship of sexual symbol identification and preference to neuroticism and extraversion–introversion, *Dissert. Abstr.*, 1965, 25, 6769.

Rokeach, M., and C. Hanley, Eysenck's tendermindedness dimension: A critique *Psychol. Bull.*, 1956, 53, 169–176.

Rosenzwieg, S., A transvaluation of psychotherapy: A reply to Hans Eysenck, *J. Abnorm. Soc. Psychol.*, 1954, 49, 298–304.

Salas, R. G., and J. F. Richardson, A further note on some characteristics of the Eysenck Personality Inventory (EPI) observed under Australian conditions *Aust. Milit. Forces Res. Rep.*, 1967, 11–67.

Siegman, A. W., A cross-cultural investigation of the relationship between intro-version–extraversion, social attitudes and anti-social behavior, *Brit. J. Soc. Clin. Psychol.*, 1963, 2, 196–208.

>No support for Eysenck's hypothesized positive correlation between extra-version and tough-minded or authoritarian attitudes.

Spence, K. W., and J. T. Spence, Relation of eyelid conditioning to manifest anxiety, extraversion, and rigidity, *J. Abnorm. Soc. Psychol.*, 1964, 68, 144–149.

>Refutes Eysenck's contention that extraversion–introversion correlates with conditioning and extinction.

Star, K. H., Reminiscence, drive and personality theroy: Replication, *Percept. Mot. Skills*, 1963, 17, 377–378.

Thorpe, J. G., A. Bardecki, and A. B. Balaguer, The reliability of the Eysenck-Withers' personality inventory for subnormal subjects, *J. Ment. Defic. Res.*, 1967, 11, 108–115.

Vingoe, F. J., Rogers' self theory and Eysenck's extraversion and neuroticism, *J. Consult. Clin. Psychol.*, 1968, 42, 618–620.

>Study supports Rogers' self theory.

Wells, W. D., H. E. Egeth, and N. P. Wray, An American application of Eysenck's short neuroticism and extraversion scales, *J. Appl. Psychol.*, 1961, 45, 271–272.

>Scales were uncorrelated when applied to 180 American housewives.

White, J. H., G. M. Stephenson, S. E. Child, and J. M. Gibbs, Validation studies of the Eysenck Personality Inventory, *Brit. J. Psychiat.*, 1968, 114, 63–68.

Yates, A. J., and J. I. Lazzlo, Learning and performance of extraverts and intro-verts on the pursuit rotor, *J. Pers. Soc. Psychol.*, 1965, 1, 79–84.

>Found no support for Eysenck's theory that there is a difference between introverts and extraverts in the rate of growth of associative connections or reactive inhibition.

Young, G. C., Personality factors and the treatment of enuresis, *Behav. Res. Ther.*, 1965, 3, 103–105.

>After treatment for enuresis, relapse rate for extraverted children was greater than for the other groups.

VII

Contributions
of Other
Theorists

PART VII of this book concerns itself with the theoretical positions of personologists whose work seems not to be as comprehensive as that of the preceding personologists; it is as valuable but not as broad in scope. The decision to place these theorists in the latter section was based primarily on three factors: completeness in dealing with *all* kinds of human behavior, current status of the theory as reflected in the opinions of other writers about personality theory, and the power and possibilities of stimulating personality research.

We have chosen, then, to include two new theorists: Kelly and Erikson.

Kelly, it seems to this author, has a true approach to human behavior, unique, and not covered by other theorists. Kelly asks a very sensible question and buttresses it with research and a measuring device, the Role Construct Repertory Test. His question is simple and necessary. Not just the scientist, as a manipulator of people, but people themselves are also concerned about their own destiny and behavior dynamics. It is a pleasure to include George Kelly's *Psychology of Personal Constructs* in the company of other personality theorists' work.

Erik Erikson takes man's behavior, in a psychoanalytic sense, and studies it through the life-span. Fortunately, we have a neo-Freudian who thinks man is important *all* his life, not just in the early formative years.

Every book has limits. It cannot cover all the material the author would like to include. Consequently, we have not dealt with the theoretical positions of Angyal, McClelland, Miller and Dollard, Rotter, Sears, or Skinner. The decision was based on the fact that their main contributions were not in personality theory. Thus, some are primarily learning theorists, some therapists, and still others show their greatest strengths as methodologists.

Chapter 14 of Part VII contains the work of Lewin as a symbolically oriented theorist, Mowrer as a learning concept theorist and representing other newer aspects of morality in theory, Maslow as an eclectically oriented theorist dealing with new yet unresearched material but provocative, and the aforementioned Kelly.

Chapter 15 concerns itself with the neo-Freudians Erikson, Sullivan, and Fromm.

14

Contributions
of Other Theorists:
General

SYMBOLICAL
[LEWIN]

She saw every personal relationship as a pair
of intersecting circles. . . . Probably perfection is reached
when the area of the two outer crescents, added
together is exactly equal to that of the leaf-shaped piece in
the middle. On paper there must be some neat,
mathematical formula for arriving at this: in life, none.

JAN STRUTHER
Mrs. Miniver

SOME BIOGRAPHICAL DATA

Kurt Lewin was born in Mongilno, Germany, on September 9, 1890. He
attended the University of Freiburg in 1908, the University of Munich in
1909, and spent the next five years at the University of Berlin, where he

received the Ph.D. in 1914. From 1914 to 1918 he served in the German Army, first as private, then as lieutenant. Lewin was married to Gertrud Weiss in October, 1928. They had four children: Esther, Reuven, Miriam, and David. In 1921 he returned to the University of Berlin Psychological Institute as an assistant. He later became professor of philosophy and psychology at the University of Berlin, 1926–1933. In 1933 he taught at Stanford University as visiting professor and became professor of psychology at Cornell University, 1933–1935. He spent the years from 1935 to 1944 at the Child Welfare Station at the University of Iowa as a professor of child psychology and directed the Research Center for Group Dynamics at MIT from 1944 until his death in 1947. He was a member of the American Psychological Association, the Midwest Psychological Association, the Society for the Psychological Study of Social Issues, the Psychometric Society, AAAS, Phi Epsilon Pi, and Sigma Xi.

INTRODUCTION

Kurt Lewin had a strong affinity for mathematical symbols. His question was not whether to use mathematics but which kind of mathematics to use. He decided that geometry with its topological dimensions best fitted the language of space in which he liked to talk. Lewin's work utilized nonmetrical symbols; that is, the size and distances of the geometric drawings or designs were not important. Lewin's devotion to using symbols almost made him a victim of his own system. Lewin did not consider himself a mathemetician, to which statement most mathemeticians would agree, but hoped that some good mathematician would come along some day and do what he could not do: prove functionally his theory. Most of Lewin's ideas about levels of aspirations, group dynamics, regression, recall in tension, satiation, and others can probably be explained without topology.

A large difficulty in writing an explanation or interpretation of Kurt Lewin's work is that one can explain what he does but cannot demonstrate it without repeating his experimental work in its entirety. (One can describe dancing or football with diagrams without actually being able to *see* it in person or on film; admittedly, much is lost with only a printed, diagrammatical description.)

Lewin felt, as many of us do, that using words to describe human behavior only obfuscates the issue of man's behavior. Many times to use a word requires the use of two more words to explain the first.

Because "words inevitably lead to using more words," Lewin substituted one kind of symbol, mathematical, for another kind of symbol, verbal. However, when one studies diagrams in lieu of words, he encounters another difficulty in interpreting Lewin's theory. The mathematical symbol by itself is usually quite meaningless; we must use words to explain the symbol, which brings us then to using words to explain symbols when the symbols were originally employed to do away with words!

This is like having a home so highly mechanized with laborsaving devices that one is constantly laboring to service the machines which are designed to save labor.

A third difficulty presents itself in the use of diagrams to explain human behavior. Lewin always regarded his diagrams as momentary, or what Mark Twain called a photograph: "A moment of petrified truth." Thus, in a diagram we have a frozen moment of human behavior but are unable to indicate past or present behavior from it.

Essentially, Kurt Lewin's topological system was a "means of communication." It became one man's language. This system of symbols, which Lewin himself felt was not real mathematics, grew out of his use of the blackboard in teaching his classes. There is a short and interesting account of this metamorphosis from the use of a pedagogical tool (the blackboard) to the sudden realization that he was dealing actually not with a pedagogical tool but with a true theory of personality (see *Principles of Topological Psychology*, p. vii).

Lewin did not go much beyond stages of definition or graphic presentation; he did not establish rules of mathematical operations with his diagrams.

Through his diagrams he was trying to introduce into psychology a shift of interest from objects or people, as such, to processes between people and from the state of being to the changes that occur in behavior.

Lewin approached the study of human personality at the level of methodology, and he appeals greatly to research and method-minded psychologists. He developed theory construction to a high degree of sophistication for his time, being most ingenious at contriving experiments with all the controls and variables accounted for. Through his emphasis upon action research, Lewin made possibly his greatest contribution in scientific methodology. His experimental methods have been more widely accepted than his theoretical views; he impressed the world of psychology as a brilliant research methodologist. Lewin's emphasis upon action research meant essentially changing social conditions. This has sometimes been misjudged as changing the objectives of research as one proceeds with the research design.

Lewin took motivation studies out of the clinic and the rat laboratory and placed them in a more natural setting. He was highly interested and involved in group dynamics causation and group dynamics research. Because of his experiences, he considered psychology essentially a social science which be based on Gestalt or social physical situations. Actually, Kurt Lewin's theory is largely unformulated. His untimely death in 1947 occurred before he had a real chance to extend and refine his theory.

Shortly before his death Lewin became associated with Norbert Wiener and others, among them Margaret Mead, in an approach designed to use

cybernetics as a communication system which would include feedback an
information theory.

Lewin firmly believed in the value of theory. Although he has been note
for saying, "Nothing is more practical than a good theory," this phras
actually was first stated at the turn of the century and should be credited t
Dorpfeld (see chap. 16). Lewin did not feel, however, that theory should b
left to the theorist; it should always be applied in a research situation whic
was as near a true life situation as possible.

THE SYSTEM, THEORY,
OR ESSENTIAL FEATURES

General Considerations

Lewin felt that developing any kind of science and especially the science c
psychology as a social science went through three stages: the speculative, th
descriptive, and the constructive.

SPECULATIVE

The speculations of Plato and Aristotle about earth, fire, and water ar
examples of this type of scientific development. To Lewin speculative cor
siderations must be seen in the light of their historical perspectives. He wa
however, a harsh critic of modern scientists who employ this type of reasor
ing. He considered it absolutely unproductive for any kind of work in today'
scientific world.

DESCRIPTIVE

The next step in the development of science, according to Lewin, was
descriptive one in which classification or taxonomic endeavors were primar
Lewin thought that, although this was a necessary step, it should not b
considered the final one.

CONSTRUCTIVE

The work of Galileo is probably the best historical example of the construc
tive foundation in developing a scientific point of view. Lewin felt that ther
can be a comfortable use of empirical theories or laws. These may be base
upon one case and need not use statistics. The primary purpose of th
constructive effort is to discover laws of behavior and especially to predic
behavior in individual cases. Lewin preferred the genotypic approach, whic
concerns itself with individuals, to the phenotypic approach, which concern
itself with statistical averages.

Lewin postulated that behavioral events revolve around three principles *elatedness*—One fact alone cannot cause a behavioral event. A behavioral 'ent must have two or more facts which are related to each other and to the 'entual behavioral pattern.

oncreteness—Behavioral events are not caused by potential facts or poten- ıl considerations which may or may not happen. Only solid facts that :tually exist in the here and now and have a concrete quality may be con- dered in the principles of behavior.

ontemporaneity—It was very important to Lewin that only present facts can ıuse present behavior. The causal factors of human behavior are contempo- ry, and facts which no longer exist cannot be considered a part of the :havioral scene.

pecific Considerations

√hat follows now is a list of terms and concepts which Lewin found it ecessary to use in describing man's personality. The list is by no means ımplete but does give the reader a strong idea of the work of Kurt Lewin.

ATHEMATICAL CONSTRUCTS

ewin's work was couched in mathematical terms but was not necessarily ıplicable to mathematical computational systems or mathematical verifica- on. He used primarily the signs and symbols of geometry but did not ısociate numbers with them. Thus, it is not possible to add, subtract, multi- ly, or divide in the Lewinian diagram system. The outstanding feature of ewin's mathematical constructs is the drawing of circles, squares, triangles, alls or membranes, arrows of force, and all types of geometrical designs both ›m original mathematical systems and from those which Lewin invented in rder to present his theory without being bound by the use of words.

ɔPOLOGY

ewin used the term *topology* as a model for describing psychological or chavioral phenomena. Behavior was classified and described in terms of :ometrical functions, which did not, however, use direct mathematical ıanipulations. A human being could be shown as a circle or a square or an liptical shape. The human being was represented as being within the figure. verything that existed outside of the figure belonged to other phenomena, ıch as environmental forces or life space.

ODOLOGY

ewin invented this term, which he found necessary in drawing the circles, liptical shapes, and pathways of behavior. *Hodology* may be thought of as a special type of geometry of paths of energy where the shortest distance between two points is the path of least resistance (not necessarily the Euclidian concept of the least distance actually traveled). In hodology a line between points A and B is not necessarily a straight line. It may be a tangential line because of forces which lie directly in the path from A to B. In hodology the direction toward or away from an object or force is important. Hodology can be construed as a tri-dimensional rather than a two-dimensional theory. That is to say, although Lewin was held to the drawings he could make on a blackboard or a sheet of paper, he did not consider that it would be impossible to go over or under an object as well as around it. To dimensions of length and breadth, the science of hodology or the science of paths of forces would also add depth.

LIFE SPACE

Assuming that one has drawn a circle, a triangle, or any enclosed figure, the area surrounding the figure is called the life space. The figure is the human personality. In the life space are all the forces that impinge upon a person and that determine his behavior. They include everything which is known and unknown at the conscious level of the individual. Inherent in the life space is the interaction between a person and the environment. The life space is the total aspect of every possible event or thing that could influence the behavior of the individual. Life space may be considered as the past, present, and future; however, it must always be *seen in the present*. Consequently, Lewin did not deny that man has a past or that he is going to have a future (he is not going to drop dead at the moment of action), but he did insist that a human's behavior can only be *seen* in its present context.

REGIONS

Regions are the additional areas within any enclosed space which represent an individual or which represent parts of his environment. The environmental parts of a region are limited in number. All regions are momentary, as previously stated. There are seven kinds of regions, as follows:

1. Connected regions. Any activity or behavior that goes on inside a region and does not affect another region is a connected region. In other words, connected regions are autonomous and are simply connected with no interplay between them.

2. Incident regions. Any activity which can go from one region to another region without entering a third region is considered an incident region. Obviously, the two incident regions are adjacent within the diagram.

3. Motoric region. The motoric region concerns itself with overt responses and outward appearances. Sometimes it is called the executive portion of the person because it gets things done. The motoric region always comes between the inner personal life space and the psychological environment. It is

at the periphery of the life space, beyond which is the psychological environment.

4. Motor-perceptual regions. Any region that forms a boundary between the environment or the area outside of the circle and the inner personal regions is a motor-perceptual region. It is a boundary which must be passed through and may approximate a barrier. It does not, however, have the drive or the executive portions of the motor region mentioned previously.

5. Neighboring regions. Any two regions that touch each other within the life space can be considered neighboring regions. Unlike incident regions, neighboring regions have somewhat common properties.

6. Psychological regions. These are regions which have similar attributes, but different from those of any other group of regions.

7. Private regions. Within the shape that one has drawn to indicate the human being, those regions which lie closest to the inner core of the shape (or person) and are most difficult to observe by others are called private regions.

$B = F(PE)$

In this oft-quoted formula of Lewin's, B means behavior, F means function or law, P means person, and E means total environment. Unfortunately, one must use many words in order to make this formula meaningful. Another way of considering the formula is to examine the function of the relationship between the person and his environment. The parentheses signify the relationship function operating as a law or condition. Environment means the total environment, which again connotes the past, present, and future although the behavior is always seen in the present. This formula is a nonmathematical one. It cannot be added, subtracted, multiplied, or divided. It consists of symbols which to Lewin expressed human behavior or were his shorthand methods of indicating behavior which includes the person, his environment, and the interaction between them.

VECTORS

Vectors (vector analysis) are forces that proceed in a given direction. Any line that has force or psychological energy behind or in it and that is outside of the person is a vector. Thus, as Lewin drew his diagrams, the length of the line, the thickness of the line, and especially the point where the front of the line in the shape of an arrowhead met the individual were quite important.

VALENCE

Lewin borrowed the term *valence* from chemistry but used in in his theory in a nonscientific way. There are two kinds of valences, one with a positive value and one with a negative value. Anything which satisfies the need of the human personality has positive valence, and any object or force which threatens the human personality has a negative valence.

NEED

Lewin defined *need* as "any desire for object possession or any desire to achieve a goal." Needs are primarily prompted by organic conditions. There may be many needs that direct their forces through the valences upon the human personality.

TENSIONS

Tensions are "any emotional states that go with, or are accompanied by needs." We may assume that if no emotion is aroused, there is no true need structure. All the tensions are within the person and do not come from the environment. Tensions are also of a temporary nature.

DIFFERENTIATION

We may define this in Lewinian terms as "the depth and richness of experience." Intelligence and variety of experiences help an individual to differentiate. It is assumed here that the more one is able to differentiate between the forces and vectors in his life space, the better personality he has. From the word root of differentiation Kurt Lewin introduced the term *de-differentiation,* which means that "the parts within a system lose their differences and return to a state of homogeneity." Balance in the personality is achieved when de-differentiation is in effect. In addition to differentiation and de-differentiation, Lewin also introduced the term *un-differentiation* to refer to states in which there is no difference between the parts of a system. In this case there is no tension, no force, no movement. It is not a return from differentiation as in de-differentiation, but is meant primarily to indicate that no differentiation, tension, or differences in parts are found in the beginning states of the organism. As an example, we may assume that a newborn baby is undifferentiated, in contrast to adults, who are highly differentiated.

EQUILIBRIUM AND DISEQUILIBRIUM

According to Lewin, the individul wants to be in a state of equilibrium. Needs, however, produce disequilibrium. It is the job of the human personality to win its way back to a state of equilibrium between the regions of the personality.

REGRESSION AND RETROGRESSION

Lewin takes the Freudian terms of *regression* and *retrogression* and treats them another way. Regression means "any behavior which is primitive behavior that has not been in the past experience of the person." Thus, to act savagely is a regression form of behavior in the person who has never before cted savagely. The term *retrogression*, however, means "a return to a previous behavior which has once been experienced by that person."

BARRIERS AND BLOCKAGES

If we were to draw an area of any shape or size and within it a perpendicular line of any thickness, this would represent a barrier, or a blockage. A barrier is a membrane or obstruction between the person and the goal he wishes to obtain. Thick barriers create frustration. Impenetrable barriers constitute a true blockage and create apathy because the person cannot pass through them. Barriers which lie between the person and his goal also may enhance the positive valence or allure of an object or a goal. "We want what we cannot have." Barriers in this sense may be a part of motivation. The very fact that a barrier exists may make it attractive to surmount or to penetrate.

LOCOMOTION

As the personality moves from one region to another within the life space, or changes position within the life space, the motive force which comes from within the person is considered to be the locomotion. Locomotion may be fast or slow depending upon individual talents.

FLUIDITY

Fluidity is the ease of locomotion between parts, between a part and the whole, or between regions.

CONFLICT

Partially from the work of others, Lewin drew three basic types of conflict: approach–approach, avoidance–avoidance, and approach–avoidance. In approach–approach conflicts, the personality desires two things and has a difficult time choosing between them. An example would be trying to decide which of two kinds of delicious chocolate bonbons one would like to consume. In the avoidance–avoidance type of conflict the individual does not want to do either of two alternatives but cannot avoid them. An example would be the unhappy husband who neither wants a divorce nor wants to continue living with a wife with whom he is unhappy. In the approach–avoidance type of conflict there is a desire to achieve a goal, but in order to do so one must go through a painful period. The traditional example is the individual with a toothache who wants to go to the dentist in order to have the tooth fixed and whose approach is to visit the dentist; however, he wishes to avoid the dentist because the dentist also may inflict pain. Thus, he has an approach–avoidance conflict.

LEVEL OF ASPIRATION

The term *level of aspiration* was originated by Tamara Dembo in 1931, and Lewin utilized it in a sense as a prediction of a future goal which will satisfy the person *at the present moment*. Lewin felt that the attainment of a goal, however, may not guarantee satisfaction. Within this rubric he considered two kinds of goals: action goals and ideal goals. The action goal is what actually will be accomplished. The ideal goal is the value derived from doing well and being praised for doing well.

■ SUMMARY

Kurt Lewin has been an important force in American psychology primarily because of his methodology. He employed geometric forms of mathematics to illustrate his concepts without the full use of the mathematical procedures.

DELIMITATION

The present treatment of Kurt Lewin's work is extremely short. Among the many things which have not been covered are the excellent experiments Lewin did with Ovsiankina, Zeigarnik, and with Lippitt and White at the Iowa Child Welfare Station. Some commentators of the psychological scene consider the Lewin-Lippitt-White studies of social climates to be more of a study of types of leadership than of social climates or of personality formation.

We also have not covered the study that Lewin did of large groups, particularly the differences he found in pre-World War II German and American populations. Also omitted are Lewin's learning theory formulations.

Undoubtedly the greatest omission of this section is the innumerable drawings and diagrams and arrows and penciled lines—which descriptive devices, however, often lose the essence of Lewin's theory on the drawing board. Lewinian diagrams need explanatory words. It is hoped this novel approach retains the essence of an interesting theory even without the "do-it-yourself" mechanics of drawing.

BIBLIOGRAPHY

PRIMARY SOURCES

BOOKS

Lewin, K., Environmental forces, in C. Murchison (ed.), *Handbook of Child Psychology*. Worcester, Mass.: Clark University Press, 1934.

Lewin, K., *A Dynamic Theory of Personality*. New York: McGraw-Hill, 1935.

Also in paperback edition.

Lewin, K., *Principles of Topological Psychology*. New York: McGraw-Hill, 1936.

Lewin, K., T. Dembo, L. Festinger, and P. S. Sears, Level of aspiration, in J. McV. Hunt (ed.), *Personality and the Behavior Disorders*. New York: Ronald Press, 1944, chap. 10.

Lewin, K., Behavior and development as a function of total situations, in L. Carmichael (ed.), *Manual of Child Psychology*. New York: Wiley, 1946, chap. 16.

Lewin, K., Group decision and social change, in T. Newcomb and E. Hartley (eds.), *Readings in Social Psychology*. New York: Holt, Rinehart & Winston, 1947.

Lewin, K., In G. W. Lewin (ed.), *Resolving Social Conflicts: Selected Papers on Group Dynamics*. New York: Harper & Row, 1948.

Foreword by G. W. Allport.

Lewin, K., Cassirer's philosophy of science and the social sciences, in P. A. Schilpp (ed.), *The Philosophy of Ernst Cassirer*. Evanston, Ill.: Living Philosophies, 1949.

Lewin, K., Will and need, in W. D. Ellis (ed.), *A Source Book of Gestalt Psychology*. New York: Humanities Press, 1950.

Lewin, K., In D. Cartwright (ed.), *Field Theory in Social Science*. New York: Harper & Row, 1951.

Lewin, K., *Principles of Topological Psychology*. New York: McGraw-Hill, 1966.

PERIODICALS

Lewin, K., Vectors, cognitive processes, and Mr. Tolman's criticism, *J. Gen. Psychol.*, 1933. 8, 318–345.

Lewin, K., Psycho-sociological problems of a minority group, *Charact. & Pers.*, 1935, 3, 175–187.

Lewin, K., Some social-psychological differences between the United States and Germany, *Charact. & Pers.*, 1936, 4, 265–293.

Lewin, K., The conceptual representation and measurement of psychological forces, in *Contr. Psychol. Theor.* (Duke Univer. Press), 1938, 1, No. 4.

    Also in *Univer. Iowa Contr. Psychol. Theor.*, 1938, 1, 1–247.

Lewin, K., R. Lippitt, and R. K. White, Patterns of aggressive behavior in experimentally created "social climates," *J. Soc. Psychol.*, 1939, 10, 271–299.

Lewin, K., Formalization and progress in psychology, *Univer. Iowa Stud. Child Welf.*, 1940, 16, No. 3, 9–42.

Barker, R., T. Dembo, and K. Lewin, Frustration and regression: An experiment with young children, *Univer. Iowa Stud. Child Welf.*, 1941, 18, No. 1.

Lewin, K., Field theory of learning, in *41st Yearb. NSSE*, 1942, 41 (Pt. II) 215–242.

Bavelas, A., and K. Lewin, Training in democratic leadership, *J. Abnorm. Soc. Psychol.*, 1942, 37, 115–119.

Lewin, K., Defining the "field at a given time," *Psychol. Rev.*, 1943, 50, 292–310.

Lewin, K., Forces behind food habits and methods of change, *The Problem of Changing Food Habits, Nat. Res. Council Bull.*, 1943, No. 108.

Lewin, K., The special case of Germany, *Publ. Opin. Quart.*, 1943, 7, 555–566.

Lewin, K., Constructs in psychology and psychological ecology, *Univer. Iowa Stud. Child Welf.*, 1944, 20, 1–29.

Lewin, K., Action research and minority problems, *J. Soc. Issues*, 1946, 2, 34–46.

Lewin, K., Frontiers in group dynamics: II. Channels of group life—social planning and action research, *Hum. Relat.*, 1947, 1, 143–153.

SUGGESTED READINGS

BOOKS

Adams, D. K., *The Anatomy of Personality*. Garden City, N.Y.: Doubleday 1954.

    Personality studied via field theory.

Bolles, R. C., *Theories of Motivation*. New York: Harper & Row, 1966.

    Includes Freud, Murray, and Lewin.

Cartwright, D., Lewinian theory as a contemporary systematic framework, in S. Koch (ed.), *Psychology: A Study of Science*, Vol. 2. New York: McGraw Hill, 1959, pp. 7–91.

Deutsch, M., Field theory in social psychology, in G. Lindzey (ed.), *Handbook of Social Psychology*. Reading, Mass.: Addison-Wesley, 1954, pp. 181–222.

Escalona, S., The influence of topological and vector psychology upon current research in child development: An addendum, in L. Carmichael (ed.), *Manual of Child Psychology*. New York: Wiley, 1954.

Hall, C. S., and G. Lindzey, *Theories of Personality*. New York: Wiley, 1957, pp. 206–256.

Excellent discussion on how to draw diagrams.

Heider, F., The Gestalt theory of motivation, in M. R. Jones (ed.), *Nebraska Symposium on Motivation*. Lincoln: University of Nebraska Press, 1960.

Kounin, J. S., Field theory in psychology: Kurt Lewin, in J. M. Wepman and R. W. Heine (eds.), *Concepts of Personality*. Chicago: Aldine, 1963, pp. 142–161.

Leeper, R. W., *Lewin's Topological and Vector Psychology: A Digest and Critique*. Eugene: University of Oregon Press, 1943.

Lippitt, P., and R. White, The "social climate" of children's groups, in R. G. Barker, J. S. Kounin, and H. F. Wright (eds.), *Child Behavior and Development*. New York: McGraw-Hill, 1943.

Wolman, B. B., *Contemporary Theories and Systems in Psychology*. New York: Harper & Row, 1960.

See especially chap. 13, "Field Theory."

PERIODICALS

Allport, G. W., The genius of Kurt Lewin, *J. Pers.*, 1947, *16*, 1–10.

Also published in *J. Soc. Issues*, 1948, *4*, 14–21, Suppl. Series I.

Berelson, B., The state of communication research, *Publ. Opin. Quart.*, 1959, *23*, 1–6.

Lewin's "small groups approach" is one of the major influences.

Brolyer, C. R., Review of Kurt Lewin's *Principles of Topological Psychology*, *Charact. & Pers.*, 1936–1937, *5*, 255–272.

Cantril, H., Review of Lewin's *Dynamic Theory of Personality*, *J. Abnorm. Soc. Psychol.*, 1935, *30*, 534–537.

Frijns, A. G., African personality structure: A critical review of bibliographical sources and of principal findings, *Gawein*, 1966, *14*, 239–248.

Uses Allport's "functional autonomy of motives" and Lewin's "principle of contemporaneity."

Freud, A., The contribution of psychoanalysis to genetic psychology, *Amer. J. Orthopsychiat.*, 1951, *21*, 476–497.

Anna Freud criticizes the Barker, Dembo, and Lewin frustration experiment.

Garrett, H. E., Lewin's "topological" psychology: An evaluation, *Psychol. Rev.*, 1939, *46*, 517–524.

Gordon, A., and W. Thurlow, Substitution with interrupted tasks of differing valence, *J. Genet. Psychol.*, 1958, *93*, 303–305.

Hearn, G., Kurt Lewin on adolescence, *Group*, 1954, *17*, 9–15.

Heider, F., On Lewin's methods and theory, *Soc. Issues*, 1959, Suppl. 13.

Koriel, H. S., Democracy unlimited: Kurt Lewin's theory, *Amer. J. Sociol.*, 1956, 62, 680–689.

Lindzey, G., Review of Lewin's *Field Theory in Social Science, J. Abnorm. Soc. Psychol.*, 1952, 47, 132–133.

Lippitt, R., Field theory and experiment in social psychology: Autocratic and democratic group atmospheres, *Amer. J. Sociol.*, 1939, 45, 26–49.

London, I. O., Psychologists' misuse of the auxiliary concepts of physics and mathematics, *Psychol. Rev.*, 1944, 51, 266–291.

McCall, S. H. A., A comparative study of the systems of Lewin and Koffka with specific reference to memory phenomena, *Contr. Psychol. Theor.* (Duke Univer. Press), 1939, 2, No. 1.

McCreary, J. K., The problem of personality definition, *J. Gen. Psychol.*, 1960, 63, 107–111.

> Reviews definitions by Allport, Lewin, Murray, and Murphy.

Mann, J. W., Adolescent marginality, *J. Genet. Psychol.*, 1965, 106, 221–235.

> Lewin's treatment of marginal man was examined in seventy-five late adolescents. Most saw adolescents as overlap of either childhood or adulthood. Only a few disclose status discrepancies, which mostly differ from the kind Lewin noted.

Moreno, J. L., How Kurt Lewin's "Research Center for Group Dynamics" started and the question of paternity, *Group Psychother.*, 1952, 5, 1–6.

Moreno, J. L., How Kurt Lewin's "Research Center for Group Dynamics" started *Sociometry*, 1953, 16, 101–106.

Smith, D. E. P., Interdisciplinary approach to the genesis of anxiety, *Educ. Theor.*, 1956, 6, 222–231.

> Compares Freud, Rank, Mowrer, Angyal, Goldstein, Lewin, Rogers Kierkegaard, and Sullivan on theories of anxiety.

Stein, G. G., B = F(P, E), *J. Proj. Techn. Pers. Assessment*, 1964, 28, 161–168

> An analysis of the dimensions associated with the parameters of Lewin' equation.

Stinnette, C. R., Human meaning of transformation in learning, *Relig. Educ* 1968, 63, 181–185.

> Insights from Lewin, Erikson and Sullivan are related to (1) languag and learning, (2) is knowing all? (3) human dimension in learning, (4 learning as transformation.

Tolman, E. C., Kurt Lewin: 1890–1947, *Psychol. Rev.*, 1948, 55, 1–4.

White, R. K., The case for the Tolman-Lewin interpretation of learning, *Psychol. Rev.*, 1943, 50, 157–186.

LEARNING
[MOWRER]

An imperfectly denatured animal intermittently
subject to the unpredictable reactions of an
unlocated, spiritual area.

RUDYARD KIPLING
Surgeons and the Soul (Definition of Man)

SOME BIOGRAPHICAL DATA[1]

Orval Hobart Mowrer was born on January 23, 1907, in Unionville, Missouri. He received his A.B. from the University of Missouri in 1929 and his Ph.D. from Johns Hopkins University in 1932. On September 9, 1931, he married Willie Mae Cook. They have three children: Linda, Kathryn, and Todd. Mowrer was a National Research Fellow at both Northwestern (1932–1933) and Princeton (1933–1934). He spent the years from 1934 to 1940 at Yale as a Sterling Fellow (1934–1936) and as an instructor in psychology and a member of the staff at the Institute of Human Relations (1936–1940). From 1940 to 1948 he was assistant professor, then associate professor of education at Harvard. Since leaving Harvard in 1948 he has been research professor at the University of Illinois. Mowrer is a fellow of the American Orthopsychiatric Association, the American Psychology Association (president, 1953–1954), and the AAAS. He is a member of the American Academy of Psychotherapists, the Linguistic Society of America, the American Association of University Professors, and Sigma Xi. Mowrer was the recipient of the Certificate of Merit from the University of Missouri. He has served as clinical psychologist for the OSS and acts as special consultant at the USPHS. While at Harvard he edited the *Harvard Educational Review*. For a highly personal account of Mowrer's life, the reader is urged to read "Abnormal Reactions or Actions?" (1966).

I am grateful to Dr. Mowrer for his suggestions regarding the preparation of this chapter.

Like Carl Rogers, Mowrer has also become highly interested in grou
therapy. Currently he spends time and energy with such lay groups :
Synanon, Alcoholics Anonymous, and Daytop Village, where he has spoke
and served as a resource person.

INTRODUCTION

As we have previously stated, there are many excellent learning theoris
whose theories could be included in this section. We have chosen to us
Mowrer's work because it seems to be more general in nature and possib
more adaptable to a general theory of behavior than are the others.

O. Hobart Mowrer is an original thinker. Some of his output is in th
vein of Miller-Dollard. The versatility of Mowrer can be seen in his rat wor
his work on enuresis, psychoanalysis, anthropology and culture, language, h
primary work in learning theory, and his current work in religion and m
rality. Mowrer is also a product of Yale University's Institute of Huma
Relations. He is not the only learning theorist who has left laboratory wor
with animals to work with people. However, he seems to have extended h
theories further than have some of the others.

THE SYSTEM, THEORY,
OR ESSENTIAL FEATURES

General Considerations

Mowrer began, as did many learning theorists, mainly within the framewor
of reinforcement theory and secondary drives. However, as early as 1947 h
moved over into a two-factor theory which he considered integrative (
dualistic. In Mowrer's own words, he gave up trying to "squeeze" all behavic
into one system. Essentially his learning theory is mediated by states of hof
and fear within the organism. Originally his learning theory work was aj
proximately in the tradition of the associationist theoretical school.

Almost all of Mowrer's work is empirically oriented. There is not muc
that is allied to many previous theories. Although Mowrer was a forme
Hullian, he deviates considerably from the Hullian position. Also after h
early experience with analysis, Mowrer deviated from the Freudian concep
of pleasure principle and reality principle. However, he has taken a genuir
research interest in proving or disproving Freud's pleasure principle an
reality principle by an empirical approach.

Mowrer's definition of personality grows out of three areas of endeavo
(1) learning theory, (2) social anthropology or cultural differences, and (3
psychoanalysis. Probably the best definition comes from the chapter (
Mowrer and Kluckhohn, "A Dynamic Theory of Personality" in J. McVicke

Hunt's, *Personality and the Behavior Disorders*, Vol. I (1944). The co-authors used four criteria in defining personality. The criteria must be considered to be integrated in the action of any individual. They are "(1) the meaning or *function*, which an individual's actions have for him, (2) the *conflicts* which exist between his various habit systems, (3) the environment or *field* to which he is accustomed, and (4) the more or less unique way in which he is held together, or *integrated*. These four criteria, derived from the four basic assumptions of dynamic theory, thus provide a comprehensive scheme for defining 'personality' in general and for identifying any 'personality' in particular" (p. 77).

Out of this framework, as we shall see later, Mowrer defines a two-factor learning theory which concerns itself with solution learning and sign learning. These he feels have a strong bearing upon personality and upon an individual's behavior.

Mowrer also believes that an individual's personality may continue and even grow for years after his death. The reference is obviously to reputation and does not mean an interacting personality. He cites, for example, painters, poets, writers, and others who are being discovered and rediscovered, whose personalities, in the interpersonal sense, continue to grow and develop despite the individual's death.

As previously stated, Mowrer has extended some of Freud's ideas. For example, he finds that in neurotic behavior the id is equivalent to primary drives; the ego, to solution learning; and the superego, to sign learning.

Specific Considerations

Mowrer's learning theory, which he finds adaptable to personality study, involves both reinforcement and contiguity. Reinforcement has and probably will continue to have innumerable meanings, but generally it represents "a strengthening of a response, whether the response is positive or negative." Contiguity means "a nearness of two objects in time or space," but it also means "a nearness of two experiences for the same organism or the human personality."

The following outline summarizes some of the more pertinent and outstanding features in Mowrer's two-factor learning theory.

SOLUTION LEARNING	SIGN LEARNING
1. Problem solving	1. Problem making
2. Drive reducing	2. Creates expectation or predispositions or a belief or set to act
3. Pleasure giving	3. Secondary drives and emotions relate or connect to new objects —so new problems exist to be solved which were not in the original organism

4. Central nervous system involved	4. Autonomic nervous system involved (contiguity)
5. Closely allied to instrumental learning	5. Goes beyond S–R bonds into cognition or learning meanings, attitudes, and sets
6. Relates to reinforcement	6. Relates to contiguity
7. Requires reward or pleasure	7. Does not require rewards but relates to higher processes (language and symbolic learning, for example)
8. Life in the past or present	8. Life in the present or future
9. Law of effect (Thorndike, Hull)	9. Classic conditioning (Pavlov)

In some of his recent work Mowrer has reintroduced the concept of habit into his two-factor theory (see especially chap. 7, "Revised Two Factor Theory and the Concept of Habit," in *Learning Theory and Behavior*, 1960). The sequel to this tome is his 1960 work *Learning Theory and the Symbolic Processes*. In actuality each book is a companion piece to the other; they could almost be read concurrently.

Essentially Mowrer is saying that the human language (symbolic processes) is learned much in the same manner as the responses of primary-drive reduction. Thus, producing responses is equally important in personality formation as reducing primary drives. The former concept (response production) relies heavily upon hope and fear within the organism. This extension of the former two-factor theory involves a newer viewpoint of the age-old concept of habit. In regard to synaptic connections Mowrer goes on to say ". . . revised two-factor theory assumes that so-called habit formulation involves a strengthening of synapses between the neurones' *connecting stimuli produced by some behavioral act and the emotion of hope and that* punishment involves a similar conditioning of fear"; i.e., you (the organism) hope to gain the reward or hope to avoid pain (*Learning Theory and Behavior*, pp. 220 ff.; italics in the original). In this way the neural connections involved in a habit formulation are not inflexible and set. In summary, then "In advancing a feedback conception of both response inhibition (punishment) and response facilitation (habit), we have emancipated behavior theory from what may be called the 'bondage' of Thorndike's scheme and also liberated it from the crass reflexology of Pavlov" (*ibid.*, p. 251).

In *The Crisis in Psychiatry and Religion* (1961) Mowrer takes an extremely intriguing side trip into the area of abnormal behavior and religious values. The book is a collection of published papers and lectures. Although Mowrer acknowledges a "major objective" in this collection as being an attempt to delineate the religious from the psychiatric, so that each can proceed to its own task, there is no major thesis or thread in the book. The following salient points are merely a random selection.

1. Biological adaptation and survival do not help us much in solving problems of psychological survival; or, how can the body best serve the mind?

2. Psychoanalysis (which Mowrer feels is on the way out as a therapy and a personality theory), and its approach to psychoneurosis, implies no sense of moral responsibility. At some point we must abandon mental "sickness" as a pessimistic approach and think also about deviant behavior and responsibility for self-action as "sin" on account of its implication of promise and hope. (Needless to say, this idea has created a thundering chorus of denial and rebuttal in the American psychological world. It is *not* popular to use the word *sin* in this country.)

3. Guilt (not just guilt feelings) is a real aspect of disturbed persons. They "are not 'disturbed' for nothing."

4. The pastoral counseling movement usurped its peripheral function and took over the whole show mainly through the overzealous acceptance of psychoanalysis and nondirective frames of reference. Theology took a back seat to therapy in seminary and in pastoral duties.

The above four points are only a small sampling of Mowrer's text, advancing the hypothesis that mental illness has a moral basis.

■ SUMMARY

In summarizing the work of O. Hobart Mowrer, we find his theory not as complete as some of the others. The theory does branch out from the two-factor learning theory with Freudian and cultural overtones. The main theme seems to be in solution learning and sign learning, and in revising his two-factor learning theory to include the states of hope and fear within the organism in an expansion of the Thorndikian habit position. The solution and sign learning systems appear to be basically different from each other. However, they are both involved in any single human being. We also find that Mowrer has moved from laboratory work with animals to people, language, and morals.

DELIMITATION

We have not treated Mowrer's work with rats, his work on enuresis and language as "tension indexes," and his experiences in psychoanalysis. We also have not mentioned the work that Mowrer and Sears and many others did in 1939 on frustration leading toward aggression. Mowrer continues, however, to expand his theory primarily from the framework of the learning theorist.

BIBLIOGRAPHY

PRIMARY SOURCES

BOOKS

Dollard, J., L. W. Doob, N. E. Miller, O. H. Mowrer, and R. R. Sears, *Frustration and Aggression*. New Haven, Conn.: Yale University Press, 1939.

Mowrer, O. H., and C. Kluckhohn, Dynamic theory of personality, in J. McV Hunt (ed.), *Personality and the Behavior Disorders*. New York: Ronald Press, 1944, chap. 3.

Mowrer, O. H., *Learning Theory and Personality Dynamics*. New York: Ronald Press, 1950.

Mowrer, O. H., Neurosis and its treatment as learning phenomena, in D. Browe and L. E. Abt (eds.), *Progress in Clinical Psychology*, Vol. 1. New York Grune & Stratton, 1952, pp. 312–323.

> Neurosis is essentially a problem of moral failure.

Mowrer, O. H., Motivation and neurosis, in J. S. Brown and others, *Current Theory and Research in Motivation: A Symposium*. Lincoln: University o Nebraska Press, 1953, pp. 162–164.

Mowrer, O. H. (ed.), *Psychotherapy: Theory and Research*. New York: Ronald Press, 1953.

Kluckhohn, C., and O. H. Mowrer, Determinants and components of personality in A. Weider (ed.), *Contributions Toward Medical Psychology*. New York Ronald Press, 1953.

Mowrer, O. H., Ego psychology, cybernetics, and learning theory, in *Learning Theory, Personality Theory and Clinical Research: Kentucky Symposium* New York: Wiley, 1954, pp. 81–90.

Mowrer, O. H., Emerging conceptions of neurosis and normality, in L. K. Hsu (ed.), *Aspects of Culture and Personality*. New York: Abelard-Schuman 1954, pp. 119–138.

Mowrer, O. H., Symposium remarks on re-evaluation in the social sciences, in Academy of Religion and Mental Health, *Religion, Science, and Mental Health*. New York: New York University Press, 1959.

Mowrer, O. H., Footnotes to a theory of psychopathology, in L. E. Abt and B. F Riess (eds.), *Progress in Clinical Psychology*, Vol. IV. New York: Grune & Stratton, 1960.

Mowrer, O. H., *Learning Theory and Behavior*. New York: Wiley, 1960.

Mowrer, O. H., *Learning Theory and the Symbolic Processes*. New York: Wiley, 1960.

Mowrer, O. H., *The Crisis in Psychiatry and Religion*. Princeton, N.J.: Van Nostrand, 1961.

Mowrer, O. H., in R. C. Birney and R. C. Teevan (eds.), *Reinforcement: An Enduring Problem in Psychology—Selected Readings*. Princeton, N.J.: Van Nostrand, 1961.

Mowrer, O. H., *The New Group Therapy*. Princeton, N.J.: Van Nostrand, 1964.

Mowrer, O. H., Learning theory and behavior therapy, in B. Wolman (ed.), *Handbook of Clinical Psychology*. New York: McGraw-Hill, 1965.

Mowrer, O. H., Stimulus-response psychology: A two factor learning theory of personality, in W. S. Sahakian (ed.), *Psychology of Personality: Readings in Theory*. Chicago: Rand McNally, 1965, pp. 462–472.

> Odds and ends of Mowrer's theory.

Mowrer, O. H., What is normal behavior? in W. D. Nunokawa (ed.), *Readings in Abnormal Psychology: Human Values and Abnormal Behavior*. Chicago: Scott, Foresman, 1965.

Mowrer, O. H., Abnormal reactions or actions? in J. A. Vernon (ed.), *Introduction to Psychology: A Self-Selection Textbook*. Dubuque, Iowa: Brown, 1966.

> Mowrer's highly personal account of his life.

Mowrer, O. H. (ed.), *Morality and Mental Health*. Chicago: Rand McNally, 1966.

> Psychopathology must be as concerned with morality per se as with personality disturbances.

Mowrer, O. H., Loss and recovery of community: A guide to the theory and practice of integrity therapy, in G. M. Gazda (ed.), *Theories and Methods of Group Psychotherapy and Counseling*. Springfield, Ill.: Thomas, 1967.

Mowrer, O. H., Ego psychology, cybernetics, and learning theory, in W. Buckley (ed.), *Modern Systems Research for the Behavioral Scientist: A Sourcebook*. Chicago: Aldine, 1968, pp. 337–342.

> Reprint of a 1954 article.

PERIODICALS

Mowrer, O. H., Apparatus for the study and treatment of enuresis, *Amer. J. Psychol.*, 1938, 51, 163–165.

Mowrer, O. H., and W. M. Mowrer, Enuresis—a method for its study and treatment, *Amer. J. Orthopsychiat.*, 1938, 8, 436–459.

Mowrer, O. H., A stimulus-response analysis of anxiety and its role as a reinforcing agent, *Psychol. Rev.*, 1939, 46, 553–565.

Mowrer, O. H., Anxiety reduction and learning, *J. Exp. Psychol.*, 1940, 27, 497–516.

Mowrer, O. H., An experimental analogue of "regression" with incidental observations on "reaction formation," *J. Abnorm. Soc. Psychol.*, 1940, 35, 56–87.

Mowrer, O. H., and R. R. Lamoreaux, Avoidance conditioning and signal dura
    tion: A study of secondary motivation and reward, *Psychol. Monogr.*, 1942
    54, No. 5.

Mowrer, O. H., and H. Jones, Extinction and behavior variability as a function o
    the effortfulness of task, *J. Exp. Psychol.*, 1943, 33, 369–386.

Whiting, J. W. M., and O. H. Mowrer, Habit progression and regression: A
    laboratory study of some factors relevant to human socialization, *J. Comp*
    Psychol., 1943, 36, 229–253.

Mowrer, O. H., and C. Kluckhohn, Personality and culture: A conceptual scheme
    Amer. Anthropol., 1944, 46, 1–29.

Mowrer, O. H., and P. Viek, Language and learning: An experimental paradigm
    Harvard Educ. Rev., 1945, 15, 35–48.

Mowrer, O. H., The law of effect and ego psychology, *Psychol. Rev.*, 1946, 53
    321–334.

Mowrer, O. H., and R. R. Lamoreaux, Fear as an intervening variable in avoid
    ance conditioning, *J. Comp. Psychol.*, 1946, 39 29–50.

Mowrer, O. H., On the dual nature of learning: A reinterpretation of "condition
    ing" and "problem solving," *Harvard Educ. Rev.*, 1947, 17, 102–148.

Dollard, J., and O. H. Mowrer, A method of measuring tension in writter
    documents, *J. Abnorm. Soc. Psychol.*, 1947, 42, 3–32.

Mowrer, O. H., Learning theory and the neurotic paradox, *Amer. J. Orthopsy*
    chiat., 1948, 18, 571–610.

Mowrer, O. H., Biological versus moral "frustration" in personality disturbances
    Progressive Educ., 1949, 26, 65–69.

Mowrer, O. H., Two-factor learning theory: Summary and comment, *Psychol*
    Rev., 1951, 58, 350–354.

Mowrer, O. H., Speech development in the young child: I. The autism theory o
    speech development and some clinical applications, *J. Speech Disorders*
    1952, 17, 263–268.

Mowrer, O. H., The therapeutic process: III. Learning theory and the neurotic
    fallacy, *Amer. J. Orthopsychiat.*, 1952, 22, 679–689.

Mowrer, O. H., Neurosis: A disorder of conditioning or problem solving, *Ann*
    N.Y. Acad. Sci., 1953, 56, 273–288.

Mowrer, O. H., Some philosophical problems in mental disorder and its treatment
    Harvard Educ. Rev., 1953, 23, 117–127.

Mowrer, O. H., Learning theory: Historical review and re-interpretation, *Harvar*
    Educ. Rev., 1954, 24, 37–58.

Mowrer, O. H., Learning theory and identification: I. Introduction, *J. Genet*
    Psychol., 1954, 84, 197–199.

Mowrer, O. H., The psychologist looks at language, *Amer. Psychologist*, 1954, 9
    660–694.

    APA presidential address.

Mowrer, O. H., Neo-analytic theory, *J. Counsel. Psychol.*, 1956, 3, 108–111.

Mowrer, O. H., Two-factor learning theory reconsidered with special references t
    secondary reinforcement and the concept of habit, *Psychol. Rev.*, 1956, 63
    114–128.

Mowrer, O. H., Some philosophical problems in psychological counseling, *J. Counsel. Psychol.*, 1957, *4*, 103–111.

Donitz, J. R., D. J. Mason, O. H. Mowrer, and P. Viek, Conditioning of fear: A function of the delay of reinforcement, *Amer. J. Psychol.*, 1957, 70, 69–74.

Mowrer, O. H., Hearing and speaking: An analysis of language learning, *J. Speech Disorders*, 1958, *23*, 143–152.

Mowrer, O. H., Symposium on relationships between religion and mental health: Discussion, *Amer. Psychologist*, 1958, *13*, 577–579.

Mowrer, O. H., and J. D. Keehn, How are intertrial "avoidance" responses reinforced? *Psychol. Rev.*, 1958, *65*, 209–221.

Mowrer, O. H., Changing conceptions of the unconscious, J. Nerv. Ment. Dis., 1959, *129*, 222–234.

Mowrer, O. H., Comments on Trude Weiss-Rosmarin's "Adler's psychology and the Jewish tradition," *J. Indiv. Psychol.*, 1959, *15*, 128–129.

Mowrer, O. H., Judgment and suffreing: Contrasting views, *Faculty Forum*, 1959, *10*.

Mowrer, O. H., Basic research methods, statistics, and decision theory, *Amer. J. Occup. Ther.*, 1960, *4*, 199–205.

Mowrer, O. H., "Sin"; the lesser of two evils, *Amer. Psychologist*, 1960, *15*, 301–304.

Mowrer, O. H., Some constructive features of the concept of sin, *J. Counsel. Psychol.*, 1960, 7, 185–188.

Also in *The Crisis in Psychiatry and Religion.*

Mowrer, O. H., Cognitive dissonance or counterconditioning? A reappraisal of certain behavioral "paradoxes," *Psychol. Rec.*, 1963, *13*, 197–211.

Mowrer, O. H., Payment or repayment: The problem of private practice, *Amer. Psychologist*, 1963, *18*, 577–580.

Mowrer, O. H., Transference and scrupulosity as reactions to unresolved guilt, *J. Relig. Hlth*, July, 1963, pp. 313–343.

Mowrer, O. H., Freudianism, behavior therapy, and "self-disclosure," *Behav. Res. Ther.*, 1964, *1*, 321–337.

Mowrer, O. H., Science, sex, and values, *Personnel Guid. J.*, 1964, *42*, 746–753.

Mowrer, O. H., Integrity therapy, *Faculty Forum*, 1965, *33*, 1–5.

Mowrer, O. H., Stage-fright and self-regard, *West. Speech*, Fall, 1965, pp. 197–201.

Mowrer, O. H., The basis of psychopathology: Malconditioning or misbehavior? *J. Nat. Assn. Women Deans*, 1966, *29*, 51–58.

Mowrer, O. H., The behavior therapies with special reference to modeling and imitation, *Amer. J. Psychother.*, 1966, *20*, 439–461.

Patients need to learn with therapist as a model.

Mowrer, O. H., Integrity therapy: A self-help approach, *Psychother.: Theor. Res. Pract.*, 1966, *3*, 114–119.

Mowrer, O. H., Civilization and its malcontents, *Psychol. Today*, 1967, *1*, 48–52.

Mowrer, O. H., Communication, conscience and the unconscious, *J. Commun. Disorders*, 1967, *1*, 109–135.

Mowrer, O. H., A revolution in integrity? *Voices,* 1967, 3, 26–33.
Mowrer, O. H., Stuttering as simultaneous admission and denial, *J. Commun Disorders,* 1967, 1, 46–50.

TAPE RECORDINGS

Mowrer, O. H., A *Re-Evaluation of Psychoanalysis,* Sound Seminars, No. 123 Cincinnati, Ohio.

SUGGESTED READINGS

BOOKS

Ard, B. N. (ed.), *Counseling and Psychotherapy: Classics on Theories and Issue* Palo Alto, Cal.: Science and Behavior Books, 1966.
Hall, C. S., and G. Lindzey, *Theories of Personality.* New York: Wiley, 1957, pp 456–465.
Kazimierz, D., *Personality-Shaping Through Positive Disintegration,* Boston Little, Brown, 1967.

    Introduction by Mowrer.

Lundin, R. W., *Personality: An Experimental Approach.* New York: Macmillan 1961.

    Personality is a valid subject for scientific study.

McClelland, D. C., *Personality.* New York: Holt, Rinehart & Winston, 1951 (Reissued as a Holt-Dryden book in 1958.)
Wolman, B. B., *Contemporary Theories and Systems.* New York: Harper & Row 1960, pp. 170–172.

PERIODICALS

Anant, S. S., Integrity therapy and the Sikh religion, *Insight: Quart. Rev. Reli, Ment. Hlth,* 1966, 5, 22–29.

    Principles of Sikh religion are examined in light of Mowrer's theory integrity therapy.

Dabrowski, K., The theory of positive disintegration, *Int. J. Psychol.,* 1966, 229–243.

    A discussion by Mowrer follows the presentation of the theory.

Eysenck, H. J., A dynamic theory of anxiety and hysteria, *J. Ment. Sci.,* 1955, 10 28–51.

    Criticizes Mowrer's theory as being more introversion–extraversion tha neuroses theory.

Feather, N. T., Mowrer's revised two-factor theory and the motive–expectancy–value model, *Psychol. Rev.*, 1963, *70*, 500–515.

>Presents alternatives to Mowrer's concepts of fear, hope, relief, and disappointment.

Funk, M. F., Moral judgments and neurosis, *Dissert. Abstr.*, 1962, *22*, 3740–3741.

Szasz, T. S., The myth of mental illness, *Amer. Psychologist*, 1960, *15*, 113–118.

Smith, D. E. P., Interdisciplinary approach to the genesis of anxiety, *Educ. Theor.*, 1956, *6*, 222–231.

>Compares Freud, Rank, Mowrer, Angyal, Goldstein, Lewin, Rogers, Kierkegaard, and Sullivan on theories of anxiety.

Swenson, C. H., Jr., Sexual behavior and psychopathology: A test of Mowrer's hypothesis, *J. Clin. Psychol.*, 1962, *18*, 406–409.

>Support of Mowrer's hypothesis of a relation between psychological distress and guilt from a violation of moral precepts. "Patients . . . have violated some well-known moral scruple more frequently than a matched group of normals."

Wolfe, L. A., Moreno and Mowrer: Or the new group therapy, *Group Psychother.*, 1965, *18*, 171–176.

>Claims Mowrer should have read Moreno first.

Yates, A. J., Symptoms and symptom substitution, *Psychol. Rev.*, 1958, *65*, 371–374.

>Criticizes Mowrer's dualistic approach.

HUMANISTIC
[MASLOW]

What you cannot as you would achieve,
You must perforce accomplish as you may.

WILLIAM SHAKESPEARE
Titus Andronicus, II, 1

SOME BIOGRAPHICAL DATA[1]

Abraham Harold Maslow was born in Brooklyn on April 1, 1908. He was educated at the University of Wisconsin, receiving his B.A. in 1930, his M.A. in 1931, and his Ph.D. in 1934. He married Bertha Goodman on December 31, 1928. They have two children, Ann and Ellen. Prior to his appointment at Brandeis in 1951, Dr. Maslow was on the faculty of the University of Wisconsin as Research Assistant in Social Psychology (1929–1930), Assistant Instructor in Psychology (1930–1934), and Teaching Fellow in Psychology (1934–1935). After serving as a Carnegie Fellow at Columbia University from 1935 to 1937, he joined the faculty of Brooklyn College as associate professor until 1951. He was plant manager at the Maslow Cooperate Corporation from 1947 to 1949. Since 1951 he has been associate professor, professor, and chairman of the Department of Psychology at Brandeis University. Dr. Maslow is a member and officer of a number of learned societies. He was president of the Massachusetts State Psychological Association and served on the council of the Society of Psychological Study of Social Issues. A member of the American Psychological Association, he was elected a Fellow of both the Association's Division of Abnormal and Clinical Psychology and the Division of Personality and Social Psychology, of which he was president. He also served as president of the Division of Esthetics. A former Fellow of the New York Academy of Sciences, he is a member of Phi Beta Kappa and

[1] The cooperation of Professor Maslow in reviewing this section and supplying additional comments is gratefully acknowledged.

Sigma Xi. Maslow is also a past president of the American Psychological Association.

INTRODUCTION

Abraham H. Maslow is a realistically oriented personality theorist. From the factual material of his studies he finds both optimistic and some pessimistic characteristics in human behavior.

Maslow has studied with and been the personal friend of some of the greatest names in psychology. He freely acknowledges his debt to his many teachers and friends. At some time in the past he has studied under or worked with Goldstein, Sheldon, Harlow, David M. Levy, Wertheimer, Koffka, Kardiner, Fromm, Horney, Adler, Ruth Benedict, Thorndike, Mittelmann, Ralph Linton, Else Frenkel-Brunswik, Tolman, Allport, and Murphy. The list is a veritable, "Who's Who" of psychology.

Some students of personality theory consider that Maslow has "done some of the best writing on motivation" (Bonner, *Psychology of Personality*, p. 267).

Maslow's theory of personality is based on a limited number of cases. Like many other theorists, he started working with primates and has ended by working with people.

THE SYSTEM, THEORY, OR ESSENTIAL FEATURES

General Considerations

Maslow's theory concerns itself primarily with growth motivation, which he feels can be gained through self-actualization. Another name given to it is *meta motivation theory*. Thus, Maslow feels that man is more interested in need gratification than in need frustration. He believes that man is essentially and innately good. The badness in man's behavior comes out of a bad environment rather than an inherent rottenness. In other words, man is more than just an animal; he is a special kind of animal. Consequently, any true motivation study concerns people, not animals only. The inner nature of self-actualization is "weak, delicate and subtle." This thin thread of the inner nature of man's self-actualization may be overcome by poor culture, bad parents, or faulty habits. But it never fully disappears. "It persists underground forever pressing for actualization" (Moustakas, ed., *The Self*, 1956, p. 233).

Maslow emphasizes growth motivation and not just deficiency motivation. Man's behavior is more than homeostasis. The human personality wants not just food but variety and differences in food. Maslow finds, for example, that happier people are oriented to growth motivation while neurotics are

oriented toward deficiency motivation. In this sense the neurotic or un
adjusted human is trying to satisfy only his basic drives and to maintain a
status quo.

Maslow's is a unified organismic theory. He freely credits the Adlerians
with understanding need structure. Much of his work is well summarized in
his chief book, *Motivation and Personality* (1954), in which he makes a
synthesis of the three approaches: holistic, dynamic or motivational, and
cultural.

In every self-actualizing personality there is a hierarchy of need priorities
These are degrees of psychological health in which one must successfully
achieve the first degree in order to go on to the second degree. Maslow does
not use the word *instinct* but coins the word *instinctoid*. We may assume
from that this is an innate or inborn capacity within the structure of man's
organism.

DEGREES OF PSYCHOLOGICAL HEALTH

Maslow proposes six degrees of need priority which lead to psychological
health. The first and second are of the lower order and are most potent. If
these first two, physiological needs and safety needs, are not met, the follow
ing four cannot be met either. Thus, belongingness, love, self-esteem, and self-
actualization are considered to be of a higher nature.

1. Physiological needs. These are needs for air, food, water, and physical
comfort, which must be met before the next needs can be approached.

2. Safety needs. Using children for an example, Maslow finds that they
have a desire for freedom from fear and insecurity. One wants to avoid
harmful or painful incidents.

3. Belongingness. Belongingness needs begin the higher order needs. The
human personality wants security. The human being wants to be somebody
even though it is in a small group. Because he is brought up by his fellow
men, he wants to belong to the group that helped to rear him.

4. Love needs. Man has had, now has, and always will have the desire to
love someone else and be loved in return.

5. Self-esteem needs. In this need man wants to know that he worthwhile, that he can master something of his own environment, that he has a
competence and an independence and a freedom and a feeling of being
recognized for some type of endeavor.

6. Self-actualization needs. These are the highest needs: for cognition
and for aesthetic reality. Man has a strong desire to know and understand not
only himself but the world about him. In addition, he does not want to live in
a stark, unbeautiful world but needs to have beauty and art, to appreciate and
to create things of an aesthetic nature.

In explaining the six needs, Maslow feels that achieving one level drives a
person on to the next higher level. However, an unsatisfied need at the lower

end of the structure will dominate the higher human need: "Bread before Bach." The physiological and safety needs are certainly of a lower order. As we have seen, neurotics have not had these needs met to a satisfactory point. Maslow believes the first two levels have been highly overemphasized by most personality theorists. The ultimate and achievable nature of man is to operate at the upper levels and especially the self-actualization level. It may be that at times society inhibits man's strivings to actualize himself. One of Maslow's most important points is that human behavior is *not* a question of normality or dichotomy between good and bad behavior but is essentially a question of self-fulfillment. Thus, what is normal is not a comparative thing; what is normal is an inner ability to make oneself the best and fullest possible personality that he is able to create.

Specific Considerations

In order to study the hierarchy of need structure, Maslow has conducted a unique type of research. He began with the concept that to study abnormal personalities is bound to prove or produce an abnormally oriented theory of personality. It would be one-sided. His next step was to find a group that he considered to be composed of actualized, successful people. *Successful* here meant possessing the ability to discover their own deepest roots of personality. With this framework, Maslow came up with forty-nine people, from public and private life. The list included personalities from history and those living who he believed possessed the characteristics of good psychological health. About two-thirds of this group of forty-nine people were truly self-actualizing personalities. Among them were Lincoln, Jefferson, Walt Whitman, Thoreau, Eleanor Roosevelt, Albert Einstein, Albert Schweitzer, and a number of Maslow's friends and acquaintances. The bulk of his findings were published in 1950 in his study "Self-Actualizing People." In order to understand better what made these individuals truly self-actualizing, we must now look at the characteristics that Maslow felt were contained in them.

OUTSTANDING CHARACTERISTICS OF SELF-ACTUALIZED PEOPLE

We have chosen to summarize in fifteen items the main characteristics of a fully self-actualized personality.

1. Oriented realistically; efficient perception; good judge of others and quick to judge them.
2. Accept selves and others and the world for what they actually are, not what they wish they would be; not hypocritical.
3. High degree of spontaneity; unaffected in behavior, act natural, may appear unconventional.
4. Problem-centered, not self-centered; work on problem, not self; not very introspective.

5. Inclined to be detached; great need for privacy at times; not entirely dependent on others; can amuse self; can detach self and concentrate alone; may appear aloof to others.
6. Autonomous within self and independent; dependent on self, serene.
7. Fresh appreciation of people and world, not dulled—not "I've been there before," but "Every sunset is as beautiful as the first," "Ten thousandth baby as miraculous as the first."
8. Somewhat mystical or profound inner experiences; seem out of this world at times.
9. Identify strongly with fellow man, but do not join in empathetic way; have older brother personality; want to help; truly interested in the welfare of man.
10. Deep and intimate relationship with only very few; have special friends or small circle of friends; highly selective in friends, give absolutely to them; easily touched and moved by children.
11. Strong democratically oriented values; can relate and learn from rich or poor; acquaintance's class or race or position not important.
12. Understand difference between means to achieve a goal and the rightful ends to be achieved; strongly ethical and highly moral, though may differ with popular idea of right and wrong; focus on ends and purposes.
13. Philosophical and whimsical inner-motivated sense of humor; do not laugh at cruelty; strong sense of incongruity; do not tell jokes as jokester but rather see jokes in everyday things spontaneously.
14. Tremendous capacity to be creative, one of *most* universal capacities in all self-actualized people; not special talent but new touches to life, creativeness of child, fresh way of doing things.
15. Swim against mainstream, very open to new experiences, resistant to conformity.[2]

Maslow does not feel that one has to be highly intelligent to do the above fifteen things. Intelligence or intellect may help, but it is not essential. Neither does he feel that one must be perfect and follow the scout code (loyal, faithful, reverent, obedient, etc.). Many of the subjects he studied whom he regarded as self-actualized were prideful, prejudiced, vain, and indeed had some sort of "surgical coldness." That is to say, they were not overly sentimental after the death of a loved one. They also had fears and doubts but did recover well from their fears and doubts. The self-actualized man is not completely happy or successful or extremely well adjusted. He has simply self-actualized his own personality to the best of his ability.

In keeping with much of the newer thinking about personality theory Maslow's *Toward a Psychology of Being* emphasizes the desire to integrate results within a scientific framework. His refreshing and nonpedantic style is

[2] The student is encouraged to read a further extension of this list in 43 "propositions" which enhances these 15 characteristics. (See chap. 14, "Some Basic Propositions of Growth and Self-Actualization Psychology," *Toward a Psychology of Being*, pp. 177–200.)

probably best seen in the above book. In some ways he almost comes out as one of the "new" voices in personality theory. He readily admits that his position is structured out of "pilot researches, bits of evidence, on personal observation, on theoretical deduction, and on sheer hunch" (*ibid.*, p. v). However, it must not be presumed that he is against the scientific approach because "Science is the only way we have of shoving truth down the reluctant throat." And "Only science can progress."

Maslow finds that human personality is far from dichotomized but that it is an integrated and integrating entity. He sees loyalty to a set position, whether it be pro- or anti-Freudian, for example, as just "plain silly." In his newer work Maslow reemphasizes the value of reconciling Being-cognition (B-psychology) with Deficiency-cognition (D-psychology), "i.e., the perfect with the imperfect, the ideal with the actual, the eupsychian with the extant, the timeless with the temporal, end-psychology with means-psychology" (*ibid.*). Some of these reconciliations may be our true "peak experiences."

One of the leading writers on personality theory finds Maslow "willing to tackle problems others leave alone" (Maddi, 1968). Like Mowrer, Fromm, and Allport, Maslow involves himself in the religious aspects of man's behavior. Almost as a neologism he has introduced the term *eupsychia* as a kind of psychological utopia, "in which all men are psychologically healthy."

◼ SUMMARY

In Maslow we find an optimistic personality theorist who desires to study normal people. Much of what he feels comes out of the degrees of psychological health begins with an "instinctoid depth." The hierarchy of the need priorities is physiological, safety, belongingness, love, self-esteem and self-actualization needs. Personality theory should concern itself with growth motivations and not deficiency motivations. Toward this end he studied forty-nine people and continues to study others to see how closely they come to being fully self-actualized and, if they are self-actualized, how they achieved this state.

DELIMITATION

We have omitted the research Abraham Maslow did on photographs of faces, good teaching, and his Security–Insecurity Test. Also because many of the studies are now well in the past, we have not included his work with hunger in animals and primates while he was studying motivation. His views on expressive behavior and coping behavior, as well as his writing in abnormal psychology, have not been included.

BIBLIOGRAPHY

PRIMARY SOURCES

BOOKS

Maslow, A. H., Personality and patterns of culture, in R. Stagner, *Psychology of Personality*. New York: McGraw-Hill, 1937.

> Also in S. Britt (ed.), *Selected Readings in Social Psychology*. New York: Holt, Rinehart & Winston, 1950.

Maslow, A. H., and B. Mittelmann, *Principles of Abnormal Psychology* (1941). New York: Harper & Row, rev. ed., 1951.

> Recorded as a talking book for the blind.

Maslow, A. H., Conflict, frustration and the theory of threat, in S. S. Tomkins, (ed.), *Contemporary Psychopathology*. Cambridge, Mass.: Harvard University Press, 1943.

Maslow, A. H., Theory of motivation, in P. L. Harriman (ed.), *Twentieth Century Psychology*. New York: Philosophical Library, 1946, pp. 22–48.

Maslow, A. H., Self-actualizing people: A study of psychological health, *Personality Symposium*, No. 1, April, 1950, in W. Wolff (ed.), *Values in Personality Research*. New York: Grune & Stratton, 1950, pp. 11–34.

> Also in Maslow's *Motivation and Personality*, 1954, pp. 199–234.
> Also in C. E. Moustakas (ed.), *The Self*. New York: Harper & Row, 1956.

Maslow, A. H., Human motivation in relation to social theory, in M. Shore (ed.), *Twentieth Century Mental Hygiene*. New York: Social Science Research Council, 1951.

> Also in K. Zerfoss (ed.), *Readings in Counseling*. New York: Association Press, 1952.

MacKinnon, D. W., and A. H. Maslow, Personality, in H. Nelson (ed.), *Theoretical Foundations of Psychology*. Princeton, N.J.: Van Nostrand, 1951, pp. 602–655.

Maslow, A. H., Love in healthy people, in M. F. A. Montagu (ed.), *The Meaning of Love*. New York: Julian Press, 1953.

Maslow, A. H., *The S–I (Security–Insecurity) Test.* Stanford, Cal.: Stanford University Press, 1953.

Maslow, A. H., *Motivation and Personality.* New York: Harper & Row, 1954.

Maslow, A. H., Deficiency motivation and growth motivation, in M. Jones (ed.), *Nebraska Symposium on Motivation.* Lincoln: University of Nebraska Press, 1955, pp. 1–39.

> Also in J. C. Coleman, *Personality Dynamics and Effective Behavior.* Chicago: Scott, Foresman, 1960, pp. 475–485.

Maslow, A. H., Personality problems and personality growth, in C. E. Moustakas, *The Self.* New York: Harper & Row, 1956.

Maslow, A. H., Power relationships and patterns of personal development, in A. Kornhauser (ed.), *Problems of Power in American Democracy.* Detroit: Wayne State University Press, 1957.

Maslow, A. H., Creativity in self-actualizing people, in H. E. Anderson (ed.), *Creativity and Its Cultivation.* New York: Harper & Row, 1959.

Maslow, A. H. (ed.), *New Knowledge in Human Values.* New York: Harper & Row, 1959.

Maslow, A. H., Symposium remarks on investigating "our best human beings," in Academy of Religion and Mental Health, *Religion, Science, and Mental Health.* New York: New York University Press, 1959.

Maslow, A. H., Resistance to being rubricized, in B. Kaplan and S. Wapner (eds.), *Perspectives in Psychological Theory.* New York: International Universities Press, 1960.

Maslow, A. H., and R. Diaz-Guerrero, Delinquency as a value disturbance, in J. G. Peatman and E. L. Hartley (eds.), *Festschrift for Gardner Murphy.* New York: Harper & Row, 1960, pp. 228–249.

Maslow, A. H., Existential psychology—What's in it for us? in R. May (ed.), *Existential Psychology.* New York: Random House, 1961.

Maslow, A. H., Some frontier problems in mental health, in A. Combs (ed.), *Personality Theory and Counseling Practice.* Coral Gables: University of Florida Press, 1961.

Maslow, A. H., Some basic propositions of a growth and self-actualization psychology, in A. Combs (ed.), *Perceiving, Behaving, Becoming: A New Focus for Education, 1962 Yearbook of the Association for Supervision and Curriculum Development* (Washington), 1962.

> Reprinted in C. Stacey and M. DeMartino (eds.), *Understanding Human Motivation,* rev. ed. New York: Howard Allen, 1963. Reprinted in G. Lindzey and L. Hall (eds.), *Theories of Personality: Primary Sources and Research.* New York: Wiley, 1965.

Maslow, A. H., *Summer Notes on Social Psychology of Industry and Management.* Delmar, Cal.: Non-Linear Systems, Inc., 1962.

> Includes papers 97, 100, 101, 105.

Maslow, A. H., *Toward a Psychology of Being.* Princeton, N.J.: Van Nostrand (Insight Books), 1962.

Maslow, A. H., Notes on innocent cognition, in L. Schenk-Danzinger and H. Thomas (eds.), *Gegenwartsprobleme der Entwicklungspsychologie: Festschrift für Charlotte Buhler*. Göttingen: Verlag fur Psychologie, 1963.

> Reprinted in *Explorations*, 1964, *1*, 2–8.

Maslow, A. H., Preface to Japanese translation of *Toward a Psychology of Being*. Tokyo: Seishin-Shobo, 1964.

Maslow, A. H., *Religions, Values and Peak-experiences*. Columbus: Ohio State University Press, 1964.

> Chap. 3 reprinted in *The Buzz Sheet*, Dec., 1964.

Maslow, A. H., Criteria for judging needs to be instinctoid, in M. R. Jones (ed.), *Human Motivation: A Symposium*. Lincoln: University of Nebraska Press, 1965, pp. 33–47.

Maslow, A. H., Critique and discussion, in J. Money (ed.), *Sex Research: New Developments*. New York: Holt, Rinehart & Winston, 1965, pp. 135–143, 144–146.

Maslow, A. H., Foreword to A. Angyal, *Neurosis and Treatment: A Holistic Theory*. New York: Wiley, 1965, pp. v–vii.

Maslow, A. H., Isomorphic interrelationships between knower and known, in G. Kepes (ed.), *Sign, Image, Symbol*. New York: Braziller, 1966.

> Reprinted in F. W. Matson and A. Montagu (eds.), *The Human Dialogue: Perspectives on Communication*. New York: Free Press, 1966.

Maslow, A. H., *The Psychology of Science: A Reconnaissance*. New York: Harper & Row, 1966.

Maslow, A. H., Foreword to Japanese translation of *Motivation and Personality*, 1967.

Maslow, A. H., Preface to Japanese translation of *Eupsychian Management*, 1967.

Maslow, A. H., Self-actualization and beyond, in J. F. T. Bugental (ed.), *Challenges of Humanistic Psychology*. New York: McGraw-Hill, 1967.

> Reprinted in D. Hamachek (ed.), *Human Dynamics in Psychology and Education*. Boston: Allyn & Bacon, 1968.

Maslow, A. H., and E. M. Drews. Dialogue on communication, in A. A. Hitchcock (ed.), *Guidance and the Utilization of New Educational Media: Report of the 1962 Conference*. Washington: American Personnel and Guidance Association, 1967, pp. 1–47, 63–68.

Maslow, A. H., Human potentialities and the healthy society, in H. Otto (ed.), *Human Potentialities*. St. Louis, Mo.: Warren H. Green, 1968.

Maslow, A. H., *Toward a Psychology of Being*, 2nd ed. Princeton, N.J.: Van Nostrand, 1968.

Maslow, A. H., Toward the study of violence, in L. Ng (ed.), *Alternatives to Violence*. New York: Time-Life Books, 1968.

Maslow, A. H., Theory Z, in W. Bennis and E. Schein (eds.), *New Development in the Human Side of Enterprise*. New York: McGraw-Hill, 1969.

Maslow, A. H., Various meanings of transcendence, in D. Cutler (ed.), *The Religious Situation*. Boston: Beacon Press, 1969.

PERIODICALS

Maslow, A. H., The "emotion" of disgust in dogs, *J. Comp. Psychol.*, 1932, *14*, 401–407.

Maslow, A. H., with H. Harlow. Delayed reaction tests on primates at Bronx Park Zoo. *J. Comp. Psychol.*, 1932, *14*, 97–107.

Maslow, A. H., with H. Harlow and H. Uehling. Delayed reaction tests on primates from the lemur to the orangoutan. *J. Comp. Psychol.*, 1932, *13*, 313–343.

Maslow, A. H., Food preferences of primates, *J. Comp. Psychol.*, 1933, *16*, 187–197.

Maslow, A. H., The effect of varying external conditions on learning, retention and reproduction, *J. Exp. Psychol.*, 1934, *17*, 36–47.

Maslow, A. H., The effect of varying time intervals between acts of learning with a note on proactive inhibition. *J. Exp. Psychol.*, 1934, *17*, 141–144.

Maslow, A. H., and E. Groshong, Influence of differential motivation on delayed reactions in monkeys, *J. Comp. Psychol.*, 1934, *18*, 75–83.

Maslow, A. H., Appetites and hungers in animal motivation, *J. Comp. Psychol.*, 1935, *20*, 75–83.

Maslow, A. H., Individual psychology and the social behavior of monkeys and apes, *Int. J. Indiv. Psychol.*, 1935, *1*, 47–59.

Maslow, A. H., The dominance drive as a determiner of the social and sexual behavior of infra-human primates, I–IV, *J. Genet. Psychol.*, 1936, *48*, 261–338; *49*, 161–198.

Maslow, A. H., The comparative approach to social behavior, *Soc. Forces*, 1937, *15*, 487–490.

Maslow, A. H., Dominance—feeling, behavior, and status, *Psychol. Rev.*, 1937, *44*, 404–429.

Maslow, A. H., The influence of familiarization on preference, *J. Exp. Psychol.*, 1937, *21*, 162–180.

Maslow, A. H., with W. Grether, An experimental study of insight in monkeys. *J. Comp. Psychol.*, 1937, *24*, 127–134.

Maslow, A. H., Dominance—feeling, personality and social behavior in women, *J. Soc. Psychol.*, 1939, *10*, 3–39.

Maslow, A. H., Dominance—quality and social behavior in infra-human primates, *J. Soc. Psychol.*, 1940, *11*, 313–324.

Maslow, A. H., A test for dominance-feeling (self-esteem) in college women, *J. Soc. Psychol.*, 1940, *12*, 255–270.

Maslow, A. H., Deprivation, threat and frustration, *Psychol. Rev.*, 1941, *48*, 364–366.

Also in T. Newcomb and E. Hartley (eds.), *Readings in Social Psychology*. New York: Holt, Rinehart & Winston, 1947.

Also in M. Marx, *Psychological Theory: Contemporary Readings*. New York: Macmillan, 1951.
Also in C. Stacey and M. DeMartino (eds.), *Understanding Human Motivation*, rev. ed. New York: Howard Allen, 1963.

Maslow, A. H., A comparative approach to the problem of destructiveness, *Psychiatry*, 1942, 5, 517–522.

Maslow, A. H., The dynamics of psychological security–insecurity, *Charact. & Pers.*, 1942, 10, 331–344.

Maslow, A. H., Liberal leadership and personality, *Freedom*, 1942, 2, 27–30.

Maslow, A. H., Self-esteem (dominance-feeling) and sexuality in women, *J. Soc Psychol.*, 1942, 16, 259–294.

Maslow, A. H., The authoritarian character structure, *J. Soc. Psychol.*, 1943, 18, 401–411.

> Also in P. Harriman (ed.), *Twentieth Century Psychology: Recent Developments in Psychology*. New York: Philosophical Library, 1946.

Maslow, A. H., Conflict, frustration and the theory of threat, *J. Abnorm. Soc. Psychol.*, 1943, 38, 81–86..

> Also in S. Tomkins (ed.), *Contemporary Psychopathology: A Source book*. Cambridge, Mass.: Harvard University Press, 1943.

Maslow, A. H., Dynamics of personality organization, I, II, *Psychol. Rev.*, 1943, 50, 514–539, 544–558.

Maslow, A. H., Preface to motivation theory, *Psychosom. Med.*, 1943, 5, 85–92.

Maslow, A. H., A theory of human motivation, *Psychol. Rev.*, 1943, 50, 370–396.

> Also in P. Harriman (ed.), *Twentieth Century Psychology*. New York: Philosophical Library, 1946.
> Also in H. Remmers *et al.* (eds.), *Growth, Teaching and Learning*. New York: Harper & Row, 1957.
> Also in C. Stacey and M. DeMartino (eds.), *Understanding Human Motivation*, rev. ed. New York: Howard Allen, 1963.
> Also in W. Lazer and E. Kelley (eds.), *Managerial Marketing*. Homewood, Ill.: Irwin, 1958.
> Also in W. Baller, *Readings in Psychology of Human Growth and Development*. New York: Holt, Rinehart & Winston, 1962.
> Also in J. Seidman (ed.), *The Child*. New York: Holt, Rinehart & Winston, 1958.
> Also in L. Gorlow and W. Katkovsky (eds.), *Readings in the Psychology of Adjustment*. New York: McGraw-Hill, 1959.

Maslow, A. H., What intelligence tests mean, *J. Gen. Psychol.*, 1944, 31, 85–93.

Maslow, A. H., Experimentalizing the clinical method, *J. Clin. Psychol.*, 1945, 1, 241–243.

Maslow, A. H., A suggested improvement in semantic usage, *Psychol. Rev.*, 1945, 53, 239–240.

Maslow, A. H., E. Birsh, M. Stein, and I. Honigman, A clinically derived test for measuring psychological security-insecurity, *J. Gen. Psychol.*, 1945, *33*, 21–41.

Maslow, A. H., Problem-centering vs. means-centering in science, *Phil. Sci.*, 1946, *13*, 326–331.

Maslow, A. H., and I. Szilagyi-Kessler, Security and breast feeding, *J. Abnorm. Soc. Psychol.*, 1946, *41*, 83–85.

Maslow, A. H., A symbol for holistic thinking, *Personality*, 1947, *1*, 24–25.

Maslow, A. H., Cognition of the particular and of the generic, *Psychol. Rev.*, 1948, *55*, 22–40.

Maslow, A. H., "Higher" and "lower" needs, *J. Psychol.*, 1948, *25*, 433–436.

> Also in C. Stacey and M. DeMartino (eds.), *Understanding Human Motivation*, rev. ed. New York: Howard Allen, 1963.
> Also in K. Schultz (ed.), *Applied Dynamic Psychology*. Berkeley: University of California Press, 1958.

Maslow, A H., Some theoretical consequences of basic-need gratification, *J. Pers.*, 1948, *16*, 402–416.

Maslow, A. H., The expressive component in behavior, *Psychol. Rev.*, 1949, *56*, 261–272.

> Also in H. Brand, *The Study of Personality: A Book of Readings*. New York: Wiley, 1954.

Maslow, A. H., Our maligned animal nature, *J. Psychol.*, 1949, *28*, 273–278.

> Also in S. Koeing *et al.* (eds.), *Sociology: A Book of Readings*. Englewood Cliffs, N.J.: Prentice-Hall, 1953.

Maslow, A. H. (ed.), American culture and personality, *J. Soc. Issues*, 1951, *7*, 1–49.

Maslow, A. H., Higher needs and personality, *Dialectica*, 1951, *5*, 257–265.

Maslow, A. H., and J. M. Sakoda, Volunteer-error in the Kinsey study, *J. Abnorm. Soc. Psychol.*, 1952, *47*, 259–262.

Maslow, A. H., and W. Zimmerman, College teaching ability, scholarly activity, and personality, *J. Educ. Psychol.*, 1953, *47*, 185–189.

Maslow, A. H., The instinctoid nature of basic needs, *J. Pers.*, 1954, *22*, 326–347.

Maslow, A. H., Normality, health and values, *Main Currents*, 1954, *10*, 75–81.

Maslow, A. H., Defense and growth, *Merrill-Palmer Quart.*, 1956, *3*, 36–37.

Maslow, A. H., A philosophy of psychology, *Main Currents*, 1956, *13*, 27–32.

> Also in *Etc. Rev. Gen. Semant.*, 1957, *14*, 10–22.
> Also in J. Fairchild (ed.), *Personal Problems and Psychological Frontiers*. New York: Sheridan Press, 1957.
> Also in S. I. Hayakawa (ed.), *Our Language and Our World*. New York: Harper & Row, 1959.

Maslow, A. H., and N. L. Mintz, Effects of esthetic surroundings: I. Initial effects of three esthetic conditions upon perceiving "energy" and "well-being" in faces, *J. Psychol.*, 1956, *41*, 247–254.

Maslow, A. H., and J. Bossom, Security of judges as a factor in impressions of warmth in others, *J. Abnorm. Soc. Psychol.*, 1957, 55, 147–148.

Maslow, A. H., Emotional blocks to creativity, *J. Indiv. Psychol.*, 1958, 14, 51–56.

> Also in *The Humanist*, 1958, 18, 325–332.
> Also in *Best Articles and Stories*, 1959, 3, 23–35.
> Also in H. Harding and S. Parnes (eds.), *Creative Problem Solving*. New York: Scribner's, 1962.

Maslow, A. H., The mission of the psychologist, *Manas*, 1958, 11, 1–8.

Maslow, A. H., Cognition of being in the peak experiences, *J. Genet. Psychol.*, 1959, 94, 43–66.

Maslow, A. H., Critique of self-actualization: I. Some dangers of being-cognition, *J. Indiv. Psychol.*, 1959, 15, 24–32.

Maslow, A. H., Remarks on existentialism and psychology, *Existentialist Inquir.*, 1960, 1, 1–5.

> Reprinted in *Religious Inquiry*, 1960, No. 28, pp. 4–7.
> Reprinted in R. May (ed.), *Existential Psychology*. New York: Random House, 1961.
> Reprinted in D. E. Hamachek (ed.), *The Self in Growth, Teaching and Learning*. Englewood Cliffs, N.J.: Prentice-Hall, 1965.

Maslow, A. H., H. Rand, and S. Newman, Some parallels between the dominance and sexual behavior of monkeys and the fantasies of patients in psychotherapy, *J. Nerv. Ment. Dis.*, 1960, 131, 202–212.

> Reprinted in M. DeMartino (ed.), *Sexual Behavior and Personality Characteristics*. New York: Citadel Press, 1963.

Maslow, A. H., Are our publications and conventions suitable for the personal sciences? *Amer. Psychologist*, 1961, 16, 318–319.

> Reprinted as WBSI Report No. 8, 1962. Reprinted in *Gen. Semant. Bull.*, 1962, 28, 29, 92–93.

Maslow, A. H., Comments on Skinner's attitude to science, *Daedalus*, 1961, 90, 572–573.

Maslow, A. H., Eupsychia—the good society, *J. Humanist. Psychol.*, 1961, 1, 1–11.

Maslow, A. H., Health as transcendence of the environment, *J. Humanist. Psychol.*, 1961, 1, 11–17.

Maslow, A. H., Peak-experiences as acute identity experiences, *Amer. J. Psychoanal.*, 1961, 21, 254–260.

> Reprinted in A. Combs (ed.), *Personality Theory and Counseling Practice*. Gainesville: University of Florida Press, 1961.

Maslow, A. H., Summary comments: Symposium on human values, *WBSI Rep.*, 1961, No. 17, pp. 41–44.

> Reprinted in *J. Humanist. Psychol.*, 1962, 2, 110–111.

Maslow, A. H., Lessons from the peak-experiences, *J. Humanist. Psychol.*, 1962, 2, 9–18.

Maslow, A. H., Notes on being-psychology, *J. Humanist. Psychol.*, 1962, 2, 47–71.

> Reprinted in H. Ruitenbeek (ed.), *Varieties of Personality Theory.* New York: Dutton, 1964.

Maslow, A. H., Was Adler a disciple of Freud? A note, *J. Indiv. Psychol.*, 1962, *18*, 125.

> Maslow says Adler said no.

Maslow, A. H., The creative attitude, *Structurist*, 1963, No. 3, pp. 4–10.

> Reprinted as a separate by *Psychosynthesis Found.*, 1963.

Maslow, A. H., Criteria for judging needs to be instinctoid, *Proc. 1963 Int. Cong. Psychol.* Amsterdam: North-Holland Publishers, 1964, pp. 86–87.

Maslow, A. H., Further notes on being-psychology, *J. Humanist. Psychol.*, 1963, 3, 120–135.

Maslow, A. H., Fusions of facts and values, *Amer. J. Psychoanal.*, 1963, 23, 117–131.

Maslow, A. H., The need to know and the fear of knowing, *J. Gen. Psychol.*, 1963, 68, 111–125.

> Excellent and readable on why we need to know things. A must for undergraduate psychology majors.

Maslow, A. H., Notes on unstructured groups, *Hum. Relat. Train. News*, 1963, 7, 1–4.

Maslow, A. H., The scientific study of values, *Proc. 7th Cong. Interamer. Soc. Psychol.*, Mexico, D.F., 1963.

Maslow, A. H., Further notes on the psychology of being, *J. Humanist. Psychol.*, 1964, 4, 45–58.

Maslow, A. H., The superior person, *Trans-action*, 1964, *1*, 10–13.

Maslow, A. H., Synergy in society and in the individual, *J. Indiv. Psychol.*, 1964, 20, 153–164.

Maslow, A. H., Humanistic science and transcendent experiences, *J. Humanist. Psychol.*, 1965, 5, 219–227.

> Reprinted in *Manas*, 1965, *18*, 1–8.
> Reprinted in *Challenge*, 1965, Nos. 21, 22.
> Reprinted in *Amer. J. Psychoanal.*, 1966, 26, 149–155.

Maslow, A. H., The need for creative people, *Personnel Admin.*, 1965, 28, 3–5, 21–22.

Maslow, A. H., Observing and reporting education experiments, *J. Humanist. Psychol.*, 1965, 5, 13.

Maslow, A. H., and R. Morant, Art judgment and the judgment of others: A preliminary study, *J. Clin. Psychol.*, 1965, 21, 389–391.

Maslow, A. H., Comments on Dr. Frankl's paper, *J. Humanist. Psychol.*, 1966, 6, 107–112.

Maslow, A. H., Toward a psychology of religious awareness, *Explorations*, 1966, No. 9, pp. 23–41.

Maslow, A. H., Neurosis as a failure of personal growth, *Humanitas*, 1967, 3, 153–169.

> Reprinted in *Relig. Hum.*, 1968, 2, 61–64.

Maslow, A. H., Synanon and Eupsychia, *J. Humanist. Psychol.*, 1967, 7, 28–35.

Maslow, A. H., A theory of metamotivation: The biological rooting of the value life, *J. Humanist. Psychol.*, 1967, 7, 92–127.

> Reprinted in *The Humanist*, 1967, 27, 83–84, 127–129.
> Reprinted in *Psychol. Today*, 1968, 2, 38–39, 58–61.

Maslow, A. H., Conversation with Abraham H. Maslow, *Psychol. Today*, 1968, 2, 35–37, 54–57.

Maslow, A. H., The farther reaches of human nature, *J. Transhumanist. Psychol.* 1968, 1.

> Reprinted in *Psychol. Scene* (South Africa), 1968, 2, 14–16.

Maslow, A. H., Music education and peak-experiences, *Music Educ. J.*, 1968, 54 72–75, 163–171.

Maslow, A. H., Some educational implications of the humanistic psychologies *Harvard Educ. Rev.*, 1968, 38, No. 4.

Maslow, A. H., Some fundamental questions that face the normative social psychologist, *J. Humanist. Psychol.*, 1968, 8.

FILM

Maslow, A. H., *Maslow and Self-Actualization.* Santa Anna, Cal.: Psychological Films, 1968.

SUGGESTED READINGS

BOOKS

Angyal, A., *Neurosis and Treatment: A Holistic Theory.* New York: Wiley, 1965

Bonner, H., *Psychology of Personality.* New York: Ronald Press, 1961, pp. 70–73 97–102, 350–352.

Coleman, J. C., *Personality Dynamics and Effective Behavior.* Chicago: Scott Foresman, 1960, pp. 475–485.

Hall, C. S., and G. Lindzey, *Theories of Personality.* New York: Wiley, 1957.

McClelland, D. C., *Personality* (1951). New York: Holt, Rinehart & Winston rev. ed. 1958, pp. 370–396, 402–416.

Maddi, S. R., *Personality Theories: A Comparative Analysis.* Homewood, Ill. Dorsey Press, 1968.

> Very fair and incisive treatment of Maslow as a "fulfillment model" in his theory.

Woodworth, R., *Dynamics of Behavior.* New York: Holt, Rinehart & Winston 1958.

> Good for motivation theory.

ERIODICALS

llen, R. M., T. D. Haupt, and R. W. Jones, Analysis of peak experiences reported by college students, *J. Clin. Psychol.*, 1964, 20, 207–212.

ranck, I., The concept of human nature: A philosophical analysis of the concept of human nature in the writings of G. W. Allport, S. E. Asch, Erich Fromm, A. H. Maslow, and C. R. Rogers, *Dissert. Abstr.*, 1966, 27, 1079.

rankl, V., Self-transcendence as a human phenomenon, *J. Humanist. Psychol.*, 1966, 6, 97–106.

oldstein, M. W., Mental health, social status, and Maslow's need system, *Dissert. Abstr.*, 1967, 28, 2123–2124.

ourevitch, V., and H. Melvin, A study of motivational development, *J. Genet. Psychol.*, 1962, 100, 361–375.

> Research on Maslow's hierarchy of motives with results confirming the theory.

Iall, M. H., A conversation with Abraham H. Maslow, President of the American Psychological Association, *Psychol. Today*, 1968, 2, 34–37, 54–57.

lavetter, R. E., and R. E. Mogar, Peak experiences: Investigation of their relationship to psychedelic therapy and self-actualization, *J. Humanist. Psychol.*, 1967, 7, 171–177.

IcKinnon, D. W., Personality and the realization of creative potential, *Amer. Psychologist*, 1965, 20, 261–281.

Iathews, W., Successful adjustment: A frame of reference, *Amer. J. Orthopsychiat.*, 1960, 30, 667–675.

Iathis, W. J., and E. W. McClain, Peak experiences of white and Negro college students, *J. Clin. Psychol.*, 1968, 24, 318–319.

orter, L. W., Job attitudes in management: Perceived deficiencies in need fulfillment as a function of job level, *J. Appl. Psychol.*, 1962, 46, 375–384.

> Self-actualization was the highest need.

ratt, S., and J. Tooley, Human actualization teams: The perspective of contract psychology, *Amer. J. Orthopsychiat.*, 1966, 36, 881–895.

tark, S., Rorschach movement, fantastic daydreaming, and Freud's concept of primary process: Interpretive commentary, *Percept. Mot. Skills*, 1966, 22, 523–532.

> Conceptual framework showing what meaning Freud's concept of primary process has for Maslow.

Vhite, R., Motivation reconsidered: The concept of competence, *Psychol. Rev.*, 1959, 66, 297–333.

PERSONAL CONSTRUCTS
[KELLY]

Let us then, instead of occupying ourselves with man-the-biological-organism or man-the-lucky-guy, have a look at man-the-scientist.

Might not the individual man, each in his own personal way, assume more of the stature of a scientist, ever seeking to predict and control the course of events with which he is involved?

George Alexander Kelly
The Psychology of Personal Constructs, pp. 4, 5

SOME BIOGRAPHICAL DATA

George Alexander Kelly was born in Perth, Kansas, on April 28, 1905. He was married in 1931 and there were two children from the marriage. Kelly's education began at Park College, where he received a Bachelor of Arts degree in 1926. In 1928 he received his Master of Arts from Kansas University.

Kelly obtained a fellowship at Edinburgh in 1930 and subsequently was awarded a Bachelor of Education degree. His formal education culminated in a Doctorate of Philosophy degree in psychology from the University of Iowa in 1931. His professional experience in nonteaching posts was wide and interesting. He served as a consultant to the Veterans Administration from 1946 until the time of his death. He was also a consultant to the Surgeon General of the United States Navy from 1948 to 1953. His further involvement with federal organizations was as follows: member, Special Medical Advisory Group for Veterans Administration, 1955–1960; Training Committee, National Institute of Mental Health, and National Institute of Health, 1958–1967; U.S. Naval Reserve, 1943–1945 with rank of lieutenant commander. George Kelly was extremely concerned with the upgrading of clinical psychologists. He helped to formulate the American Board of Examiners for Professional Psychologists, being one of its first members and serving as its president from 1951 through 1953. As we shall see, his primary interests were in personality theory and in the training of clinical psychologists. His earliest teaching experience was as an associate professor in psychology at Kansas State College, Fort Hayes, from 1931 to 1943. He then went to the University of Maryland as an associate professor of psychology, 1945 through 1946. In 1946 he went as a full professor to Ohio State University, where he was also Director of the Psychological Clinic. George Kelly left Ohio State and went to Brandeis University in 1965. His untimely death on March 6, 1967, ended the career of a brilliant and concerned clinical psychologist.

INTRODUCTION

George Kelly's personality theory of personal constructs is one of the most recent, if not the most recent, personality theories we have. Erikson, of course, would be the second most recent theorist since his major work dates from 1950.

Like Rogers, Freud, Jung, and practically every theorist in this book, George Alexander Kelly's major theoretical formulations grew out of his experiences as a therapist. He presents his main statements in two books. One is a two-volume work published in 1955 called *The Psychology of Personal Constructs*. The other, published in 1963, consists of the first three chapters of the 1955 book and is called *A Theory of Personality: A Psychology of Personal Constructs*. Actually, Kelly did not publish very much in comparison with other famous and contemporary psychologists, the two books and about a dozen articles being his total output. He spent the major part of his career in university settings directing psychological clinics and training clinical psychology students. Other than his publications, therefore, and his work in the American Psychological Association, Kelly's chief impact seems to have been through his doctoral student candidates. He not only trained them well but must have influenced them greatly. For example, from 1952 through 1955 twelve doctoral dissertations from Ohio State University owe their main thesis to Kelly's concept of the personal construct: J. Bieri, 1953; R. E. Fager, 1954; R. E. Jones, 1954; F. E. Lemcke, 1959; L. H. Levy, 1954; R. M. Lundy, 1954; W. H. Lyle, 1954; D. K. Newman, 1956; D. E. Payne, 1956; S. M. Poch, 1952; L. B. Sechrest, 1956; D. J. Shoemaker, 1955. Some of these men then went to other universities, and we have other doctoral dissertations around the concept of the personal construct.

It is obvious from the effect Kelly had upon his graduate students and his delightful writing style that he had a personality well worth knowing. His verbal expressions were devoid of pompous style. As evidence we quote the dedication of his 1963 book: "To a lot of people I know, and some I don't, most of whom I like, and some I don't; but acquaintances or strangers, friends or scoundrels, I must confess I am indebted to them all."

George Kelly's effect upon personality theory and research in personality dynamics appears to be spotty. On the one hand, for example, in the issues of the *Annual Review of Psychology*, 1964 through 1969, only one issue, that of 1968, Vol. 19, includes Kelly in the index. Moreover, in a huge volume of 1232 pages edited by Borgatta and Lambert, *Handbook of Personality Theory and Research*, 1968, there is no mention of any work by Kelly. On the other hand, as the reader can see by glancing at "Delimitations," at the end of this section, there has been an enormous concern with research on higher cognitive processes. Much of the interest in Kelly's personal constructs has been aroused through use of his test, Role Construct Repertory Test, almost always called the REP test. Also, we find Bonarius in a valuable review of research on personality construct psychology very thoroughly going through Kelly's concepts and ending with a ninety-four-item bibliography which is indicative of Kelly's effect upon research in personology (Maher, 1965).

Two well-known psychologists (Bruner and Rogers) seem to be ambivalent about Kelly's work, particularly in a review of his 1955 book, *The Psychology of Personal Constructs*. "Critics of Kelly feel he has placed too great an emphasis upon cognition." In Jerome S. Bruner's view, Kelly's theory is inadequate because it ignores man's emotions in order to do full justice to man's intellect. Carl R. Rogers' criticism addresses itself to the method of psychotherapy that Kelly derives from his personality theory. Rogers also takes Kelly to task for his exclusive emphasis on intellect but mainly "deplores the lack of attention paid to the emotional relationship between the therapist and the patient." However, despite these comments, we find that "These excellent, original, and infuriatingly prolix two volumes easily nominate themselves for the *distinction of being the single greatest contribution of the past decade to the theory of personality function. Professor Kelly has written a major work*" (Southwell and Merbaum, 1964; italics added).

Maddi, a dedicated student of personality theory, finds some relationship between Kelly's concepts of the personal construct and Leon Festinger's concept of cognitive dissonance (Maddi, 1968).

Before we get into the general and specific considerations of his system of theory, the reader can get the essence of what Kelly is trying to do, even though the quotations are out of context, by the following:

Viewed in the perspective of the centuries man might be seen as an incipient scientist and . . . each individual man formulates in his own way constructs through which he views the world of events. . . . *We assume that all of our present interpretations of the universe are subject to revision or replacement* . . . . We take the stand that there are always some alternative constructions available to choose among in dealing with the world. No one needs to paint himself into a corner; no one needs to be completely hemmed in by circumstances; no one needs to be the victim of his biography. We call this philosophical position *constructive alternativism*. . . . A person is not necessarily articulate about the construction he places on his world. . . . We insist that man can erect his own alternative approaches to reality (A *Theory of Personality*).

THE SYSTEM, THEORY,
OR ESSENTIAL FEATURES

General Considerations

Like most personality theorists, George Kelly is concerned about theory formulation. In his 1963 book, A *Theory of Personality: The Psychology of Personal Constructs*, we find at least fourteen comments in a section called "The Function of a Theory" (pp. 18–44):

1. "A theory need not be highly scientific in order to be useful."

2. "A theory binds or determines the events which are subordinated to It is not determined by the events themselves; it is determined by the perordinating point of view of the theorist. Yet it must conform to events order to predict them."

3. "Theories are the thinking of men who speak freedom amid swirling ents."

4. ". . . a theory may be considered as a way of binding together a ultitude of facts. But a good theory also performs more active functions."

5. ". . . theory acts as a tool for the man who actively seeks to anticipate e future and to explore its possibilities."

6. ". . . a good scientific theory is its fertility in producing new ideas."

7. "Another criterion of a good psychological theory is its production of potheses which are testable."

8. "A good psychological theory should be expressed in terms of abstracns which are of a sufficiently high order to be traced through nearly all of e phenomena with which psychology must deal."

9. "A theory should be considered as modifiable and ultimately exndable."

10. "The function of a scientific theory is to provide a basis for making ecise predictions."

11. "Any psychological theory is therefore somewhat reflexive; it must o account for itself as a product of psychological processes. Thus, if the eory is to account for the way in which a man turns, it should also account r the way its author turned when he wrote it."

12. "A good psychological theory has an appropriate focus and range of nvenience."

13. "A good psychological theory should be expressed in terms of abactions which can be traced through most of the phenomena with which ychology must deal."

14. "A psychological theory should be considered ultimately expendable

Thus, psychoanalysis "takes no consistent theoretical stand with respe to the issue. It is perhaps best described as a theory of compromises: t compromise between the reality principle and the pleasure principle." And conclusion, "Indeed, it is almost impossible to give any comprehensive theo the final coup de grace" (*ibid.*, p. 25).

In regard to formulating hypotheses, George Kelly finds there are esse tially three methods, all of which psychology employs. The first he calls t hypothetico-deductive method, which he likens to Hull's learning theory. T second, called the clinico-inductive method, he finds represented in psych analysts who are scientifically minded. The third is the statistical-dragn method, which may be found in personnel test research, such as that of t Minnesota Multiphasic Personality Inventory. "As long as good scienti methodology is used in checking the hypotheses, all three methods are a ceptable. In using them, however, one should be aware of the bias literalism of the hypothetico-deductive method, the personal bias in t clinico-inductive method, and the popular bias in the statistical-dragn method" (*ibid.*, p. 34).

Probably the most central theme of George Kelly's personal construc theory of personality is the idea that each man is essentially and can be ar should be his own theory constructor. Kelly finds it curious indeed that ps chologists will rarely credit the human subjects upon whom they are expe menting with having the same aspirations as the so-called scientific psycho gist. "It is as though the psychologist were saying to himself, 'I, being *psychologist,* and therefore a *scientist,* am performing this experiment order to improve the prediction control of certain human phenomena; but i subject, being merely a human organism, is obviously propelled by inexoral drives welling up within him, or else he is in gluttonous pursuit of sustenan and shelter.' " Kelly rejects this tunnel-vision concept that only the psycho gist wearing a white coat and acting like a scientist is concerned with hum behavior. He asks, therefore, is not the individual man also interested in l own future and predicting and controlling the course of events for his ov life? The question is a good one.

Out of this fabric Kelly contrives the concept of personal construc meaning the person constructing his own world perceptions and exerti cognitive control over his own environment, which means of course predi ing and controlling his own and others' behavior to some degree. Thus t personality psychology researcher is not the only person who is concern with or manipulates human behavior. In a sense this is something like Kar Horney's suggestion that man solved some of his problems throughout t ages before the clinical psychologist came on the scene. In Horney's terr however, what does the clinical psychologist or therapist or psychoanalyst d

One gets the impression that he eases the pain and reduces the time of suffering but is not the sole agent for reducing emotional turmoil in the individual. In another sense, a talented student of Kelly's, Sechrest, finds that Kelly's theory is both cognitive and phenomenological as well as thoroughly based "on intellectual models of behavior" (Sechrest, 1963).

In still another but parallel sense, "A person's processes are psychologically channelized by the ways in which he anticipates events." Kelly's use of the word *channelized* is not, however, in the same frame of reference as Gardner Murphy's use of *canalized* because by *channelized* Kelly means a network. Also in anticipating events we find some similarity to Adler's idea that in his fictional goals man is prompted by the future.

Another essential feature in George Kelly's system of personal constructs very similar to Freud's and Jung's dividing life into polarities or dualities. Kelly feels that all choices, all behaviors, all concepts are dichotomous and gives this phenomenon the name *constructive alternativism*. For example, man's higher cognitive processes may be complex or simple. Kelly titles his entire first chapter "Constructive Alternativism." Maddi comments, "Kelly feels that constructs are inherently dichotomous in nature. This is not changed for him by the fact that a person may seem to be using only one pole of a construct. If a person is, for example, talking only in terms of the goodness of people, without reference to badness at all, this merely means that the badness pole of the goodness–badness construct is implicit. It does not mean it is nonexistent. *There are no unipolar constructs*" (Maddi, 1968; italics added). As we have previously stated, this is very like the Jungian idea that whatever exists, its opposite must exist. For example, the opposite of chair would be no chair.

In reference to defining the term *personality*, "Nowhere in his two volumes does Kelly define the term personality, but he has discussed the concept in general terms in a later article in which he states that personality is, 'Our abstraction of the activity of a person and our subsequent generalization of this abstraction to all matters of his relationship to other persons, known and unknown, as well as to anything else that may seem particularly valuable' " (Sechrest, 1963, p. 229).

George Kelly is frank—almost blunt—in advising the student of personality theory what his concept of the personal construct does not include: ". . . it is only fair to warn the reader that he will find missing many of the familiar landmarks of psychological theory. In this new way of thinking about psychology, there is no *learning*, no *motivation*, no *emotion*, no *cognition* (?), no *stimulus*, no *response*, no *ego*, no *unconscious*, no *need*, no *reinforcement*, no *drive*. It is not only that these terms are abandoned; what is more important, the concepts themselves evaporate" (Kelly, 1963a).

We now proceed to the specific considerations of George Kelly's personal

constructs theory wherein we shall find one basic postulate and eleven corollaries which expand and clarify that postulate.

Specific Considerations

The primary, the essential, the *fundamental postulate* around which Kell
frames the remainder of his personal construct theory of personality is a
follows: "A person's processes are psychologically channelized by the ways i
which he anticipates events." This, then, casts the mold for the eleve
corollaries which substantiate this position.

1. *Construction:* "A person anticipates events by construing their repl
cations."

2. *Individuality:* "Persons differ from each other in their construction o
events."

3. *Organization:* "Each person characteristically evolves, for his co
venience in anticipating events, a construction system embracing ordina
relationships between constructs."

4. *Dichotomy:* "A person's construction system is composed of a finit
number of dichotomous constructs."

5. *Choice:* "A person chooses for himself that alternative in a dichoto
mized construct through which he anticipates the greater possibilities fo
extension and definition of his system."

6. *Range:* "A construct is convenient for the anticipation of a finit
range of events only."

7. *Experience:* "A person's construction system varies as he successivel
construes the replications of events."

8. *Modulation:* "The variation in a person's construction system i
limited by the permeability of the constructs within whose ranges of con
venience the variants lie."

9. *Fragmentation:* "A person may successively employ a variety of con
structions subsystems which are inferentially incompatible with each other.

10. *Commonality:* "To the extent that one person employs a construc
tion of experience which is similar to that employed by another, his psycho
logical processes are similar to those of the other person."

11. *Sociality:* "To the extent that one person construes the constructio
processes of another, he may play a role in a social process involving the othe
person."

Having presented his primary or fundamental postulate and its eleve
corollaries, Kelly carefully defines almost every word in this "assumptive stru
ture." The reader is invited, if he wishes to pursue the definition structure, t
read particularly Chapter II of Kelly's *Theory of Personality: The Psycholog
of Personal Constructs.*

DELIMITATIONS

The present treatment of George Alexander Kelly's personality theory, called personal constructs, does not include considerable material which can be found in his 1955 book, *The Psychology of Personal Constructs*. Omitted material concerns itself primarily with Kelly's scientific methodology and particularly his statistical work, his work on the mathematical construction of psychological space (in which he is dealing mainly with nonparametric factor analysis), and particularly his therapeutic approach, which he at times called "multifaceted ways of coping with human distress"; this would also include his "fixed role therapy."

We have also omitted the enormous amount of research which has been done with his test, Role Construct Repertory Test (RCRT) or, as it is generally known in the psychological literature, REP. We have likewise not treated the revisions of REP and particularly the cognitive complexity research allied to Kelly's work.

Students and interested readers who wish to pursue the research in these areas are directed particularly to the work of the following experimenters (see bibliography): Crockett, 1965; Harrison, 1966; Harvey *et al.*, 1961; Irwin *et al.*, 1967; Leventhal and Singer, 1964; Miller and Bieri, 1965; Rigney *et al.*, 1964; Schroder and Streufert, 1967; Signell, 1966; Todd and Rappoport, 1964; Tripodi and Bieri, 1966.

BIBLIOGRAPHY

PRIMARY SOURCES

BOOKS

Kelly, G. A., *The Psychology of Personal Constructs*. New York: Norton, 1955, 2 vols.

> "Twenty-year collection of impacted ideas about a new theory of personality."

Kelly, G. A., Man's construction of his alternatives, in G. Lindzey (ed.), *Assessment of Human Motives*. New York: Holt, Rinehart & Winston, 1958.

Kelly, G. A., Europe's matrix of decision, in M. R. Jones (ed.), *Nebraska Symposium on Motivation*, 1962, pp. 83–125.

Kelly, G. A., A *Theory of Personality: The Psychology of Personal Constructs* New York: Norton, 1963a.

> First three chapters of the two-volume 1955 book.

PERIODICALS

Kelly, G. A., The abstraction of human processes, *Proc. 14th Int. Cong. Appl. Psychol.*, Copenhagen, Munksgaard, 1961.

Kelly, G. A., Nonparametric factor analysis of personality theories, *J. Indiv. Psychol.*, 1963b, *19*, 115–147.

> The Q-sorts of an Adlerian, a Freudian, a Jungian, a nondirectivist, a personal constructionist, and a Sullivanian are examined.

Kelly, G. A., The language of hypotheses: Man's psychological instrument, *J. Indiv. Psychol.*, 1964, *20*, 137–152.

Kelly, G. A., Personal construct theory as a line of inference, *J. Psychol.* (Lahore), 1964, *1*, 80–93.

Kelly, G. A., A threat of aggression, *J. Humanist. Psychol.*, 1965, *5*, 195–201.

SUGGESTED READINGS

BOOKS

Bannister, D., A new theory of personality, in B. M. Foss (ed.), *New Horizons in Psychology*. Baltimore: Penguin Books, 1966.

> Applications and extensions of Kelly's concepts.

Bonarius, J. C., Research in the personal construct theory of George A. Kelly: Role Construct Repertory Test and basic theory, in B. A. Maher (ed.). *Progress in Experimental Personality Research*, Vol. 2. New York: Academic Press, 1965.

> Most complete summary of Kelly's personal construct theory from 1955 to 1964; ninety-four-item bibliography.

Bieri, J., Complexity–simplicity as a personality variable in cognitive and preferential behavior, in D. W. Fiske and S. R. Maddi (eds.), *Functions of Varied Experience*. Homewood, Ill.: Dorsey Press, 1961.

Bieri, J., A. L. Atkins, S. Briar, R. L. Leaman, H. Miller, and T. Tripodi, *Clinical and Social Judgment: The Discrimination of Behavioral Information*. New York: Wiley, 1966.

> Some extensions and applications of G. A. Kelly's work.

Crockett, W. H., Cognitive complexity and impression formation, in B. A. Maher (ed.), *Progress in Experimental Personality Research*, Vol. 2. New York: Academic Press, 1965.

arvey, O. J., D. E. Hunt, and H. M. Schroder, *Conceptual Systems and Personality Organization*. New York: Wiley, 1961.

Models of cognitive complexity.

Iaddi, S., *Personality Theories: A Comparative Analysis*. Homewood, Ill.: Dorsey Press, 1968.

Core personality and how cognitive dissonance fit in with personal constructs.

Iaher, B. A. (ed.), *Progress in Experimental Personality Research*, Vol. 2. New York: Academic Press, 1965.

Exceedingly thorough review of research on personal constructs theory and measurement.

Iehrabian, A., *An Analysis of Personality Theories*. Englewood Cliffs, N.J.: Prentice-Hall, 1968.

How to modify the REP test using Bieri's methods.

Iinton, H. L., Power as a personality construct, in B. A. Maher (ed.), *Progress in Experimental Personality Research*, Vol. 4. New York: Academic Press, 1968.

chroder, H. M., and S. Streufert, *Human Information Processing: Individuals and Groups in Complex Social Situations*. New York: Holt, Rinehart & Winston, 1967.

echest, L., The psychology of personal constructs: George Kelly, in J. M. Wepman and R. W. Heine (eds.), *Concepts of Personality*. Chicago: Aldine, 1963, pp. 206–233.

Probably the best short summary and evaluation of Kelly's theory.

outhwell, E. A., and M. Merbaum (eds.), *Personality: Readings in Theory and Research*. Belmont, Cal.: Wadsworth, 1964.

Kelly on how man constructs alternatives, Bieri on cognitive complexity and predictive accuracy, and Rogers' and Bruner's appraisals of Kelly—he is good and bad.

ERIODICALS

llard, M. J., and E. R. Carlson, The generality of cognitive complexity, *J. Soc. Psychol.*, 1963, 59, 73–75.

Substantiates REP test.

runer, J. S., You are your constructs, *Contemp. Psychol.*, 1956, 1, 355–357.

Iarrison, R., Cognitive change and participation in a sensitivity-training laboratory, *J. Consult. Psychol.*, 1966, 30, 517–520.

rwin, M., T. Tripodi, and J. Bieri, Affective stimulus value and cognitive complexity, *J. Pers. Soc. Psychol.*, 1967, 5, 444–448.

eventhal, H., and D. L. Singer, Cognitive complexity, impression formation, and impression change, *J. Pers.*, 1964, 32, 210–226.

Mair, J. M., Prediction of grid scores, *Brit. J. Psychol.*, 1966, 57, 187–192.

> Supports Kelly's grid method of providing meaningful measurements of the relation between the constructs that any individual uses.

Miller, H., and J. Bieri, Cognitive complexity as a function of the significance of the stimulus objects being judged, *Psychol. Rep.*, 1965, 16, 1203–1204.

Mischel, T., Personal constructs, rules, and the logic of clinical activity, *Psychol. Rev.*, 1964, 71, 180–192.

Oliver, W. D., and A. W. Landfield, Reflexivity: An unfaced issue of psychology, *J. Indiv. Psychol.*, 1963, 20, 187–201.

> Models for cognitive control.

Rigney, J., J. Bieri, and T. Tripodi, Social concept attainment and cognitive complexity, *Psychol. Rep.*, 1964, 15, 503–509.

Runkel, P. J., and D. E. Damrin, Effects of training and anxiety upon teachers' preferences for information about students, *J. Educ. Psychol.*, 1961, 52, 254–261.

> "Higher-order cognitive constructs determine the direction and organization of behavior."

Signell, K. A., Cognitive complexity in person perception and notion perception: A developmental approach, *J. Pers.*, 1966, 34, 517–537.

Thompson, G. G., George Alexander Kelly (1905–1967), *J. Gen. Psychol.*, 1968, 79, 19–24.

> "Reviews the personal and professional attributes of a pioneer in clinical psychology."

Todd, F. J., and L. A. Rappoport, A cognitive structure approach to person perception: A comparison of two models, *J. Abnorm. Soc. Psychol.*, 1964, 68, 469–478.

Tripodi, T., and J. Bieri, Cognitive complexity, perceived conflict, and certainty, *J. Pers.*, 1966, 34, 144–153.

15

Contributions
of Other Theorists:
Neo-Freudian

DEVELOPMENTAL
[ERIKSON]

I shall present human growth from the point of view of
the conflicts, inner and outer, which the vital personality
weathers, re-emerging from each crisis with an increased sense
of inner unity, with an increase of good judgment, and an increase
in the capacity "to do well" according to his own standards
and to the standards of those who are significant to him.

ERIK HOMBURGER ERIKSON
Identity: Youth and Crisis, pp. 91–92

SOME BIOGRAPHICAL DATA

Erik Homburger Erikson was born in Frankfurt, Germany, on June 15, 1902.
After coming to this country in the mid-1930s, he became a naturalized
United States citizen. He was married in 1930, and he and his wife Joan have

three children. Erikson credits his wife with "Always editing his books," and he apparently looks forward to her editorial assistance. Mrs. Erikson has also been a coworker with him in the Austen-Riggs Center in the Berkshires.

Erik Erikson is a trained lay analyst in the Freudian tradition. He received his training and was graduated from the Vienna Psychoanalytic Institute, where his teachers were Anna Freud and August Aichorn. From 1936 to 1939 Erikson was a research assistant in psychoanalysis in the Department of Psychiatry at the Yale University Medical School. From 1939 to 1951 he was a research associate in the Institute of Child Welfare and later he became a professor of psychology and a lecturer in psychiatry at the University of California. For the next nine years Erikson held a dual role as Senior Staff Consultant in the Austen-Riggs Center and as a professor in the Department of Psychiatry at the University of Pittsburgh School of Medicine. In 1960 he moved to Harvard University Medical School, where he is currently employed. At Harvard he is professor of human development and also a lecturer in the Medical School.

Erikson continues his involvement with the Austen-Riggs Center as a staff consultant. Since 1942 he has been highly involved as a training psychoanalyst in all the professional positions he has held. At the present time he is a Fellow in the American Psychological Association, the American Psychoanalytical Association, and the American Academy of Psycho-Social Development. Most of Erikson's research has been conducted under the auspices of the following agencies: the Harvard Psychological Clinic, the Yale Institute of Human Relations, the Institute of Child Welfare at the University of California, and the Western Psychiatric Institute in Pittsburgh.

INTRODUCTION

Erik Erikson and his neo-Freudian ego developmental theory of personality has become known largely through his four books, his research, his wide lecturing, and about a dozen journal articles, not all of which are in the bibliography at the end of this section. The primary impact of his theory on personality comes largely through his first book, *Childhood and Society* Issued first in 1950, it was revised and reissued in 1963. Well over 300,000 copies of this book have been sold since 1950. Erikson's second book is a very interesting psychoanalysis and history and study of leadership through the character of Martin Luther: *Young Man Luther*, 1962. In 1964 came Erikson's third book, *Insight and Responsibility*, which is a collection of previous lectures. *Identity: Youth and Crisis*, published in 1968, is based on his previous writings and expanded notes which he has incorporated into his treatment of adolescence and its problems in current society. Erikson has also edited *The Challenge of Youth*, first issued in 1963 and reissued as a pocket book in 1965. As a writer, Erikson is interesting and at times quite dramatic, perhaps because, as he states, "I came to psychology from art, which may explain, if not justify, the fact that at times the reader will find me painting contexts and backgrounds where he would rather have me point to facts and concepts." Obviously, any author who has written a book which has sold over 300,000 copies is an effective writer.

As we have seen from his biographical data, Erikson has been largely influenced by Anna Freud, under whom he studied in Vienna. In fact, *Insight and Responsibility* is dedicated to Anna Freud.

Erikson also acknowledges his intellectual debt to and feels he has been particularly influenced by the late David Rapaport, who was the research director while Erikson was at the Riggs Center. He likewise pays respect to the value of having worked with Margaret Mead. In addition to these well-known names in the field of psychology, Erikson has worked with Gregory Bateson, Ruth Benedict, and Henry Murray, in whose Yale Clinic he first gained experience in the United States.

The reaction to and evaluation of Erikson's work, particularly of the developmental aspects and the extension of the Freudian viewpoint on youth, has been mostly favorable. The following five sources may help the reader evaluate the status and esteem that Erikson has held in the world of personology.

One leading writer feels that "various character types are integrated into Erikson's theory, rather than simply representing descriptions of his observations of people. While his position has an unfinished quality, there being many loose ends, it is certainly a brave beginning" (Maddi, 1968, p. 258).

Mehrabian uses Erikson's work as follows: "In this presentation of the longitudinal analysis, we shall use Erikson's 1963 version of Freud's model. Although this shift in thought may result in a less coherent presentation of Freud's thinking, it does have the advantage of including concepts which are more easily amenable to observation and measurement. Since, according to our general introductory comments, the measurement of the concepts of any theory constitutes a very essential step in the further elaboration and pragmatic use of the theory, Erikson's formulation is preferred" (Mehrabian, 1968).

Heinz Hartmann's *Essays on Ego Psychology* in many ways parallels and illuminates the work of Erikson (Hartmann, 1964).

In *Handbook of Personality Theory and Research* (1968), edited by E. F. Borgatta and W. W. Lambert, one of the writers, G. H. Elder, comments, "Erikson's and Sullivan's theories are widely admired as two of the first truly developmental formulations of personality structure and processes. The contemporary psycho-social problems of selfhood, mastery, and fidelity among youth in complex, rapidly changing societies, are assessed in Erikson's analysis of the identity crisis at the point where life history and social history inter-sect. . . . Erikson's psycho-social theory of ego development covers the entire life span, although identity formation and role confusion in late adolescence have been most fully elaborated."

And finally we turn to Jane Loevinger's insightful discussion of ego development as additional evidence of the significance of Erikson's ego development theory of personality (Loevinger, 1966): "Ego development has two quite different types of manifestations, milestone sequences and polar aspects. The distinction is a crucial one for measurement" (p. 202). "I am defending ego development as a construct of central importance for psychology, one that summarizes and helps to account for many diverse phenomena" (p. 203). "Ego development has been presented not only as one interesting personality trait among many, but as the *master trait*. It is second only to intelligence in accounting for human variability" (p. 205). "On this basis, ego development must become a focal construct in psychological theory and research" (p. 206). (Italics added.)

Erik H. Erikson continues to be productive and inventive. At present he is deeply engaged in research and in studying the life of Mahatma Gandhi. In addition to this work he continues to analyze the relationships between socialization, development, and perception, particularly between age groups and between generations.

THE SYSTEM, THEORY, OR ESSENTIAL FEATURES

General Considerations

Erikson is a neo-Freudian trained as a lay psychoanalyst, and still continues largely in the tradition of the Freudian theory. However, we note in some of his work extensions of the psychoanalytic frame of reference. For example, in contrast to Freud's position, he does not feel that personality is set after childhood. As we shall see, he considers personality to be still flexible throughout the adult years.

As an example of his Freudian position, we find the first four ages of ego development closely parallel to the oral, anal, phallic, and latency stages that Freud wrote about. Furthermore, in some sense the first four ages have more components of unconscious behavior, though not exclusively so, than the last four ages, which are more on the conscious levels of mental activity. Erikson also uses the polar or dichotomized principles which Freud used—and which of course, Jung used. An illustration is his eighth age of ego development, in which the individual ends life, either as a success or as a failure—in Erikson's words, integrity *vs.* despair.

At least for the purposes of this book and its emphasis on personality

heory, probably the most outstanding contribution of Erikson is the eight
ges of ego development. He focuses on adolescence in the life-span approach:
'Adolescence is the interaction of life history and social history." There is a
trong parallel between Erikson's eight ages of ego development and Havig-
urst's six levels of developmental tasks. Both consider the process to be
ifelong. Both consider that failure at an early stage is difficult to make up for
vithout stress and anxiety. Both believe that failure at an early stage
eopardizes a full development at a later stage. As Erikson stated, "Ego
trength develops from an interplay of personal and social structure." How-
ver, Erikson's concept is his own, not borrowed from Havighurst, and
Erikson feels that fulfillment at any one stage does not automatically guaran-
ee success and, specifically, that the individual may backslide after having
uccessfully passed an earlier stage.

Erikson's eight ages of ego development toward maturity are character-
zed by "critical periods" and "milestone solutions" in which the social in-
luences, both in the first four and in the last four ages, are undeniable. "Ego
dentity is never gained nor maintained once and for all." An example of
ritical period and milestone solution may be seen when the youth is con-
ronted by "A combination of experiences which demand his simultaneous
ommitment to (1) *physical intimacy* (not by any means overtly sexual), (2)
decisive occupational choice, (3) through energetic *competition*, and (4) to
scho-social self-definition" (Erikson, 1950, p. 57). If the individual, infant,
adolescent, or adult fails to adapt adequately to the ego development there
vill necessarily be a "negative identity."

In trying to understand human growth and development, Erikson frequently uses the term *epigenetic principle*. "Whenever we try to understand
growth, it is well to remember the *epigenetic principle* which is derived from
he growth of organisms *in utero*. Somewhat generalized, this principle states
hat anything that grows has a ground plan, and that out of this ground plan
he parts arise, each part having its special ascendency, until all parts have
arisen to form a functioning whole" (Erikson, 1968, p. 92). Apparently to
Erikson the epigenetic principle is crucial to understanding the whole frame-
vork of his personality theory. English and English define epigenesis as
omething like the emerging during development of newer phenomena or
newer properties which were not necessarily contained in the original egg or
original organism. Thus, these newer properties which were not in existence
at a prior stage of the organism ultimately emerge as functional parts of the
organism.

Erik Erikson has a longtime interest in anthropological studies. In what
he prefers to call "cultural relativity" we find the ages of ego development
may be applied to men throughout the globe.

Finally, Erikson acknowledges the difficulties in doing research, particu-
arly with his theory. "Attempts at transverting clinical concepts into quanti-

fiable items subject to experimental verification are always undertaken at the risk of the experimenter." By this he means it is not necessarily the sole responsibility of the theory to help the experimenter in his methodology. Whatever method the experimenter or researcher chooses to use is his own responsibility, and if it doesn't work, he, the experimenter, should not exclusively blame the theory.

The following section, more fully spells out the details of Erikson's eight ages of ego development.

Specific Considerations

ERIKSON'S EIGHT AGES OF MAN'S EGO DEVELOPMENT

Success brings   *Failure brings*

1st Age
Early Infancy
(birth to about one year)
(corollary to Freudian oral sensory stage)

BASIC TRUST	*vs.*	MISTRUST
Result of affection and gratification of needs, mutual recognition.		Result of consistent abuse, neglect, deprivation of love; too early or harsh weaning, autistic isolation.

2nd Age
Later Infancy
(about ages one to three years)
(corollary to Freudian muscular anal stage)

AUTONOMY	*vs.*	SHAME AND DOUBT
Child views self as person in his own right apart from parents but still dependent.		Feels inadequate, doubts self, curtails learning basic skills like walking, talking, wants to "hide" inadequacies.

3rd Age
Early Childhood
(about ages four to five years)
(corollary to Freudian genital locomotor stage)

INITIATIVE	*vs.*	GUILT
Lively imagination, vigorous reality testing, imitates adults, anticipates roles.		Lacks spontaneity, infantile jealousy "castration complex," suspicious, evasive, role inhibition.

4th Age
Middle Childhood
(about ages six to eleven years)
(corollary to Freudian latency stage)

INDUSTRY	vs.	INFERIORITY
Has sense of duty and accomplishment, develops scholastic and social competencies, undertakes real tasks, puts fantasy and play in better perspective, learns world of tools, task identification.		Poor work habits, avoids strong competition, feels doomed to mediocrity; lull before the storms of puberty, may conform as slavish behavior, sense of futility.

5th Age
Puberty and Adolescence
(about ages twelve to twenty years)

EGO IDENTITY	vs.	ROLE CONFUSION
Temporal perspective		Time confusion
Self-certain		Self-conscious
Role experimenter		Role fixation
Apprenticeship		Work paralysis
Sexual polarization		Bisexual confusion
Leader–followership		Authority confusion
Ideological commitment.		Value confusion.

6th Age
Early Adulthood

INTIMACY	vs.	ISOLATION
Capacity to commit self to others, "true genitability" now possible, *Lieben und Arbeiten*—"to love and to work"; "mutuality of genital orgasm."		Avoids intimacy, "character problems," promiscuous behavior; repudiates, isolates, destroys seemingly dangerous forces.

7th Age
Middle Adulthood

GENERATIVITY	vs.	STAGNATION
Productive and creative for self and others, parental pride and pleasure, mature, enriches life, establishes and guides next generation.		Egocentric, nonproductive, early invalidism, excessive self-love, personal impoverishment, self-indulgence.

579

8th Age
Late Adulthood

INTEGRITY	*vs.*	DESPAIR
Appreciates continuity of past, present, and future, acceptance of life cycle and life style, has learned to cooperate with inevitabilities of life, "state or quality of being complete, undivided, or unbroken; entirety" (Webster's Dictionary); "death loses its sting."		Time is too short; finds no meaning in human existence, has lost faith in self and others, wants second chance at life cycle with more advantages, no feeling of world order or spiritual sense, "fear of death."

Perhaps at this point it is wise to repeat Erikson's disenchantment with interpretations of his theory in which the eight ages are considered as achievements, being secured once and for all at a given state. For those who do use Erikson's eight ages of ego development, he prefers not having them referred to as achievement stages or scales or traits or aspirations unless the material is thoroughly understood, primarily because others "blithely omit" the negative parts which the reader finds on the right hand of the description of the eight stages. "The personality is engaged with the hazards of existence continuously, even as the body's metabolism copes with decay." In some ways it is as important for the infant also to learn a basic mistrust in life as a basic trust. It is as valuable to learn what not to trust as to learn what to trust.

The following are what Erikson calls basic virtues which appear to reemerge from generation to generation (Jungian): (1) drive and hope (coming out of succeeding and basic trust), (2) self-control and willpower (emerging from autonomy), (3) direction and purpose (emerging from initiative), (4) method and competence (coming from industry), (5) devotion and fidelity (as a result of gaining true identity), (6) affiliation and love (coming from the age of intimacy), (7) production and care (emerging from generativity), and at the end of life (8) renunciation and wisdom, which will come from the individual who has real ego integrity in later adulthood.

Erik Erikson is extremely interested in the cycle of generations and the human strength which he hopes comes from virtues. He names some of the basic virtues which he has found in working with humans, particularly in a therapeutic situation.

I will, therefore, speak of *Hope, Will, Purpose,* and *Competence* as the rudiments of virtue developed in childhood; of *Fidelity* as the adolescent virtue; and of *Love, Care,* and *Wisdom* as the central virtues of adulthood. In all their seeming discontinuity, these qualities depend on each other. Will cannot be trained until hope is secure, nor can love become reciprocal until fidelity has proven reliable. Also, each virtue and its place in the schedule of all virtues is vitally interrelated to other segments of human development such as the stages of psychosexuality which are so thoroughly explored in the whole of psychoanalytic literature, the psychosocial crises, and the steps of cognitive maturation. These schedules I must take for granted, as I restrict myself to a parallel timetable of the evolving virtues.

Erikson goes on then to describe and define the eight virtues:

1. "*Hope* is the enduring belief in the obtainability of fervent wishes, in spite of the dark urges and rages which mark the beginning of existence."

2. "*Will*, therefore, is the unbroken determination to exercise free choice as well as self-restraint, in spite of the unavoidable experience of shame and doubt in infancy."

3. "*Purpose*, then, is the courage to envisage and pursue valued goals uninhibited by the defeat of infantile fantasies, by guilt and by the foiling fear of punishment."

4. "*Competence*, then, is the free exercise of dexterity and intelligence in the completion of tasks, unimpaired by infantile inferiority."

5. "*Fidelity* is the ability to sustain loyalties freely pledged in spite of the inevitable contradictions of value systems."

6. "*Love*, then, is mutuality of devotion forever subduing the antagonisms inherent in divided function."

7. "*Care* is the widening concern for what has been generated by love, necessity, or accident; it overcomes the ambivalence adhering to irreversible obligation."

8. "*Wisdom*, then, is detached concern with life itself, in the face of death itself" (Erikson, 1963).

DELIMITATIONS

The present author has not covered many of Erikson's contributions. For example, we have not included his book on Luther, *Young Man Luther*, or discussed his therapeutic techniques or the many case studies of which a number are extremely interesting—for example, his analysis of George Bernard Shaw and Hitler. Nor have we included any of the anthropological studies that Erikson made, such as a comparison of the Sioux Indian and American cultures and his definitive work of the Yurok Indians of California.

BIBLIOGRAPHY

PRIMARY SOURCES

BOOKS

Erikson, E. H., Identity and the life cycle, *Psychological Issues*, Monograph #1. New York: International Universities Press, 1959.

Erikson, E. H., The course of health personality development, in J. M. Seidman (ed.), *The Adolescent: A Book of Readings*. New York: Holt, Rinehart & Winston, 1960, pp. 218–237.

Erikson, E. H., *Young Man Luther: A Study in Psychoanalysis and History*. New York: Norton, 1962.

Recriprocity between men, institutions, and leaders.

Erikson, E. H., *Childhood and Society*, 2nd ed. New York: Norton, 1963.

First issued in 1950.

Erikson, E. H., Growth and crises of the "healthy personality," in C. Kluckhohn and H. A. Murray (eds.), *Personality: In Nature, Society, and Culture*, 2nd ed. New York: Knopf, 1964, pp. 185–225.

Short and easily understood essay on the eight stages.

Erikson, E. H., *Insight and Responsibility*. New York: Norton, 1964.

Six of Erikson's previous lectures reviewed and expanded.

Erikson, E. H. (ed.), *The Challenge of Youth*. Garden City, N.Y.: Doubleday (Anchor), 1965.

Originally *Youth: Change and Challenge*. New York: Basic Books, 1963.

Erikson, E. H., Generativity and ego integrity, in B. L. Neugarten (ed.), *Middle Age and Aging: A Reader in Social Psychology*. Chicago: University of Chicago Press, 1968, pp. 85–87.

Erikson, E. H., *Identity: Youth and Crisis*. New York: Norton, 1968.

"Each chapter of this book, then, is a revision of a major essay of the last two decades, supplemented by excerpts from papers written at about the same time."

Erikson, E. H., Youth and the life cycle, in D. E. Hamachek (ed.), *Human Dynamics in Psychology and Education: Selected Readings*. Boston: Allyn & Bacon, 1968, pp. 305–316.

PERIODICALS

Erikson, E. H., The problem of ego identity, *J. Amer. Psychoanal. Ass.*, 1956, 4, 56–121.

Erikson, E. H., Reality and actuality, *J. Amer. Psychoanal. Ass.*, 1962, 10, 451–474.

> Reality is the world of "phenomenal experience perceived with a minimum of idiosyncratic distortion and with a maximum of joint validation; while actuality is the world of participation, shared with a minimum of defensive maneuvers and a maximum of mutual activation."

Erikson, E. H., A memorandum on identity and Negro youth, *J. Soc. Issues*, 1964, 20, 29–42.

Erikson, E. H., Psychoanalysis and ongoing history: Problems of identity, hatred and nonviolence, *Amer. J. Psychiat.*, 1965, 122, 241–253.

> A "counterpart to the author's *Young Man Luther*."

Erikson, E. H., Eight ages of man, *Int. J. Psychiat.*, 1966, 2, 281–300. Reprinted from *Childhood and Society*, 2nd ed.

> "8 stages of psychosocial development are distinguished, and the specific nuclear conflicts for each stage are indicated. The solution of each nuclear conflict is based on the integration of earlier ones."

Erikson, E. H., Memorandum on youth, *Daedalus*, 1967, 96, 860–870.

> Erikson believes that "the fabric of traditional authority has been torn so severely in the last decades that the re-establishment of certain earlier forms of convention is all but unlikely."

SUGGESTED READINGS

BOOKS

Elder, G. H., Adolescent socialization and development, in E. F. Borgatta and W. W. Lambert (eds.), *Handbook of Personality Theory and Research*. Chicago: Rand McNally, 1968, pp. 239–364.

Erikson, J. M., Eye to eye, in G. Kepes (ed.), *The Man Made Object*. New York: Braziller, 1966.

> Mrs. Erikson on how a baby and mother meet.

Evans, R. I., *Dialogue with Erik Erikson*. New York: Harper & Row, 1967.

> Erikson corrects some interpretations of his work.

Hartmann, H., *Essays on Ego Psychology*. New York: International Universities Press, 1964.

> The coping and integrative functions of the ego derived from psycho-analysis.

Helson, H., *Adaptation-Level Theory: An Experimental and Systematic Approach to Behavior*. New York: Harper & Row, 1964.

Lynd, H. M., *On Shame and the Search for Identity*. New York: Science Editions, 1961.

Maddi, S., *Personality Theories: A Comparative Analysis*, Homewood, Ill.: Dorsey Press, 1968.

> Erikson as an ego psychologist.

Maier, H. W., *Three Theories of Child Development: The Contributions of Erik H. Erikson, Jean Piaget and Robert R. Sears and Their Applications*. New York: Harper & Row, 1965.

Mehrabian, A., *An Analysis of Personality Theories*, Englewood Cliffs, N.J.: Prentice-Hall, 1968, pp. 63–78, 144–152.

> Longitudinal analysis of Erikson's critical periods of development.

Smart, M. S., and R. C. Smart, *Children: Development and Relationships*. New York: Macmillan, 1968.

PERIODICALS

Cornyetz, P., Panel discussion: Psychoanalysis and social reality, *Psychoanal. Rev.*, 1967, 54, 61–65.

> Freud's theories are necessary.

Howard, S. M., and J. F. Kubis, Ego identity and some aspects of personal adjustment, *J. Psychol.*, 1964, 58, 459–466.

> Tested hypothesis derived from Erikson's psychosocial theory of ego development. Found ego identity had consistent negative relationship to manifest anxiety.

Loevinger, J., The meaning and measurement of ego development, *Amer. Psychologist*, 1966, 21, 195–206.

> The polar and the milestone sequences in life: important but different.

Marcia, J. E., Determination and construct validity of ego identity status, *Dissert. Abstr.*, 1965, 25, 6763.

Murrac, J. B., The identity image of the college student, *Psychol. Rep.*, 1964, 14, 267–271.

> Erikson's concept of identity image and some of the crises in its development are applied to college students.

Rasmussen, J. E., Relationship of ego identity to psychosocial effectiveness, *Psychol. Rep.*, 1964, *15*, 815–825.

> Compares well adjusted and poorly adjusted students. The former had more adequate ego identity. Also present evidence for construct validity.

Sommers, V. S., The impact of dual membership on identity, *Psychiatry*, 1964, *27*, 332–349.

> An Eriksonian analysis of self-image problems of sociocultural and psychological identity.

Stinnette, C. R., Human meaning of transformation in learning, *Relig. Educ.*, 1968, *63*, 181–185.

> Insights from Lewin, Erikson, and Sullivan are related to (1) language and learning, (2) is knowing all? (3) human dimension in learning, (4) learning as transformation.

INTERPERSONAL
[SULLIVAN]

No man is an island, entire of itself—
John Donne
Devotions XVII

SOME BIOGRAPHICAL DATA

Harry Stack Sullivan was born and educated in America and always remained dedicated to his country. He was born in New York State on February 21 1892, of farm parents. Like many other personality theorists, he first trained as a medical doctor and was graduated from the Chicago College of Medicine and Surgery in 1917, just in time to enter World War I as a medical officer After being demobilized, and until 1922, he worked for the federal government, first as a medical officer in the federal Board of Vocational Education and later with the Public Health Service. In 1923 he went to St. Elizabeth Hospital in Washington, D.C., for a year and the following year joined the staff of the medical school at the University of Maryland, where he remained until 1930. During this period his affiliation with the Pratt Hospital in Towson, Maryland, gave him his opportunity to conduct research concerning schizophrenia. His close contact with William Alanson White and the strong influence White had on his work brought Sullivan the presidency of the William Alanson White Foundation in 1933. Sullivan continued in the presidency until 1943.

Sullivan served in many capacities during the later years of his professional life. He helped found and until his death was a director of the Washington School of Psychiatry; he became editor of the journal *Psychiatry* which advanced his public recognition; he served as consultant for the Selective Service Board in the early years of World War II and acted as consultant to the United Nations UNESCO project on tensions. He was returning from an executive board meeting of the World Federation for Mental Health held in Amsterdam when, on January 14, 1949, he died suddenly in Paris, France

During his lifetime many people influenced Sullivan. Other than White, Sigmund Freud, George Herbert Mead, Adolph Meyer, Leonard Cotrell, Ruth Benedict, and especially Edward Sapir all affected the formulation of Sullivan's work and theory on man's personality. Those Sullivan influenced have in turn created many valuable concepts beyond his own valuable work. Through his editorship of the journal *Psychiatry*, the Washington School of Psychiatry, his innumerable consultancies for federal and international agencies, and his students in the medical school of the University of Maryland, Sullivan's impact on the world of psychiatry and the field of human behavior has been notable. His untimely death cut too short a productive life dedicated to making the human race run an easier and less anxious course.

INTRODUCTION

Harry Stack Sullivan's theory is much easier to categorize than that of other theorists, according to the organization of this text. Whereas other theorists' works, such as Freud's, are vast and encyclopedic, Sullivan's is neater, more orderly in arrangement. Another feature lending itself to the treatment of this text is the high sense of prediction that arises from Sullivan's theory. His work is not as fully spelled out as some other theorists' (he died at the age of fifty-six), nor is it as fully developed as a system of thought. However, others have continued to develop it to a high and more inclusive degree. Sullivan's theories have made a definite contribution to the further understanding of man's behavior.

With no levity or disrespect intended, Sullivan could be called the "anxious" theorist. As will be discussed later, a great central theme of his theory revolves around anxiety in man: anxiety as a prime mover, as the builder of a self-system, and as the great educator in life. The word *anxiety* itself has become popular coinage in the writings of many psychologists and psychiatrists. It has been given many meanings. Sullivan's emphasis on anxiety also has some wide variations in theme as he uses the term in describing man's behavior.

Sullivan began his professional work as a somewhat Freudian-oriented psychiatrist. However, while others such as Fromm and Horney are considered renovators of Freudian theory, Sullivan is often credited with being a highly original innovator of Freudian theory. As a psychiatrist Sullivan worked primarily with emotionally disturbed people. His theory, then, is based, as were so many others, on the deviant type of personality as the raw material for theorization. Out of his beginnings as a Freudian-flavored psychiatrist into his highly original and valuable work with schizophrenics, Sullivan evolved what he called the *interpersonal theory of psychiatry*. It has been allied, therefore, to the field of psychiatry, but psychologists, and sociologists as well, have made heavy use of his work. Out of all this came a further impetus for the field of social psychology. The end result of Sullivan's work is far removed from its earlier flavor of Freudianism.

Sullivan, like Adler, followed the precepts of his own theory in his personal living. He felt, because man was a socially created animal and society was doing a poor job of creating, that society as it exists today was in dire need of help. He was a strong critic of modern society and its effect upon man's development. As a consequence he spent time, energy, and money working for world peace causes. His contribution to these organizations was immense.

Part of Sullivan's appeal to the field of sociology is the emphasis he placed on society as the creator of man's personality. Another attraction of the interpersonal theory is the tenet that man can change, that man does change, and even that man *has* to change in his basic personality pattern as he grows to and through maturity. This has helped other societally oriented theorists to substantiate their belief in the forces of the environment as a molder of man. Part of Sullivan's theory states that man lives in a tension system. Tension exists within a single individual and between himself and all other individuals. These forces of tension within self and between selves make man what he is. In addition, life itself is a tension system, according to Sullivan. The analogy of Freud's work was that of a building constructed brick by brick and quite unchangeable after the foundation is constructed. The analogy of the interpersonal theory of Sullivan's is that of a kite, which is held together by the tension between its parts. The entire structure, although retaining a basic shape, may be altered and changed depending upon the tensions within the system.

Harry Stack Sullivan was not a prolific writer. He did not have to be in promulgating his theories. Although in his lifetime he wrote one full treatise on his theory, *Conceptions of Modern Psychiatry* (1947), his main influence came through his work in UNESCO, his vivid lectures, his devoted students, and the many highly competent professional friends he made by his own pleasant personality.

In addition to his brilliant intellect and his influence on the psychiatric and psychological world, Sullivan had a high degree of empathy for his fellow man. He felt many times so keenly attuned to the sufferings and tribulation of his patients that he incorporated part of these feelings of sympathy into his techniques of psychiatric interviewing. Sullivan was no passive student of humanity. He was a dedicated student of life as it is lived by all types of people. He felt a responsibility toward man.

Sullivan considered his theory (as a good environmentalist should) a product of the society that he, Sullivan, knew. He acknowledged that it was unique to the Western world and might be altered by being applied in other cultures, particularly as regards the stages of development.

THE SYSTEM, THEORY,
OR ESSENTIAL FEATURES

General Considerations

Personality was a word to Sullivan rather than an entity for study. His theory stressed the relationships between personalities and not the study of the single personality. The human being does not exist as a single personality. His personality can exist only as it is related to others.

Sullivan does not deny the influence of man's biological system. In fact he bases his theory on man as an operating organic system. Man's body does condition his personality but only to the extent that the body is necessary to life. At times, man may even subvert his biological needs to the more powerful needs of his social system. He may diet, or end his life, or overcome tremendous physical obstacles if the pressures and tensions of society so demand.

Of primary importance to the interpersonal theory of personality is the way the human being develops in infancy, childhood, and adolescence. This is not to say that the formative years permanently stamp the personality. It does indicate that the interpersonal patterns of early life are extremely important to the personality. These patterns continue to exert the crucial influence on man's behavior. They do not, however, mandate the elimination of current social determiners of personality. If one lives in a stable environment, his personality is stable. If one lives in an unstable environment, his personality will be unstable. This effect continues throughout life.

It is pointless, Sullivan declares, to discuss or even think about one human personality by itself. It must always be considered and studied and seen in relationship to one, two, or more personalities. No one can have a personality all by himself exclusive of the world about him. Sullivan believes this interpersonal relationship is the foundation of personality. The moment man is born into the world he is in contact with at least one other personality who sees that he stays alive. Contact with other personalities persists throughout life, either in actual or in vestigial forms.

The human personality can display itself only in relationship to other personalities. The reciprocity is a key structure in the theories of Sullivan. Not all contacts have to be between living beings. The interaction may take place between a living person and a fictional character; Santa Claus, children's cowboy television heroes, and other nonexisting human prototypes may serve as the other interacting personality. In such cases the fictional figure is based upon the personification of a live human being, who strengthens the fictional image, and the fictional figure affects in some degree the behavior of the living personality. The living personality creates and changes the fictional personality as time goes on. Once having constructed a fictional personality, man finds it has the power to affect his own behavior. Pygmalion-like, the interaction takes place. Santa Claus may be Kris Kringle or St. Nicholas or Father Christmas, depending upon the ethnic group. Each group, having started essentially with the same figure, has modified it to suit its needs and in turn has been affected to some degree by the now self-created image.

In addition to legendary images conceived as personalities with an inter-active effect, there may also be an interacting dream image which bears no direct relationship to any known human being. The principle of interperson-ality relationships still operates even in dreams, and analogously, in this case, to the created image.

Even basic psychological mental activities are considered by Sullivan to be involved in interpersonal relationships. For example, the mental activities of imagining, perceiving, remembering, and thinking are connected with other personalities and are not exclusively inner dynamics of behavior void of influence from other personalities. Everything we do is the result of the social order in which we live. Other personalities have had some effect upon our behavior no matter how intrapersonal it seems to be. In imagination we have dreams and images that revolve about other people. We dream of success, not over trees, but in terms of what we can do to trees that will impress other people. The astronaut imagines himself in outer space with all of its unknown qualities and apparently nonhuman features, but the culmination of his imagined journey is his coming back. He wants to come back not only for life's sake but because that is where people are. His outer space behavior will be partially determined by what other personalities did to him before he went aloft. It can further be assumed that his behavior in space will be affected by concern for the opinions of others upon his return.

Perception is highly involved in interpersonal relationships. The person reared in circumstances of wealth walks through a smart shopping district and perceives the expensive displays as obtainable merchandise fitting his interests and desires. The person reared in poverty walks along the same street, sees the same glittering displays, and is bound to perceive them in a different light. He either covets, resents, or plans some day to achieve these symbols of wealth. In any case, his perceptive system is different from that of the wealthy indi-vidual. Perception differs in this case because of background and training, gained through life with other personalities.

Remembering is influenced by others too. What is important or unim-portant to remember depends on parents, friends, and other personalities deemed worthy of imitation. Whether one remembers baseball scores or musical scores and considers either one or the other to be worth remembering is the product of contact with other personalities. Even the methods and mnemonic devices employed are the result of influence from teachers, par-ents, or friends. And lastly, it is well established that people from Oriental and Occidental cultures are inclined to think differently from each other. The human neural systems (ganglia, dendrites, neurons, synaptic gaps, etc.) may be identical, but the end products of the thinking process may be just the opposite.

The preceding discourse does not imply that Sullivan categorically rejected the study of individual personalities. Later concepts in this chapter, like dynamisms, personifications, and cognitive experiences, are indeed directed toward the individual personality. Such study is necessary, Sullivan feels, if one is to comprehend the nature of man, but it is equally necessary not to lose sight of the interactive systems which always operate within and around the single personality.

Like numerous other theorists, Sullivan feels that man strives to reduce the tensions in his life. From the level of complete lack of tension, which he calls *euphoria* (a psychiatric term generally used to describe delusional feelings of well-being), to the state of excessive tension akin to psychosis, an important aspect of man's personality is the reduction of tensions which threaten his security.

Tension arises from two sources, organic needs and social insecurity, which lead to anxiety. Organic needs, basic to all personalities, are both general and specific. Needs for air and water are general organic needs. Specific organic needs may be for pine-scented, perfumed, or at least non-obnoxious air, or for coffee, soft drinks, or alcoholic beverages. The general need is often satisfied and tension reduced by satisfying the socially indoctrinated specific need. Hunger, for example, may be assuaged by sucking, smoking, or using the lips and mouth as one would in eating. In addition to the general and specific categories, organic needs may also be arranged in hierarchical order from most important in reducing tension to least important. An illustration of the subordination of one biological need to another may be found in our habit of eating a sweet dessert after the main meal instead of before. Or we may wish for pure sweet air to breathe before we wish for scented air. One need must be met before the other becomes important.

Much can be said concerning the reduction of tensions from man's social behavior. For the present we find that man is surrounded by feelings of anxiety the moment he enters life. From his mother's anxious intent that he survive and be fed and clothed properly, to the precautions that society takes to keep its constituents safe from injury, pain, or death (polio drives, heart disease campaigns, auto safety measures, etc.) the individual prolongs and develops the anxiety he first met at birth. The threats to his security may be either real or imagined. In either case, anxiety situations may be met by tension-reducing behavior. Whether he has actually had a serious automobile accident on a frantic metropolitan throughway or has only seen pictures and heard accounts of accidents on the same throughway, the driver in traffic will be anxious about avoiding an accident. Similarly, lightning may never have struck the individual, but he exercises caution on the golf course in a thunderstorm, and his behavior is anxiety centered. In all cases, his behavior of anxiety may be modified and disguised by the presence of others.

Increased feelings of anxiety may also accrue from real or imagined social rebuffs. The college freshman may hesitate to ask for a dancing partner at his first college mixer because of the imagined refusal. He may never have been refused before and may be an accomplished social dancer, but the imagined threat of refusal is stultifying enough to keep him on the sidelines, wistfully eyeing the proceedings and possible dance partners for the entire evening. He gives all the manifestations of being anxious to guard his ego from blunt refusal. Tension and ambivalence ensue as he wants neither to deny himself the pleasures of college social life nor to risk damage to his ego. He may avoid further similar social occasions until he acquires a coed friend who gives him the security he has learned from early infancy to need.

GENERAL CONDITIONS

Harry Stack Sullivan placed a great deal of emphasis upon the fact that man is an anxious animal. Although anxiety is so closely associated with the tension systems as actually to be a part of them, it is also more than an adjunct of another system. It is one of the prime motivators in life. It is both productive and destructive. Slight anxiety is good for man; it moves him off dead center. Total anxiety leads him to utter confusion and renders him incapable of intelligent action. Anxiety, therefore, varies in intensity, sometimes causing the personality to make greater effort to keep tensions in hand and at other times causing psychotic or neurotic behavior in the attempt to straighten out the twisted strands of existence. Sullivan believed that tension systems are similar among men but that each man has his own peculiar method of handling them. Individuality is manifested in the way men meet their stresses.

The child's first educative experience comes out of his feelings of anxiety transmitted by his mother. Her behavior, looks, and general demeanor reveal anxious moments in his care and welfare. The infant soon notices that he is worried about and that he is cautioned about fire, high places, and all the other dangers against which measures must be taken in raising a child. Through empathy and emulation the infant takes on the feelings of anxiety concerning health and safety which he first noticed in the mother. In the beginning he knew only pain and pleasure. Something hurt or it felt good. Gradually as he received sympathy and ministrations for his cuts and bruises, he began to exercise caution, and with caution grew the realization that he was surrounded by a world which could harm him. Through the cognitive experience of parataxic thinking he associates many activities not necessarily anxiety-producing with what he considers an anxiety-packed situation. Some anxiety helps him to learn what is good and what is harmful. Too much anxiety makes him withdraw into a shell of security.

Out of early life experiences the personality constructs the self system, creates personifications, and maintains a tension system.

SELF SYSTEM

One of the results of the anxious childhood is the creation of the self system. Emerging from the mother-fed feelings of anxiety regarding himself and later from attempts to construct a system which will secure him from tension, the human personality gradually builds a self system to protect himself. Conforming to the social rules of his parents allows him to avoid anxiety: being a good little boy brings praise; being a bad little boy brings punishment. The good me–bad me dichotomy has opposite rewards. Conformity prevents anxiety; nonconformity produces anxiety. Anxiety begets tension. Tension is painful. By the process of evolutionary development, the child can create a system of doing things according to conformity, but it seldom represents his true self. Once the self system proves its worth in avoiding anxiety ("Do what you are told and never mind how you feel"), it is likely to become isolated from the real self, which often feels contrary to what the self system is doing to conform.

Having once been instituted in childhood, a self system tends to persist and be reinforced as life progresses, even though conformity not in tune with the real self is demanded. The personality considers the self system to be highly valuable in reducing anxiety. Any valuable item is guarded and held in high esteem. The personality continues to use the self system especially to protect it from criticism by its real self. The wider the gulf and the greater the use of the self system, the more complex and independent it becomes. A schizoid situation develops if the distance between the self system and the true self continues to widen. It is possible, therefore, for the true self to be unable ultimately to control the self system with its devious ways.

Sullivan felt, however, that some self system was essential to avoid or at least reduce anxiety in the modern world. One of the problems in life, then, is to use but control one's self system. Frank analysis and criticism of the self system by the real self may help in providing controls to a schizoid situation.

SEVEN LIFE PERIODS

Table 15.1 is designed to help the student make a short survey of Sullivan's contribution to developmental psychology through the avenue of anxiety periods. Sullivan proposed seven states, possibly more applicable to western European cultures, which he knew best, than to other cultures. The period of adolescence was of such importance to Sullivan that he made three groupings within it rather than a single grouping entitled *adolescence*. This approach

TABLE 15.1. *Seven Life Periods According to Sullivan's Theory*

PERIOD	APPROXIMATE AGES	BODY ZONE	SELF SYSTEM	COGNITIVE EXPERIENCES	PERTINENT INTERPERSONAL EXPERIENCES
Infancy	0–18 mo. (birth to articulate speech)	Oral	Barely emerging	Largely prototaxic	1. Nursing—breast or bottle; great stress on nipple orientation 2. Fearing the good–bad mother 3. Occasional success at satisfying self independent of mother 4. Completely dependent on paternal–maternal care
Childhood	18–20 mo. to age 4–5 (speech to needing playmates)		Sex role recognition	Largely parataxic emerging to syntaxic	1. Personifications 2. Dramatizations—plays at being adult 3. Possible "malevolent transformations"—feeling the world is against you—create isolation 4. Dependent
Juvenile	5–6 to 11 (elementary school)	Dormant genital	Integrating needs—internal controls	Syntaxic most of the time, fascination with symbols	1. Socialization—cooperation and competition 2. Learning controls 3. Orientation in how to live 4. Dependent

594

Preadolescence	11–13 (jr. high school)	Emerging genital	Somewhat stabilized	Syntaxic	1. Outstanding need for peer of same sex 2. Begins genuine human relationships 3. Needs opportunity for equality—mutuality and particularly reciprocity in interpersonal relationships 4. Emerging and confusing independence
Early adolescence	12–17 (high school)	Fully genital	Confused, but continuingly stabilized	Syntaxic (highly sexually oriented)	1. Strongly lustful 2. Double social needs: erotic for opposite sex and intimacy for like-sexed peer (confusion leads to homosexuality) 3. Highly independent
Late adolescence	17–19 to early 20s (college)	Fully matured	Integrated and stabilized	Fully syntaxic	1. Strong security against anxiety 2. Prolonged period 3. Full member of social group 4. Fully independent
Adulthood	20–30 etc. (parenthood)	Completely heterosexual	Completely stabilized	Syntaxic and completely symbolic	1. Society has now created a fully social animal from a human animal 2. Completely independent of paternal control

may seem strange to readers familiar with the more traditional groupings of life stages. (See Gesell, Hurlock, Erikson, Havighurst.)

Specific Considerations

A dynamism is any recurring, habitual action, attitude, or feeling that one person has about one or more other persons. It is the smallest unit of human behavior that can be analyzed and studied profitably by another human. It is a relatively enduring behavior pattern. It can be closely associated with habit.

Dynamisms accumulate throughout life as the human being experiences more and more social contacts. The wider the variety of experiences one has, the greater the number of dynamisms he will possess. The total group of dynamisms may become so complex as to constitute a particular style of living. The self system previously mentioned is a complex of dynamisms built around the potent energizing emotion of anxiety.

A dynamism changes only when there has been an accumulation of different dynamisms crowding upon it. The ancient problem of differences in degree and differences in kind is involved in changing a dynamism. Differences of degree do not alter the basic properties of a dynamism, whereas differences in kind do. Exactly what constitutes a difference in degree and a difference in kind is most troublesome to define. Apparently, and in some manner not explicitly stated by Sullivan, the difference of kind is decided by the self. What may appear as a difference of degree to some personalities will be construed as a difference of kind by others. However it may be, only the differences in kind of dynamisms alter preceding and currently operating dynamisms. We may further assume that the trick in therapy, if we are to change the basic behavior pattern of the client, is to make him accept dynamisms which are different in kind.

Dynamisms may be openly expressed (overt) or secretly practiced within the self system (covert). Such activities as laughing, talking, and dancing are examples of the former, while autistic thinking and reasoning are examples of the latter.

Most dynamisms serve a basic need of the body, however remote that may seem as the dynamisms operate. Sullivan reveals his early Freudian influence by associating many dynamisms with the erotogenic zones of the body. The mouth, anus, and genitals are involved at times with dynamisms, although other parts of the body, too, such as the hands, feet, and back may be involved.

Some examples of dynamisms follow: The dynamism of lust would be indicated by excessive gambling; dreading new situations would be considered the dynamism of fear; and the dynamism of aggression would reveal itself in fighting or strongly exerting the self at the expense of others.

Personifications are the images one has first of self and then of others. In sense they represent a stereotype of self. Personifications shared by many thers become the stereotype as it is generally known. In the main, however, ersonifications are the pictures of others which the person carries in his own nind. Accuracy is not necessarily involved in a personification of someone lse. "Love is blind," "My child can do no wrong; he must be understood rst"—these are examples of the prejudicial characteristics of a personification.

As the child develops, he first gains an impression of the thing he knows est: himself. From the good–bad nature of himself he notices and empa-hizes with the good–bad nature of others as he interprets their behavior. hese impressions grow into a complicated personification of many persons. ach person then is a composite, or complex personification, of the previous xperiences the child has had with similar personalities. By adopting per-onifications of others, the self hopes to protect itself from anxiety. On the rejudged basis that some people are harmful and thus to be avoided or ontrolled, the personification serves as a tool to decrease the tensions in life. ny person resembling the original personified concept gains the reputation, ood or bad, of the original personification. Consequently, although personifi-ations are highly instrumental in interpersonal processes, they may not be ccurate estimations of another's qualities.

Cognitive experiences consist of three hierarchical forms of thinking hich relate one to other human beings. The lowest level is the prototaxic xperience. The next higher and more involved experience is parataxic. The ighest mental experience man attains is the syntaxic mode of interacting ith others.

ROTOTAXIC

n the beginning, man's conscious mental processes consist of raw sensations f a momentary nature. Fleeting through the infantile mind, Sullivan be-eves, are sensations, feelings, and fragmentary images, none of which are of ng duration. Prototaxic experiences of a mental nature (it can hardly be alled thinking in the popular sense) are rarely, if ever, connected with each ther. They occur at random, are vivid experiences during their duration, ave memory traces, and are a necessary prelude to the next two modes of ental processes. No logical behavior ensues from the impact of prototaxic ental experiences. The baby follows one clue to another with apparently ompletely random responses. The important factor is that in this manner he radually becomes aware of his surroundings, and particularly of the human eings who constitute his environment. In a haphazard way, then, man begins get some impressions of the world beyond his own physical and mental lf.

PARATAXIC

Parataxic thinking sees causal relationships between two simultaneous phe
nomena whether there is really any causality or not. The parataxically
oriented person confuses correlation with causation. Because two things
happen at the same time, he is inclined to believe that one activity created or
caused the other. The author recalls an intriguingly titled paper, "Superstition
in the Pigeon," which was presented at a Midwestern Psychological Associa
tion meeting. The paper clearly indicated that a pigeon had made a random
movement at the exact moment that a food pellet was introduced into the
cage. The pigeon "thought" that his queer sideways gesture of the head had
caused the food pellet to appear. The one reinforcement was sufficient to
perpetuate the head jerk in the pigeon, which always assumed that food
would be gained by the movement. This is a perfect example of parataxic
thinking. Another and oft-told example from basic psychology classes serve
well to illustrate parataxic thinking: A certain gentleman stated that every
time he heard the fire engine there also happened to be a fire. Ergo, fire
engines cause fires!

This type of thinking may do a disservice to the child's sense of interper
sonal relations, and hence it becomes important to Sullivan's theory. Part of
the self system, as well as personifications, may be formed by the child's
inability to separate two concurrent factors. He may feel, for example, that
wherever there is a police officer there is crime or trouble. Failing to make the
proper association between the officer's function and the occurrence of
trouble, he may attribute the trouble to the police. In his childish mind police
officers cause trouble. Unfortunately, this type of parataxical thinking is
frequently the foundation for adult prejudices and superstitious beliefs
Sullivan felt that too much of modern man's thinking does not progress
beyond parataxic thinking. It must be admitted that there is strong evidence
to substantiate his claim.

SYNTAXIC

The highest of the three types of thinking as Sullivan incorporated them into
his theoretical system, syntaxic thinking uses symbols as its basis. The symbol
may be verbal or numerical, but they must have been accepted by enough
people for them to have an agreed-upon meaning. Private symbols convey
nothing to the uninitiated, as witness the rituals of a fraternity or sorority
Public symbols, Sullivan felt, are absolutely necessary for man to carry on an
interpersonal relationship with other men. The complexities of society remove
the ancient possibility of human contact by gestures or even rudimentary
speech. In a sense, man can only progress in his relationships with other men
as he creates and employs more meaningful symbols.

The value of syntaxic thinking based upon symbology is increased by its aiding man to a greater degree of logical quality in his personal thinking, as well as by the invaluable avenue it gives him for communication with others.

SUMMARY

Interpersonal relations are the basic core of Sullivan's theory. He believed that the human personality is never separate from all other human personalities. All that the individual's personality has been, is, and will be is the product of the interpersonal contacts he makes through life. One may study a single personality just as one may study the human heart separately from the body only if he keeps always in mind that the heart or the personality cannot exist alone. Even man's innermost thoughts and mental processes are products of the interhuman environment. Dreams, thinking, remembering, and other introspective processes are couched in terms of interpersonal experiences and forces. The reciprocity of personalities is a key theme in Sullivan's theory.

Life consists of a series of interwoven and sequential tensions for the human animal. The tensions may be of the basic, organic, biological type and may later incorporate the tremendous tensions of societal living. To reduce tension is a primary task of living. At no time in his life is man free for any appreciable time from the pressures of tension. Tension may be considered in two ways: as an interior system which holds man together to face the struggles of life, and externally as man is the recipient of pressures from the world outside himself.

The essential connotation of tension, however, as employed by Sullivan is that man comes into a world of tension at birth and soon learns to adapt to the conditions of this state of existence. As he develops, he learns through dynamisms to reduce the tensions of life, using for this purpose the self system, personification, dramatizations, and cognitive experiences.

To Sullivan the world is an anxious place. Anxiety and tension are so uniquely interwoven in his theory that at times cause and effect are not readily distinguishable. Fundamentally, the world of anxiety causes tension, although it also seems that tension creates anxiety.

Out of anxiety grows much of the formulation of the basic fabric of man's personality. The self system is a cardinal feature of the personality and one which Sullivan utilized heavily in studying schizophrenic behavior. Man creates a self system which is a false portion of his personality in that it exists only to protect the real self from anxiety. Because the self system knows no insight, it contains no self-corrective powers and at times may take control of the true self. The result is a split personality dominated by a system concerned only with the preservation of self.

A dynamism is the smallest unit of human contact with another human being. It is cumulative and can be considered much like a habit formation. Dynamisms are difficult to change. They may be expressed overtly or covertly. Sullivan felt that most dynamisms are associated with various parts of the body. Dynamisms related to the oral zone are created early in life and tend to persist strongly throughout the remainder of life.

Personifications are the images one has first of the self and later of other human beings. A personification shared by a majority of people in an environment becomes a stereotype. One does not necessarily create accurate pictures of others through personifications.

The three levels of cognitive experiences are prototaxic, parataxic, and syntaxic. The first is a form of mental reaction to stimuli which is primarily sensory in nature. The second sees causal relationships between simultaneous phenomena whether there is a degree of causality or not. The third and highest form of cognitive experience employs symbols to express relationship and to retain the knowledge gained from this type of thinking.

DELIMITATION

The primary omission in this section is Sullivan's insightful work in psycho therapy and interviewing.

BIBLIOGRAPHY

PRIMARY SOURCES

BOOKS

Sullivan, H. S., Tensions interpersonal and international: A psychiatrist's view, H. Cantril (ed.), *Tensions That Cause War*. Urbana: University of Illino Press, 1950, pp. 79–138.

Sullivan, H. S., *Conceptions of Modern Psychiatry*. New York: Norton, 1953.

> Based on W. A. White lectures on five essays of 1940.

Sullivan, H. S., *The Interpersonal Theory of Psychiatry*. New York: Norton 1953.

> Primarily from lectures given in the winter of 1946–1947.

Sullivan, H. S., *The Psychiatric Interview*. New York: Norton, 1954.

> Based on two lecture series given in 1944–1945.

Sullivan, H. S., *The Psychiatric Interview*. New York: Norton, 1956.

> Based on 1943 lectures.

Sullivan, H. S. In H. S. Perry (ed.), *Schizophrenia as a Human Process*. New York: Norton, 1962.

> Covers *all* his major articles from 1924 to 1935.

PERIODICALS

See above, *Schizophrenia as a Human Process*.

SUGGESTED READINGS

BOOKS

Blitsten, D. R., *The Social Theories of Harry Stack Sullivan*. New York: William-Frederick, 1953.

> Selection of his papers from 1892 to 1949.

Brown, I. A. C., *Freud and the Post-Freudians*. Baltimore: Penguin Books, 1961.

> Horney, Fromm, and Sullivan also included.

Kardiner, B., Some problems of personality development among Negro children, in *Personality in Nature, Society, and Culture*, 2nd ed., C. Kluckhohn and H. A. Murray (eds.), New York: Knopf, 1964, pp. 545–566.

> Basic theoretical orientation very close to that of H. S. Sullivan.

Deutsch, F., and W. F. Murphy, *The Clinical Interview*. New York: International Universities Press, 1955.

Maccoby, E. E., and N. Maccoby, The interview: A tool of social science, in G. Lindzey (ed.), *Handbook of Social Psychology*, Vol. I. Reading, Mass.: Addison-Wesley, 1954, pp. 449–487.

Maddi, S. R., *Personality Theories: A Comparative Analysis*. Homewood, Ill.: Dorsey Press, 1968.

> Sullivan position in Maddi's model methods: conflict, consistency, and fulfillment.

Mullahy, P., *Oedipus—Myth and Complex*. New York: Hermitage Press, 1948.

Mullahy, P. (ed.), *A Study of Interpersonal Relations*. New York: Hermitage Press, 1949.

Mullahy, P. (ed.), *The Contributions of Harry Stack Sullivan: A Symposium on Interpersonal Theory in Psychiatry and Social Science*. New York: Hermitage Press, 1952.

> Seven articles appraising Sullivan's contributions plus a photograph and full bibliography of his writings.

Munroe, R. L., *Schools of Psychoanalytic Thought.* New York: Holt, Rinehart & Winston, 1955.

> Analysis and integration of Freud, Adler, Jung, Rank, Fromm, Horney, Sullivan, *et al.*

Pearce, J., and S. Newton, *The Conditions of Human Growth.* New York: Citadel Press, 1963.

> A contemporary statement of Harry Stack Sullivan's interpersonal theory of personality.

Perry, H. S., and M. L. Gawel (eds.), *The Collected Works of Harry Stack Sullivan, M.D.,* Vol. I. New York: Norton, 1953.

Perry, H. S., M. L. Gawel, and M. Gibbon (eds.), *The Collected Works of Harry Stack Sullivan, M.D.,* Vol. II. New York: Norton, 1956.

Ruesch, J., and G. Bateson, *Communication: The Social Matrix of Society.* New York: Norton, 1951.

Sahakian, W. S. (ed.), *Psychology of Personality: Readings in Theory.* Chicago: Rand McNally, 1965.

> Excerpts from Sullivan's theory.

Saltzman, L., *Developments in Psychoanalysis.* New York: Grune & Stratton, 1962.

> The innovations of Horney and Sullivan.

Sarason, I. G., *Personality: An Objective Approach.* New York: Wiley, 1966.

> Sullivan a neo-Freudian.

PERIODICALS

Arieti, S., The double methodology in the study of personality and its disorders, *Amer. J. Psychother.,* 1957, *11,* 532–547.

> Fromm and Sullivan on the idiographic–historical and nomothetic–scientific approaches to personality study.

Blitsten, D. R., Harry Stack Sullivan's suggestions concerning the place of small groups in personality development, *Autonomous Groups Bull.,* 1954, 9, 3–12.

Chrzanowski, G., What is psychotherapy? The viewpoint of the Sullivanian school, *Ann. Psychother. Monogr.,* 1959, No. 1, pp. 31–36.

Goldman, G. D., Group psychotherapy from the point of view of various schools of psychology: III. Some applications of Harry Stack Sullivan's theories to group psychotherapy, *Int. J. Group Psychother.,* 1957, 7, 385–391.

> Use of parataxis in group work.

Green, M. R., Prelogical processes and participant communication, *Psychiat. Quart.,* 1961, *35,* 726–740.

> Sullivan on prelogical processes.

Green, M. R., The roots of Sullivan's concept of self, *Psychiat. Quart.*, 1962, 36, 271–282.

Harris, C., Sullivan's concept of scientific method as applied to psychiatry, *Phil. Sci.*, 1954, 21, 33–43.

Kates, S. L., First-impression formation and authoritarianism, *Hum. Relat.*, 1959, 12, 277–286.

> One aspect of. Sullivan's concept of perceiving others in terms of self proves to be correct.

Mumford, R. S., Traditional psychiatry, Freud, and H. S. Sullivan, *Compr. Psychiat.*, 1961, 2, 1–10.

Nydes, J., Interpersonal relations: Personal and depersonalized, *Psychoanalysis*, 1951, 1, 36–47.

> A critique of Sullivan's theory as being very limited.

Rose, L. A. R., A test of three stages of Harry Stack Sullivan's developmental theory of personality: Juvenile era, preadolescence, and early adolescence stages, *Dissert. Abstr.*, 1965, 25, 6800–6801.

Siberman, H. L., The psychology and psychiatry of Harry Stack Sullivan, *Psychiat. Quart. Suppl.*, 1955, 29, 7–22.

Smith, D. E. P., Interdisciplinary approach to the genesis of anxiety, *Educ. Theor.*, 1956, 6, 222–231.

> Compares Freud, Rank, Mowrer, Angyal, Goldstein, Lewin, Rogers, Kierkegaard, and Sullivan on theories of anxiety.

Strupp, H. H., Infantile sexuality in the theories of Freud and Sullivan, *Complex*, 1952, 7, 51–62.

Thompson, C., Concepts of the self in interpersonal theory, *Amer. J. Psychother.*, 1958, 12, 5–17.

> Examines confusion of self system and concept of self in Sullivanian terms.

SOCIAL-ANALYTICAL
[FROMM]

*He who knows nothing, loves nothing. He who can do
nothing understands nothing. He who understands nothing
is worthless. But he who understands also loves, notices,
sees. . . . The more knowledge is inherent in a thing, the
greater the love. . . . Anyone who imagines that all fruits
ripen at the same time as strawberries, knows nothing
about grapes.*

Paracelsus

SOME BIOGRAPHICAL DATA

Erich Fromm was born in Frankfurt, Germany, on March 23, 1900. The
University of Heidelberg awarded him the Ph.D. in 1922. He married Frieda
Reichmann on June 16, 1926. After being divorced from her he was married
to Henny Gurland on July 24, 1944. Following her death, he married Annis
Freeman on December 18, 1953. After receiving his degree from the Univer-
sity of Heidelberg he studied at the University of Munich and later at the
Psychoanalytic Institute in Berlin. He served as lecturer at the Psychoanalytic
Institute of Frankfurt, the Institute for Social Research, and the University of
Frankfurt during the period from 1929 to 1932. In 1934 he went to the
International Institute for Social Research in New York City and stayed until
1939. Fromm was guest lecturer at Columbia during the years 1940–1941, was
a member of the faculty at Bennington College, 1941–1950, and delivered the
Terry Lectures at Yale in 1949. He was a Fellow on the faculty at the
William Alanson White Institute of Psychiatry in New York.

Fromm has been Professor National at the University of Mexico since
1951 and he is the Director of the Mexican Psychoanalytic Institute in
Mexico City. He has also been on the staff at Michigan State University since
1957. He is a Fellow of the New York Academy of Science and a member of
the Washington Psychoanalytical Society and of the Mexican National
Academy of Medicine.

INTRODUCTION

Erich Fromm is a "socio-psychoanalyst." He is well trained as an analyst. Fromm has had an optimistic approach to the human personality, feeling that all men are ultimately idealists and hope for a life beyond pure physical satisfaction. However, Fromm is not a dreamer. In *May Man Prevail?* (1961) he reveals a tremendous sense of urgency about the atomic-nuclear threat. Although he is not directly against current psychological research, he does wonder whether it will do any good in saving mankind. While the comparative psychologists and the factor analysts crank out their new data, he feels the world may blow apart around them.

Individual behavior is shaped by society. But counter to the Freudians, Fromm feels that there is hope because man has the capacity to solve his own problems. Since man has created most of his problems beyond those of weather and natural phenomena, he can solve these problems. In short, man can unwind what he has wound up, but it will take just as long to unwind his problems as it took to wind them up. Consequently, Erich Fromm does not look for quick solutions.

Since his arrival in the United States Fromm has been an exceedingly popular symposium speaker. He has at different times spoken on creativity, appeared at many APA meetings, and discussed Zen Buddhism, and psychoanalysis. He is in demand as a platform speaker.

Fromm considers man to be an animal, but with certain differences. "Man is the only animal who finds his own existence a problem which he has to solve and from which he cannot escape. In the same sense man is the only animal who knows he must die" (*The Sane Society*, pp. 23–24).

THE SYSTEM, THEORY, OR ESSENTIAL FEATURES

General Considerations

Erich Fromm thinks in broad historical terms, as did Jung. He uses human history as a laboratory in his own study of human personality. He feels that man is a history-made animal, primarily the product of social influences. In contrast to Freud, who believed that personalities make society, Fromm feels that society in general makes the personality. He thus reverses the causal order of Freud. Fromm sees the differences in man's personality as being due to social processes. All men must eat, drink, breathe, defecate, sleep, rest, and exercise, but society molds basic behavior into different forms. The most beautiful and ugly of man's actions do not spring from his biological system but from environmental forces. As a consequence, man has transformed himself into a thing. He now worships the products of his own hand. Erich Fromm feels that this is the idolatry of materialism. Man even worships the mechanisms of war that he has created, such as the atomic bomb. Quoting Emerson, who felt that "Things are in the saddle and ride mankind," Fromm thinks we can still put man back in the saddle and let him decide his own destiny.

In regard to democratic order, Erich Fromm feels we have mistaken democracy and equality as "sameness" rather than "one-ness" (*The Art of Loving*, p. 15). He does not believe that because man has a democratic way of living we must homogenize humanity, but rather that each variant human being can be directed toward the same goal but not always along the same path.

Man is not instinctual even though he may have a general or uniform mode of behavior. Also, man does not satisfy his physiological needs in an animal-like way. He cooks his meat; he does not eat it raw. The higher the species, the better developed is the brain and the less instinctual, therefore, is the behavior. Thus, it is possible that more learning, reasoning, and adaptable behavior can be and have been achieved by the human animal. The development of each human personality, as the human being goes through childhood Fromm believes, somewhat recapitulates what the human race has gone through. Out of experience with his fellow men, through the prime psychological agent of the family, the child emerges into adulthood and has a social character. Fromm believes the family is an overpowering and extremely strong force in the formation of any personality.

Specific Considerations

DICHOTOMIES OF EXISTENCE

Erich Fromm feels that man is surrounded by contradictions which are of a polar nature. These contradictions are man-made and hence can be man solved. Thus, with one exception, our problems in life are not insoluble. The problem of *existential dichotomies* he feels has no solution. Fromm is referring primarily to religion. Some of the dichotomies of existence are these man lives but he must die; man is part of nature but he also transcends it man loves peace but wages war; in some societies man has abundance, but through inequality of wealth many people face starvation; man has a future but he cannot achieve his future personally (he must do it through a social order); man wants freedom but he also wants security; and man likes to believe that he behaves rationally but he is also unreasonable and immoral and has a strong urge to behave emotionally. Other dichotomies of existence are that man wishes both to submit and to dominate. He wants to be alone but has an inexpressible urge to be with others. He denies his identity with nature as a natural animal but is part of nature, and always will be. He wants governmental protection but chafes under governmental restrictions. He wants to be fully individualized and be himself, but he also wants strongly to be socialized and to be like everyone else. Therefore, there is a strong dichotomy in man's existence and a split between the intellect and the emotions. Erich Fromm has taken considerable trouble to spell out his ideas in his well-known book *Escape from Freedom.* Man now has a portion of negative freedom. He is "free from" certain things, but he is definitely not "free to" do as he wishes. In the progress of human society mankind has developed a "marketing orientation" or "what he is worth," but he also wants a "productive orientation." Man should create out of his own individual capacities a productive way of life. Unfortunately he strives for "what he is worth" rather than "what he can do." The pleasure of satiation is not differentiated from the pleasure of production. Mann finds himself gluttonous rather than creative.

Fromm feels that humanity's problems may be resolved by restoring the unity of man and nature. Man needs an orientation, a devotion, and ideals which are beyond his own selfish purposes. Witthout an aim, an objective, an ideal, man will continue to be lost in the dichotomies of existence. Looking back at the history of man, Fromm believes that nature is a continuing process, and it has always involved a creative activity. Thus man may still continue to emerge and resolve his dichotomies because he has continued throughout thousands of years to move beyond a pure animal state.

The name Fromm gives to the total social order which may achieve the resolvement of the dichotomies is Humanistic Communitarian Socialism. He is not referring to any political party by this label, nor even any national structure. He means rather a total world order which uses the humanistic approach, shares in a communal way, produces in a socialistic order, and will thus achieve the best possible state of existence for the human race.

MECHANISMS OF ESCAPE

There are four mechanisms of escape from the dichotomies of existence. The first is sadism toward others who are dependent upon one. He may destroy them or try to swallow up all of his problems. The second mechanism is masochism, in which the single personality gives up or submits to a stronger personality or a stronger group and in so doing tries to escape loneliness. The lonely masochistic personality may even ignore the bestiality of the group in order to belong to it, have it engulf him, and identify with its strength, even though it hurts him in the process. The third mechanism is wanton destructiveness. The human personality may try to escape the feeling of powerlessness by crushing any outside force. The adolescent delinquent who senselessly destroys property is using this form of escape mechanism. The fourth mechanism, which many people follow, is automaton conformity. The

automaton personality simply has a blind acceptance of all of the dichotomies
of life. If he can't beat them, he must join them. He totally lacks any spontaneity and has no true experience of what is really his own life. In a social
group he is full of meaningless chatter, which carries over to much of his
thinking and takes the place of true communication with his fellow men.

TEMPERAMENT AND CHARACTER

Fromm believes that all therapy and all of life, too, must stand on moral
issues. Ultimately value judgments always determine action. There are problems of right and wrong in personality dynamics, in life itself, in religion, in
any ethical consideration of behavior. Fromm does not believe there are good
and bad people; there are people who do good and bad things. The human
personality is made up of temperament and character. The temperament is
the basic constitutional organic stuff with which one is born. Character,
however, is formed through social pressures and influence. Character may
have and usually does have two parts: the individual character and the social
character. The individual character comes primarily out of man's innate
biological makeup plus the valuable things his family may or may not do for
him. The social character is molded by society, and man shares his social
character with society. The considerations of temperament and character may
be much like Adler's style of life. In man's orientation to the world he may
follow the primary path of assimilation, or being oriented toward things. The
second kind of orientation would be that of socialization, or being oriented
toward people. This is another example of the dichotomy of existence.

LOVE

In the final analysis of man's troubled existence, Fromm fervently feels that
the answer to the problem is the capacity of man to love. All of humanity is
starved for love, but being loved is no more important than loving someone.
The need to love and be loved is reciprocal. To Fromm love is a faculty or
function of behavior, not an object cathexis. We do not speak of true love,
therefore, if we speak of a love object as if something were possessed. Love is
an art and must be practiced and mastered like an art. In any art form the
artist must do two things: master the theory of his art and master the practice
of it. Of all the potentials and dynamics in man's behavior, love is probably
the most active and will continue to be so.

Fromm mentions four basic elements to love: care, responsibility, respect, and knowledge. All must be interdependent. None is more important
than any other.

In his powerfully written book *The Art of Loving* Fromm proposes five
types of love. They are described below:

Brotherly love is the most fundamental, the strongest, and the most
underlying kind of love. It is a love between equals.

Motherly love is the love and care for the helpless, the wanting to make them strong and independent; the greatest test of motherly love is the capacity to let go or to wean; it is a love between unequals.

Erotic love is usually allied with sexual experience, a "craving for complete fusion," and is what most consider the only kind of love. It is exclusive and inclined toward jealousy. (Fromm doubts it has anything to do with true love, because love is basically a phenomenon not of sexual satisfaction or discharge but of intimacy.) It is a love between equals.

Self-love is the care, responsibility, respect, and knowledge of self (not sinful as often assumed because of Calvinistic rigidity). Self-love and love for others are not mutually exclusive; one must love self in order to be able to love others. Selfish people are not capable of self-love, but only of vanity.

Love of God has the highest value, is the most desirable good, and emphasizes care, respect, responsibility, and especially knowledge. It must be remembered that love is an act or a function, not an object cathexis. It is essential to human existence because man must have something perfect to aspire to. Fromm quotes Meister Eckhart: "By knowing God I take him to myself. By loving God, I penetrate him" (*Art of Loving*, p. 81).

FIVE HUMAN NEEDS

Erich Fromm says there are at least five human needs which must be met in order for man to fulfill completely a true personality. They are as follows:

Transcendence: to go above being just an animal, to improve and learn, to increase in material things.
Identity: knowing one's true self, being able to identify with others.
Rootedness: return to nature or a natural way of existence and not artificial symbols, gaining satisfaction from work and not just working for money.
Frame of orientation: a consistent, good way of life, to be creative and aware and respond, live a reasonable life in a reasoning world.
Relatedness: feeling a oneness with fellow men and with self.

SUMMARY

Erich Fromm is a trained psychoanalyst who uses history for his psychological data. He feels that personality begins out of organic nature which very soon merges with, and is organized and molded by, society. Because man so highly prizes security, he has given up some of his freedom, so that he now has freedom from pain and threat but has lost the greater freedom to do things as he wishes. Fromm places extreme importance on the capacity to love and be loved. He feels that without love a personality cannot exist satisfactorily. And in the final analysis, Fromm continues to be an optimist. He maintains that man has inherent in his own personality and in the social systems he organizes the capacity to solve the problems he himself has created.

DELIMITATIONS

There are no gross omissions from Fromm's work, except that Fromm's writing and thinking and speaking have been extremely abbreviated in the above treatment.

BIBLIOGRAPHY

PRIMARY SOURCES

BOOKS

Fromm, E., *Escape from Freedom*. New York: Holt, Rinehart & Winston, 1941.
Fromm, E., Hitler and the Nazi authoritarian character structure, in T. M. Newcomb and E. S. Hartley (eds.), *Readings in Social Psychology*. New York: Holt, Rinehart & Winston, 1947.
Fromm, E., *Man for Himself: An Inquiry into the Psychology of Ethics*. New York: Holt, Rinehart & Winston, 1947.
Fromm, E., Individual and social origins in neurosis, in C. Kluckhohn and H. A. Murray (eds.), *Personality in Nature, Society and Culture*. New York Knopf, 1948 and 1953.
Fromm, E., The Oedipus Complex and the Oedipus Myth, in R. N. Anshen (ed.), *The Family: Its Functions and Destiny*. New York: Harper & Row 1948, pp. 334–358.
Fromm, E., Psychoanalytic characterology and its application to the understanding of culture, in S. S. Sargent and M. W. Smith (eds.), *Culture and Personality*. New York: Viking Press, 1949.
Fromm, E., *Psychoanalysis and Religion*. New Haven, Conn.: Yale University Press, 1950.
Fromm, E., *The Forgotten Language*. New York: Holt, Rinehart & Winston 1951.
Fromm, E., Man-woman, in M. M. Hughes (ed.), *The People in Your Life*. New York: Knopf, 1951, pp. 3–27.
Fromm, E., *The Sane Society*. New York: Holt, Rinehart & Winston, 1955.

Fromm, E., *The Art of Loving*. New York: Harper & Row, 1956.

Fromm, E., *Sigmund Freud's Mission: An Analysis of His Personality and Influence*. New York: Harper & Row, 1959.

Fromm, E., Values, psychology, and human existence, in A. H. Maslow (ed.), *New Knowledge in Human Values*. New York: Harper & Row, 1959, pp. 151–164.

> Also in J. C. Coleman, *Personality Dynamics and Effective Behavior*. Chicago: Scott, Foresman, 1960, pp. 522–527.

Fromm, E., D. T. Suzuki, and R. DeMartino, *Zen Buddhism and Psychoanalysis*. New York: Harper & Row, 1960.

Fromm, E., *Marx's Concept of Man*. New York: Ungar, 1961.

> Marx and the alienation of man from himself.

Fromm, E., *May Man Prevail?: An Inquiry into the Facts and Fiction of Foreign Policy*. Garden City, N.Y.: Doubleday, 1961.

> Also published in hardback and paperback editions.

Fromm, E., Rational and irrational faith, in A. E. Kuenzli (ed.), *Reconstruction in Religion: A Symposium*. Boston: Beacon Press, 1961.

Fromm, E., *The Heart of Man: Its Genius for Good and Evil*. New York: Harper & Row, 1964.

> Edited by R. N. Anshen.

Fromm, E., Are we sane? in W. D. Nunokawa (ed.), *Readings in Abnormal Psychology: Human Values and Abnormal Behavior*. Chicago: Scott, Foresman, 1965.

Fromm, E., Character and the social process, in G. Lindzey and C. S. Hall (eds.), *Theories of Personality: Primary Sources and Research*. New York: Wiley, 1965, pp. 117–124.

> A short selection from his 1941 book, *Escape from Freedom*.

Fromm, E., Humanistic psychoanalysis, in W. S. Sahakian (ed.), *Psychology of Personality: Readings in Theory*. Chicago: Rand McNally, 1965, pp. 117–133.

> Bits and pieces of Fromm's writings.

Fromm, E., *The Dogma of Christ and Other Essays on Religion, Psychology and Culture*. Garden City, N.Y.: Doubleday, 1966.

> An anchor book.

Fromm, E., Values, psychology and human existence, in D. E. Hamachek (ed.), *Human Dynamics in Psychology and Education: Selected Readings*. Boston: Allyn & Bacon, 1968, pp. 665–673.

PERIODICALS

Fromm, E., Selfishness and self-love, *Psychiatry*, 1939, 2, 507–523.

Fromm, E., Sex and character, *Psychiatry*, 1943, 6, 21–31.

Fromm, E., Individual and social origins of neurosis, *Amer. Sociol. Rev.*, 1944, 9, 380–384.

Fromm, E., The contribution of social sciences to mental hygiene, *Proc. 4th Int. Congr. Ment. Hlth*, 1951, pp. 38–42.

Fromm, E., Remarks on the problem of free association, *Psychiat. Res. Rep.*, 1955, 2, 1–6.

Fromm, E., Love and its disintegration, *Pastoral Psychol.*, 1956, 7(68), 37–44.

Fromm, E., El carácter revolucionario (The revolutionary personality), *Rev. Psicoanal. Psiquiat. Psicol.*, 1966, 3, 25–35.

> Revolutionary is the independent personality capable of disobedience; identifies with humanity.

Fromm, E., *et al.*, El complijo de Edipo: Comentarios al "Analisis de la fobia de un niño de cinco años" (The Oedipus complex: Commentaries on the "analysis of a five year old child's phobia"), *Rev. Psicoanal. Psiquiat. Psicol.*, 1966, 4, 26–33.

Fromm, E., Psychological problems of aging, *J. Rehabilit.*, 1966, 32, 10–12, 51–57.

Fromm, E., La situación psicologica del hombre en la mundo moderno (The psychological situation of modern man), *Rev. Psicoanal. Psiquiat. Psicol.*, 1967, 5, 6–16.

Fromm, E., Teoria freudiana de la agresividad y la destructividad (Freudian theory of aggressiveness and destructiveness), *Rev. Psicoanal. Psiquiat. Psicol.*, 1968, 8, 19–48.

> Challenges Freud's assumption of the presence of a constant amount of aggressive–destructive behavior between individuals and between different groups.

SUGGESTED READINGS

BOOKS

Arastch, A. R., *Rumi the Persian: Rebirth in Creativity and Love*. Lahore, Kistan Sl: Muhammad Ashraf, 1965.

> Preface by Erich Fromm.

Brown, I. A. C., *Freud and the Post-Freudians*. Baltimore: Penguin Books, 1961

> Horney, Fromm, and Sullivan also included.

Coleman, J. C., *Personality Dynamics and Effective Behavior*. Chicago: Scott Foresman, 1960.

Evans, R. I., *Dialogue with Erich Fromm*. New York: Harper & Row, 1966.

Fromm, E., *Sigmund Freud's Mission: An Analysis of His Personality and Influence*. New York: Grove Press, 1963.

Hammond, G. B., *Man in Estrangement: A Comparison of the Thought of Paul Tillich and Erich Fromm.* Nashville, Tenn.: Vanderbilt University Press, 1965.

Maddi, S., *Personality Theories: A Comparative Analysis.* Homewood, Ill.: Dorsey Press, 1968.

> Excellent précise of Fromm as a perfection and fulfillment model theorist.

Munroe, R. L., *Schools of Psychoanalytic Thought.* New York: Holt, Rinehart & Winston, 1955.

> Analysis and integration of Freud, Adler, Jung, Rank, Fromm, Horney, Sullivan, *et al.*

Sarason, I. G., *Personality: An Objective Approach.* New York: Wiley, 1966.

> Treats Fromm and Horney as equals.

Schaar, J. H., *Escape from Authority: The Perspectives of Erich Fromm.* New York: Basic Books, 1961.

Wells, H. K., *The Failure of Psychoanalysis: From Freud to Fromm.* New York: International Publishers, 1963.

PERIODICALS

Arieti, S., The double methodology in the study of personality and its disorders, *Amer. J. Psychother.*, 1957, *11*, 532–547.

> Fromm and Sullivan on the idiographic–historical and nomothetic–scientific approaches to personality study.

Brams, J., From Freud to Fromm, *Psychol. Today*, 1968, *1*, 32–35, 64–65.

> Freud was primarily the psychologist, while Fromm is more the social philosopher.

Franck, I., The concept of human nature: A philosophical analysis of the concept of human nature in the writings of G. W. Allport, S. E. Asch, Erich Fromm, A. H. Maslow, and C. R. Rogers, *Dissert. Abstr.*, 1966, *27*, 1079.

de la Fuente-Muniz, R., Fromm's approach to the study of personality, *Psychiat. Res. Rep.*, 1955, *2*, 7–14.

James, W. T., Karen Horney and Erich Fromm in relation to Alfred Adler, *Indiv. Psychol. Bull.*, 1947, *6*, 105–116.

Kaplan, M. F., and E. Singer, Dogmatism and sensory alienation: An empirical investigation, *J. Consult. Psychol.*, 1953, *27*, 486–491.

> Investigates certain aspects of the concept of "alienation" as employed by Fromm.

Yonker, H. J., Ambiguities of love: An inquiry into the psychology of Erich Fromm, *Dissert. Abstr.*, 1961, *22*, 1245.

VIII

Prospects for Personality Theory

PART VIII consists of one chapter which deals with a synopsis or summary of the material covered in the present book and with speculations for the future of personality theory. The first section is a pedagogical device for students and instructors. The second section is open to all. What will the next two decades bring for personality theory? What will personologists probably be doing twenty years from now? The reader, as well as this writer, can prognosticate to their hearts' desire since the prediction of the future is everyone's game.

16

PERSONALITY THEORY:
SYNOPSIS
AND SPECULATIONS

INTRODUCTION

What can we say now after examining the work of nineteen theorists? One thing is certain. None of the theories are identical, yet all are the same in some way. To any reader who has had the energy and interest to follow through all of the nineteen theorists in this book, it should be apparent upon reviewing them that personality theories are more complementary than contradictory. There are more areas in which they agree than in which they disagree. This is not a particularly startling discovery since personality theories are dealing with behavior and humans can behave only in circumscribed ways (Mehrabian, 1968).

The recognition but obviously not the formulation of the personality theories themselves is relatively new in psychology. Some of the theories, of course, particularly Freud's, go back to the turn of the century. However, starting around the mid-1930s personality theory began to find its place as an academic field in the preparation of psychologists. Thus, personality theory has become a part of the curriculum only since approximately 1935. In 1957 an interesting development took place. Prior to that time, personality theory was usually taught as a psychoanalytic theory, or one or two—at the most six—theorists were studied during the semester. When Hall and Lindzey's book *Theories of Personality* came out, although not written as a textbook, it became enormously popular because it was the only thing of its kind. Thus, this monumental work almost by itself created a course which began to be called Theories of Personality. Since 1957 many other excellent books have appeared, expanding the number of theorists and the treatment of each theory.

We still hear the almost plaintive request for an all-encompassing theory of personality which will finally serve as a neat, inclusive theory of human behavior. Of course, this is not possible and for more than the usual reason given, which is that personality theory has not progressed far enough and does not have sufficient methodology. The other reasons are not in rebuttal to having a single theory, but apply more to the question of whether a single theory is all that necessary. We refer again to Cattell's observation that because there is one word (in this case two words, personality theory) there must then be one concept or one overall idea. This is sophistry. Have other fields of endeavor been hampered because they do not have one theory which gives most or all the answers? Obviously not. We have but to look at politics, sociology, medicine and all its ramifications, law, and many, many other behavioral systems, none of which have a singular theory yet all of which appear to be productive and important to human existence. And how about the field of psychology itself, wherein are many learning theories, theories of therapy, testing theories, theories of perception, and so on? Perhaps the personologists or those most interested in personality theory are asking for something which never could or even should exist: a single, all-embracing, unified theory of personality.

Again, in retrospect, one finds a good deal of difficulty in generalizing about the material in this book. Thus we have problems in generalizing from animals to people and in generalizing from one theory to another theory. And most emphatically we cannot generalize from one human being to another human being without falling into many traps.

Finally, in looking back over the chapters of this book we discover frequently that a theory of personality is not necessarily a theory of therapy. Or saying it in reverse, a theory of therapy is not necessarily a good theory of personality (Maddi, 1968).

SYNOPSIS

As we have stated briefly before, all theories seem to be right at times and all theories seem to be wrong at times. Why? Perhaps for the same reason that a stopped clock does tell the time accurately twice a day, providing, of course, that the viewer looks at it at precisely the proper times.

One of the most difficult problems in studying personality theories is to ascertain first whether the theory is asking the right type of question and second whether we as students of personality theory are asking the right type of question of the theory? Theories cannot be all things to all men; they can only be what man himself constructs out of necessity. Rychlak in discussing theory at the end of his book wisely states, "In a tactic of this sort *we ask the right type of question*. We begin tying this theorist to that intellectual tradition, no matter how he might wiggle to free himself and shout in the name of purity that he will be his own man. As a cultural product, man's knowledge is the knowledge of men. The more we study our supposedly unique natures and decry our unique problems—and also read history—the more we see that there have been men like us, saying the same sorts of 'unique' things for centuries, only in different contexts" (Rychlak, 1968; p. 455, italics added).

One of the best suggestions for review and synopsis purposes, which too few students take, is to reread the first chapter of any book. Perhaps that is the way to find out what the reader has learned now that he is at the end of this book. It should be recalled that the first chapter dealt with four problems: problems of definition, problems of using and constructing personality theories, problems of theory testing, and problems of research methodology. Now it should be obvious that the problems still exist—they have not been solved—but many, many approaches to them are being taken. In other words, there are better ways of thinking about theories and their usefulness, particularly as we look up the research which each theory has promoted and which is conducted to test that particular theory. The suggestion here is a serious one. Reread Chapter 1.

Various methods may be employed in summarizing the work of the preceding theorists. One method is listing the principles, which has been done in the following outline. Having noted the principles, we must ask ourselves, "Are all the principles equally important?"

Freud: Pleasure, Reality, Tension Reduction, Polarity, Repetition, Compulsion (6).

Murray: Regnancy, Motivation, Longitudinal, Physiological Processes, Abstract, Uniqueness, Role (7).

Jung: Polarity, Equivalence, Entropy, Self-Actualization, Unconscious States, Teleology (6).

Adler: Inferiority, Superiority, Style of Life, Creative Self, Conscious Self, Fictional Goals, Social Interest (7).

Horney: Optimism–Positivism, Society–Culture, Character Structure, Self-Concept, Complementation–Conflict, Self-Analysis (6).

Moreno: Social Atom, Tele, Warming Up, Role Playing, Spontaneity, Creativity, Cultural Conserve, Group Development, Sociogenetic Law, Measurement (10).

Allport: Motivation, Learning, Contemporaneity, Uniqueness, Ego or Self, Continuity–Discontinuity, Traits–Trends–Tendency–Temperament (7).

Rogers: Self, Self-Actualization, Self-Maintenance, Self-Enhancement (4).

Murphy: (Themes) Biological Personality, Emerging and Integrating Personality, Socialized Personality, Human Potentialities or New Perspectives (4).

Sheldon: Body–Temperament, Continuous Variable, Inductive–Empirical, Objective Measurement, Consistency of Somatotype, Behavioral Environment (6).

Cattell: Methodology, Dynamic/Structural, Developmental, Social (4).

Eysenck: Biological, Methodological, Dynamic/Structural, Empirical/Learning (4).

The student of personality theory may now summarize these seventy-one principles according to their importance, their necessity, or the completeness with which they treat each personality theory.

A second method of summarizing personality theories is suggesting explanations of behavioral phenomena which are not mentioned in the present chapters. For example, is the individual now sophisticated enough to be able to explain at least to himself with some degree of satisfaction why an individual forgets, loses his temper, saves his money, becomes ashamed, gets a divorce, etc.? It is frequently interesting to have students match their explanations whith those of other students. Often this is more a test of the student's ability to understand the theory rather than of the usefulness of the theory to explain behavior. It is for the former reason that explanation has been included in each of the major chapters.

Another method in which personality theories may be summarized would be to rearrange the theories from the most significant to the least significant according to a number of criteria. Thus, we may rearrange the theories on the basis of their emphasizing one or all of the following: heredity, which would include instincts; the developmental process from infancy to old age; idio-graphic *vs.* nomothetic concepts; the use and concept of self; what social forces are considered to impinge upon the individual's behavior; simplicity—i.e., going from the most complex, convoluted theories to the simplest theories; and, most meaningful of all, how applicable the theory is to research.

Theories may also be compared as to their terminology. How well or adequately does the theory use the vast concept of self or self-enhancement or self-concept? How well does the theory employ the term *ego* or *polarity* or *homeostasis* or *introversion/extraversion* or *life-style* or *needs* or *cognition*, etc.?

Theories may be rearranged in accordance with Rychlak's concept of the dialectic *vs.* the demonstrative traditional concepts. Rychlak suggests, for example, that we may use the dialectic tradition or clinically oriented tradi-tion to study the theory's emphasis or components in regard to such as the following: idiographic quality, R–R laws, stressing of theory, degree of subjectiveness, ethics of freedom, the life-style or developmental line, tender-minded qualities, the nature of applied research, soft determinism, behavior as being active and stimulating, the question of nurture, or the degree to which the theory uses hypothetical constructs. In contrast to this, we may judge a theory on the opposite end of the continuum, in which we would find demonstrative or experimentally oriented theories, in terms of: degree of nomothetic emphasis, S–R laws in experimentation, stressing of method, degree of objectivity, ethics of control, emphasis on short-line development rather than life-style development, tough-mindedness, the basic nature of research, degree of hard determinism, the fact that behavior is passive in responding, the degree of nature in the behaving organism, or the use of intervening variables. The above adaptation of Rychlak's list may help the student of personality theory to get a better synopsis of that which he is studying (Rychlak, 1968, p. 456).

Theories may be studied from the point of view of their proneness to fit into one of two streams. The first is correlational psychology, in which the factors are correlated with one another, and the second is experimental psychology, in which the behaving organism is manipulated to some extent (Cronbach, 1966).

Finally, as was suggested before, one may return to Chapter 1 to be confronted with the questions: What should a theory do? What should it promote? How should it arrange the data? How should it function? Maddi finds there are six functions that a personality theory should perform: impor-tant, operational, parsimonious, stimulating, usable, and empirically valid (Maddi, 1968). Back in 1957, Hall and Lindzey suggested five functions that a personality theory should perform: It should be simple and understandable, it should be useful, it should help to arrange the data in orderly fashion, it should clarify thinking, and above all it should predict human behavior accurately (Hall and Lindzey, 1957). Rychlak suggests four functions for a theory: descriptive, delimiting, generative, and intergrative (Rychlak, 1968)

SPECULATIONS

What will be the future of personality theories? We suggest sixteen possibil ities, all or none of which may happen within the next twenty years.

1. If the world continues as it has, the layman will become more and more interested in his own behavior and what the psychologist has to offer in explaining it. Therefore, it seems to us that the lay individual will want to know what we are doing, what the results are, and whether it is worth his money to support psychological research in personality theory.

2. Will behavior theory supplant or displace personality theory? There are two ways of looking at this question. Farber, in Lindzey and Hall, states ". . . one may anticipate that as behavior theories become more precise and more comprehensive they will encompass more and more phenomena now referred to under the rubric of personality." "I, for one, look forward to the day, which I do not expect to see myself, when personality theories are regarded as historical curiosities" (Lindzey and Hall, 1965, p. 442). On the other hand, Berlyne, in a long and sophisticated chapter on behavior theory a personality theory, concludes his remarks with "If behavior theory as person ality theory belongs largely to the future, the same future may present us with personality theory as behavior theory!" (Berlyne, 1968, p. 682).

3. It is interesting to note the progression of ideas as personality theorist work longer and longer in the field and become older. We refer here to their growing interest in religion. Some theorists have turned in their later years to the study and importance of religion in human behavior. It should be remembered that Jung, Allport, and Fromm have always considered religiou behavior a fundamental part of human existence. However, in the work of Horney and Maslow and to some degree Erikson, particularly in the eighth age of ego development, and finally in the great emphasis that Mowrer place on religion in his integrity therapy viewpoints, there is ample evidence that religion may become more and more an important part of personality theory This, of course, will not make some of the experimentally oriented person ologists particularly happy.

4. Computer simulation is looming larger and larger in personality theory. However, how long will computer simulation and the ramifications of it continue to titillate the personologist? What one can do with a computer in simulating personality problems and behavioral paradigms has captured the interest of some very talented experimentalists (Abelson and Carroll, 1965 Colby, 1967; Coleman, 1961; Green, 1963; Gullahorn and Gullahorn, 1963 Loehlin, 1965, 1968; Simon and Newell, 1962, 1964; Tomkins and Messick 1963).

5. Along with the ability to handle statistical data more sophisticatedly, accurately, and quickly, we may also assume that measurement techniques of the personologist will definitely improve. If nothing else happens, at least the techniques and devices that the research-oriented psychologist uses will become more and more refined. Whether new ideas emerge from them or not is, of course, a moot point (Shontz, 1965).

6. If current trends continue, we may feel quite assured that there will be in the field of personality theory more and more interdisciplinary research in which the biologist, the sociologist, the social worker, the psychiatrist, and the psychologist will work in a team or group approach.

7. Following the leads of Cattell and Eysenck, there certainly will be, apropos of the computer work mentioned above, more and more multivariate handling of data rather than the simple correlational statistics of one-to-one relationships (Byrne, 1966).

8. Mathematical models are coming to the fore. How well they handle the complications of personality theory only the future can tell. However, the earlier work and suggestions of von Bertalanffy may be an indicator: ". . . the attempt to give a general definition of the concept of organized system to classify logically the various types of systems and work out mathematical models for describing them," may be part of the future for personality theory (von Bertalanffy, 1968).

9. Some psychologists believe that the developmental aspects of personality have been inadequately treated. The feeling is that adults and the elderly have as much personality as any child or adolescent and that human personality does not stop its dynamics simply because psychology doesn't study it. Thus, we may assume that personality theory will become more and more interested in the older adult (Bischof, 1969; Norbeck et al., 1968).

10. It seems obvious that whatever differences may exist between racial groups will have to be studied if for no other reason than the pressure and unrest concerning blacks and whites. Thus, the future of personality theory may also concern itself with racial differences if and wherever they exist.

11. We may also find differences between cultural and ethnic groups and the personalities that seem to emerge from these factors.

12. Current trends in psychobiological and biochemical components of human behavior offer still another possibility for future efforts in the study of man's personality.

13. Following the suggestion of Mehrabian, perhaps personality theories are going more in the direction of "theories of the middle ground." Thus, this type of theory has a limited area of specialization rather than the all-encompassing areas of earlier theories of personality (Mehrabian, 1968, p. 180).

14. There appears to be more and more emphasis, particularly from the clinicians, on gathering quantities of data simply to describe one person. Byrne acknowledges this by saying, "In the future, when all basic personality

dimensions have been identified and an enormous body of data has been assembled, the task of producing a complete personality description of just one subject will be a formidable one. Very likely the need for such a description will be limited. Possibly the only justifiable use will be when a key individual is being selected for a position in which his behavior in response to a variety of situations has widespread consequences for others" (Byrne, 1966, p. 500).

15. Probably there will always be at least a parallel between theories of personality as the psychologist studies and views them and the entire panoply of work done in the arts through drama, literature, and painting and sculpture. Whether the research-oriented psychologist approves of this or not, it appears to be in the future.

16. And, if history tells us anything, the entire field of personology will repeat itself over and over even back to the work of William James. It may, however, use more statistical finesse and thus give new names to old truths.

Are personality theories worth knowing about? Worth studying? Worth the time and trouble to research their concepts? Gardner Murphy concludes that they are. "Lack of knowledge about human beings is not a trivial but a major threat to life. *Lack of knowledge about personality is perhaps the central core of the issue that is most relevant for us today:* the issue of understanding what human beings can become under a new set of social arrangements" (Norbeck *et al.*, 1968, p. 38; italics added).

The present author can think of no more appropriate method to end this book on personality theories than to quote Dorpfeld's dictum, *"There is nothing more practical than a good theory."*

BIBLIOGRAPHY

PRIMARY SOURCES

BOOKS

Allport, G. W., *Personality and Social Encounter*. Boston: Beacon Press, 1960.
Berlyne, D. E., Behavior theory as personality theory, in E. F. Borgatta and W. W. Lambert, *Handbook of Personality Theory and Research*. Chicago: Rand McNally, 1968.

Bischof, L. J., *Adult Psychology*. New York: Harper & Row, 1969.

Byrne, D., *An Introduction to Personality: A Research Approach*. Englewood Cliffs, N.J.: Prentice-Hall, 1966.

Cronbach, L. J., The two disciplines of scientific psychology, in D. Byrne and M. L. Hamilton, *Personality Research: A Book of Readings*. Englewood Cliffs, N.J.: Prentice-Hall, 1966.

Green, B. F., *Digital Computers in Research: An Introduction for Behavioral and Social Scientists*. New York: McGraw-Hill, 1963.

> Written by a psychologist.

Gullahorn, J. T., and J. E. Gullahorn, A computer model of elementary social behavior, in E. A. Feigenbaum and J. Feldman (eds.), *Computers and Thought*. New York: McGraw-Hill, 1963.

> The model's name is Homunculus who engages in social interaction as created by a husband (sociologist) and wife (psychologist) team.

Hall, C. S., and G. Lindzey, *Theories of Personality*. New York: Wiley, 1957.

Lindzey, G., and C. S. Hall, *Theories of Personality: Primary Resources and Research*. New York: Wiley, 1965.

Loehlin, J. C., *Computer Models of Personality*. New York: Random House, 1968.

> A delightful book on computers. One of the easiest and best to read.

Maddi, S., *Personality Theories: A Comparative Analysis*. Homewood, Ill.: Dorsey Press, 1968.

Mehrabian, A., *An Analysis of Personality Theories*. Englewood Cliffs, N.J.: Prentice-Hall, 1968.

Norbeck, E., D. Price-Williams, and W. M. McCord (eds.), *The Study of Personality: An Interdisciplinary Approach*. New York: Holt, Rinehart & Winston, 1968.

Rychlak, J. F., *A Philosophy of Science for Personality Theory*. Boston: Houghton Mifflin, 1968.

Shontz, F. C., *Research Methods in Personality*. New York: Appleton-Century-Crofts, 1965.

> Personality research needs methods that are unique.

Simon, H. A., and A. Newell, Simulation of human thinking, in M. Greenberg (ed.), *Computers and the World of the Future*. Cambridge, Mass.: M.I.T. Press, 1962.

Tomkins, S. S., and S. Messick (eds.), *Computer Simulation of Personality*. New York: Wiley, 1963.

> Thoughts and ideas from a 1962 conference.

von Bertalanffy, L., General system theory, in W. Buckley (ed.), *Modern Systems Research for the Behavioral Scientist*. Chicago: Aldine, 1968.

Wepman, J. M., and R. W. Heine (eds.), *Concepts of Personality*. Chicago: Aldine, 1963.

PERIODICALS

Abelson, R. P., and J. D. Carroll, Computer simulation of individual belief systems, *Behav. Sci.*, 1965, 8, 24–30.

Colby, K. M., Computer simulation of change in personal belief systems, *Behav Sci.*, 1967, 12, 248–253.

Coleman, J. S., Analysis of social structures and simulation of social processes with electronic computers, *Educ. Psychol.* 1961, 21, 203–218.

Loehlin, J. C., "Interpersonal" experiments with a computer model of personality *J. Pers. Soc. Psychol.*, 1965, 2, 580–584.

Simon, H. A., and A. Newell, Information processing in computer and man *Amer. Sci.*, 1964, 52, 281–300.

SUGGESTED READINGS

BOOKS

Adams, D. K., *The Anatomy of Personality.* Garden City, N.Y.: Doubleday 1954.

Babladelis, G., and S. Adams, *The Shaping of Personality.* Englewood Cliffs, N.J. Prentice-Hall, 1967.

>   The social-learning viewpoint in human development.

Bandura, A., and R. H. Walters, *Social Learning and Personality Development* New York: Holt, Rinehart & Winston, 1963.

>   Social variables and social learning theories.

Baughman, E. E., and G. S. Welsh, *Personality a Behavioral Science,* Englewood Cliffs, N.J.: Prentice-Hall, 1962.

>   Progress in prediction; see chap. 15.

Blum, G. S., *Psychoanalytic Theories of Personality.* New York: McGraw-Hill 1953.

>   A classic on Freud and the neo-Freudians.

Bonner, H., *Psychology of Personality.* New York: Ronald Press, 1961.

Brand, H., *The Study of Personality: A Book of Readings.* New York: Wiley 1954.

Bronfenbrenner, U., Toward an integrated theory of personality, in R. R. Blake and G. V. Ramsey (eds.), *Perception: An Approach to Personality.* New York: Ronald Press, 1951, chap. 9.

Coleman, J. C., *Personality Dynamics and Effective Behavior.* Chicago: Scott Foresman, 1960.

Based on the premise that man has "inborn capacity for responsible self-direction."

Coopersmith, S., *Frontiers of Psychological Research: Reading from Scientific American.* San Francisco: Freeman, 1966.

David, H. P., and H. von Bracken (eds.), *Perspectives in Personality Theory.* New York: Basic Books, 1957.

The international touch—twenty-two authors from ten countries.

Diamond, S., *Personality and Temperament.* New York: Harper & Row, 1957.

Development of individuality in the normal person.

Dollard, J., and N. E. Miller, *Personality and Psychotherapy.* New York: McGraw-Hill, 1950.

Dreger, R. M., *Fundamentals of Personality.* Philadelphia: Lippincott, 1962.

Dustin, D. S., *How Psychologists do Research: The Example of Anxiety.* Englewood Cliffs, N.J.: Prentice-Hall, 1969.

Fiske, D. W., Problems in measuring personality, in J. M. Wepman and R. W. Heine (eds.), *Concepts of Personality.* Chicago: Aldine, 1963.

Grinker, R. R. (ed.), *Toward a Unified Theory of Human Behavior.* New York: Basic Books, 1956.

Excellent source.

Guilford, J. P., *Personality.* New York: McGraw-Hill, 1959.

Heavy emphasis on factor analytic approach to personality study.

Hall, C. S., and G. Lindzey, *Theories of Personality.* New York: Wiley, 1957.

One of the best overall treatments of personality theory for resource purposes.

Harsh, C. M., and H. G. Schrickel, *Personality: Development and Assessment* (1950), 2nd ed. New York: Ronald Press, 1959.

Horst, P., *Personality: Measurement of Dimensions.* San Francisco: Jossey-Bass, 1968.

Janis, I. L., G. F. Mahl, J. Kagan, and R. R. Holt, *Personality: Dynamics, Development, and Assessment.* New York: Harcourt, Brace & World, 1969.

Discusses stress and frustration, conflict and defense, development, and assessment.

Johnson, P. E., *Personality and Religion.* Nashville, Tenn.: Abingdon Press, 1957.

Uses Freud, Lewin, Sullivan, and Allport views in studying a girl's development.

Kentucky Symposium, *Learning Theory, Personality Theory, and Clinical Research.* New York: Wiley, 1954.

Eleven lectures at the University of Kentucky, March, 1953, by such notables as Cattell, Harlow, Mowrer, Snygg, Spence, and Wickens.

Klein, G. S., and D. Krech, *Theoretical Models and Personality Theory*. Durham N.C.: Duke University Press, 1952.

Personality theory must be unified and explanatory.

Kleinmuntz, B., *Personality Measurement*. Homewood, Ill.: Dorsey Press, 1967.

Covers exclusively research on personality measurement.

Kluckhohn, C., H. A. Murray, and D. M. Schneider (eds.), *Personality in Nature Society, and Culture*, 2nd ed. New York: Knopf, 1964.

A compilation of all the approaches, revised and enlarged.

Leary, T., *Interpersonal Diagnosis of Personality: A Functional Theory and Methodology for Personality Evaluation*. New York: Ronald Press, 1957.

Interpersonal behavior and personality theory in the therapeutic setting

Leeper, R., Theories of personality, in W. Dennis (ed.), *Current Trends in Psychological Theory*. Pittsburgh: University of Pittsburgh Press, 1951.

Lundin, R. W., *Personality: An Experimental Approach*. New York: Macmillan 1961.

Experiments, many of them animal, on personality.

Lundin, R. W., *Personality: A Behavioral Analysis*. New York: Macmillan, 1969

Application of operant conditioning techniques to human behavior.

McClelland, D. C., Toward a science of personality psychology, in H. P. David and H. von Bracken (eds.), *Perspectives in Personality Theory*. New York Basic Books, 1957.

Highly recommended for the student of personality theory who is dis couraged or confused—so are others.

McClelland, D. C., *Personality*. New York: Holt, Rinehart & Winston, 1951 Reissued 1958.

Intensive study of one personality.

McCrary, J. L. (ed.), *Psychology of Personality: Six Modern Approaches*. New York: Logos Press, 1956.

Symposium, University of Houston, 1954.

McCurdy, H. G., *The Personal World: An Introduction to the Study of Personality*. New York: Harcourt, Brace & World, 1961.

An undergraduate text.

Maher, B. A. (ed.), *Progress in Experimental Personality Research*, Vol. 2. New York: Academic Press, 1965.

Synthesizes and integrates research in personality.

Mednick, M. T., and S. A. Mednick, *Research in Personality*. New York: Holt Rinehart & Winston, 1963.

Iillon, T. (ed.), *Approaches to Personality*. New York: Pitman, 1968.

> Explores theory, development, assessment, and research by forty-two authors.

ielson, G. (ed.), *Personality Research, Proc. 14th Int. Congr, Appl. Psychol.*, Vol. 2. Copenhagen, Denmark: Munskgaard, 1962.

Iotcutt, B., *The Psychology of Personality*. New York: Philosophical Library, 1953.

Iuttin, J., *Psychoanalysis and Personality: A Dynamic Theory of Normal Personality*. New York: Sheed & Ward, 1953.

> Father Nuttin, a Belgian, in a refreshing approach.

oback, A. A., *Personality in Theory and Practice*. Cambridge, Mass.: Sci-Art, 1950.

oback, A. A., Personality study at crossroads, in A. A. Roback (ed.), *Present Day Psychology*. New York: Philosophical Library, 1955, pp. 189–238.

otter, J. B., *Social Learning and Clinical Psychology*. Englewood Cliffs, N.J.: Prentice-Hall, 1954.

> Systematic theory for clinical psychologists.

arason, I. (ed.), *Contemporary Research in Personality: A Reader*, 2nd ed. Cincinnati, Van Nostrand/Reinhold, 1969.

> Stresses research in personality assessment and development, deviant behavior, and experimental studies.

arason, I. (ed.), *Contemporary Research in Personality*, 2nd ed. Princeton, N.J.: Van Nostrand, 1969.

> Armchair theorizing is speculation; this book of readings treats of joint application of assessment and experimental methods to studying personality.

arnoff, I., *Personality Dynamics and Development*. New York: Wiley, 1962.

> Integrates psychoanalytic theory and research for normal individuals.

aul, L. J., *The Development and Dynamics of Personality: Emotional Maturity*, 2nd ed. Philadelphia: Lippincott, 1960.

> A developmental theory of personality—based on psychoanalysis—combines biological, psychological, and sociological.

ears, R. R., Social behavior and personality development, in T. Parsons and E. A. Shils (eds.), *Toward a General Theory of Action*. Cambridge, Mass.: Harvard University Press, 1951, pp. 465–476.

nygg, D., and A. W. Combs, *Individual Behavior*. New York: Harper & Row, 1949.

> A much-quoted classic in its field.

Thorpe, L. P., and A. M. Schmuller, *Personality: An Interdisciplinary Approac* Princeton, N.J.: Van Nostrand, 1958.

>A "patterned eclecticism" is the rationale.

Wallace, A. F. C., *Culture and Personality*. New York: Random House, 1961.

>Analysis of personality research and personality theory.

White, R. W., *Lives in Progress: A Study of the Natural Growth of Personalit* New York: Holt, Rinehart & Winston, 1952.

>Highly readable, interesting account of three lives: those of a physicia a businessman, and a housewife.

Wolman, B. J., *Contemporary Theories and Systems in Psychology*. New Yor Harper & Row, 1960.

>Excellent source book—almost encyclopedic.

Worchel, P., and D. Byrne, *Personality Change*. New York: Wiley, 1964.

Young, K., *Personality and Problems of Adjustment*, 2nd ed. New York: Appleto Century-Crofts, 1952.

>A traditional author in the field of sociology.

PERIODICALS

Allen, D. A., Aptitudes and personality, *Harvard Educ. Rev.*, 1956, 26, 17–23.

>Aptitudes emerge from personality factors.

Beck, S. J., Personality research and theories of personality structure: Some co vergences, *J. Proj. Tech.*, 1955, 19, 361–371.

>Jackson's neurological theories, Freud's psychological, and Rorschach theory are compatible, consistent, and logical.

Crowne, D. P., Review of R. B. Cattell, *The Scientific Analysis of Personalit Contemp. Psychol.*, 1967, 12, 40–41.

Falk, J. L., Issues distinguishing idiographic from nomothetic approaches to pe sonality theory, *Psychol. Rev.*, 1956, 63, 53–62.

Freides, D., Toward the elimination of the concept of normality, *J. Consu Psychol.*, 1960, 24, 128–133.

>Normality in personality theory is criticized.

Gilbert, A. R., Intentionalism, *J. Psychol.*, 1959, 48, 181–190.

>The author tries for a "unified theory of personality" to avoid "sm: package theories."

Greenspoon, J., Perspectives in psychology: XIX. Private experience revisite *Psychol. Rec.*, 1961, 11, 373–381.

>Private experience is a false point of departure—start with behavior.

Iayakawa, S. I., The fully functioning personality, *ETC, Rev. Gen. Semant.*, 1956, *13*, 169–181.

> Uses Rogers, Maslow, D. H. Lawrence, and Korzybski in discussing the healthy personality.

Ielson, H., An experimental approach to personality, *Psychiat. Res. Rep.*, 1955, 2, 89–99.

> Personality and perception viewed in the same light.

Iunt, J. McV., Traditional personality theory in the light of recent evidence, *Amer. Sci.*, 1965, *53*, 80–96.

> "A recent brief critical evaluation that stresses the value of the interaction view."

anner, L., Centripetal forces in personality development, *Amer. J. Psychoanal.*, 1959, 19, 123–133.

> Freud is to integrate centrifugal (internal) and centripetal (external) forces.

Ielly, E. L., Consistency of the adult personality, *Amer. Psychologist*, 1955, *10*, 659–681.

> Test of 600 persons, ages sixteen to eighteen and retested later. People don't give up—"adults may hope for continued psychological growth."

IcGriegan, F. J., Confirmation of theories in psychology, *Psychol. Rev.*, 1956, 63, 98–104.

Iaier, N. R. F., Maier's law, *Amer. Psychologist*, 1960, *15*, 208–212.

> Any theory that cannot be quantified is inadequate, even if it works.

Iailloux, N., The contribution of clinical research to personality theory, *Canad. J. Psychol.*, 1955, 9, 133–143.

> Restricted interpretation of method has delayed theory development. Methodologists are stopping ideas before they get started.

Iilner, E., New frontiers in personality theory, *J. Nat. Ass. Deans of Women*, March, 1954, pp. 105–119.

Iogar, R. E., Value orientations of college students: Preliminary data and review of the literature, *Psychol. Rep.*, 1964, *15*, 739–770.

> Interprets value orientation in terms of personality theory, research, and social factors.

oby, T. B., An opinion on the construction of behavior theory, *Amer. Psychologist*, 1959, *14*, 129–134.

> Natural sciences are ahead of the behavioral sciences—the latter are far from satisfactory.

Sears, R. R., Personality theory: The next forty years, *Monogr. Soc. Res. Chil* Develpm., 1959, 24, 37–48.

Secord, P. F., and C. W. Backman, Personality theory and the problem of stabi ity change in individual behavior: An interpersonal approach, *Psychol. Rev* 1961, 68, 21–32.

Shaklee, A. B., Optional stopping and theory making, *Psychol. Rep.*, 1958, 4 17.

> The value of terminating observations in theory construction.

Van Kaam, A., Existential psychology as a comprehensive theory of personality *Rev. Existential Psychol. Psychiat.*, 1963, 3, 11–26.

> Because it is so complex, existential psychology is valuable as a personalit theory.

Winthrop, H., Scientism is psychology, *J. Indiv. Psychol.*, 1959, 15, 112–120.

> Because methods and assumptions work in the physical sciences does no mean they will, can, or should in psychology.

Indexes

INDEX OF NAMES

INDEX OF SUBJECTS

70 71 72 73   7 6 5 4 3 2 1